楊英風全集
YUYU YANG CORPUS

創作篇　第二卷　Volume 2

版畫　Print
繪畫　Painting
雷射　Laser
攝影　Photograph

策畫／國立交通大學
主編／國立交通大學楊英風藝術研究中心
　　　財團法人楊英風藝術教育基金會
出版／藝術家出版社

感謝 APPRECIATE

國立交通大學	National Chiao Tung University
朱銘文教基金會	Nonprofit Organization Juming Culture and Education Foundation
新竹法源講寺	Hsinchu Fa Yuan Temple
張榮發基金會	Yung-fa Chang Foundation
高雄麗晶診所	Kaohsiung Li-ching Clinic
典藏藝術家庭	Art & Collection Group
謝金河	Chin-ho Shieh
葉榮嘉	Yung-chia Yeh
麗寶文教基金會	Lihpao Foundation
許順良	Shun-liang Shu
許雅玲	Ya-Ling Hsu
杜隆欽	Long-Chin Tu
洪美銀	Mei-Yin Hong

對《楊英風全集》的大力支持及贊助

For your great advocacy and support to *Yuyu Yang Corpus*

楊英風全集

YUYU YANG CORPUS

創作篇　第二卷　Volume 2

版畫　Print

繪畫　Painting

雷射　Laser

攝影　Photograph

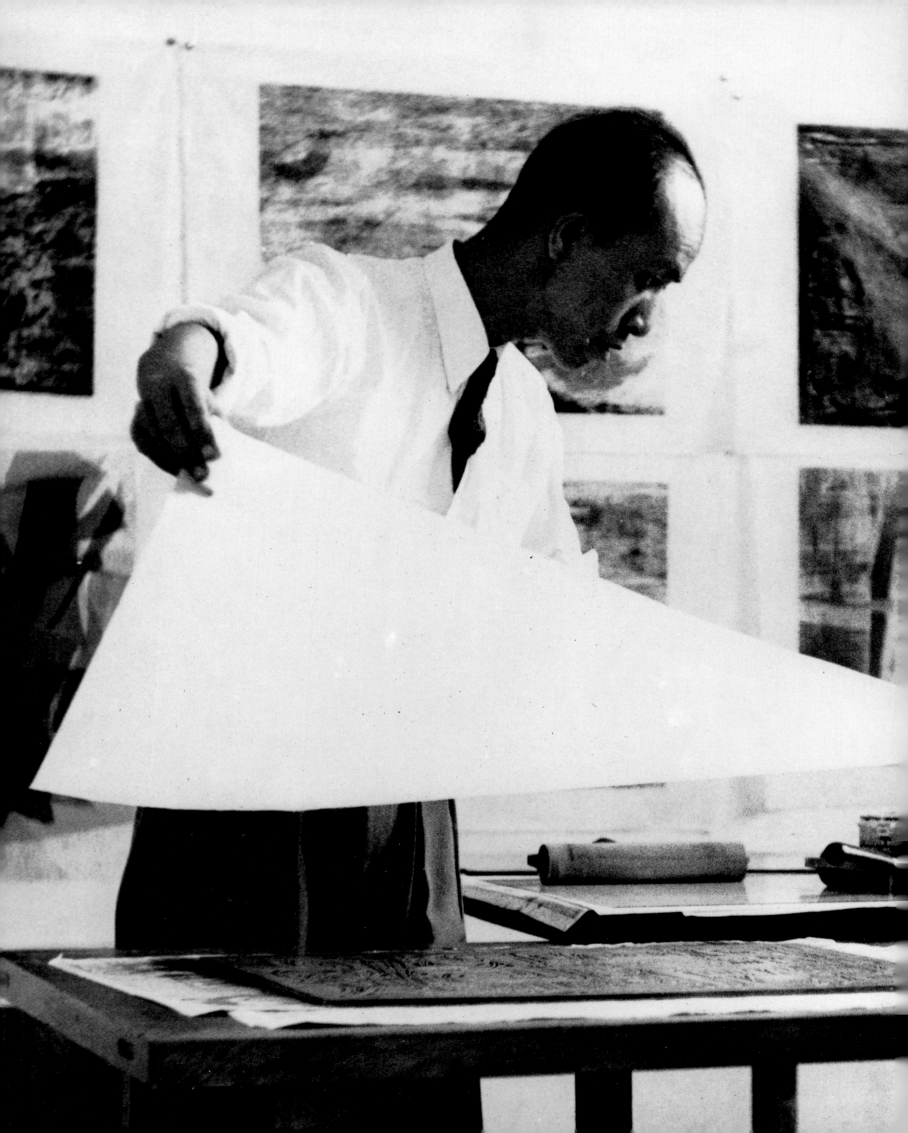

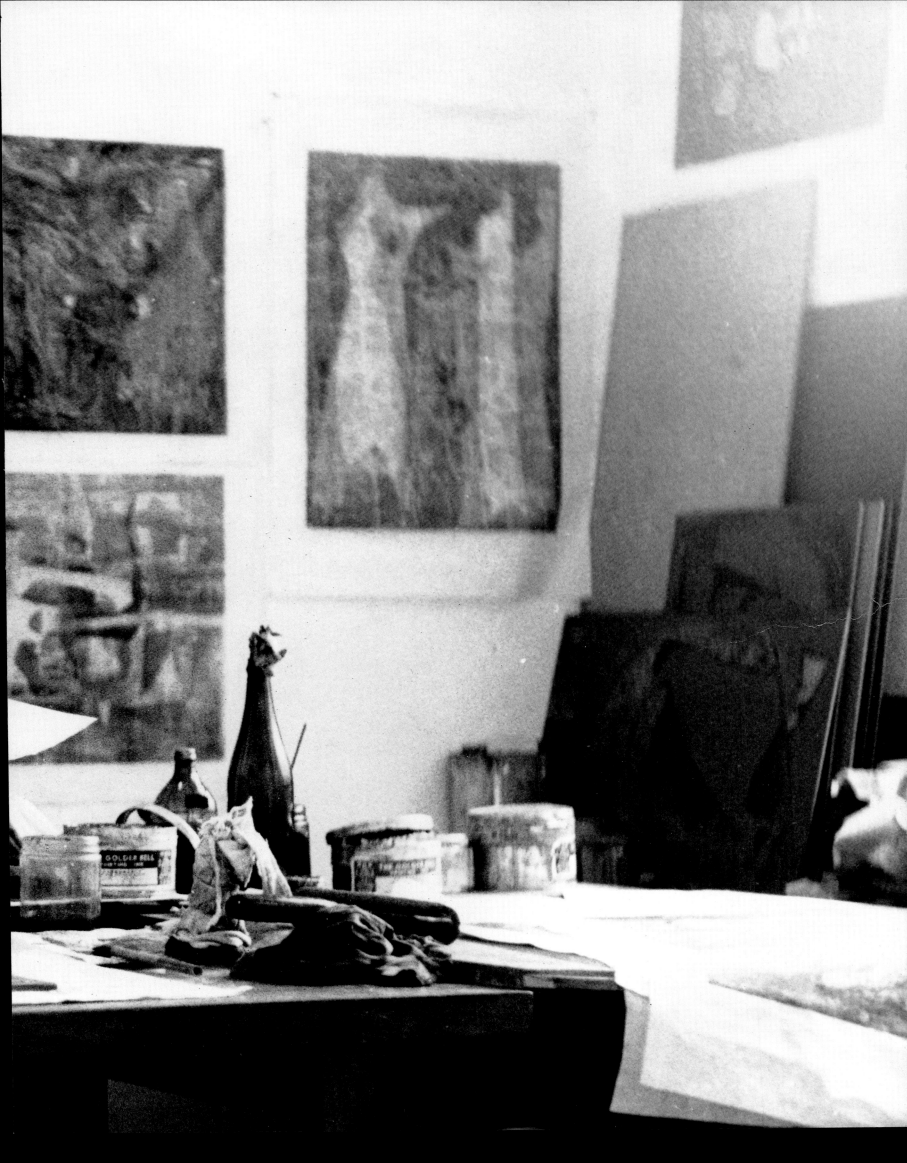

目 次

Contents

序

　　國立交通大學向來以理工聞名，是眾所皆知的事，但在二十一世紀展開的今天，科技必須和人文融合，才能創造新的價值，帶動文明的提昇。

　　我主持校務以來，孜孜於如何將人文引入科技領域，使成為科技創發的動力，也成為心靈豐美的泉源。

　　一九九四年，本校新建圖書館大樓接近完工，偌大的資訊廣場，需要一些藝術景觀的調和，我和雕塑大師楊英風教授相識十多年，遂推薦大師為交大作出曠世作品，終於一九九六年完成以不銹鋼成型的巨大景觀雕塑〔緣慧潤生〕，也成為本校建校百周年的精神標竿。

　　隔年，楊教授即因病辭世，一九九九年蒙楊教授家屬同意，將其畢生創作思維的各種文獻史料，移交本校圖書館，成立「楊英風藝術研究中心」，並於二○○○年舉辦「人文‧藝術與科技——楊英風國際學術研討會」及回顧展。這是本校類似藝術研究中心，最先成立的一個；也激發了日後「漫畫研究中心」、「科技藝術研究中心」、「陳慧坤藝術研究中心」的陸續成立。

　　「楊英風藝術研究中心」正式成立以來，在財團法人楊英風文教基金會董事長寬謙師父的協助配合下，陸續完成「楊英風數位美術館」、「楊英風文獻典藏室」及「楊英風電子資料庫」的建置；而規模龐大的《楊英風全集》，構想始於二○○一年，原本希望在二○○二年年底完成，作為教授逝世五周年的獻禮。但由於內容的豐碩龐大，經歷近五年的持續工作，終於在二○○五年年底完成樣書編輯，正式出版。而這個時間，也正逢楊教授八十誕辰的日子，意義非凡。

　　這件歷史性的工作，感謝本校諸多同仁的支持、參與，尤其原先擔任校外諮詢委員也是國內知名的美術史學者蕭瓊瑞教授，同意出任《楊英風全集》總主編的工作，以其歷史的專業，使這件工作，更具史料編輯的系統性與邏輯性，在此一併致上謝忱。

　　希望這套史無前例的《楊英風全集》的編成出版，能為這塊土地的文化累積，貢獻一份心力，也讓年輕學子，對文化的堅持、創生，有相當多的啟發與省思。

國立交通大學校長　張俊彥

Preface

National Chiao Tung University is renowned for its sciences. As the 21st century begins, technology should be integrated with humanities and it should create its own value to promote the progress of civilization.

Since I led the school administration several years ago, I have been seeking for many ways to lead humanities into technical field in order to make the cultural element a driving force to technical innovation and make it a fountain to spiritual richness.

In 1994, as the library building construction was going to be finished, its spacious information square needed some artistic grace. Since I knew the master of sculpture Prof. Yuyu Yang for more than ten years, he was commissioned this project. The magnificent stainless steel environmental sculpture "Grace Bestowed on Human Beings" was completed in 1996, symbolizing the NCTU's centennial spirit.

The next year, Prof. Yuyu Yang left our world due to his illness. In 1999, owing to his beloved family's generosity, the professor's creative legacy in literary records was entrusted to our library. Subsequently, Yuyu Yang Art Research Center was established. A seminar entitled "Humanities, Art and Technology - Yuyu Yang International Seminar" and another retrospective exhibition were held in 2000. This was the first art-oriented research center in our school, and it inspired several other research centers to be set up, including Caricature Research Center, Technological Art Research Center, and Hui-kun Chen Art Research Center.

After the Yuyu Yang Art Research Center was set up, the buildings of Yuyu Yang Digital Art Museum, Yuyu Yang Literature Archives and Yuyu Yang Electronic Databases have been systematically completed under the assistance of Kuan-chian Shi, the President of Yuyu Yang Foundation. The prodigious task of publishing the *Yuyu Yang Corpus* was conceived in 2001, and was scheduled to be completed by the and of 2002 as a memorial gift to mark the fifth anniversary of the passing of Prof. Yuyu Yang. However, it lasted five years to finish it and was published in the and of 2005 because of his prolific works.

The achievement of this historical task is indebted to the great support and participation of many members of this institution, especially the outside counselor and also the well-known art history Prof. Chong-ray Hsiao, who agreed to serve as the chief editor and whose specialty in history makes the historical records more systematical and logical.

We hope the unprecedented publication of the *Yuyu Yang Corpus* will help to preserve and accumulate cultural assets in Taiwan art history and will inspire our young adults to have more reflection and contemplation on culture insistency and creativity.

President of
Nation Chiao Tung University
Chun-yen Chang

9

涓滴成海

　　楊英風先生是我們兄弟姊妹所摯愛的父親，但是我們小時候卻很少享受到這份天倫之樂。父親他永遠像個老師，隨時教導著一群共住在一起的學生，順便告訴我們做人處世的道理，從來不勉強我們必須學習與他相關的領域。誠如父親當年教導朱銘，告訴他：「你不要當第二個楊英風，而是當朱銘你自己」！

　　記得有位學生回憶那段時期，他說每天都努力著盡學生本分：「醒師前，睡師後」，卻是一直無法達成。因為父親整天充沛的工作狂勁，竟然在年輕的學生輩都還找不到對手呢！這樣努力不懈的工作熱誠，可以說維持到他逝世之前，終其一生始終如此，這不禁使我們想到：「一分天才，仍須九十九分的努力」這句至理名言！

　　父親的感情世界是豐富的，但卻是內斂而深沉的。應該是源自於孩提時期對母親不在身邊而充滿深厚的期待，直至小學畢業終於可以投向母親懷抱時，卻得先與表姊定親，又將少男奔放的情懷給鎖住了。無怪乎當父親被震懾在大同雲崗大佛的腳底下的際遇，從此縱情於佛法的領域。從父親晚年回顧展中「向來回首雲崗處，宏觀震懾六十載」的標題，及畢生最後一篇論文〈大乘景觀論〉，更確切地明白佛法思想是他創作的活水源頭。我的出家，彌補了父親未了的心願，出家後我們父女竟然由於佛法獲得深度的溝通，我也經常慨歎出家後我才更理解我的父親，原來他是透過內觀修行，掘到生命的泉源，所以創作簡直是隨手捻來，件件皆是具有生命力的作品。

　　面對上千件作品，背後上萬件的文獻圖像資料，這是父親畢生創作，幾經遷徙殘留下來的珍貴資料，見證著台灣美術史發展中，不可或缺的一塊重要領域。身為子女的我們，正愁不知如何正確地將這份寶貴的公共文化財，奉獻給社會與眾生之際，國立交通大學張俊彥校長適時地出現，慨然應允與我們基金會合作成立「楊英風藝術研究中心」，企圖將資訊科技與人文藝術作最緊密的結合。先後完成了「楊英風數位美術館」、「楊英風文獻典藏室」與「楊英風電子資料庫」，而規模最龐大、最複雜的是《楊英風全集》，則整整戮力近五年。

　　在此深深地感恩著這一切的因緣和合，張校長俊彥、蔡前副校長文祥、楊前館長維邦、林前教務長振德的全力支援，編輯小組諮詢委員會十二位專家學者的指導。蕭瓊瑞教授擔任總主編，李振明教授及助理張俊哲先生擔任美編指導，本研究中心的同仁鈴如、珊珊、瑋鈴擔任分冊主編，還有過去如海、怡勳、美璟、秀惠與盈龍的投入，以及家兄嫂奉琛及維妮與法源講寺的支持和幕後默默的耕耘者，更感謝朱銘先生在得知我們面對《楊英風全集》龐大的印刷經費相當困難時，慨然捐出十三件作品，價值新台幣六百萬元整，以供義賣。還有在義賣過程中所有贊助者的慷慨解囊，更促成了這幾乎不可能的任務，才有機會將一池靜靜的湖水，逐漸匯集成大海般的壯闊。

楊英風藝術教育基金會
董事長　釋寬謙

Little Drops Make An Ocean

Yuyu Yang was our beloved father, yet we seldom enjoyed our happy family hours in our childhoods. Father was always like a teacher, and was constantly teaching us proper morals, and values of the world. He never forced us to learn the knowledge of his field, but allowed us to develop our own interests. He also told Ju Ming, a renowned sculptor, the same thing that "Don't be a second Yuyu Yang, but be yourself !"

One of my father's students recalled that period of time. He endeavored to do his responsibility - awake before the teacher and asleep after the teacher. However, it was not easy to achieve because of my father's energetic in work and none of the student is his rival. He kept this enthusiasm till his death. It reminds me of a proverb that one percent of genius and ninety nine percent of hard work leads to success.

My father was rich in emotions, but his feelings were deeply internalized. It must be some reasons of his childhood. He looked forward to be with his mother, but he couldn't until he graduated from the elementary school. But at that moment, he was obliged to be engaged with his cousin that somehow curtailed the natural passion of a young boy. Therefore, it is understandable that he indulged himself with Buddhism. We could clearly understand that the Buddha dharma is the fountain of his artistic creation from the headline - "Looking Back at Yuen-gang, Touching Heart for Sixty Years" of his retrospective exhibition and from his last essay "Landscape Thesis". My forsaking of the world made up his uncompleted wishes. I could have deep communication through Buddhism with my father after that and I began to understand that my father found his fountain of life through introspection and Buddhist practice. So every piece of his work is vivid and shows the vitality of life.

Father left behind nearly a thousand pieces of artwork and tens of thousands of relevant documents and graphics, which are preciously preserved after the migration. These works are the painstaking efforts in his lifetime and they constitute a significant part of contemporary art history. While we were worrying about how to donate these precious cultural legacies to the society, Mr. Chun-yen Chang, President of National Chiao Tung University, agreed to collaborate with our foundation in setting up Yung Yang Art Research Center with the intention of integrating information technology with art. As a result, Yuyu Yang Digital Art Museum, Yuyu Yang Literature Archives and Yuyu Yang Electronic Databases have been set up. But the most complex and prodigious was the *Yuyu Yang Corpus*; it took three whole years.

We owe a great deal to the support of NCTU's president Chun-yen Chang, former vice president Wen-hsiang Tsai, former library director Wei-bang Yang and former dean of academic Cheng-te Lin as well as the direction of the twelve scholars and experts that served as the editing consultation. Prof. Chong-ray Hsiao is the chief editor. Prof. Cheng-ming Lee and assistant Jun-che Chang are the art editor guides. Ling-ju, Shan-shan and Wei-ling in the research center are volume editors. Ru-hai, Yi-hsun, Mei-jing, Xiu-hui and Ying-long also joined us, together with the support of my brother Fong-sheng, sister-in-law Wei-ni, Fa Yuan Temple, and many other contributors. Moreover, we must thank Mr. Ju Ming. When he knew that we had difficulty in facing the huge expense of printing *Yuyu Yang Corpus*, he donated thirteen works that the entire value was NTD 6,000,000 liberally for a charity bazaar. Furthermore, in the process of the bazaar, all of the sponsors that made generous contributions helped to bring about this almost impossible mission. Thus scattered bits and pieces have been flocked together to form the great majesty.

President of
Yuyu Yang Art Education Foundation
Kuan-Chian Shi

Kuan - Chian Shi

為歷史立一巨石──關於《楊英風全集》

　　在戰後台灣美術史上，以藝術材料嘗試之新、創作領域橫跨之廣、對各種新知識、新思想探討之勤，並因此形成獨特見解、創生鮮明藝術風貌，且留下數量龐大的藝術作品與資料者，楊英風無疑是獨一無二的一位。在國立交通大學支持下編纂的《楊英風全集》，將證明這個事實。

　　視楊英風為台灣的藝術家，恐怕還只是一種方便的說法。從他的生平經歷來看，這位出生成長於時代交替夾縫中的藝術家，事實上，足跡橫跨海峽兩岸以及東南亞、日本、歐洲、美國等地。儘管在戰後初期，他曾任職於以振興台灣農村經濟為主旨的《豐年》雜誌，因此深入農村，也創作了為數可觀的各種類型的作品，包括水彩、油畫、雕塑，和大批的漫畫、美術設計等等；但在思想上，楊英風絕不是一位狹隘的鄉土主義者，他的思想恢宏、關懷廣闊，是一位具有世界性視野與氣度的傑出藝術家。

　　一九二六年出生於台灣宜蘭的楊英風，因父母長年在大陸經商，因此將他託付給姨父母撫養照顧。一九四〇年楊英風十五歲，隨父母前往中國北京，就讀北京日本中等學校，並先後隨日籍老師淺井武、寒川典美，以及旅居北京的台籍畫家郭柏川等習畫。一九四四年，前往日本東京，考入東京美術學校建築科；不過未久，就因戰爭結束，政局變遷，而重回北京，一面在京華美術學校西畫系，繼續接受郭柏川的指導，同時也考取輔仁大學教育學院美術系。唯戰後的世局變動，未及等到輔大畢業，就在一九四七年返台，自此與大陸的父母兩岸相隔，無法見面，並失去經濟上的奧援，長達三十多年時間。隻身在台的楊英風，短暫在台灣大學植物系從事繪製植物標本工作後，一九四八年，考入台灣省立師範學院藝術系（今台灣師大美術系），受教溥心畬等傳統水墨畫家，對中國傳統繪畫思想，開始有了瞭解。唯命運多舛的楊英風，仍因經濟問題，無法在師院完成學業。一九五一年，自師院輟學，應同鄉畫壇前輩藍蔭鼎之邀，至農復會《豐年》雜誌擔任美術編輯，此一工作，長達十一年；不過在這段時間，透過他個人的努力，開始在台灣藝壇展露頭角，先後獲聘為中國文藝協會民俗文藝委員會常務委員（1955-）、教育部美育委員會委員（1957-）、國立歷史博物館推廣委員（1957-）、巴西聖保羅雙年展參展作品評審委員（1957-）、第四屆全國美展雕塑組審查委員（1957-）等等，並在一九五九年，與一些具創新思想的年輕人組成日後影響深遠的「現代版畫會」。且以其聲望，被推舉為當時由國內現代繪畫團體所籌組成立的「中國現代藝術中心」召集人；可惜這個藝術中心，因著名的政治疑雲「秦松事件」（作品被疑為與「反蔣」有關），而宣告夭折（1960）。不過楊英風仍在當年，盛大舉辦他個人首次重要個展於國立歷史博物館，並在隔年（1961），獲中國文藝協會雕塑獎，也完成他的成名大作──台中日月潭教師會館大型浮雕壁畫群。

　　一九六一年，楊英風辭去《豐年》雜誌美編工作，一九六二年受聘擔任國立台灣藝術專科學校（今台灣藝大）美術科兼任教授，培養了一批日後活躍於台灣藝術界的年輕雕塑家。一九六三年，他以北平輔仁大學校友會代表身份，前往義大利羅馬，並陪同于斌主教晉見教宗保祿六世；此後，旅居義大利，直至一九六六年。期間，他創作了大批極為精采

的街頭速寫作品，並在米蘭舉辦個展，展出四十多幅版畫與十件雕塑，均具相當突出的現代風格。此外，他又進入義大利國立造幣雕刻專門學校研究銅章雕刻；返國後，舉辦「義大利銅章雕刻展」於國立歷史博物館，是台灣引進銅章雕刻的先驅人物。同年（1966），獲得第四屆全國十大傑出青年金手獎榮譽。

隔年（1967），楊英風受聘擔任花蓮大理石工廠顧問，此一機緣，對他日後大批精采創作，如「山水」系列的激發，具直接的影響；但更重要者，是開啓了日後花蓮石雕藝術發展的契機，對台灣東部文化產業的提升，具有重大且深遠的貢獻。

一九六九年，楊英風臨危受命，在極短的時間，和有限的財力、人力限制下，接受政府委託，創作完成日本大阪萬國博覽會中華民國館的大型景觀雕塑〔鳳凰來儀〕。這件作品，是他一生重要的代表作之一，以大型的鋼鐵材質，形塑出一種飛翔、上揚的鳳凰意象。這件作品的完成，也奠定了爾後和著名華人建築師貝聿銘一系列的合作。貝聿銘正是當年中華民國館的設計者。

〔鳳凰來儀〕一作的完成，也促使楊氏的創作進入一個新的階段，許多來自中國傳統文化思想的作品，一一湧現。

一九七七年，楊英風受到日本京都觀賞雷射藝術的感動，開始在台灣推動雷射藝術，並和陳奇祿、毛高文等人，發起成立「中華民國雷射科藝推廣協會」，大力推廣科技導入藝術創作的觀念，並成立「大漢雷射科藝研究所」，完成於一九八〇的〔生命之火〕，就是台灣第一件以雷射切割機完成的雕刻作品。這件工作，引發了相當多年輕藝術家的投入參與，並在一九八一年，於圓山飯店及圓山天文台舉辦盛大的「第一屆中華民國國際雷射景觀雕塑大展」。

一九八六年，由於夫人李定的去世，與愛女漢珩的出家，楊英風的生命，也轉入一個更為深沈內蘊的階段。一九八八年，他重遊洛陽龍門與大同雲岡等佛像石窟，並於一九九〇年，發表〈中國生態美學的未來性〉於北京大學「中國東方文化國際研討會」；〈楊英風教授生態美學語錄〉也在《中時晚報》、《民眾日報》等媒體連載。同時，他更花費大量的時間、精力，為美國萬佛城的景觀、建築，進行規劃設計與修建工程。

一九九三年，行政院頒發國家文化獎章，肯定其終生的文化成就與貢獻。同年，台灣省立美術館為其舉辦「楊英風一甲子工作紀錄展」，回顧其一生創作的思維與軌跡。一九九六年，大型的「呦呦楊英風景觀雕塑特展」，在英國皇家雕塑家學會邀請下，於倫敦查爾西港區戶外盛大舉行。

一九九七年八月，「楊英風大乘景觀雕塑展」在著名的日本箱根雕刻之森美術館舉行。兩個月後，這位將一生生命完全貢獻給藝術的傑出藝術家，因病在女兒出家的新竹法源講寺，安靜地離開他所摯愛的人間，回歸宇宙渾沌無垠的太初。

楊英風一生的藝術追求，有其明顯的思維路向與踏實豐碩的創作成果。一般人或許對其景觀雕塑有較多的認識，事實上在版畫、繪畫、雷射、攝影，乃至美術設計、漫畫、景觀設計各方面，楊英風均具前衛且重要的地位。例如在版畫

方面，早在一九五九年，他和陳庭詩、李錫奇、秦松等人創立「現代版畫會」以前，便展現出各種造型思維與媒材實驗的強烈企圖與成就，稱他為「中國現代版畫的先驅者」，絕非過語。尤其他對台灣特有媒材「甘蔗板」的開發，這可能和他服務《豐年社》的地利之便有關，不但增美了版畫印刷畫面的豐富質感，也影響了陳庭詩後來膾炙人口的宇宙版畫系列。

當他留學義大利時，結合中西媒材與畫法所創作的一批繪畫作品，也可窺見他在調和中西、解決傳統與現代衝突此一課題上的努力與成績。

而對雷射藝術的開發、實驗與創作，更是國內僅見的前衛藝術家。目前收存近七十幅的作品，其實只是現場創作的部份記錄；楊英風創作雷射藝術的理想，其實是結合音樂、景觀，形成一種占有360度空間，波濤洶湧、潛流迴盪的奇異感受。

至於對攝影藝術的接觸，他也是戰後台灣投入較早的一位；包括最早和郎靜山等人一起進行女性裸體的拍攝，也持續到一九七○年代後期，大批美國萬佛城的風景照，甚至一九七八年，還假台北國立歷史博物館舉行「美國萬佛城自然景觀攝影展」。顯示楊英風作為一個全能藝術家，對各種表現媒材與手法高度的熱忱與投入。

一九九四年，楊英風受邀為國立交通大學新建圖書館資訊廣場，規劃設計大型景觀雕塑〔緣慧潤生〕，這件作品在一九九六年完成，作為交大建校百週年紀念。

一九九九年，也是楊氏辭世的第二年，交通大學正式成立「楊英風藝術研究中心」，並與財團法人楊英風藝術教育基金會合作，在國科會的專案補助下，於二○○○年開始進行「楊英風數位美術館」建置計劃；隔年，進一步進行「楊英風文獻典藏室」與「楊英風電子資料庫」的建置工作，並著手《楊英風全集》的編纂計劃。

二○○二年元月，個人以校外諮詢委員身份，和林保堯、顏娟英等教授，受邀參與全集的第一次諮詢委員會；美麗的校園中，散置著許多楊英風各個時期的作品。初步的《全集》構想，有三巨冊，上、中冊為作品圖錄，下冊為楊氏日記、工作週記與評論文字的選輯和年表。委員們一致認為：以楊氏一生龐大的創作成果和文獻史料，採取選輯的方式，有違《全集》的精神，也對未來史料的保存與研究，有所不足，乃建議進行更全面且詳細的搜羅、整理與編輯。

由於這是一件龐大的工作，楊英風藝術教育教基金會的董事長寬謙法師，也是楊英風的三女，考量林保堯、顏娟英教授的工作繁重，乃商洽個人前往交大支援，並徵得校方同意，擔任《全集》總主編的工作。

個人自二○○二年二月起，每月最少一次由台南北上，參與這項工作的進行。研究室位於圖書館地下室，與藝文空間比鄰，雖是地下室，但空曠的設計，使得空氣、陽光充足。研究室內，現代化的文件櫃與電腦設備，顯示交大相關單位對這項工作的支持。幾位學有專精的專任研究員和校方支援的工讀生，面對龐大的資料，進行耐心的整理與歸檔。工作的計劃，原訂於二○○二年年底告一段落，但資料的陸續出土，從埔里楊氏舊宅和台北的工作室，又搬回來大批的圖稿、文件

與照片。楊氏對資料的蒐集、記錄與存檔，直如一位有心的歷史學者，恐怕是台灣，甚至海峽兩岸少見的一人。他的史料，也幾乎就是台灣現代藝術運動最重要的一手史料，將提供未來研究者，瞭解他個人和這個時代最重要的依據與參考。

《全集》最後的規模，超出所有參與者原先的想像。全部內容包括兩大部份：即創作篇與文件篇。創作篇的第1至5卷，是巨型圖版畫冊，包括第1卷的浮雕、景觀浮雕、雕塑、景觀雕塑，與獎座，第2卷的版畫、繪畫、雷射，與攝影；第3卷的速寫；第4卷的美術設計、插畫與漫畫；第5卷除大事年表和一篇介紹楊氏創作經歷的專文外，則是有關楊英風的一些評論文字、日記、剪報、工作週記、書信，與雕塑創作過程、景觀規劃案、史料、照片等等的精華選錄。事實上，第5卷的內容，也正是第二部份文件篇的內容的選輯，而文卷篇的詳細內容，總數多達二十冊，包括：文集三冊、研究集五冊、早年日記一冊、工作札記二冊、書信六冊、史料圖片二冊，及一冊較為詳細的生平年譜。至於創作篇的第6至10卷，則完全是景觀規劃案；楊英風一生亟力推動「景觀雕塑」的觀念，因此他的景觀規劃，許多都是「景觀雕塑」觀念下的一種延伸與擴大。這些規劃案有完成的，也有未完成的，但都是楊氏心血的結晶，保存下來，做為後進研究參考的資料，也期待某些案子，可以獲得再生、實現的契機。

類如《楊英風全集》這樣一套在藝術史界，還未見前例的大部頭書籍的編纂，工作的困難與成敗，還不只在全書的架構和分類；最困難的，還在美術的編輯與安排，如何將大小不一、種類材質繁複的圖像、資料，有條不紊，以優美的視覺方式呈現出來？是一個巨大的挑戰。好友台灣師大美術系教授李振明和他的傑出弟子，也是曾經獲得一九九七年國際青年設計大賽台灣區金牌獎的張俊哲先生，可謂不計酬勞地以一種文化貢獻的心情，共同參與了這件工作的進行，在此表達誠摯的謝意。當然藝術家出版社何政廣先生的應允出版，和他堅強的團隊，尤其是柯美麗小姐辛勞的付出，也應在此致上深深的謝意。

個人參與交大楊英風藝術研究中心的《全集》編纂，是一次美好的經歷。許多個美麗的夜晚，住在圖書館旁招待所，多風的新竹、起伏有緻的交大校園，從初春到寒冬，都帶給個人難忘的回憶。而幾次和張校長俊彥院士夫婦與學校相關主管的集會或餐聚，也讓個人對這個歷史悠久而生命常青的學校，留下深刻的印象。在對人文高度憧憬與尊重的治校理念下，張校長和相關主管大力支持《楊英風全集》的編纂工作，已為台灣美術史，甚至文化史，留下一座珍貴的寶藏；也像在茂密的藝術森林中，立下一塊巨大的磐石，美麗的「夢之塔」，將在這塊巨石上，昂然矗立。

個人以能參與這件歷史性的工程而深感驕傲，尤其感謝研究中心同仁，包括鈴如、珊珊、瑋鈴，和已經離職的怡勳、美璟、如海、盈龍、秀惠的全力投入與配合。而八師父（寬謙法師）、奉琛、維妮，為父親所付出的一切，成果歸於全民共有，更應致上最深沈的敬意。

總主編

蕭瓊瑞

15

A Monolith in History :
About The *Yuyu Yang Corpus*

The attempt of new art materials, the width of the innovative works, the diligence of probing into new knowledge and new thoughts, the uniqueness of the ideas, the style of vivid art, and the collections of the great amount of art works prove that Yuyu Yang was undoubtedly the unique one In Taiwan art history of post World War II. We can see many proofs in *Yuyu Yang Corpus*, which was compiled with the support of the National Chiao Tung University.

Regarding Yuyu Yang as a Taiwanese artist is only a rough description. Judging from his background, he was born and grew up at the juncture of the changing times and actually traversed both sides of the Taiwan Straits, Japan, Europe and America. He used to be an employee at Harvest, a magazine dedicated to fostering Taiwan agricultural economy. He walked into the agricultural society to have a clear understanding of their lives and created numerous types of works, such as watercolor, oil paintings, sculptures, comics and graphic designs. But Yuyu Yang is not just a narrow minded localism in thinking. On the contrary, his great thinking and his open-minded makes him an outstanding artist with global vision and manner.

Yuyu Yang was born in Yilan, Taiwan, 1926, and was fostered by his aunt because his parents ran a business in China. In 1940, at the age of 15, he was leaving Beijing with his parents, and enrolled in a Japanese middle school there. He learned with Japanese teachers Asai Takesi, Samukawa Norimi, and Taiwanese painter Bo-chuan Kuo. He went to Japan in 1944, and was accepted to the Architecture Department of Tokyo School of Art, but soon returned to Beijing because of the political situation. In Beijing, he studied Western painting with Mr. Bo-chuan Kuo at Jin Hua School of Art. At this time, he was also accepted to the Art Department of Fu Jen University. Because of the war, he returned to Taiwan without completing his studies at Fu Jen University. Since then, he was separated from his parents and lost any financial support for more than three decades. Being alone in Taiwan, Yuyu Yang temporarily drew specimens at the Botany Department of National Taiwan University, and was accepted to the Fine Art Department of Taiwan Provincial Academy for Teachers (is today known as National Taiwan Normal University) in 1948. He learned traditional ink paintings from Mr. Hsin-yu Fu and started to know about Chinese traditional paintings. However, it's a pity that he couldn't complete his academic studies for the difficulties in economy. He dropped out school in 1951 and went to work as an art editor at *Harvest* magazine under the invitation of Mr. Ying-ding Lan, his hometown artist predecessor, for eleven years. During this period, because of his endeavor, he gradually gained attention in the art field and was nominated as a member of the standing committee of China Literary Society Folk Art Council (1955-), the Ministry of Education's Art Education Committee (1957-), the National Museum of History's Outreach Committee (1957-), the Sao Paulo Biennial Exhibition's Evaluation Committee (1957-), and the 4th Annual National Art Exhibition, Sculpture Division's Judging Committee (1957-), etc. In 1959, he founded the Modern Printmaking Society with a few innovative young artists. By this prestige, he was nominated the convener of Chinese Modern Art Center. Regrettably, the art center came to an end in 1960 due to the notorious political shadow - a so-called Qin-song

Event (works were alleged of anti-Chiang). Nonetheless, he held his solo exhibition at the National Museum of History that year and won an award from the ROC Literary Association in 1961. At the same time, he completed the masterpiece of mural paintings at Taichung Sun Moon Lake Teachers Hall.

Yuyu Yang quit his editorial job of *Harvest* magazine in 1961 and was employed as an adjunct professor in Art Department of National Taiwan Academy of Arts (is today known as National Taiwan University of Arts) in 1962 and brought up some active young sculptors in Taiwan. In 1963, he accompanied Cardinal Bing Yu to visit Pope Paul VI in Italy, in the name of the delegation of Beijing Fu Jen University alumni society. Thereafter he lived in Italy until 1966. During his stay in Italy, he produced a great number of marvelous street sketches and had a solo exhibition in Milan. The forty prints and ten sculptures showed the outstanding Modern style. He also took the opportunity to study bronze medal carving at Italy National Sculpture Academy. Upon returning to Taiwan, he held the exhibition of bronze medal carving at the National Museum of History. He became the pioneer to introduce bronze medal carving and won the Golden Hand Award of 4th Ten Outstanding Youth Persons in 1966.

In 1967, Yuyu Yang was a consultant at a Hualien marble factory and this working experience had a great impact on his creation of Lifescape Series hereafter. But the most important of all, he started the development of stone carving in Hualien and had a profound contribution on promoting the Eastern Taiwan culture business.

In 1969, Yuyu Yang was called by the government to create a sculpture under limited financial support and manpower in such a short time for exhibiting at the ROC Gallery at Osaka World Exposition. The outcome of a large environmental sculpture, "Advent of the Phoenix" was made of stainless steel and had a symbolic meaning of rising upward as Phoenix. This work also paved the way for his collaboration with the internationally renowned Chinese architect I.M. Pei, who designed the ROC Gallery.

The completion of "Advent of the Phoenix" marked a new stage of Yuyu Yang's creation. Many works come from the Chinese traditional thinking showed up one by one.

In 1977, Yuyu Yang was touched and inspired by the laser music performance in Kyoto, Japan, and began to advocate laser art. He founded the Chinese Laser Association with Chi-lu Chen and Kao-wen Mao and China Laser Association, and pushed the concept of blending technology and art. "Fire of Life" in 1980, was the first sculpture combined with technology and art and it drew many young artists to participate in it. In 1981, the 1st Exhibition & Congress of the International Society for Laser Artland at the Grand Hotel and Observatory was held in Taipei.

In 1986, Yuyu Yang's wife Ding Lee passed away and her daughter Han-Yen became a nun. Yuyu Yang's life was transformed to an inner stage. He revisited the Buddha stone caves at Loyang Long-men and Datung Yuen-gang in 1988, and two years later, he published a paper entitled "The Future of Environmental Art in China" in a Chinese Oriental Culture International Seminar at

Beijing University. The "Yuyu Yang on Ecological Aesthetics" was published in installments in China Times Express Column and Min Chung Daily. Meanwhile, he spent most time and energy on planning, designing, and constructing the landscapes and buildings of Wan-fo City in the USA.

In 1993, the Executive Yuan awarded him the National Culture Medal, recognizing his lifetime achievement and contribution to culture. Taiwan Museum of Fine Arts held the "The Retrospective of Yuyu Yang" to trace back the thoughts and footprints of his artistic career. In 1996, "Lifescape - The Sculpture of Yuyu Yang" was held in west Chelsea Harbor, London, under the invitation of the England's Royal Society of British Sculptors.

In August 1997, "Lifescape Sculpture of Yuyu Yang" was held at The Hakone Open-Air Museum in Japan. Two months later, the remarkable man who had dedicated his entire life to art, died of illness at Fayuan Temple in Hsinchu where his beloved daughter became a nun there.

Yuyu Yang's endeavor on art creation through his life had his apparent thinking points and great accomplishments. Many people may know more about his lifescapes, however, Yuyu Yang led an advancing and important way on prints, paintings, laser , photographs, art designs, comics, and lifescapes. Take his prints for example. As early as 1959, the time before Modern Print Association was set up by Ting-shi Chen, Xi-qi Li, Qin-song and Yuyu Yang himself, he showed his strong attempts and achievements on various creations and on trying materials, especially the invention of peculiar bagasse plywood in Taiwan. It had close relation to his working experience in *Harvest* Magazine. Therefore, he deserved the name of "The Pioneer of Chinese Modern Prints." The use of bagasse plywood not only enriched the appearance of prints but affected Ting-shi Chen's famous prints of "The Cosmos Series. "

During his studying in Italy, we could also see his efforts and outcome on harmonizing conflicts between the East and the West, tradition and modern times though some of his works blending eastern and western materials.

As for artistic development, experiment and creation, Yuyu Yang was a rare fashionable artist in Taiwan. The seventy preserved works so far were actually part of his live creations. In fact, Yuyu Yang's ideal creation on laser art was to combine music, views and formed a stereo space with a magnificent view and was worth pondering.

He was also one of the earliest people who contacted photographic art. In the beginning, Yuyu Yang and Jing-shan Lang took photos of naked women together. Till late 1970s, there were a large number of scenic photos of The City of Ten Thousand Buddhas in USA. Even in 1978, a photo exhibition of landscape of The City of Ten Thousand Buddhas in USA was held in National Taipei Fine Art Museum. As an almighty artist, these achievements proved Yuyu Yang's enthusiasm and devotion on trying artistic materials and his exquisite idiosyncrasy.

In 1994, Yuyu Yang was invited to design a Lifescape for the new library information plaza of National Chiao Tung University. This "Grace Bestowed on Human Beings", completed in 1996, was for NCTU's centennial anniversary.

In 1999, two years after his death, National Chiao Tung University formally set up Yuyu Yang Art Research Center, and cooperated with Yuyu Yang Foundation. Under special subsidies from the National Science Council, the project of building Yuyu Yang Digital Art Museum was going on in 2000. In 2001, Yuyu Yang Literature Archives and Yuyu Yang Electronic Databases were under construction. Besides, *Yuyu Yang Corpus* was also compiled at the same time.

At the beginning of 2002, as outside counselors, Prof. Bao-yao Lin, Juan-ying Yan and I were invited to the first advisory meeting for the publication. Works of each period were scattered in the campus. The initial idea of the corpus was to be presented in three massive volumes - the first and the second one contains photos of pieces, and the third one contains his journals, work notes, commentaries and critiques. The committee reached into consensus that the form of selection was against the spirit of a complete collection, and will be deficient in further studying and preserving; therefore, we were going to have a whole search and detailed arrangement for Yuyu Yang's works.

It is a tremendous work. Considering the heavy workload of Prof. Bao-yao Lin and Juan-ying Yan, Kuan-chian Shih, the President of Yuyu Yang Art Education Foundation and the third daughter of Yuyu Yang, recruited me to help out. With the permission of the NCTU, I was served as the chief editor of *Yuyu Yang Corpus*.

I have traveled northward from Tainan to Hsinchu at least once a month to participate in the task since February 2002. Though the research room is at the basement of the library building, adjacent to the art gallery, its spacious design brings in sufficient air and sunlight. The research room equipped with modern filing cabinets and computer facilities shows the great support of the NCTU. Several specialized researchers and part-time students were buried in massive amount of papers, and were filing all the data patiently. The work was originally scheduled to be done by the end of 2002, but numerous documents, sketches and photos were sequentially uncovered from the workroom in Taipei and the Yang's residence in Puli. Yang is like a dedicated historian, filing, recording, and saving all these data so carefully. He must be the only one to do so on both sides of the Straits. The historical archives he compiled are the most important firsthand records of Taiwanese Modern Art movement. And they will provide the researchers the references to have a clear understanding of the era as well as him.

The final version of the *Yuyu Yang Corpus* far surpassed the original imagination. It comprises two major parts - Artistic Creation and Archives. Volume I to V in Artistic Creation Section is a large album of paintings and drawings, including Volume I of embossment, lifescape embossment, sculptures, lifescapes, and trophies; Volume II of prints, drawings, laser works and photos; Volume III of sketches; Volume IV of graphic designs, illustrations and comics; Volume V of chronology charts, an essay about his creative experience and some selections of Yang's critiques, journals, newspaper clippings, weekly notes, correspondence, process of sculpture creation, projects, historical documents, and photos. In fact, the content of Volume V is exactly a selective collection of Archives Section, which consists of 20 detailed Books altogether, including 3 Books of literature, 5 Books of research, 1 Book of early journals, 2 Books of working notes, 6 Books of correspondence, 2 Books of historical pictures, and 1 Book of biographic chronology. Volumes VI to X in Artistic Creation Section are about lifescape projects. Throughout his life, Yuyu Yang advocated the concept of "lifescape" and many of his projects are the extension and augmentation of such concept. Some of these projects were completed, others not, but they are all fruitfulness of his creativity. The preserved documents can be the reference for further study. Maybe some of these projects may come true some day.

Editing such extensive corpus like the *Yuyu Yang Corpus* is unprecedented in Taiwan art history field. The challenge lies not merely in the structure and classification, but the greatest difficulty in art editing and arrangement. It would be a great challenge to set these diverse graphics and data into systematic order and display them in an elegant way. Prof. Cheng-ming Lee, my good friend of the Fine Art Department of Taiwan National Normal University, and his pupil Mr. Jun-che Chang, winner of the 1997 International Youth Design Contest of Taiwan region, devoted themselves to the project in spite of the meager remuneration. To whom I would like to show my grateful appreciation. Of course, Mr. Cheng-kuang He of The Artist Publishing House consented to publish our works, and his strong team, especially the toil of Ms. Mei-li Ke, here we show our great gratitude for you.

It was a wonderful experience to participate in editing the Corpus for Yuyu Yang Art Research Center. I spent several beautiful nights at the guesthouse next to the library. From cold winter to early spring, the wind of Hsin-chu and the undulating campus of National Chiao Tung University left me an unforgettable memory. Many times I had the pleasure of getting together or dining with the school president Chun-yen Chang and his wife and other related administrative officers. The school's long history and its vitality made a deep impression on me. Under the humane principles, the president Chun-yen Chang and related administrative officers support to the Yuyu Yang Corpus. This corpus has left the precious treasure of art and culture history in Taiwan. It is like laying a big stone in the art forest. The "Tower of Dreams" will stand erect on this huge stone.

I am so proud to take part in this historical undertaking, and I appreciated the staff in the research center, including Ling-ju, Shan-shan, Wei-ling, and those who left the office, Yi-hsun, Mei-jing, Lu-hai, Ying-long and Xiu-hui. Their dedication to the work impressed me a lot. What Master Kuan-chian Shih, Fong-sheng, and Wei-ni have done for their father belongs to the people and should be highly appreciated.

Chief Editor of the Yuyu Yung Corpus
Chong-ray Hsiao

Chong-ray Hsiao

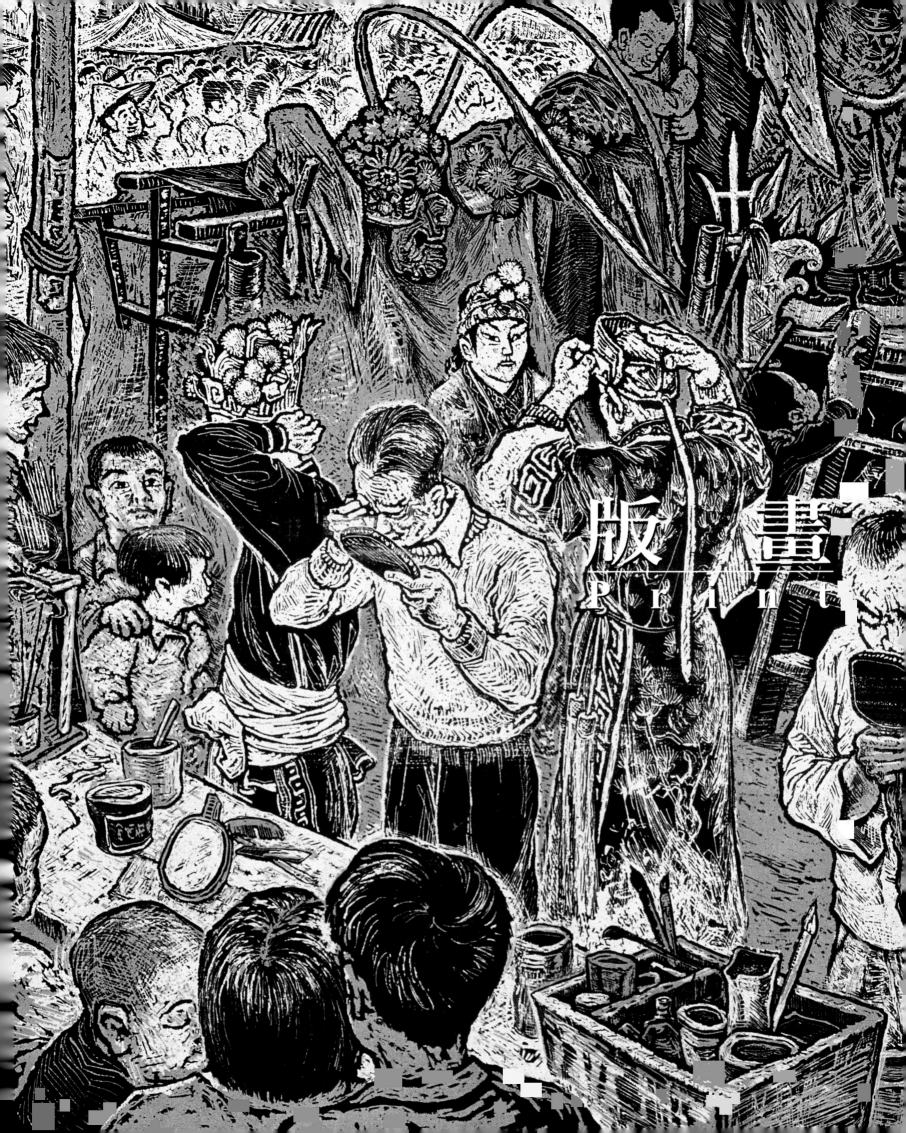

版畫
Print

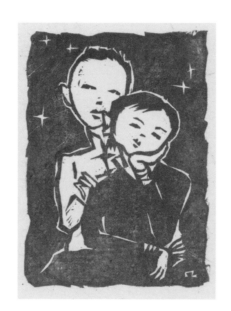

相依　SIMPLICITY　1946　木刻版畫　7.1×4.9cm（原寸）

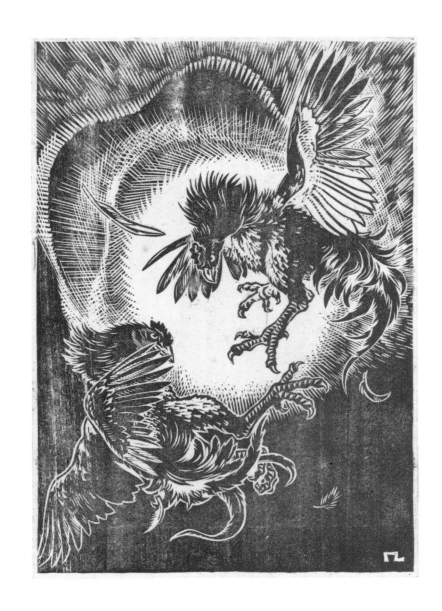

鬥雞　COCK FIGHTING　1946　木刻版畫　14.6×10cm（原寸）

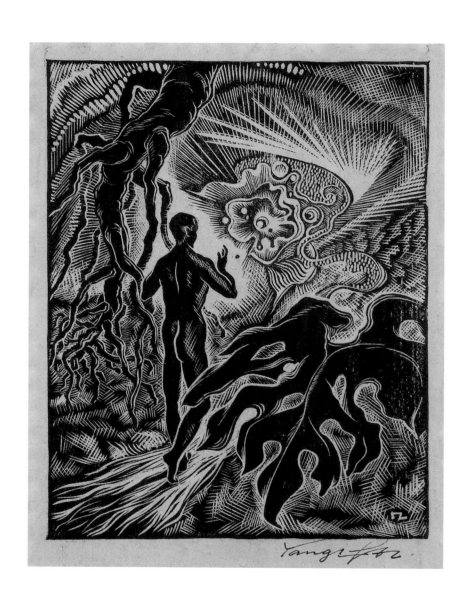

探索　THE　QUEST　1946　木刻版畫　13.1×10.2cm（原寸）

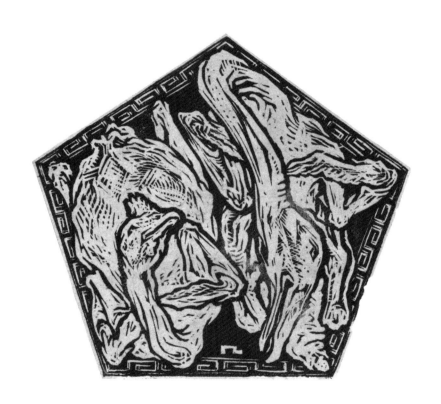

邂逅　MEET BY CHANCE　1946　木刻版畫　9.6×10cm（原寸）

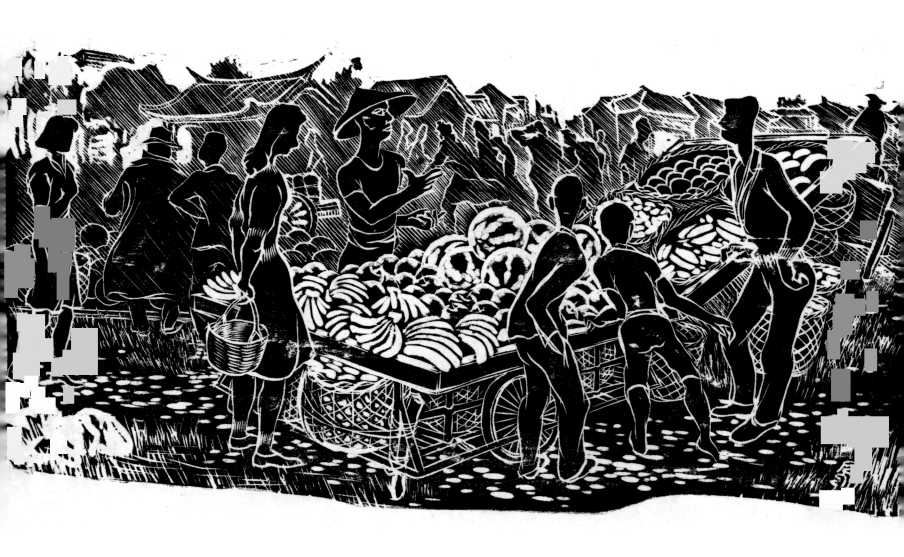

青果市場　THE　MARKET　1946　木刻版畫　13×24cm（原寸）

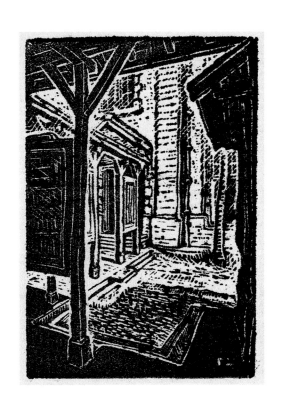

校園走廊　SCHOOL CORRIDOR　1947　木刻版畫　9.4×6.2cm（原寸）

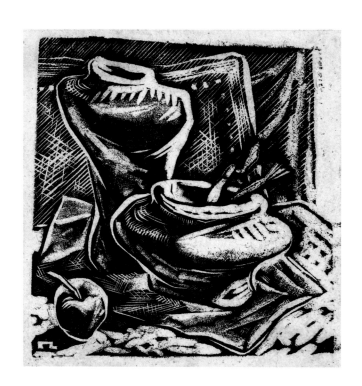

靜物　STILL　LIFE　1947　木刻版畫　8.7×8cm（原寸）

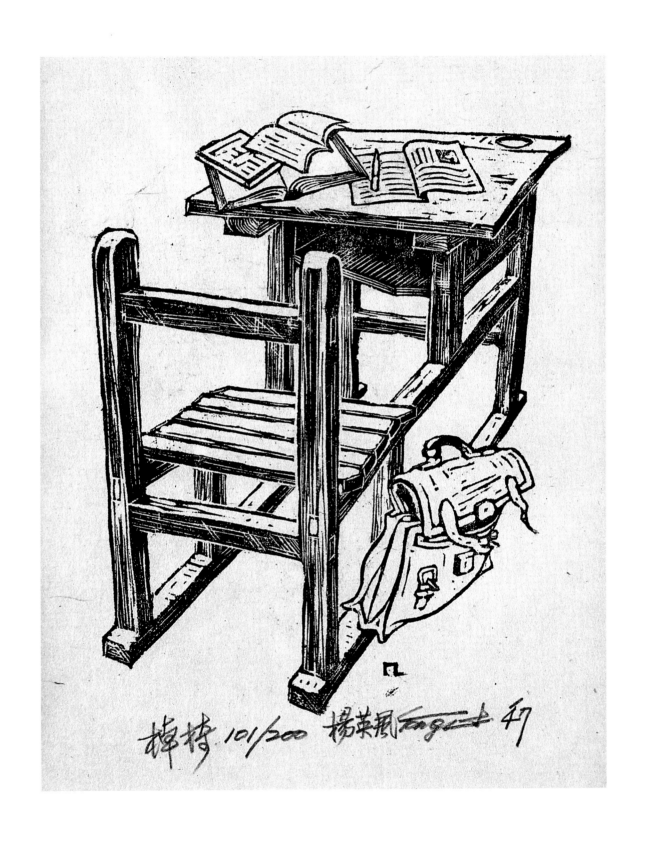

桌椅　TABLE　1947　木刻版畫　16.5×14cm（原寸）

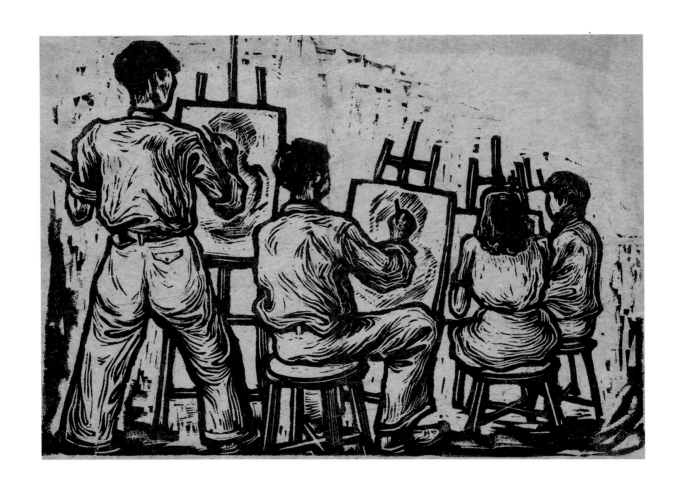

繪畫教室　PAINTING CLASSROOM　1947　木刻版畫　11.6×16cm（原寸）

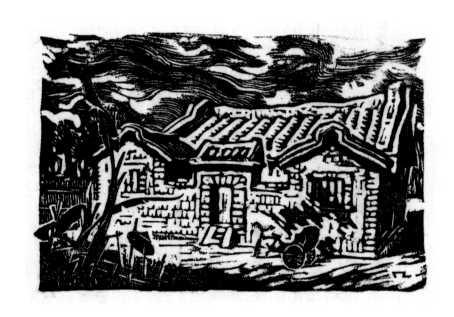

台灣農家　TAIWAN FARM HOUSE　1947　木刻版畫　7.5×11cm(原寸)

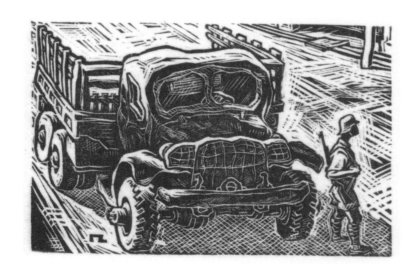

國軍　SOLDIER　1947　木刻版畫　6.3×9.5cm（原寸）

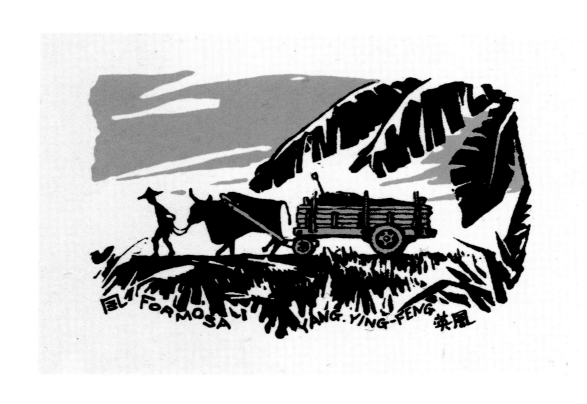

歸　RETURN　1948　木刻版畫　7.5×12cm（原寸）

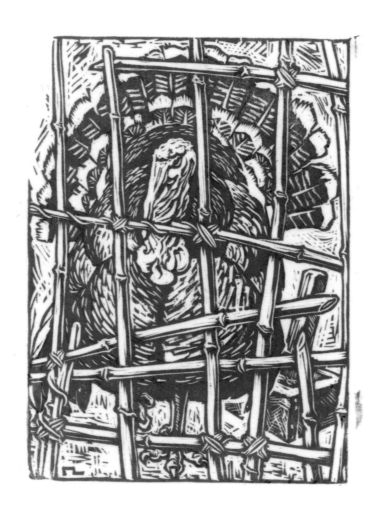

爭脫牢籠　STRUGGLE　1948　木刻版畫　12.1×8.3cm(原寸)

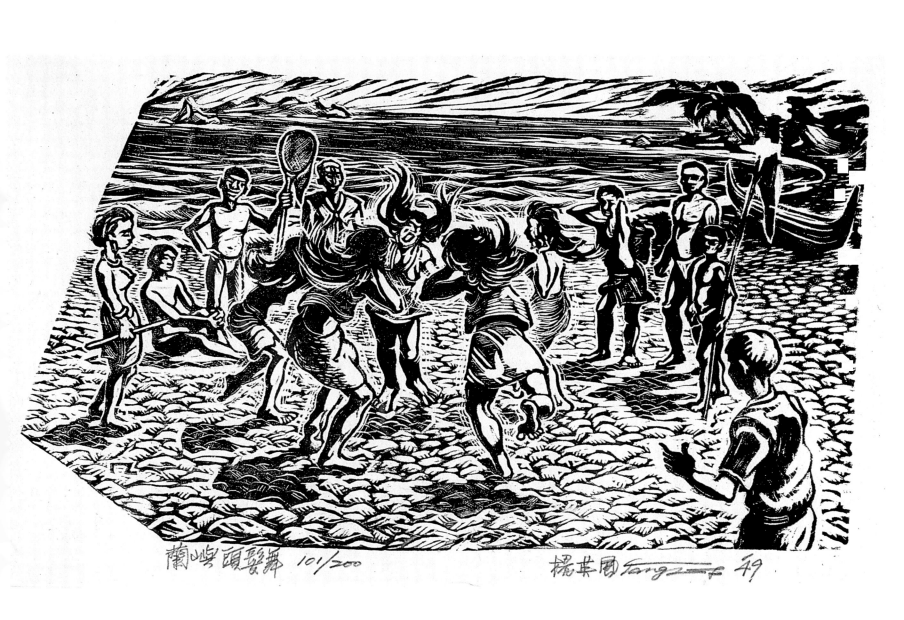

蘭嶼頭髮舞　HAIR DANCE OF ORCHID ISLAND　1949　木刻版畫　15.5×25cm

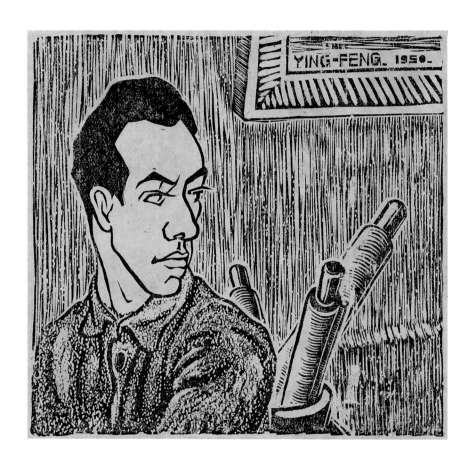

自刻像　SELF-PORTRAIT　1950　木刻版畫　11×11cm（原寸）

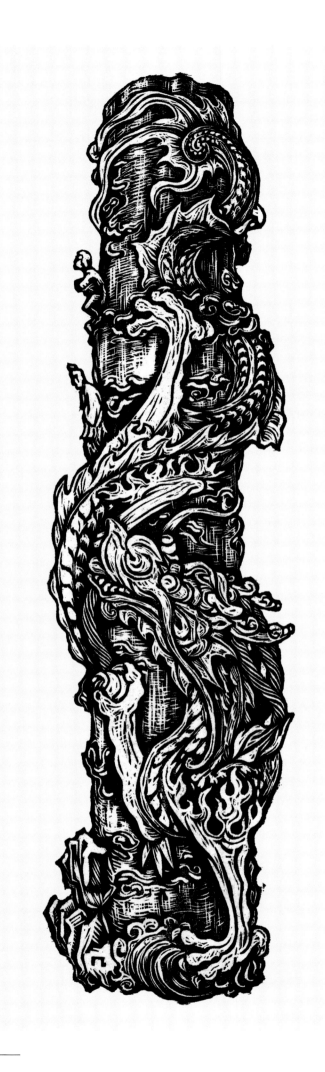

石龍柱　DRAGON PILLAR　1950　木刻版畫　30×8cm

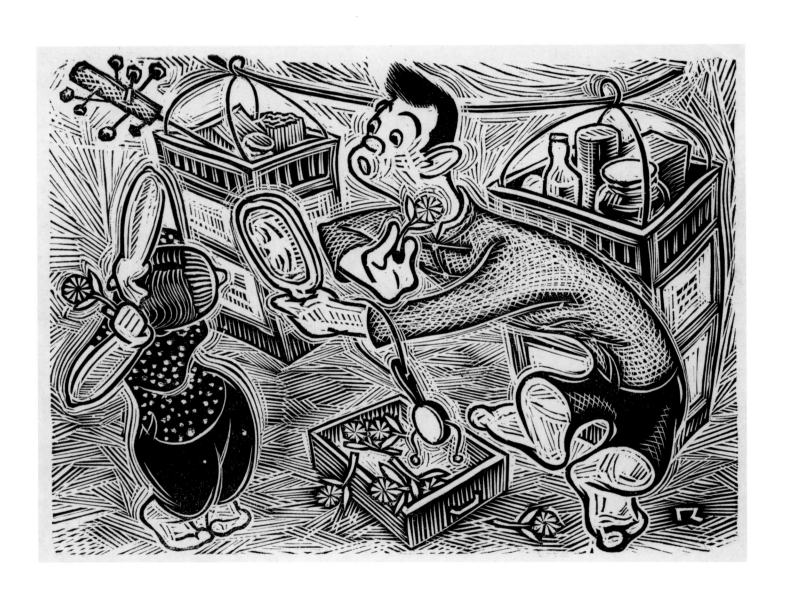

賣雜細　PEDDLER　1951　木刻版畫　13.5×18.3cm

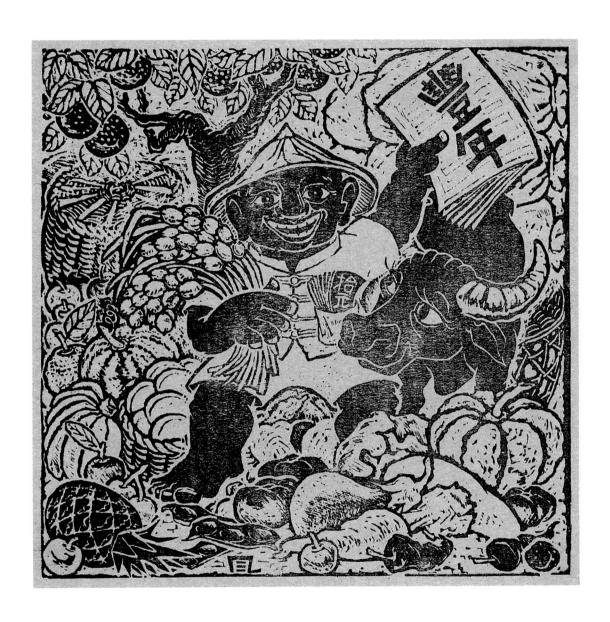

豐年　HARVEST　1951　木刻版畫　14×14.5cm（原寸）

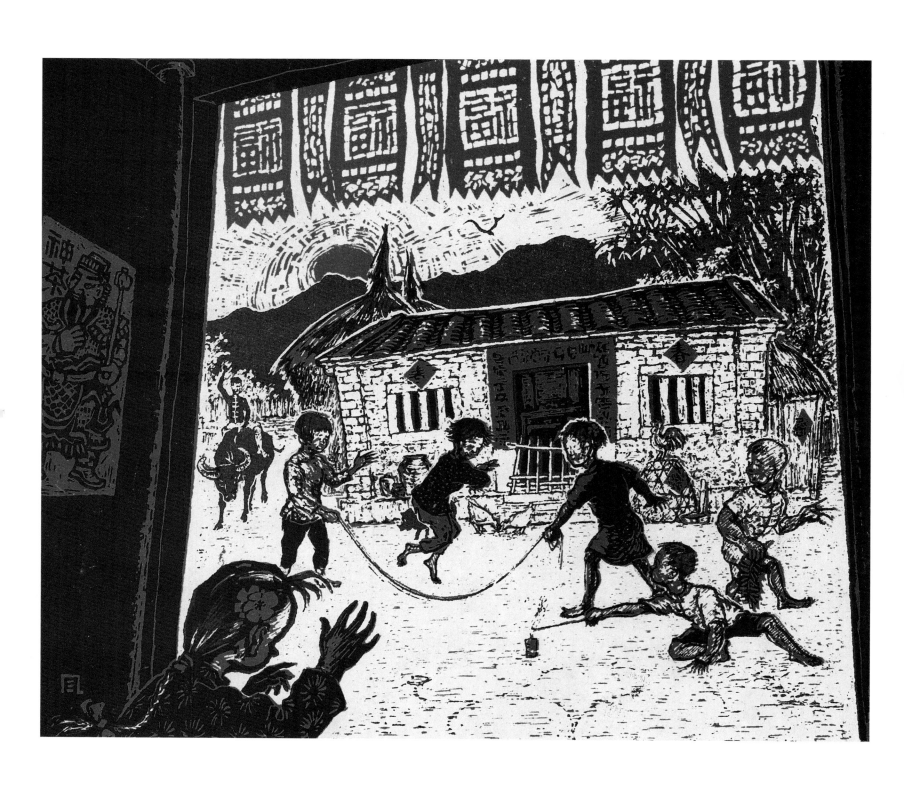

嬉春　OUTDOOR PLEASURE IN SPRING TIME　1951　木刻版畫　20.8×24cm

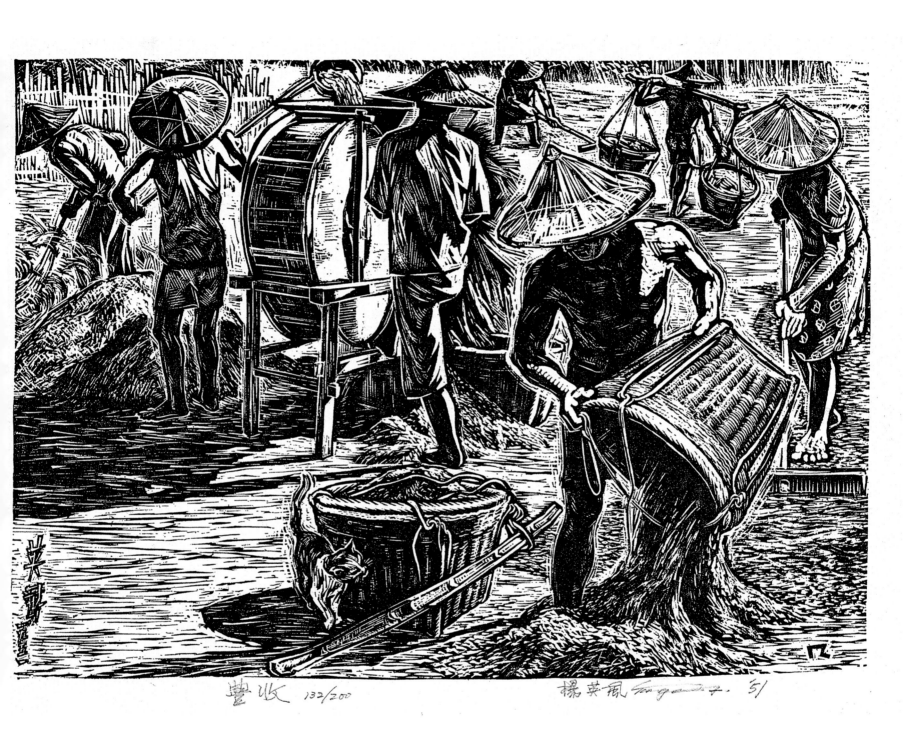

豐收　HARVEST ABUNDANT　1951　木刻版畫　32×41cm

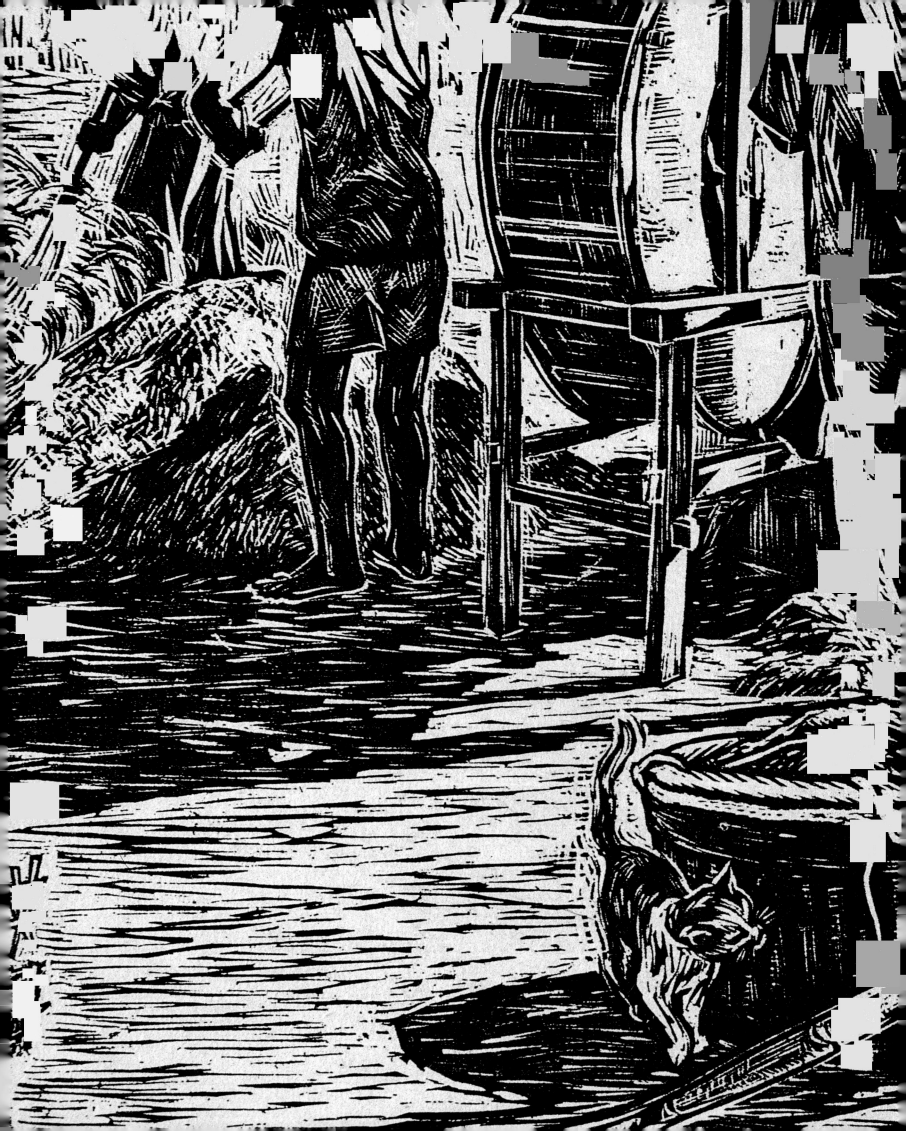

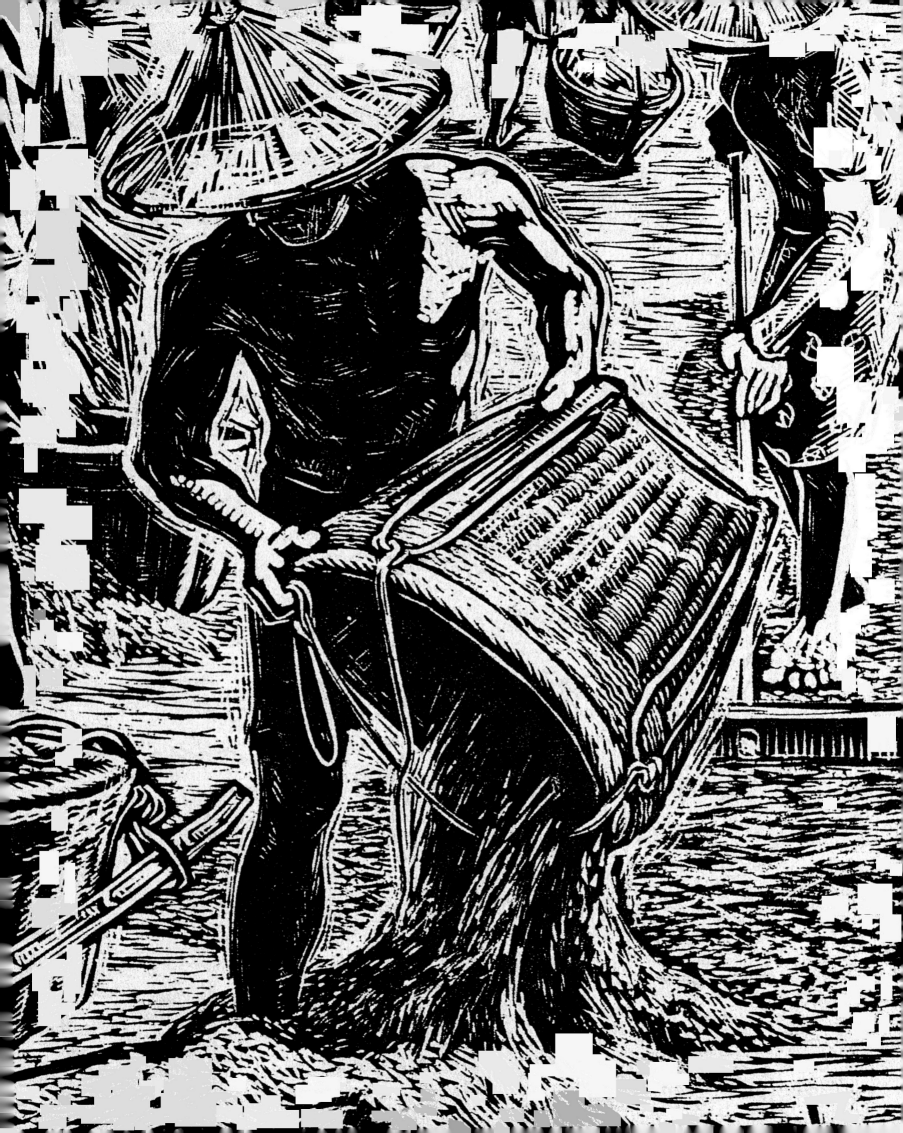

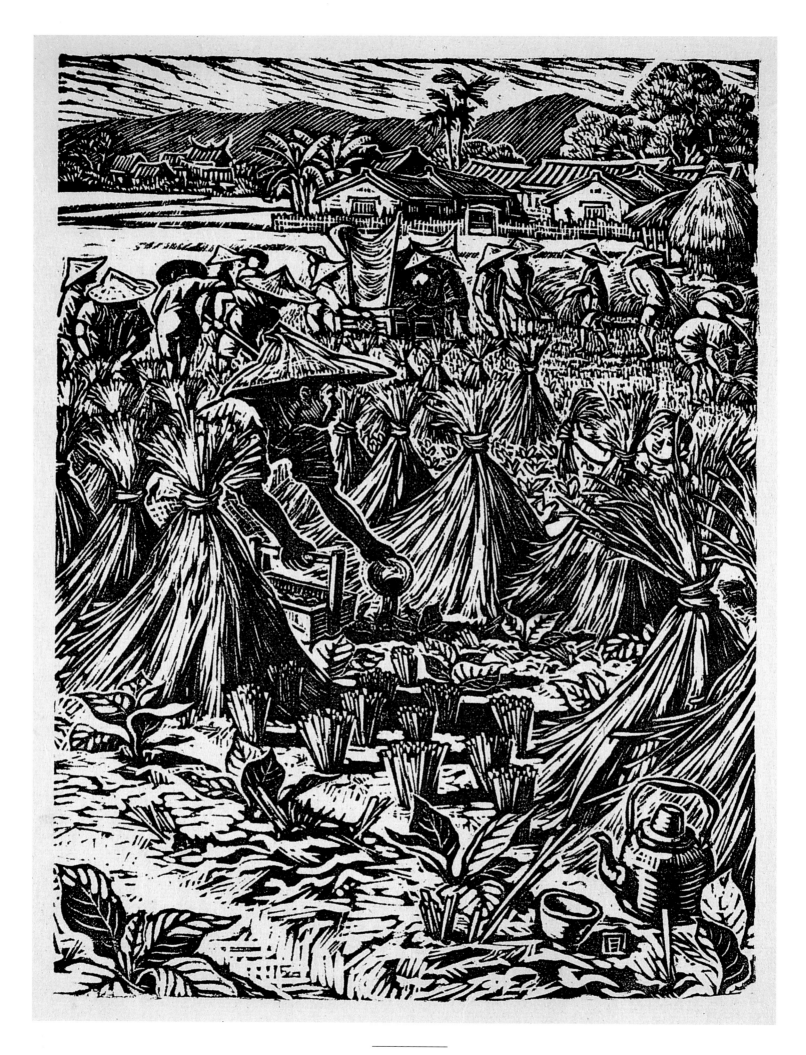

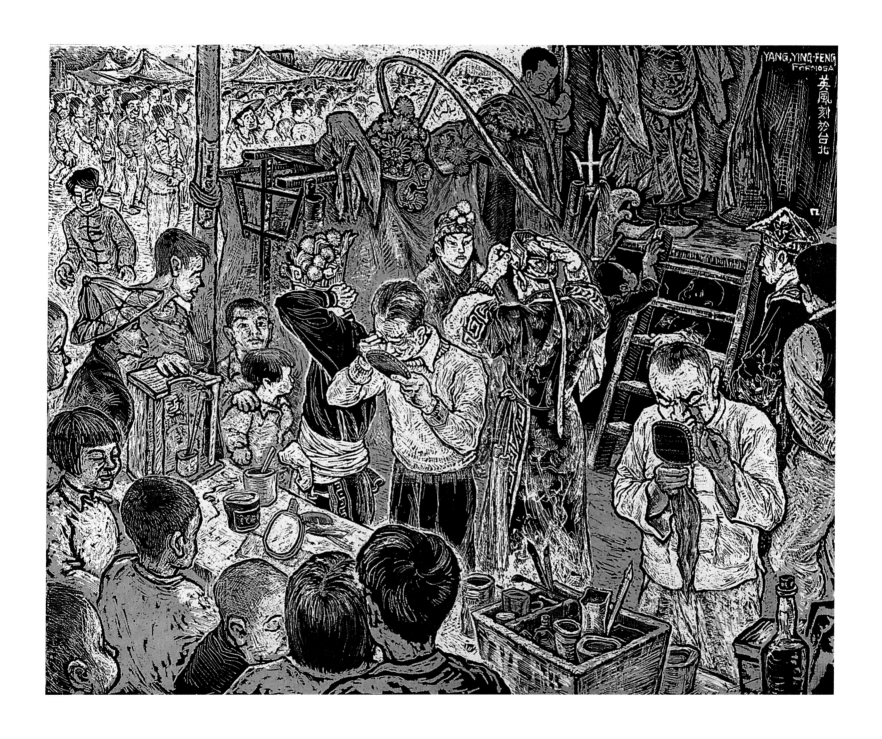

間作　BETWEEN CROPS　1952　木刻版畫　29×21cm（左頁圖）

後台　BACKSTAGE　1952　木刻版畫　48×56cm

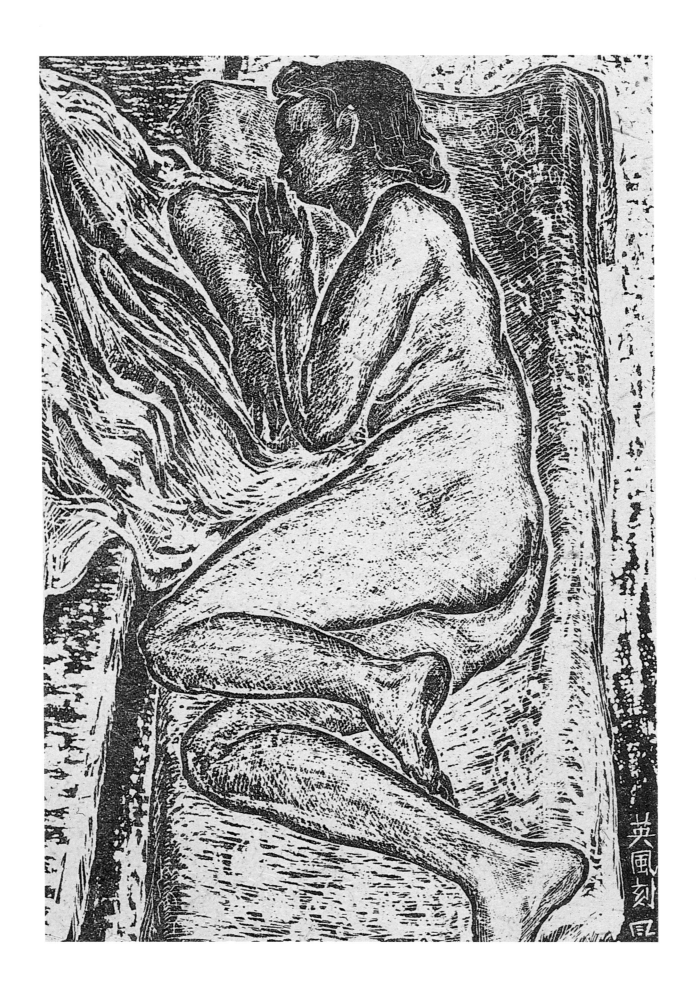

假寢　SIESTA　1952　木刻版畫　42.5×30cm

神農氏　SHEN-NONG　1952　木刻版畫　49×37.5cm(右頁圖)

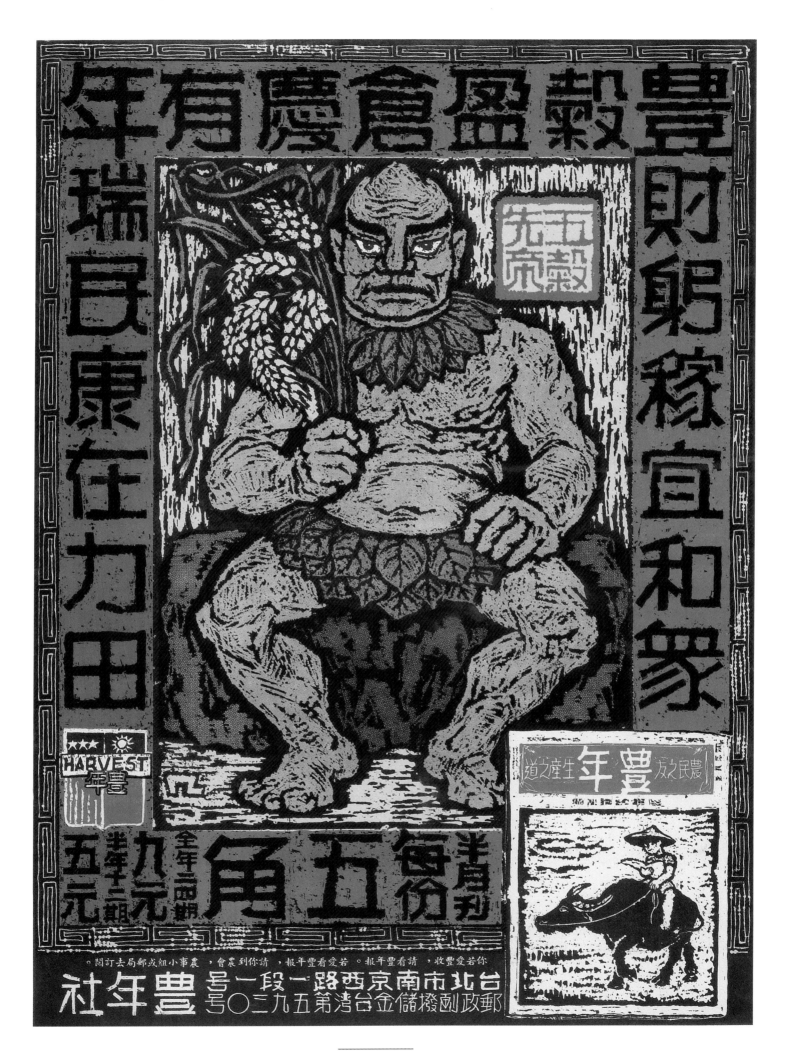

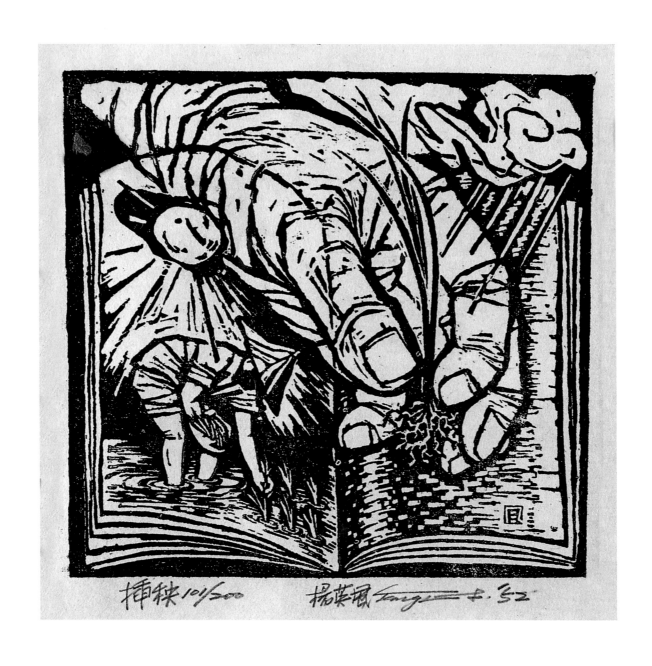

插秧　PLANTING　1952　木刻版畫　14×14cm（原寸）

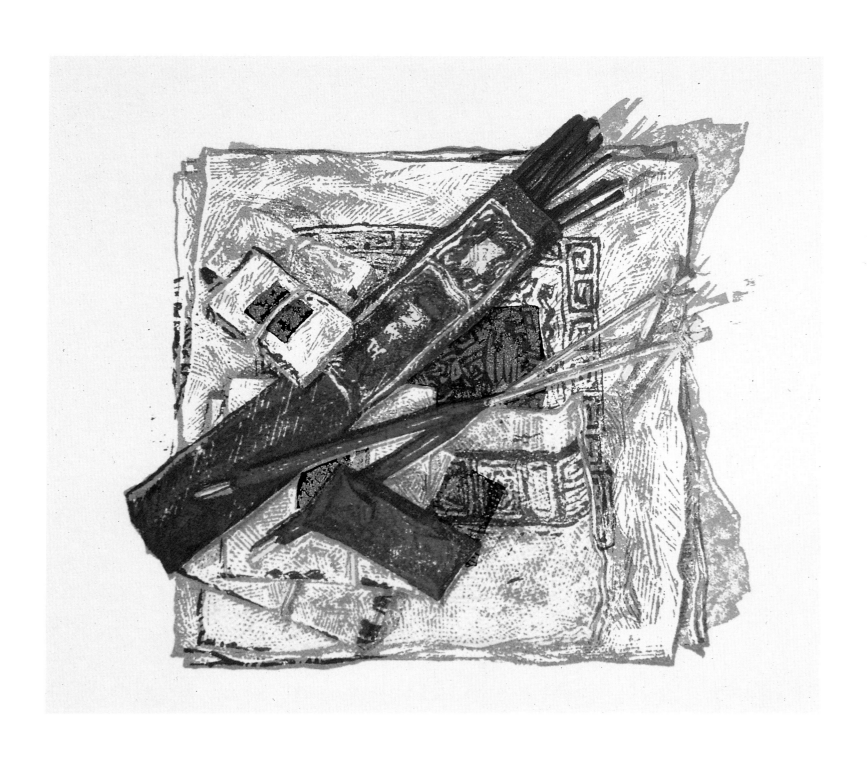

糕仔金紙　REMEMBERANCE　1953　木刻版畫　15.5×17cm（原寸）

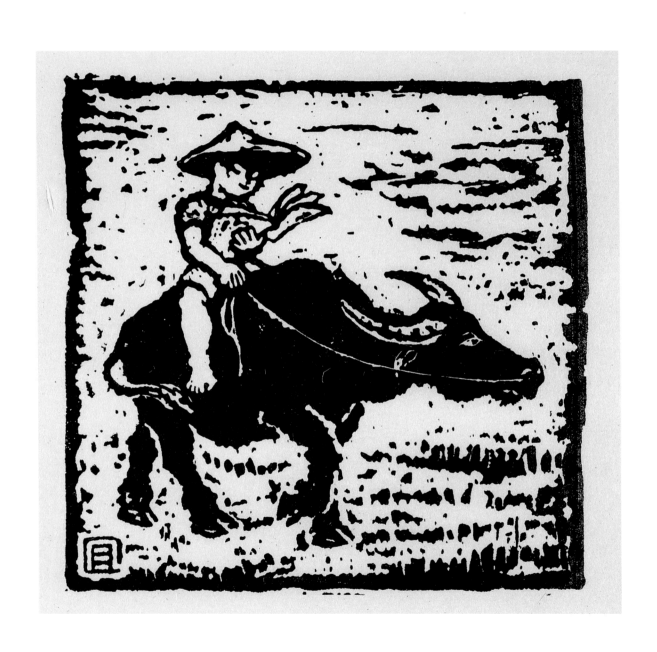

悠遊　ENJOY　THE　RIDE　1953　木刻版畫　14.5×14cm（原寸）

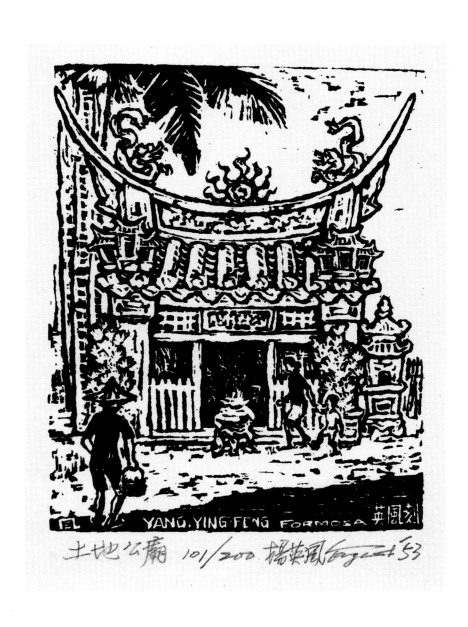

土地公廟　THE TEMPLE OF GOD TUTALA　1953　木刻版畫　13×10cm（原寸）

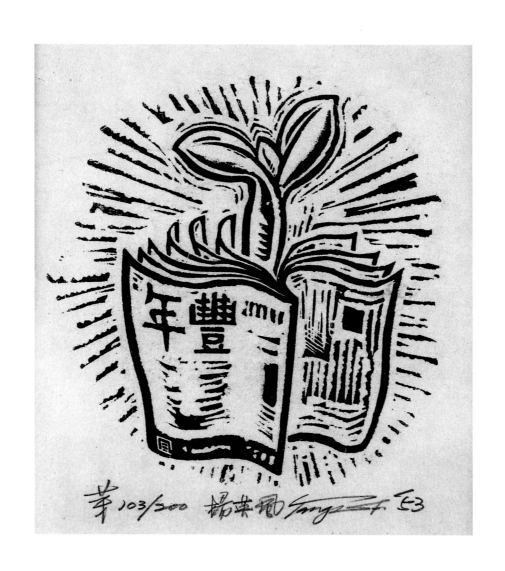

芽　BUD　1953　木刻版畫　11×10cm（原寸）

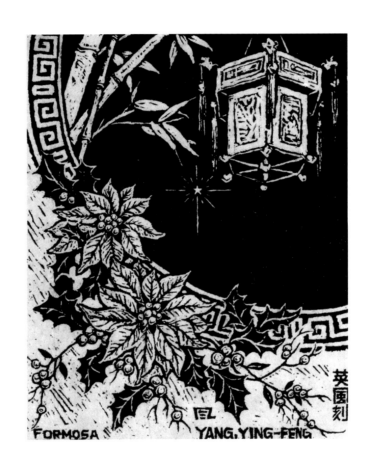

聖誕夜　THE CHRISTMAS EVE　1953　木刻版畫　11×8.5cm（原寸）

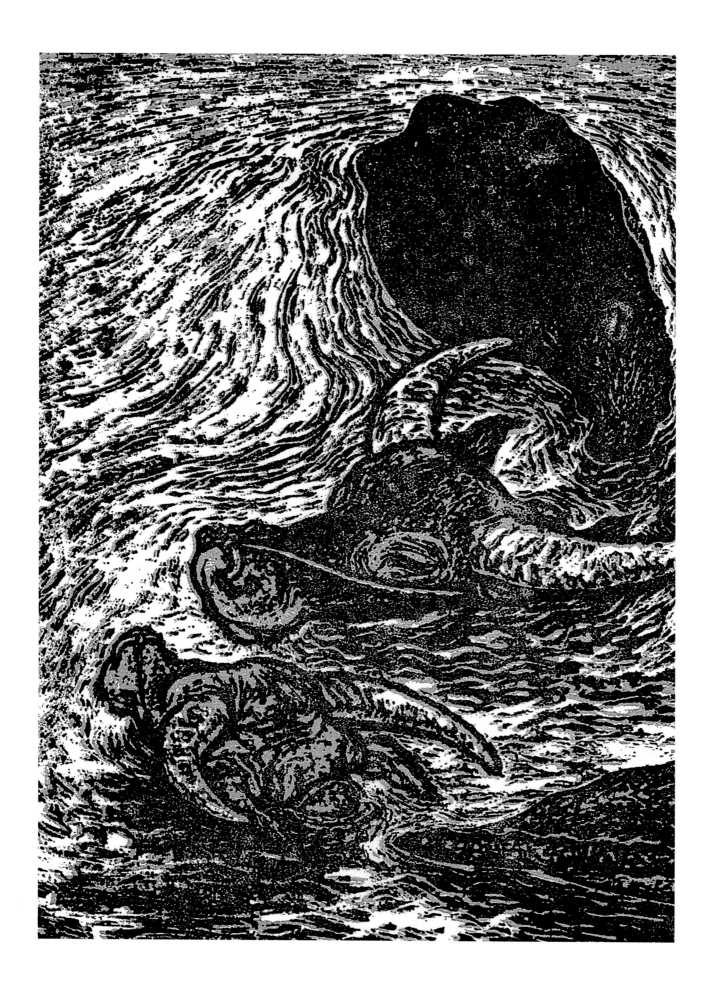

水牛　BUFFALO　1953　木刻版畫　24.3×17cm（原寸）

舞龍　DRAGON DANCE　1955　玻璃版畫　26.5×19cm（右頁圖）

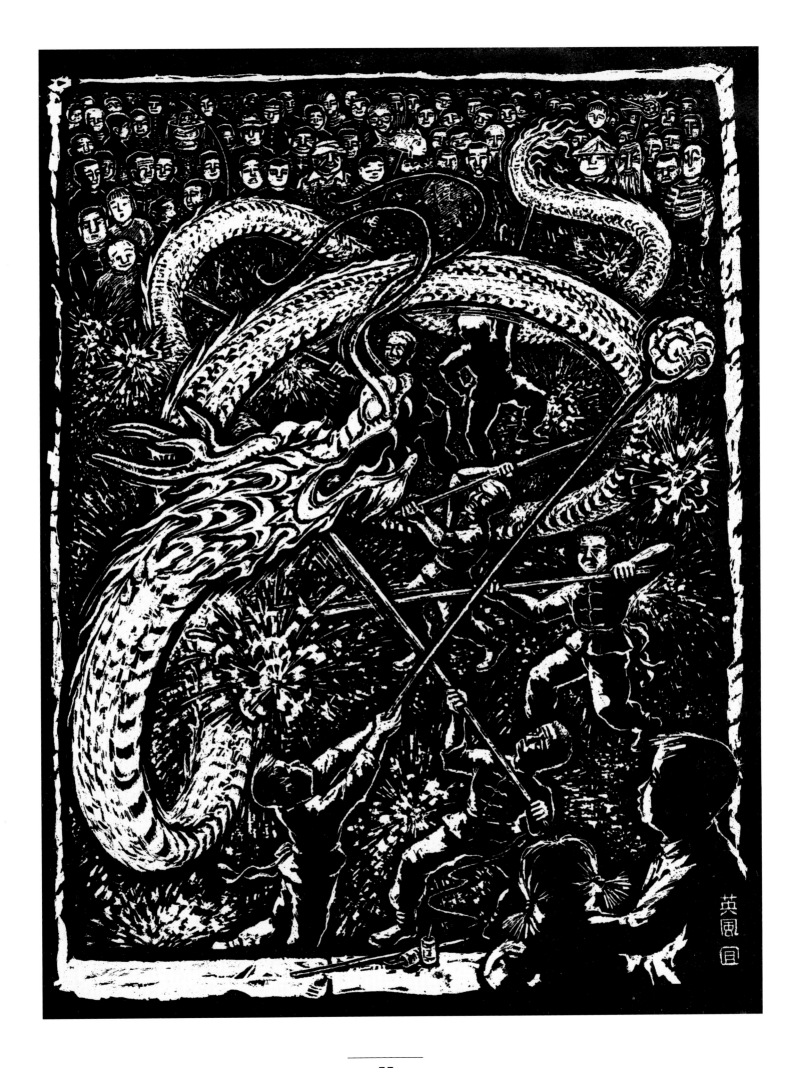

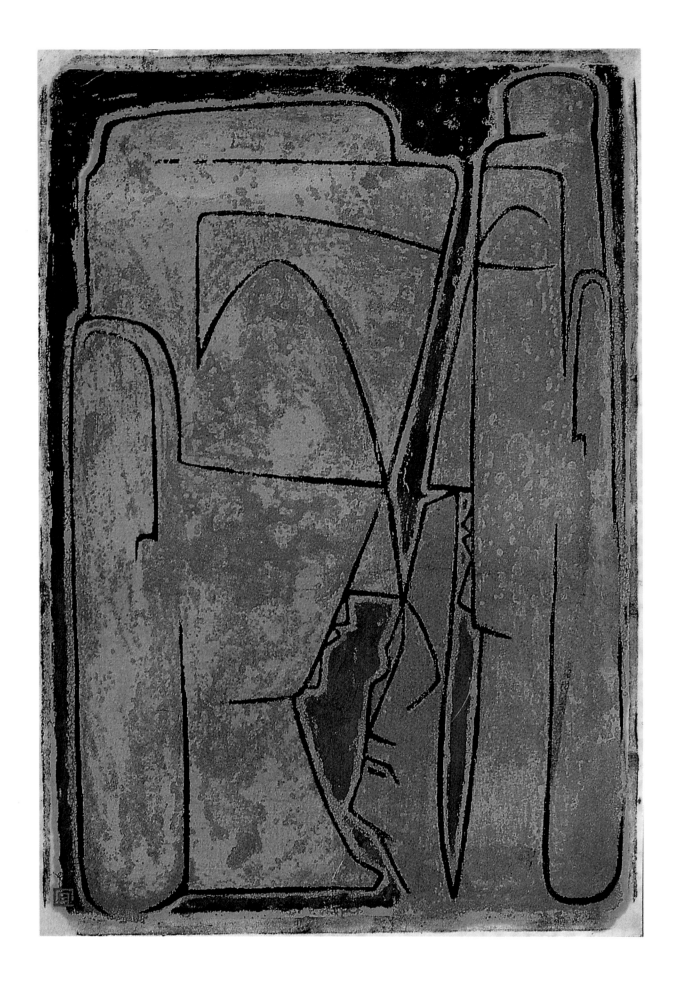

慈悲（一）　MERCY（1）　1955　網板版畫　37×25cm

慈悲（二）　MERCY（2）　1995　電腦合成版畫　88.5×69cm（右頁圖）

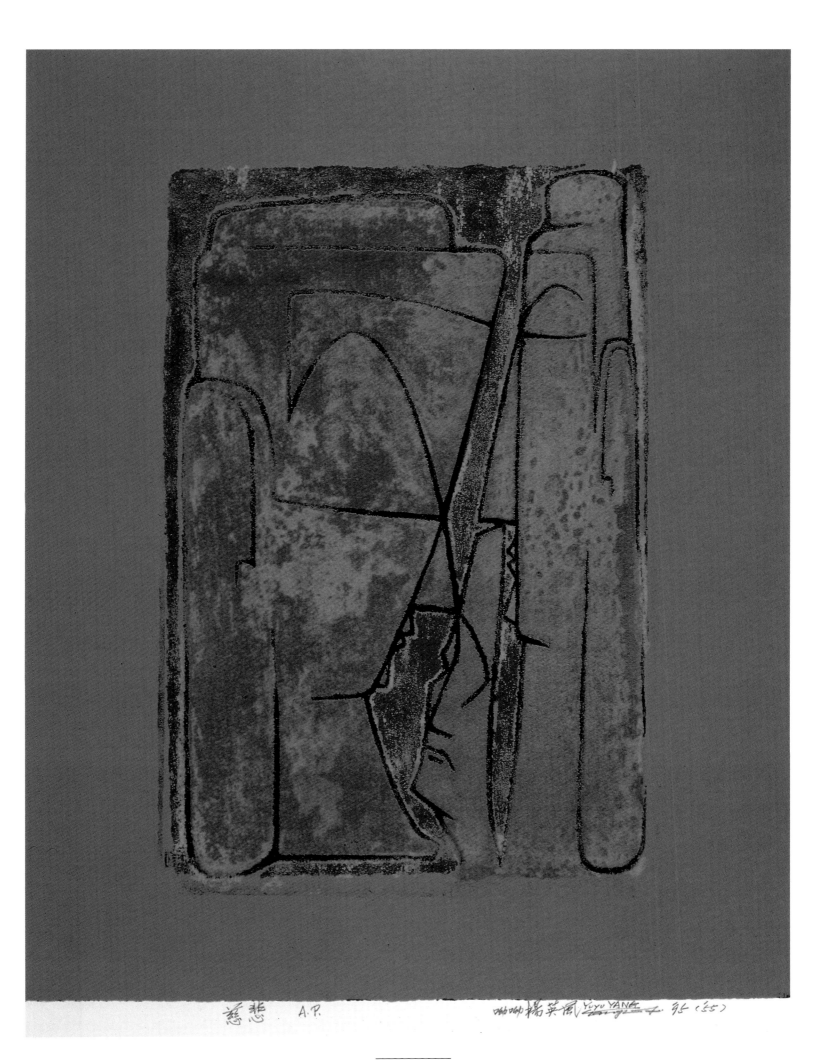

慈悲　A.P.　　　　　　　　呦呦楊英風 YUYU YANG 弋 〈55〉

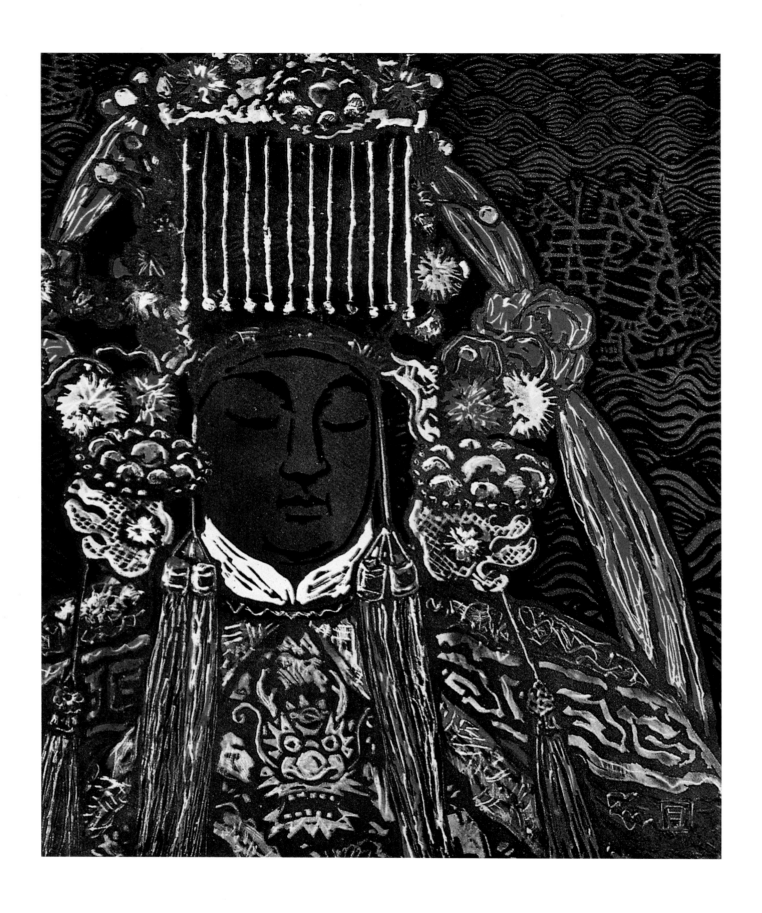

媽祖　MASU　1956　玻璃版畫　22×18cm（原寸）

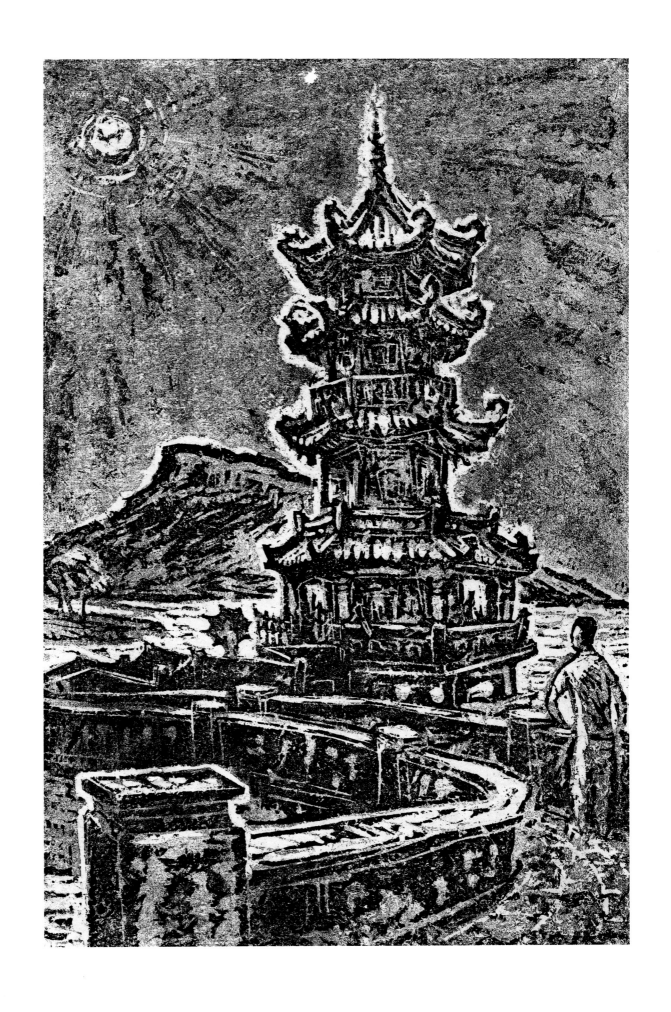

春秋閣　CHUN-QIU PAVILION　1957　木刻版畫　33×21cm

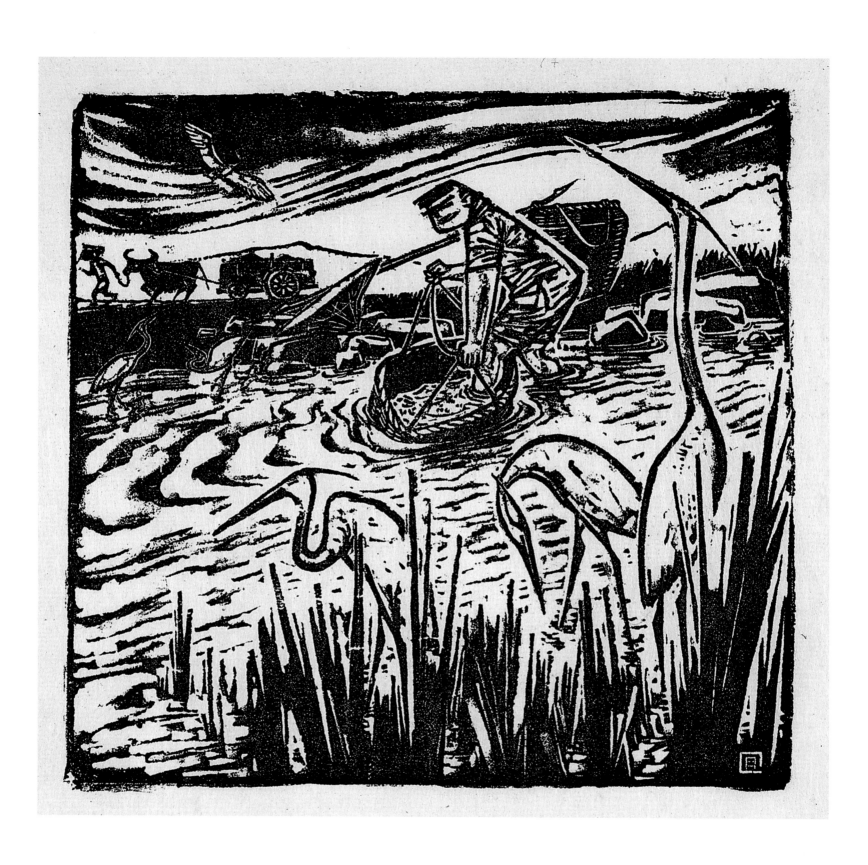

浸種　WATER TREATMENT　1957　木刻版畫　21×20cm

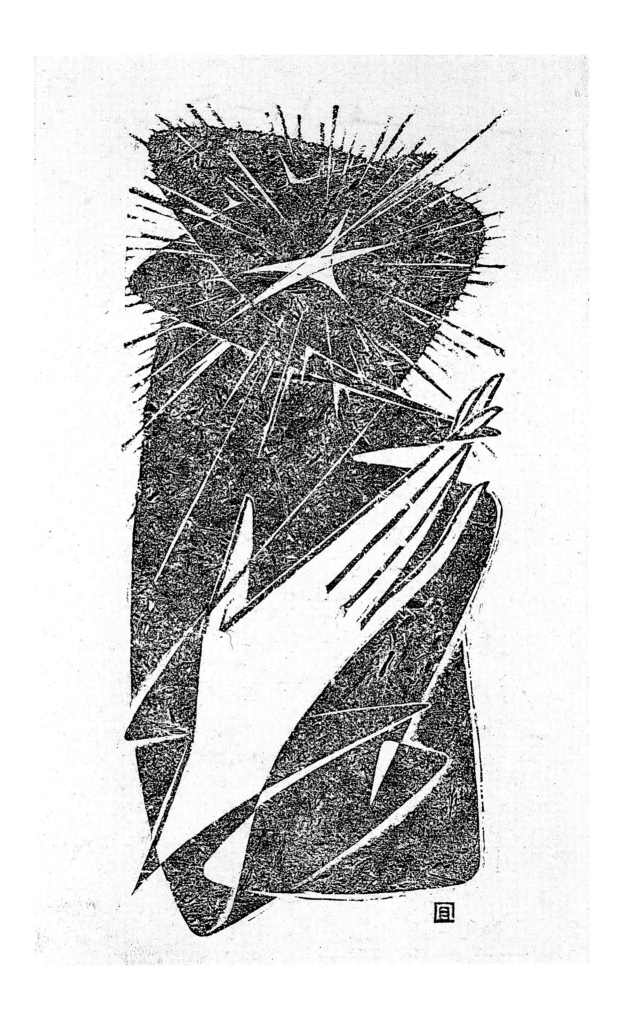

藍星　BLUE STAR　1957　木刻版畫　37×18cm

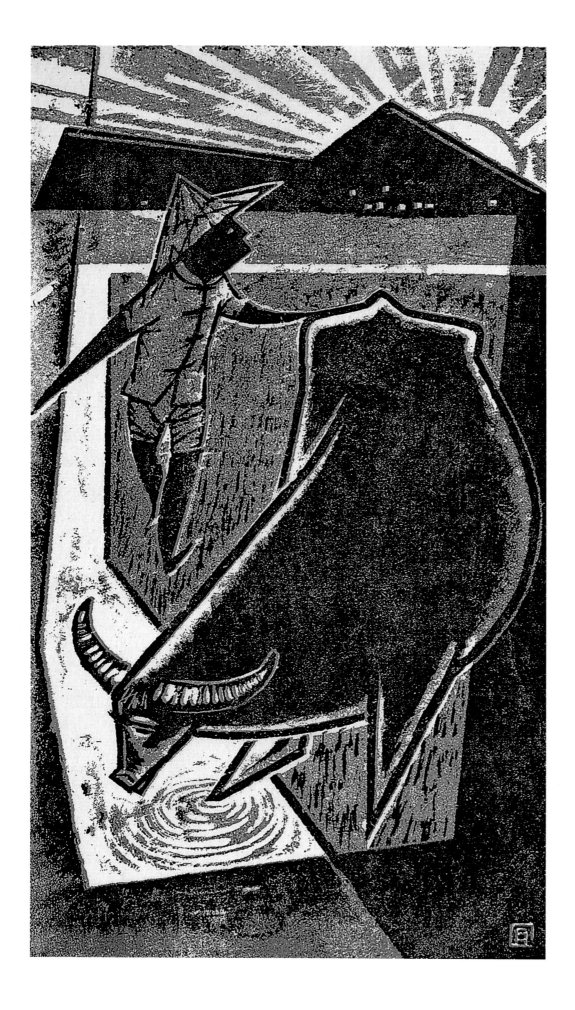

日出而作　DAY'S LABOR　1957　木刻版畫　32×17cm

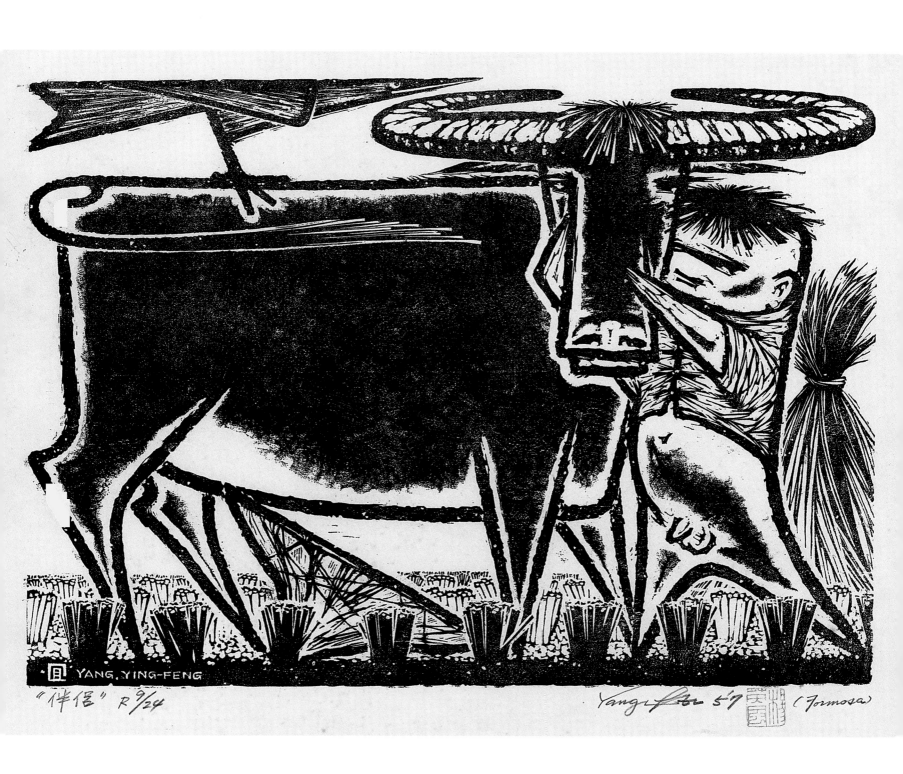

伴侶　COMPANIONSHIP　1957　木刻版畫　29.5×40cm

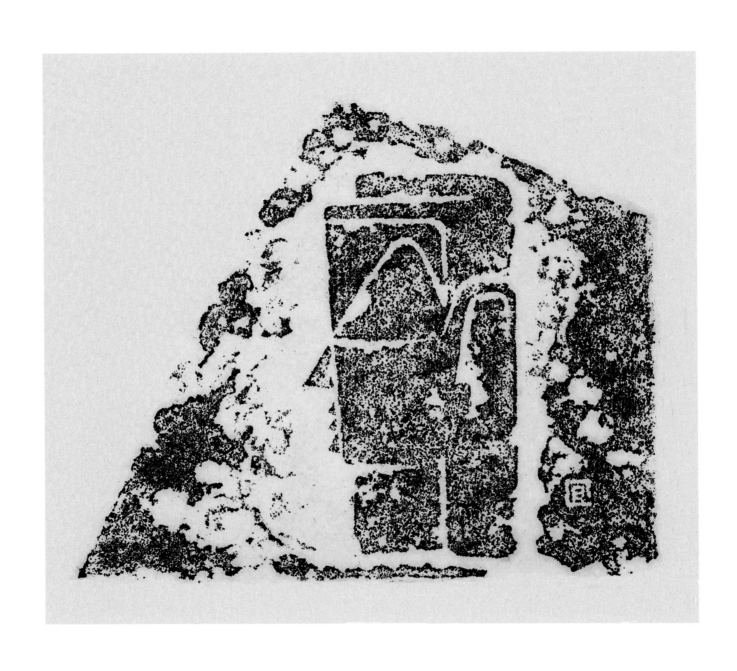

英風造佛供養　WORSHIPPING BUDDHA　1958　石膏版畫　13.2×15.2cm（原寸）

燈　LIGHT　1958　木刻版畫　35×23cm（右頁圖）

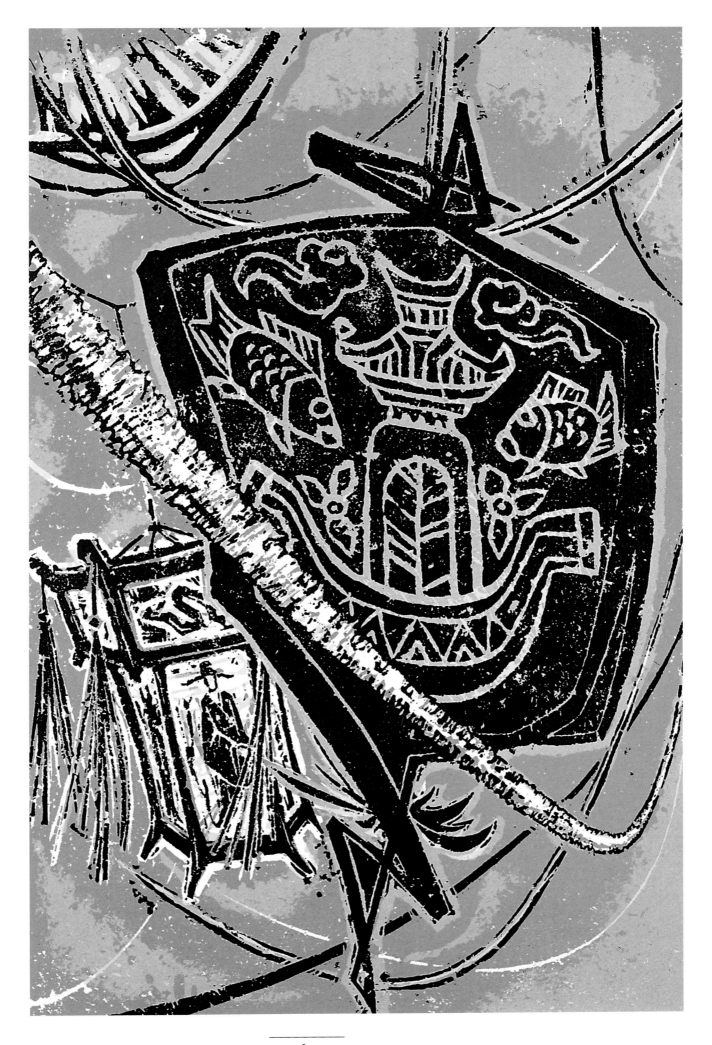

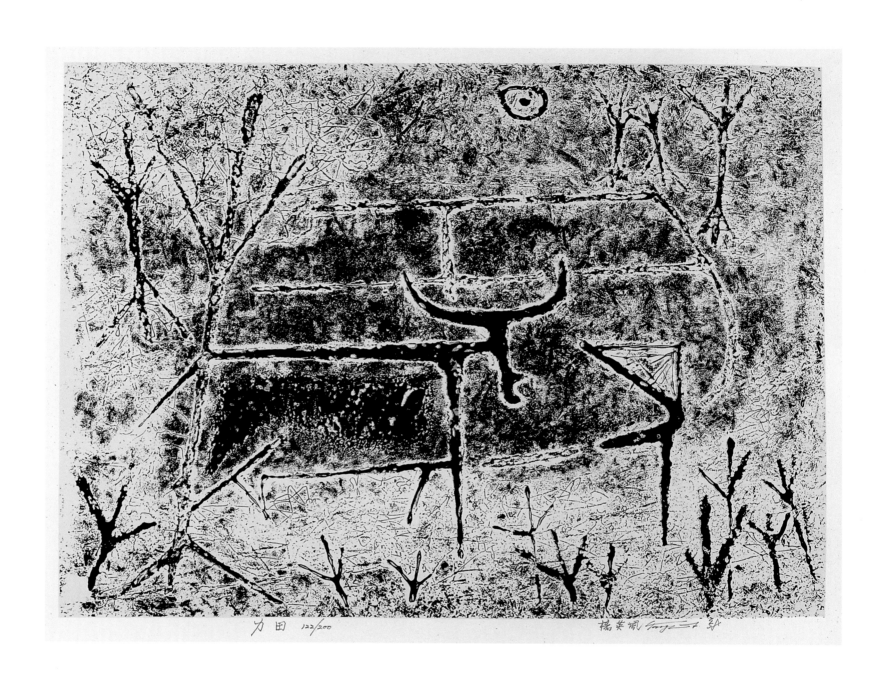

力田（一）　THE　POWER　OF　SOW（1）　1958　蔗板版畫　45.5×60cm

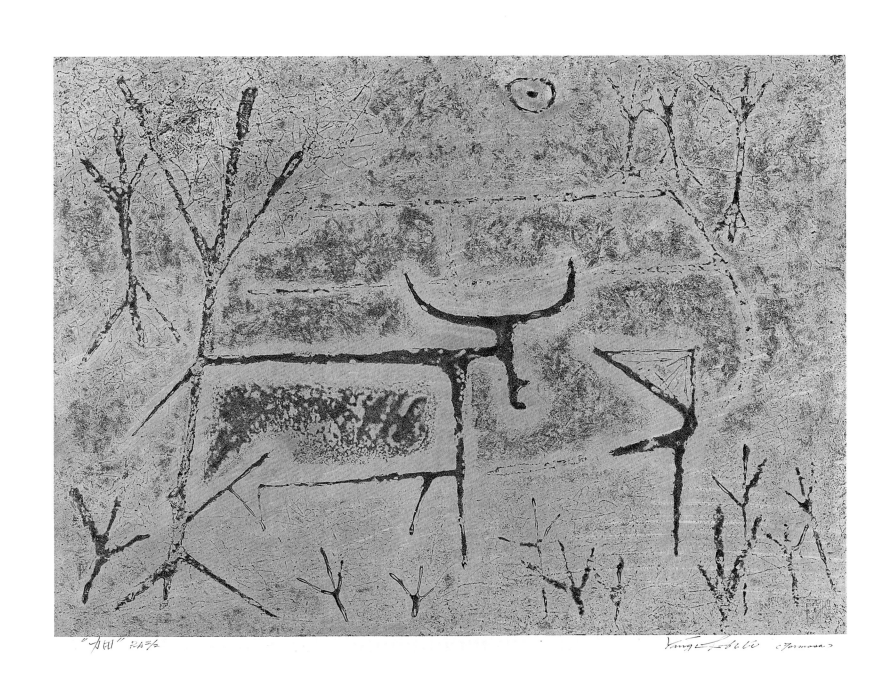

力田（二）　THE　POWER　OF　SOW（2）　1960　蔗板版畫　45.5×60cm

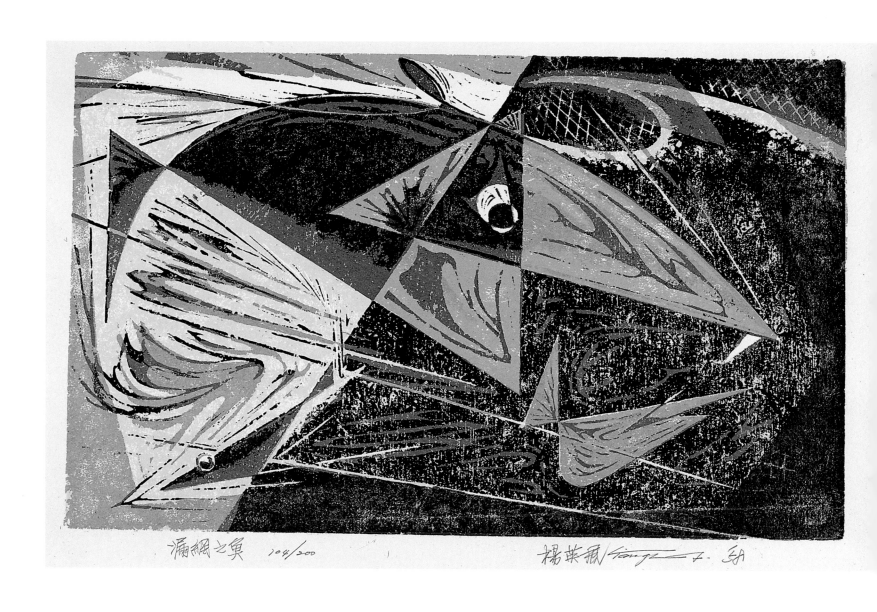

漏網之魚（一）　ESCAPED FISH（1）　1958　複合版畫　21×33cm

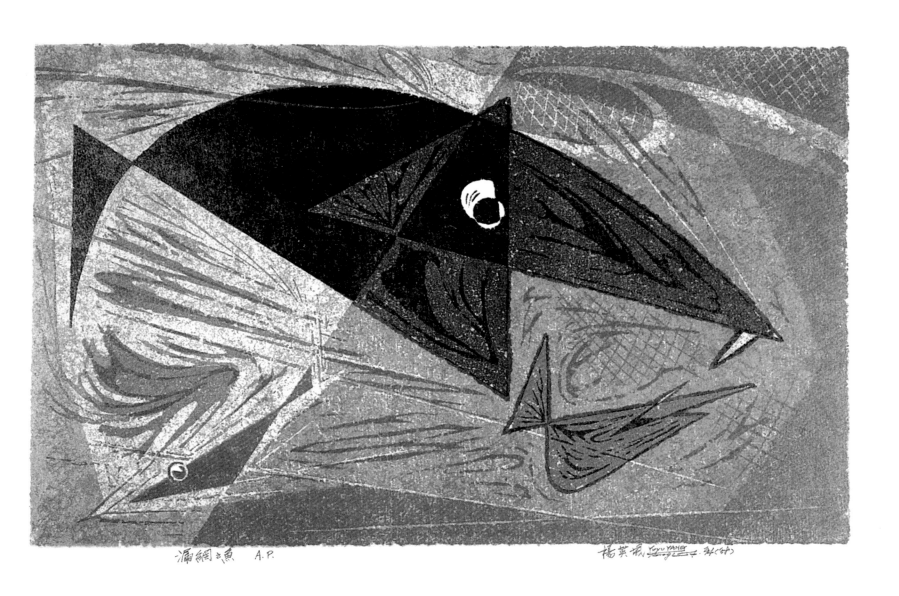

漏網之魚　A.P.

漏網之魚（二）　ESCAPED FISH（2）　1994　電腦合成版畫　尺寸未詳

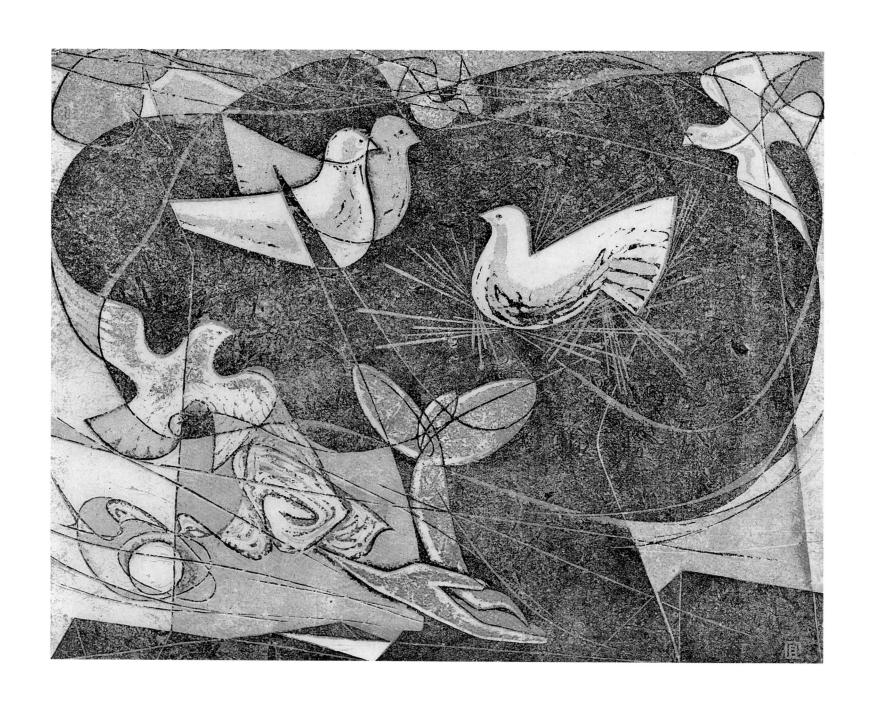

成長（一）　GROWTH（1）　1958　木刻版畫　35.5×43.5cm

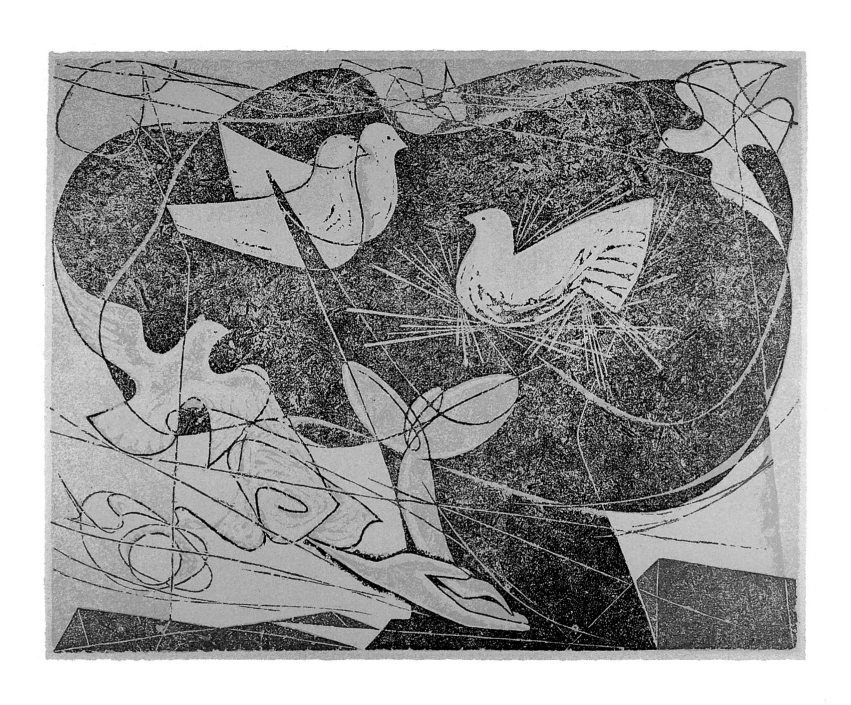

成長（二）　GROWTH（2）　1995　電腦合成版畫　55×66cm

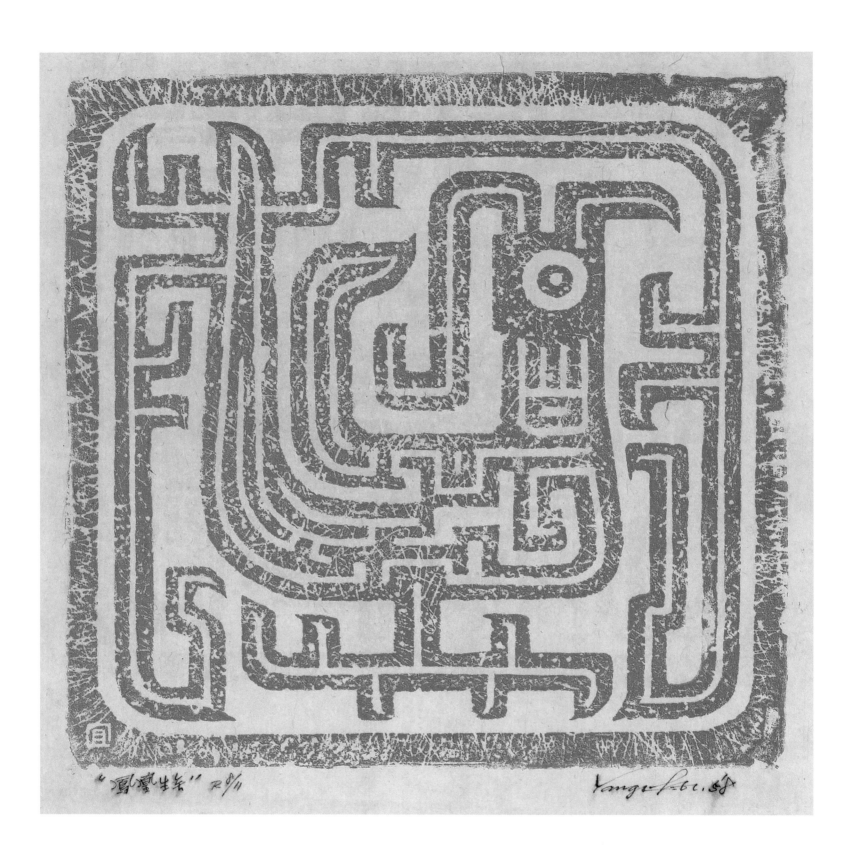

鳳凰生矣　PHOENIX　1958　石膏版畫　34.5×34.5cm

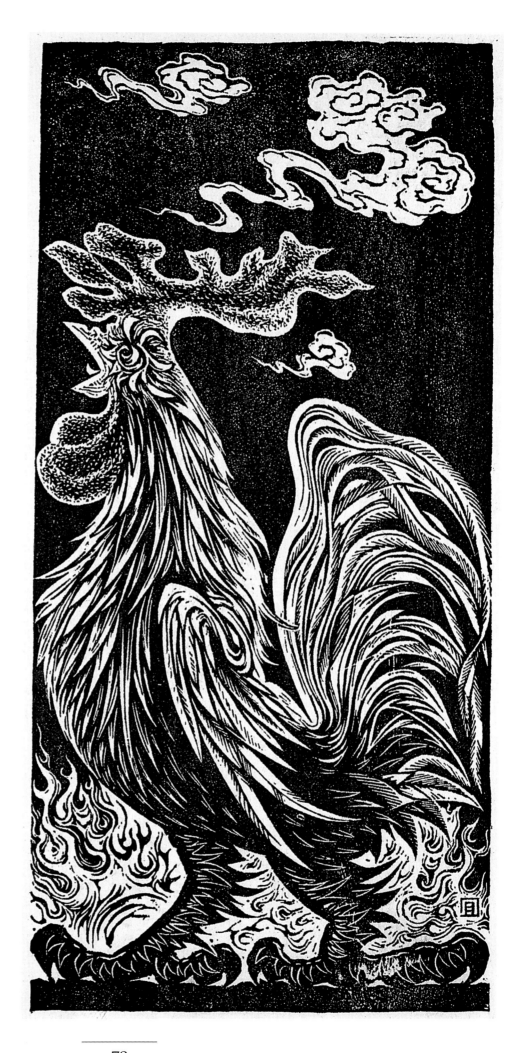

司晨　MORNING CALL

1959　木刻版畫　32×15cm

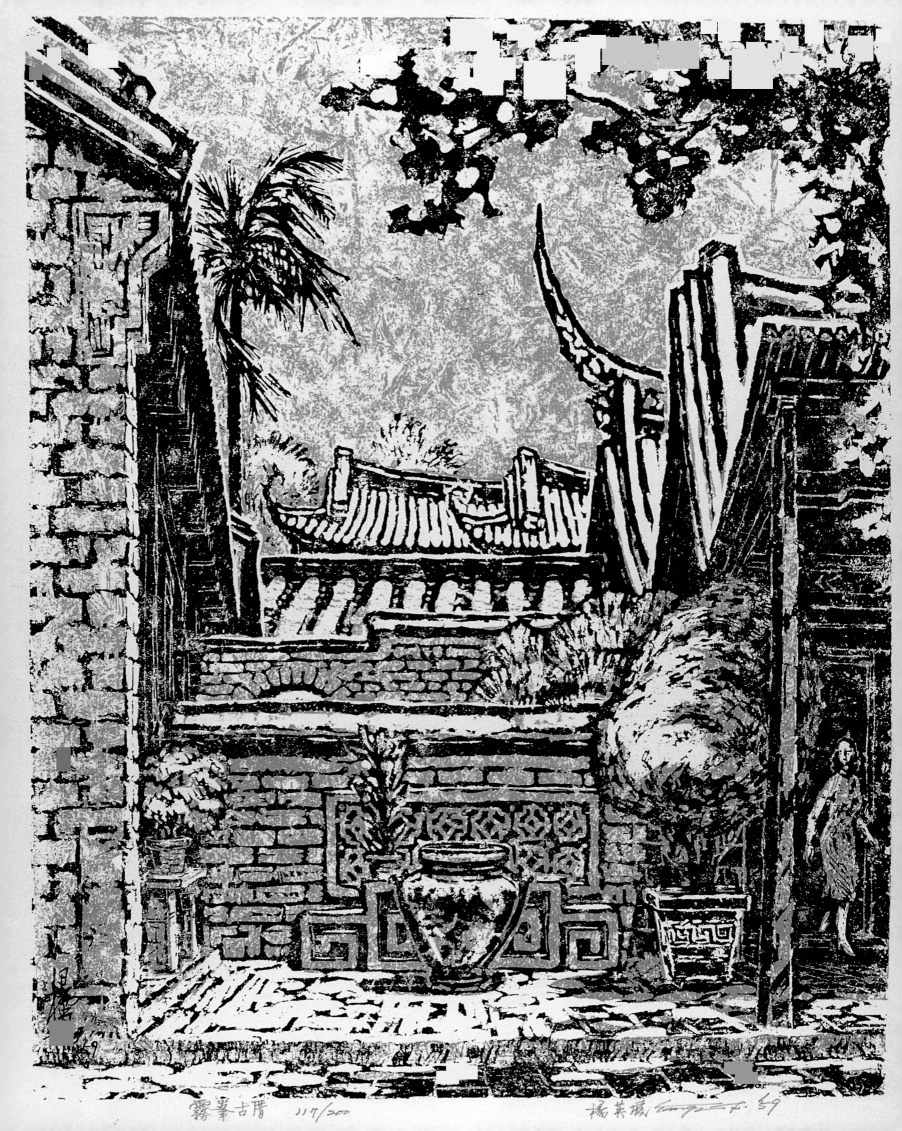

霧峰古厝　117/200　　　　楊英風 Yuyu Yang 59

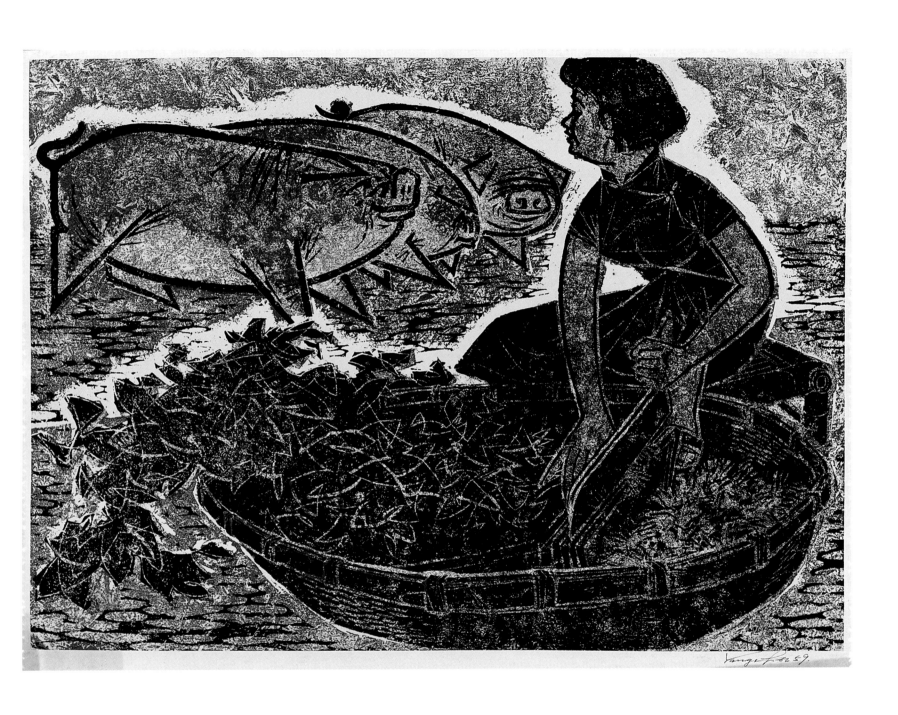

霧峰古厝　ANCIENT HOUSE IN WUFENG　1959　蔗版版畫　60.5×46.5cm（左頁圖）

嬉　PLAYING　1959　蔗版版畫　49×62.5cm

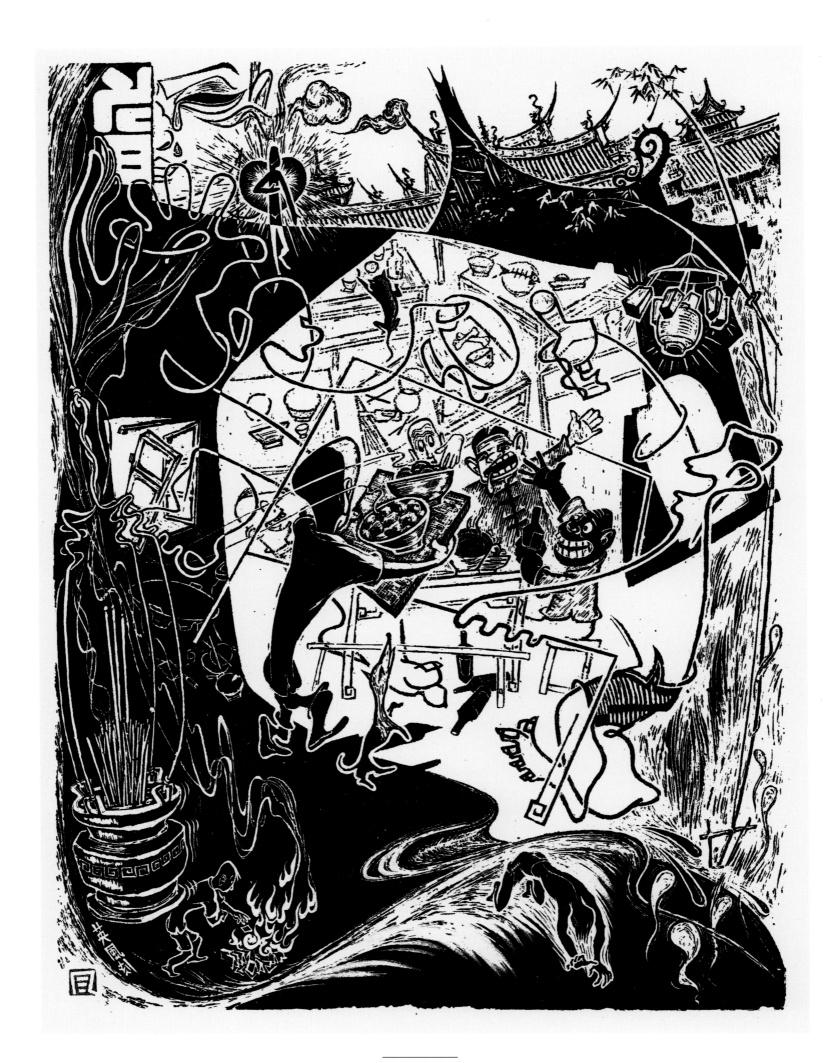

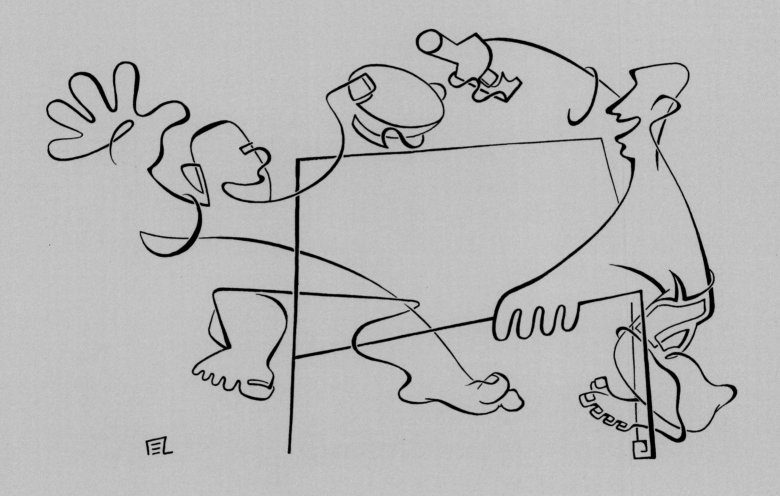

吃拜拜　FEAST AFTER WORSHIPING　1959　木刻版畫　46×34cm（左頁圖）

拜拜　WORSHIP　1959　版畫底稿　24×35.5cm

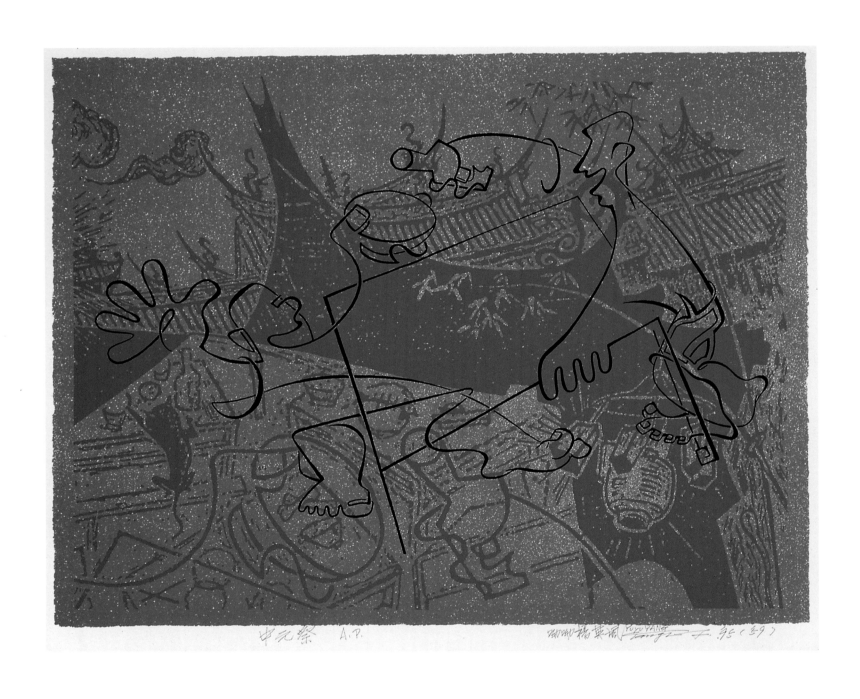

中元祭　CHINESE LANTERN FESTIVAL　1995　電腦合成版畫　72.8×56.6cm

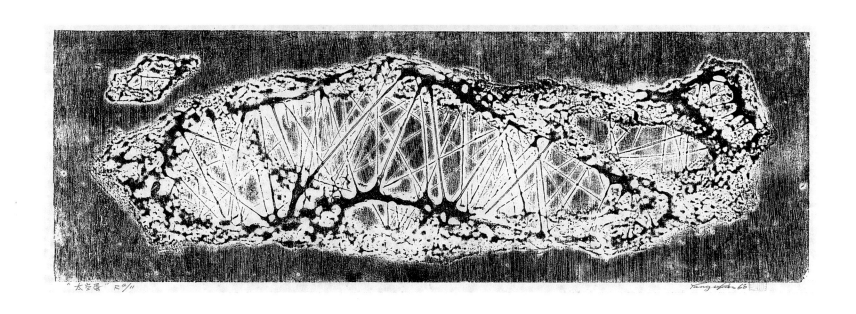

太空蛋（一） SPACE EGG（1） 1959 木板版畫 26×75.5cm

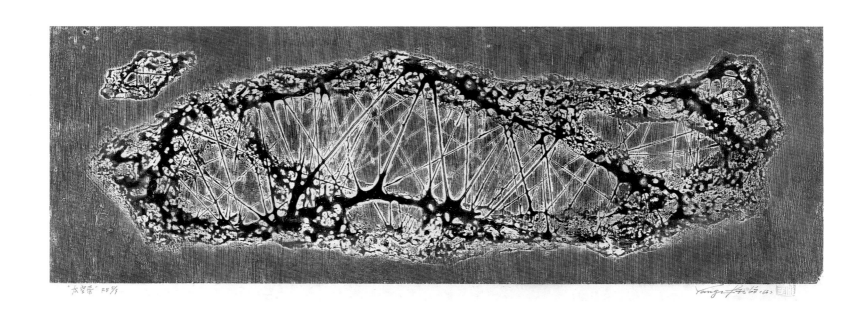

太空蛋（二）　SPACE　EGG（2）　1963　木板版畫　27.5×75.5cm

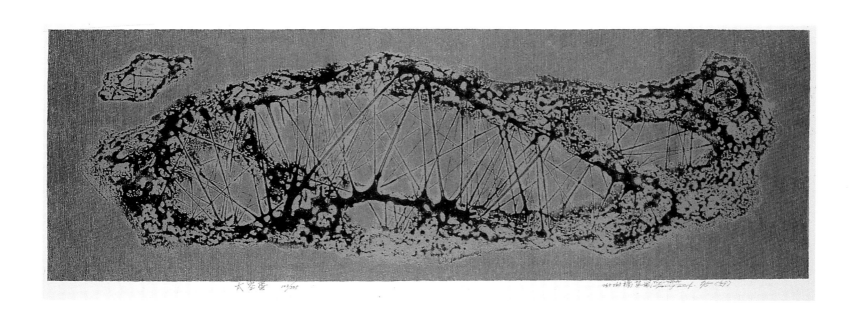

太空蛋(三)　SPACE　EGG(3)　1995　電腦合成版畫　42×122cm

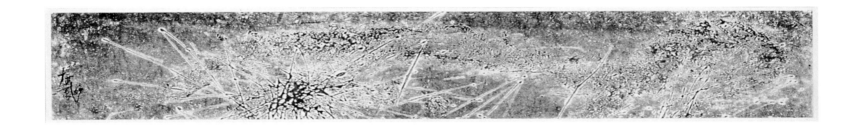

生命智慧的凝結（一）　COAGULATION　OF　WISDOM（1）　1959　蔗板版畫　14×70cm

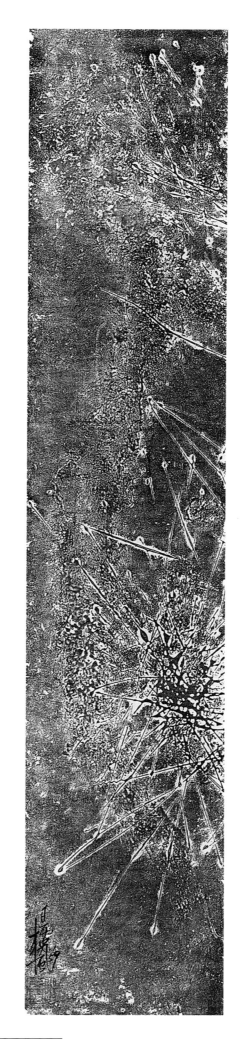

生命智慧的凝結（二）　COAGULATION OF WISDOM（2）

1959　蔗板版畫　70×14cm

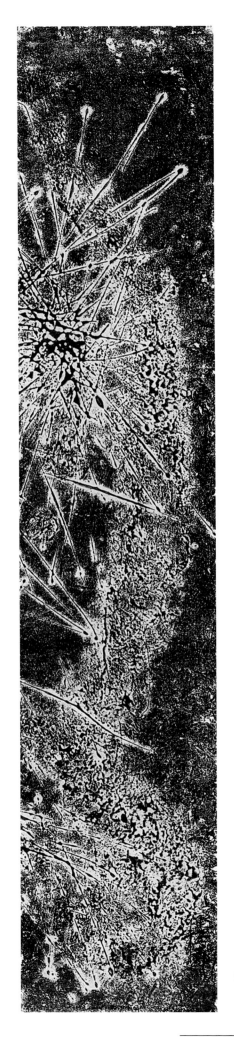

生命智慧的凝結(三)　COAGULATION OF WISDOM(3)
1959　蔗板版畫　70×14cm

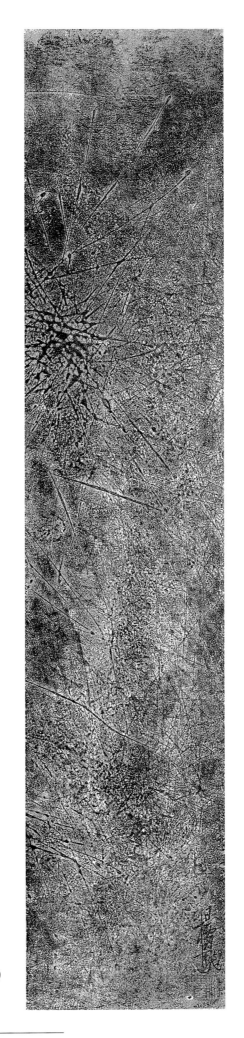

生命智慧的凝結(四)　COAGULATION OF WISDOM(4)
1959　蔗板版畫　70×14cm

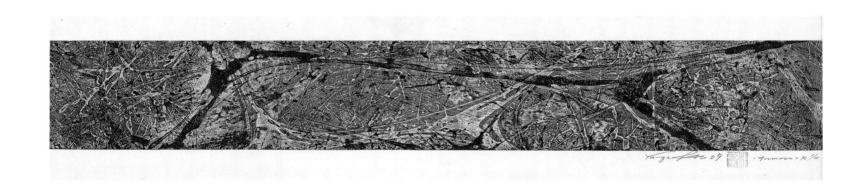

生命的訊息（一） MESSAGE OF LIFE（1） 1959 蔗板版畫 14×70cm

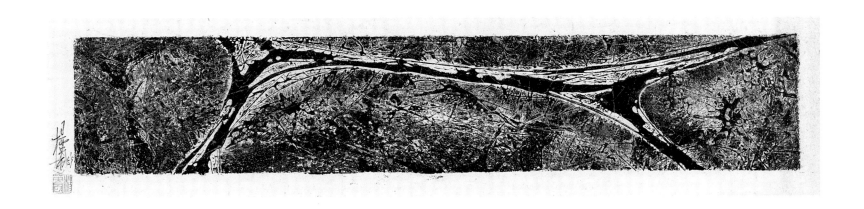

生命的訊息（二） MESSAGE OF LIFE（2） 1959 蔗板版畫 14×70cm

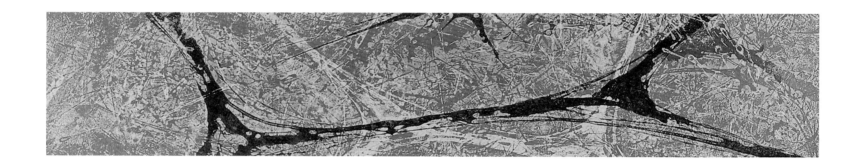

生命的訊息（三）　MESSAGE　OF　LIFE（3）　1995　電腦合成版畫　20×104cm

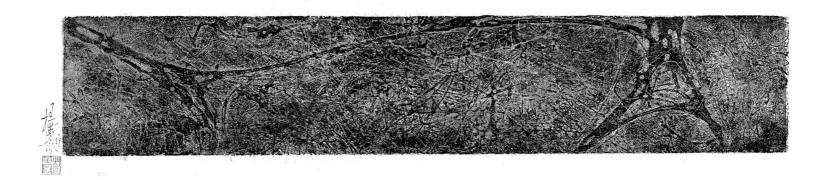

抽象版畫59-01　ABSTRACT PRINT 59-01　1959　蔗板版畫　14×70cm

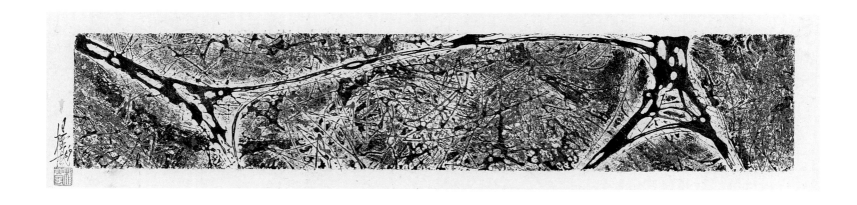

抽象版畫59-02　ABSTRACT PRINT 59-02　1959　蔗板版畫　14×70cm

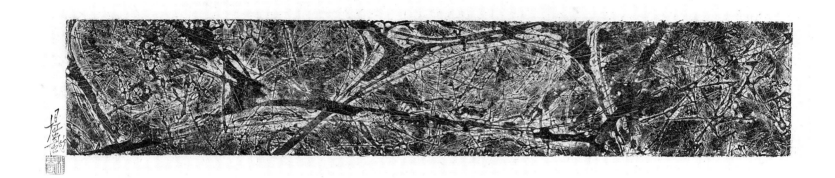

抽象版畫59-03　ABSTRACT PRINT 59-03　1959　蔗板版畫　14×70cm

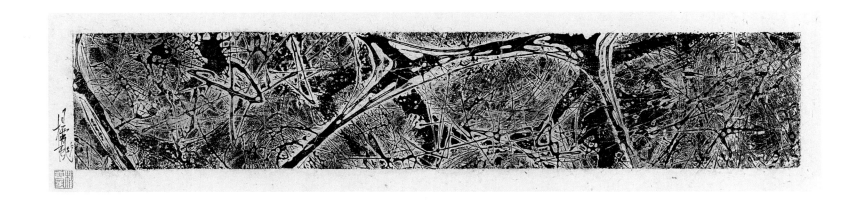

抽象版畫59-04　ABSTRACT PRINT 59-04　1959　蔗板版畫　14×70cm

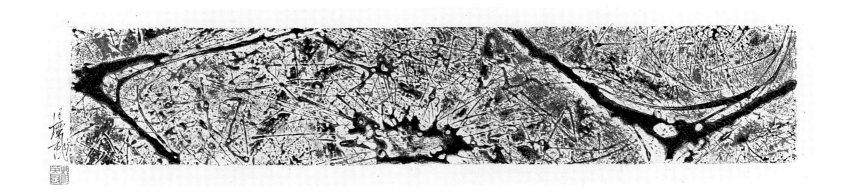

抽象版畫59-05　ABSTRACT PRINT 59-05　1959　蔗板版畫　14×70cm

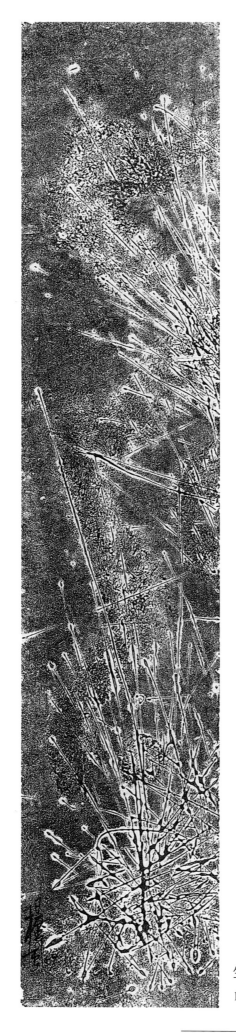

生命初放的茁壯（一）　STRIKING MOMENT OF BIRTH（1）

1959　蔗板版畫　70×14cm

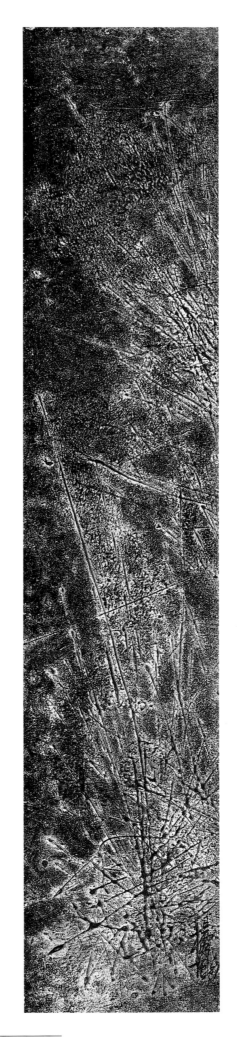

生命初放的茁壯(二)　STRIKING MOMENT OF BIRTH(2)
1959　蔗板版畫　70×14cm

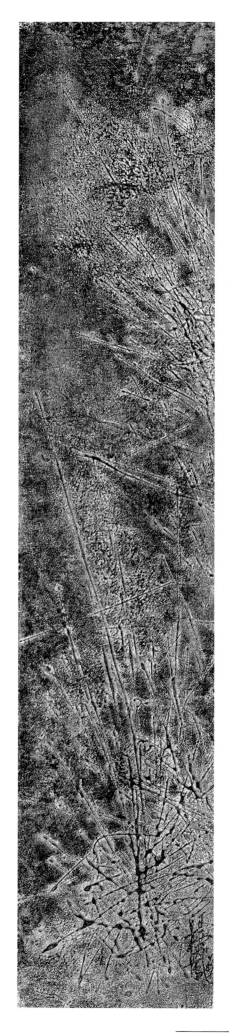

生命初放的茁壯（三）　STRIKING MOMENT OF BIRTH（3）

1959　蔗板版畫　70×14cm

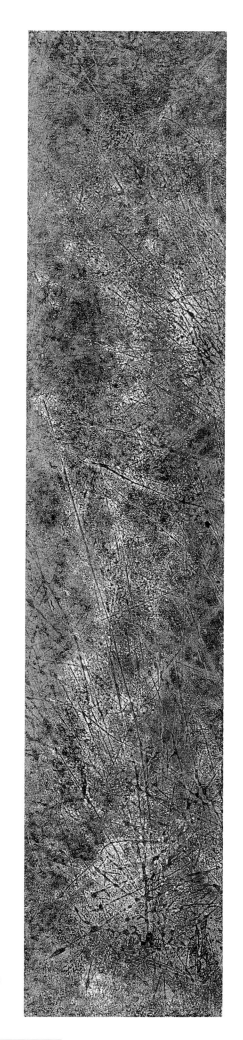

生命初放的茁壯（四） STRIKING MOMENT OF BIRTH（4）
1959　蔗板版畫　70×14cm

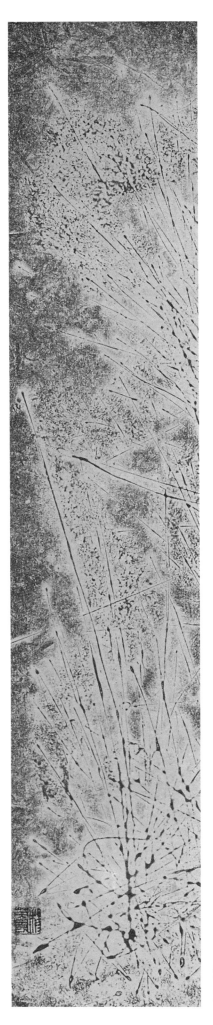

生命初放的茁壯（五）　STRIKING MOMENT OF BIRTH（5）
1959　蔗板版畫　69.5×13.5cm

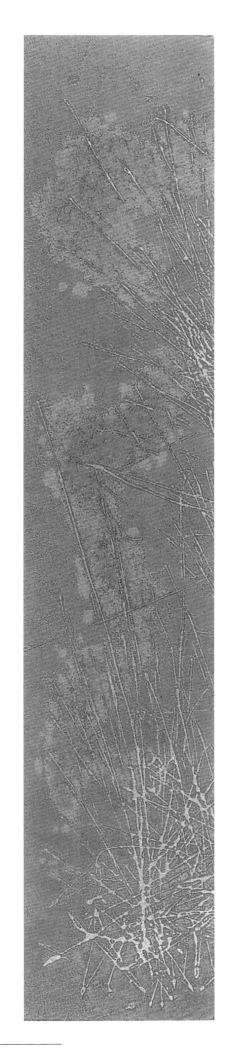

美麗的矜驕　ALOOFNESS

1995　電腦合成版畫　104×20cm

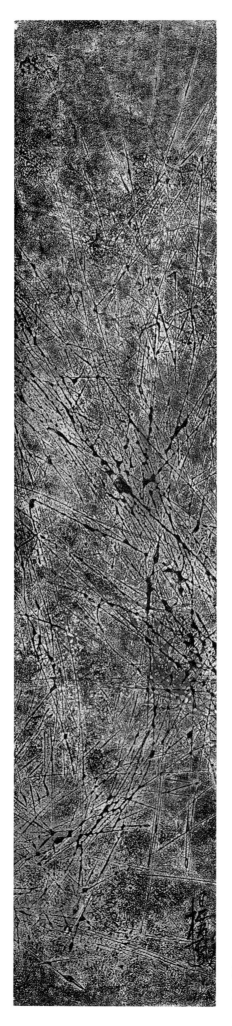

抽象版畫59-06　ABSTRACT PRIANT 59-06

1959　蔗板版畫　70×14cm

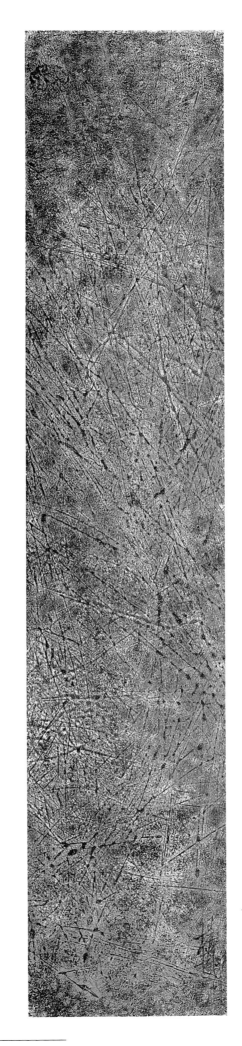

抽象版畫59-07　ABSTRACT PRIANT 59-07
1959　蔗板版畫　70×14cm

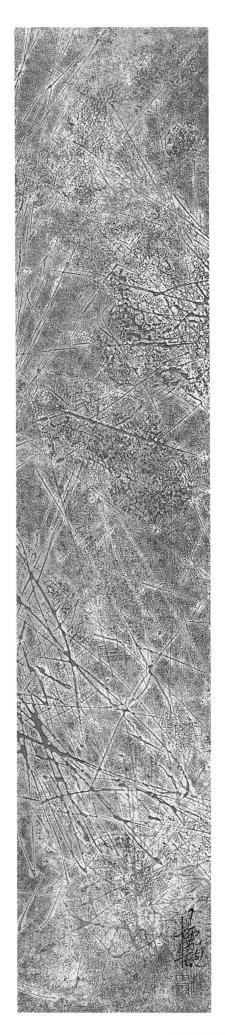

抽象版畫59-08　ABSTRACT PRIANT 59-08

1959　蔗板版畫　70×14cm

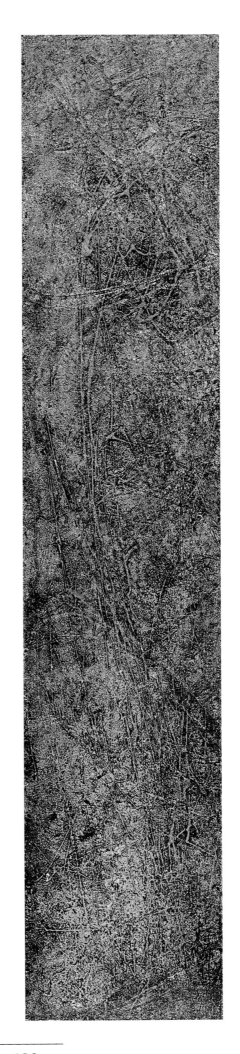

抽象版畫59-09　ABSTRACT PRIANT 59-09
1959　蔗板版畫　70×14cm

森林（一） FOREST（1） 1959 木板版畫 59.5×40cm

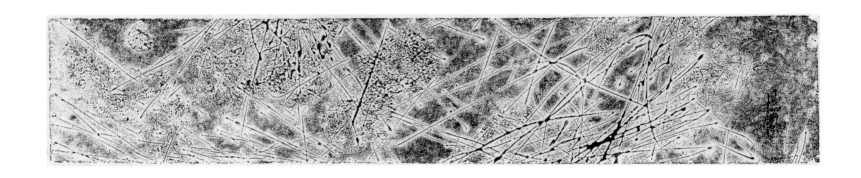

不眠之夜　SLEEPLESS NIGHT　1959　蔗板版畫　14×69.6cm

雛鳳　BABY PHOENIX　1959　蔗板版畫　60×46cm（右頁圖）

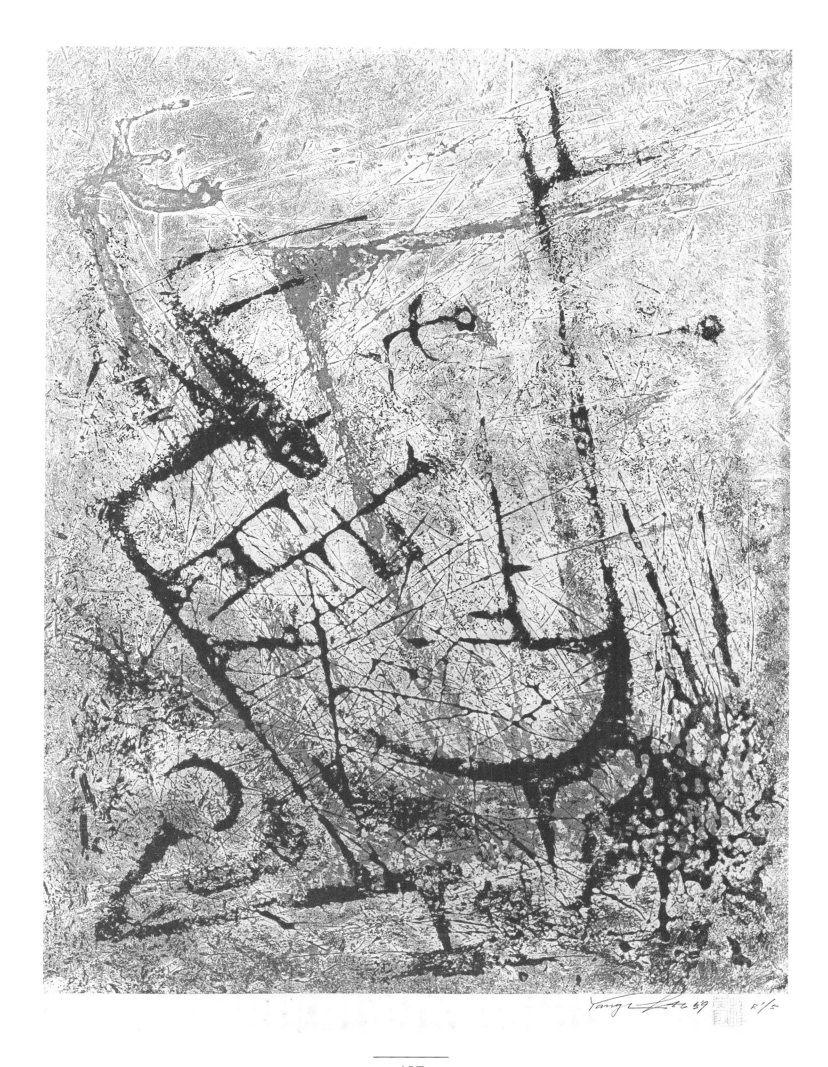

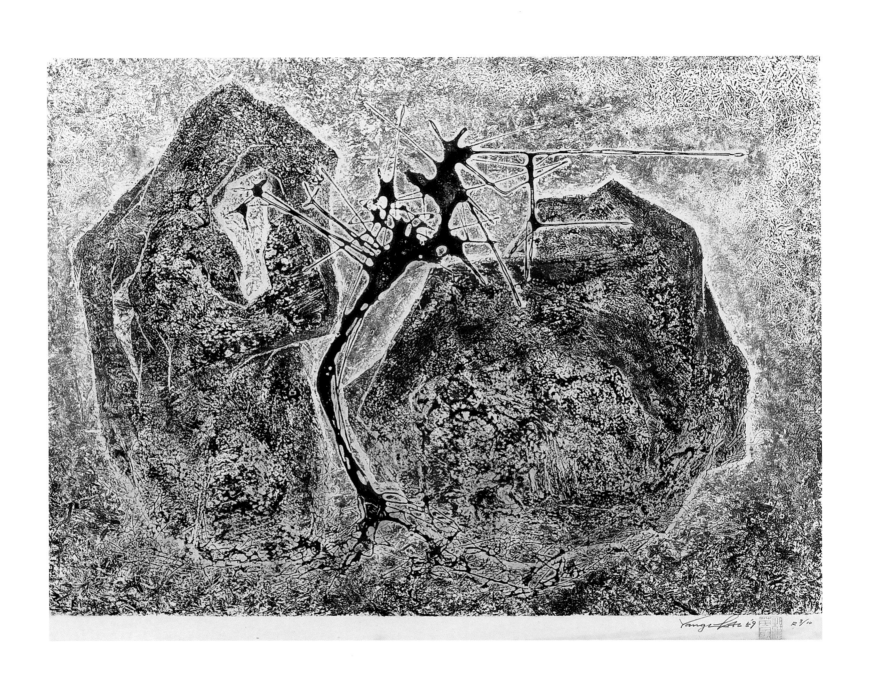

文化的起源　ORIGION OF CULTURE　1959　蔗板版畫　45.5×60.5cm

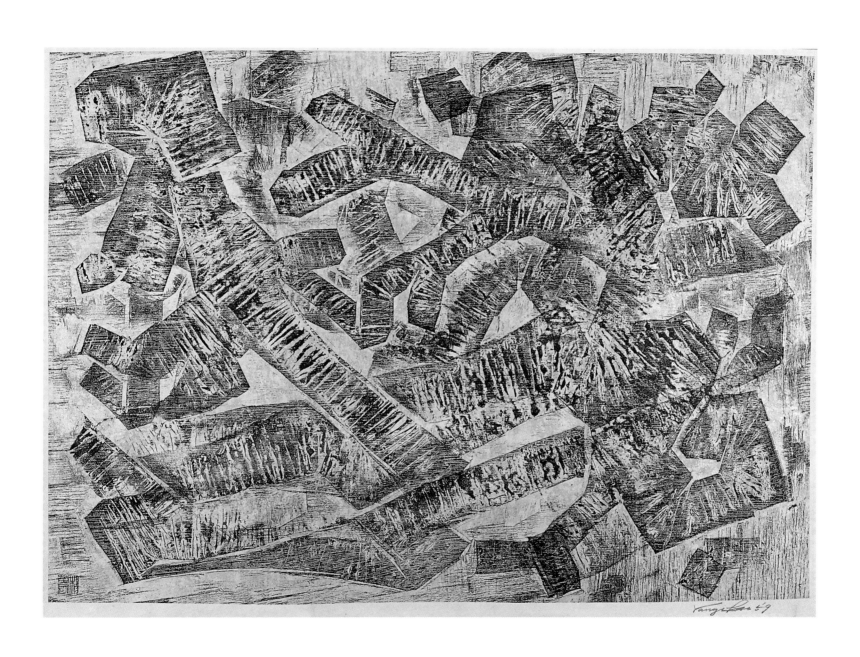

抽象版畫59-10　ABSTRACT PRINT 59-10　1959　木板版畫　51×69cm

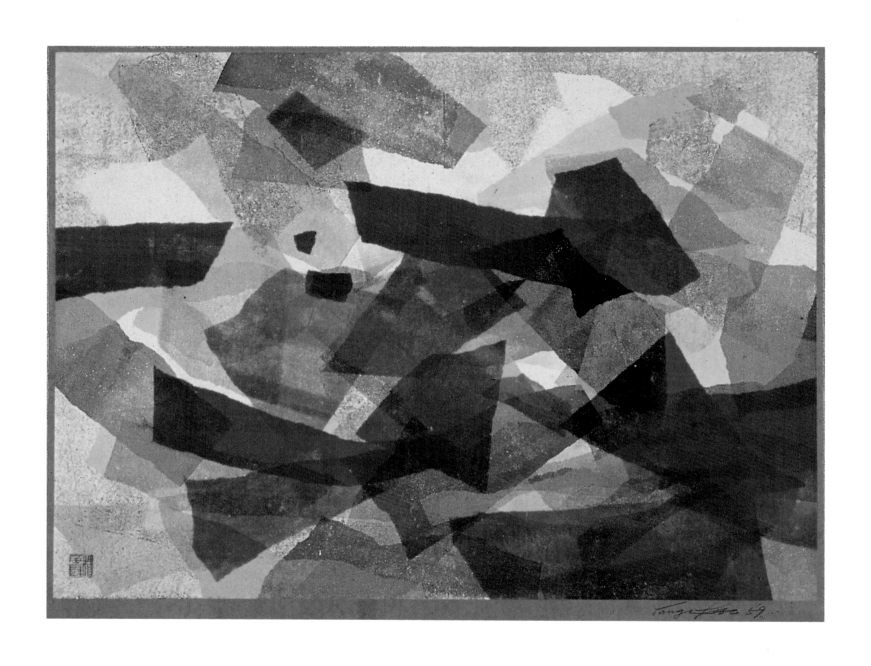

豐實的歡欣　HAPPY HARVEST　1959　紙板版畫　44.5×60cm

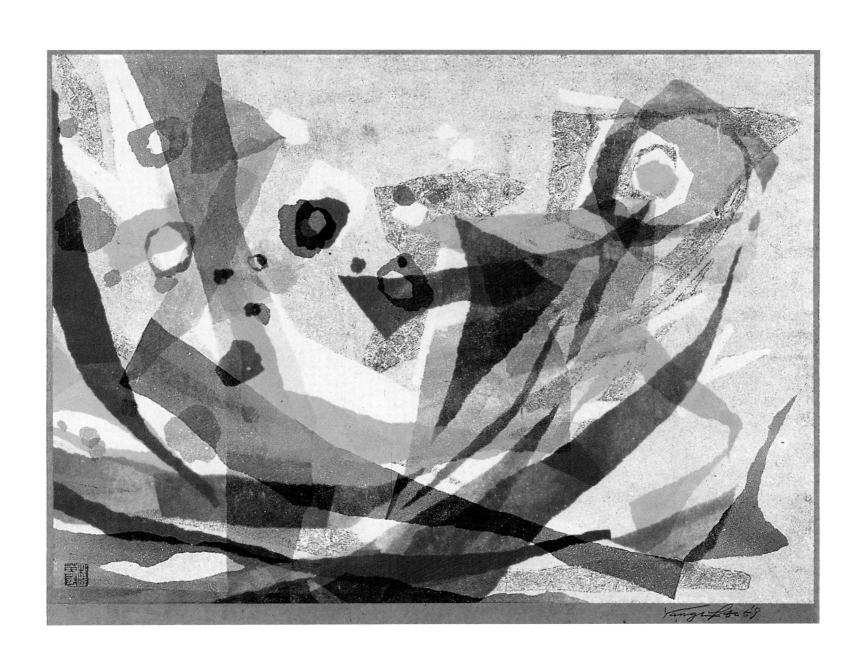

節慶的喜悅　JOY OF FESTIVAL　1959　紙板版畫　44.5×60cm

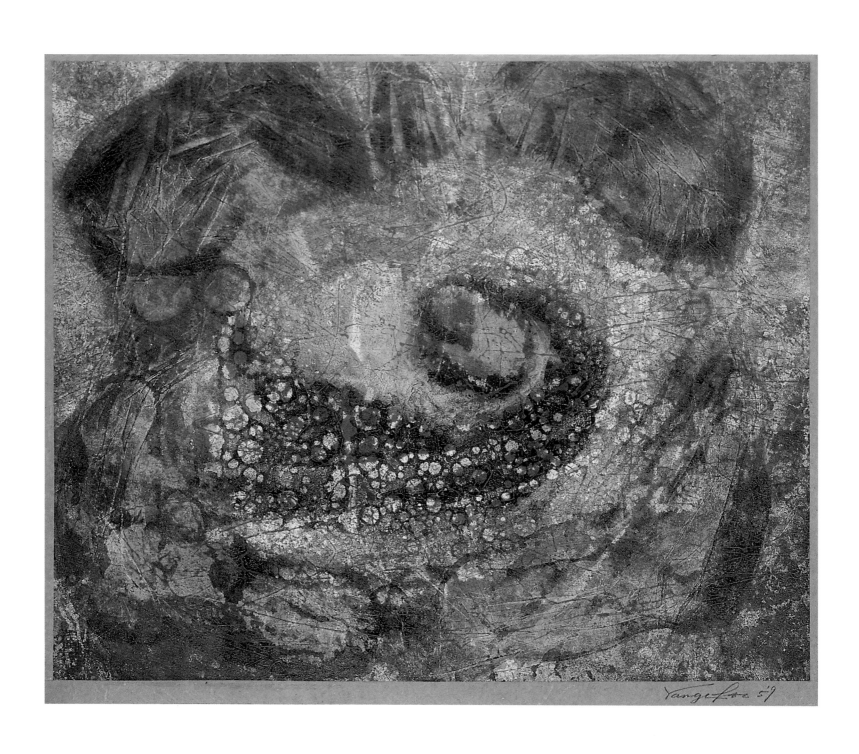

抽象版畫59-11　ABSTRACT PRINT 59-11　1959　複合版畫　44.7×52.7cm

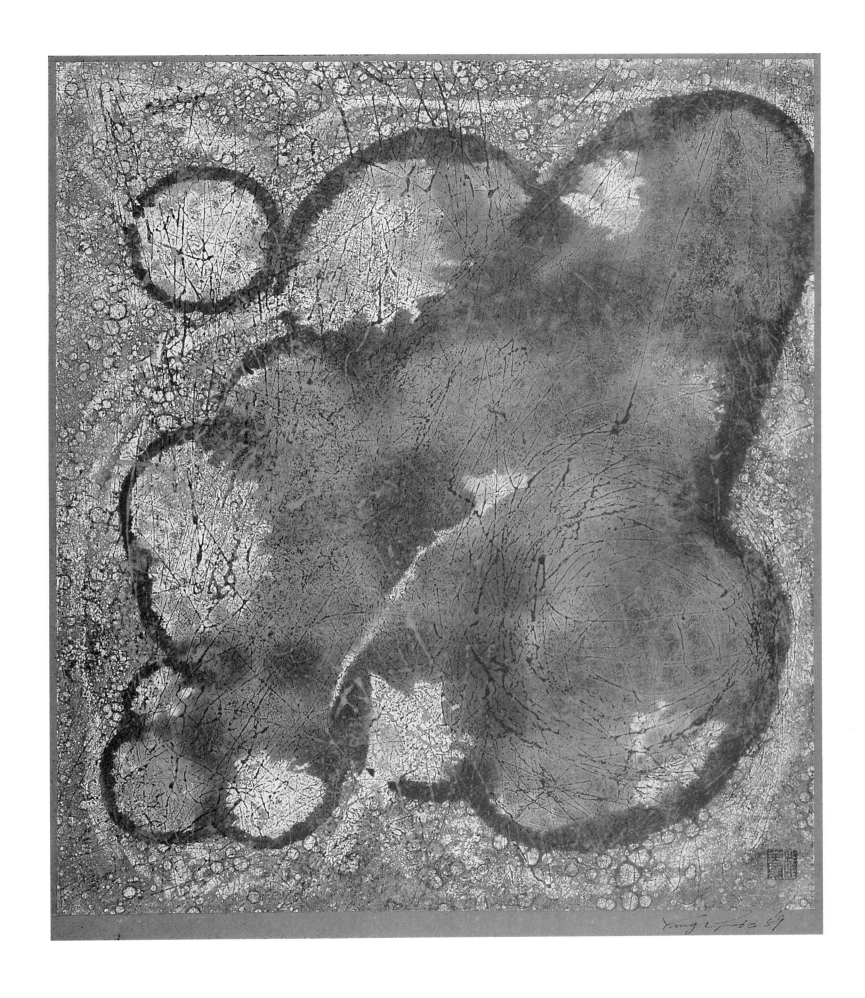

抽象版畫59-12　ABSTRACT PRINT 59-12　1959　複合版畫　54×46.2cm

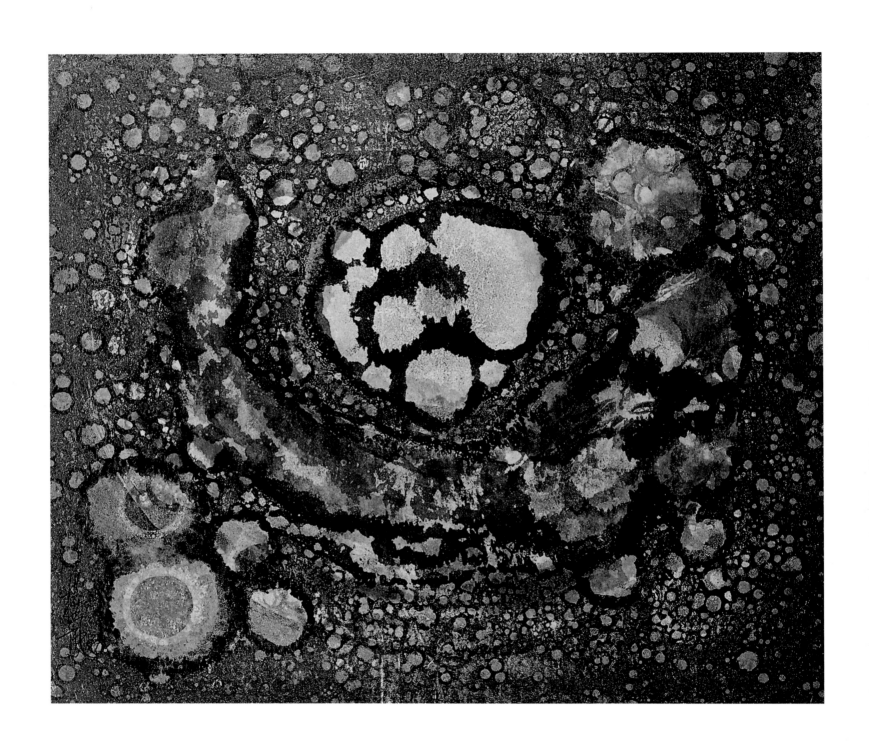

金　THE FIVE ELEMENTS-METAL　1959　複合版畫　46×52cm

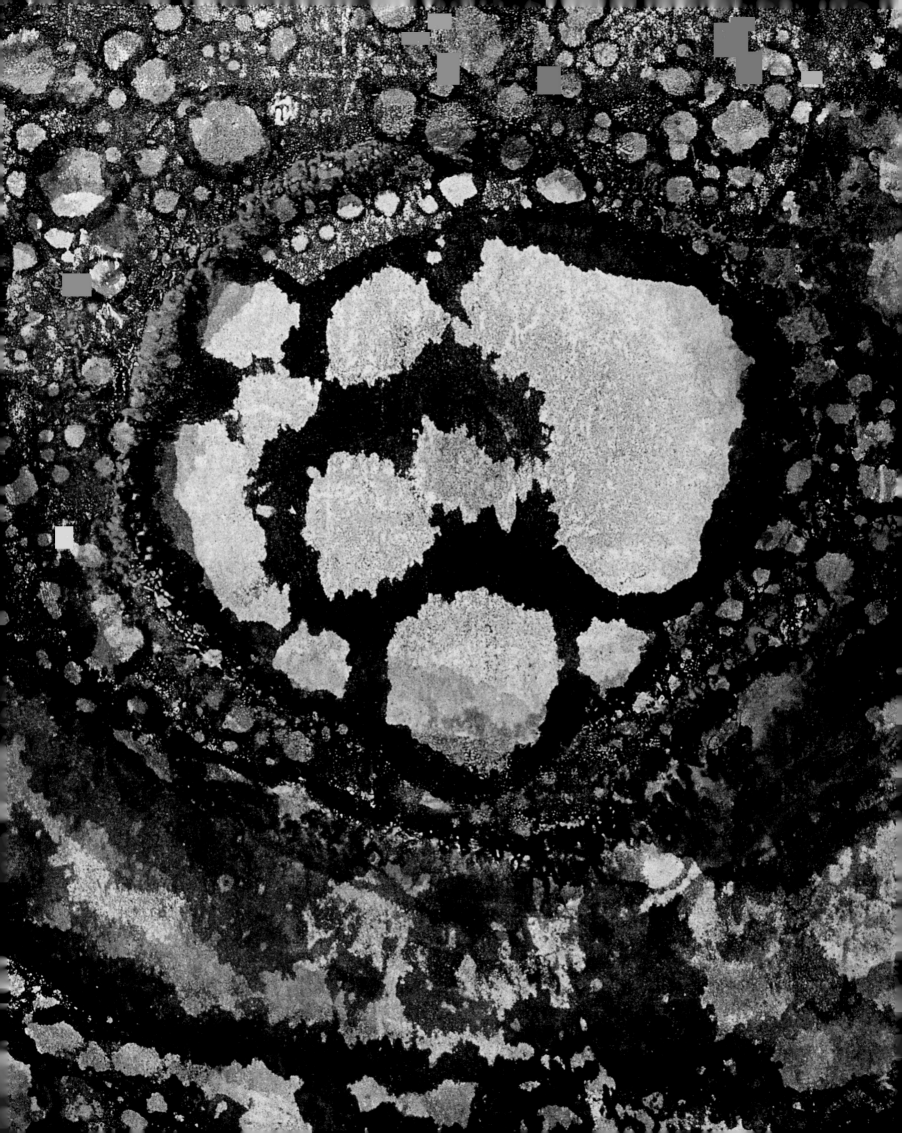

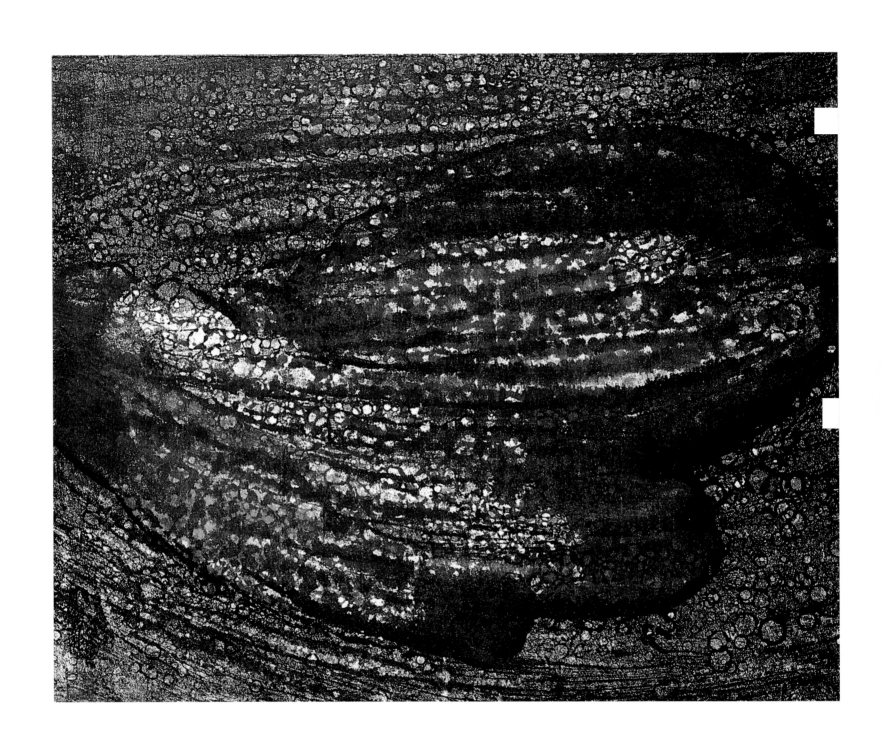

木　THE FIVE ELEMENTS-WOOD　1959　複合版畫　46×52cm

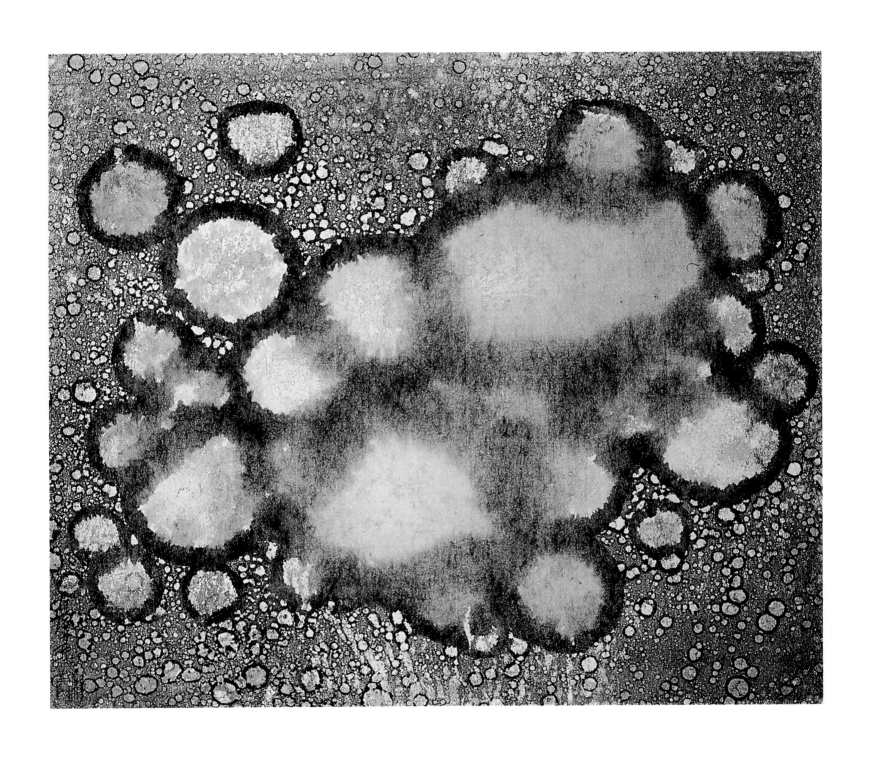

水　THE FIVE ELEMENTS-WATER　1959　複合版畫　46×52cm

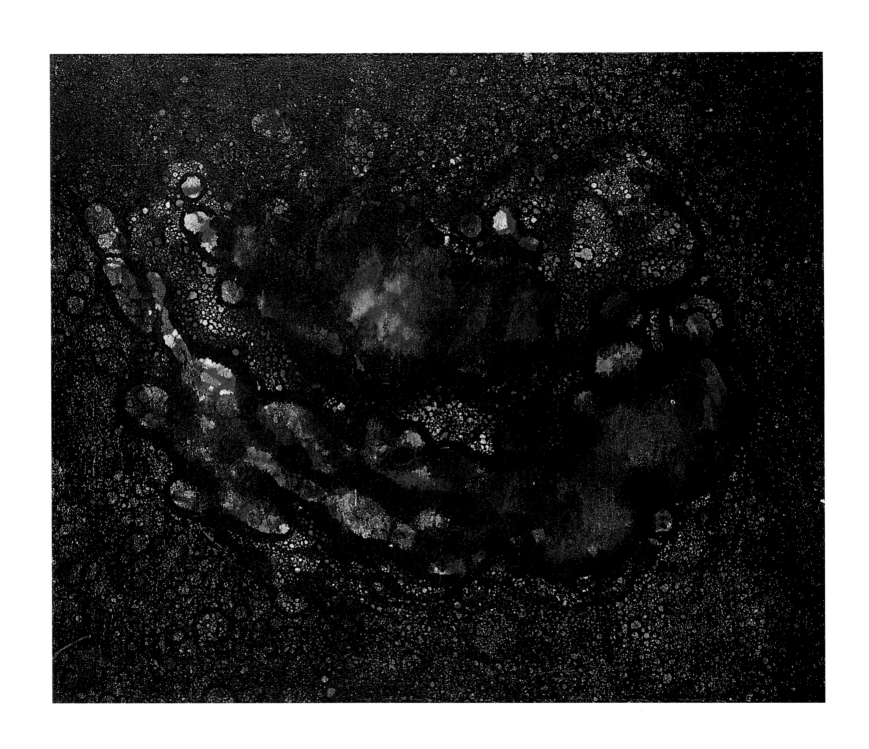

火　THE FIVE ELEMENTS-FIRE　1959　複合版畫　46×52cm

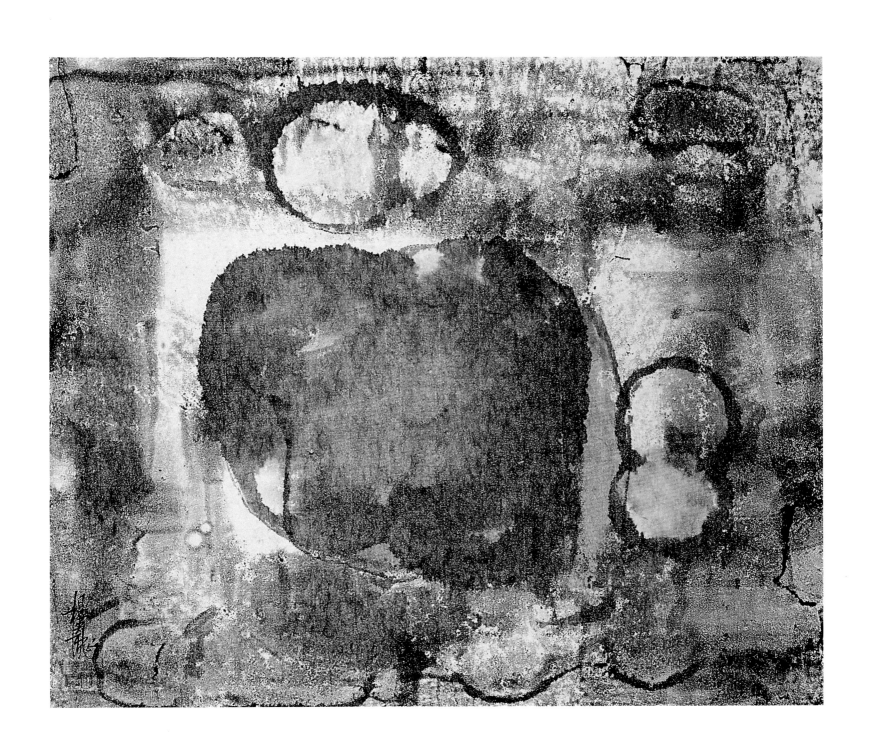

土　THE FIVE ELEMENTS-EARTH　1959　複合版畫　46×52cm

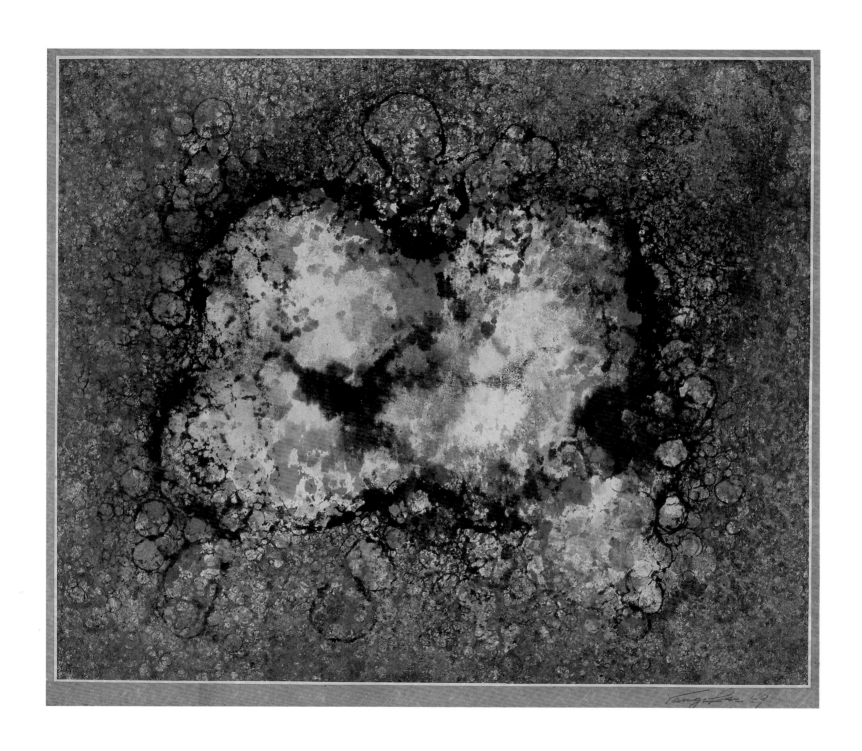

抽象版畫59-13　ABSTRACT PRINT 59-13　1959　蔗板版畫　45×52.3cm

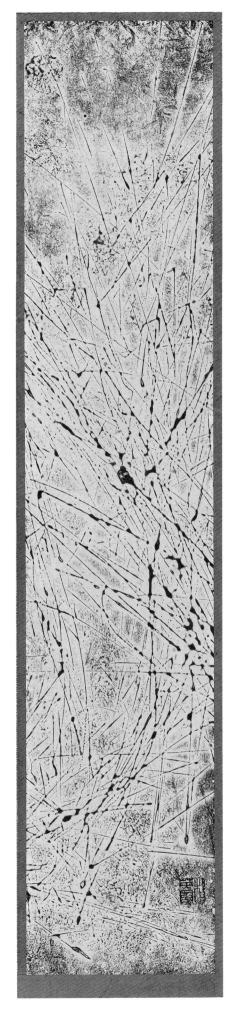

抽象版畫59-14　ABSTRACT PRINT 59-14

1959　複合版畫　69.3×13.3cm

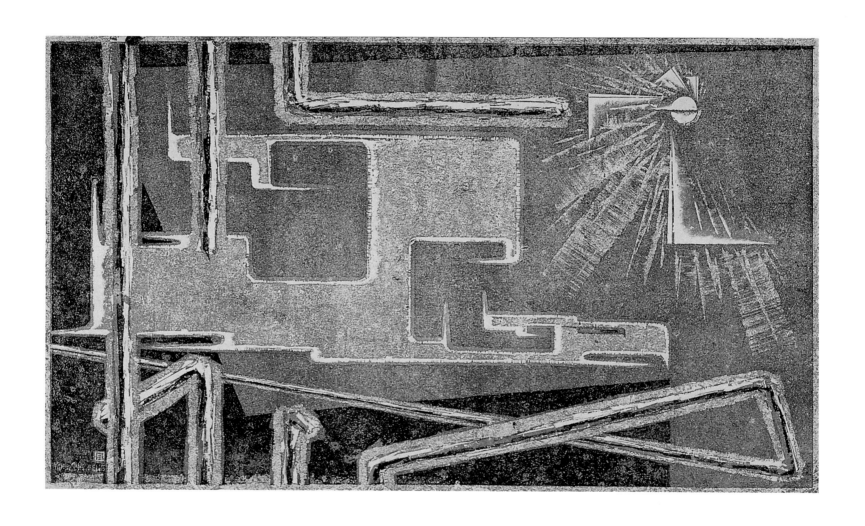

自由　FREEDOM　1959　木刻版畫　36.6×60.6cm

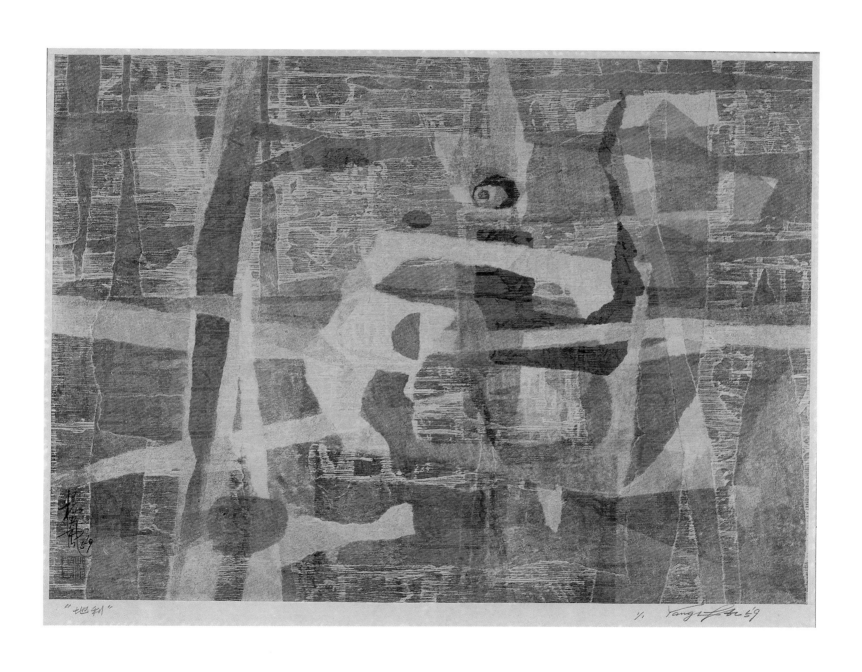

地利　ADVANTAGES OF SITUATION　1959　複合版畫　44.3×59.6cm

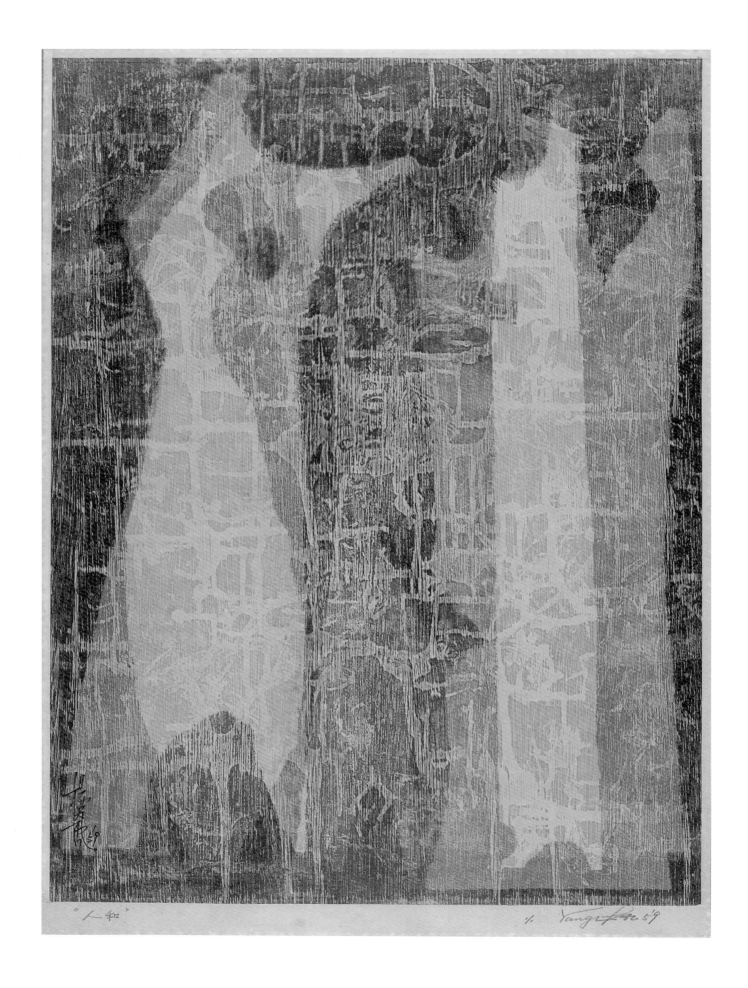

人和　INTER-PERSONAL HARMONY　1959　複合版畫　59.8×44.5cm

傳教者　MISSIONARY　1959　複合版畫　59.6×44.6cm

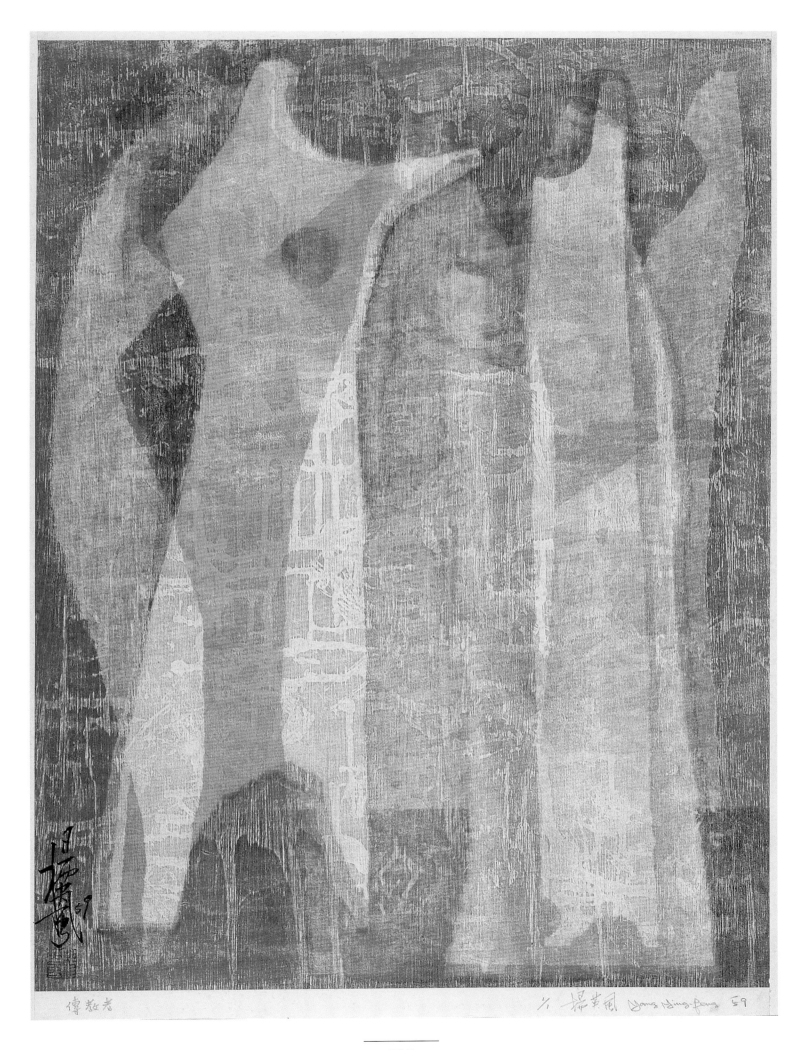

傳教者　　　　　　　　　　　　　　　　　　½　楊英風 Yang Ying-feng 59

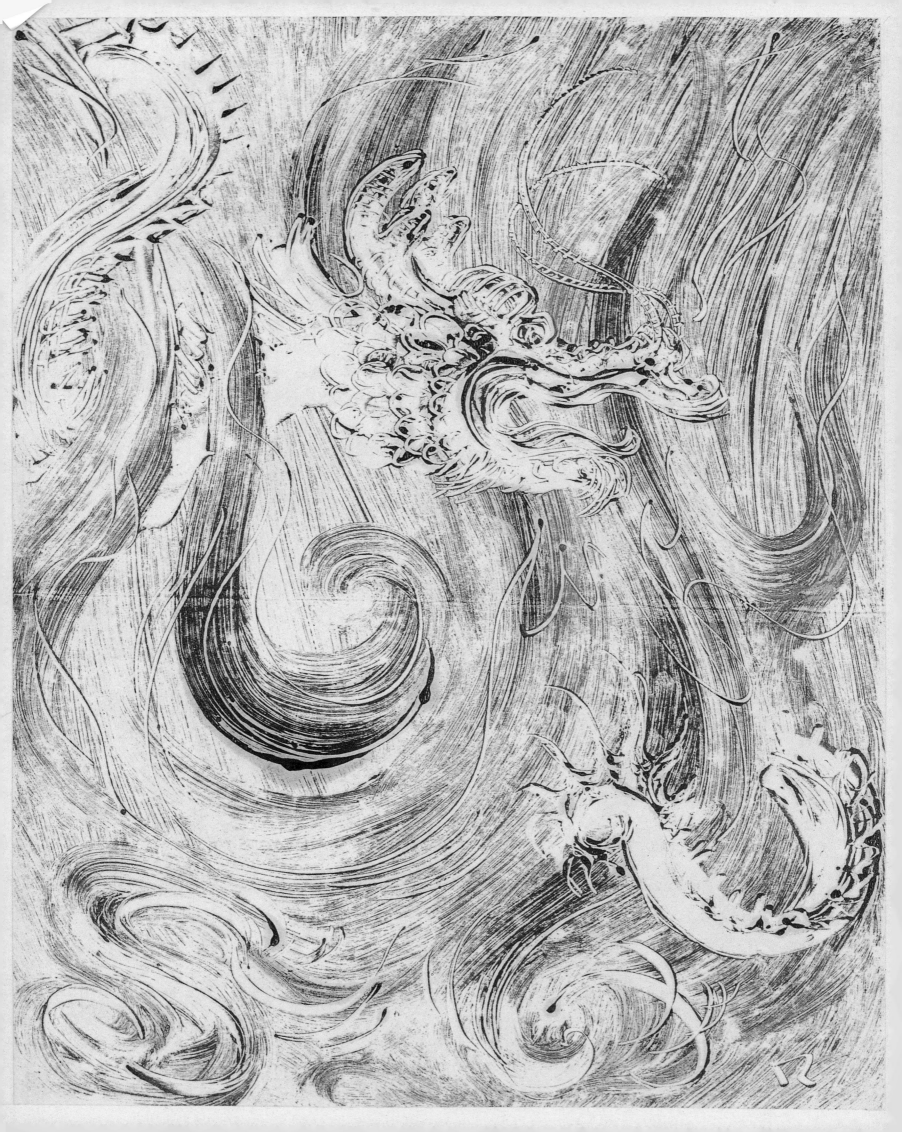

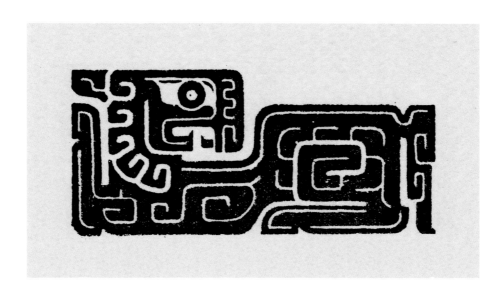

龍　DRAGON　約1950年代　玻璃版畫　27.5×21.2cm（左頁圖）

幼獅　LITTLE LION　1960　石膏版畫　4.5×9.5cm（原寸）

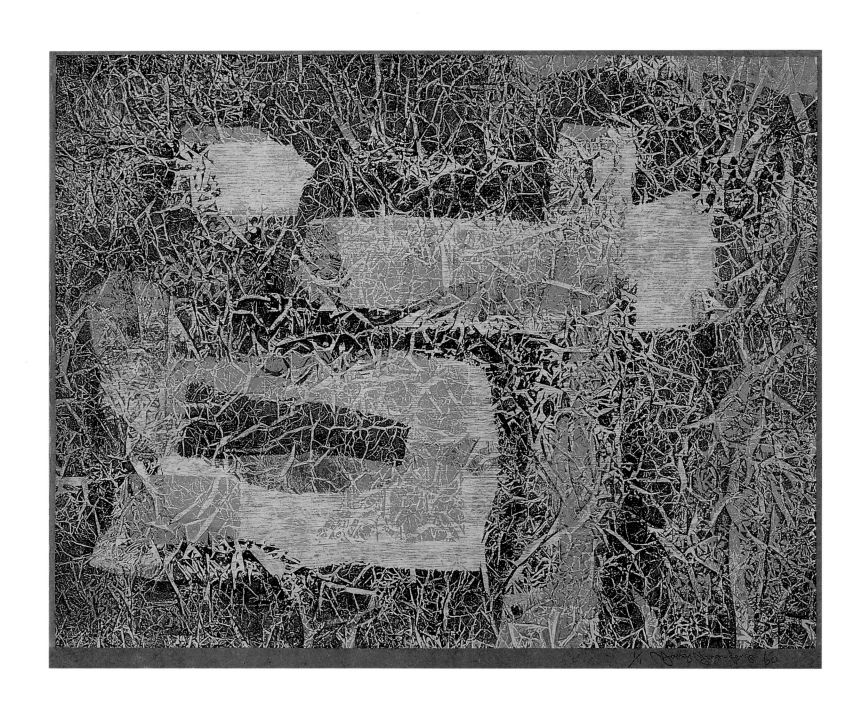

抽象版畫60-01　ABSTRACT PRINT 60-01　1960　複合版畫　18×59.6cm

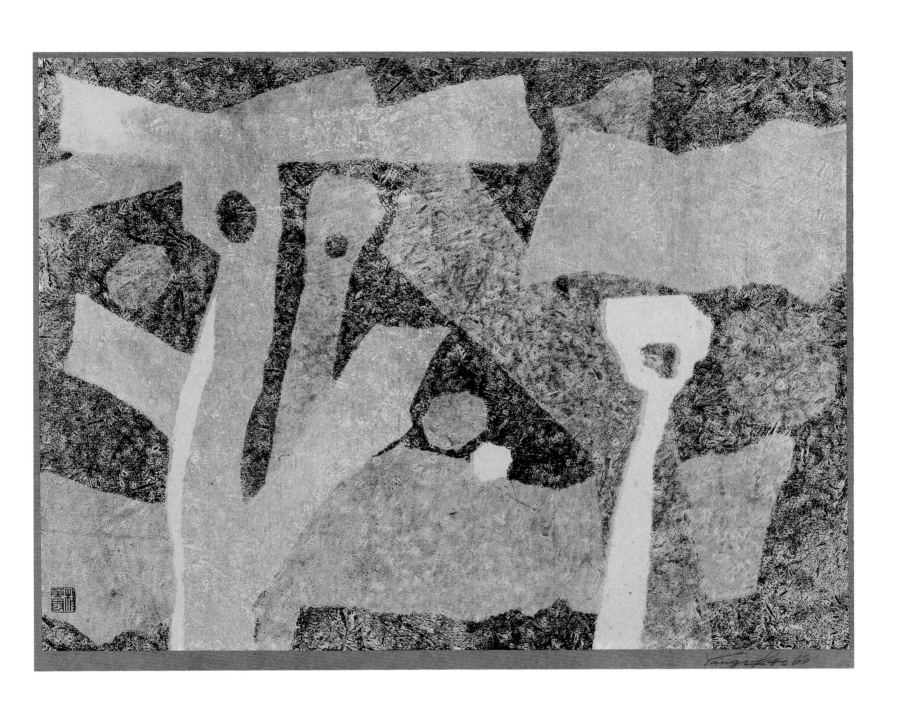

抽象版畫60-02　ABSTRACT PRINT 60-02　1960　複合版畫　45.2×59.8cm

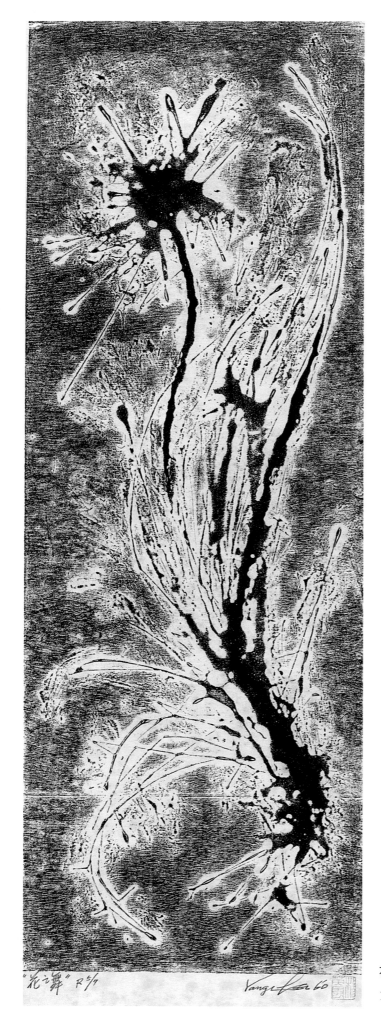

"花之舞" P5/7   Vange Fan 60

花之舞（一）　FLOWERS' DANCE（1）
1960　木板版畫　75.5×26cm

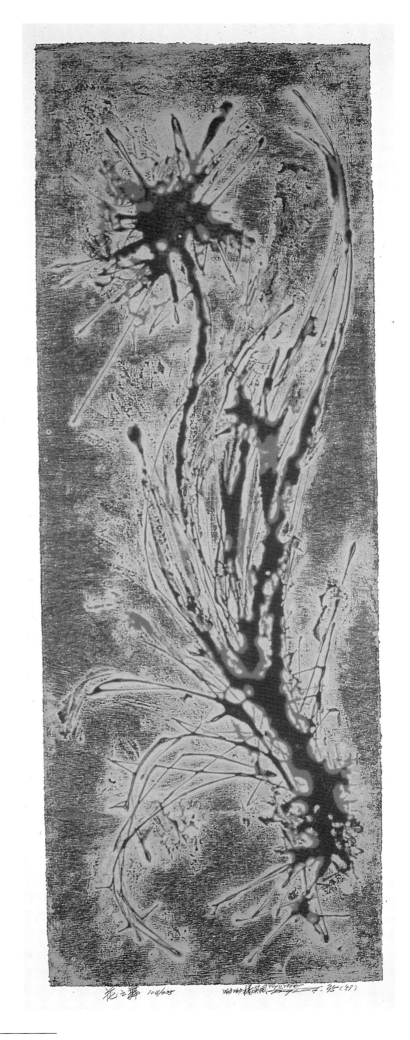

花之舞（二）　FLOWERS' DANCE（2）
1995　電腦合成版畫　125×43cm

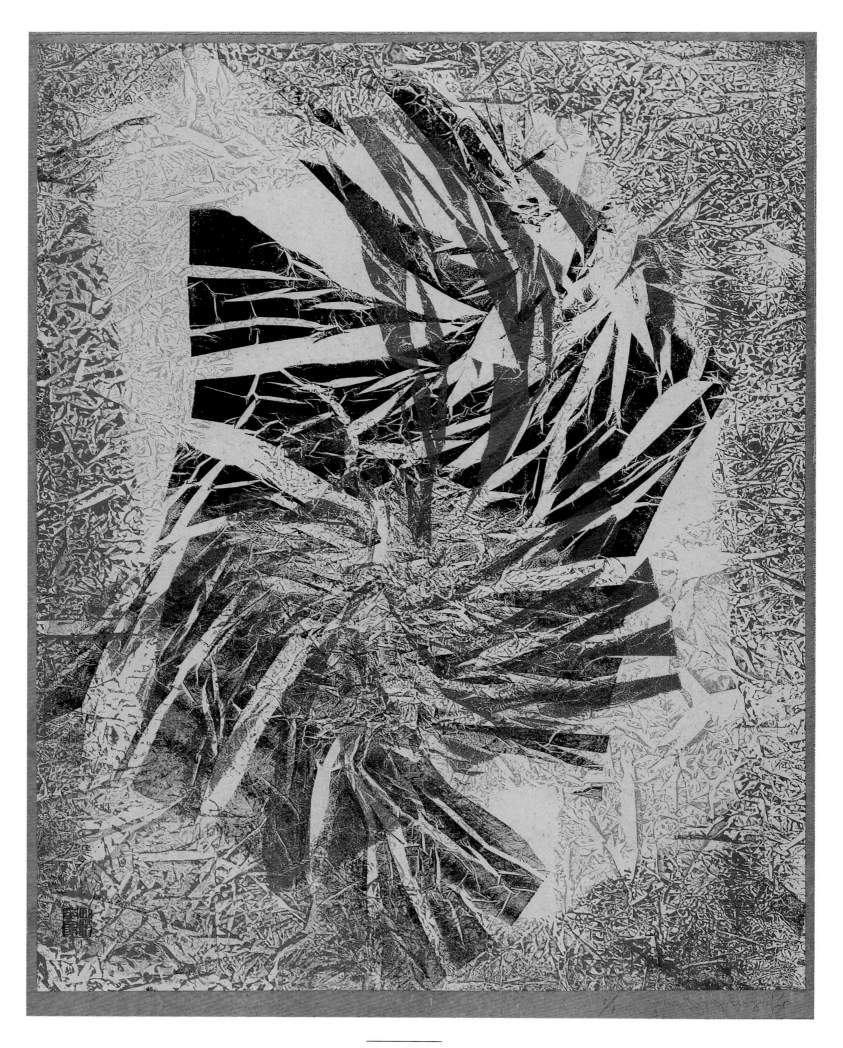

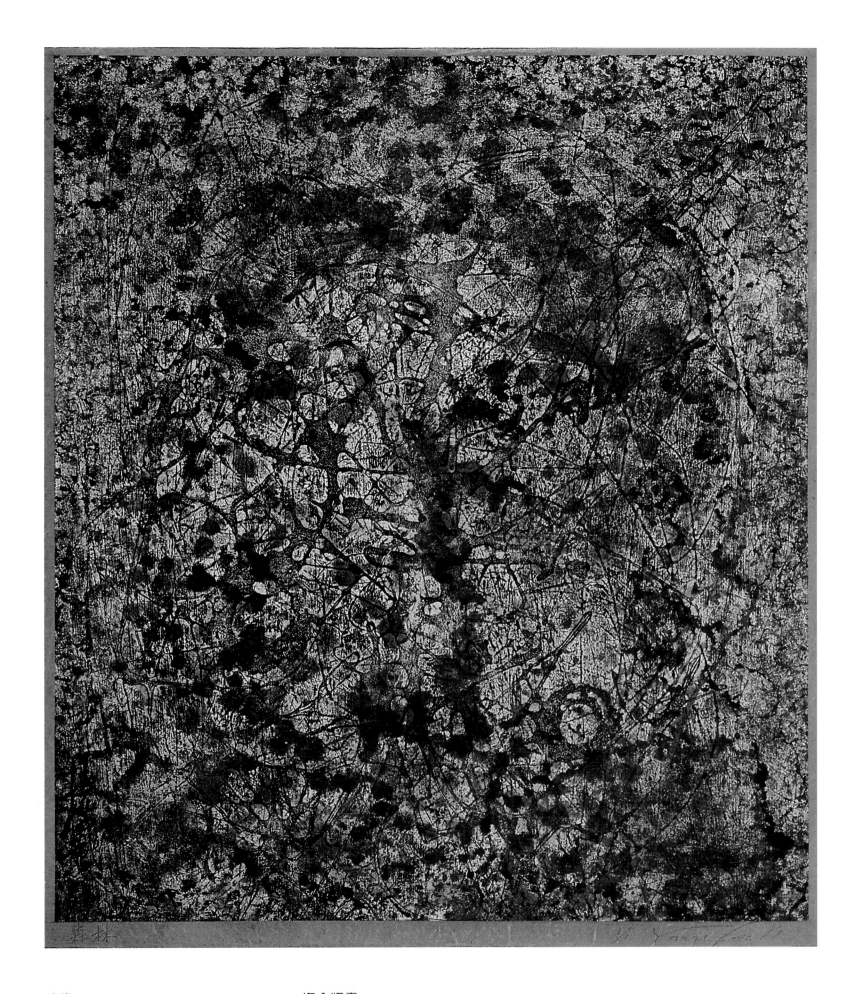

時代 THE MARCH OF TIME 1960 複合版畫 61.4×48.2cm（左頁圖）

森林（二） FOREST（2） 1961 木板版畫 53×44.5cm

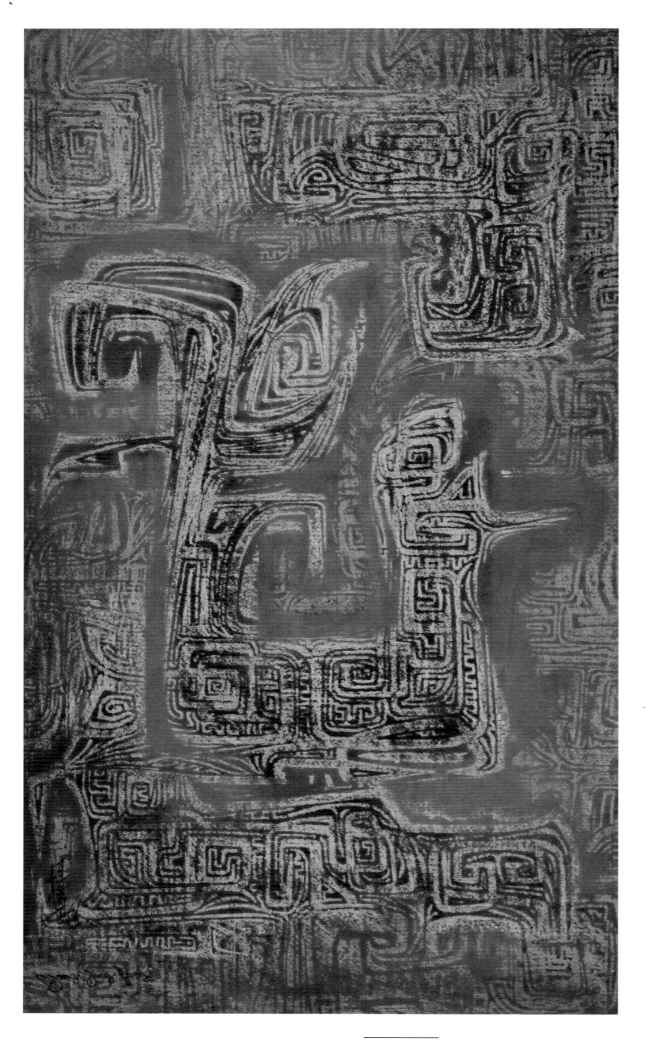

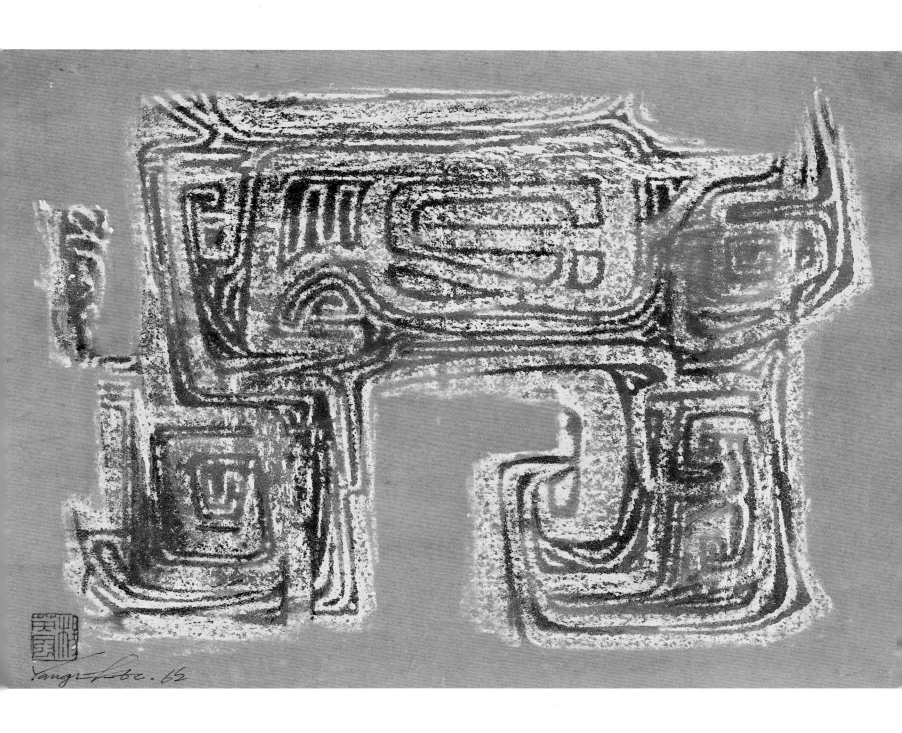

鳳凰生矣　BIRTH OF A PHOENIX　1961　複合版畫　77×45cm（左頁圖）

動中靜　MOTION IN TRANQUILITY　1962　木刻版畫　26×37cm

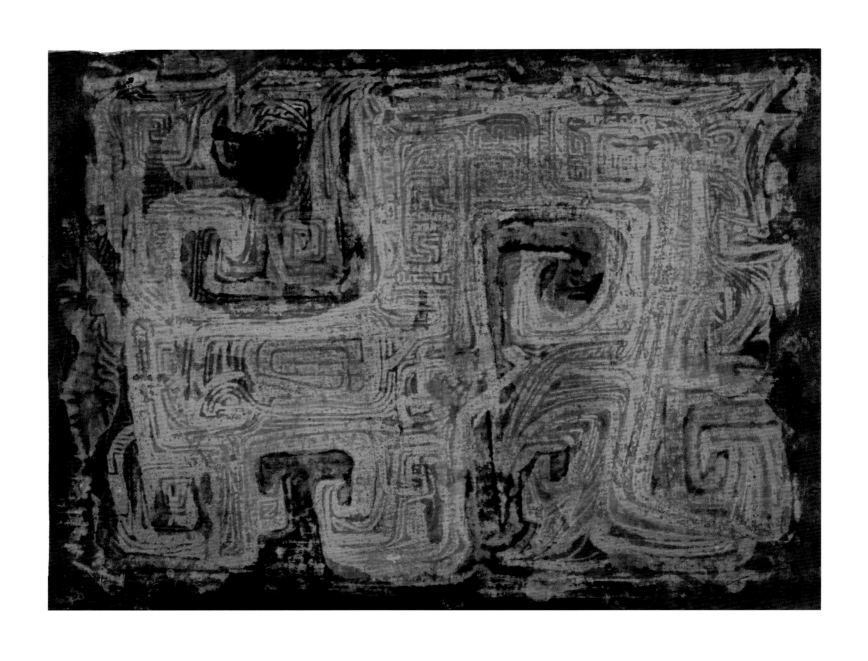

龍種　DRAGON SEEDS　1962　複合版畫　47×62cm

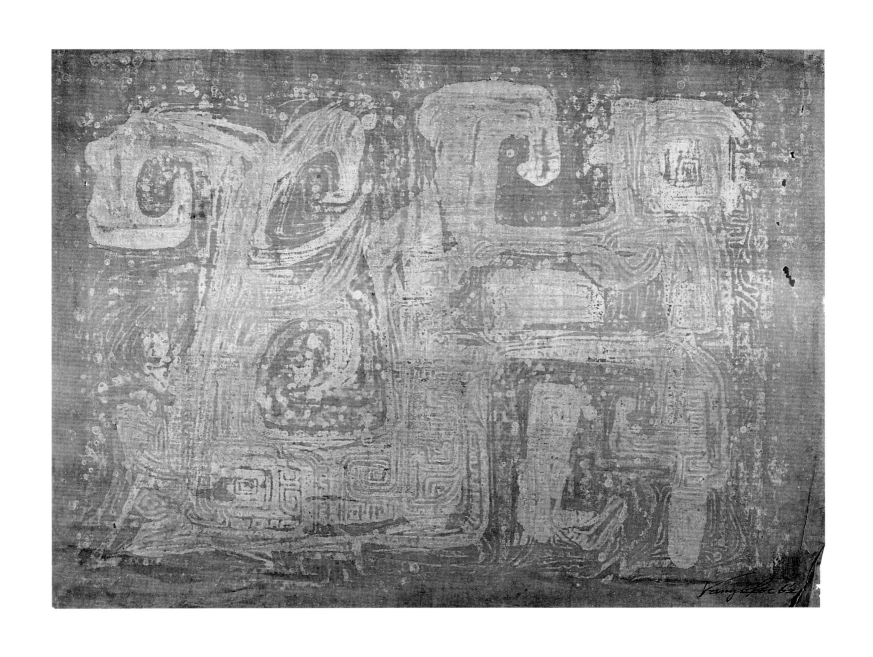

抽象版畫 62-01　ABSTRACT PRINT 62-01　1962　複合版畫　48×64.5cm

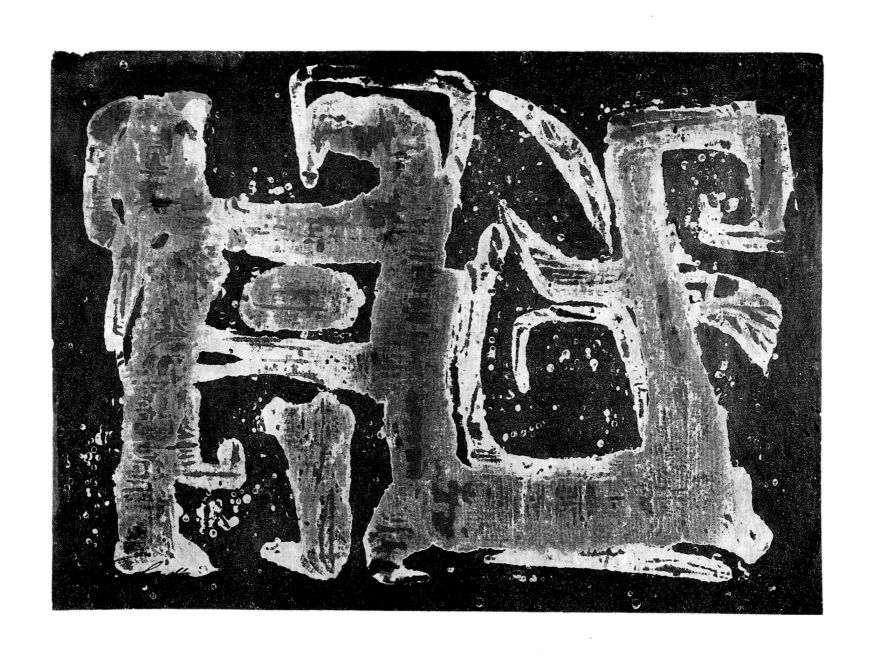

抽象版畫 62-02　ABSTRACT PRINT 62-02　1962　複合版畫　44.7×59.7cm

抽象版畫 62-03　ABSTRACT PRINT 62-03　約1962　木板版畫　45×60cm(右頁圖)

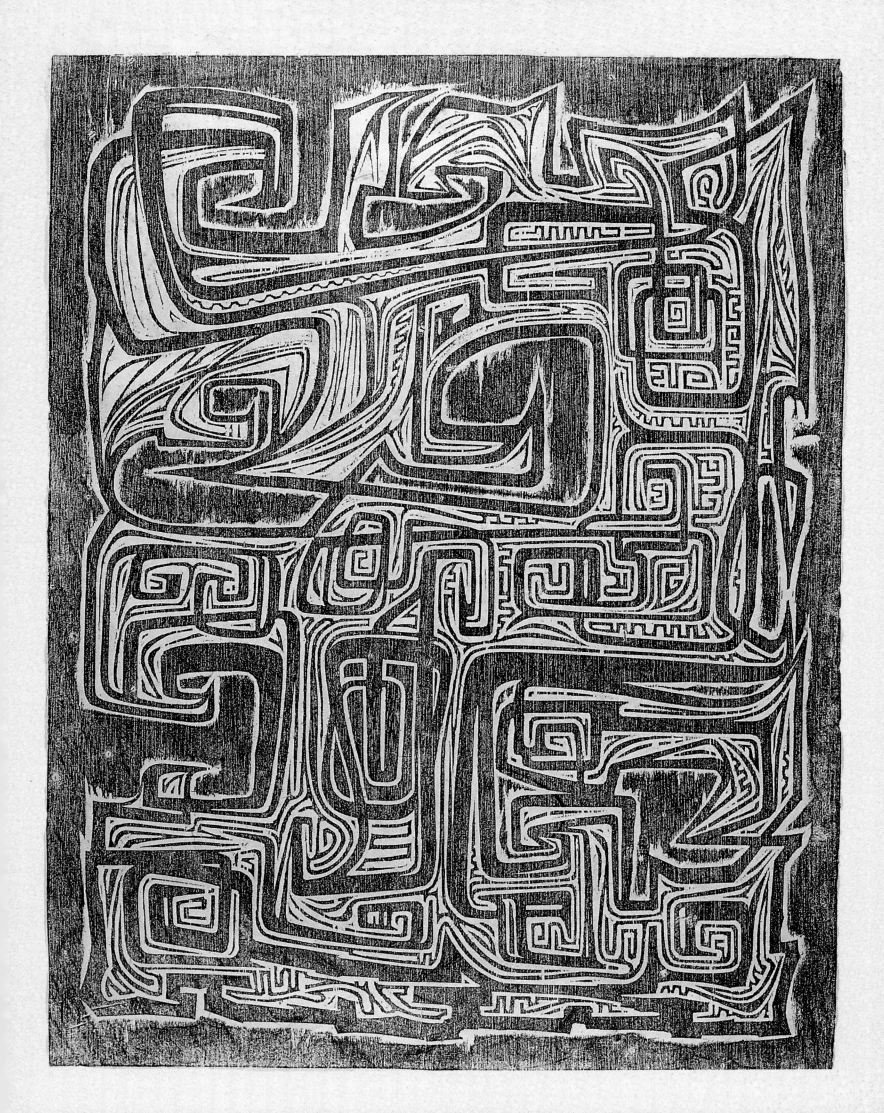

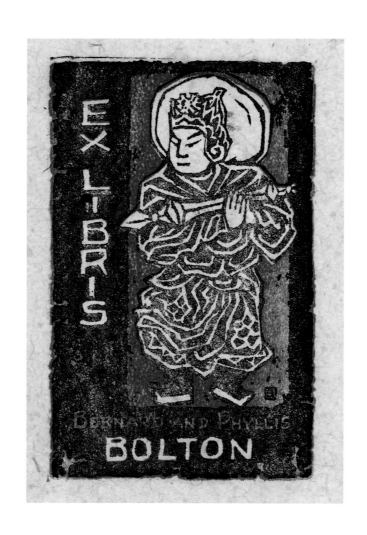

飛龍　FLYING　DRAGON　1962　木刻版畫　11.5×7cm（原寸）

狐狸的詭計　SCHEMING　FOX　1962　木刻版畫　38×25cm（右頁圖）

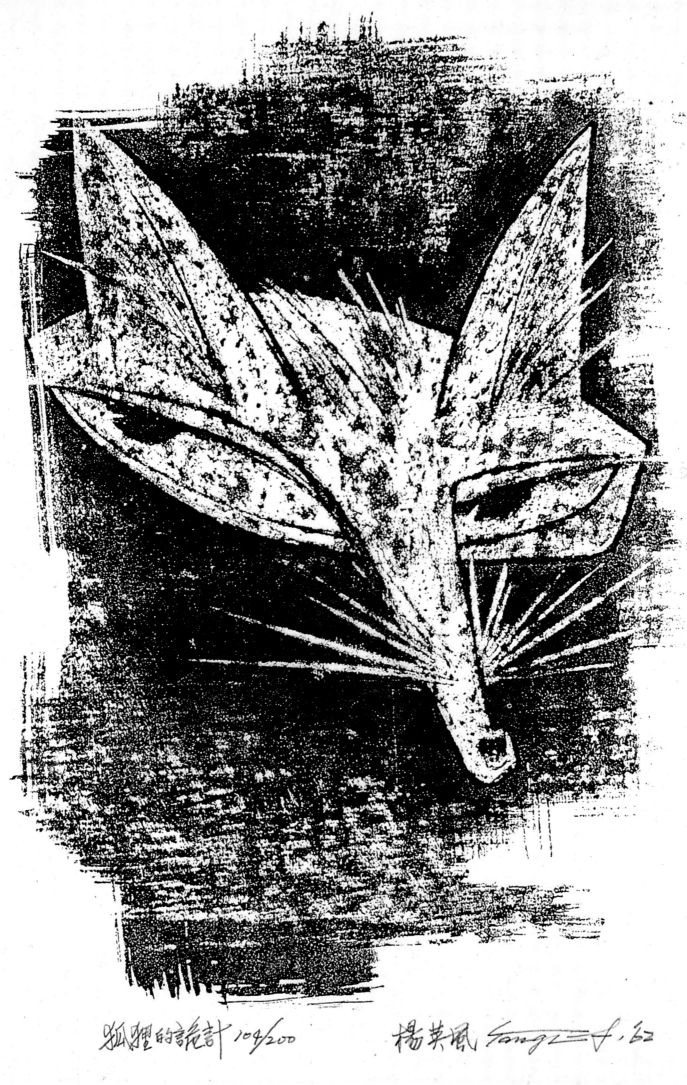

狐狸的詭計 104/200　　　　楊英風 Yang

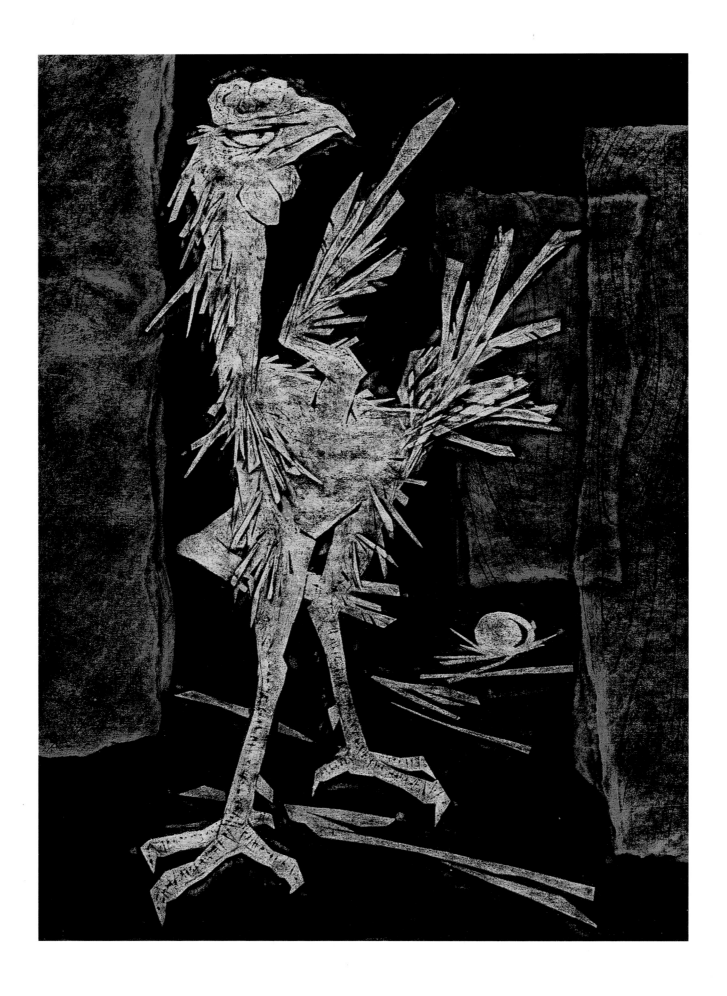

公雞生蛋（一）　ROOSTER'S EGG（1）　1962　木刻版畫　62×44cm

公雞生蛋（二）　ROOSTER'S EGG（2）　1995　電腦合成版畫　115.5×83cm（右頁圖）

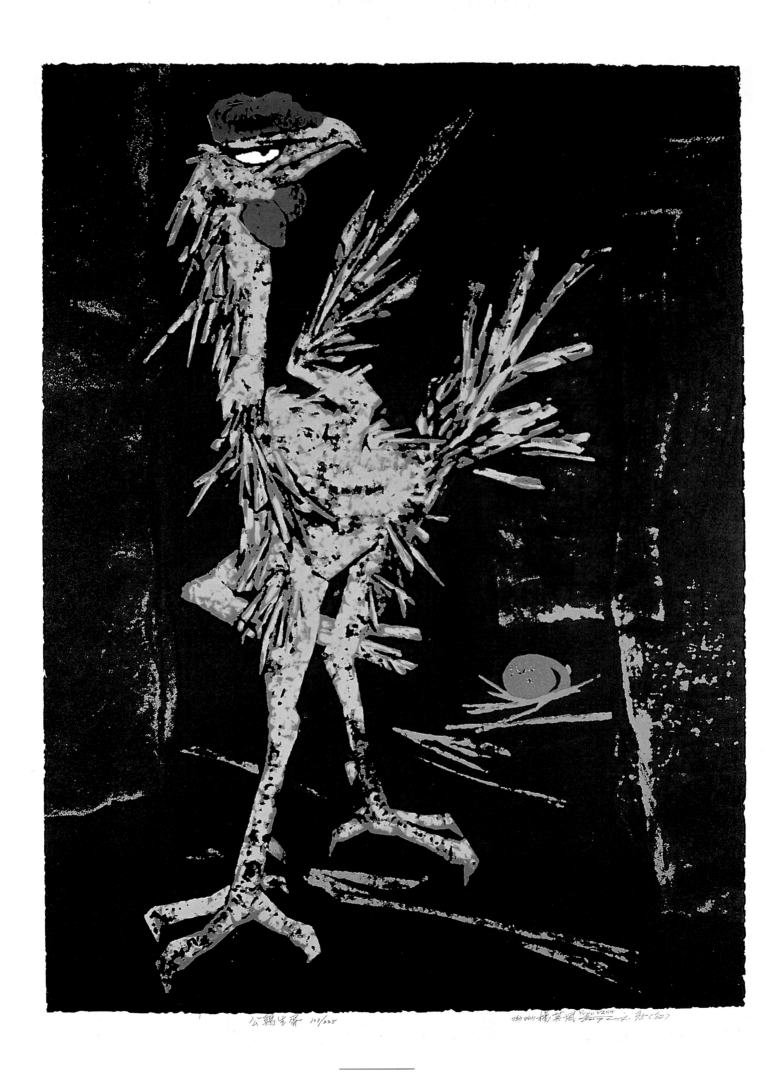

公雞生蛋 103/225　　　　　喇喇橋英風 YUYU YANG 一九八二水.經（紀）

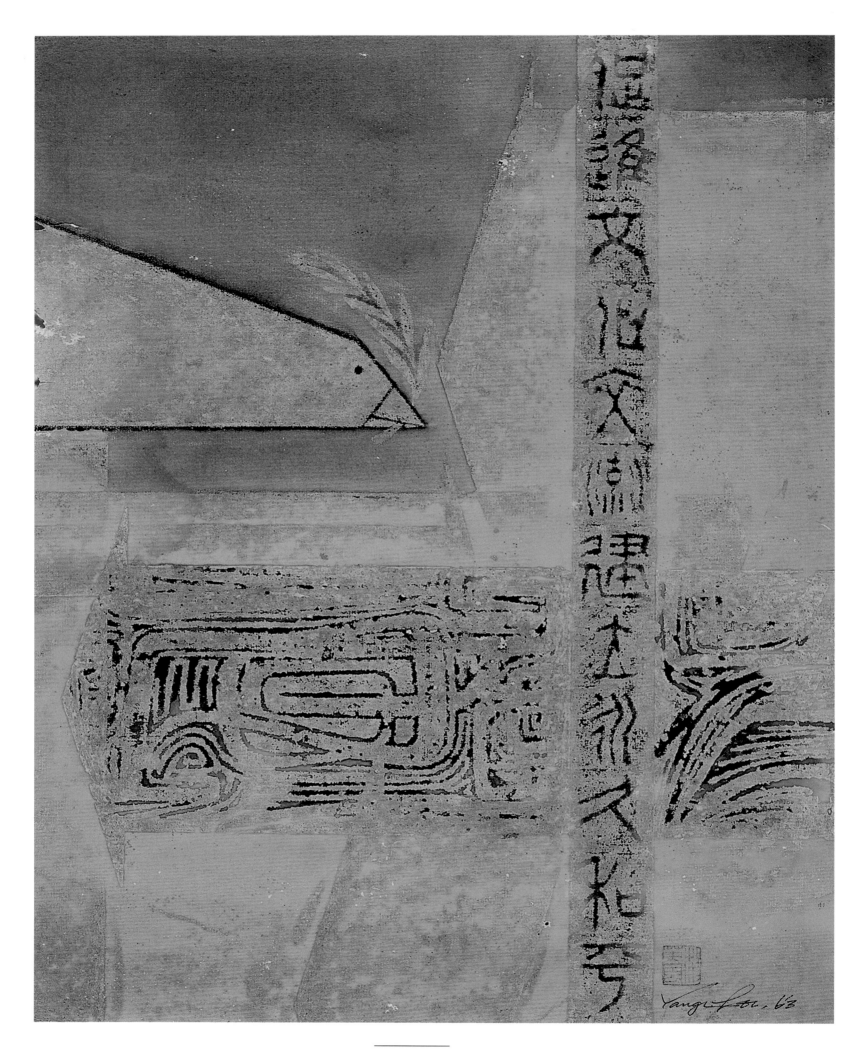

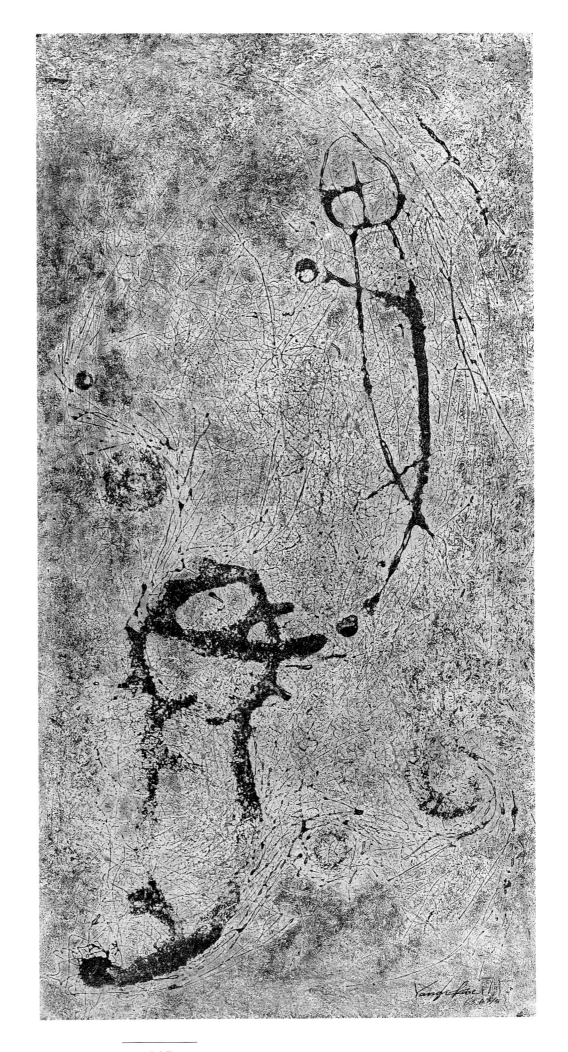

文化交流　CULTURE EXCHANGE
1963　複合版畫　39×48.5cm（左頁圖）

春（一）　SPRING（1）
1963　蔗板版畫　102×50cm

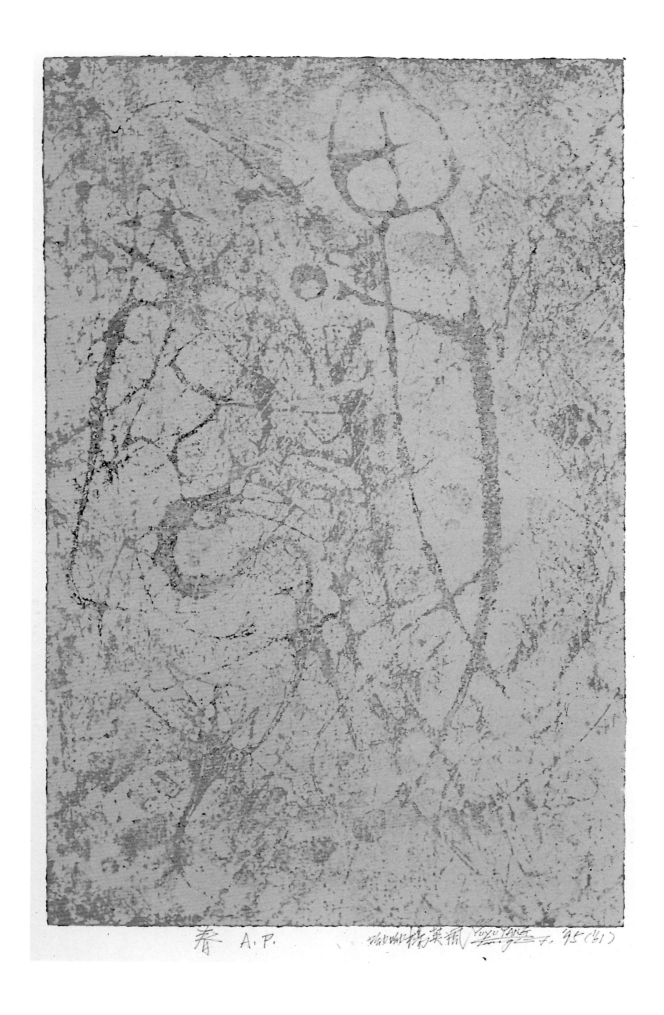

春（二）　SPRING（2）　1995　電腦合成版畫　56×35.5cm

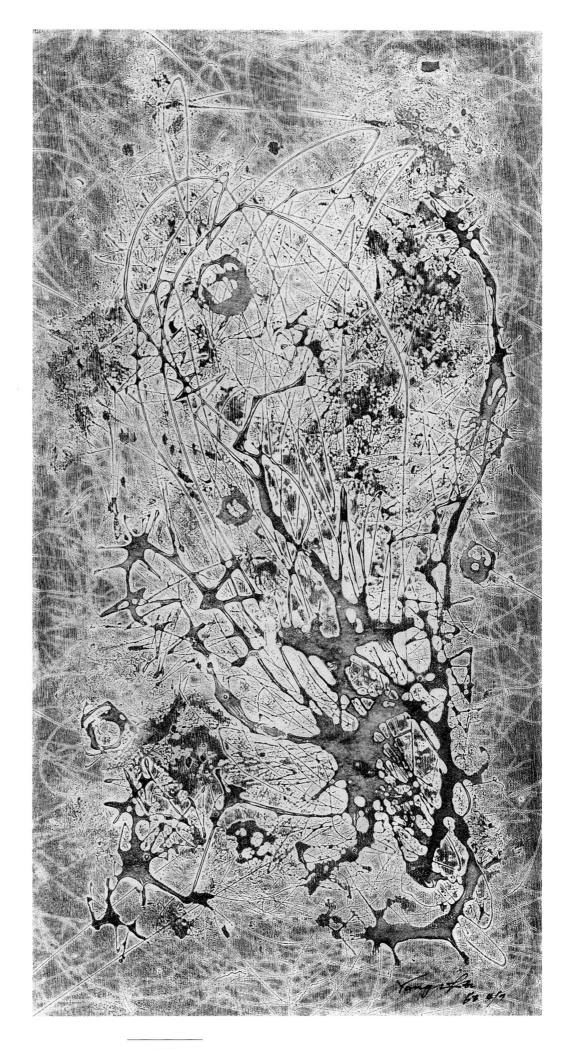

秋（一）　AUTUMN（1）

1963　木板版畫　91×45.5cm

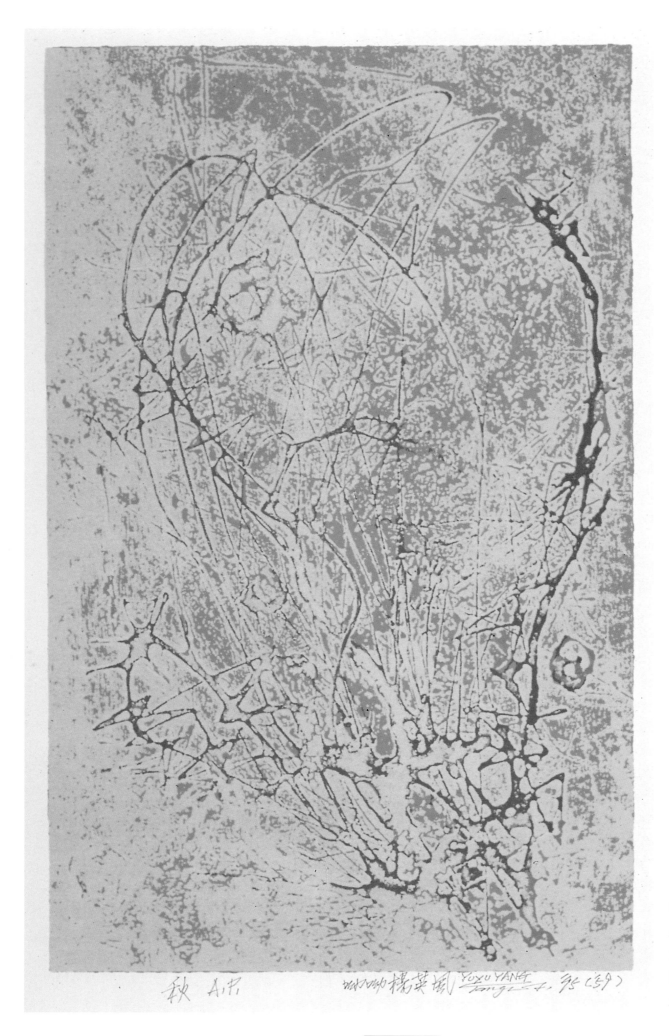

秋（二）
AUTUMN（2）
1995
電腦合成版畫
54.5×32.5cm

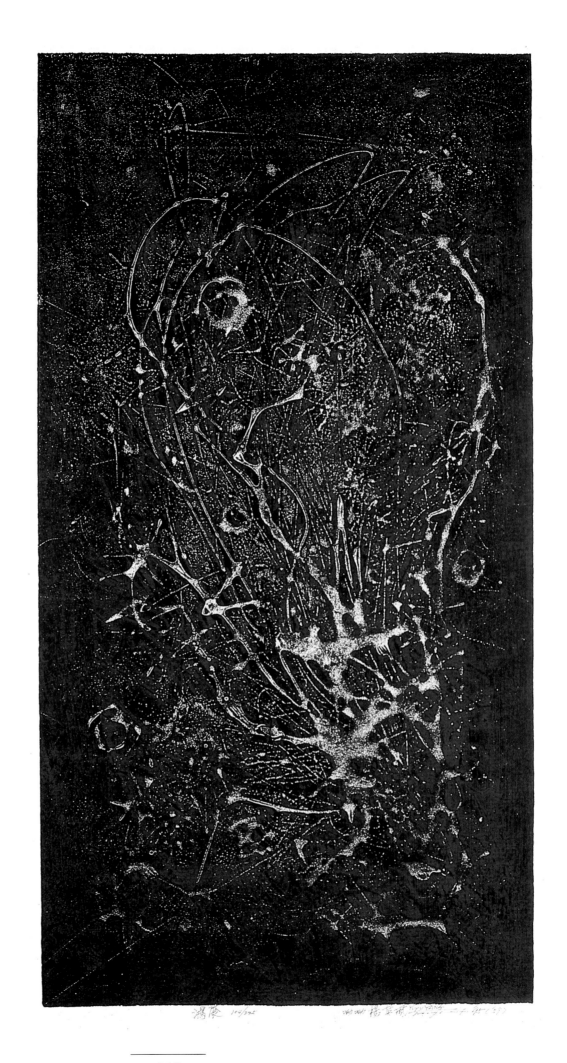

鴻展　GLORY

1995　電腦合成版畫　122×61cm

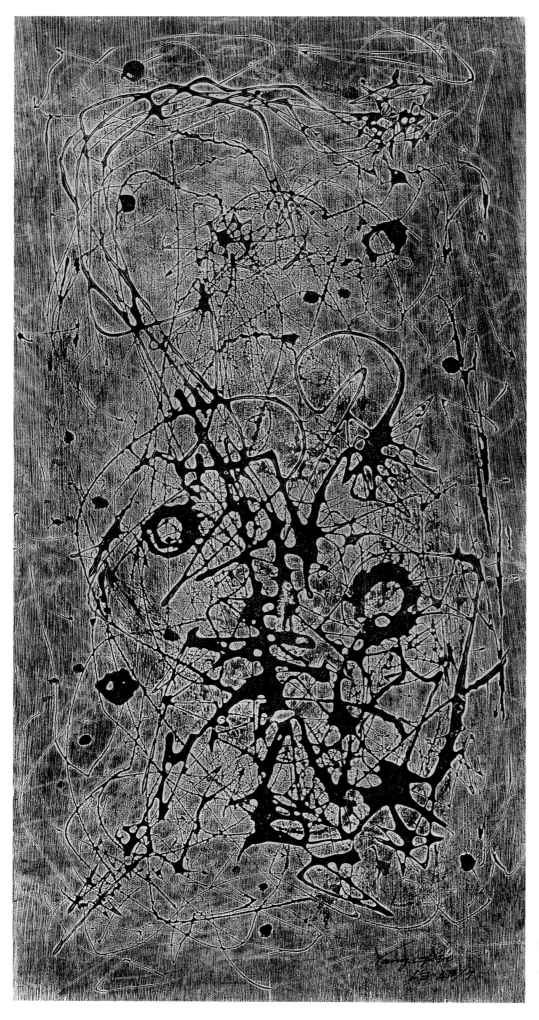

抽象版畫63-01

ABSTRACT PRINT 63-01

1963 木板版畫 91×45.5cm

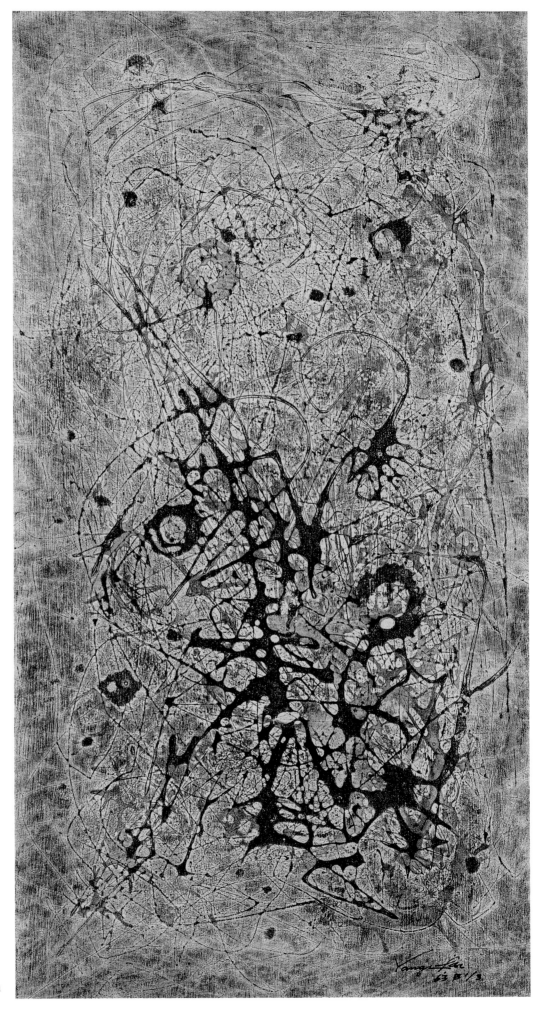

抽象版畫63-02

ABSTRACT PRINT 63-02

1963　木板版畫　91×45.5cm

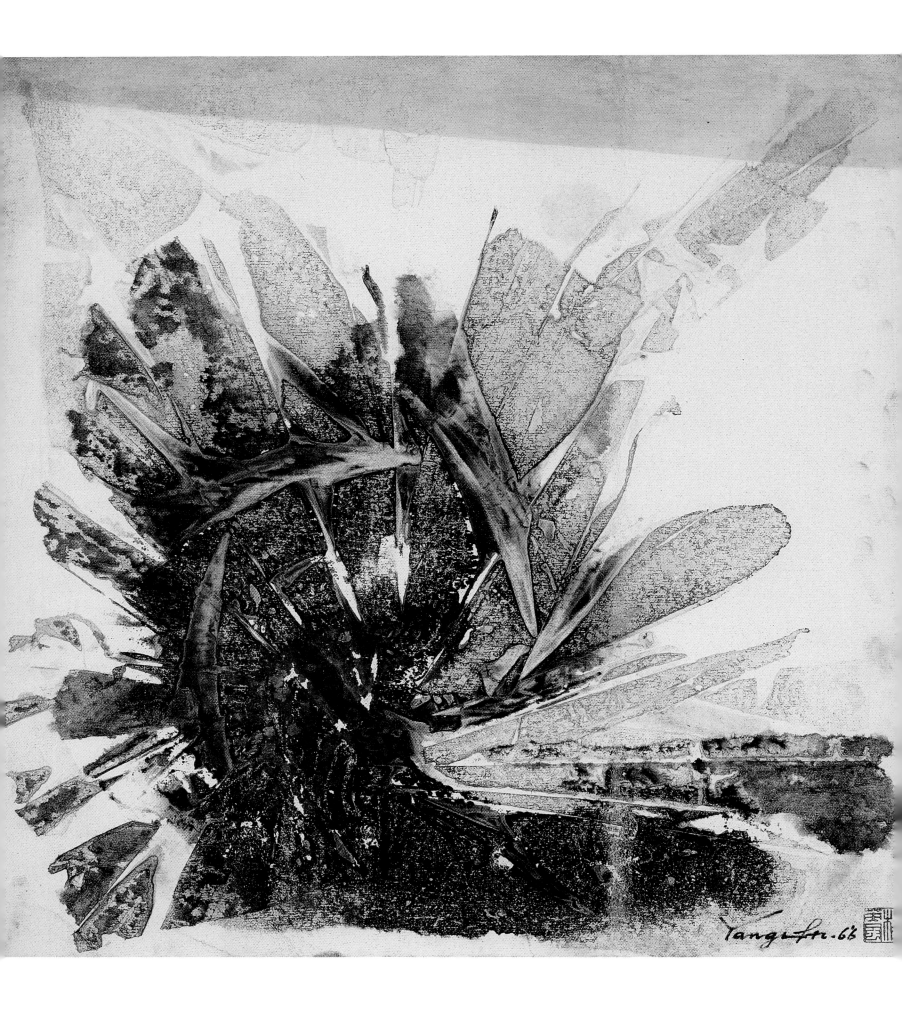

力　FORCE　1963　複合版畫　50×50cm

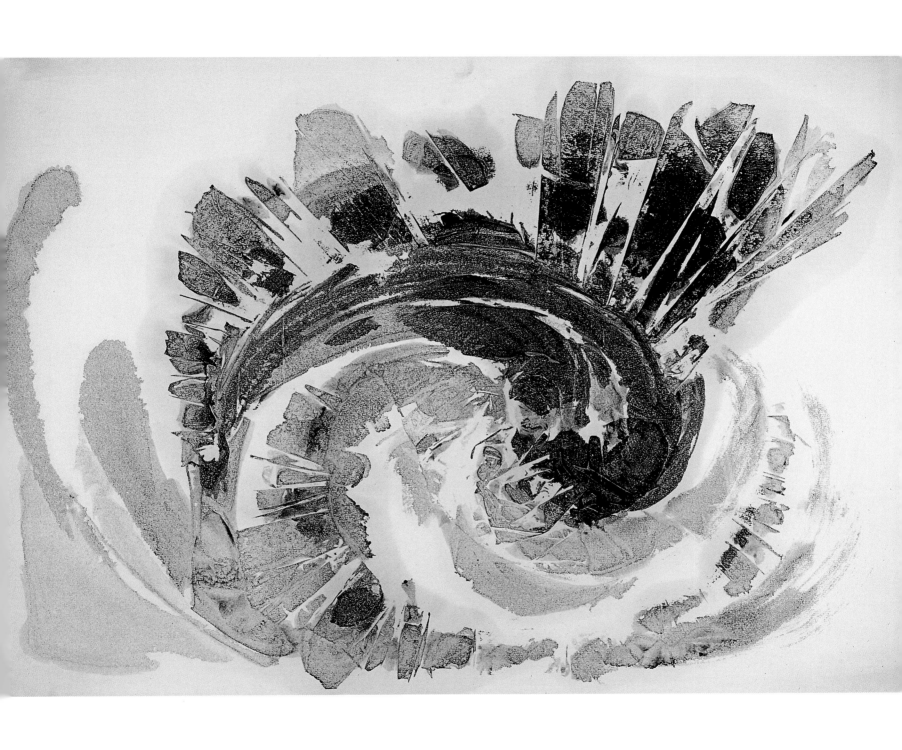

抽象版畫63-03　　ABSTRACT PRINT 63-03　　約1963-1966　　複合版畫　　60×86cm

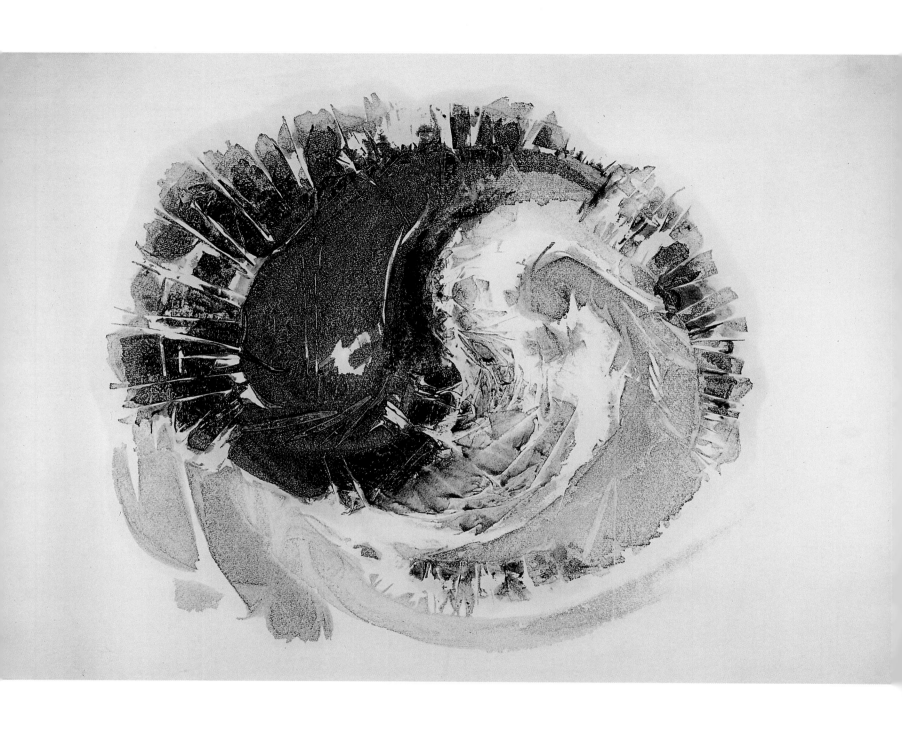

抽象版畫63-04　ABSTRACT PRINT 63-04　約1963-1966　複合版畫　55×65cm

抽象版畫64-01　ABSTRACT PRINT 64-01　1964　複合版畫　62×42cm（右頁圖）

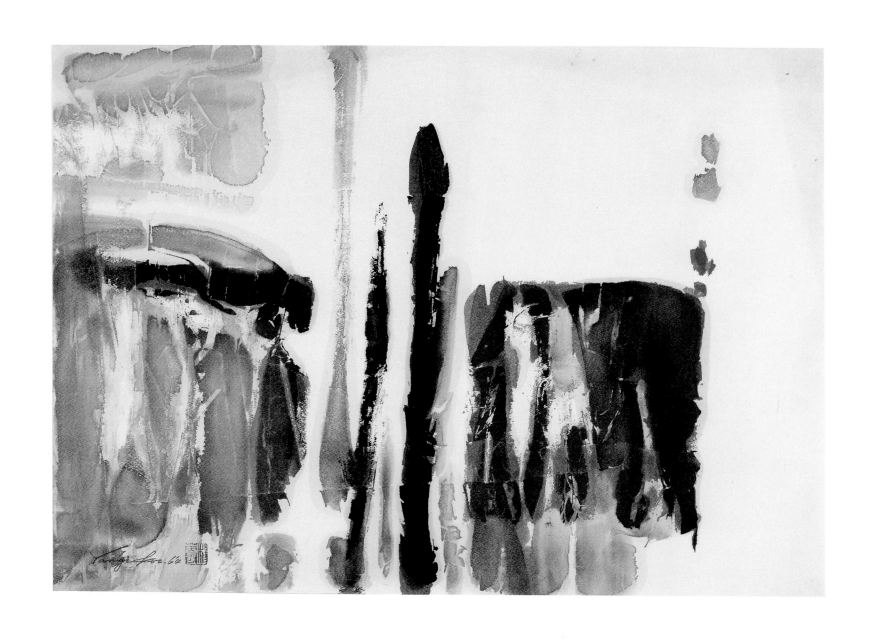

抽象版畫64-02　ABSTRACT PRINT 64-02　1964　複合版畫　47×64cm

抽象版畫64-03　ABSTRACT PRINT 64-03　約1964-1966　複合版畫　47×64.5cm

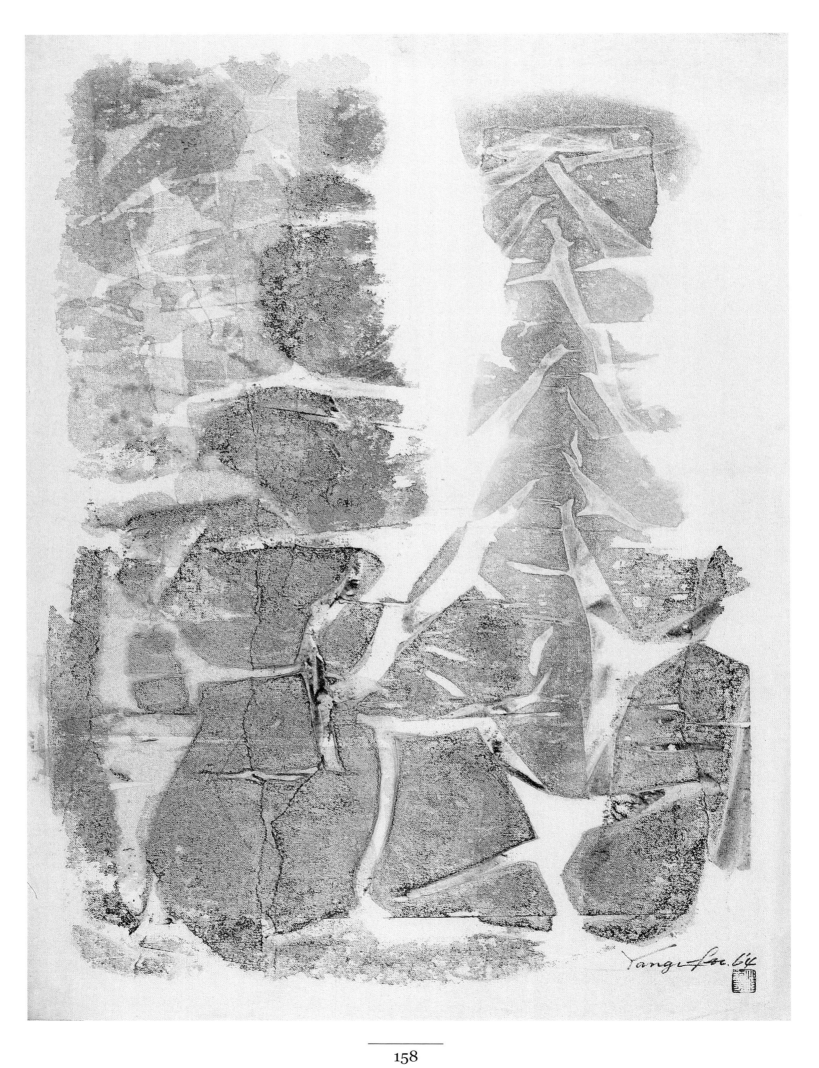

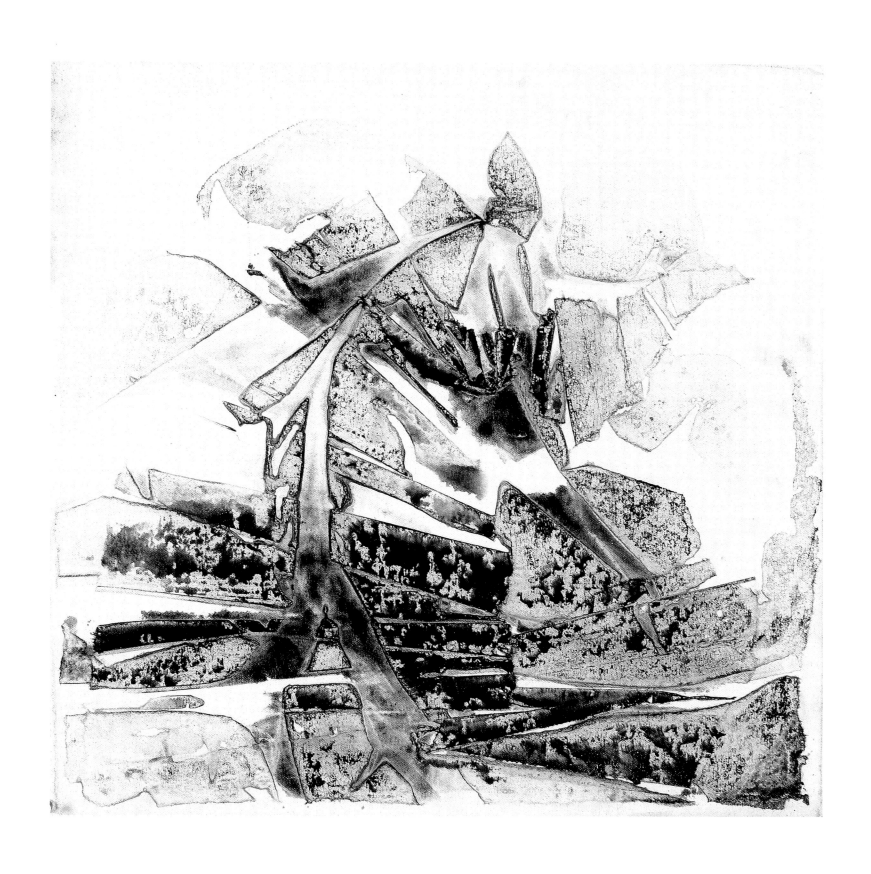

抽象版畫64-04　ABSTRACT PRINT 64-04　1964　複合版畫　77.7×59.5cm（左頁圖）

抽象版畫64-05　ABSTRACT PRINT 64-05　約1964-1966　複合版畫　48.3×48.3cm

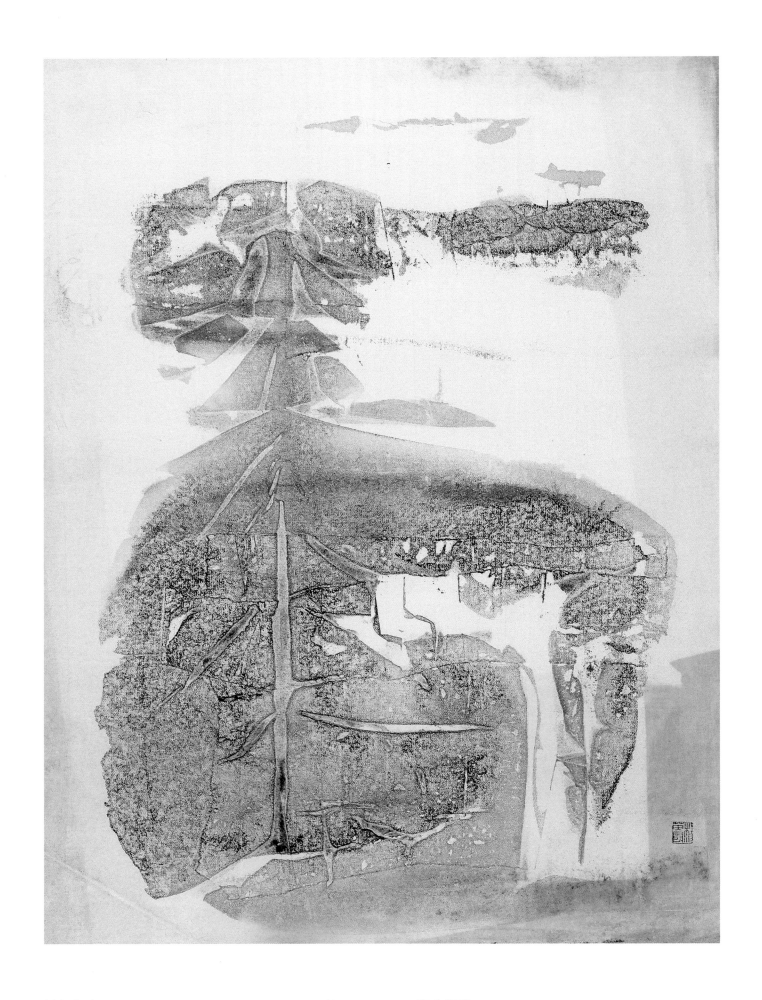

抽象版畫64-06　ABSTRACT PRINT 64-06　約1964-1966　複合版畫　79×57.5cm

抽象版畫64-07　ABSTRACT PRINT 64-07　約1964-1966　複合版畫　59×78cm(右頁圖)

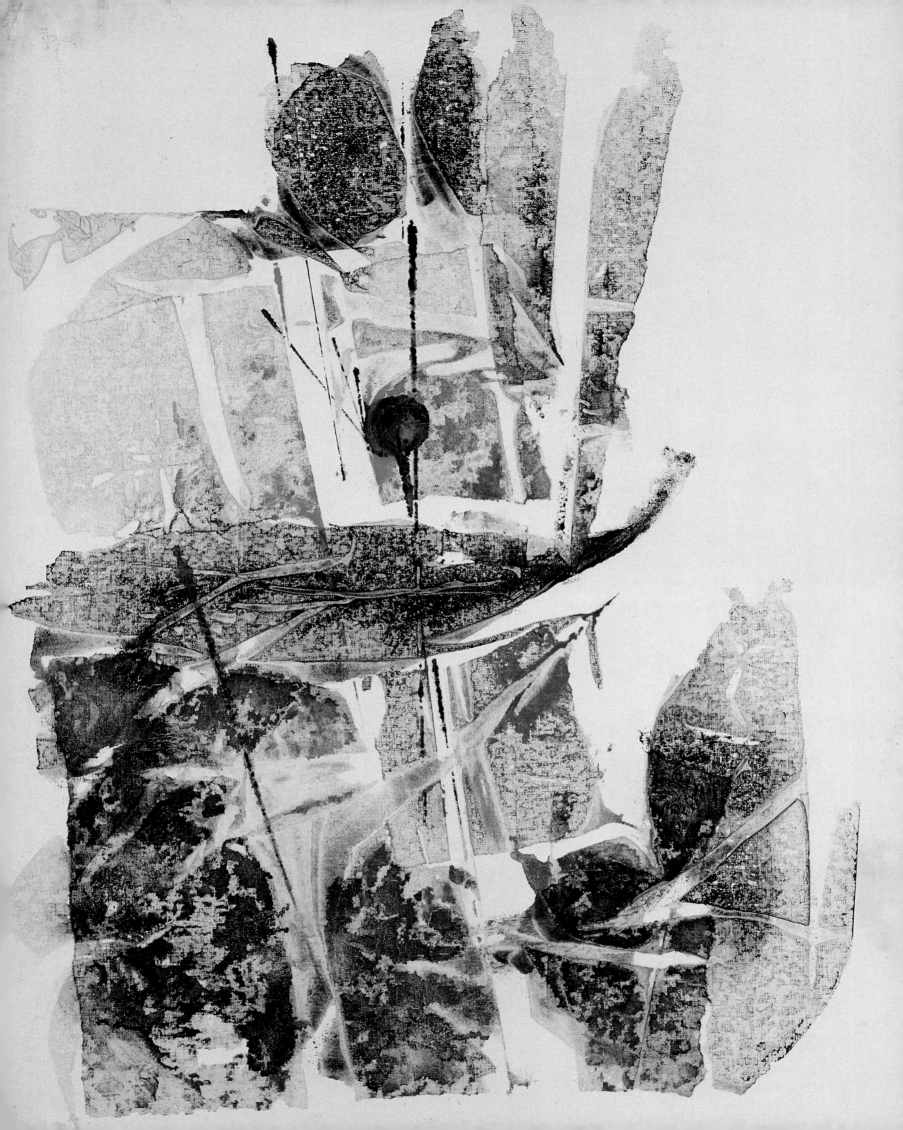

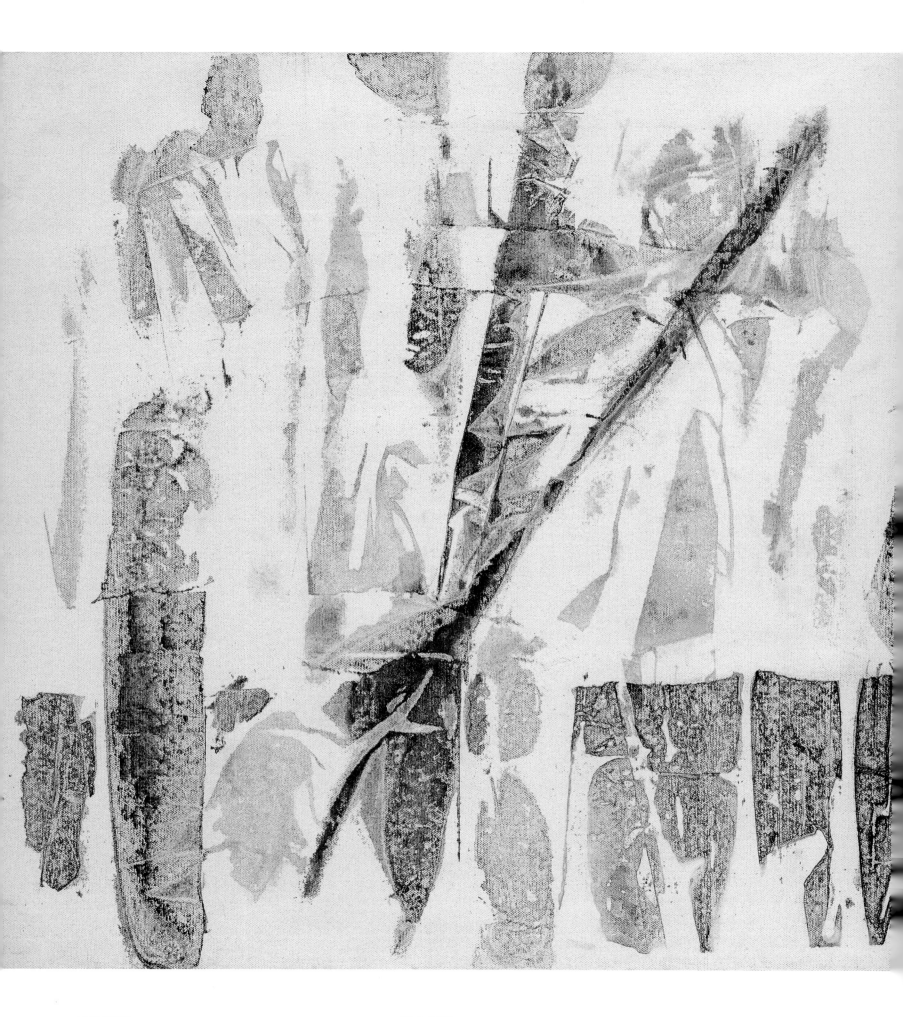

抽象版畫64-08　ABSTRACT PRINT 64-08　1964　複合版畫　59×118cm

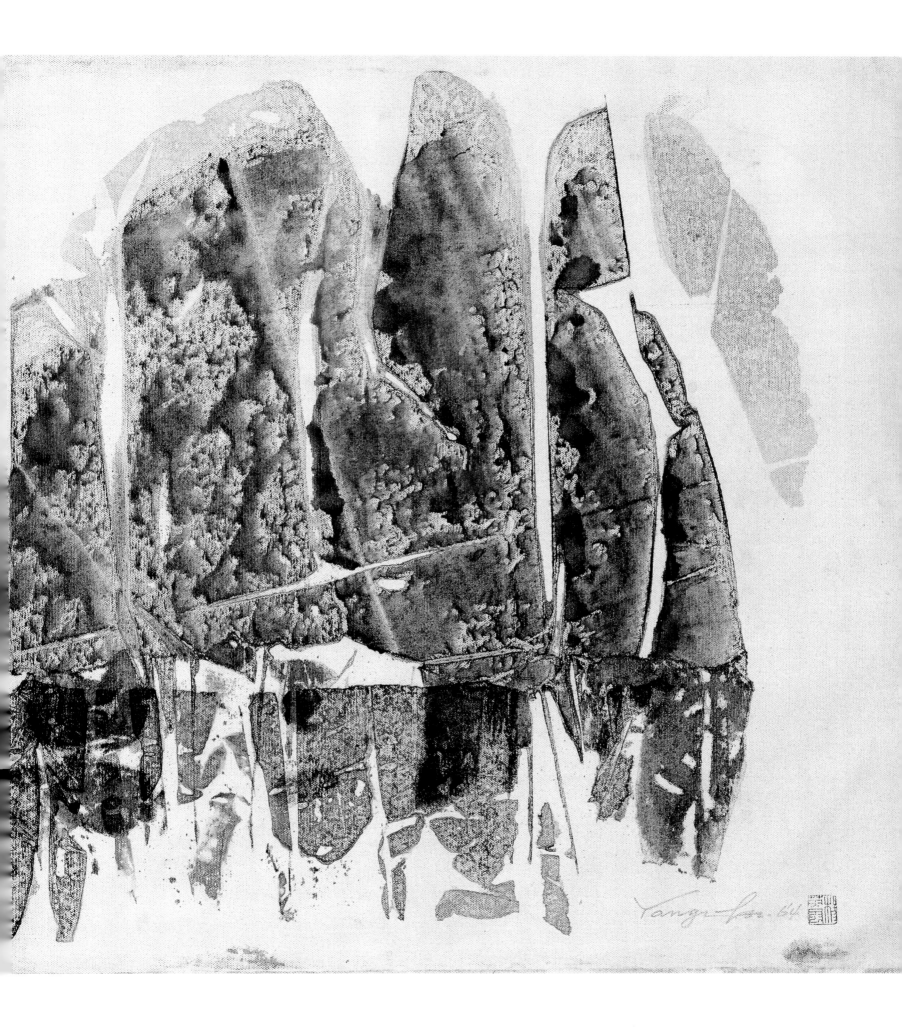

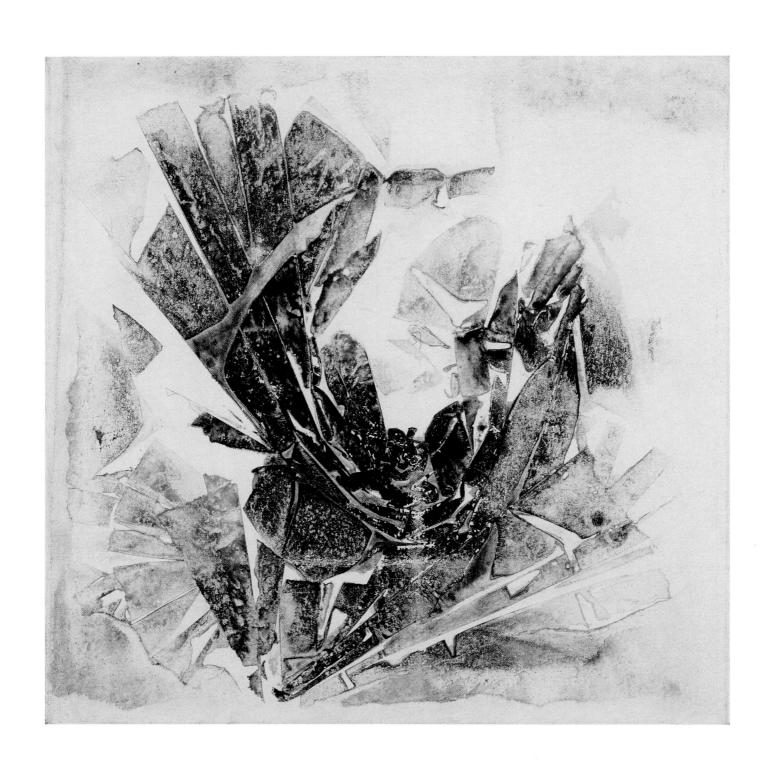

抽象版畫64-09　ABSTRACT PRINT 64-09　約1964-1966　複合版畫　49.5×48cm

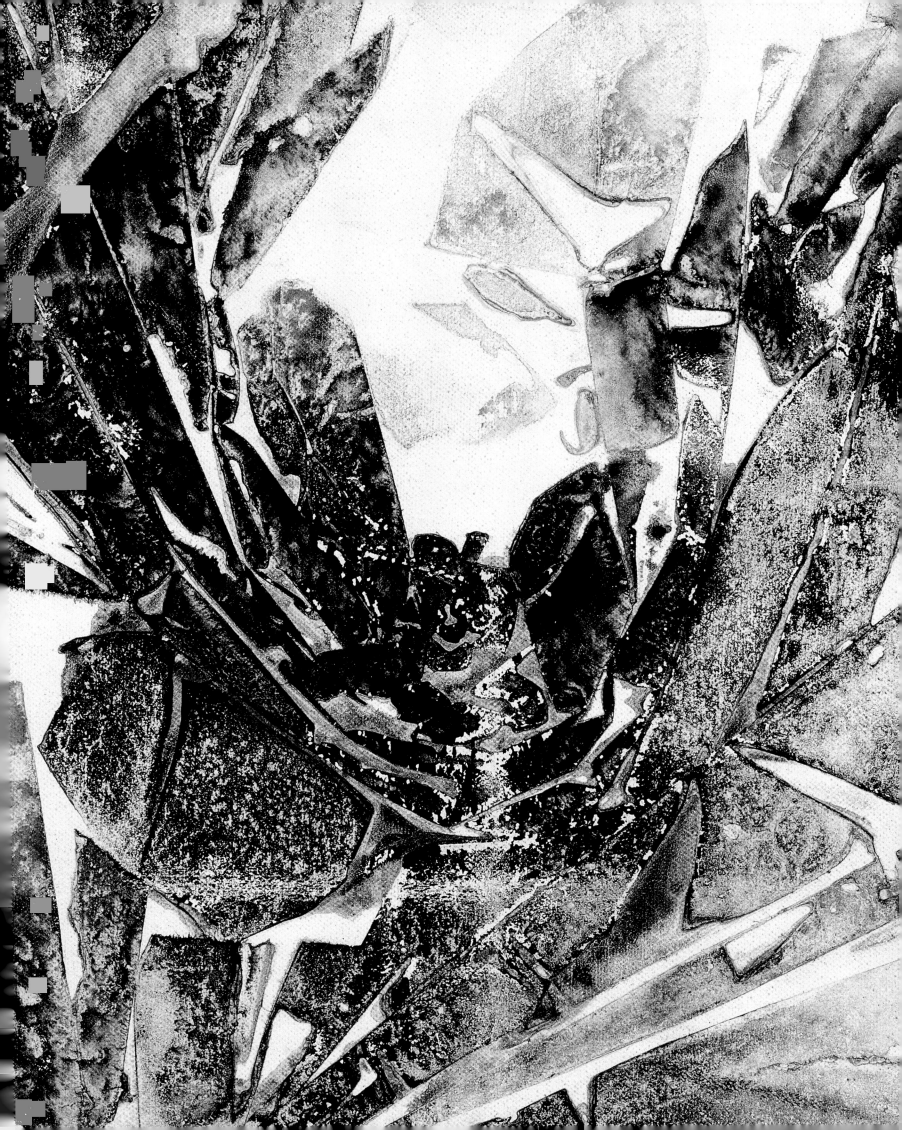

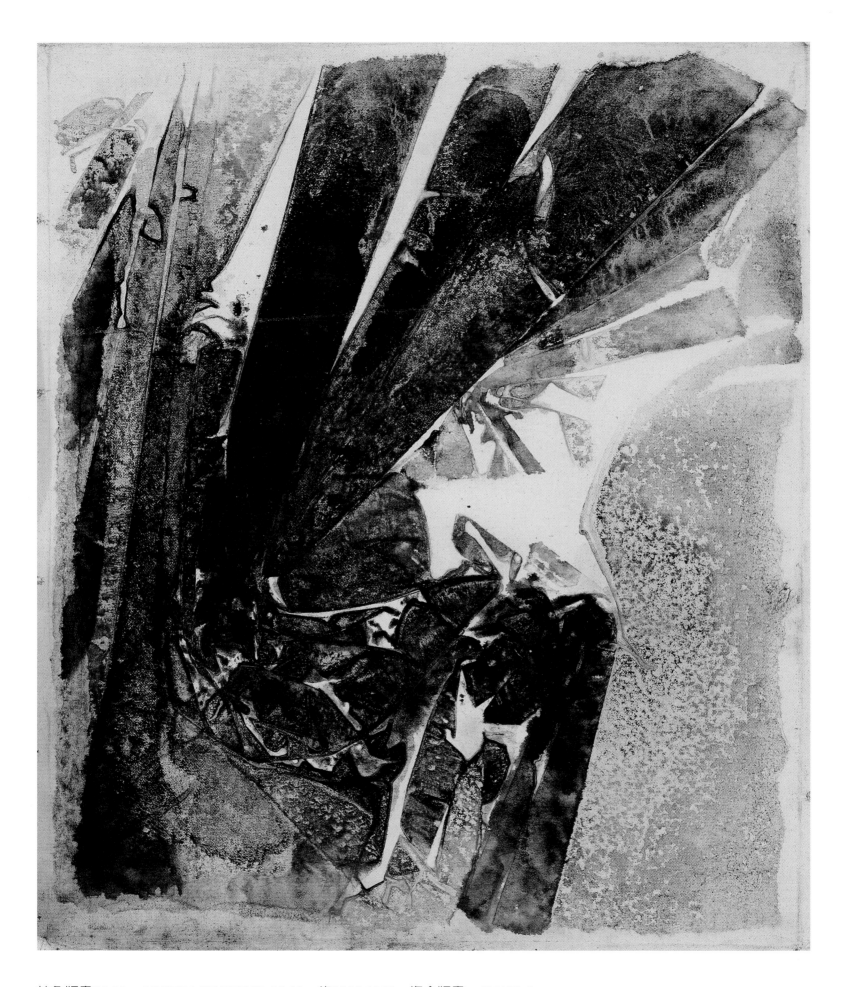

抽象版畫64-10　ABSTRACT PRINT 64-10　約1964-1966　複合版畫　49×39.5cm

虛靜觀其反覆・羅第55號　CHANGES PRESERVED IN SILENCE：R.55　1966　複合版畫　78.2×59cm（右頁圖）

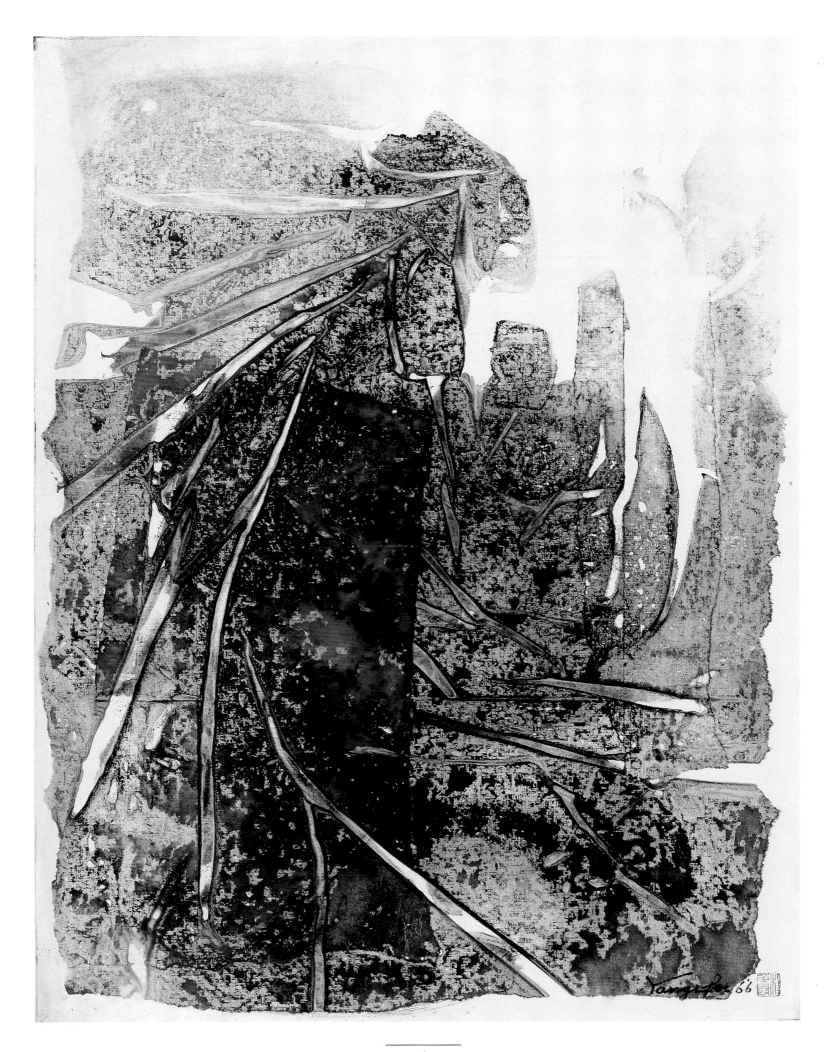

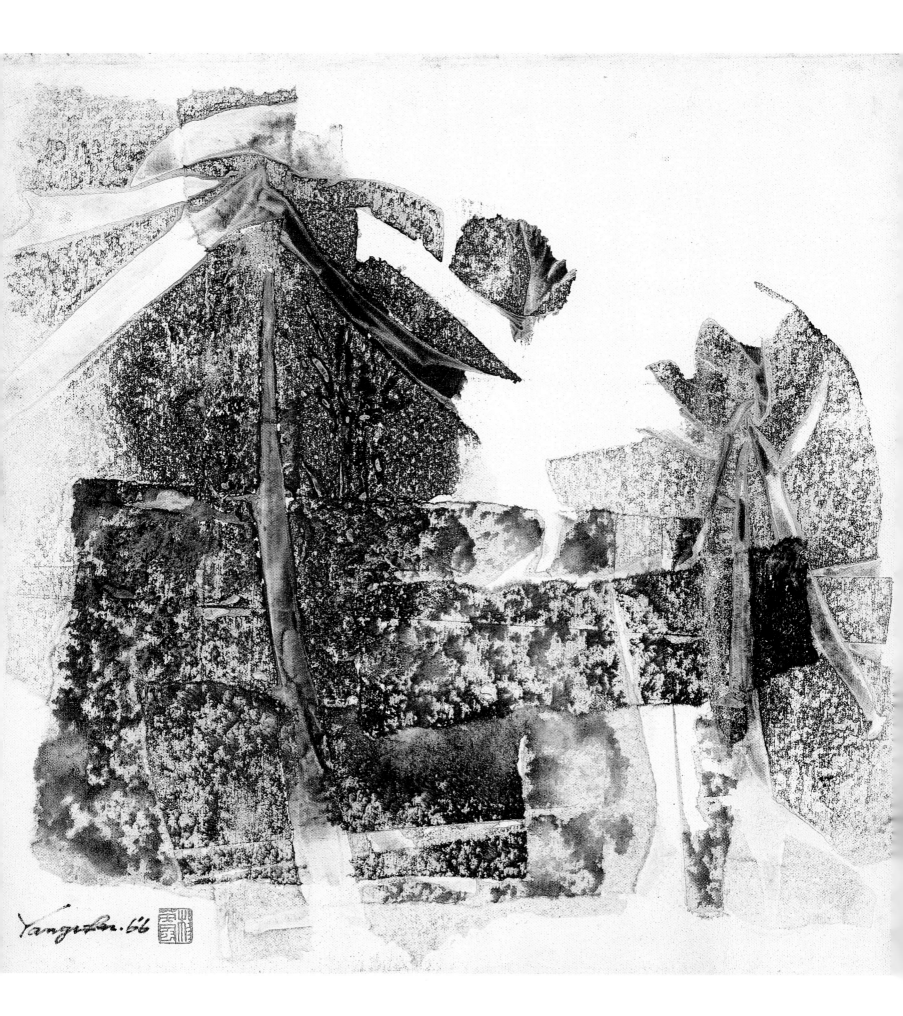

抽象版畫66-01　ABSTRACT PRINT 66-01　1966　複合版畫　49.5×49cm

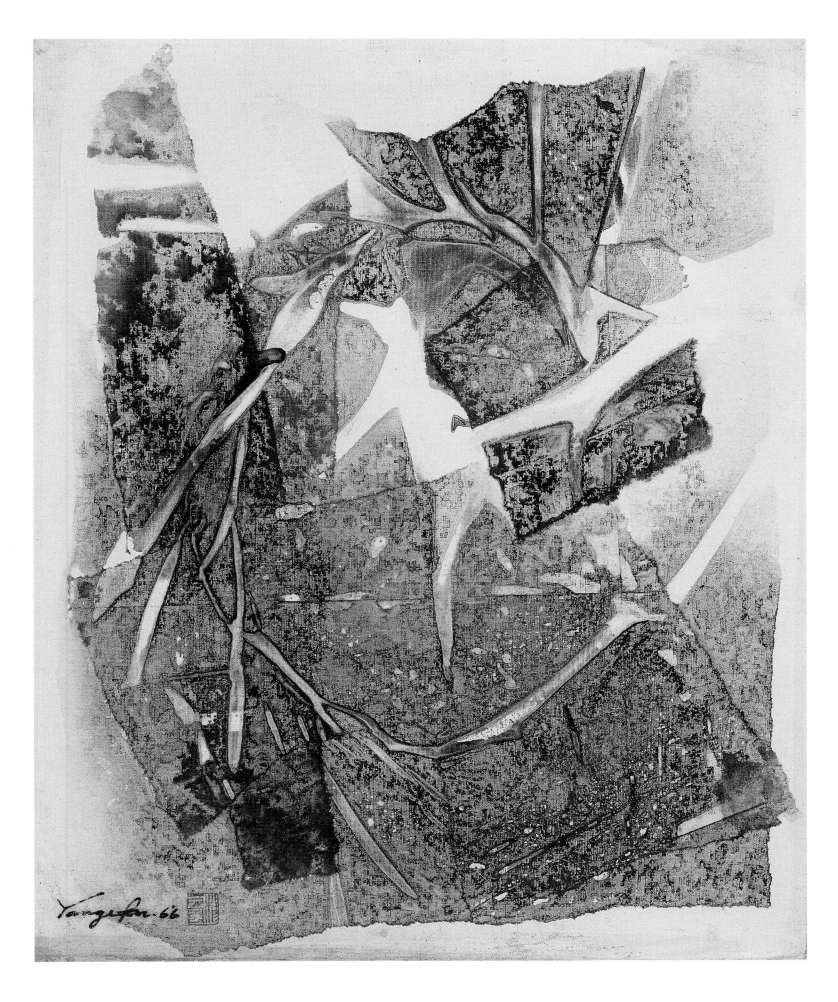

抽象版畫66-02　ABSTRACT PRINT 66-02　1966　複合版畫　53×44cm

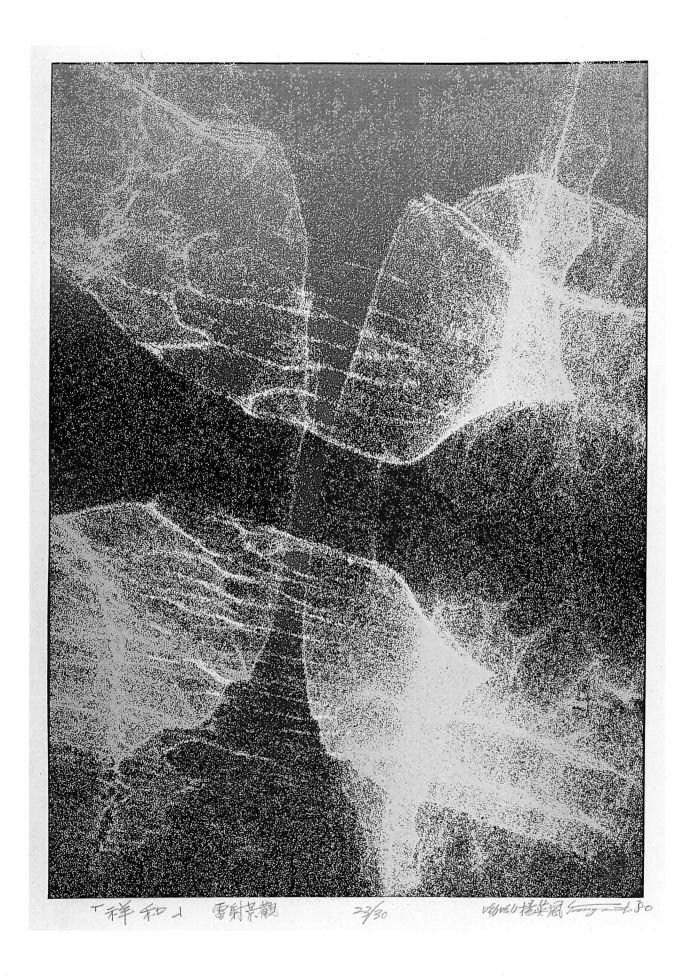

祥和　HARMONY　1980　絹版版畫　51×35cm

禪　ZEN　1980　絹版版畫　51×35cm（右頁圖）

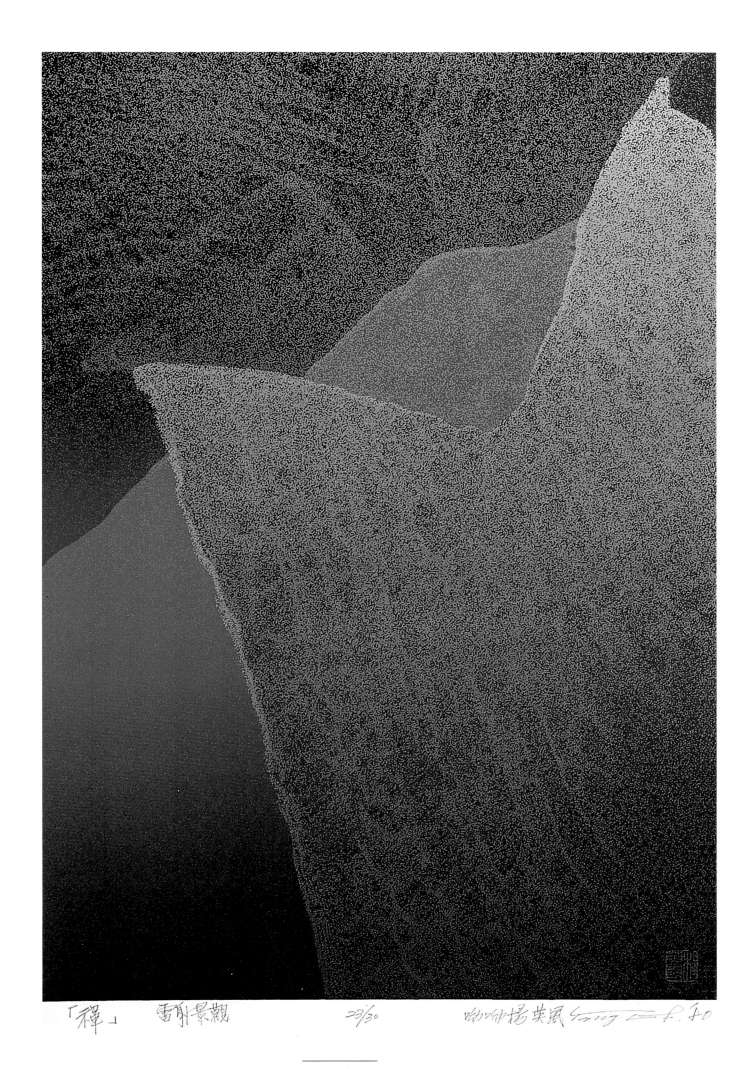

「禪」　雷射景觀　　　　　23/30　　　　　呦呦楊英風 ⋯⋯ P.40

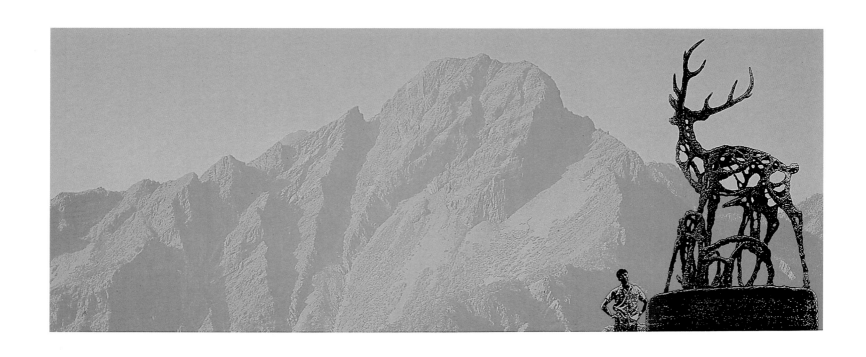

玉山春曉　DEER & JADE MOUNTAIN　1994　電腦合成版畫　35×89cm

福祿　DEER'S EAGERNESS　1994　電腦合成版畫　45×45cm（右頁圖）

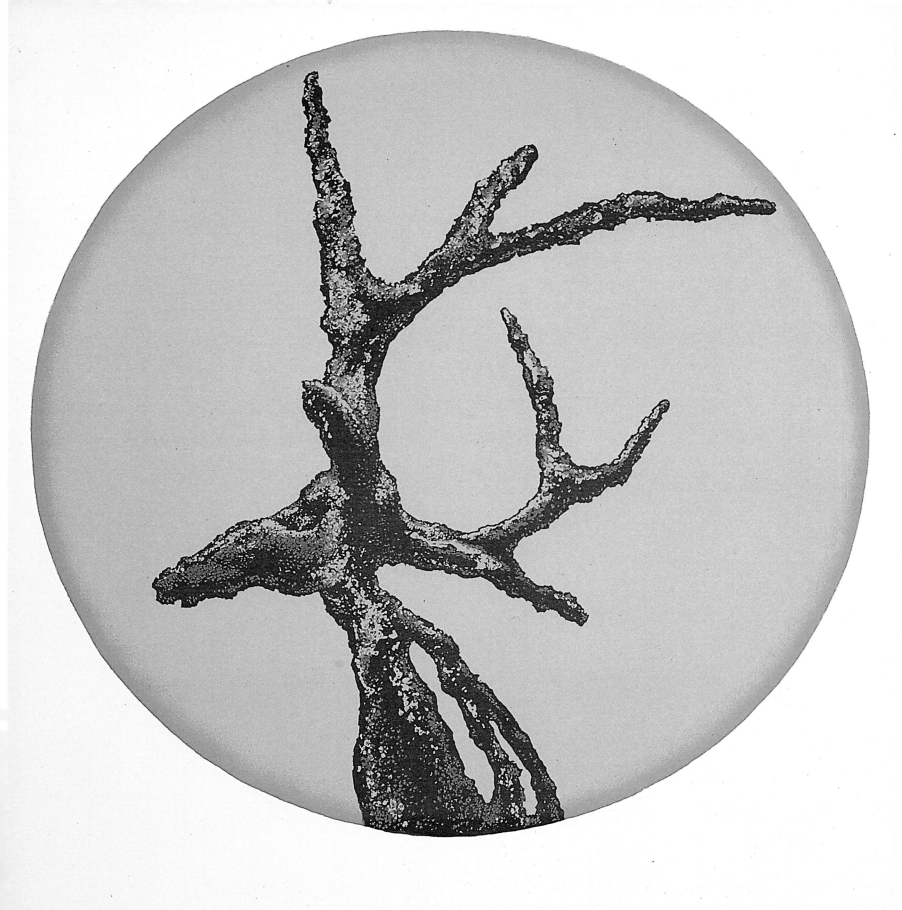

福祿　102/225　　　　　　　呦呦楊英風 YUYU YANG 呦呦 75 (63)

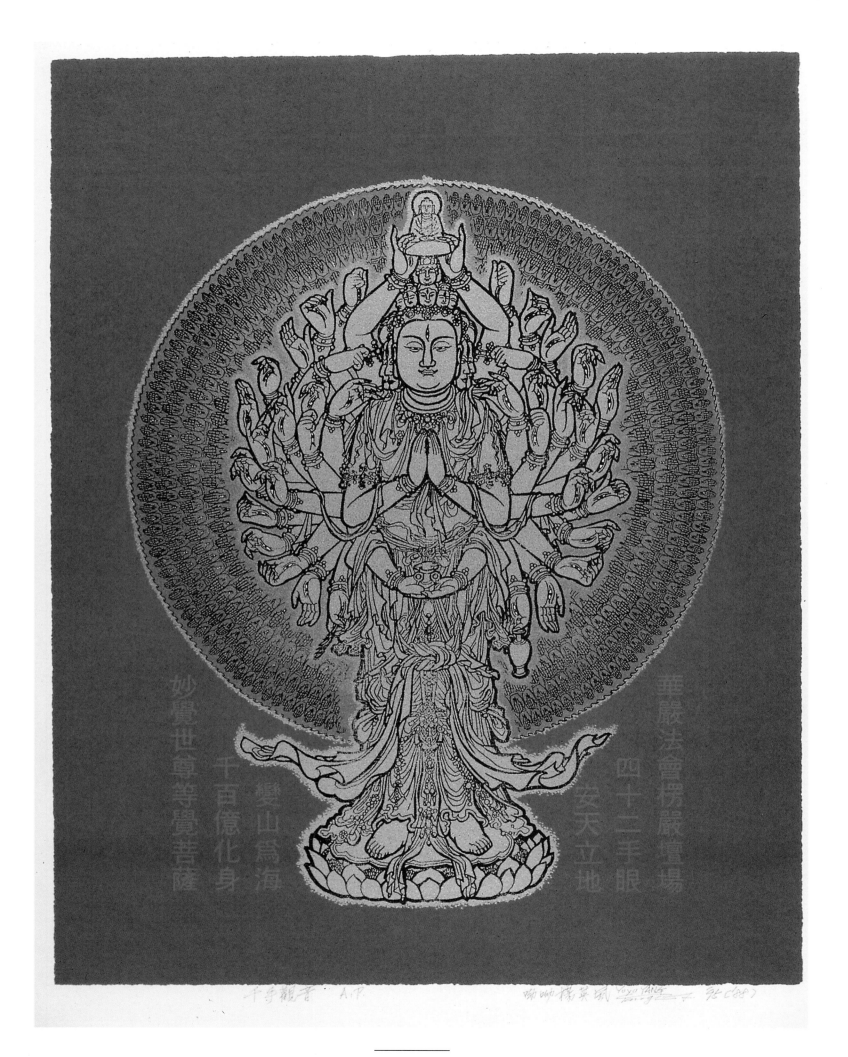

華嚴法會楞嚴壇場
四十二手眼
安天立地

妙覺世尊等覺菩薩
變山為海
千百億化身

千手觀音　A.P.
嗡嗡楊菜斌　Yoyu Yange　　死（88）

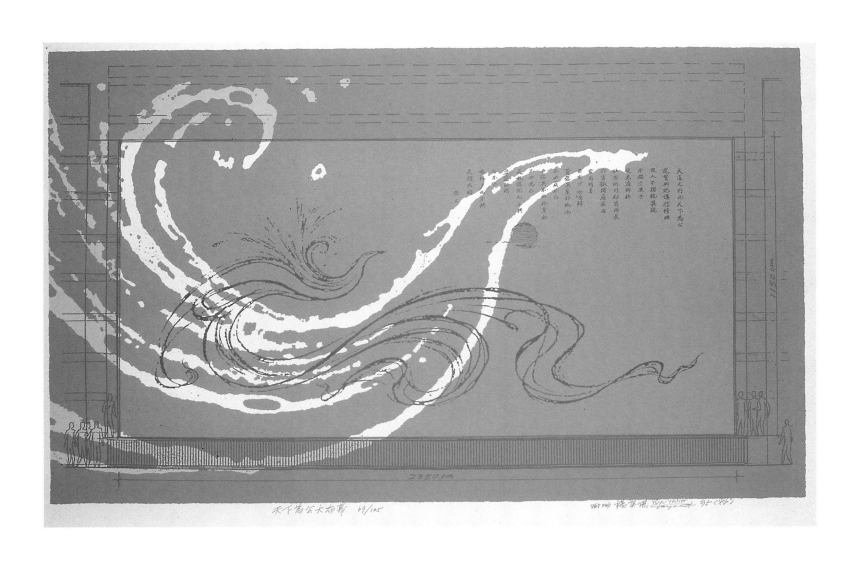

千手觀音　THE THOUSAND HAND GODDNESS-KUANYIN　1995　電腦合成版畫　88.5×69cm（左頁圖）

天下為公大布幕　JUSTICE　1995　電腦合成版畫　63×102cm

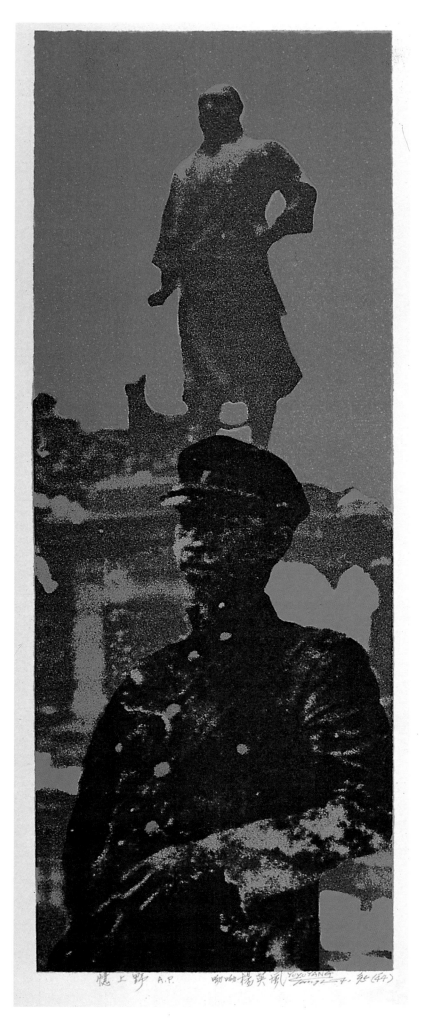

憶上野　RECALL THE SHANG-YE PARK

1995　電腦合成版畫　89×32cm

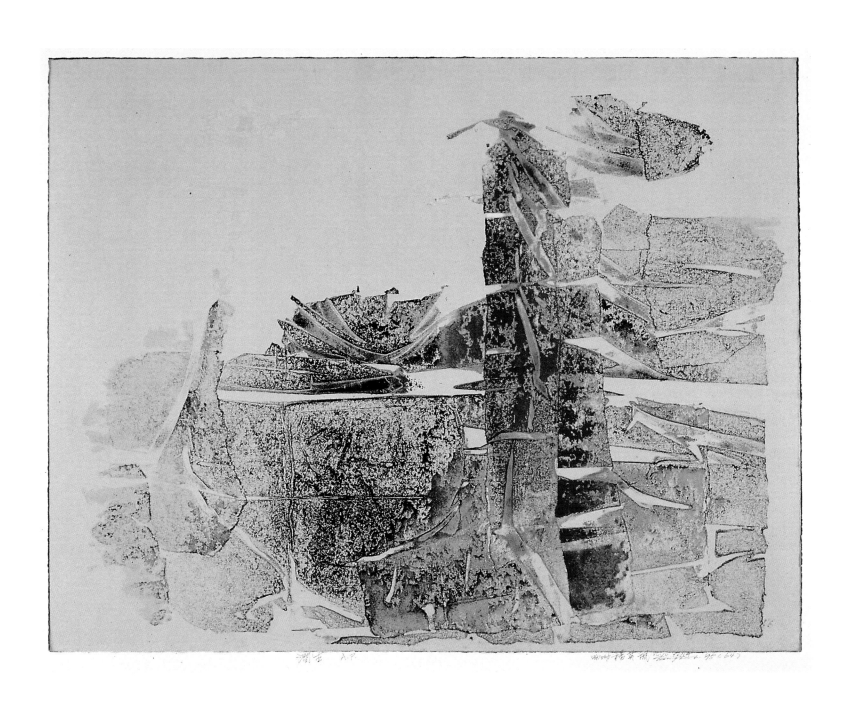

潤生　JOY OF LIFE　1995　電腦合成版畫　112×92cm

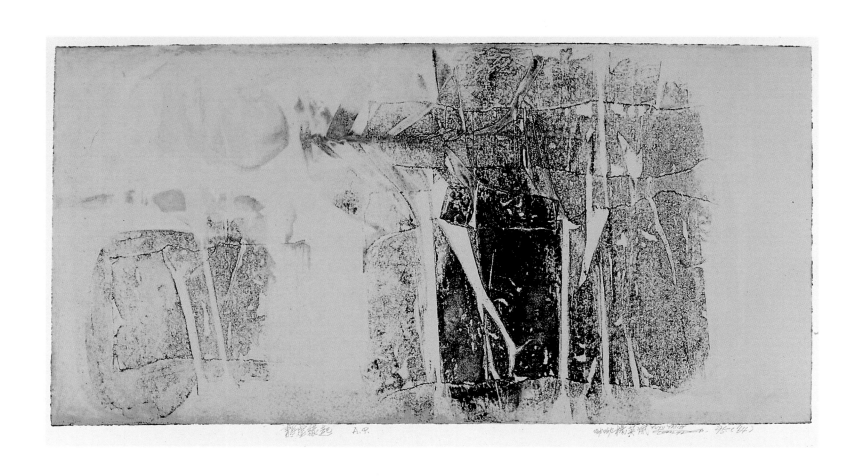

靜虛緣起　ORIGIN　1995　電腦合成版畫　55×107cm

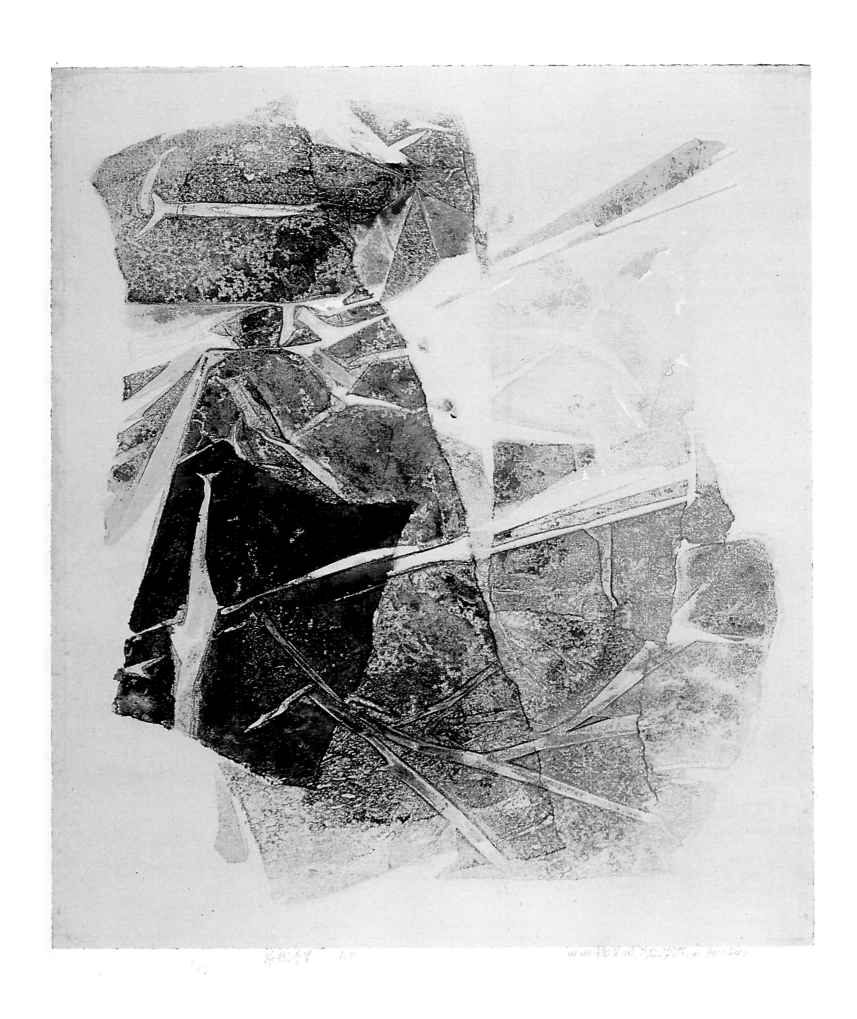

昂然千里　ADVANCE　1995　電腦合成版畫　106×88cm

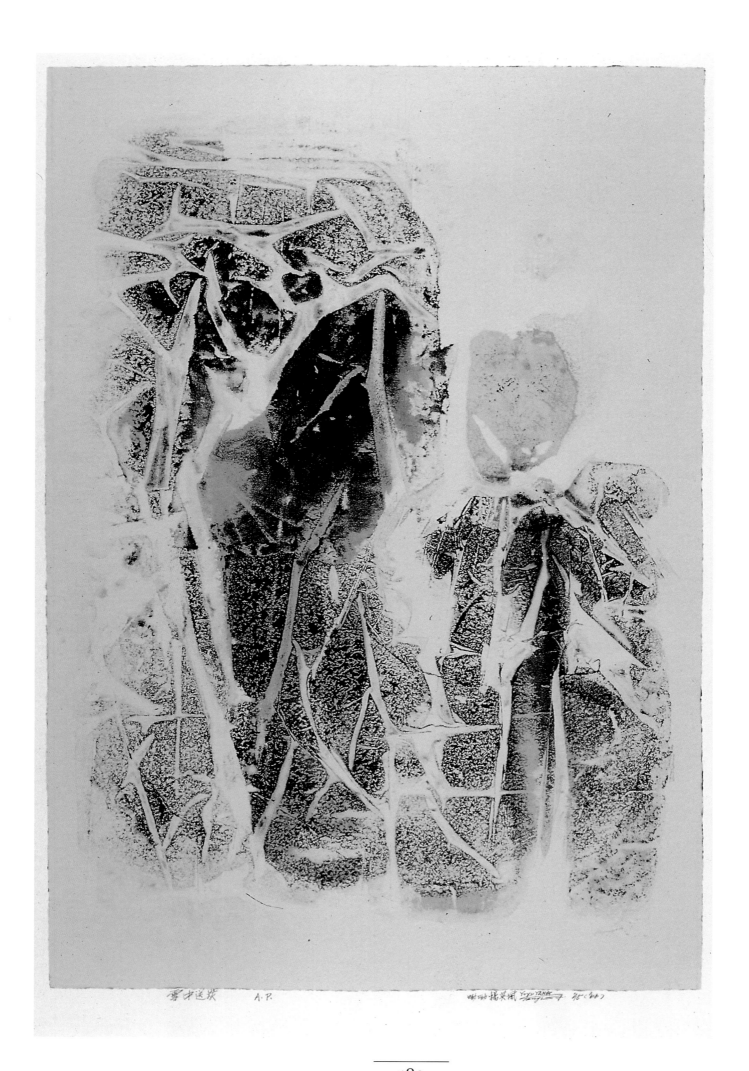

雾中送葬　　A.P.　　　　　　　嘟嘟撈荚域 YUI YANG　　　95（366）

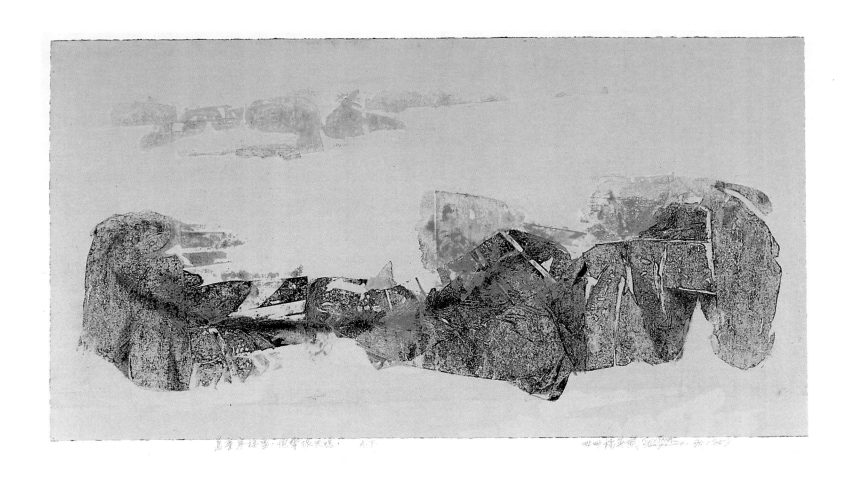

雪中送炭　HELPING　1995　電腦合成版畫　131×90cm（左頁圖）

島慶寒梅盛·砲響振天鳴　CELEBRATION　1995　電腦合成版畫　58×107cm

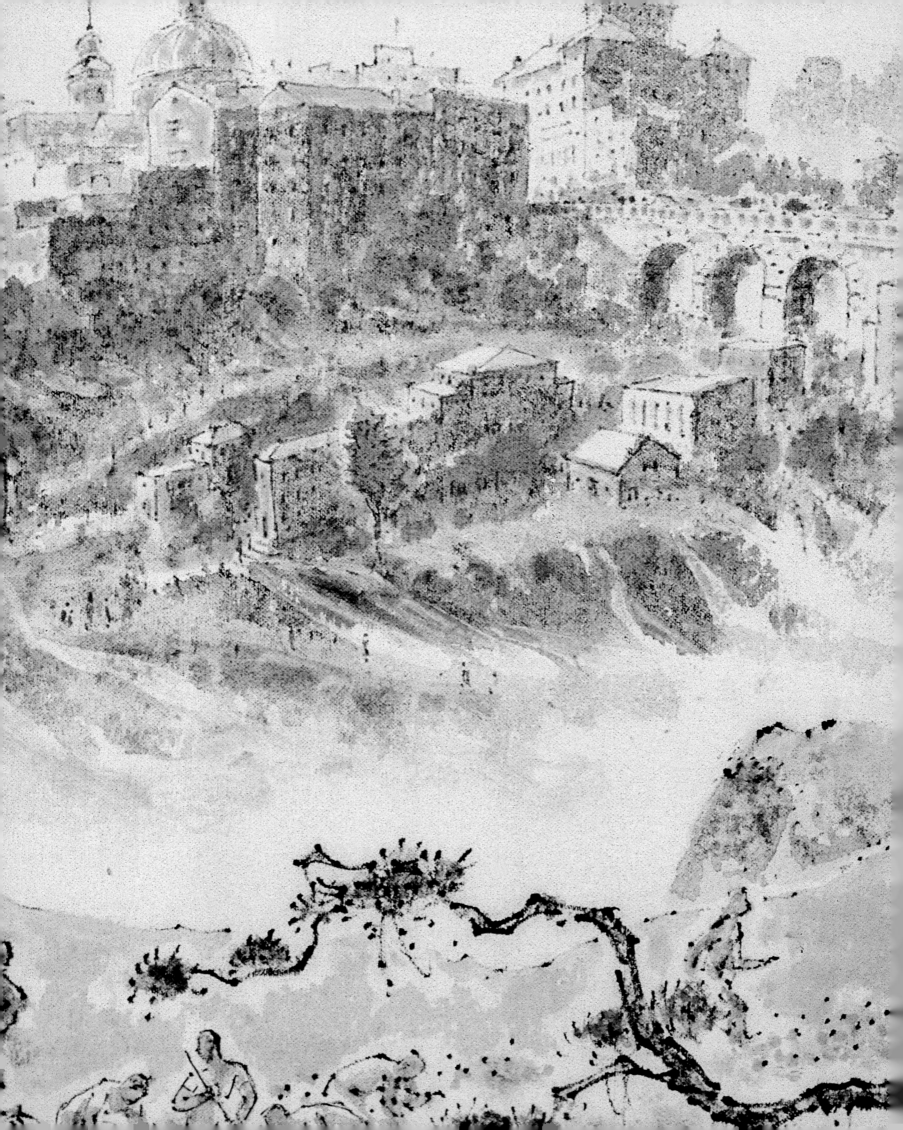

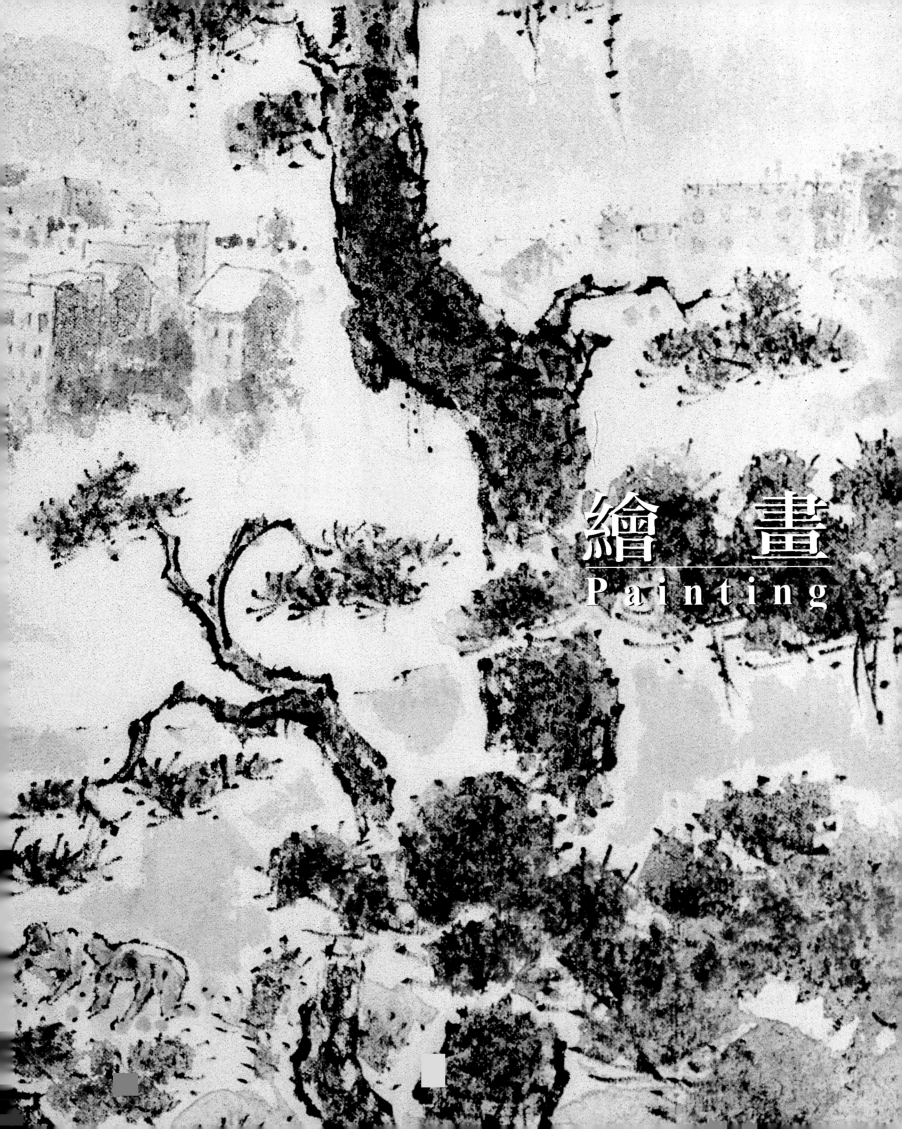

繪　畫
Painting

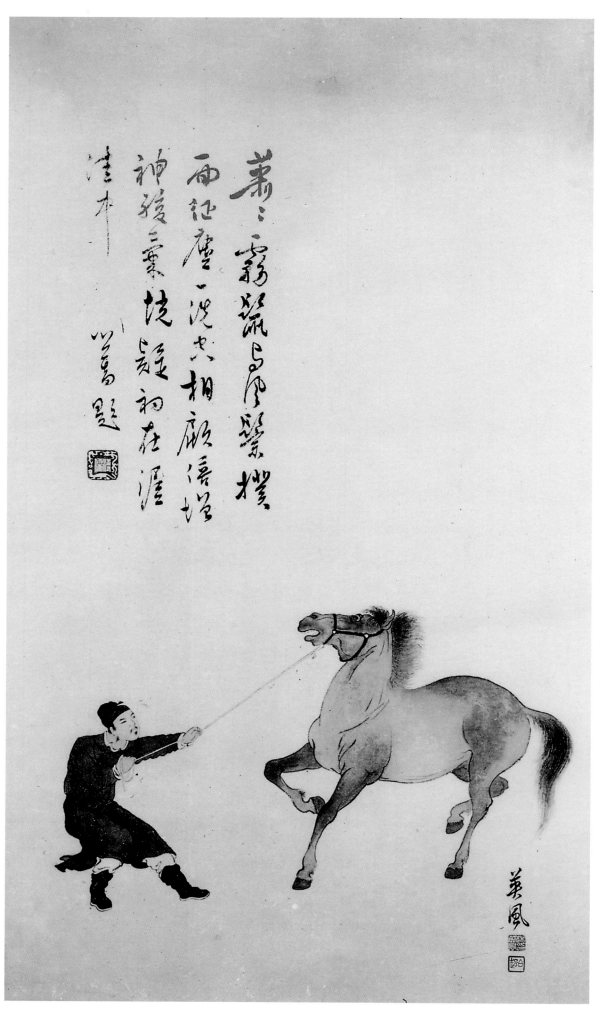

玉花驄圖　STALLION
1948　紙本水墨
76×101.5cm

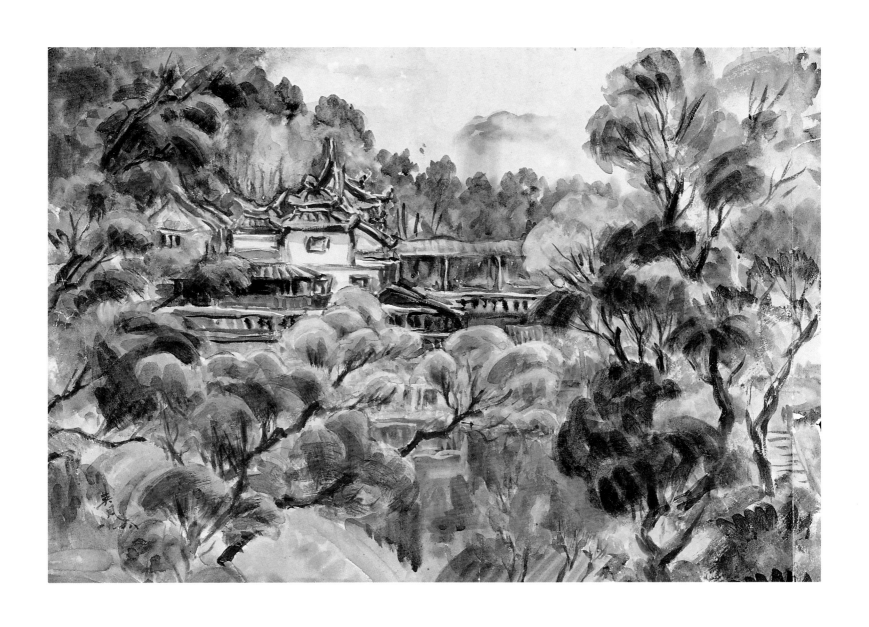

風景　SCENERY　1948　紙本水彩　34.5×49cm

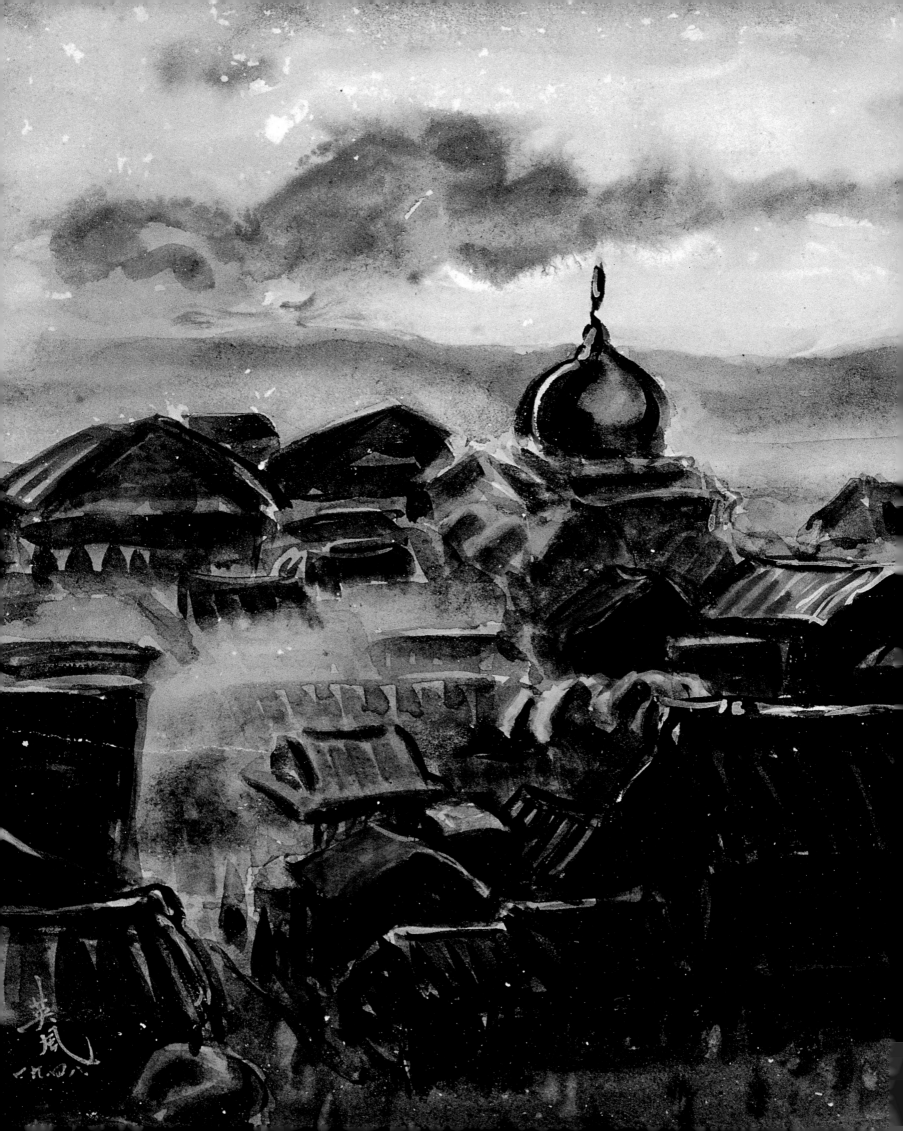

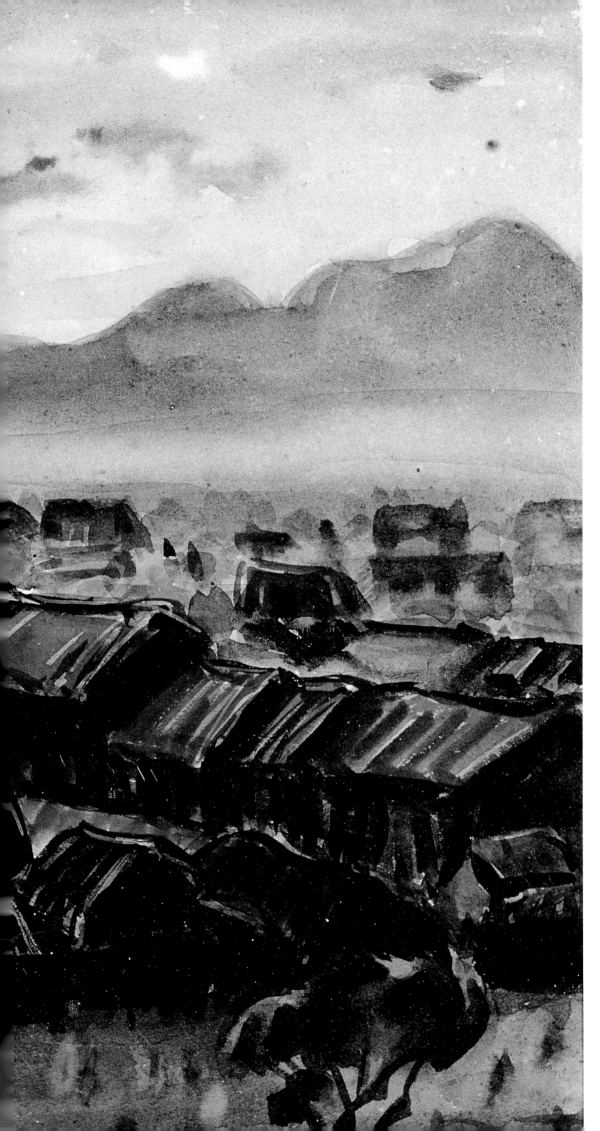

傍晚
EVENING
1948
紙本水彩
29×36.5cm

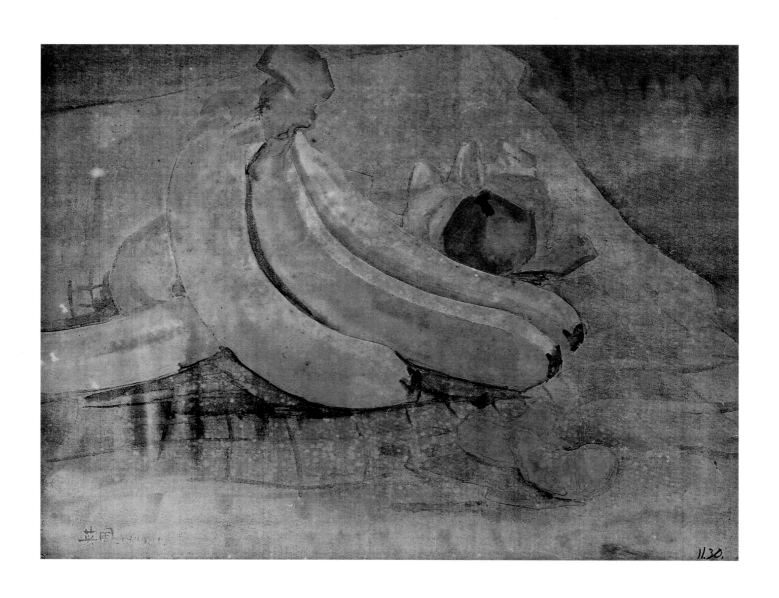

香蕉　BANANA　1949　紙本水彩　29×36.8cm

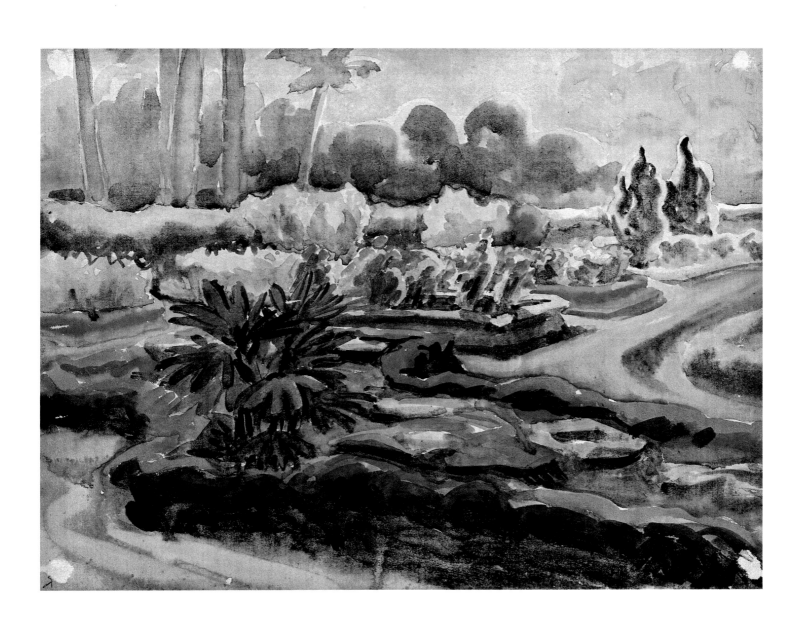

花園　GARDEN　1949　紙本水彩　29×36.8cm

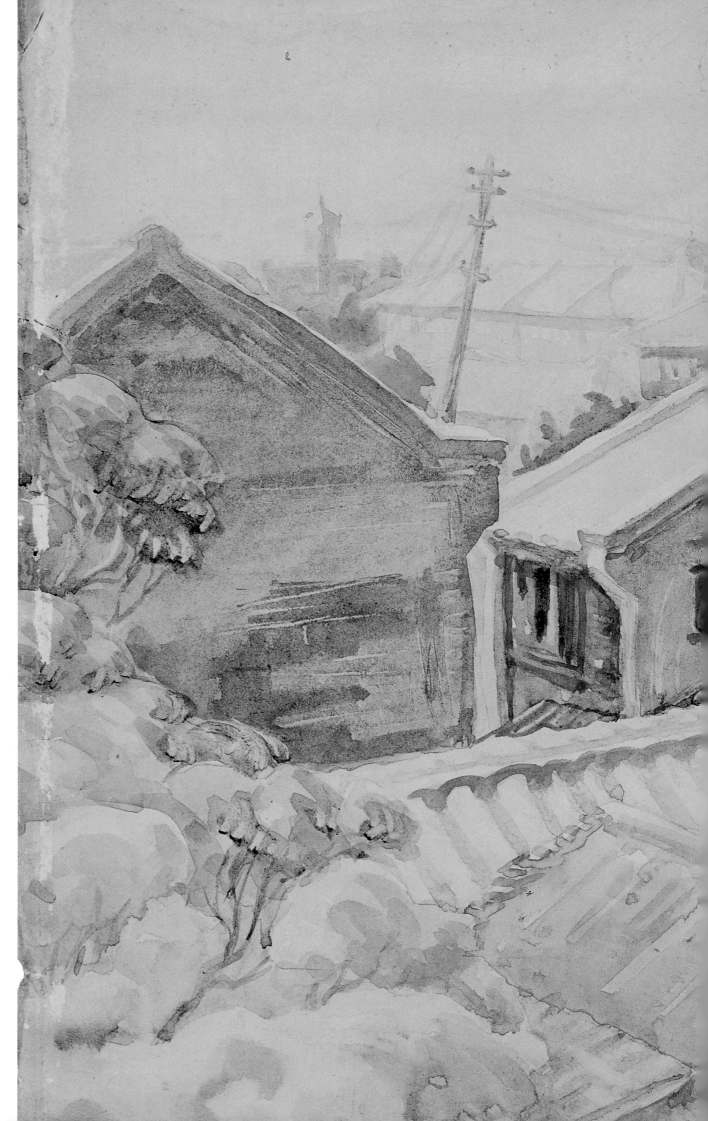

屋頂
ROOF
1949
紙本水彩
37.3×51.7cm

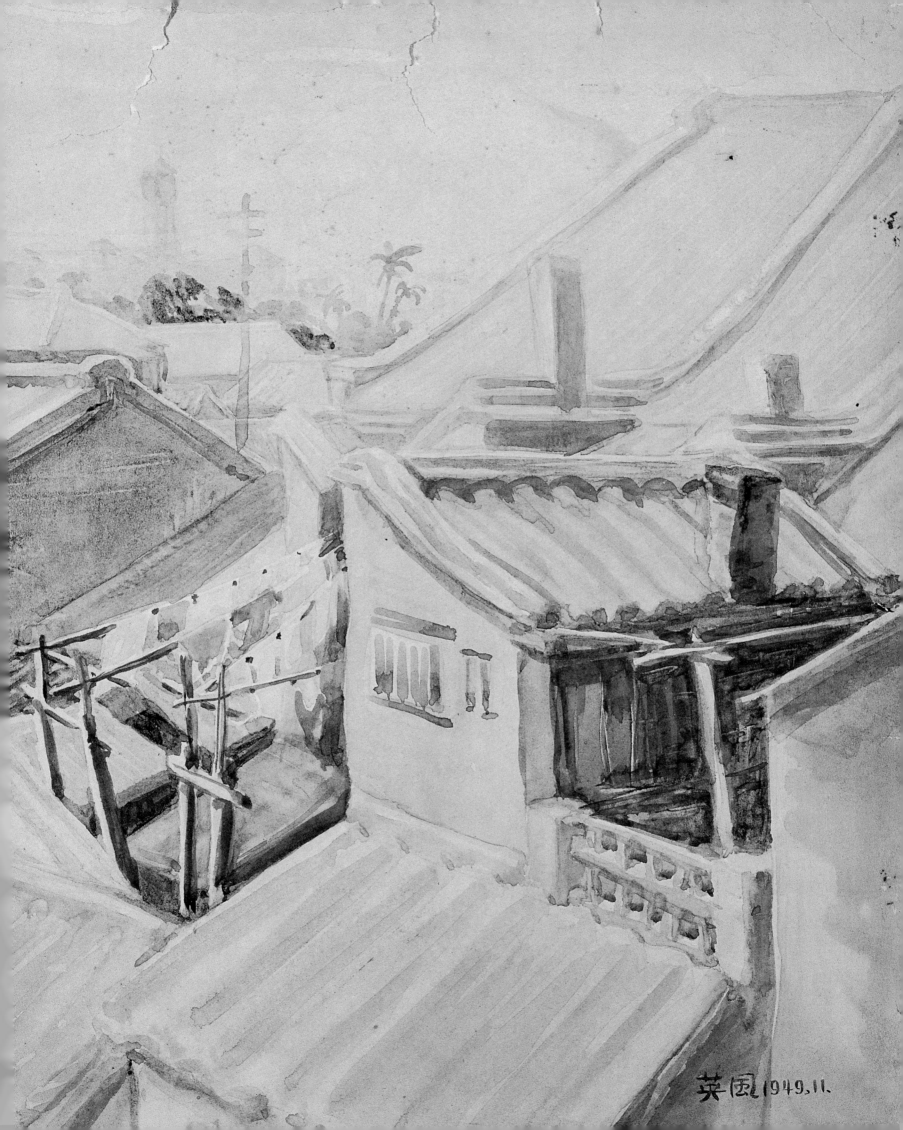

英国 1949.11.

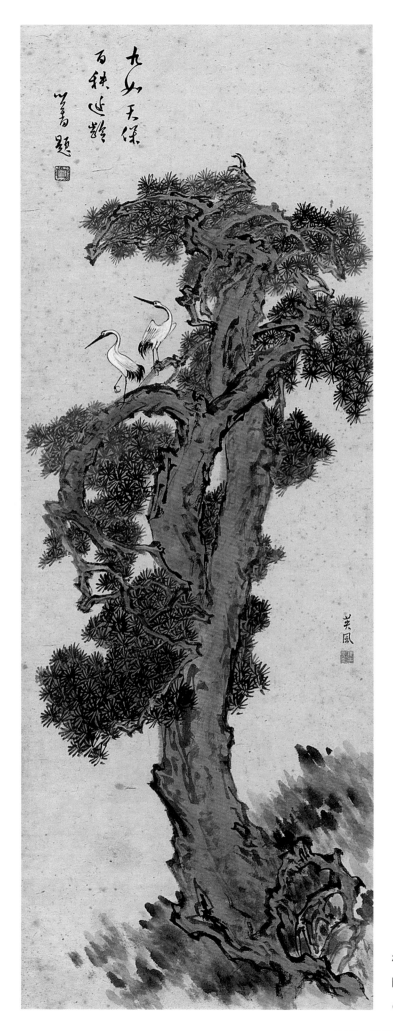

松鶴延齡　LONGEVITY　1951　紙本設色　58.5×155cm
印刷工人　PRINTER　約1950年代　紙本水彩　29.5×21cm
（右頁圖）

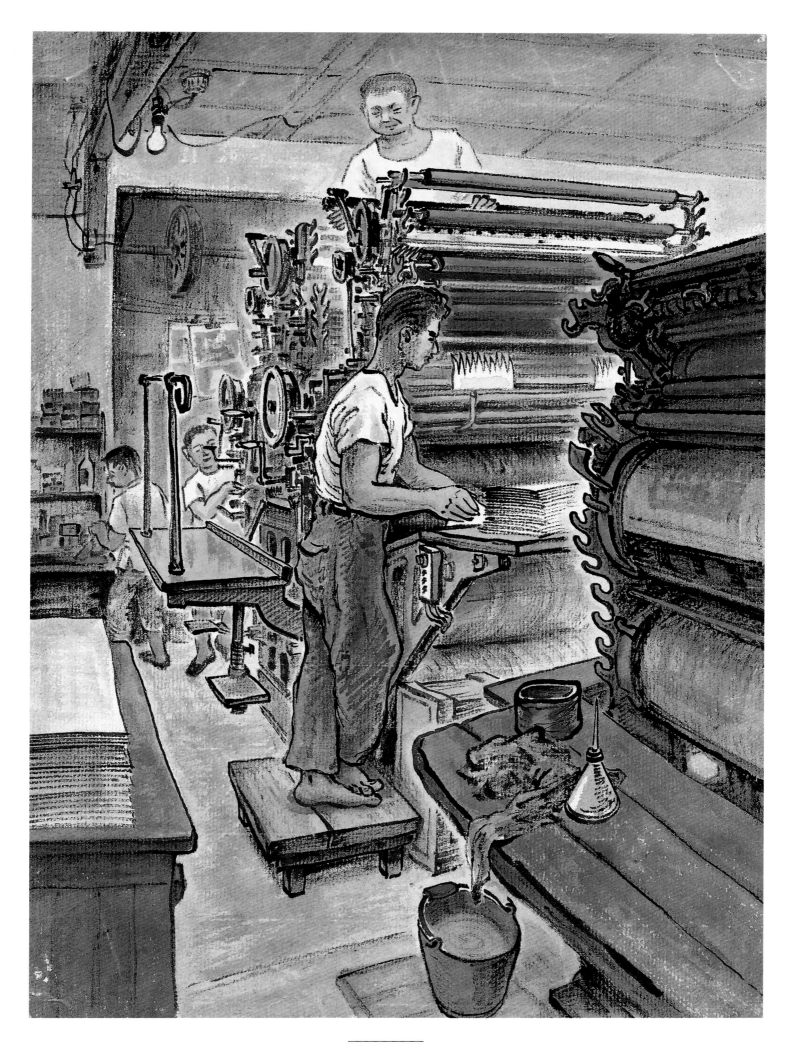

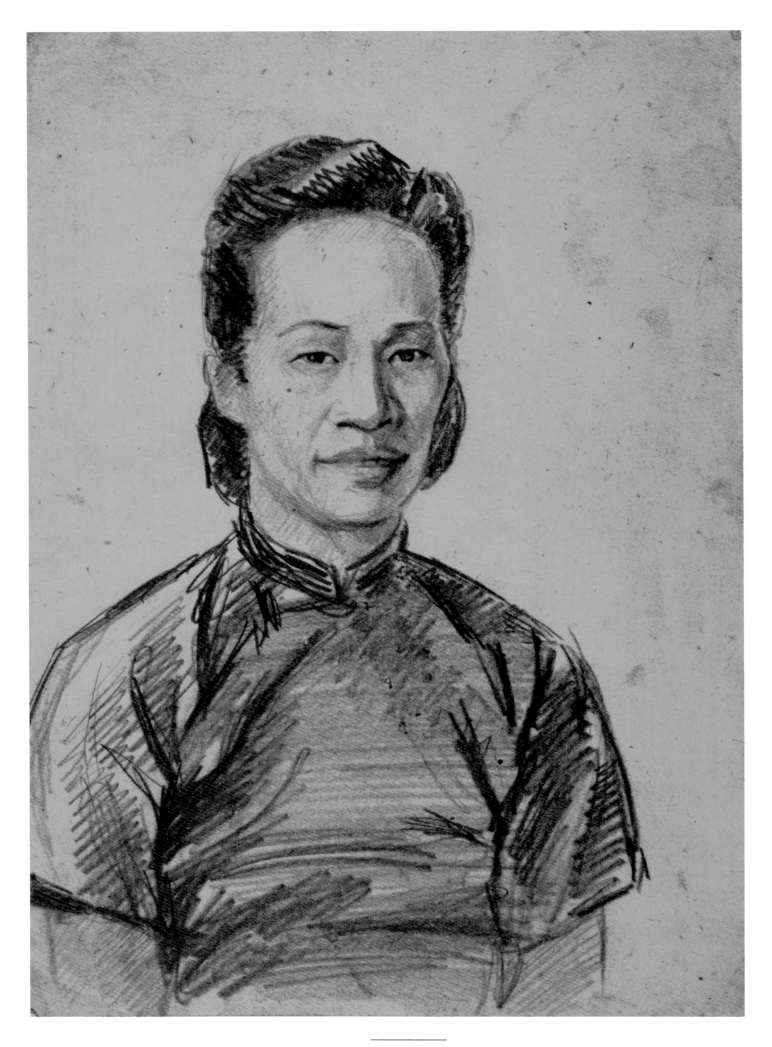

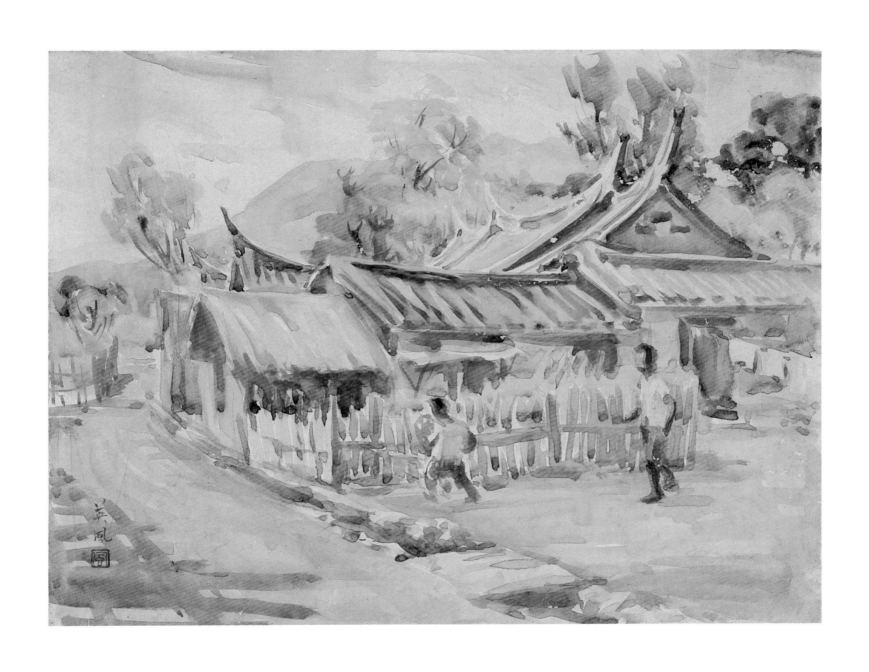

母親　MOTHER　年代未詳　紙本鉛筆　26×18cm（左頁圖）

芝山巖農家　JHIHSHANYAN FARM HOUSE　1953　紙本水彩　25.4×33cm

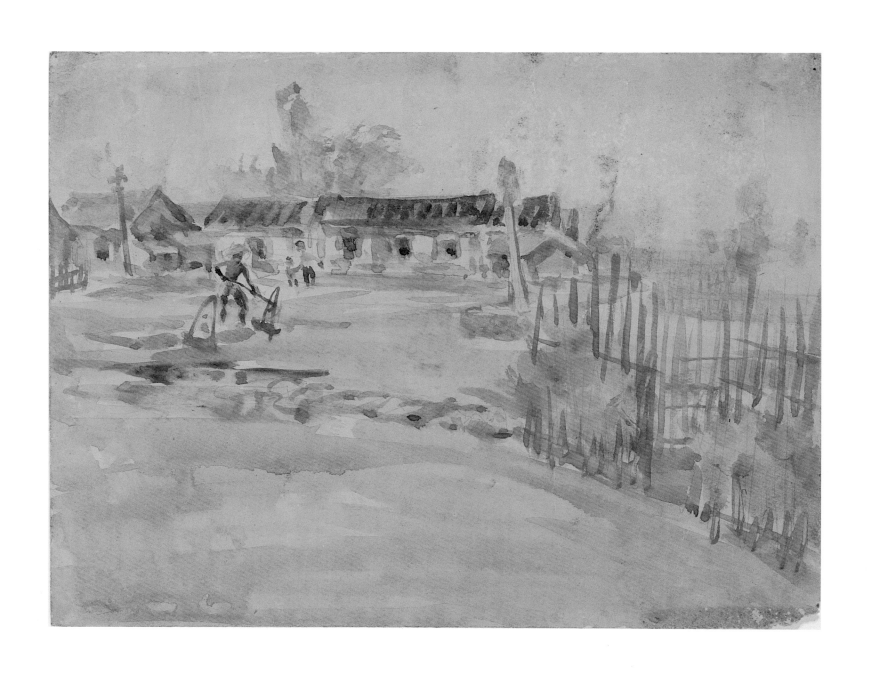

台灣農家　TAIWAN FARM HOUSE　約1950年代　紙本水彩　25.5×32.8cm

閱讀少女　READING　約1950年代　紙本水彩　56.8×49.1cm（右頁圖）

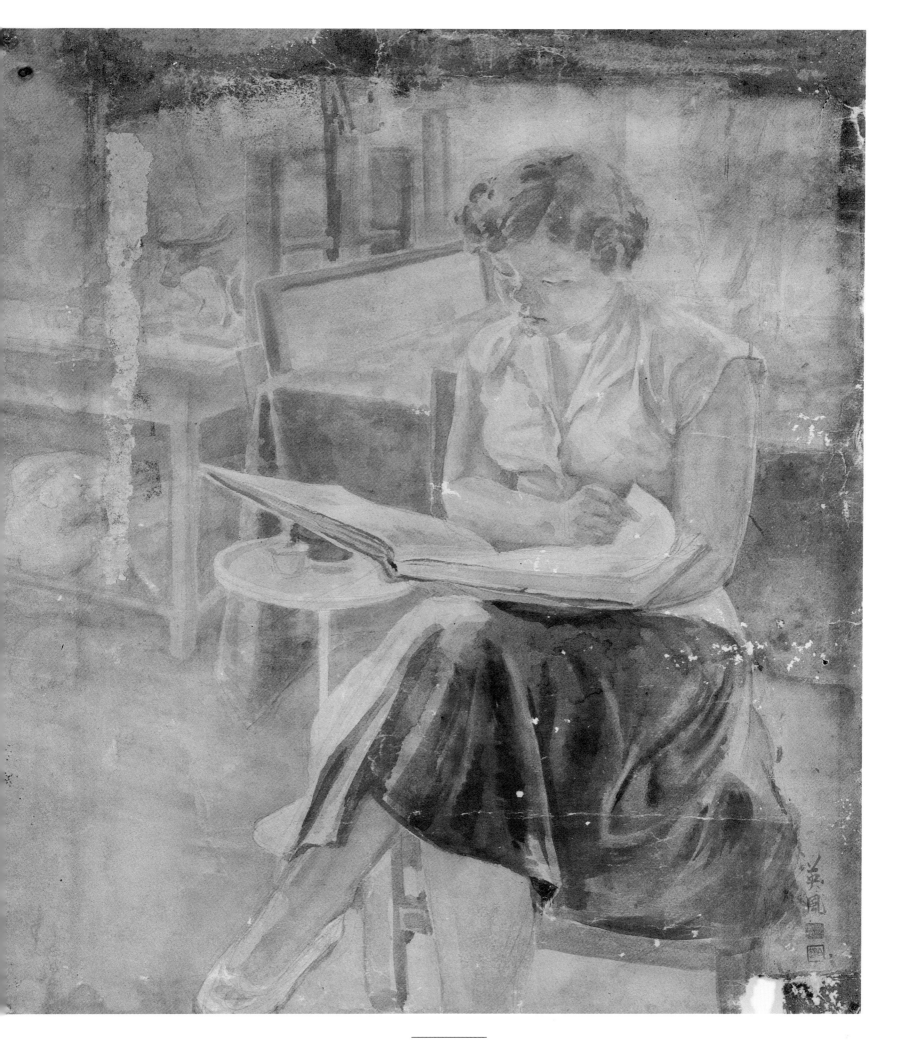

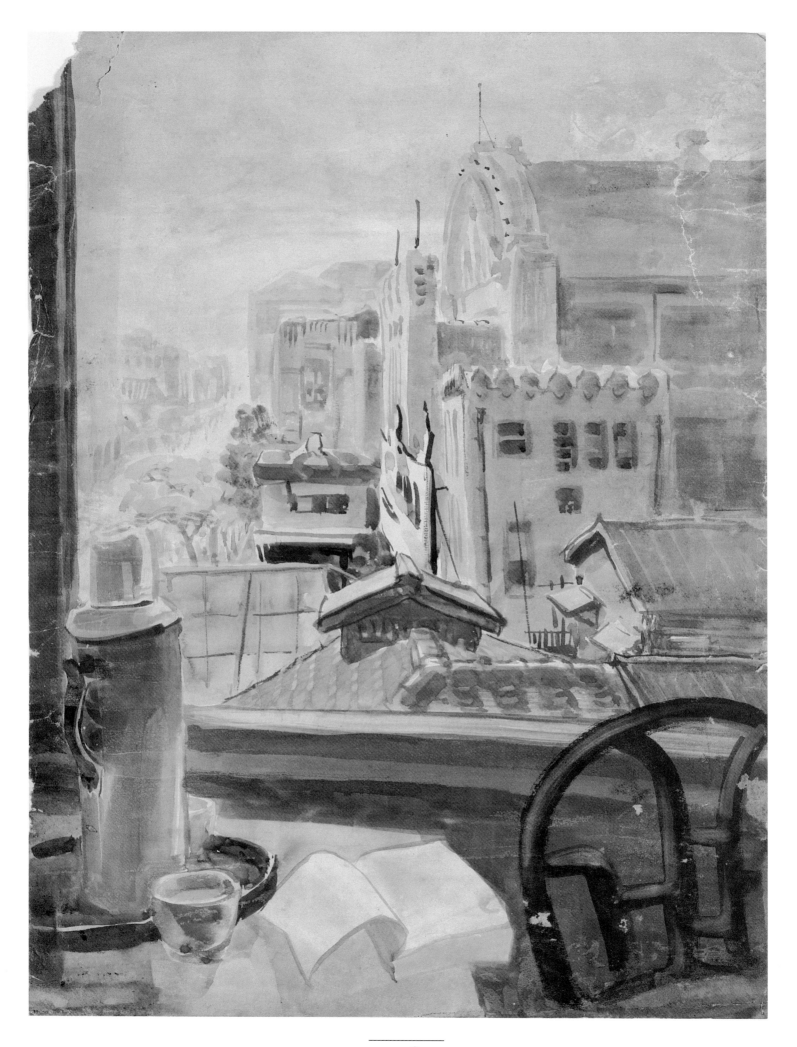

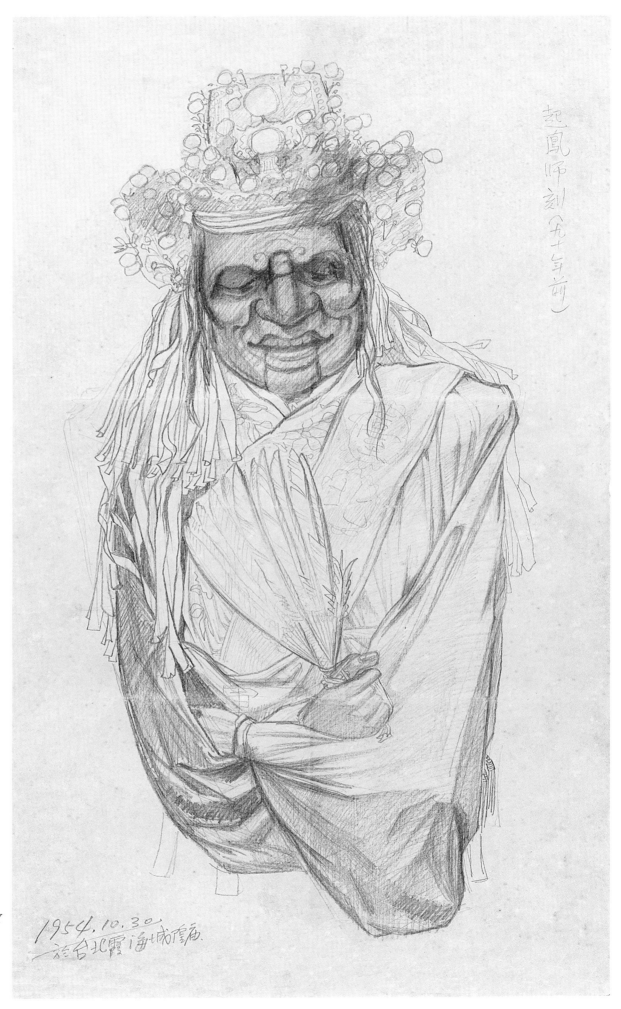

起鳳師刻（五十年前）

1954.10.30
於台北霞海城隍廟

窗外
OUTSIDE THE WINDOW
約1950年代　紙本水彩
52.3 × 37.9cm（左頁圖）

台北霞海城隍廟之七爺
GUARDING DEITIES OF
THE TAIPEI SIAHAI CITY
GOD TEMPLE
1954　紙本鉛筆
56 × 32cm

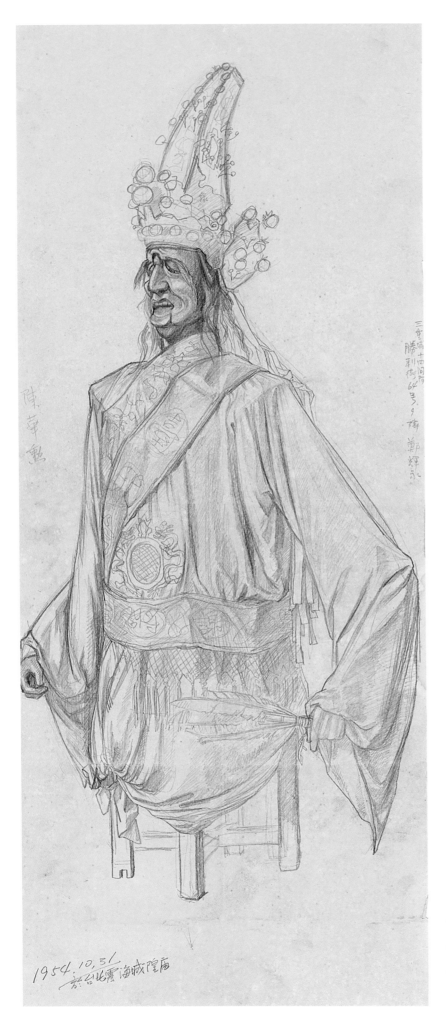

台北霞海城隍廟之八爺

GUARDING DEITIES OF THE TAIPEI

SIAHAI CITY GOD TEMPLE

1954　紙本鉛筆　86×32cm

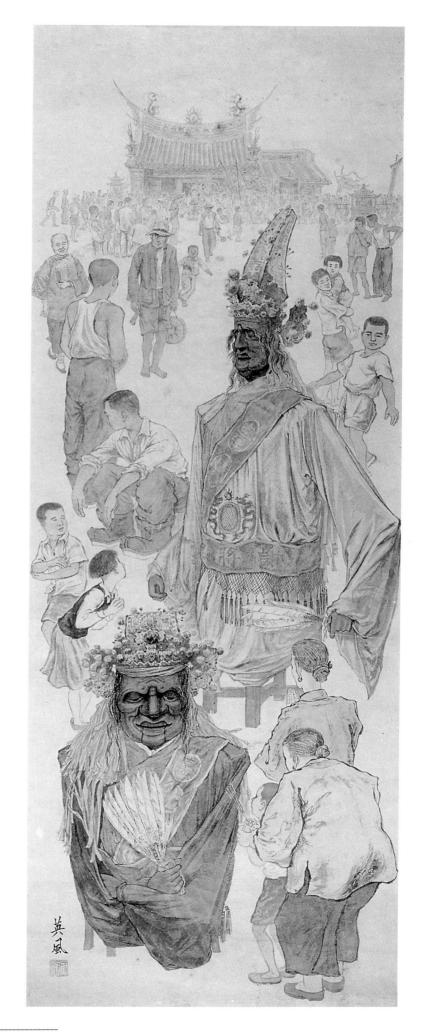

范謝兩將軍　GUARDING DEITIES

1954　紙本水彩　130×49cm

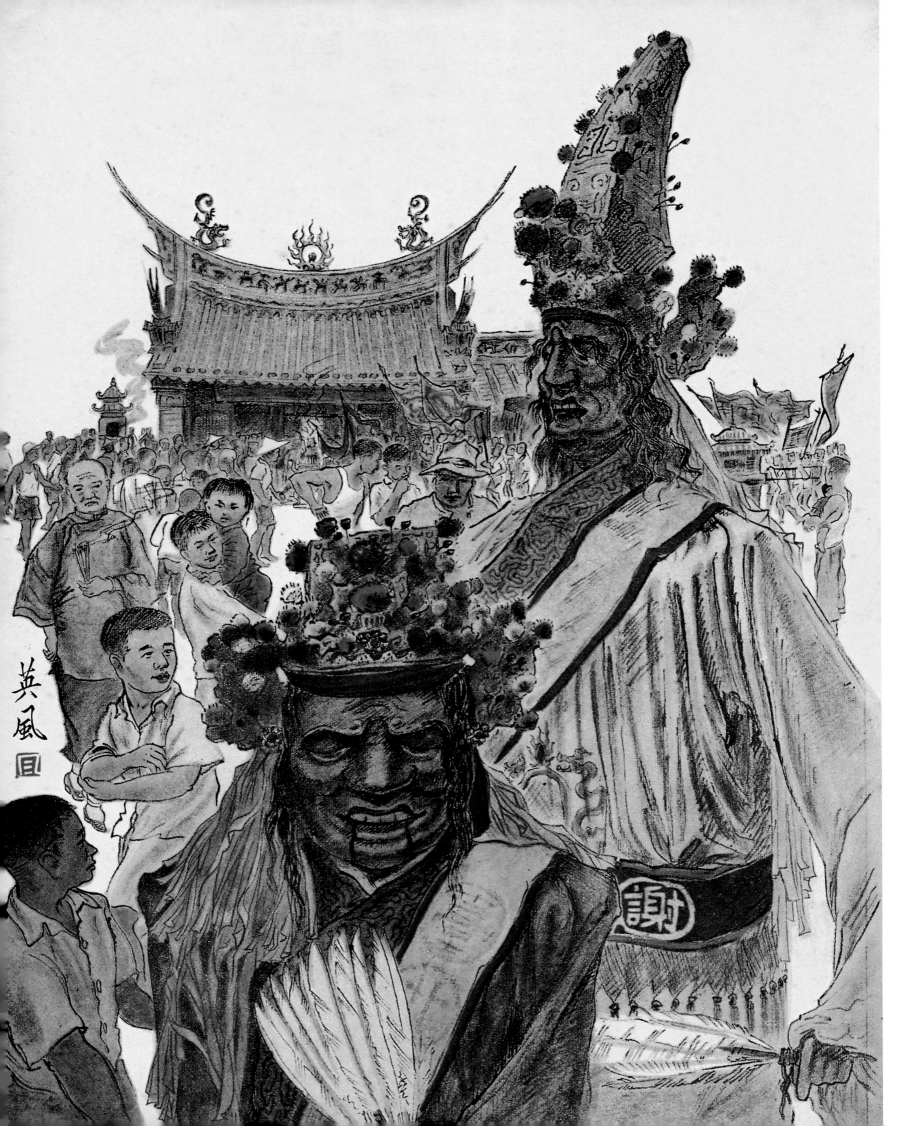

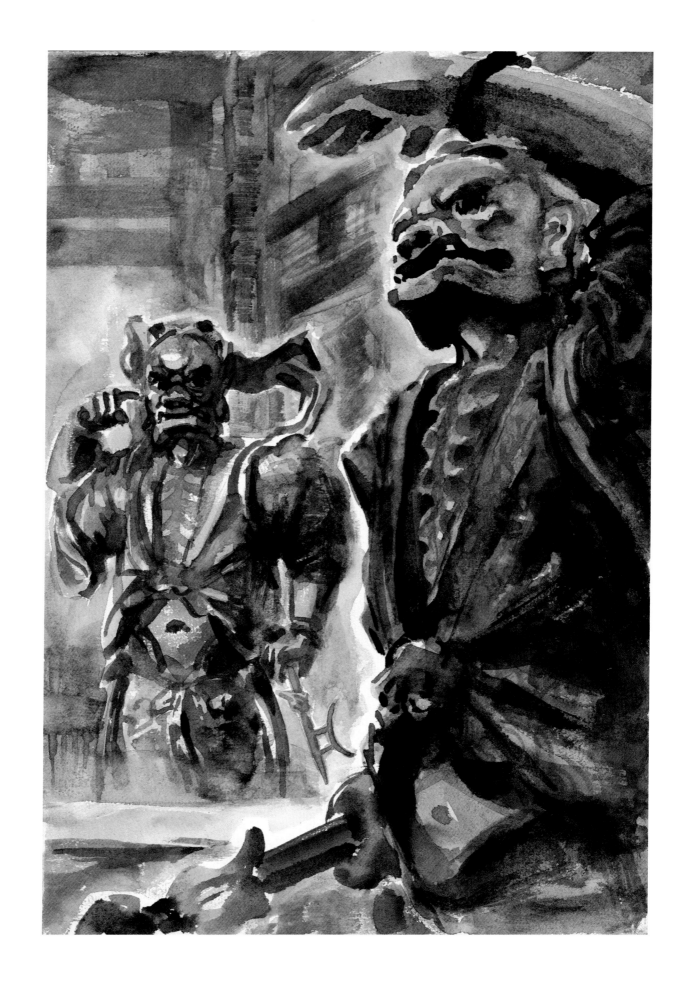

霞海城隍誕辰　TAIPEI SIAHAI CITY GOD'S BIRTHDAY　1955　紙本水彩　56×13cm（左頁圖）

千里眼順風耳　SCOUTING DEITIES　1955　紙本水彩　31.5×21.2cm

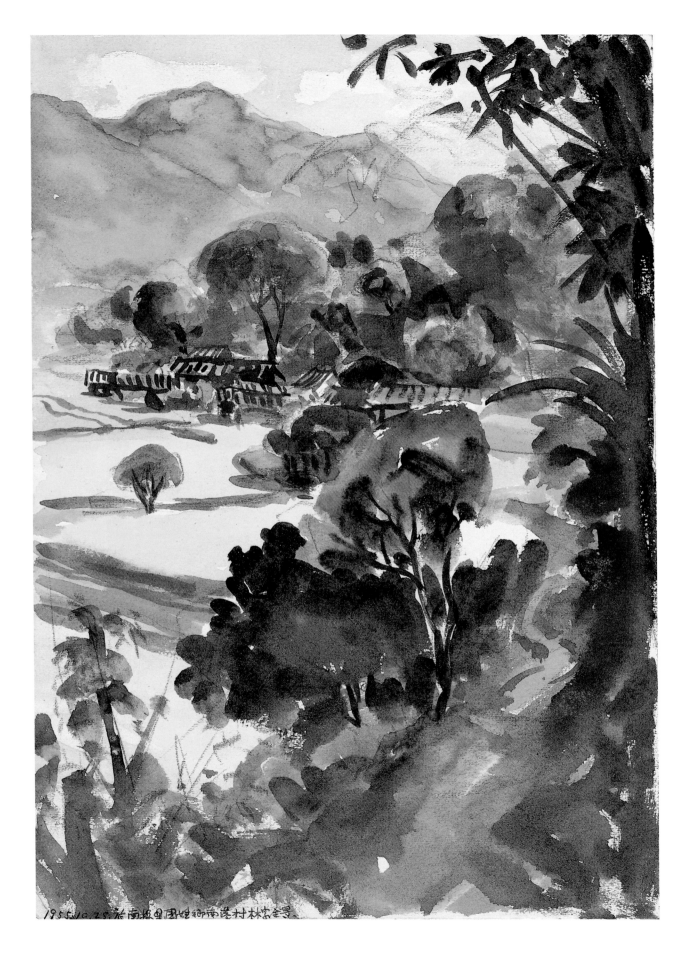

1955.10.25 於南投里國姓鄉南港村林宅全景

國姓鄉南港村林家全景　WHOLE IMAGE OF THE LIN FAMILY AT NANGANG VILLAGE, GUOSING HSIAN
1955　紙本水彩　32.5×21.5cm
太平雲海　SEA OF CLOUDS IN TAIPING MOUNTAIN　1956　紙本水墨　21.5×32.5cm（右頁圖）

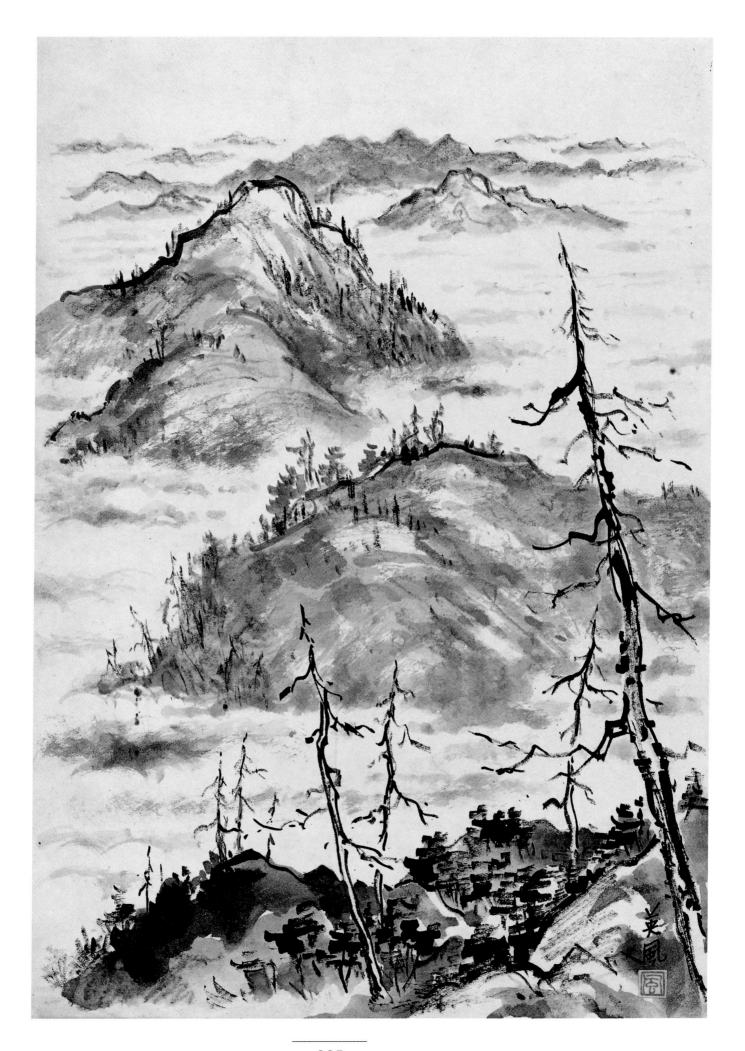

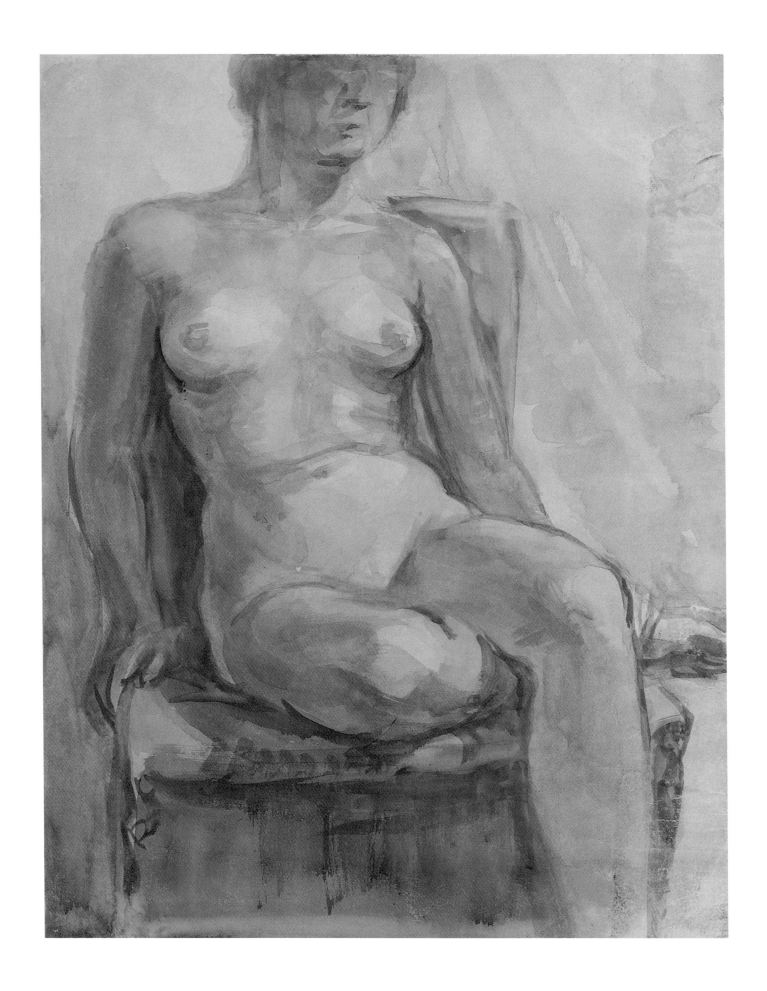

紅椅佳人　LADY ON A RED CHAIR　1956　紙本水彩　41.3×30.5cm

指南仙宮　JHIHNAN TEMPLE　1956　紙本水彩　68.5×51cm（右頁圖）

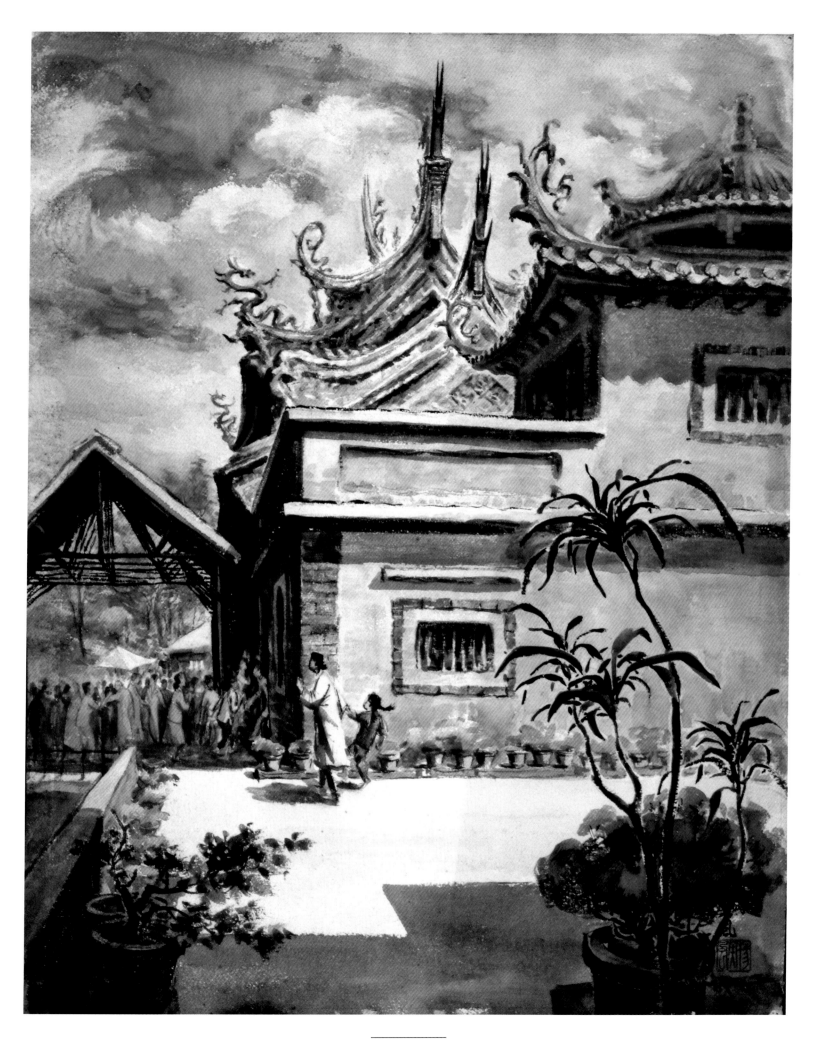

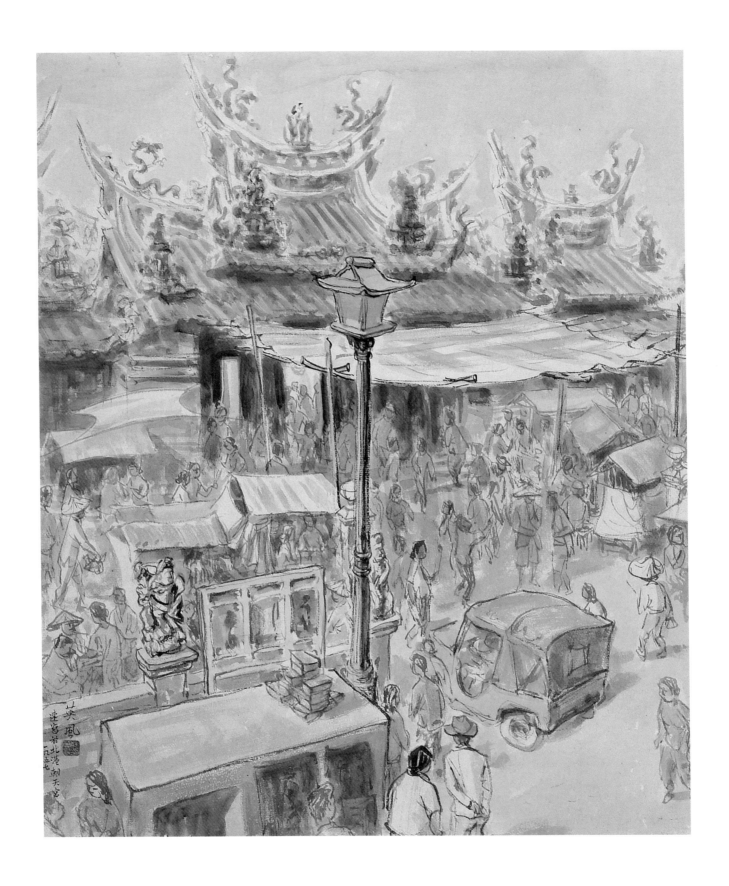

北港朝天宮　MATSU-TEMPLE AT BEI-KANG　1957　紙本水彩　47×37.5cm

台南孔廟　CONFUCIAN TEMPLE IN TAINAN　1957　紙本水彩　54×39cm（右頁圖）

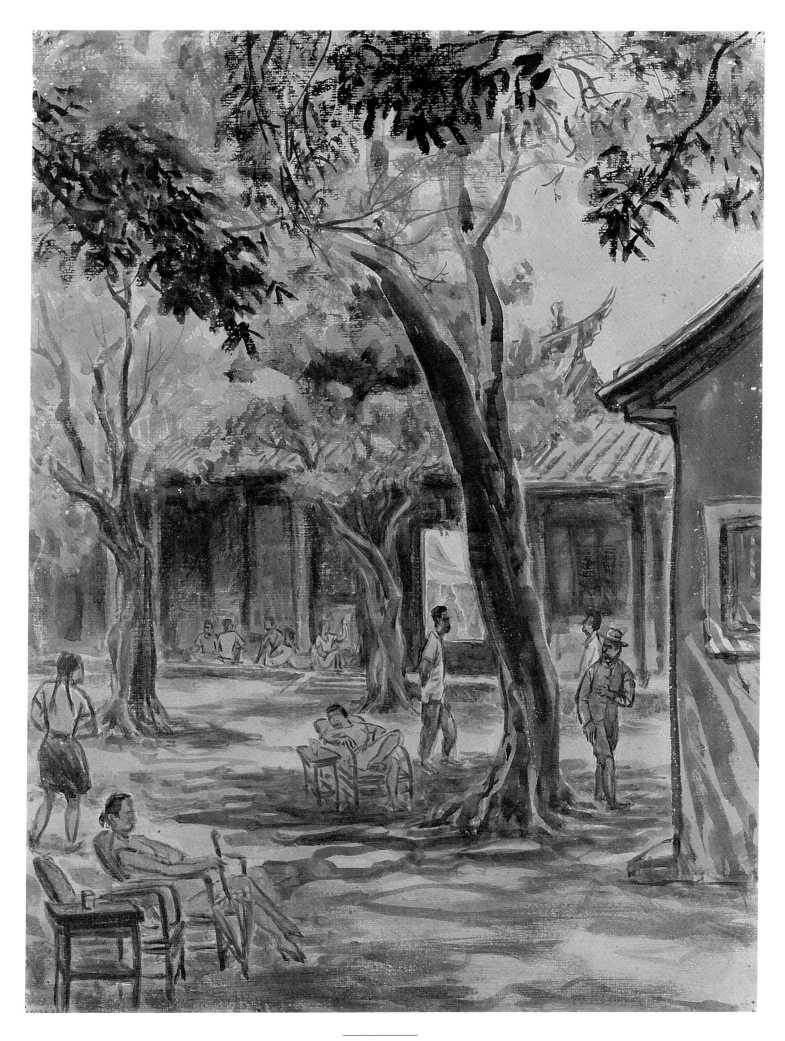

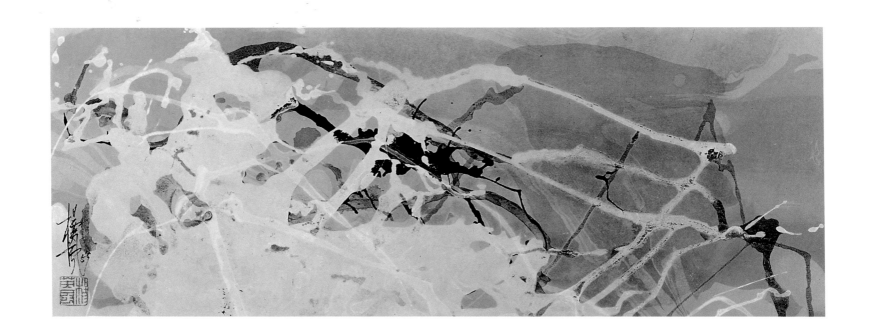

抽象繪畫59-01　　ABSTRACT PAINTING 59-01　　1959　　紙本水彩　　19.3×49.8cm

抽象繪畫59-02　　ABSTRACT PAINTING 59-02　　1959　　紙本水彩　　43×29.5cm（右頁圖）

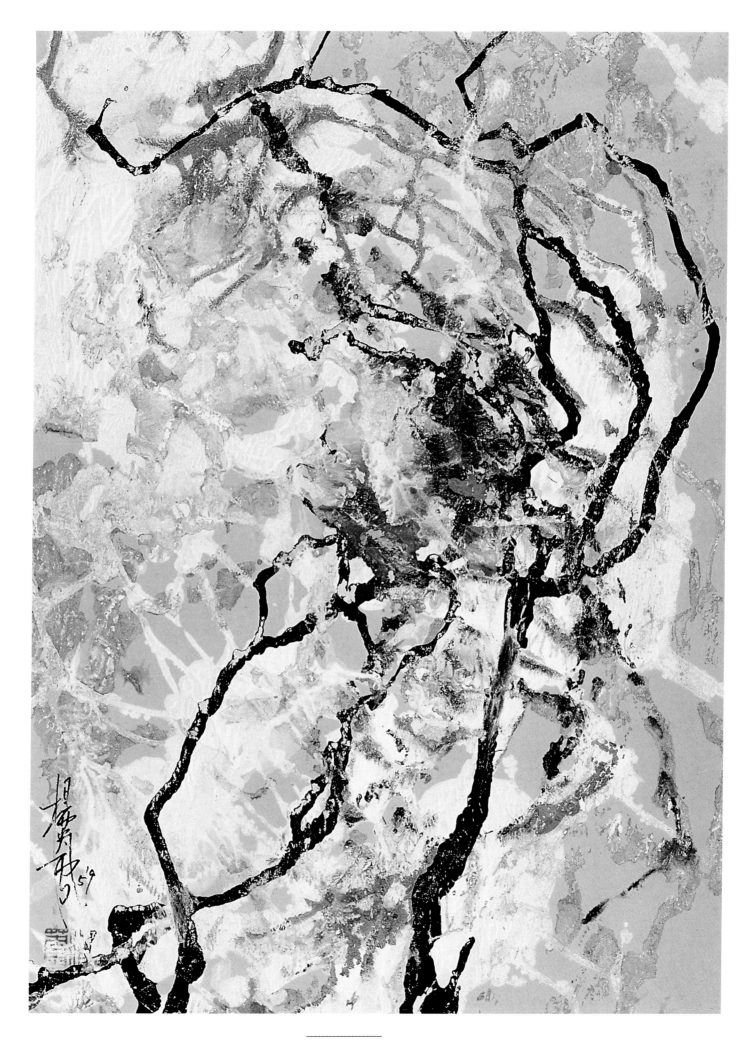

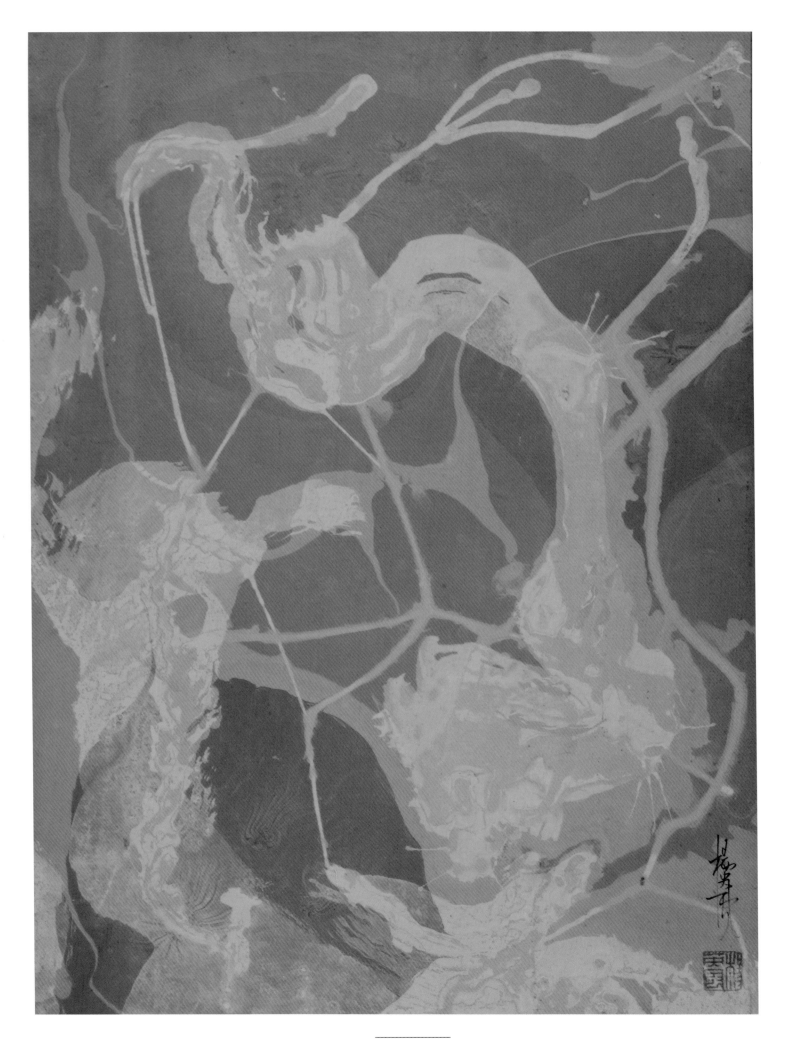

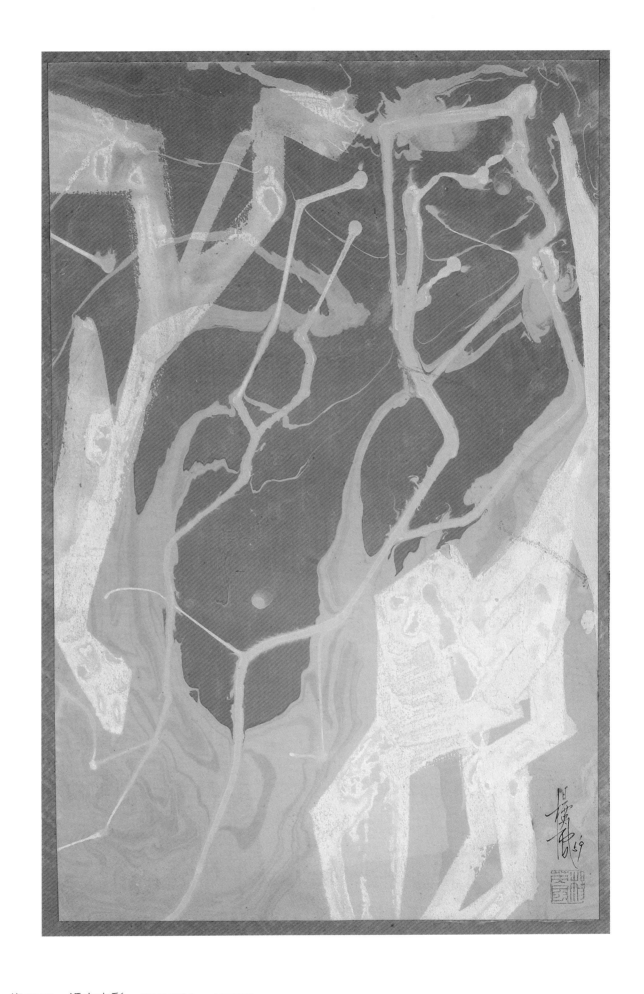

龍種　DRAGON SEEDS　約1959　紙本水彩　47.7×34cm（左頁圖）

抽象繪畫59-03　ABSTRACT PAINTING 59-03　1959　紙本水彩　47.8×29.2cm

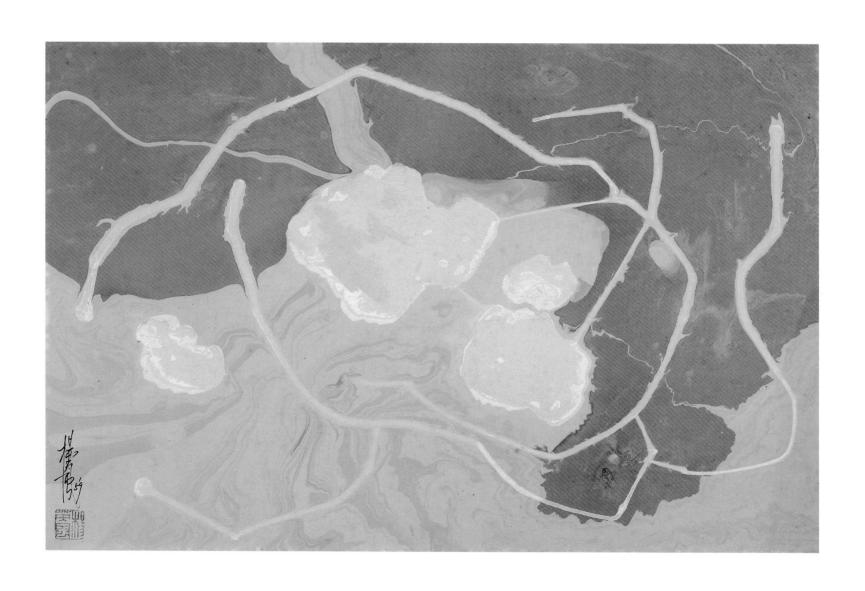

抽象繪畫59-04　　ABSTRACT PAINTING 59-04　　1959　　紙本水彩　　33.1×48.6cm

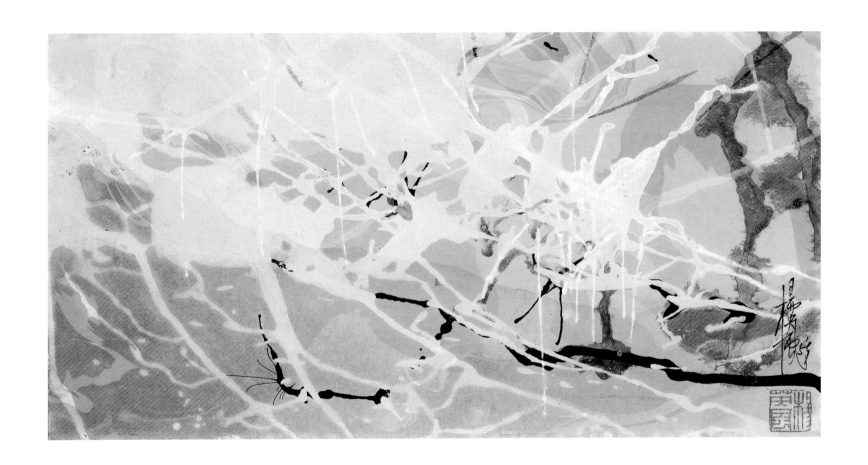

抽象繪畫59-05　ABSTRACT PAINTING 59-05　1959　紙本水彩　18.7×34.3cm

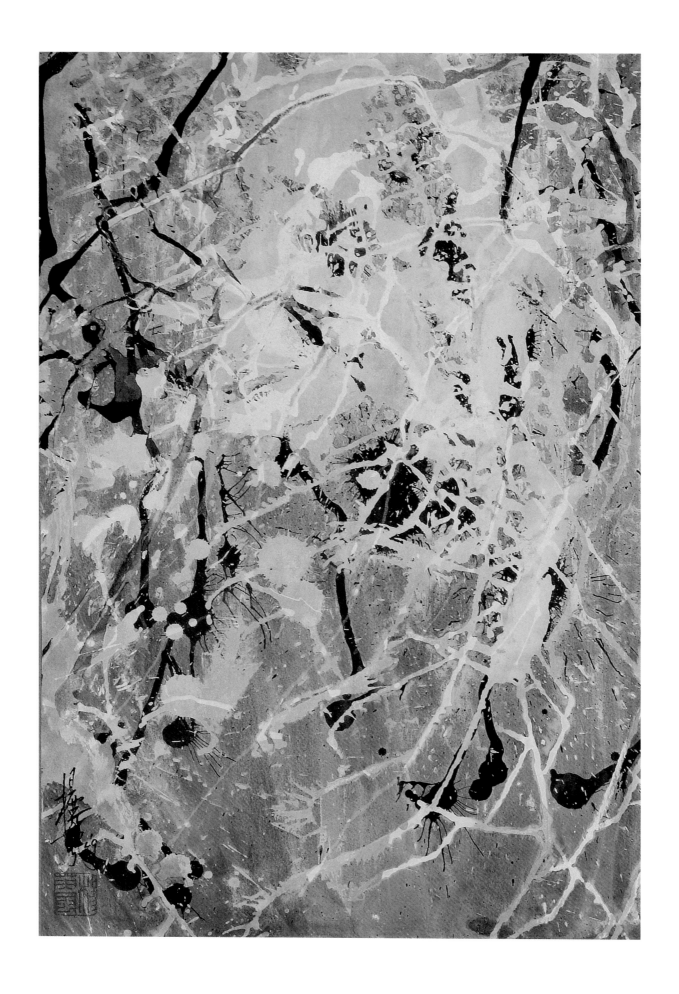

抽象繪畫59-06　ABSTRACT PAINTING 59-06　1959　紙本水彩　38.8×25.4cm

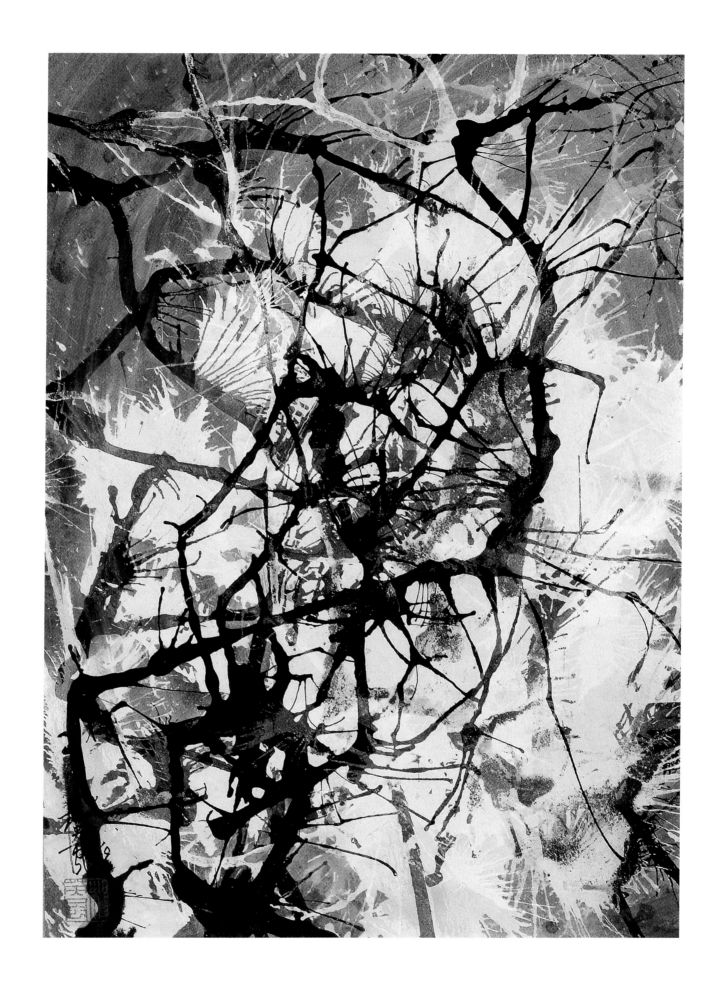

抽象繪畫59-07　ABSTRACT PAINTING 59-07　1959　紙本水彩　38.4×26.4cm

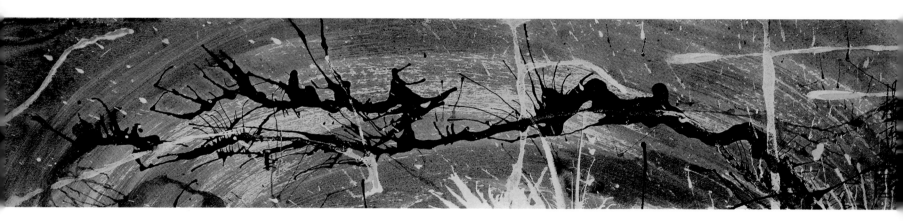

抽象繪畫59-08　ABSTRACT PAINTING 59-08　1959　紙本水彩　8.7×41.2cm

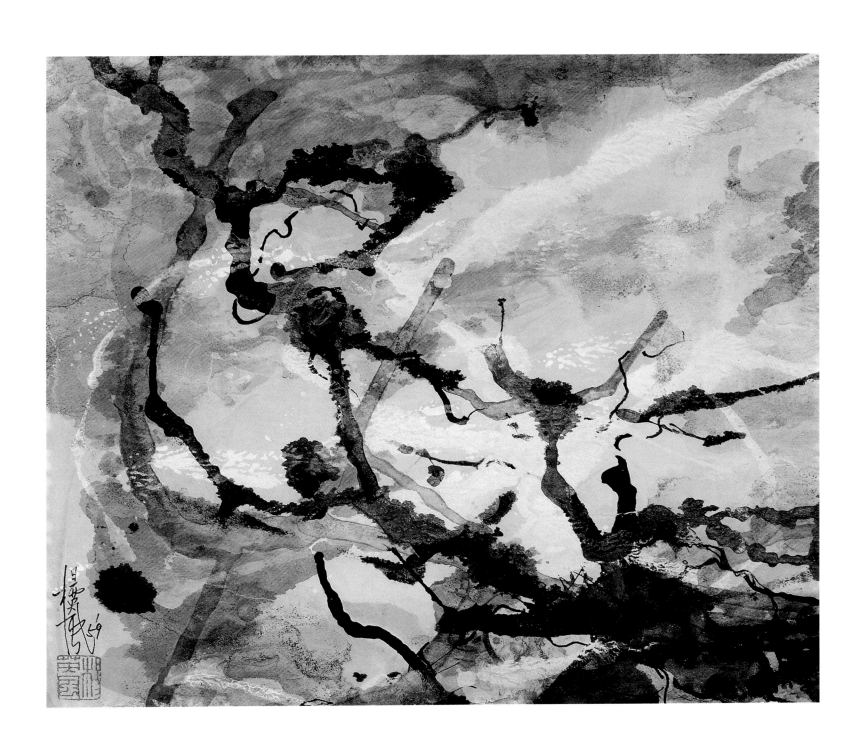

抽象繪畫59-09　ABSTRACT PAINTING 59-09　1959　紙本水彩　28×32cm

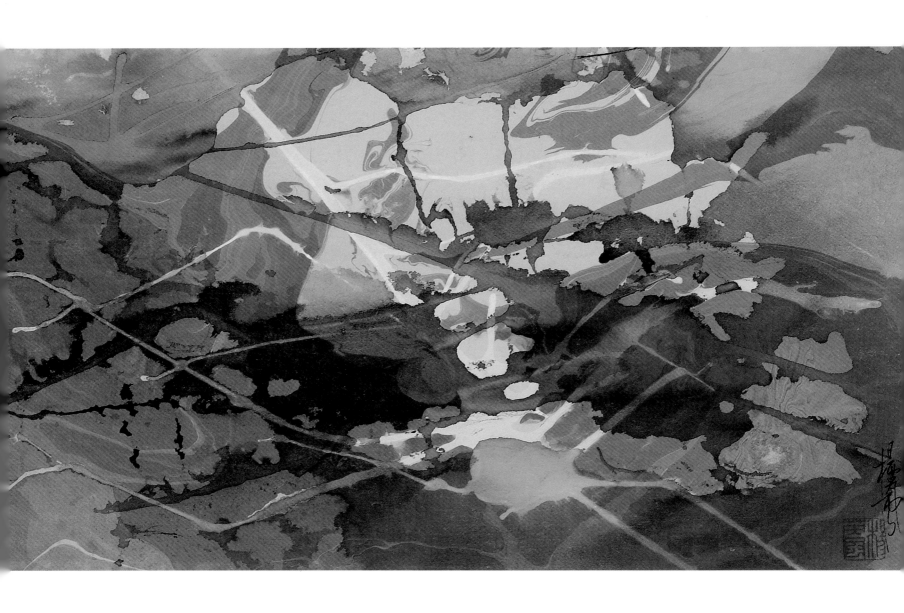

抽象繪畫59-10　ABSTRACT PAINTING 59-10　1959　紙本水彩　23.7×41cm

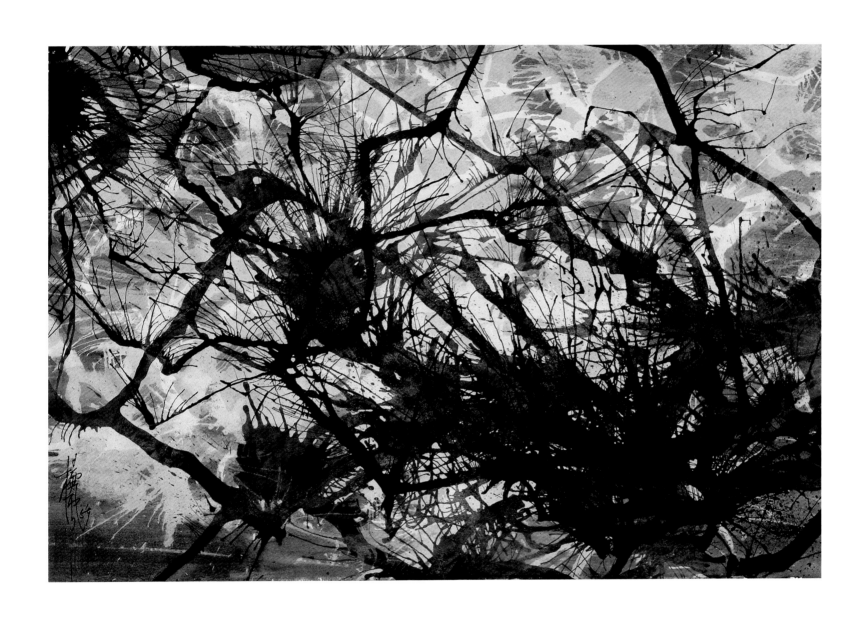

抽象繪畫59-11　ABSTRACT PAINTING 59-11　1959　紙本水彩　29×40.5cm

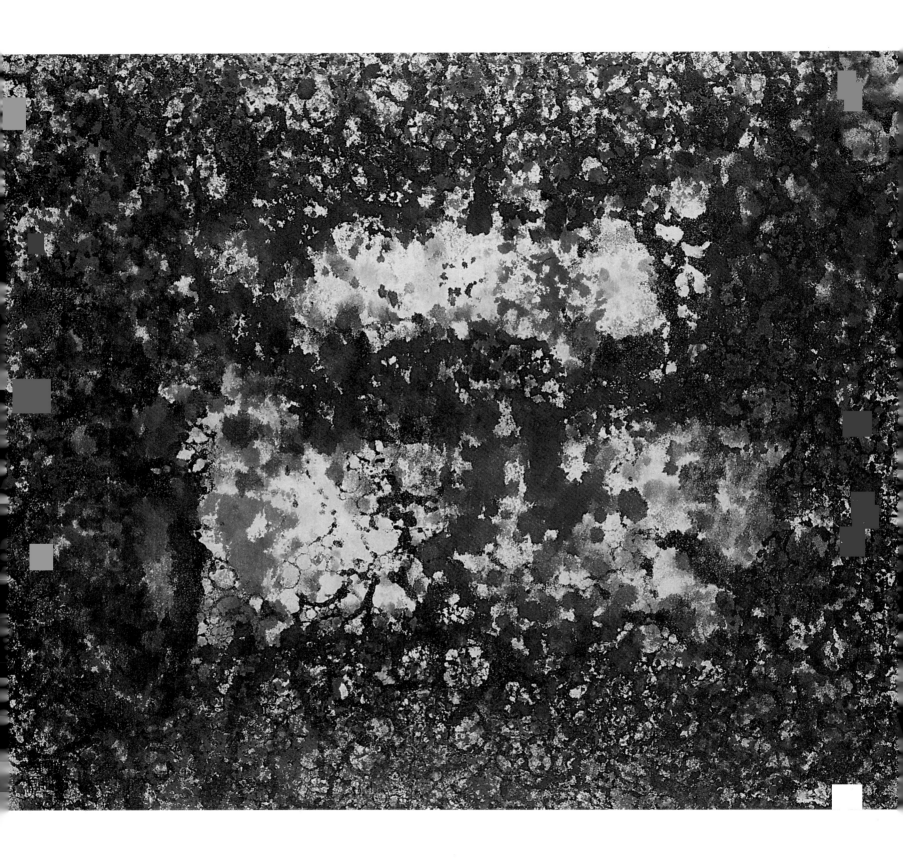

抽象繪畫59-12　ABSTRACT PAINTING 59-12　1959　紙本水彩　45×54cm

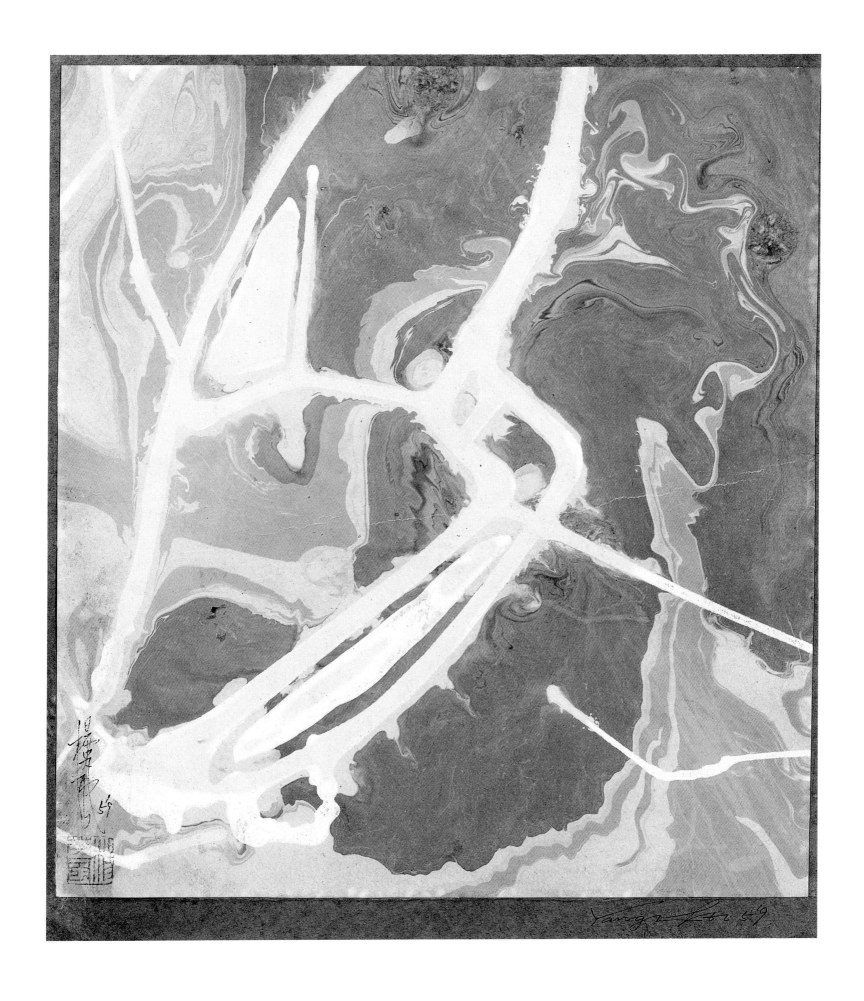

抽象繪畫59-13　ABSTRACT PAINTING 59-13　1959　紙本水彩　33×20.9cm

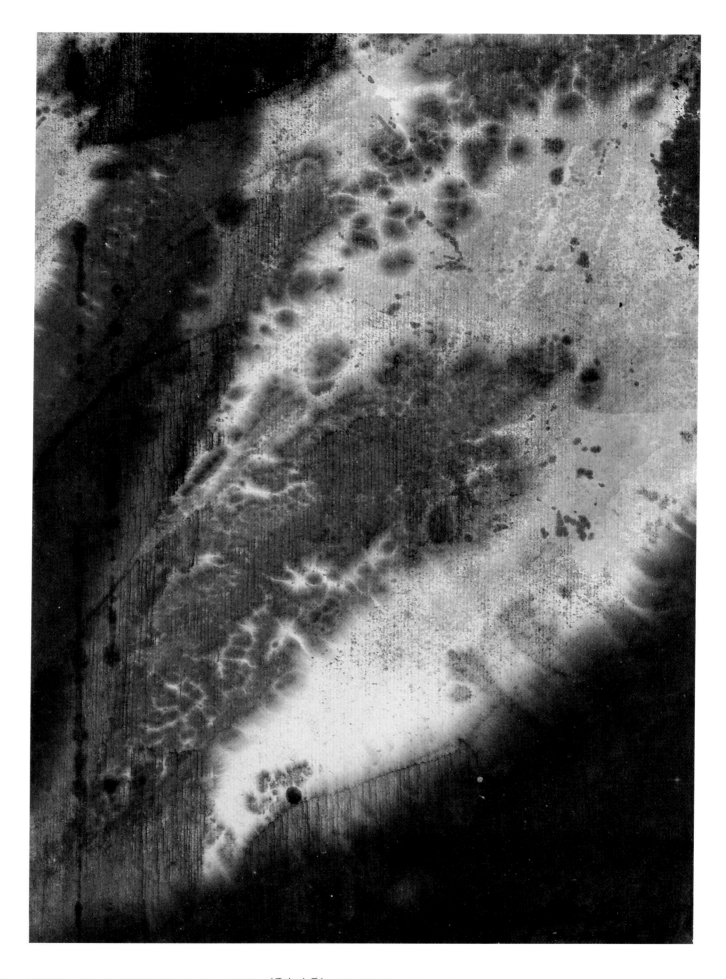

抽象繪畫62-01　ABSTRACT PAINTING 62-01　1962　紙本水彩　64.5×42cm（左頁圖）

抽象繪畫62-02　ABSTRACT PAINTING 62-02　1962　紙本設色　31.5×22.3cm

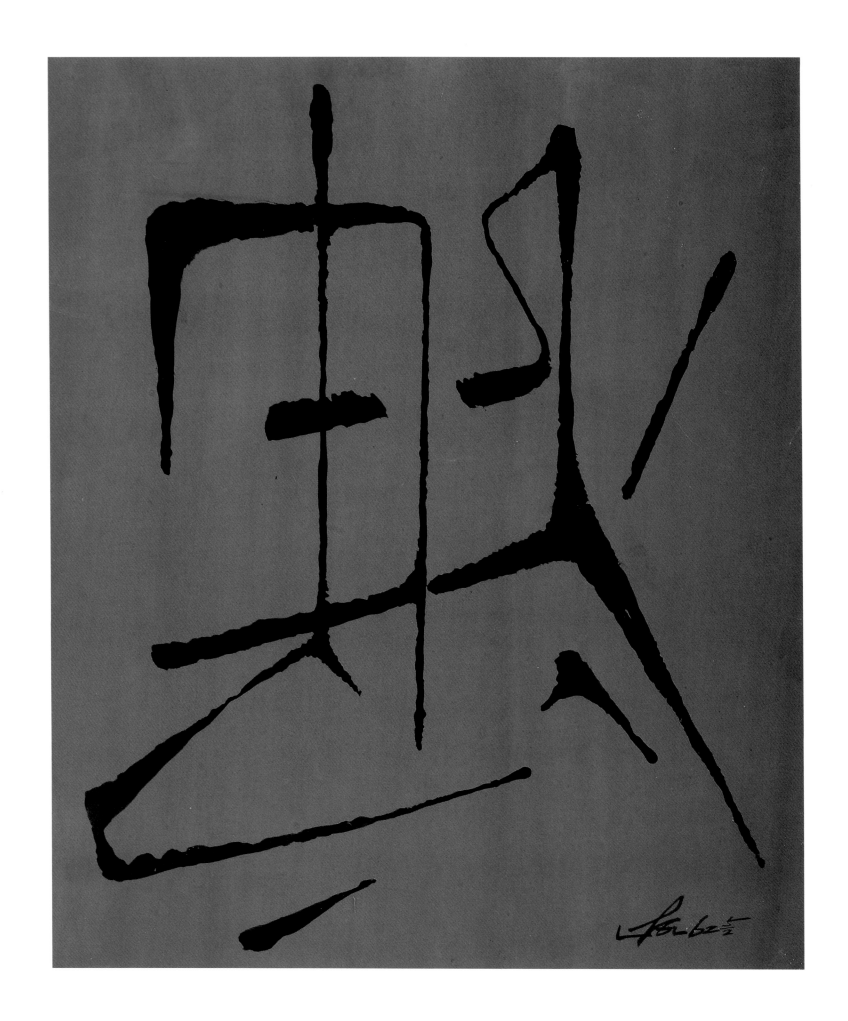

抽象繪畫62-03　ABSTRACT PAINTING 62-03　1962　紙本水墨　63.2×51.3cm

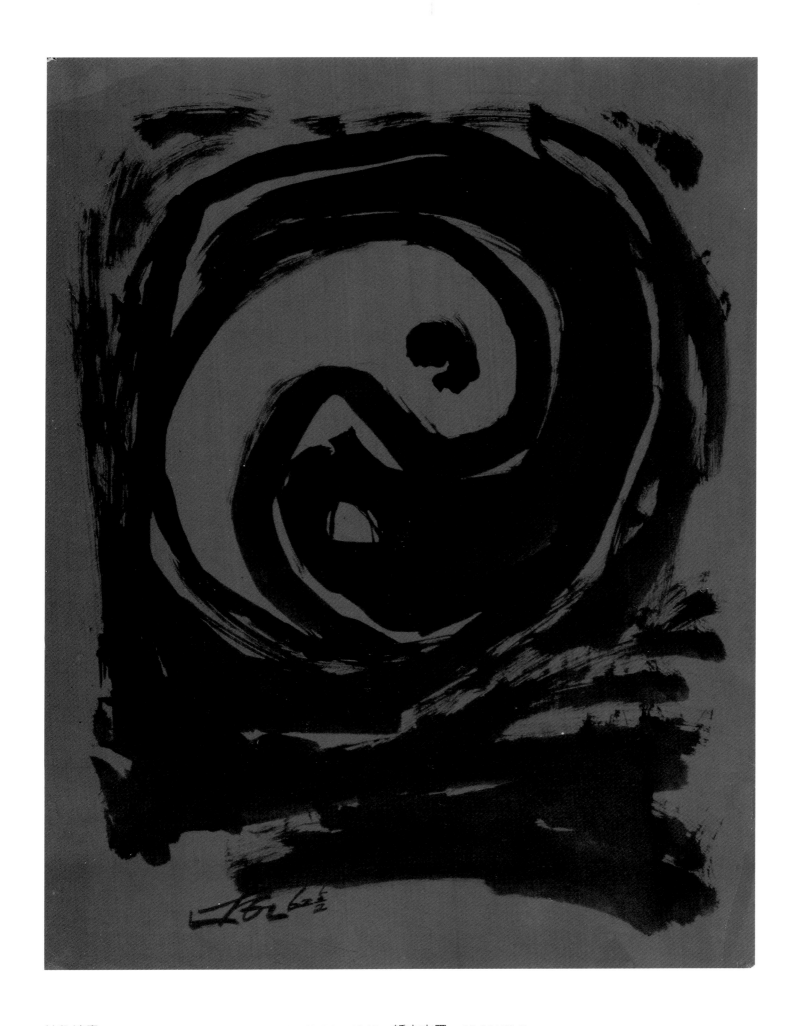

抽象繪畫62-04　ABSTRACT PAINTING 62-04　1962　紙本水墨　69.8×53.3cm

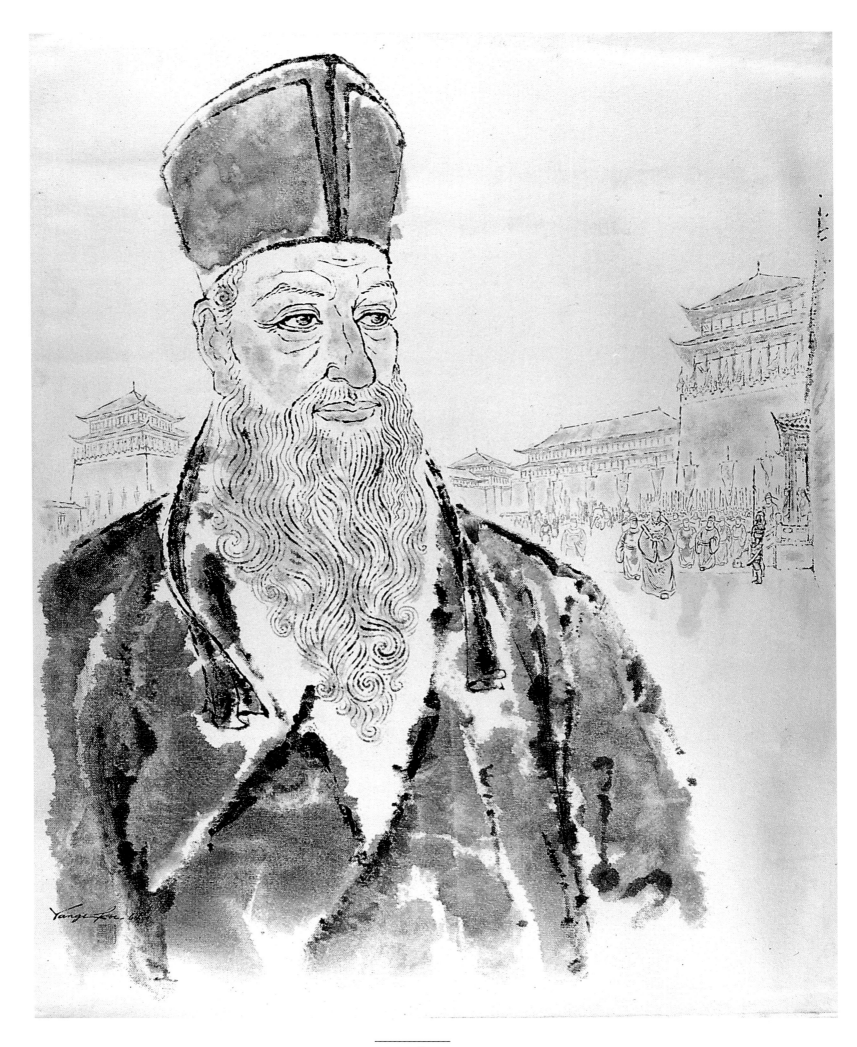

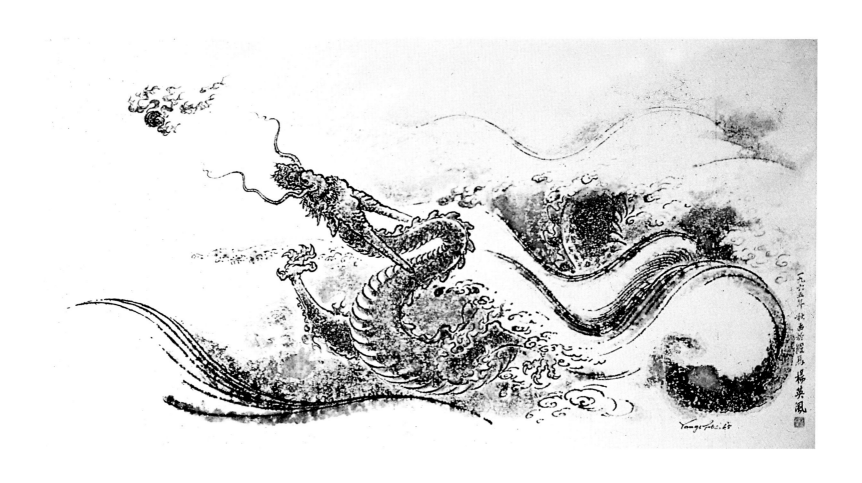

利馬竇在故宮　POPE MATTEO　1964　布上油彩　97×76cm（左頁圖）

龍　DRAGON　1965　布上油彩　尺寸未詳

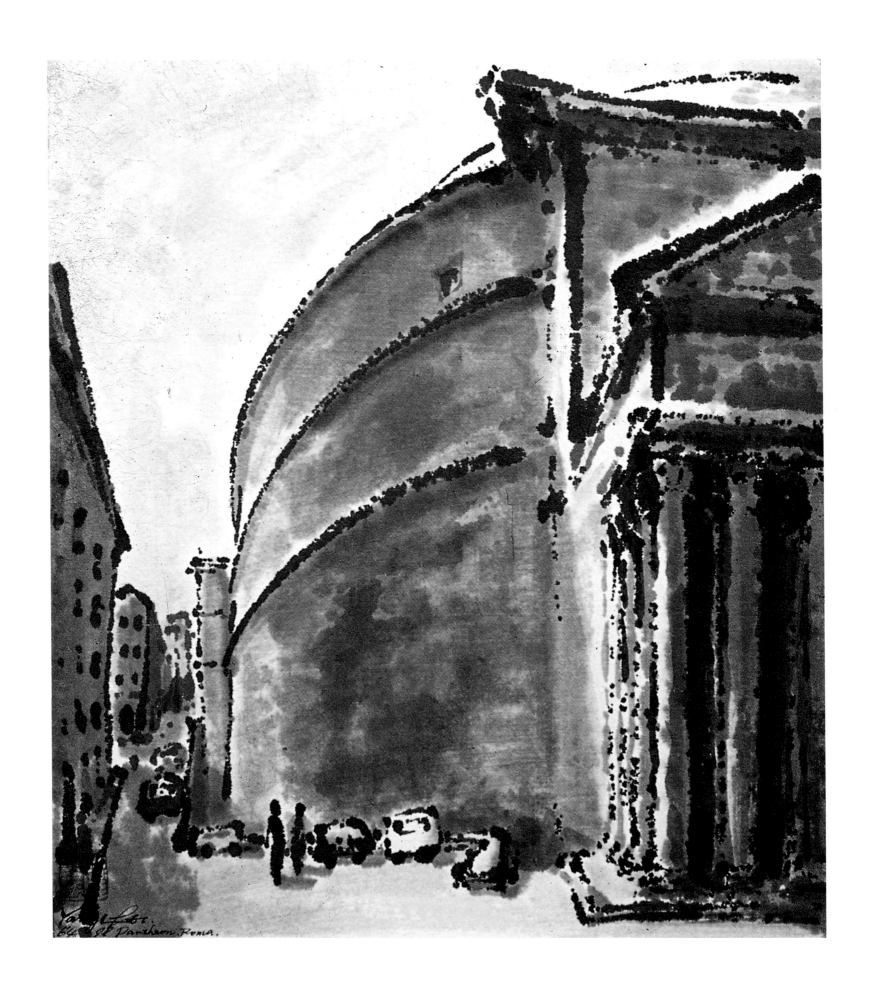

羅馬萬神殿　IL PANTHEON,ROMA　1964　紙本水彩　尺寸未詳

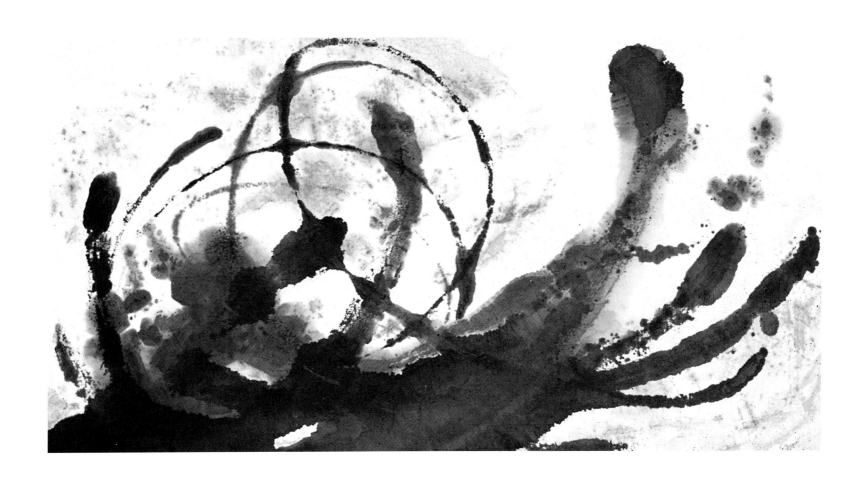

抽象繪畫64-01　ABSTRACT PAINTING 64-01　1964　紙本水彩　尺寸未詳

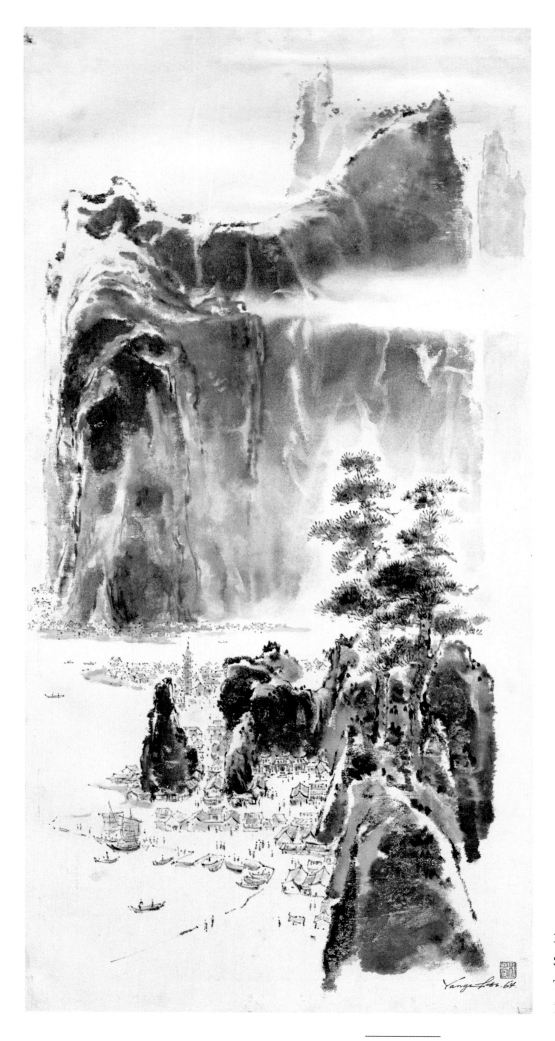

大地回春

SPRING AGAIN OVER

THE GOOD EARTH

1964　布上油彩　120×60cm

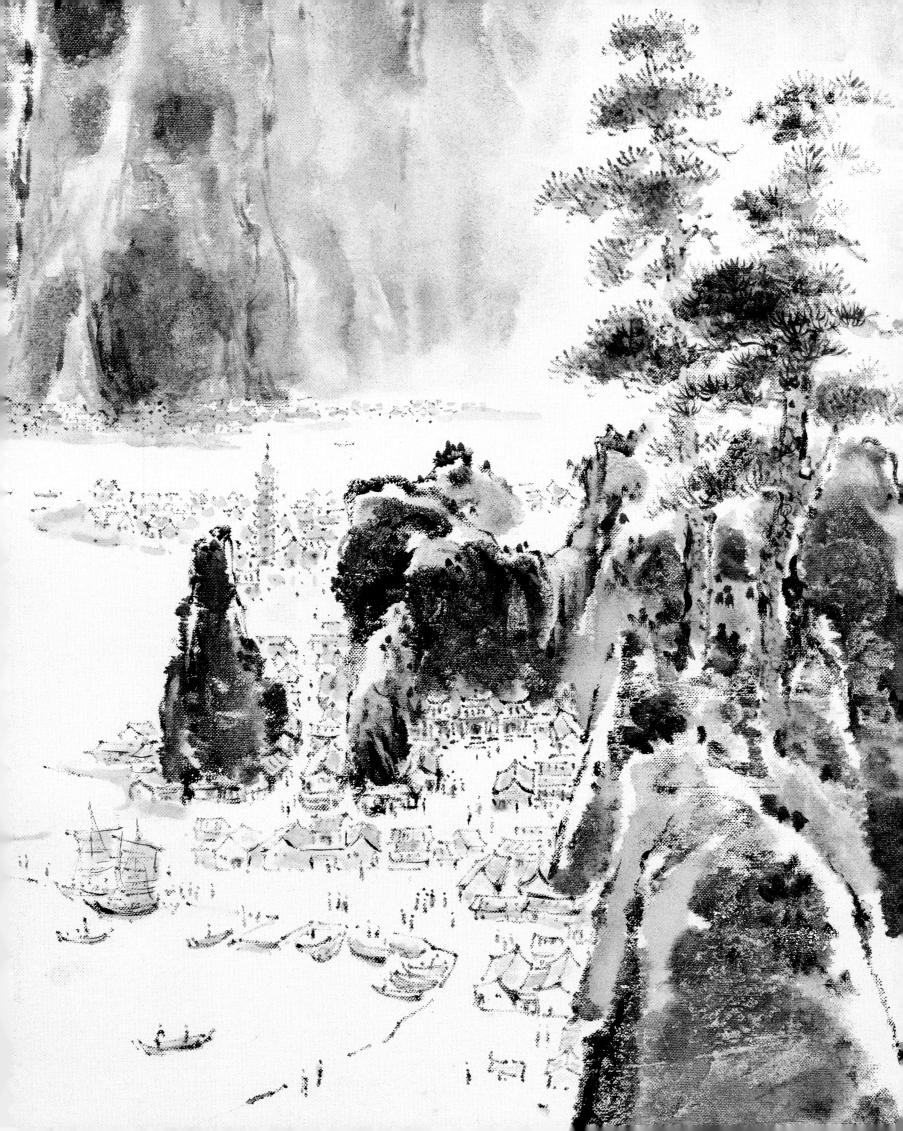

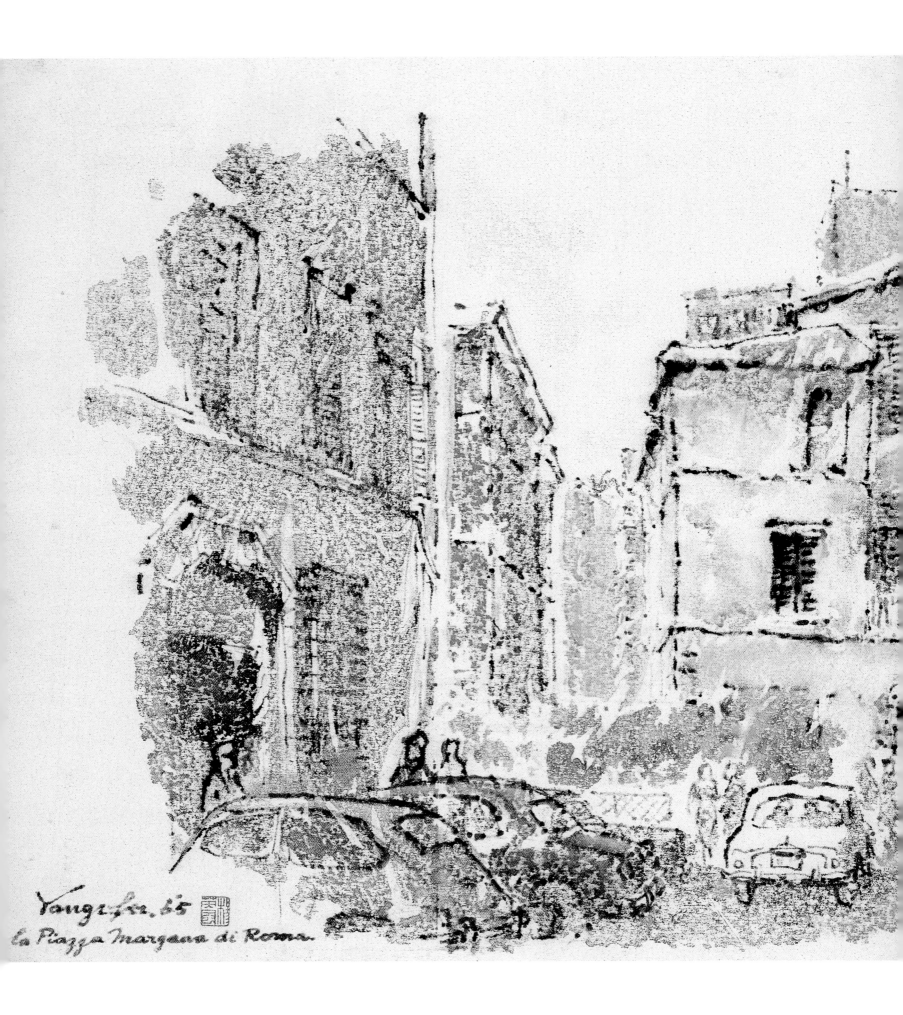

羅馬瑪歌娜廣場　LA PIAZZA MARGANA DI ROMA　1965　布上油彩　59×118cm

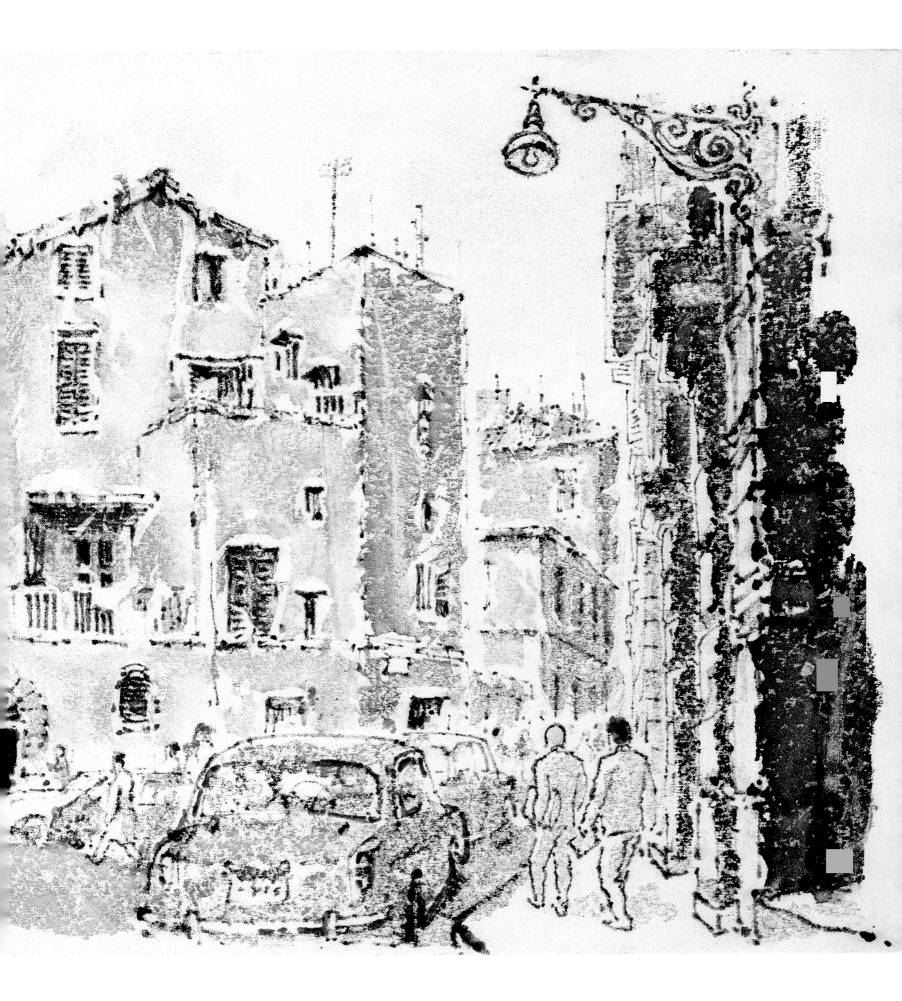

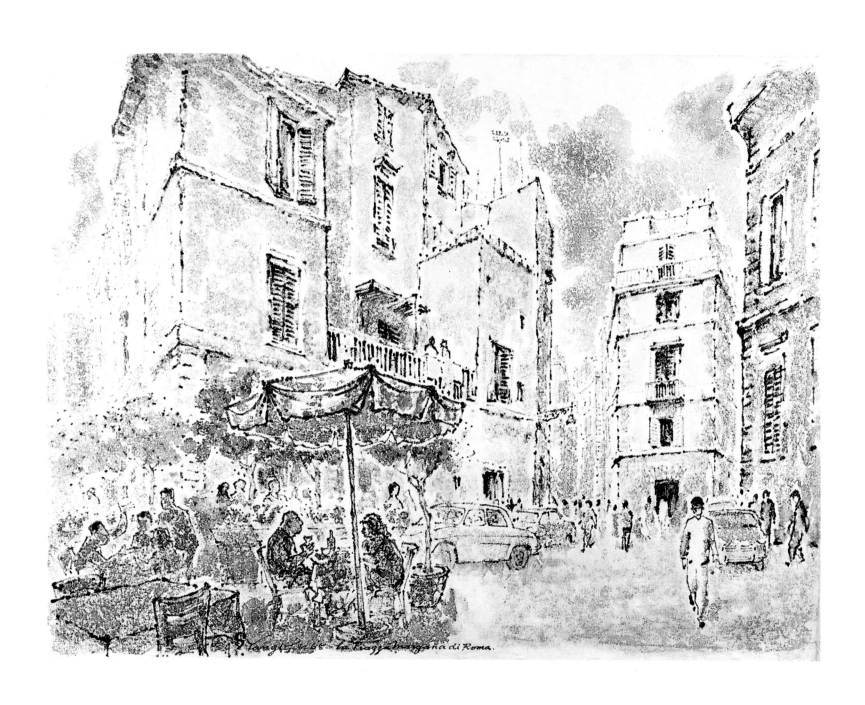

羅馬茶座　ROMAN ROADSIDE TEA-STALL　1965　布上油彩　76×97cm

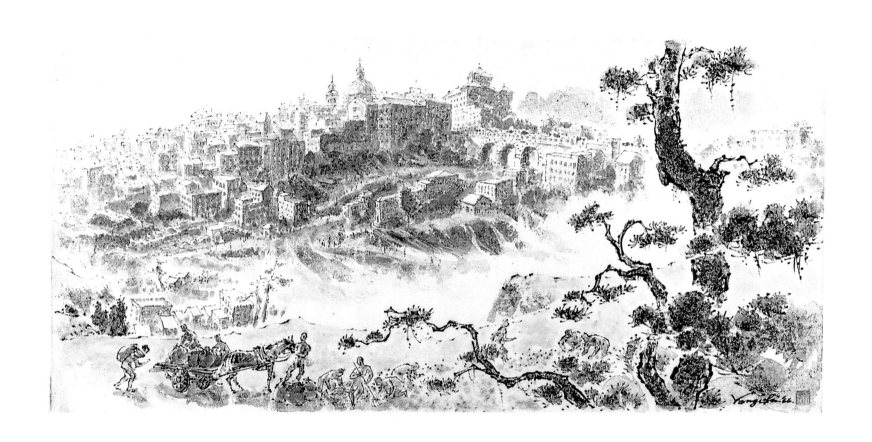

羅馬郊外　SUBURB OF ROME　1966　布上油彩　49.5×92.5cm

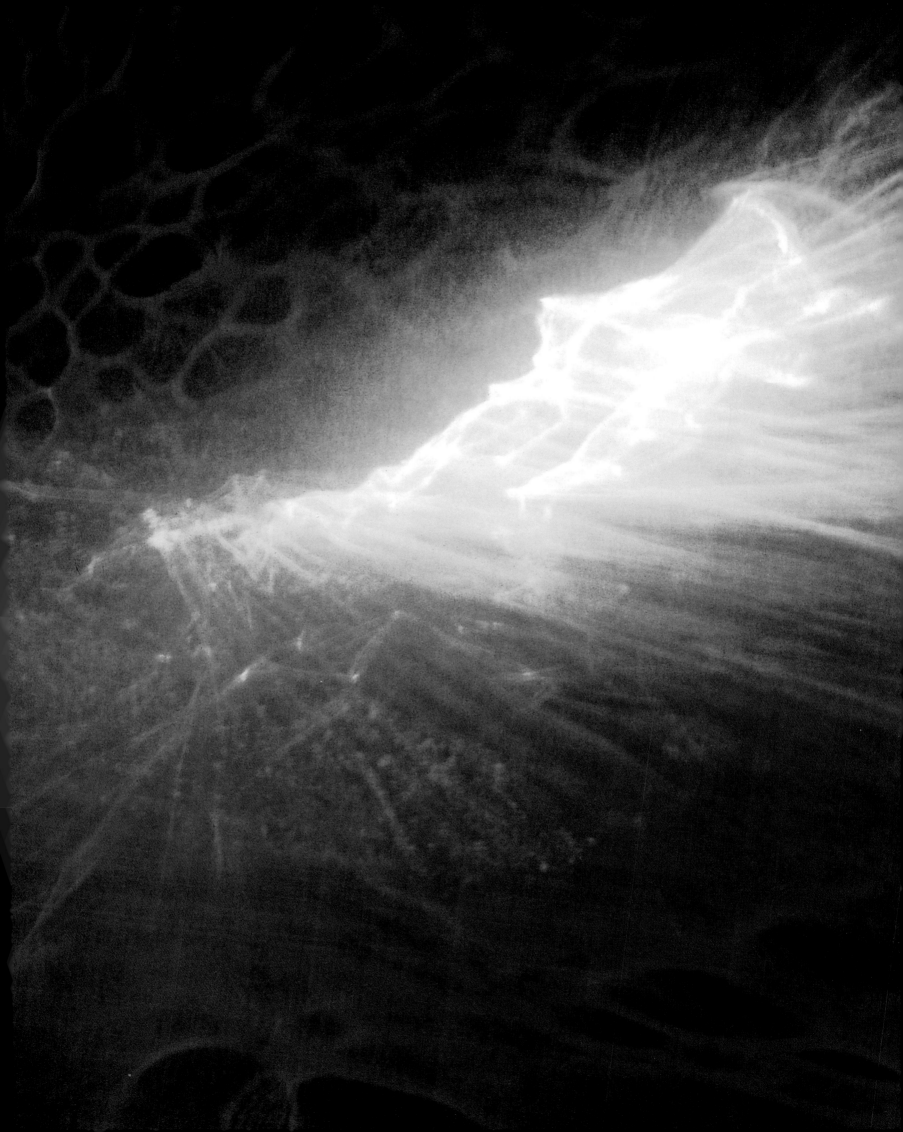

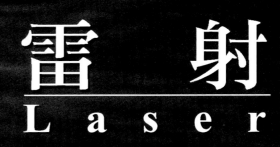

雷射
Laser

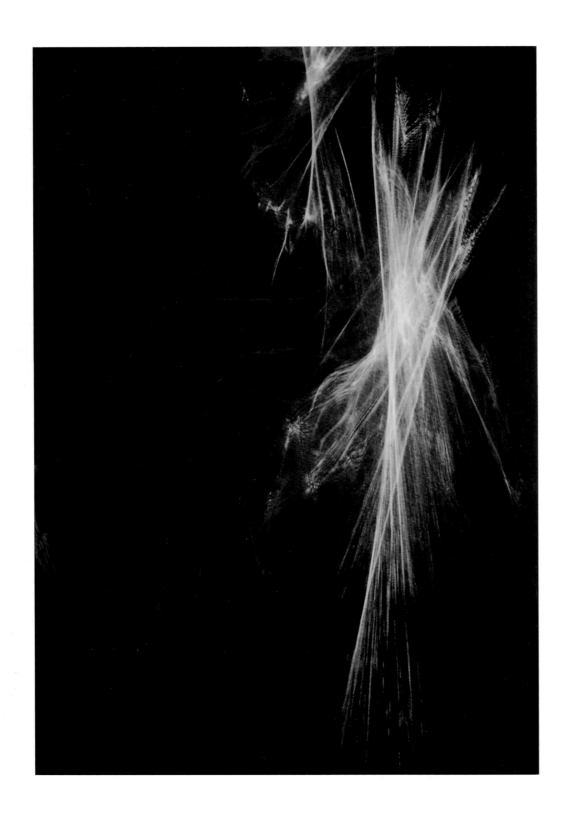

面紗（一）　VEIL（1）　1980　雷射
面紗（二）　VEIL（2）　1980　雷射（右頁圖）

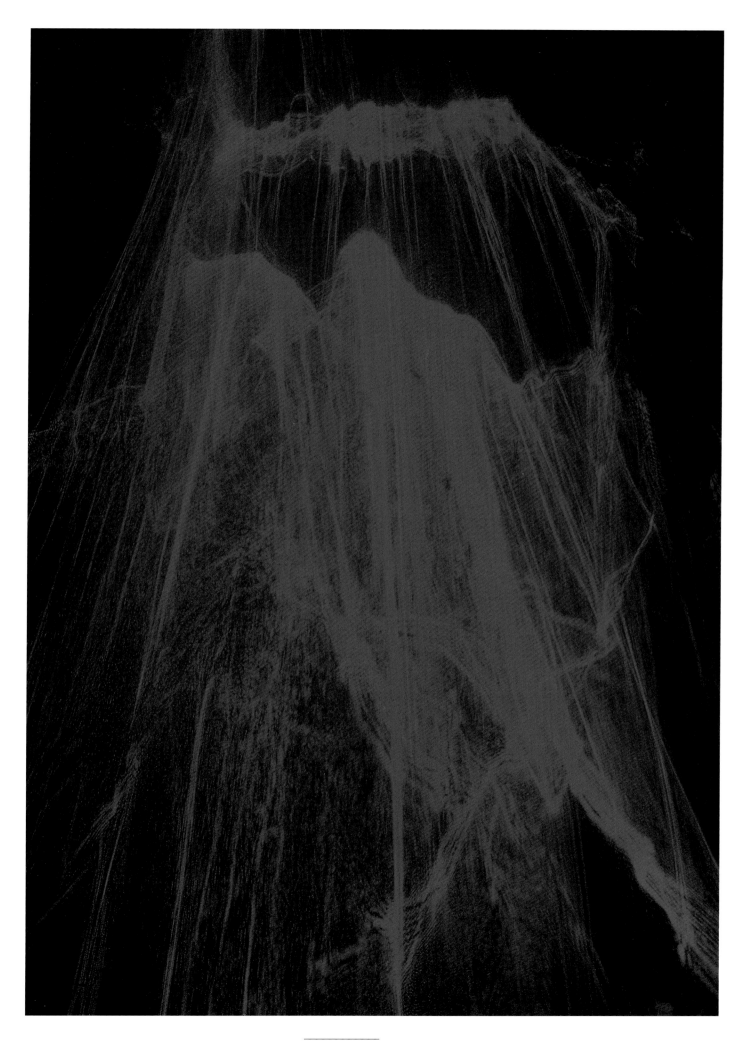

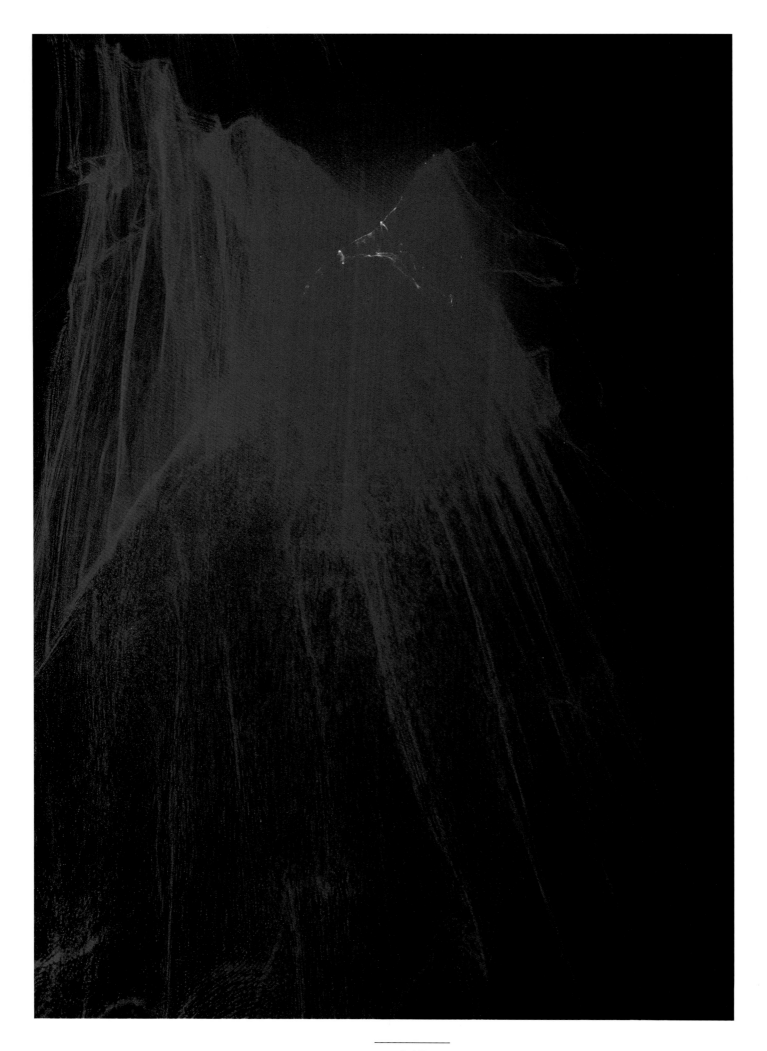

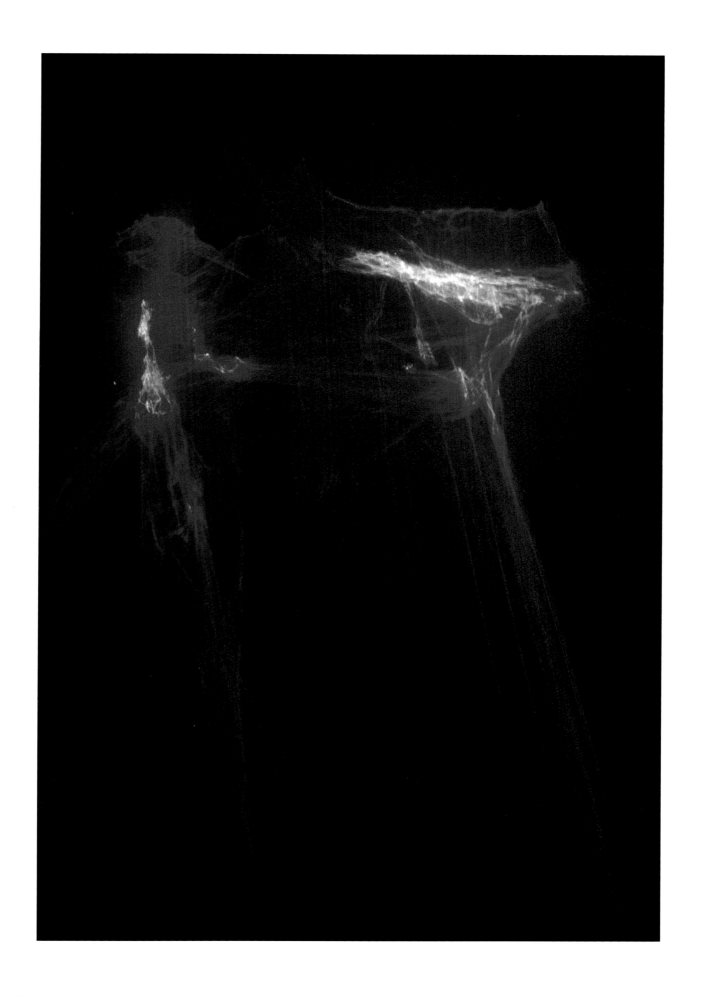

243

面紗（三） VEIL（3） 1980 雷射 （左頁圖）

面紗（四） VEIL（4） 1980 雷射

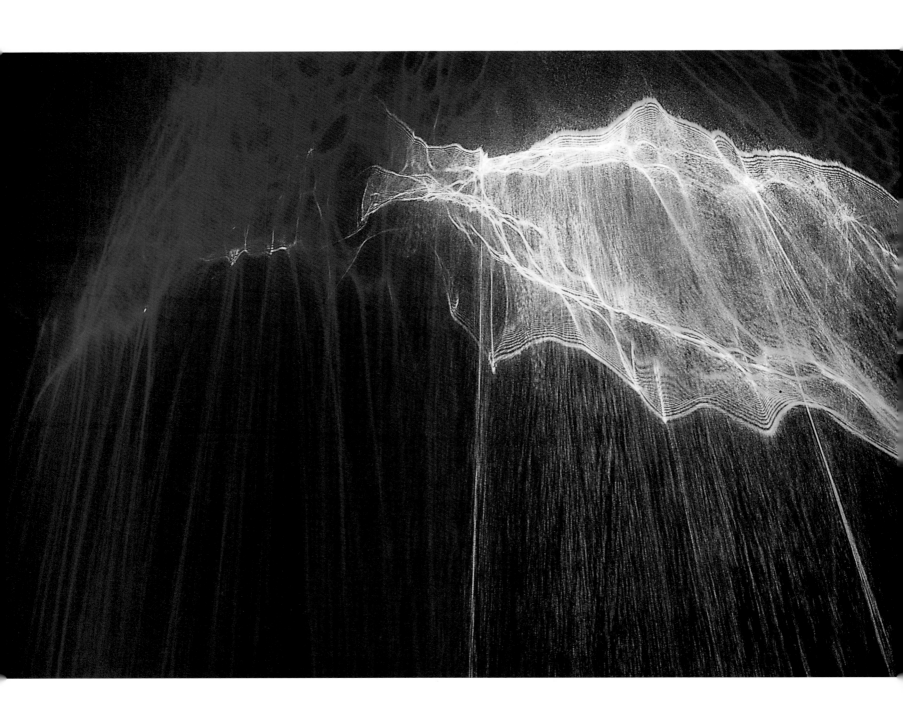

面紗（五）　VEIL（5）　1980　雷射
面紗（六）　VEIL（6）　1980　雷射（右頁圖）

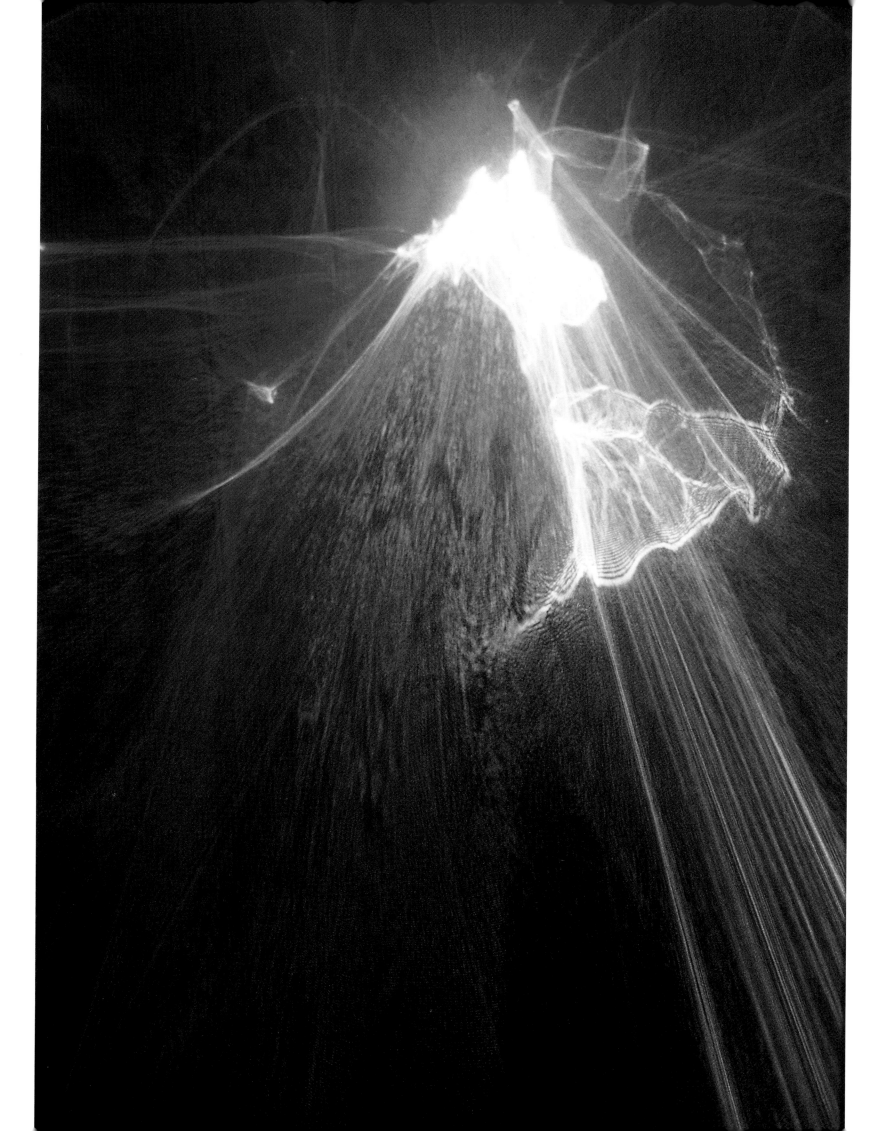

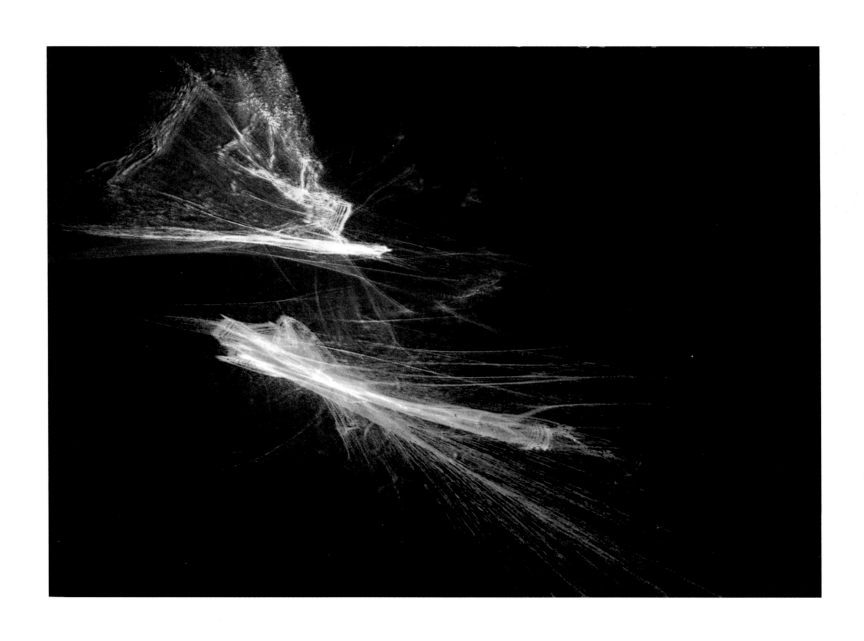

鳳凰（一）　THE　PHOENIX（1）　1980　雷射

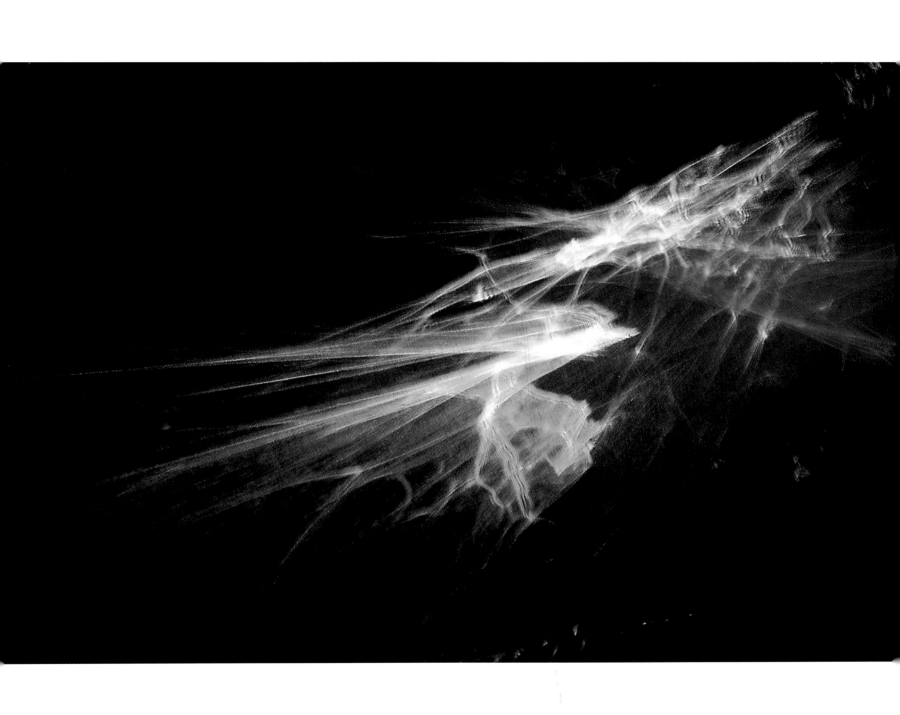

鳳凰（二） THE PHOENIX（2） 1980 雷射

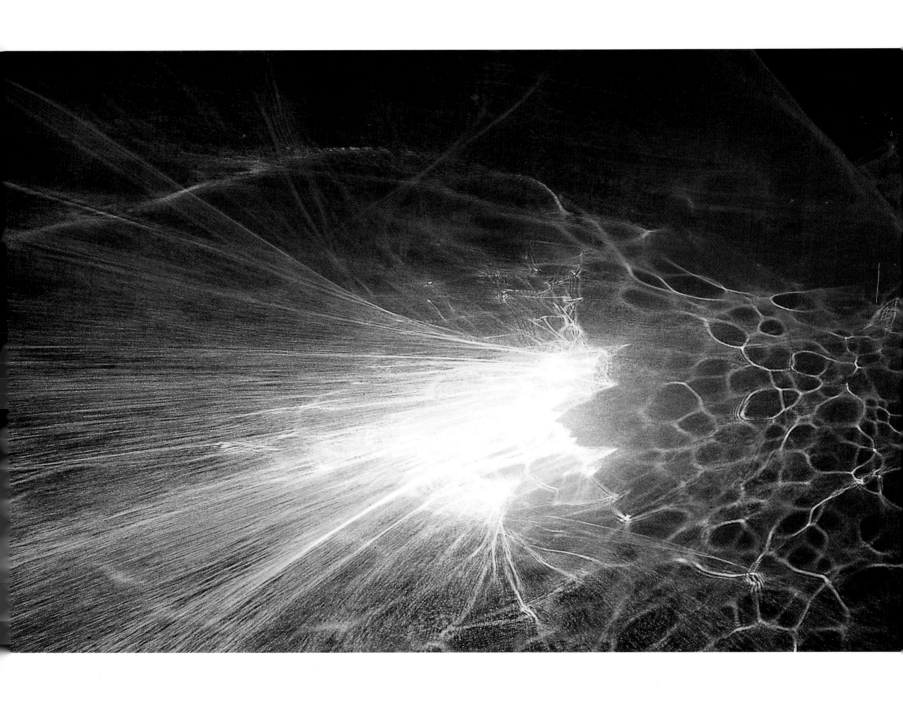

鳳凰（三）　THE PHOENIX（3）　1980　雷射

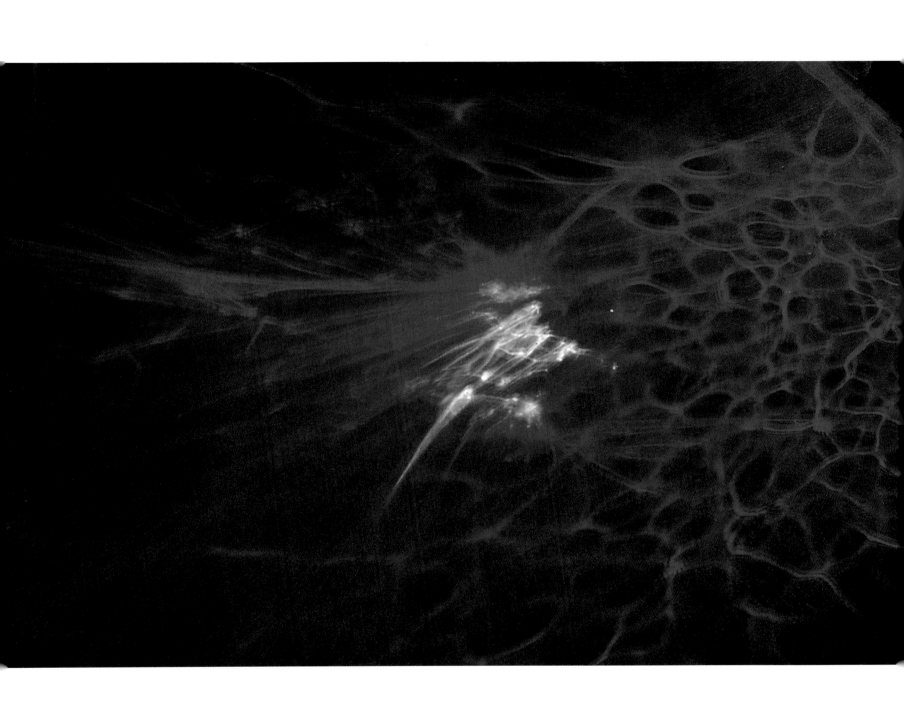

鳳凰（四）　THE　PHOENIX（4）　1980　雷射

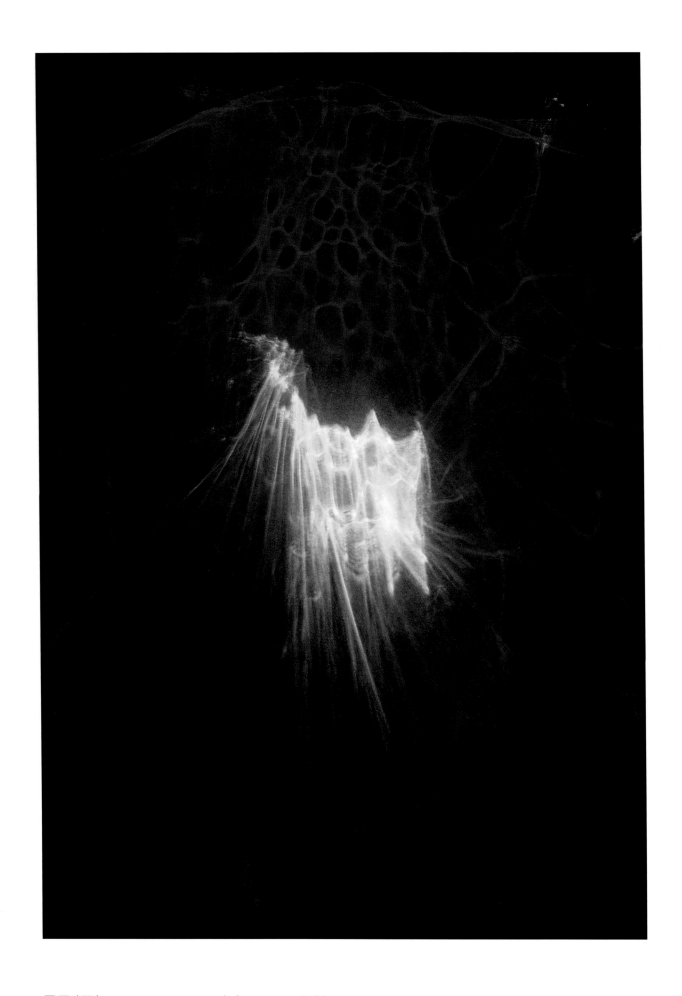

鳳凰（五）　THE　PHOENIX（5）　1980　雷射

鳳凰（六）　THE　PHOENIX（6）　1980　雷射 （右頁圖）

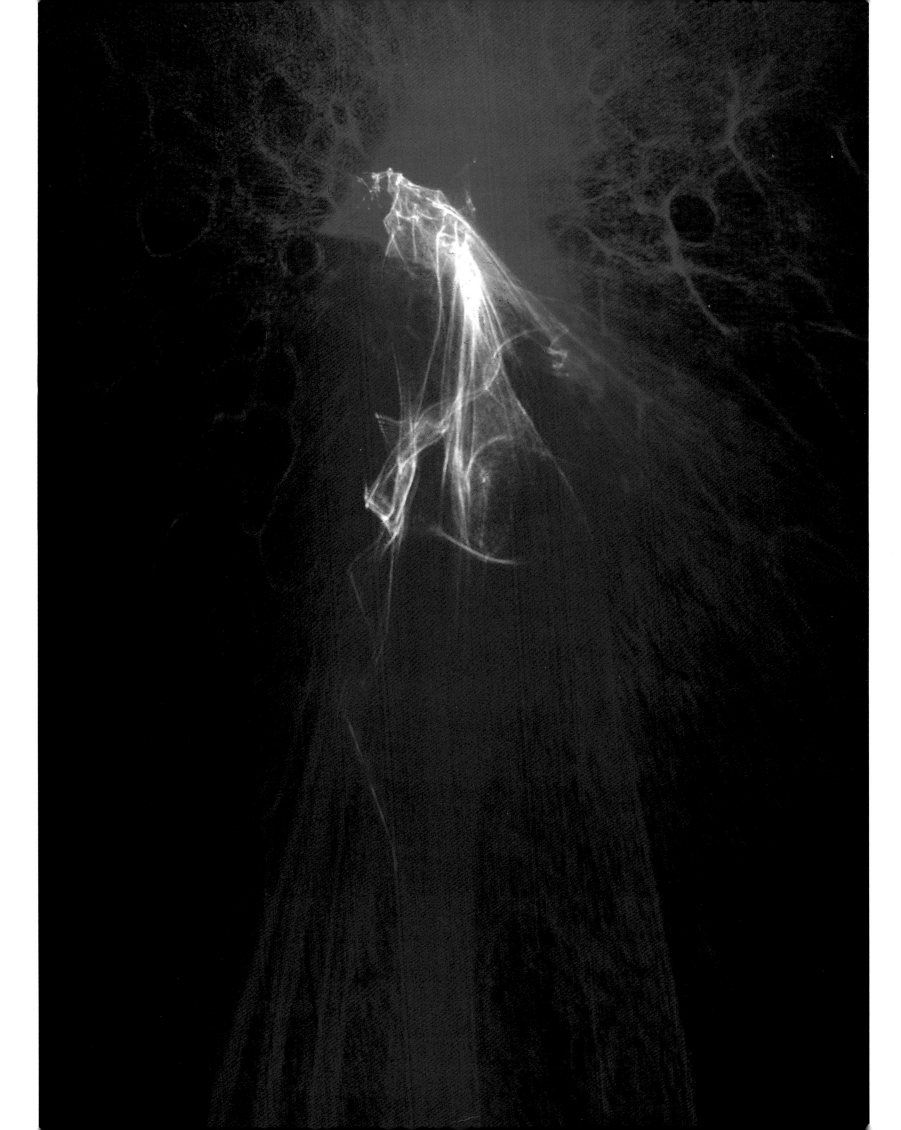

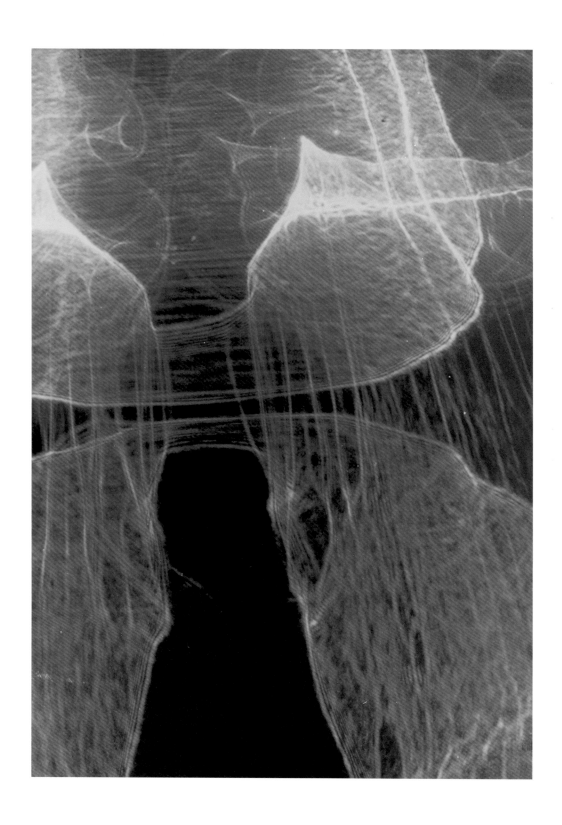

聖架　THE CROSS　1980　雷射
聖衣（一）　HOLY　ROBE（1）　1980　雷射（右頁圖）

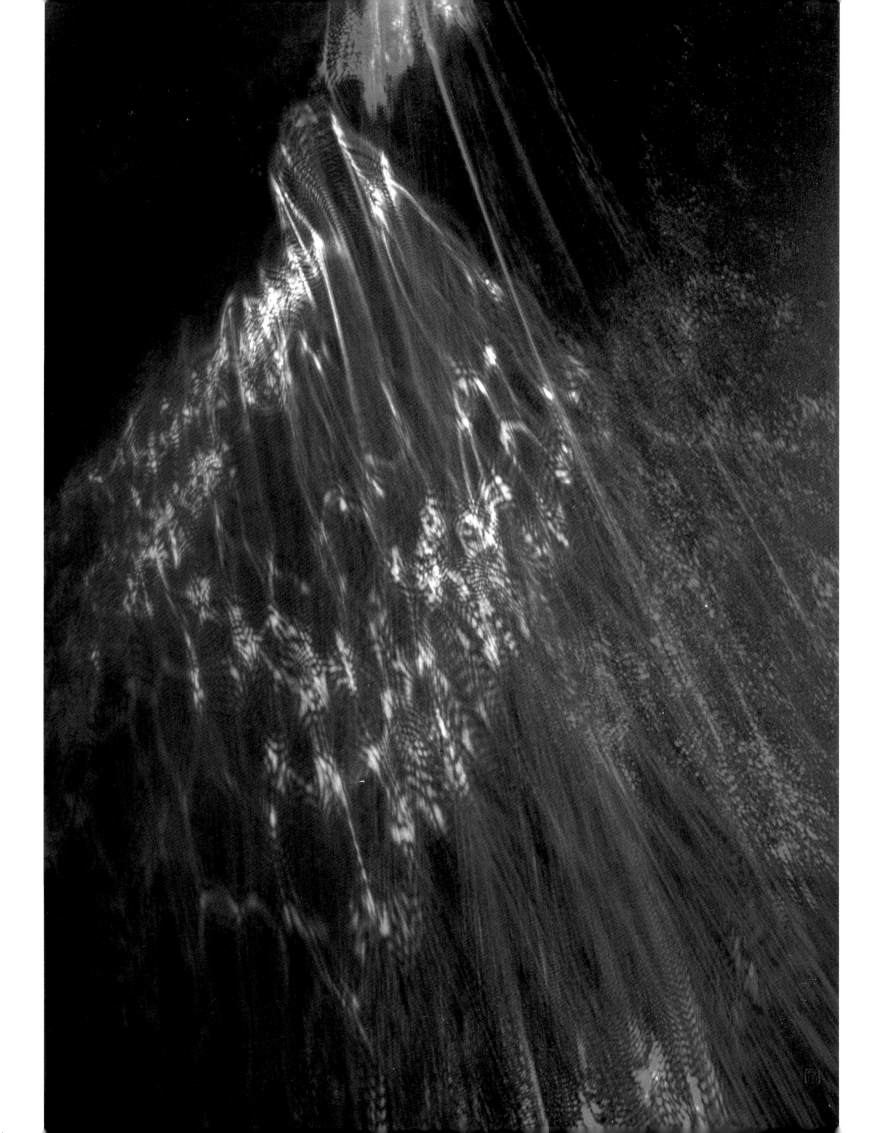

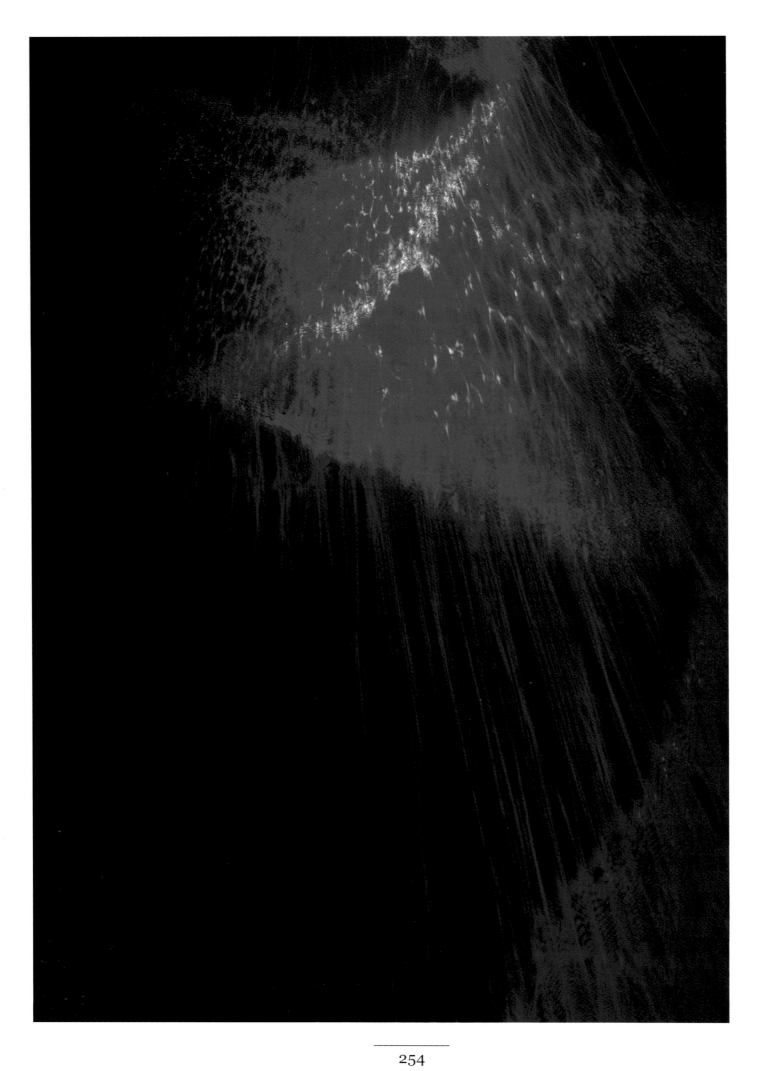

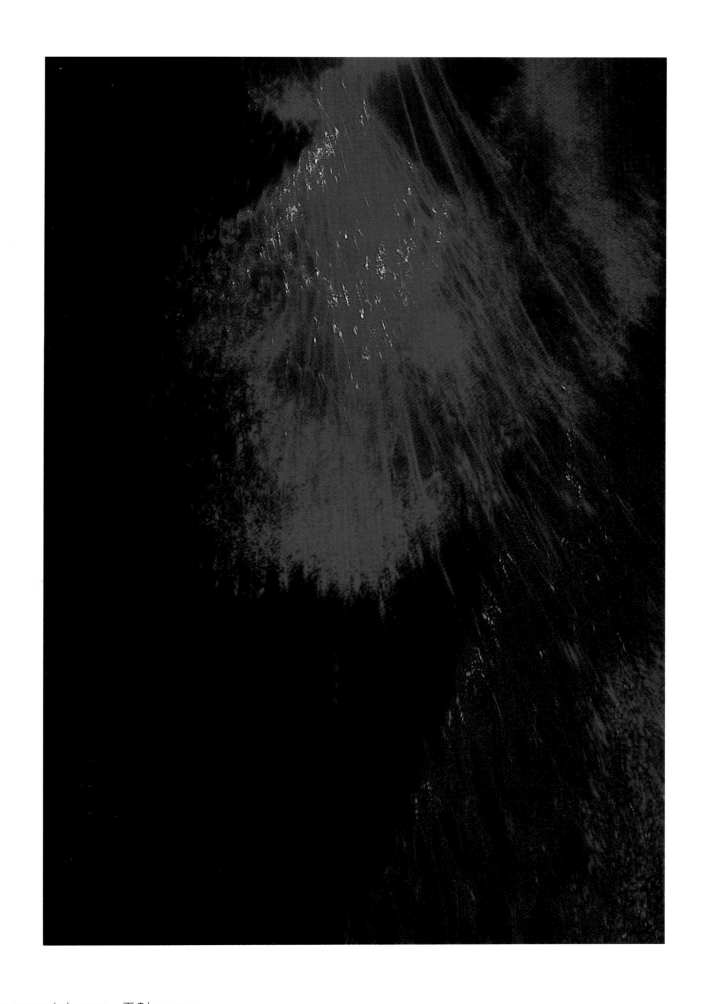

聖衣（二）HOLY ROBE（2） 1980 雷射 <small>（左頁圖）</small>

聖衣（三）HOLY ROBE（3） 1980 雷射

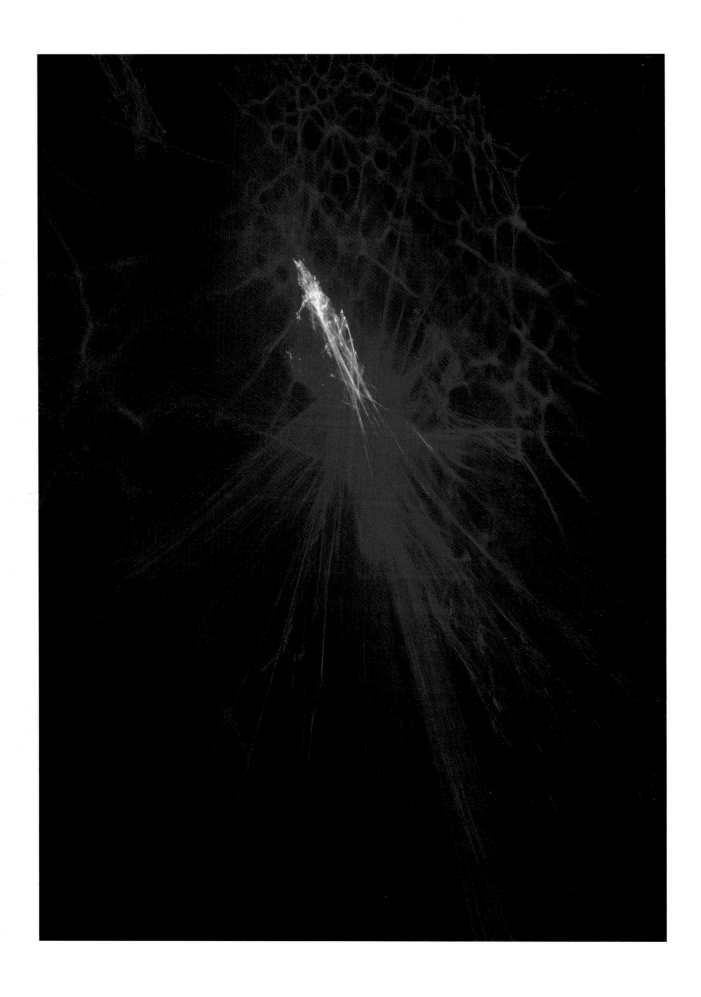

聖者（一） SAINT（1） 1980 雷射

聖者（二） SAINT（2） 1980 雷射 （右頁圖）

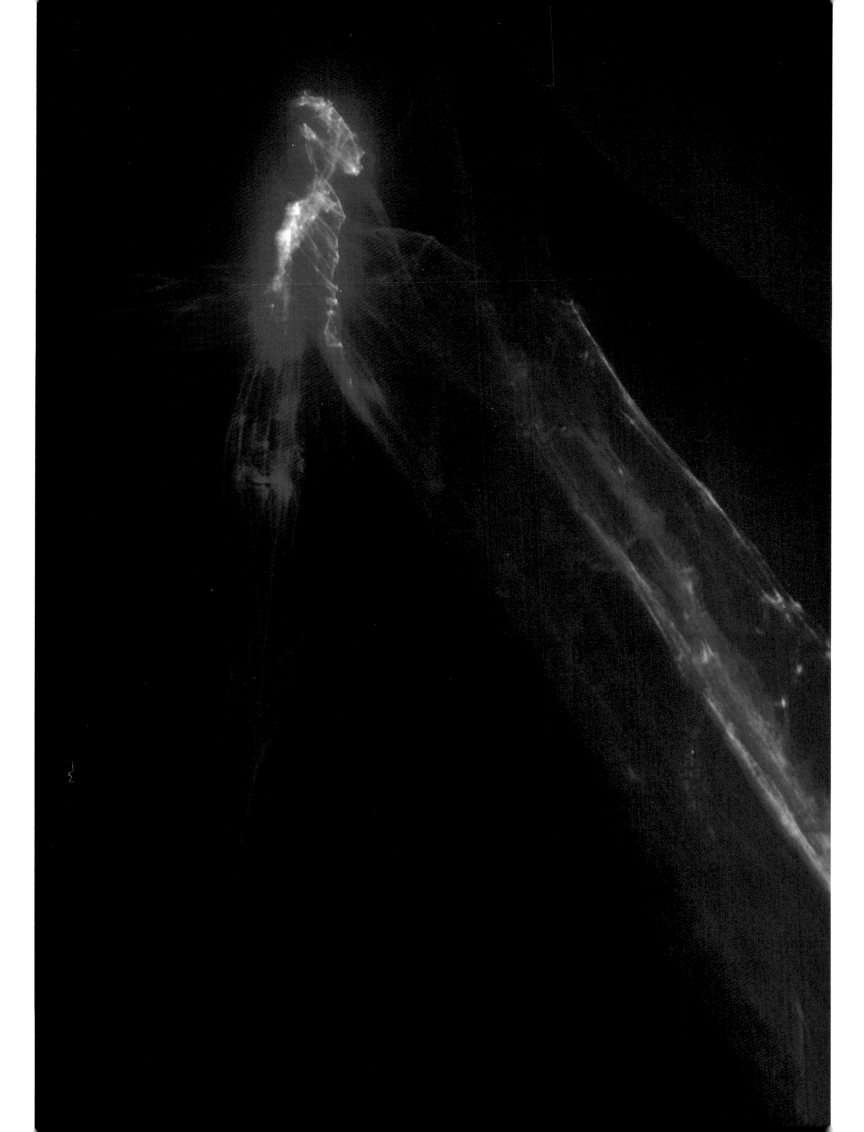

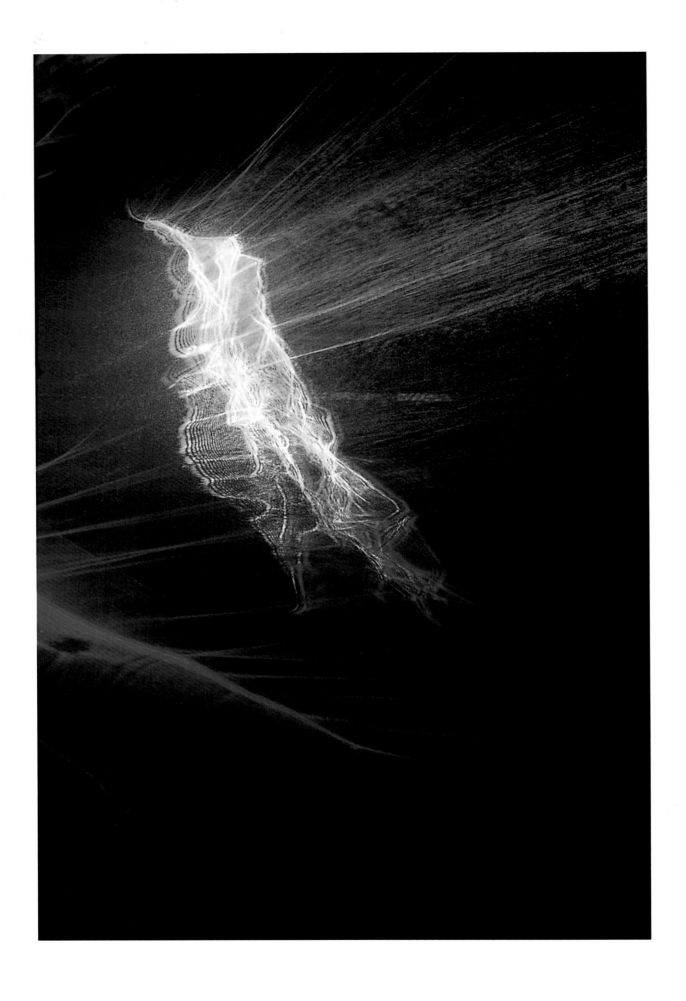

聖者（三）SAINT（3） 1980　雷射

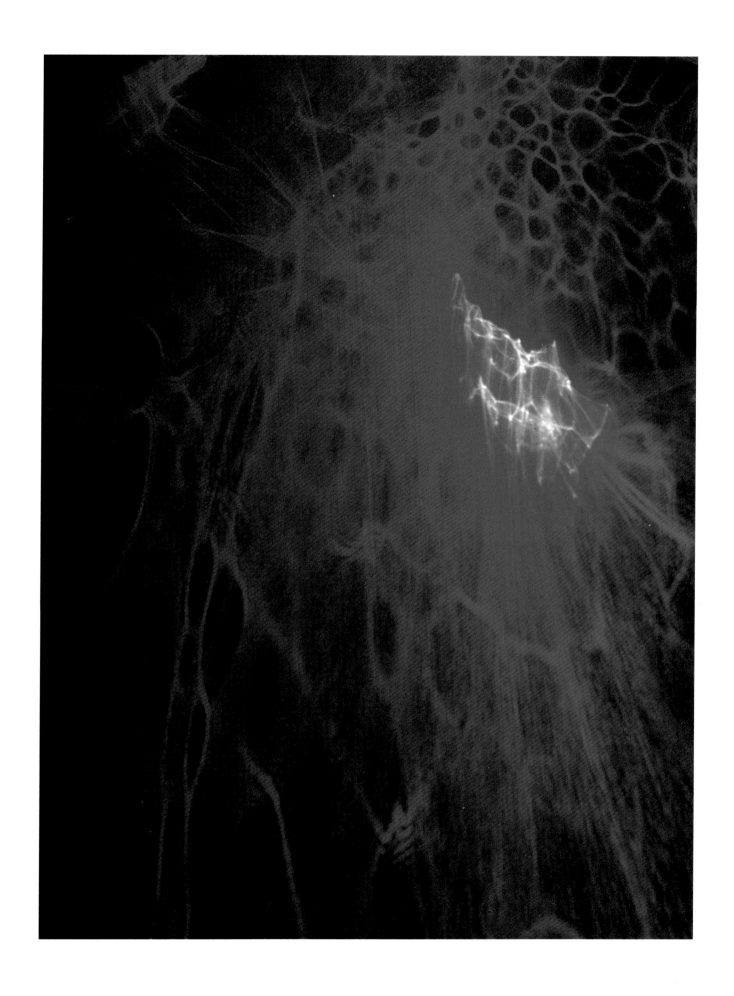

聖者（四）　SAINT（4）　1980　雷射

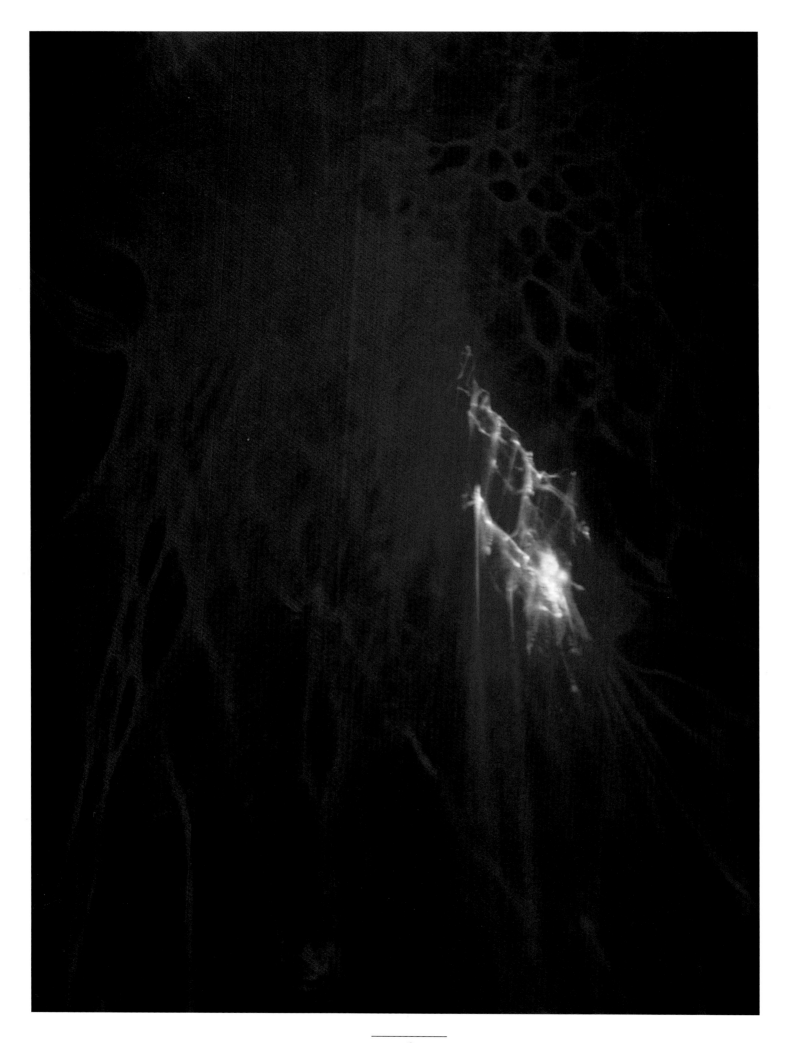

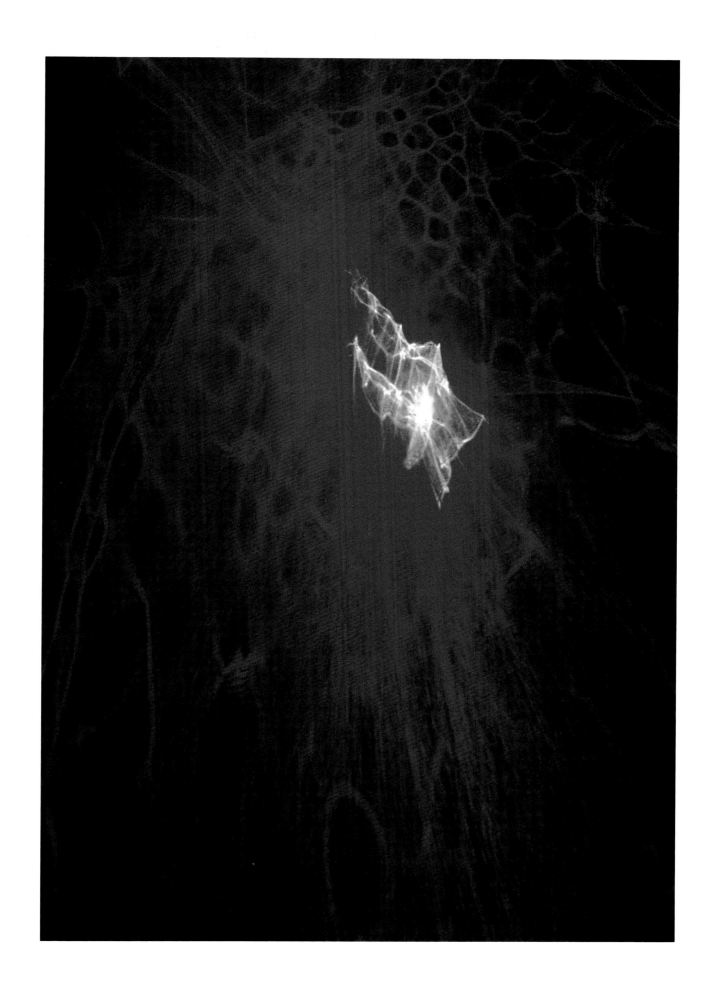

聖者（五） SAINT（5） 1980 雷射 _{（左頁圖）}
聖者（六） SAINT（6） 1980 雷射

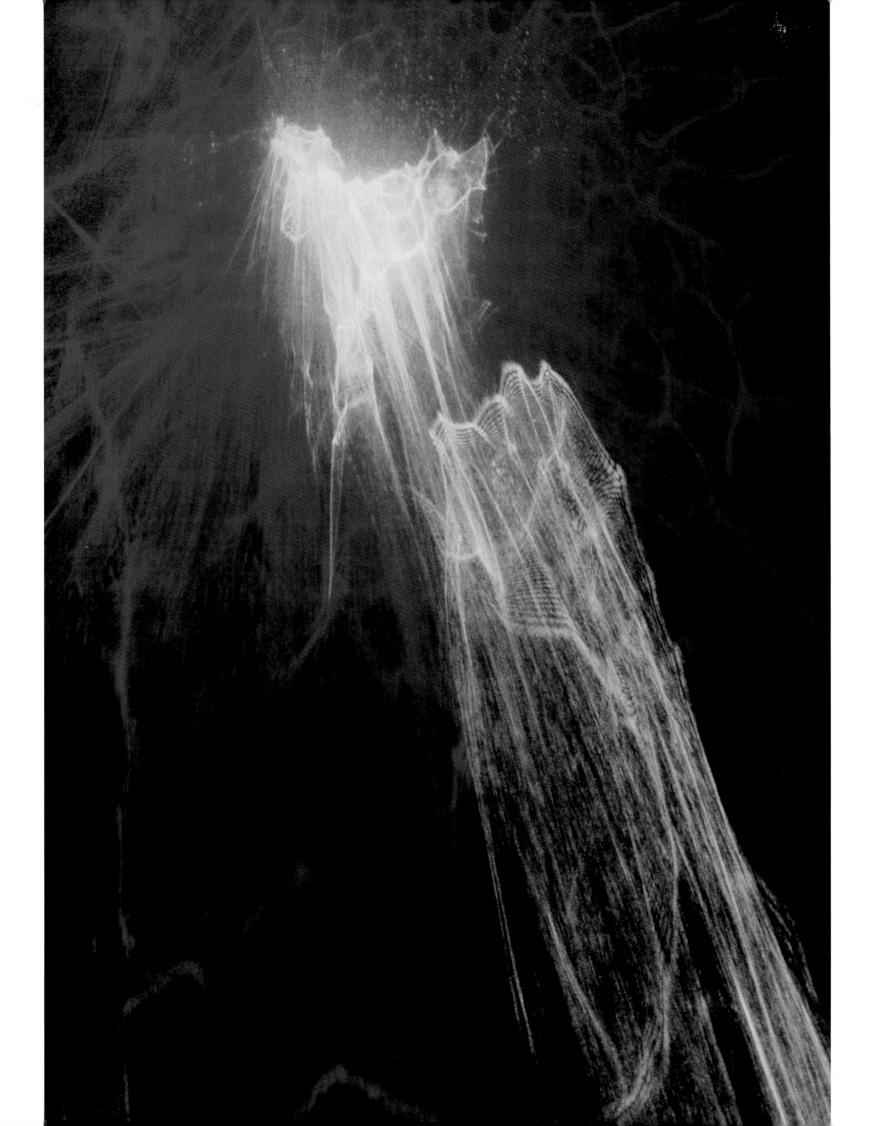

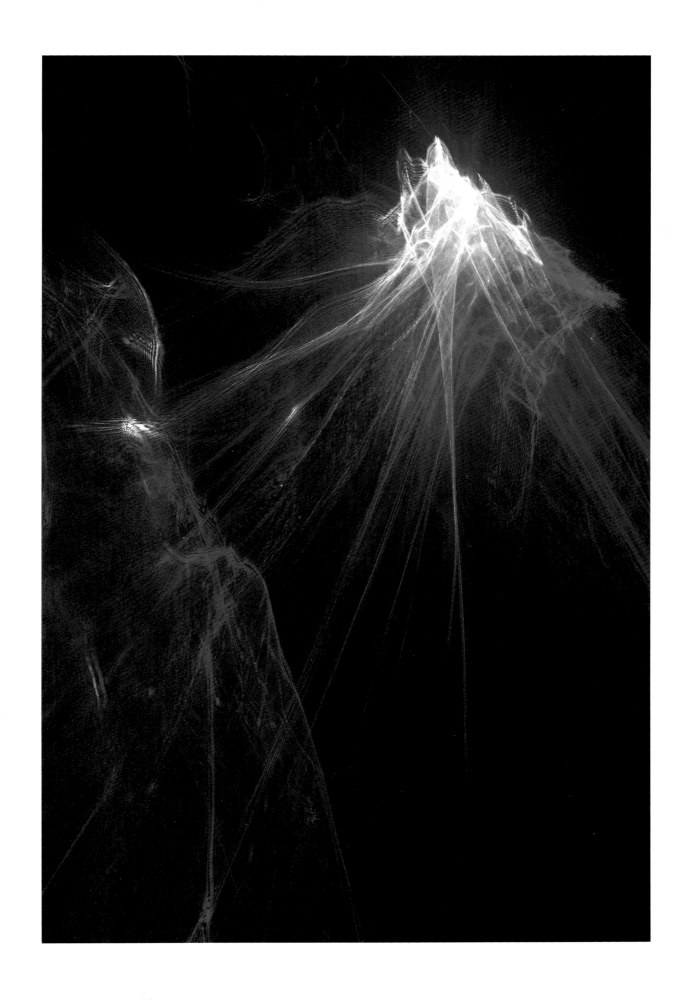

聖光（一）　HOLY LIGHT(1)　1980　雷射 _{（左頁圖）}

聖光（二）　HOLY LIGHT(2)　1980　雷射

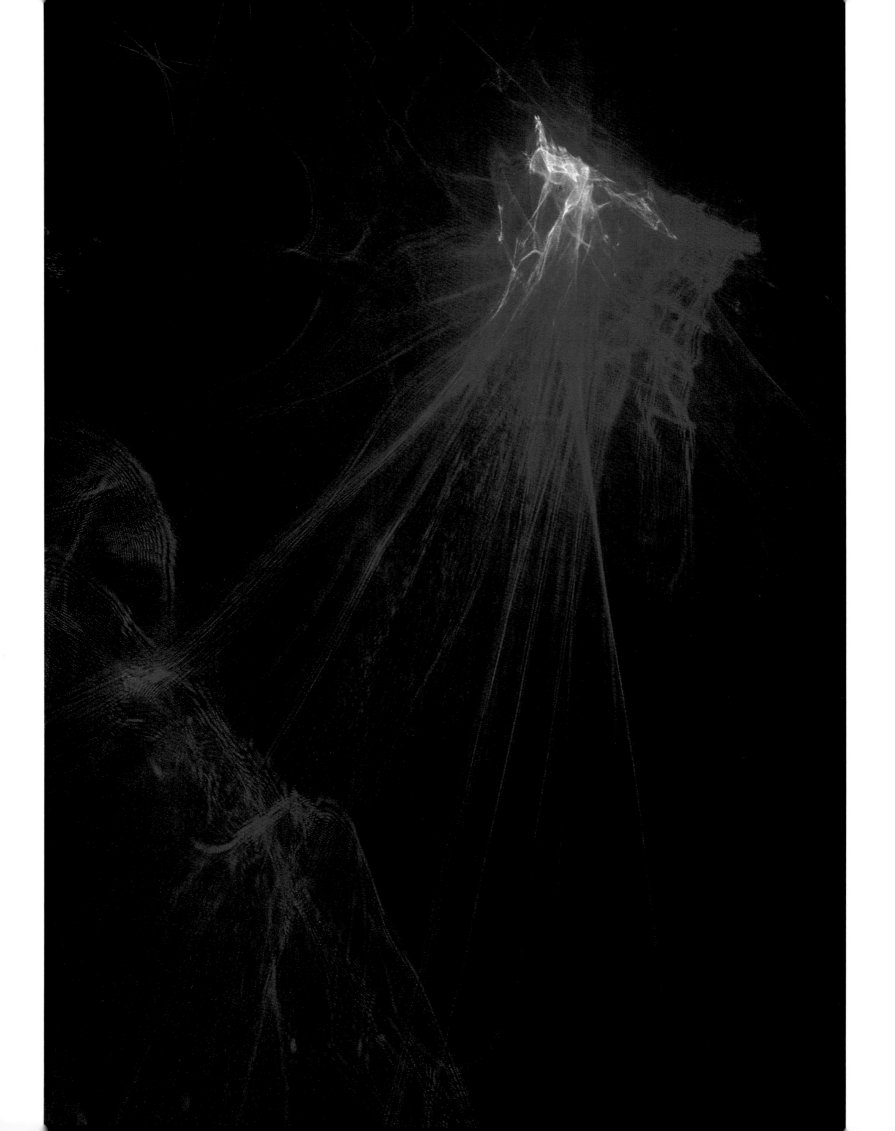

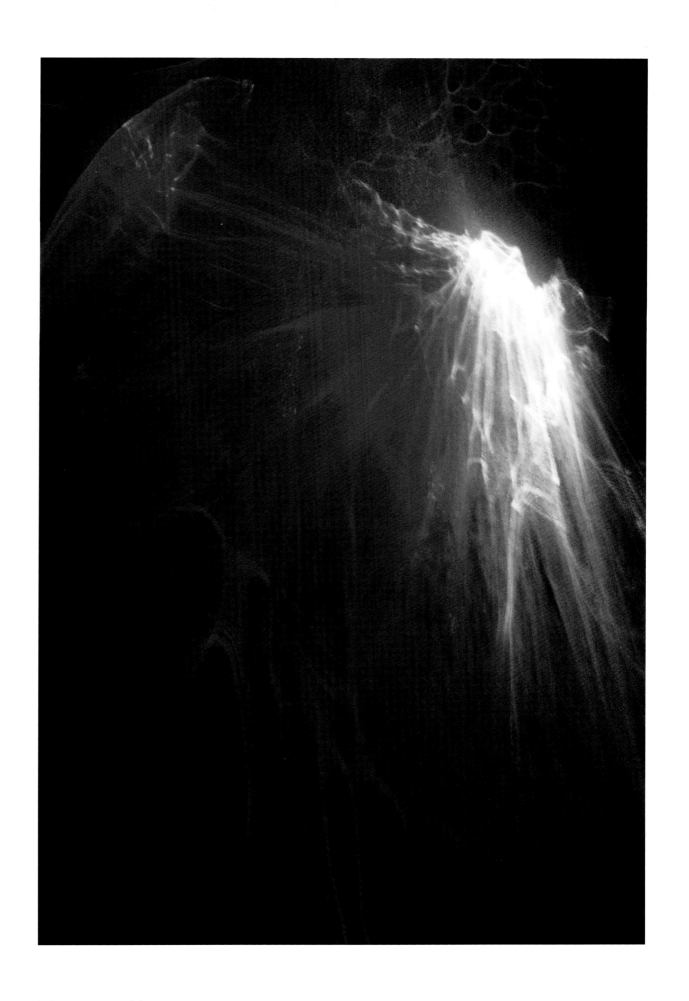

聖光（三）HOLY LIGHT（3） 1980 雷射（左頁圖）

聖光（四）HOLY LIGHT（4） 1980 雷射

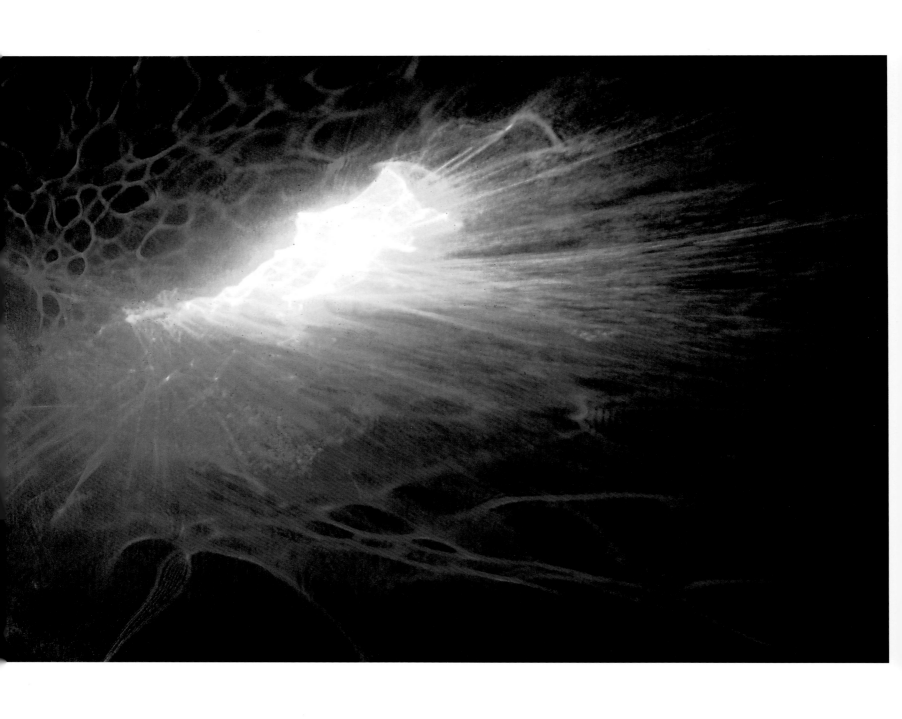

聖光（五）HOLY LIGHT(5)　1980　雷射

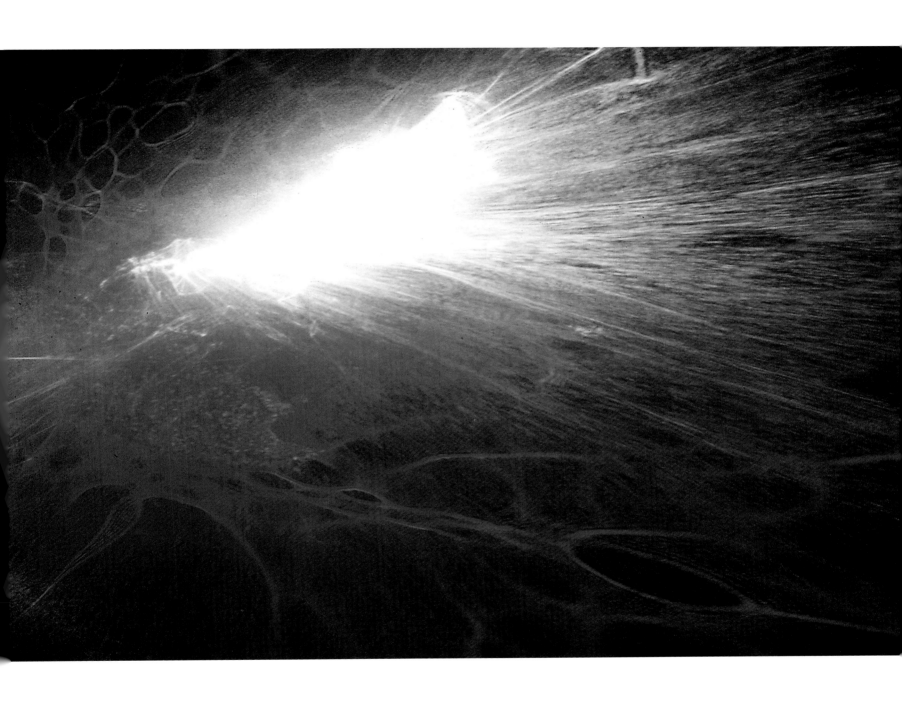

聖光（六）　HOLY LIGHT（6）　1980　雷射

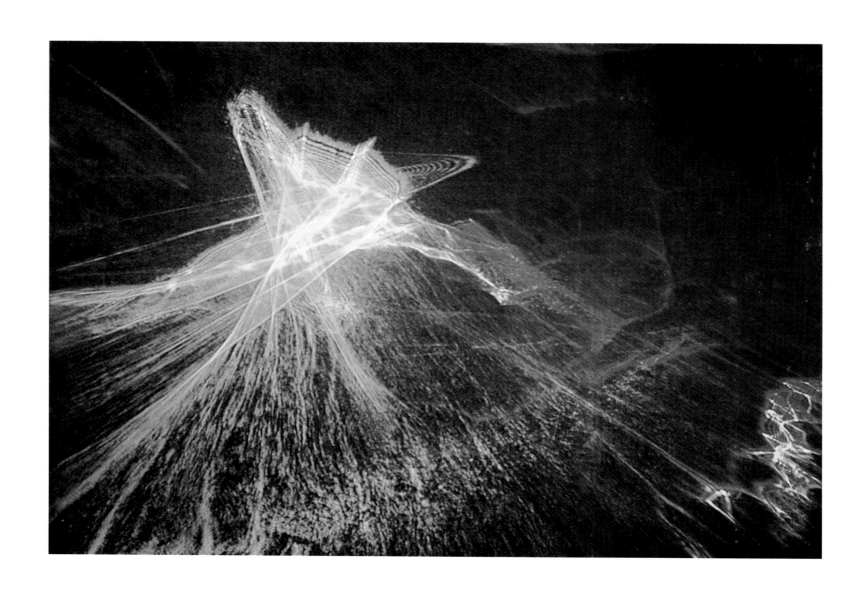

乾坤袋　THE MAGNIFICENT UNIVERSE　1980　雷射

驚蟄　AWAKENING OF SPRING　1980　雷射（右頁圖）

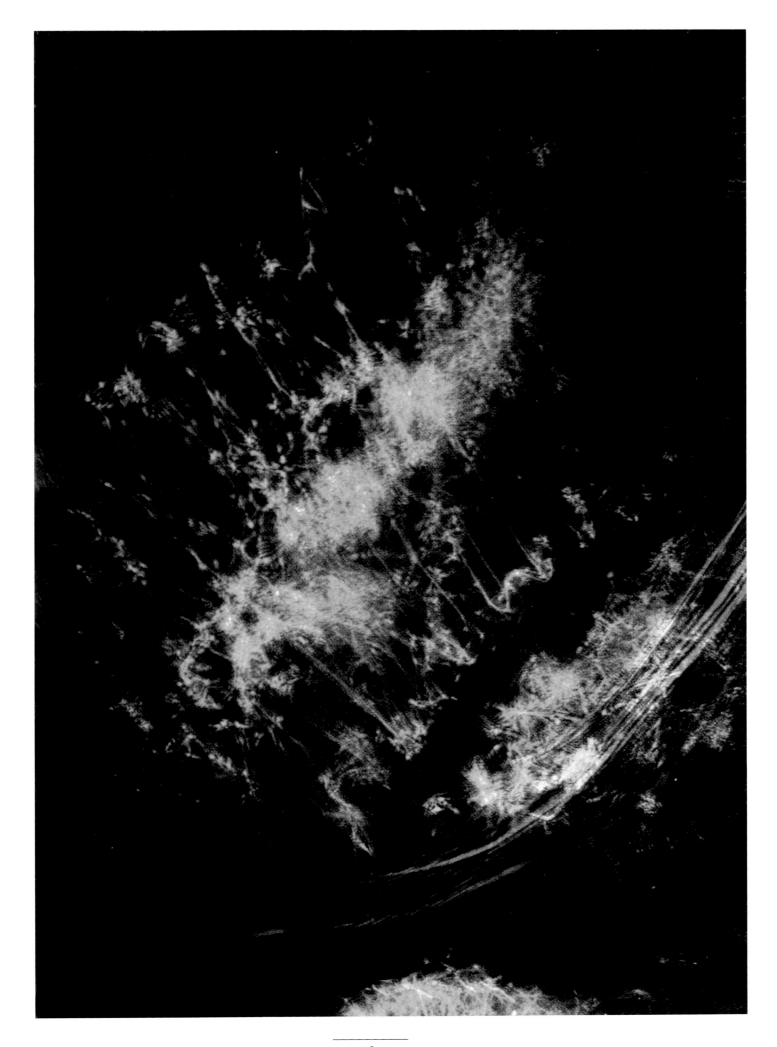

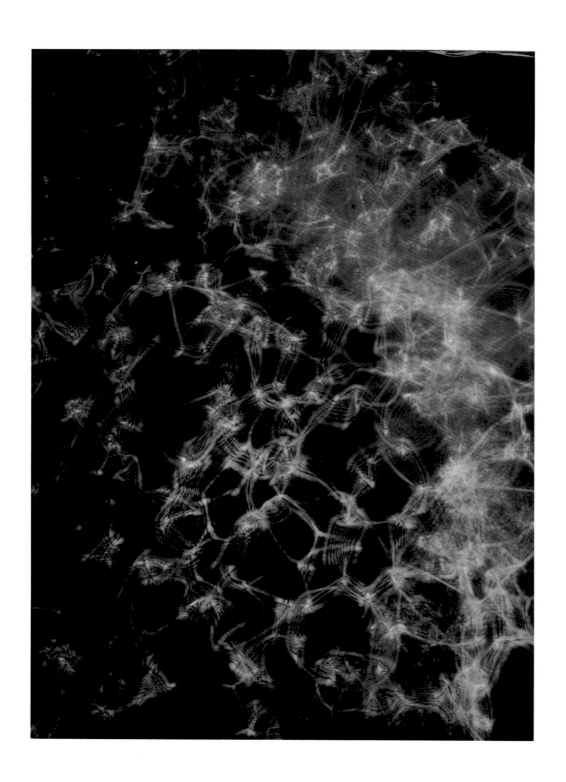

春滿大地　SPRING HAS ARRIVED　1980　雷射

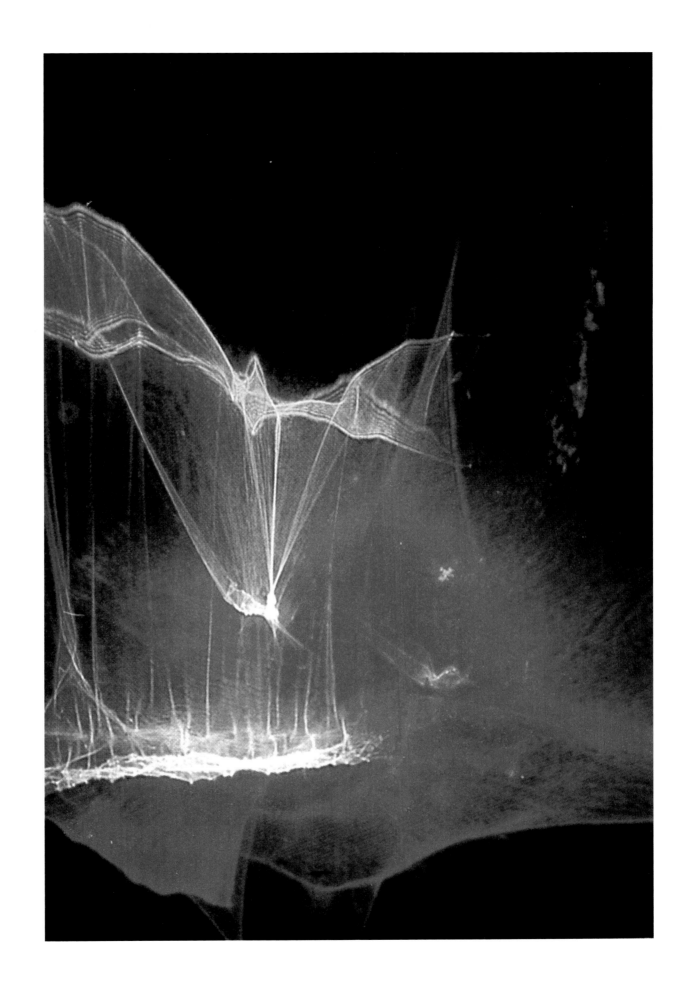

芽　THE SPROUT　1980　雷射

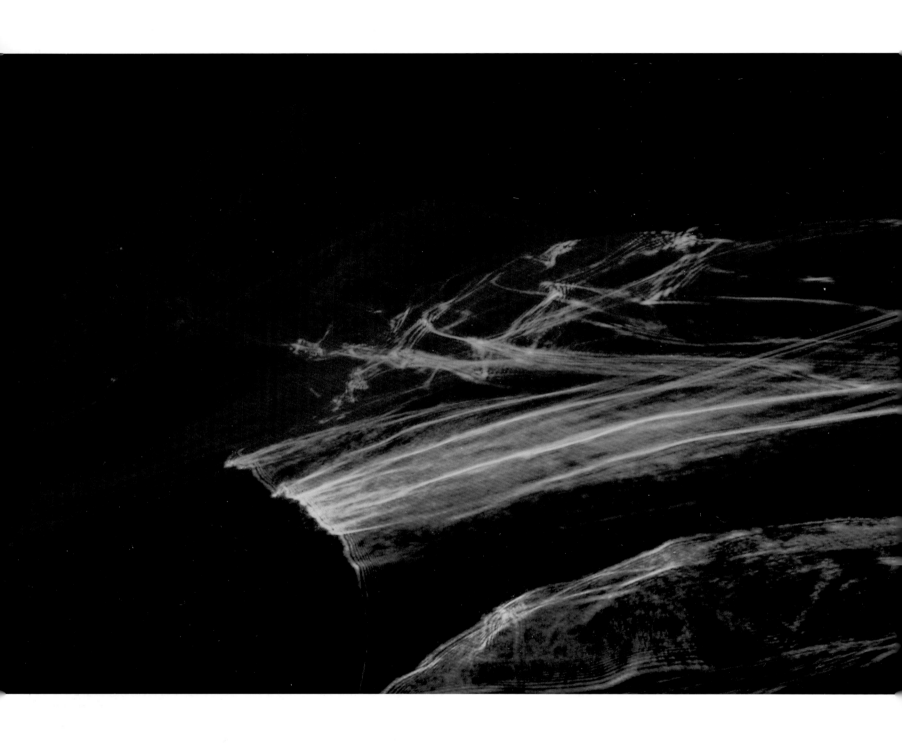

遠山夕照　SUNSHINE　1980　雷射
蘇花公路　SU-HUA　FREEWAY　1980　雷射(右頁圖)

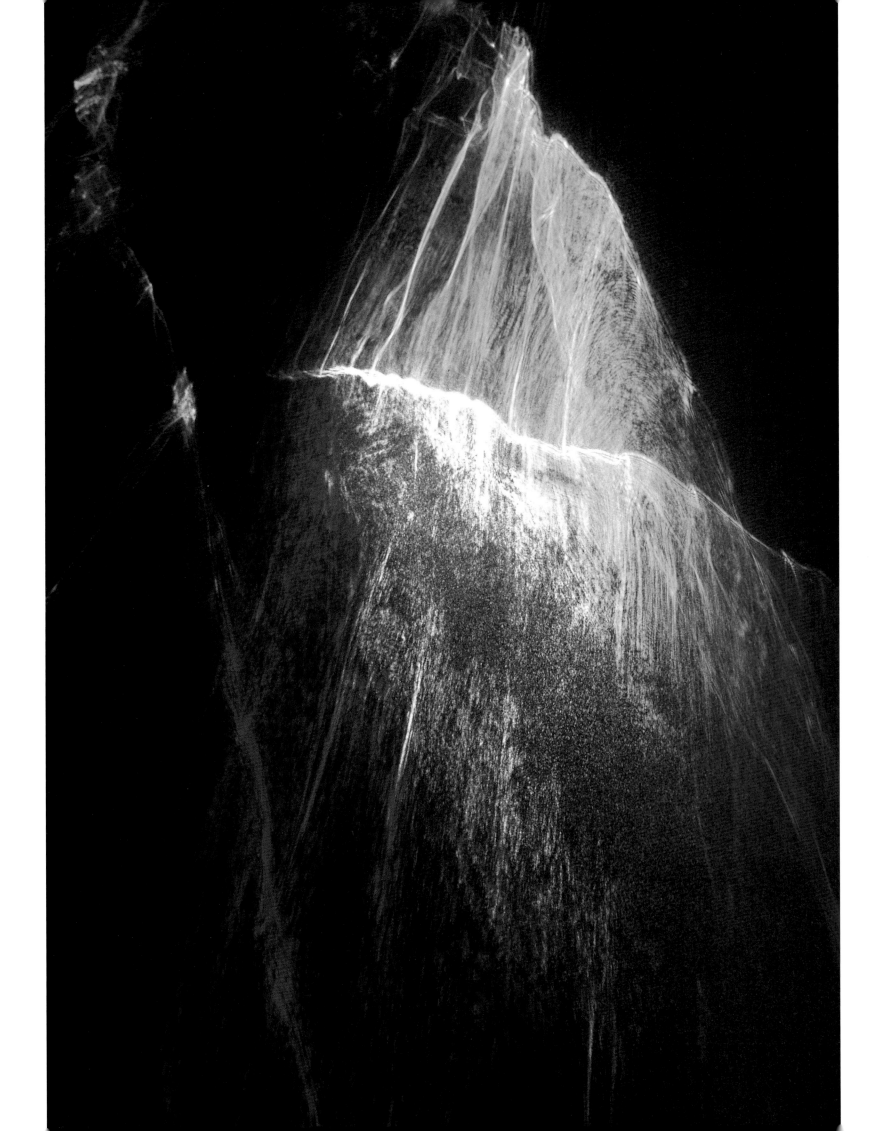

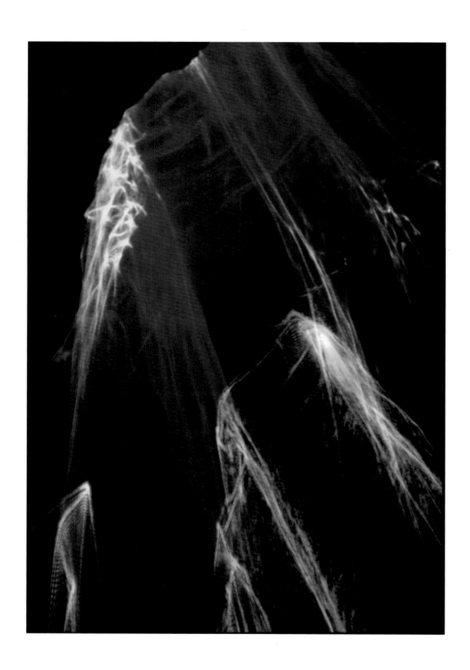

山岳（一）MOUNTAINS AND HILLS（1）1980　雷射
山岳（二）MOUNTAINS AND HILLS（2）1980　雷射（右頁圖）

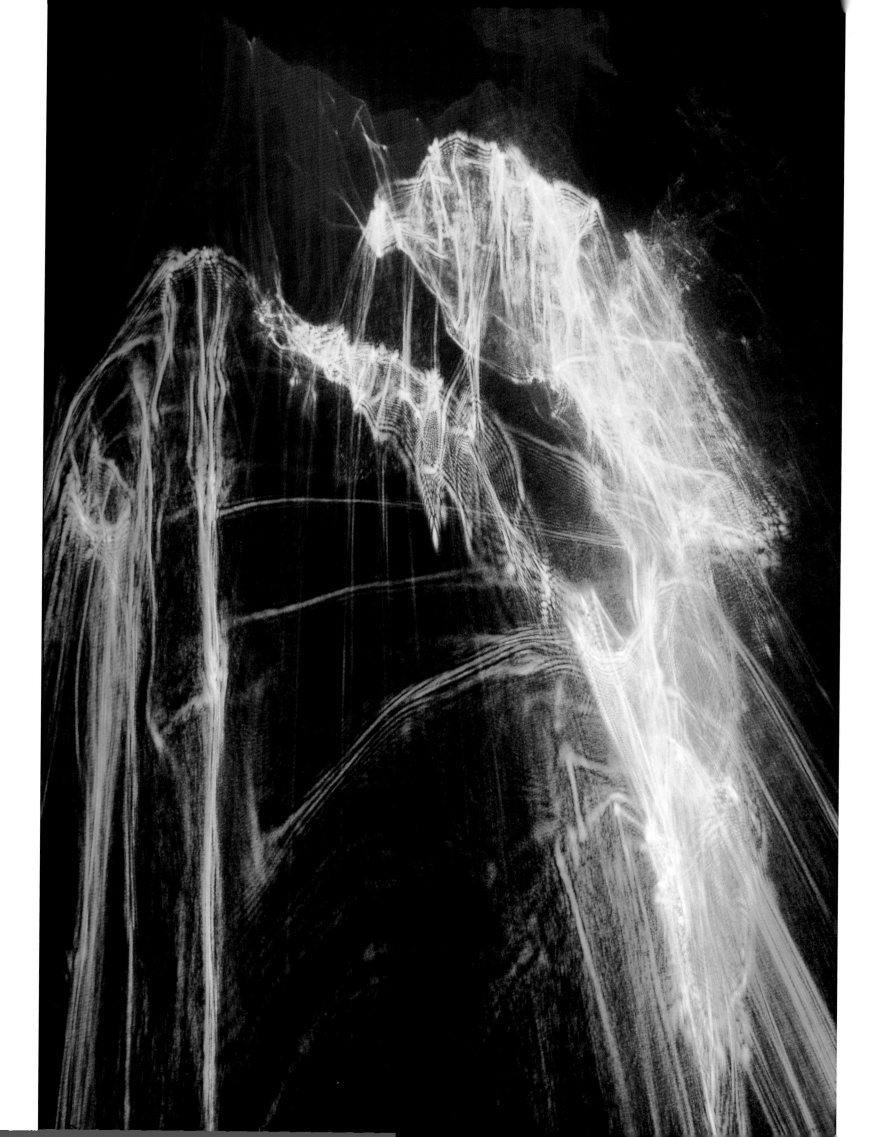

山岳（三）　MOUNTAINS　AND　HILLS（3）　1980　雷射

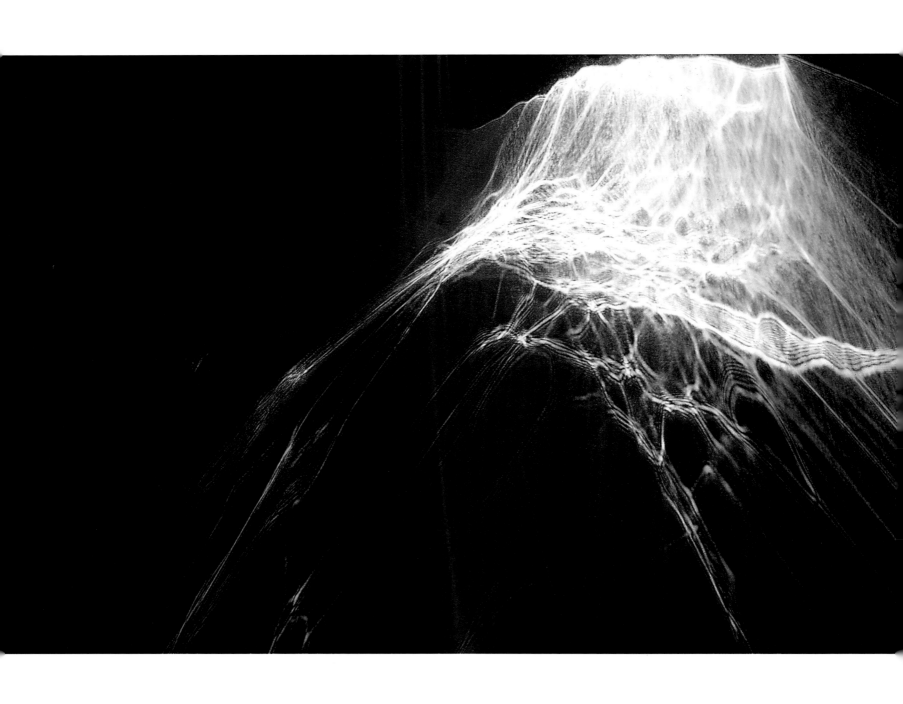

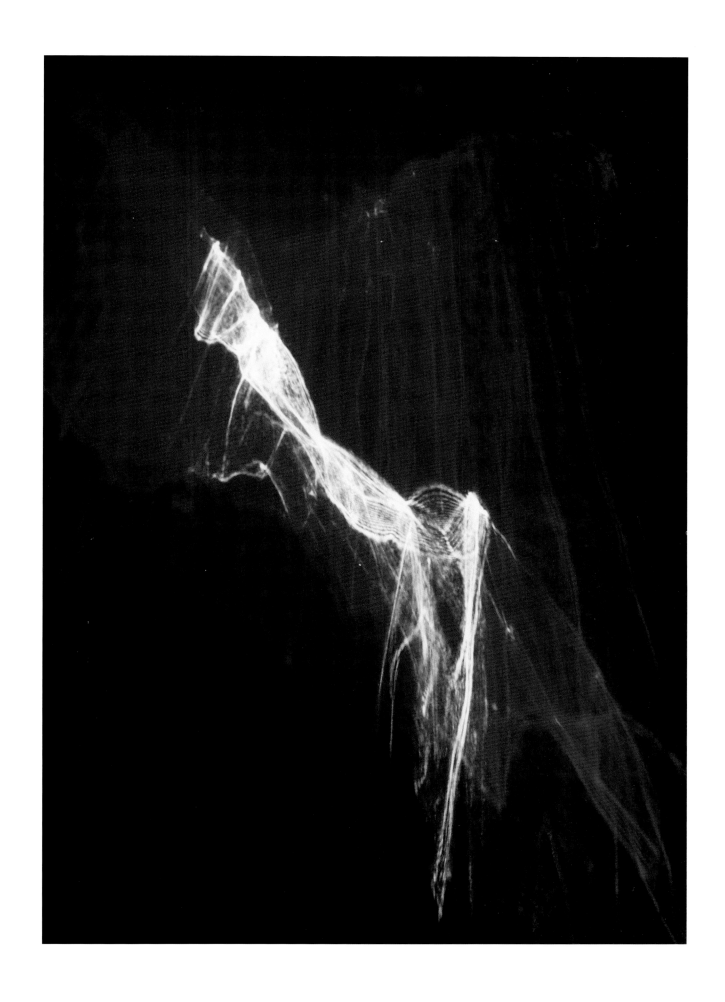

峽谷（一）　VALLEY（1）　1980　雷射

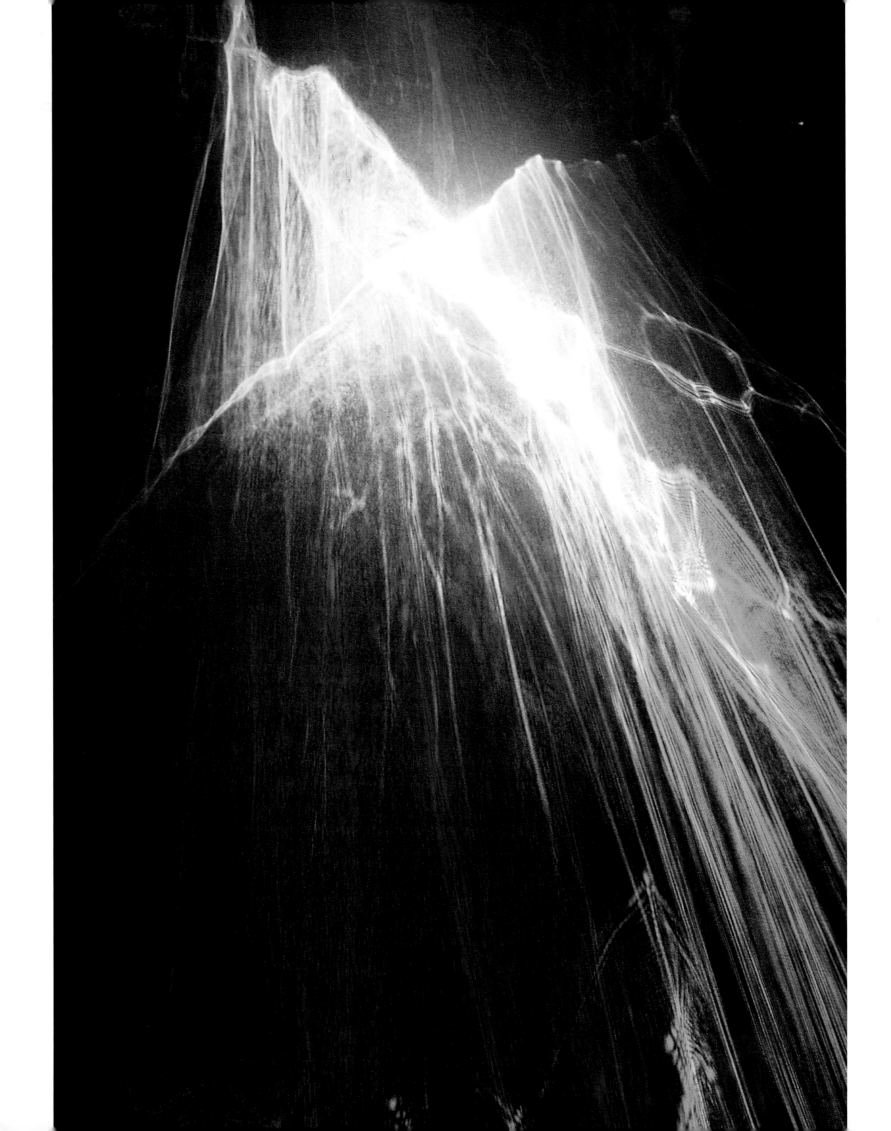

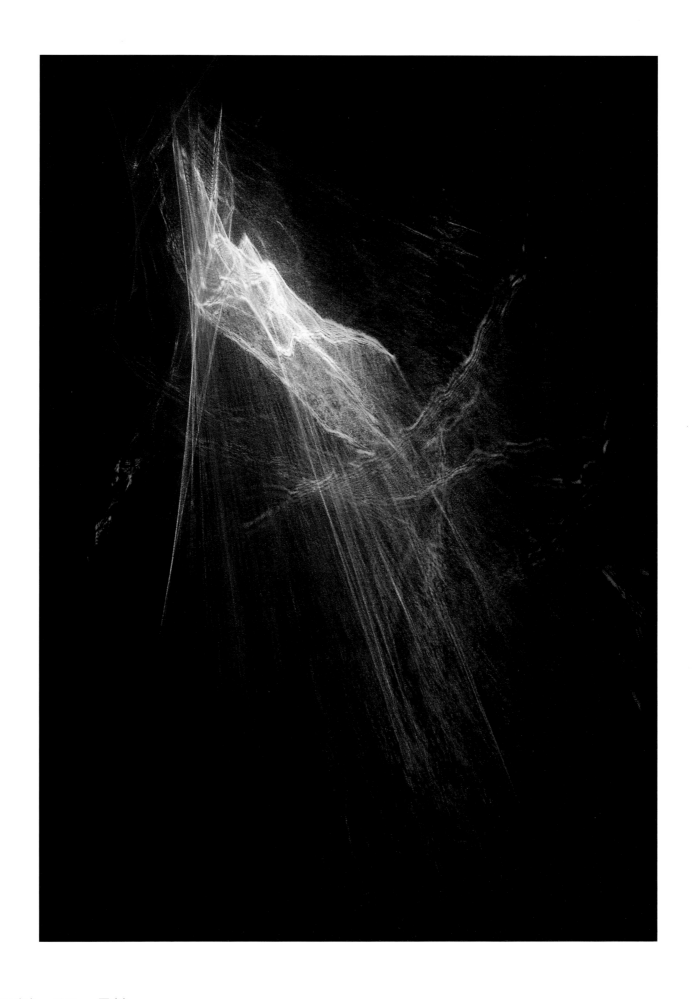

峽谷（二）VALLEY（2） 1980 雷射（左頁圖）
峽谷（三）VALLEY（3） 1980 雷射

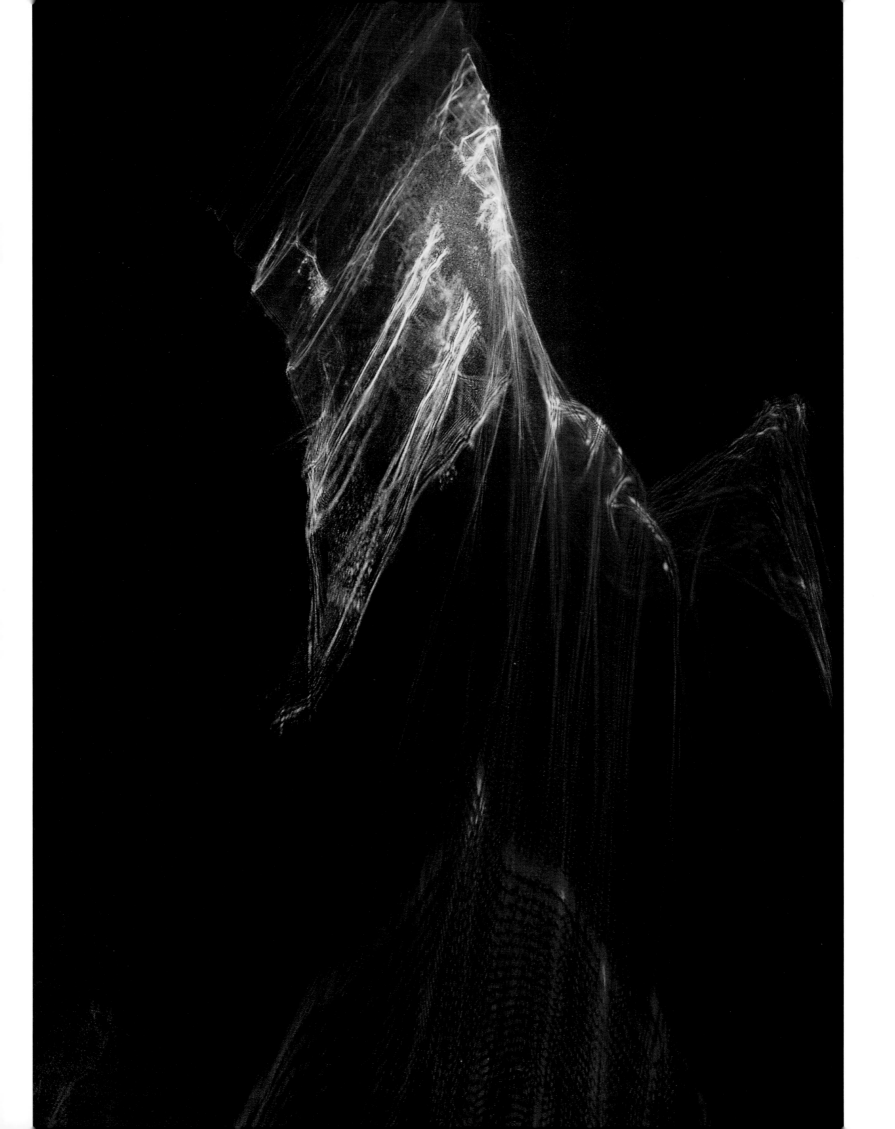

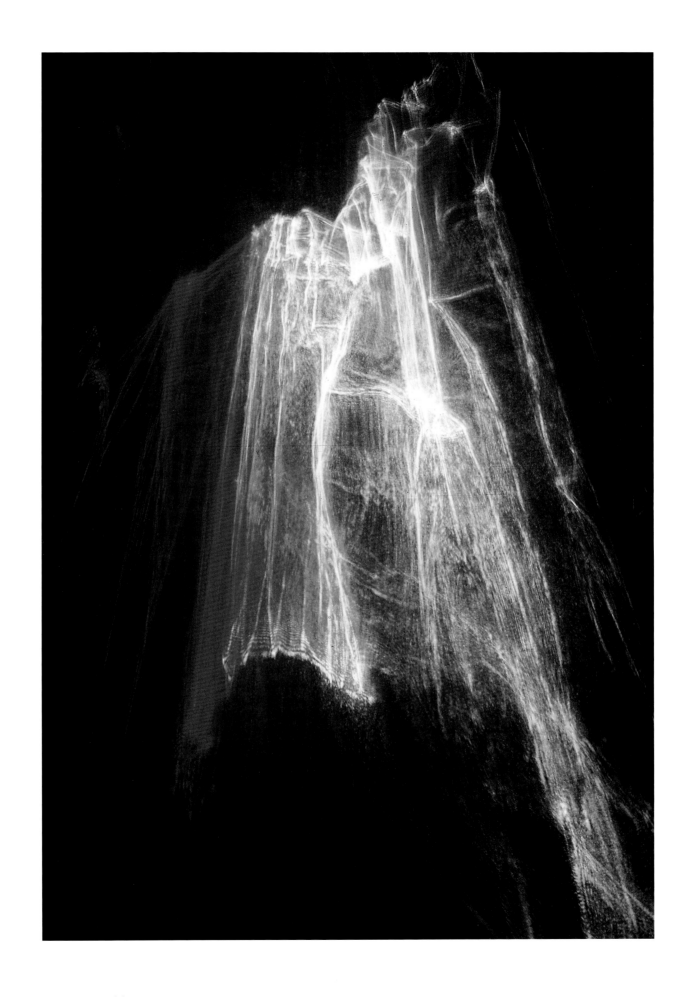

峽谷（四） VALLEY（4） 1980 雷射（左頁圖）

絕壁（一） PRECIPICE（1） 1980 雷射

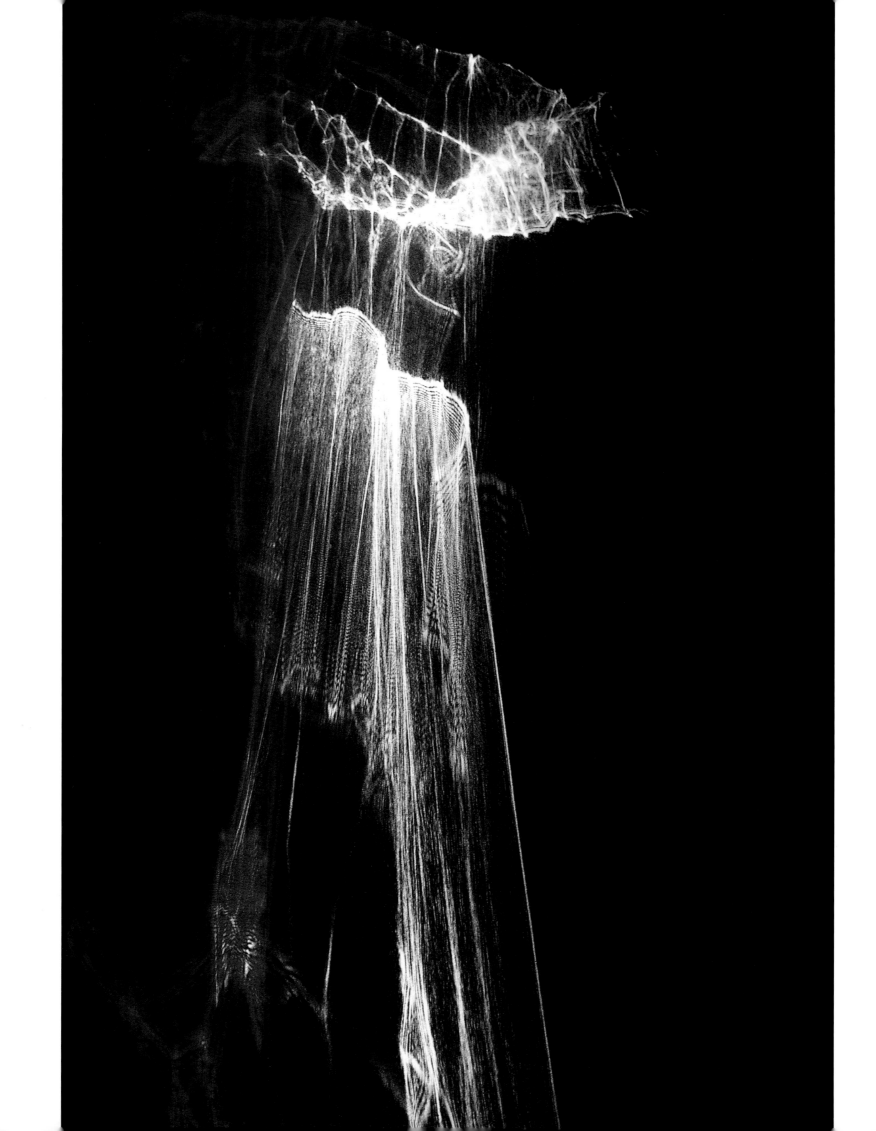

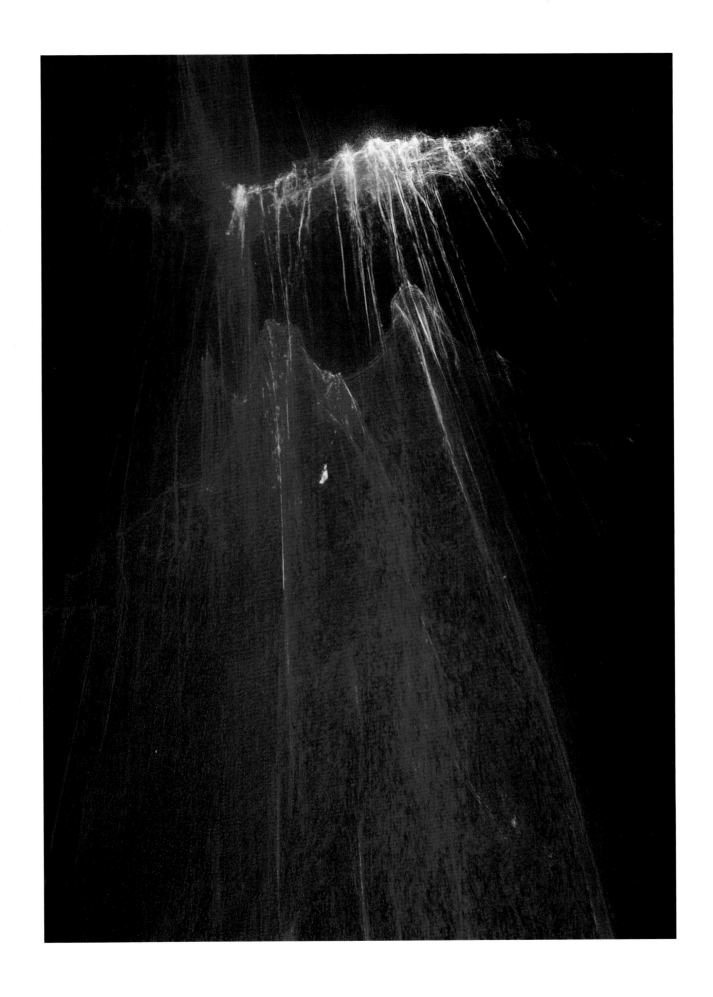

絶壁（二）　PRECIPICE（2）　1980　雷射（左頁圖）

絶壁（三）　PRECIPICE（3）　1980　雷射

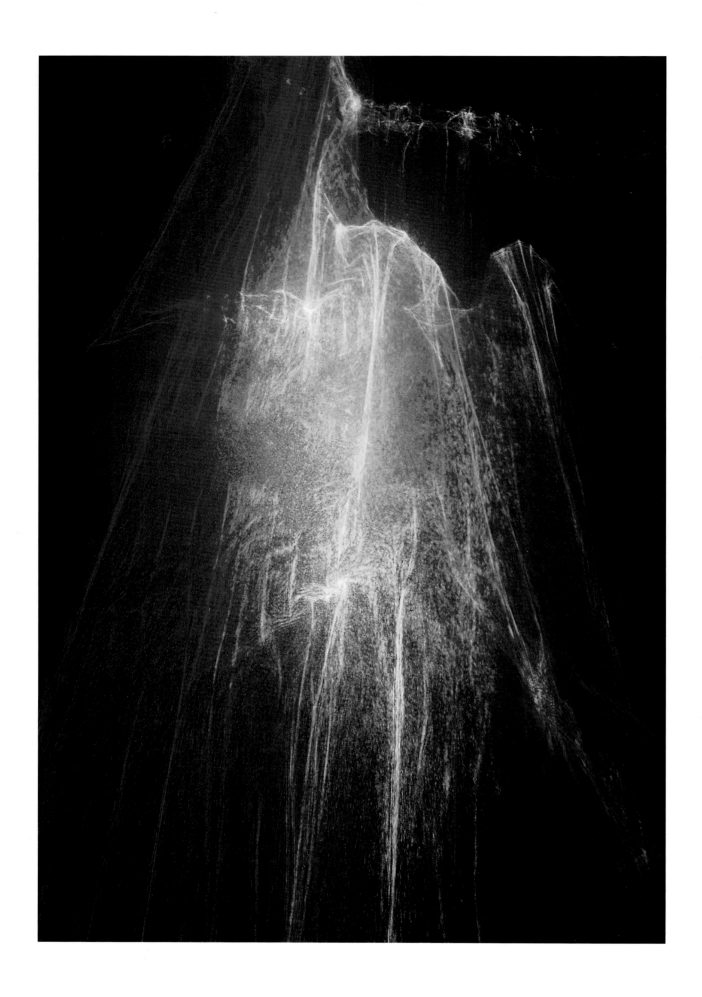

絶壁（四）　PRECIPICE（4）　1980　雷射

瀑布（一）　WATERFALL（1）　1980　雷射（右頁圖）

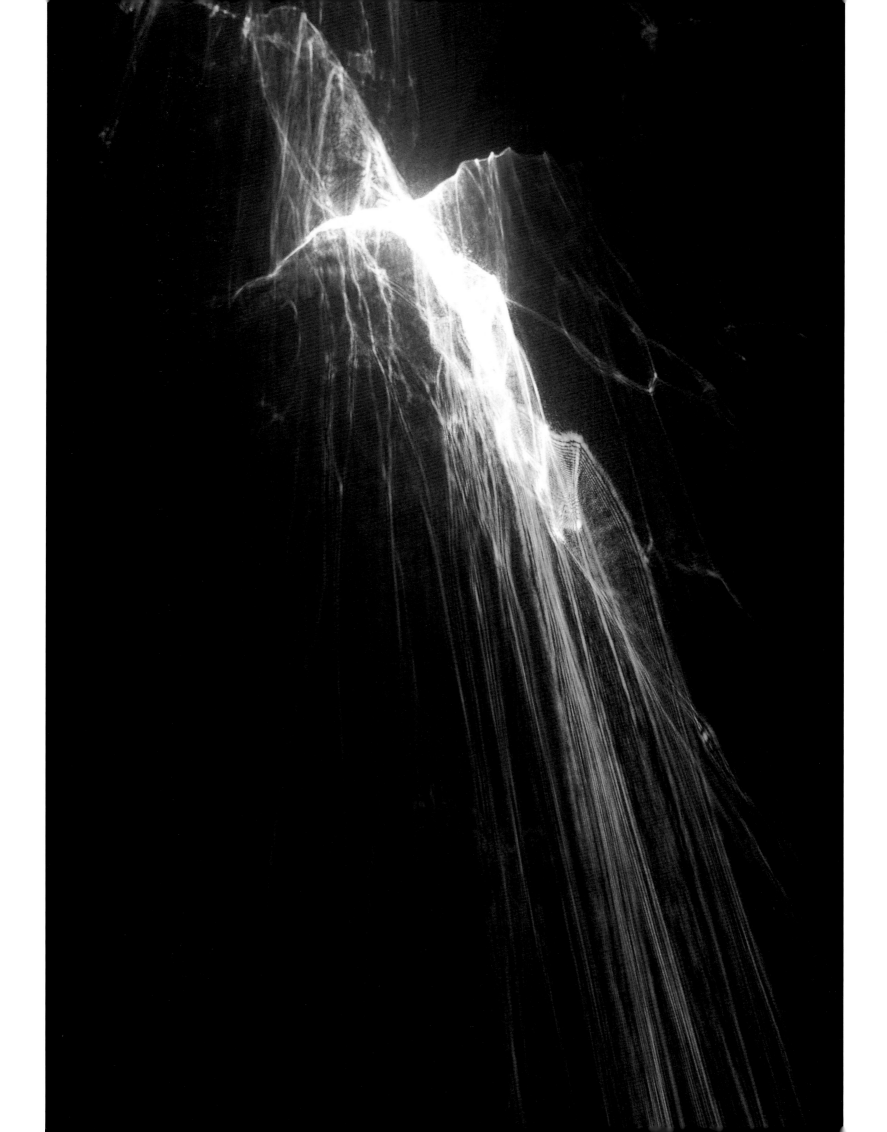

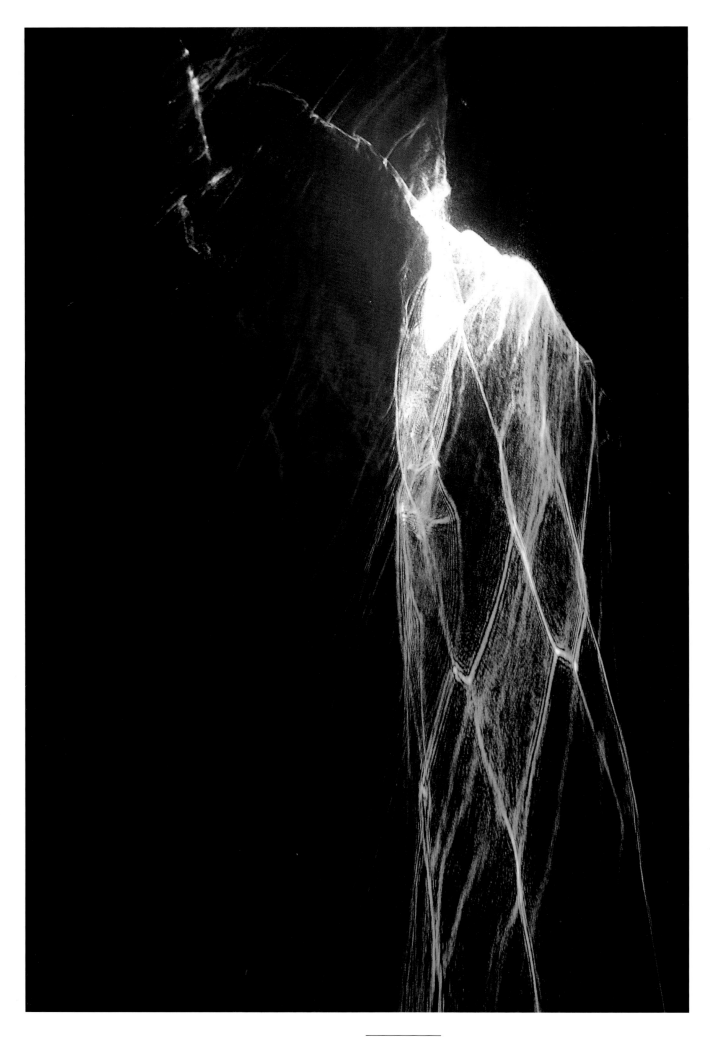

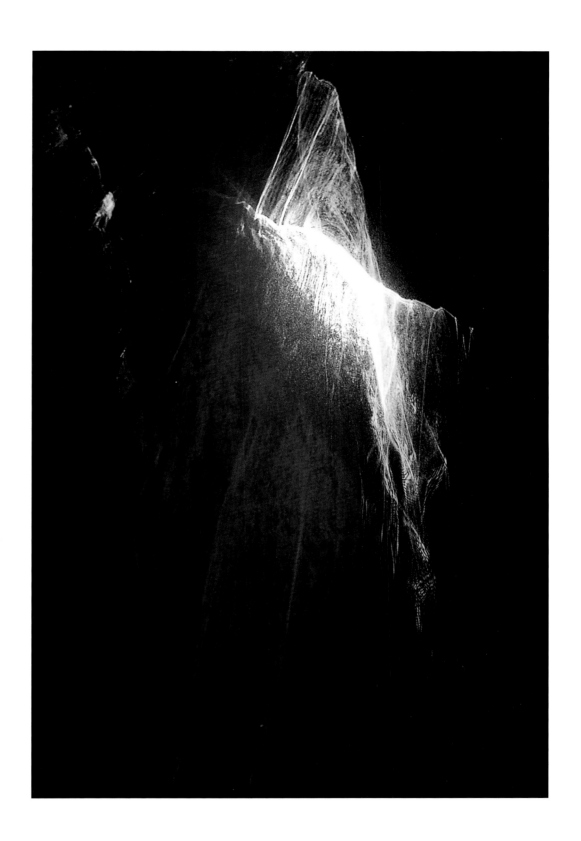

瀑布（二）　WATERFALL（2）　1980　雷射（左頁圖）

瀑布（三）　WATERFALL（3）　1980　雷射

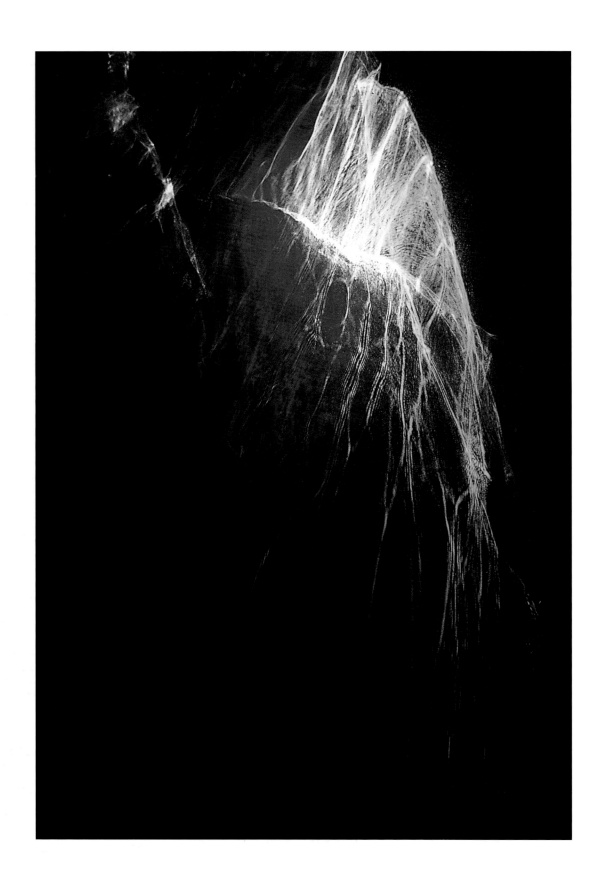

瀑布（四）　WATERFALL（4）　1980　雷射
瀑布（五）　WATERFALL（5）　1980　雷射<small>（右頁圖）</small>

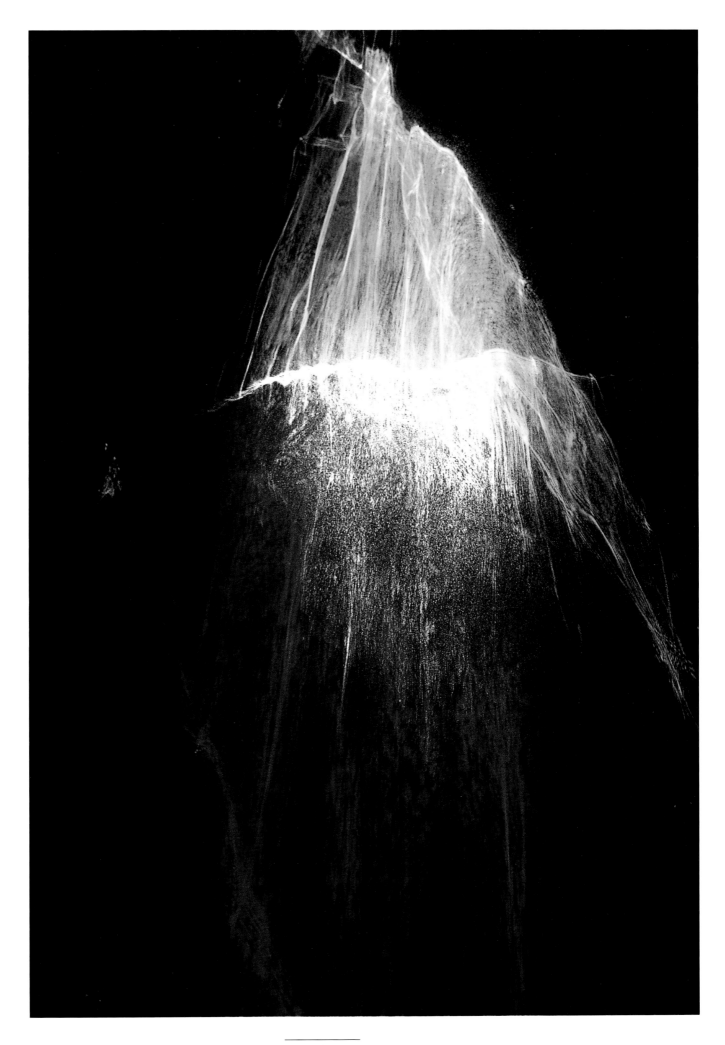

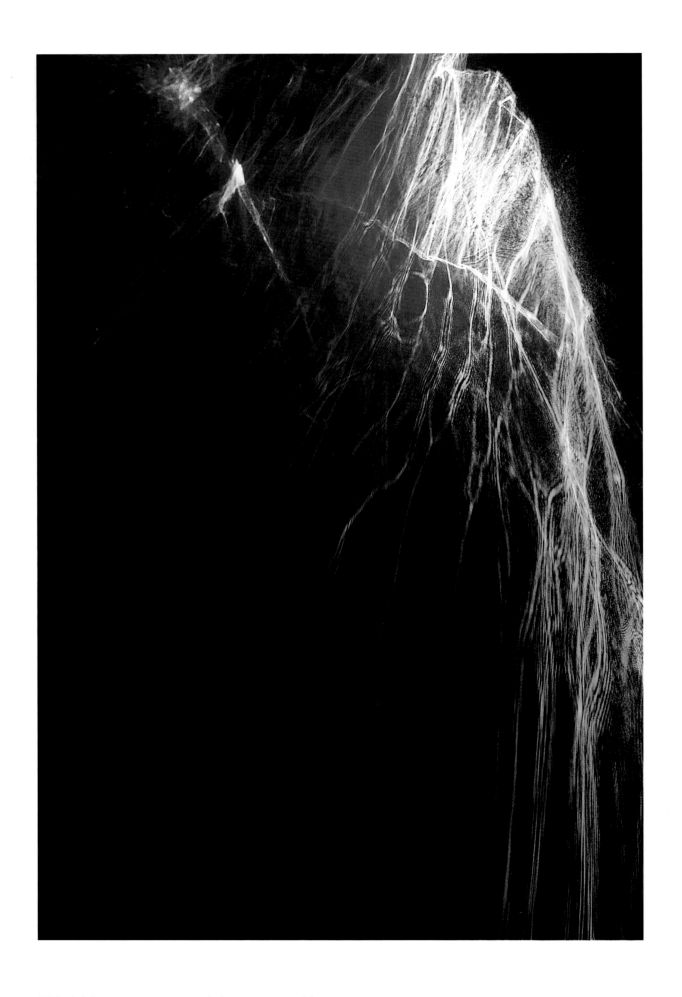

瀑布（六）　WATERFALL（6）　1980　雷射

水火伴遊　FIRE　AND　WATER　1980　雷射（右頁圖）

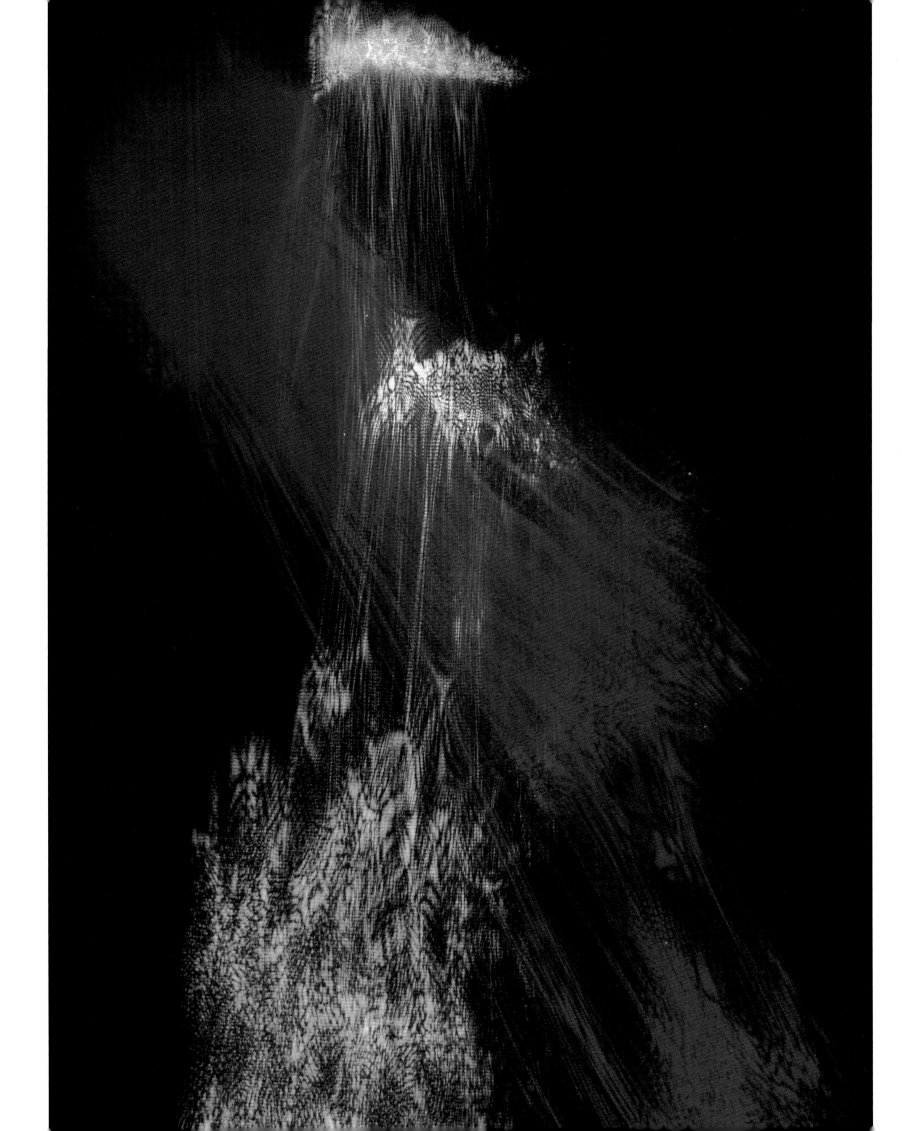

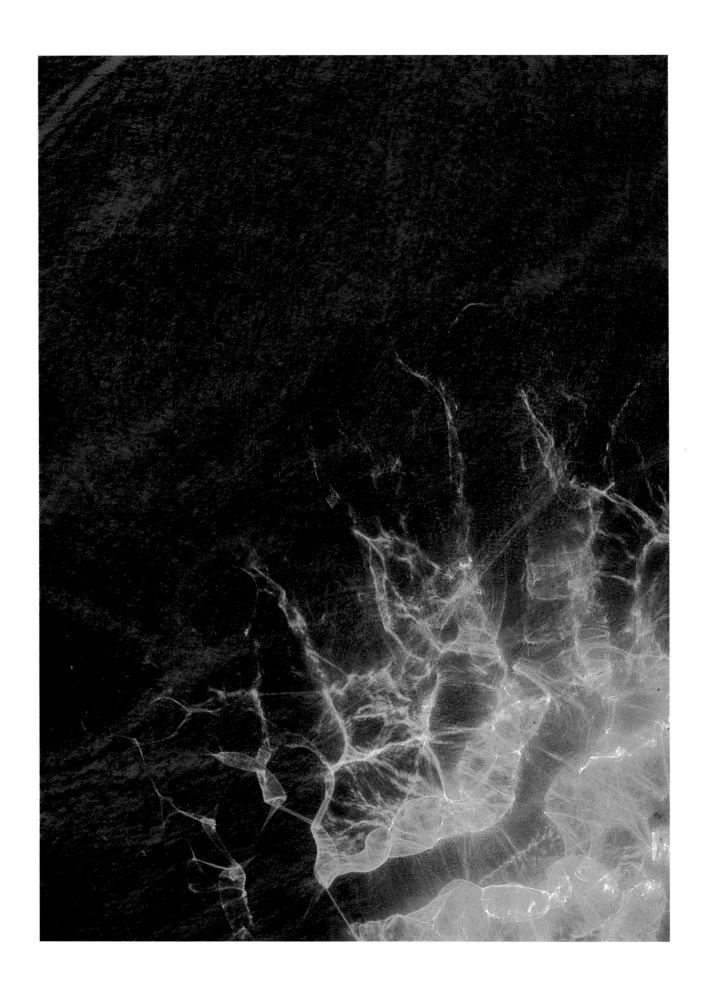

火水　FIRE AND WATER　1980　雷射

遠山（一）　FARAWAY MOUNTAINS（1）　1980　雷射（右頁圖）

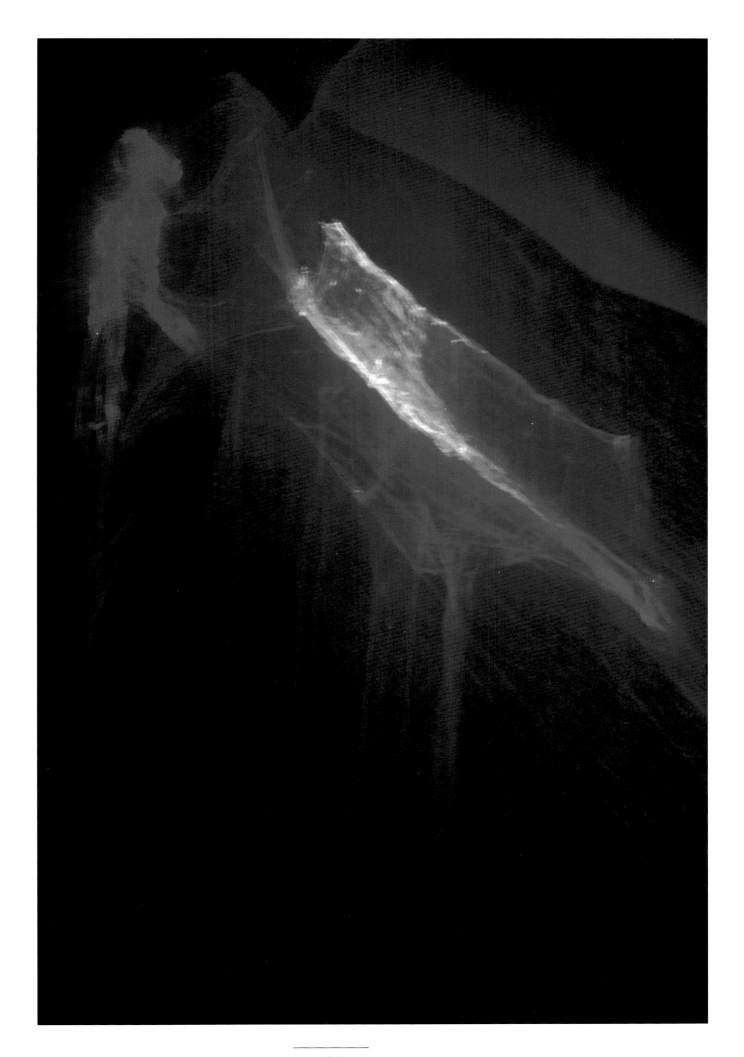

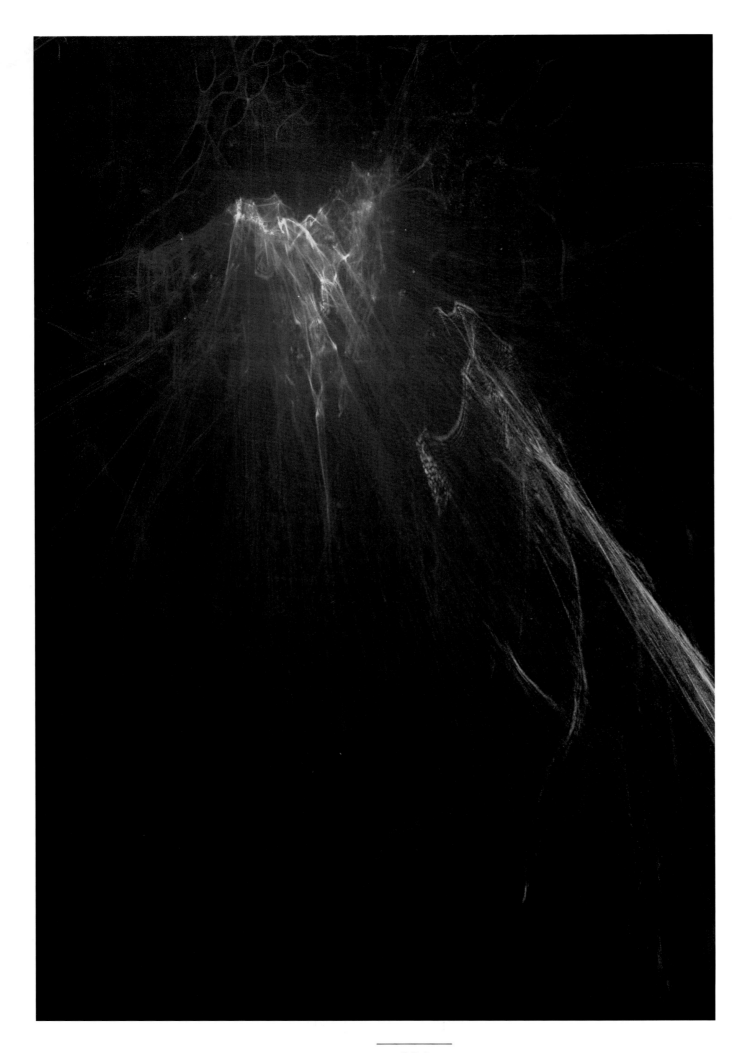

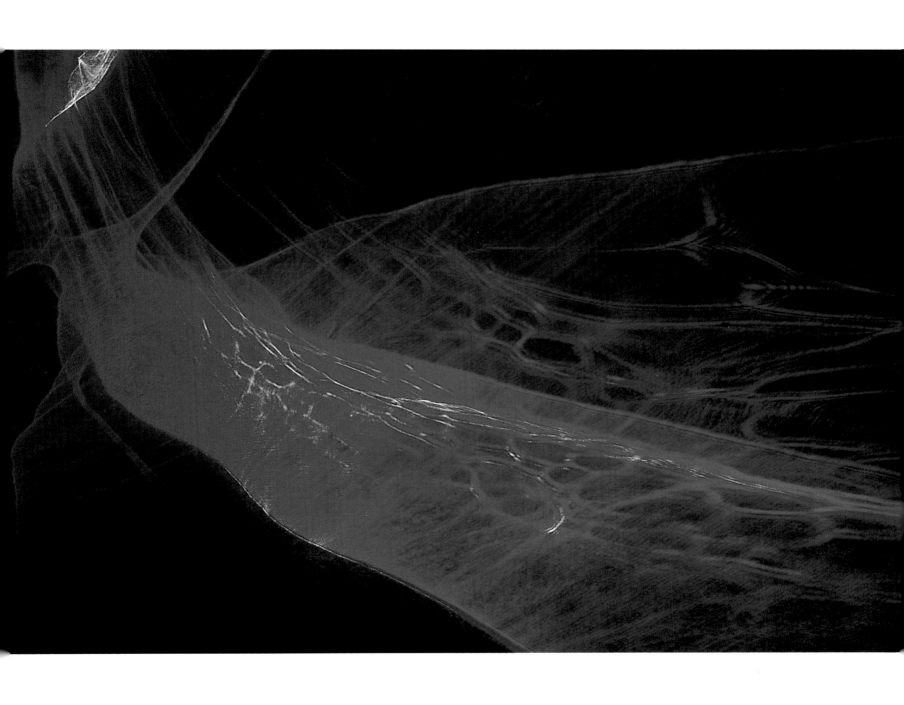

遠山（二）　FARAWAY　MOUNTAINS（2）　1980　雷射（左頁圖）

遠流（一）　FLOW（1）　1980　雷射

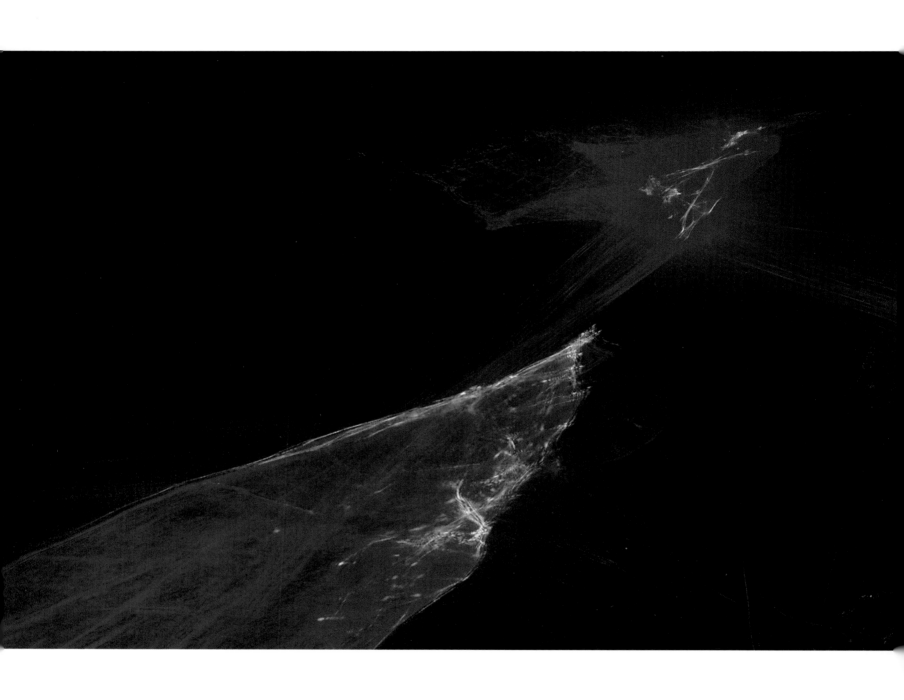

遠流（二）　FLOW（2）　1980　雷射

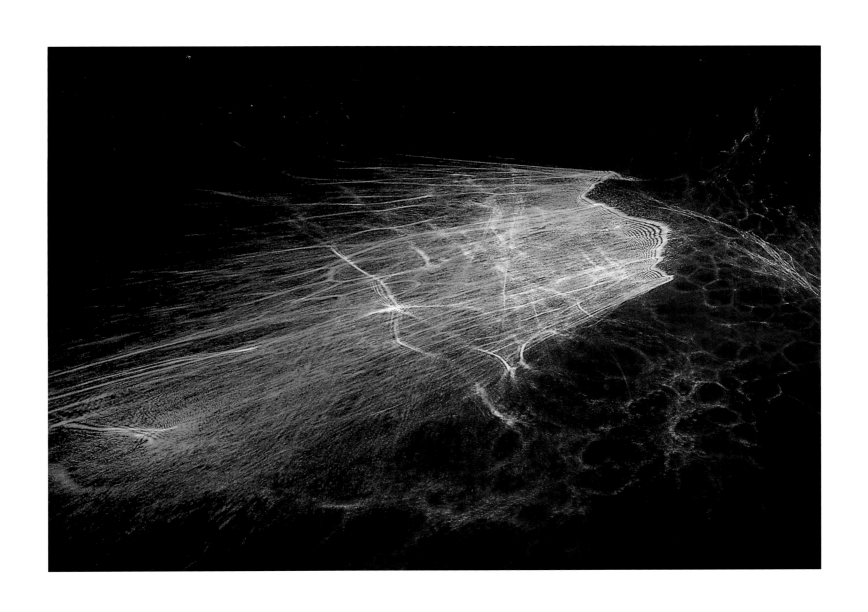

激浪（一）　WAVES（1）　1980　雷射

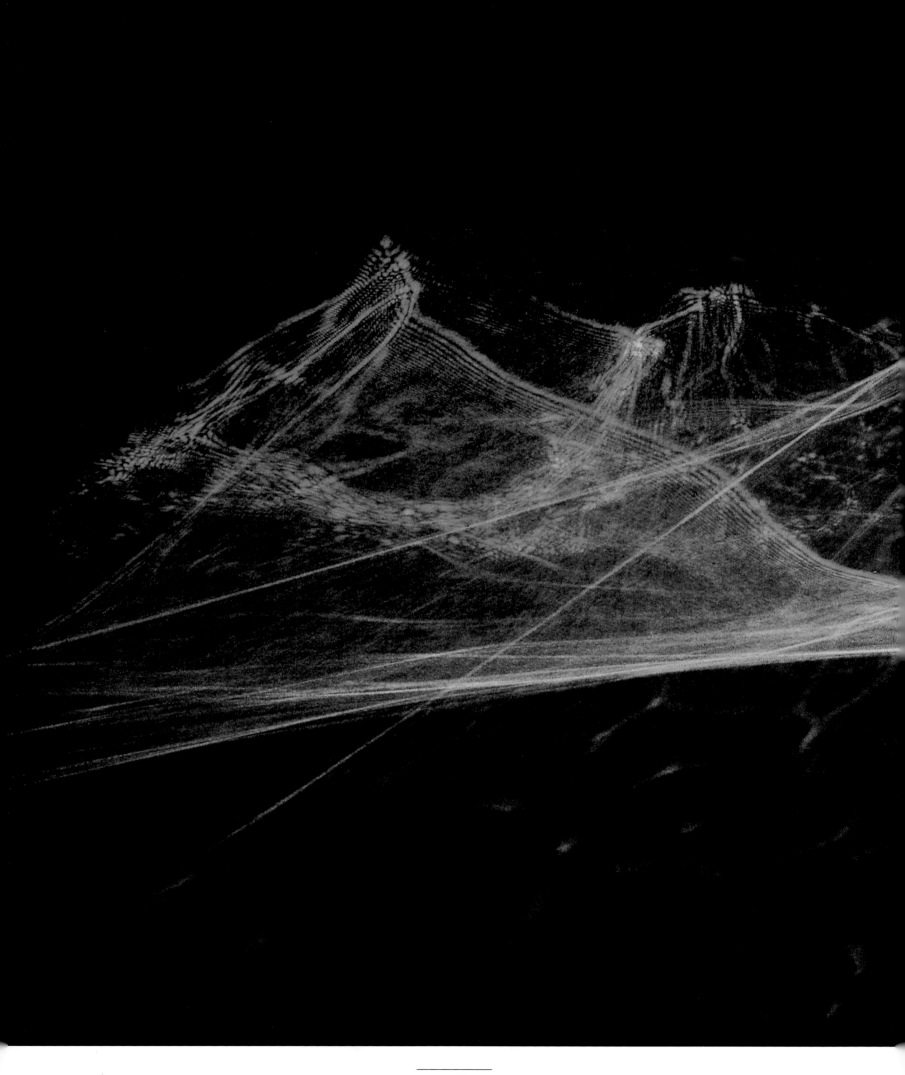

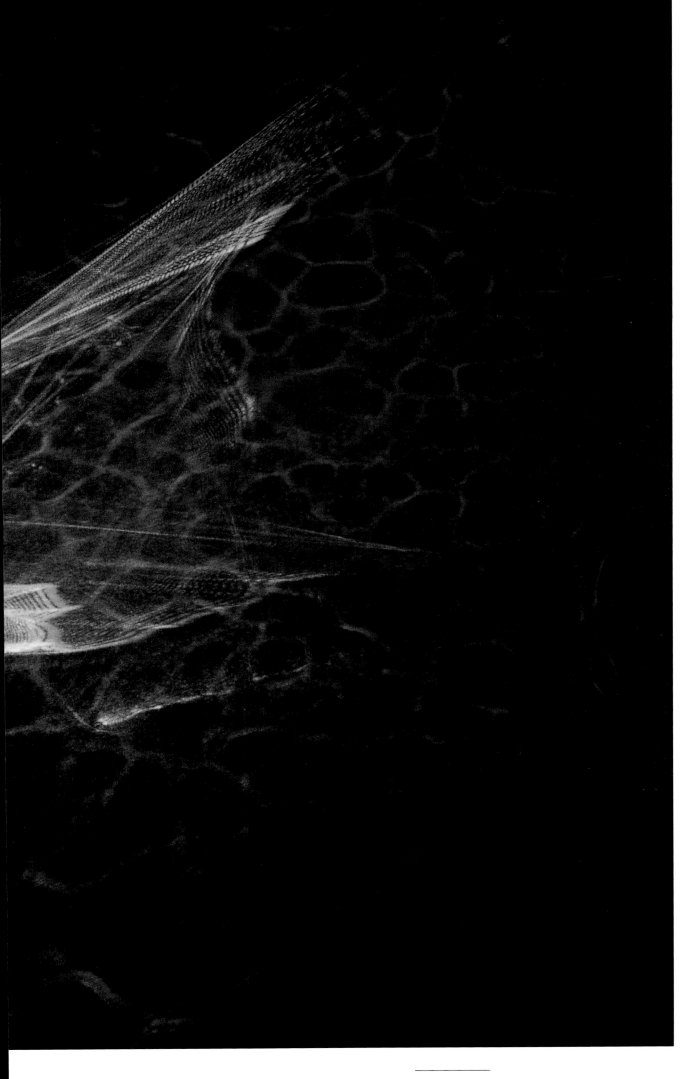

激浪（二）
WAVES(2)
1980
雷射

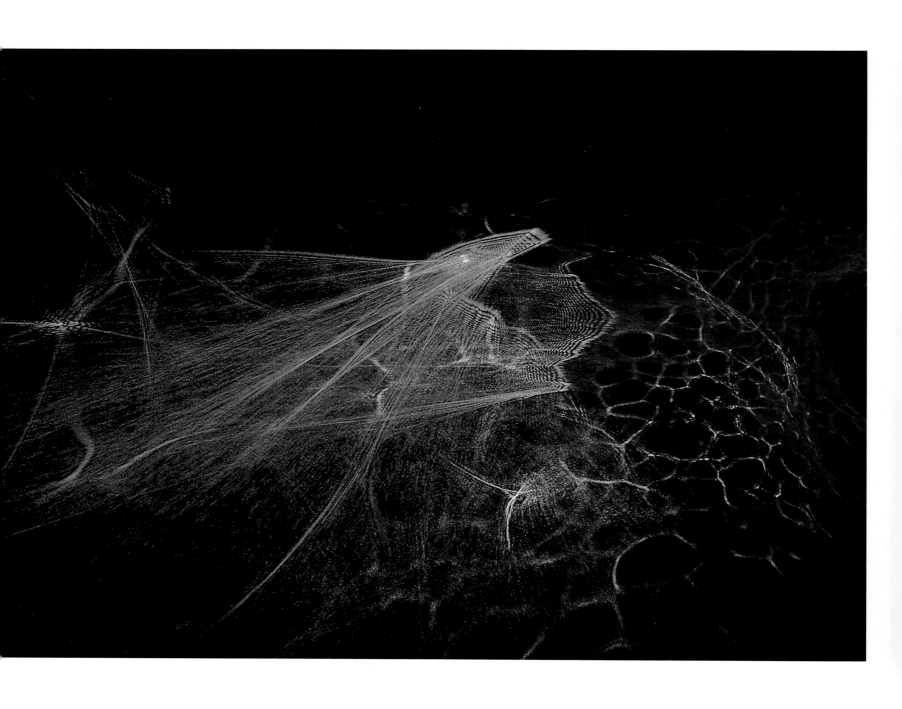

激浪（三）　WAVES（3）　1980　雷射

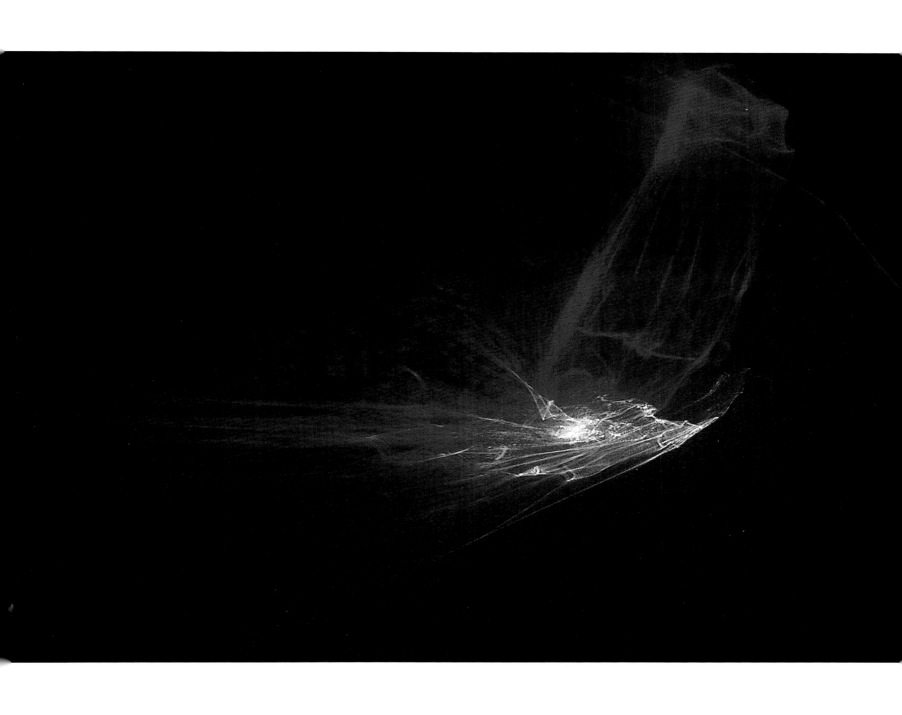

極光（一）　POLAR LIGHTS（1）　1980　雷射

極光（二）
POLAR LIGHTS（2）
1980
雷射

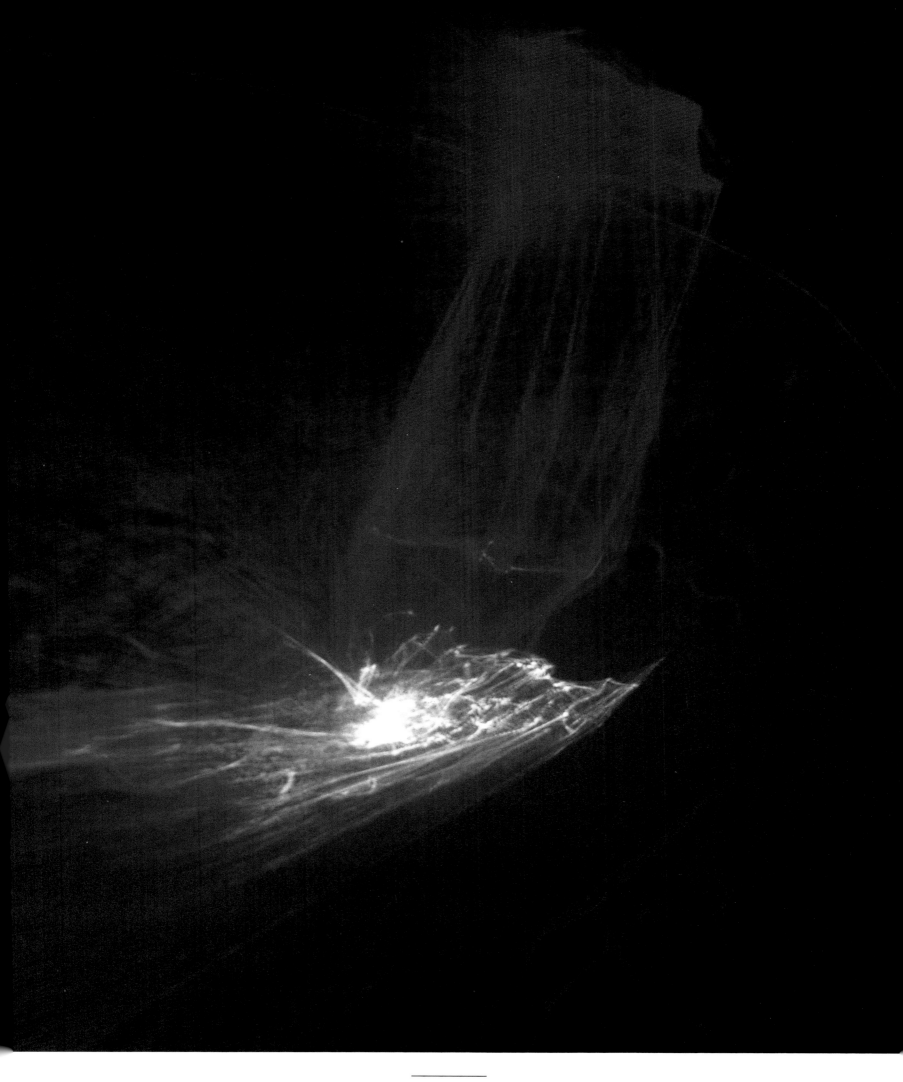

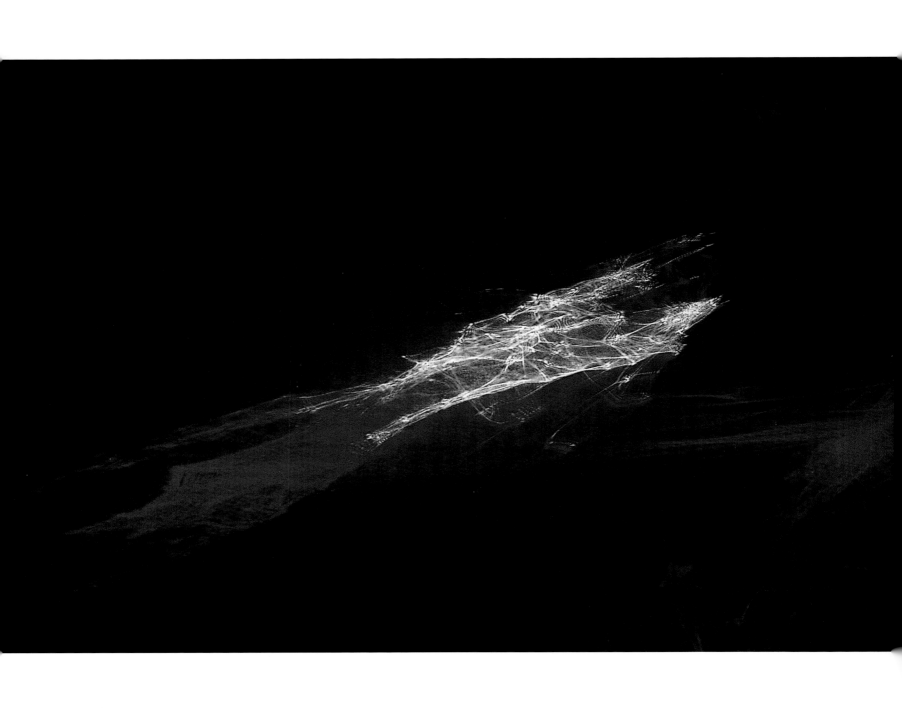

極光（三）　POLAR　LIGHTS（3）　1980　雷射

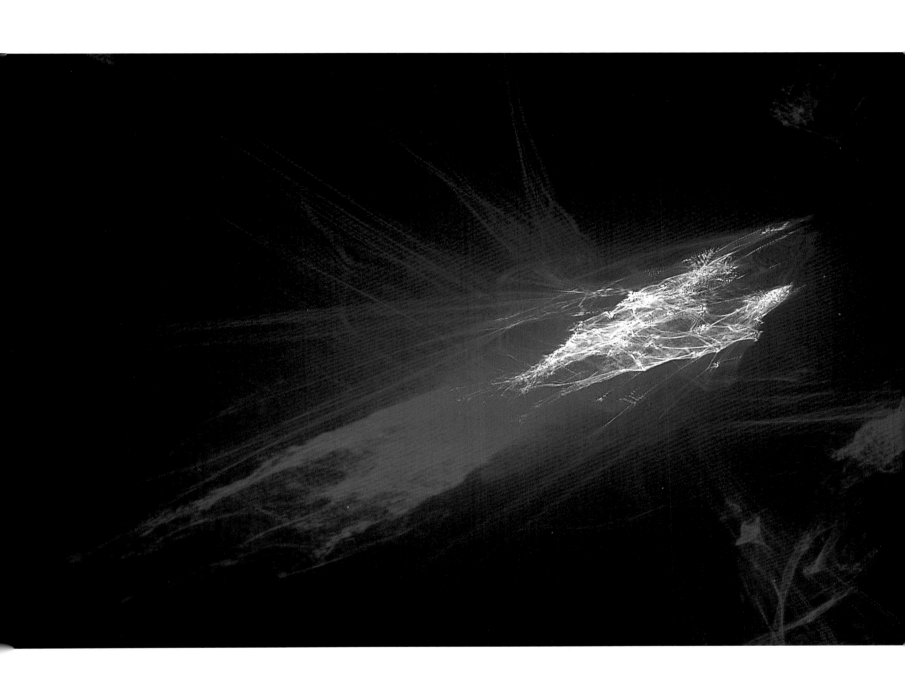

極光（四）　POLAR LIGHTS（4）　1980　雷射

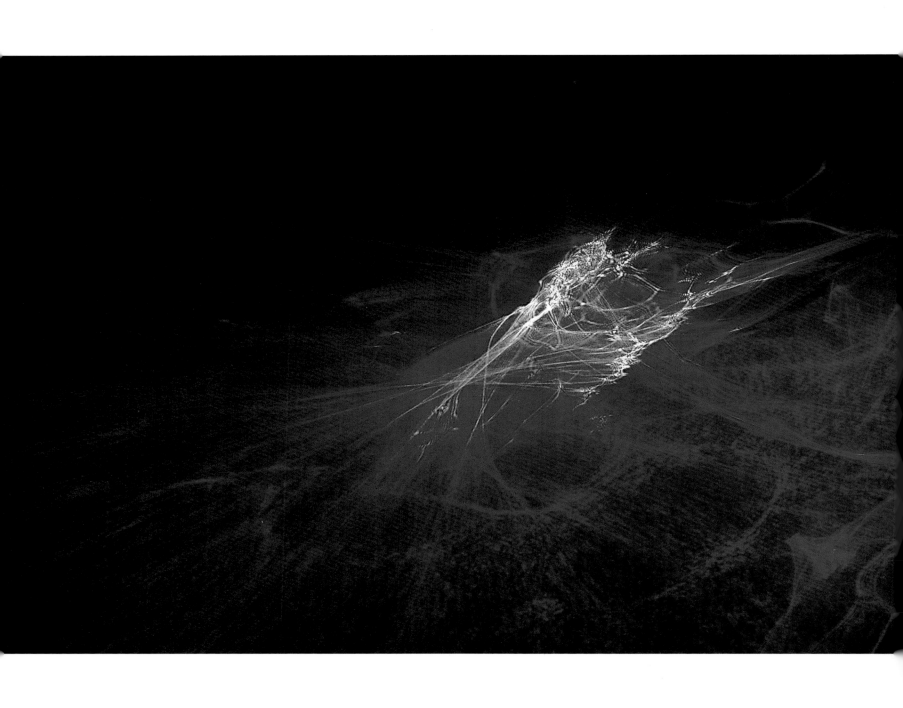

極光（五）　POLAR　LIGHTS（5）　1980　雷射

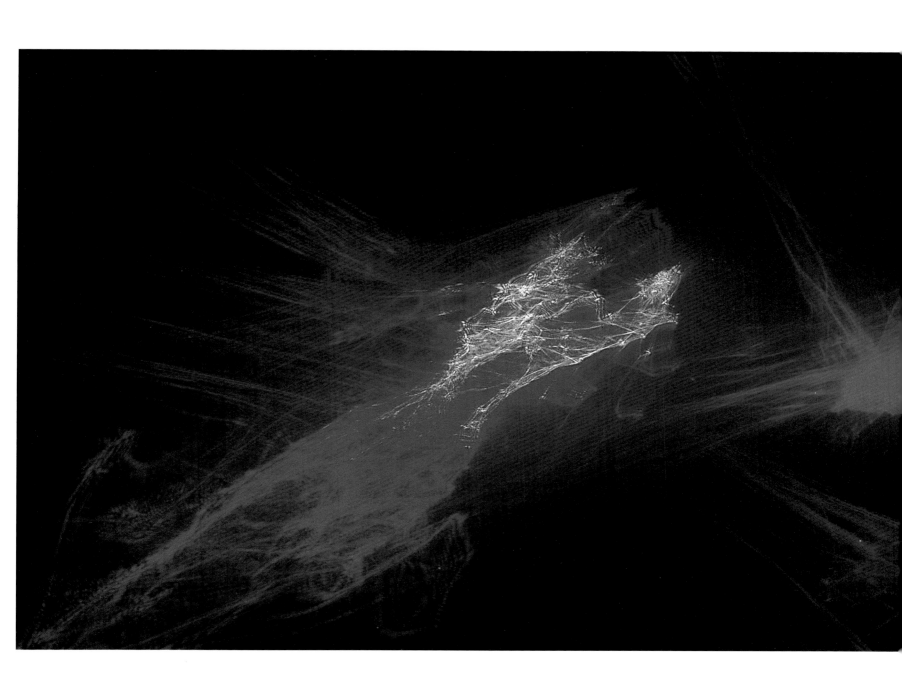

極光（六）　POLAR LIGHTS（6）　1980　雷射

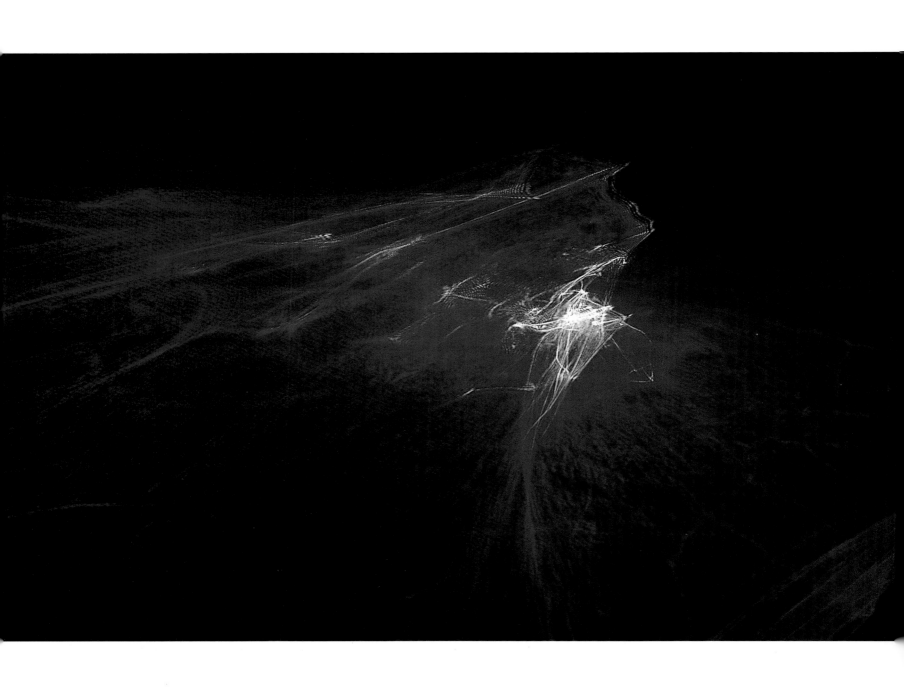

極光（七）　POLAR LIGHTS（7）　1980　雷射

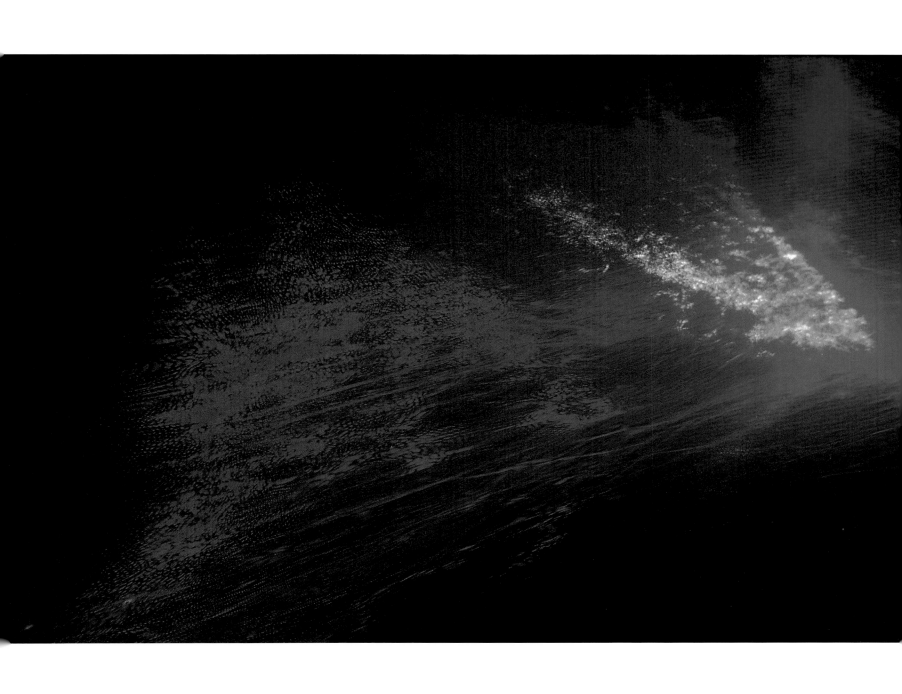

極光（八）　POLAR　LIGHTS（8）　1980　雷射

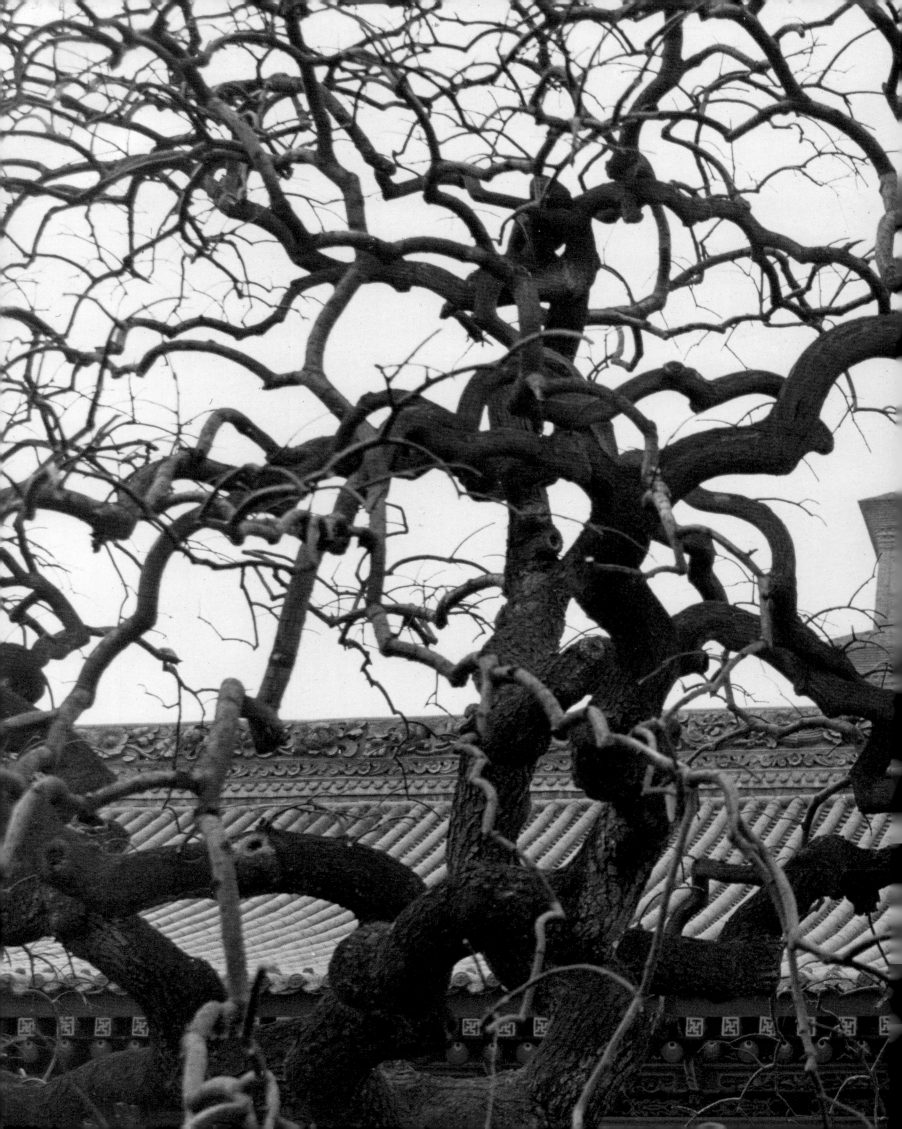

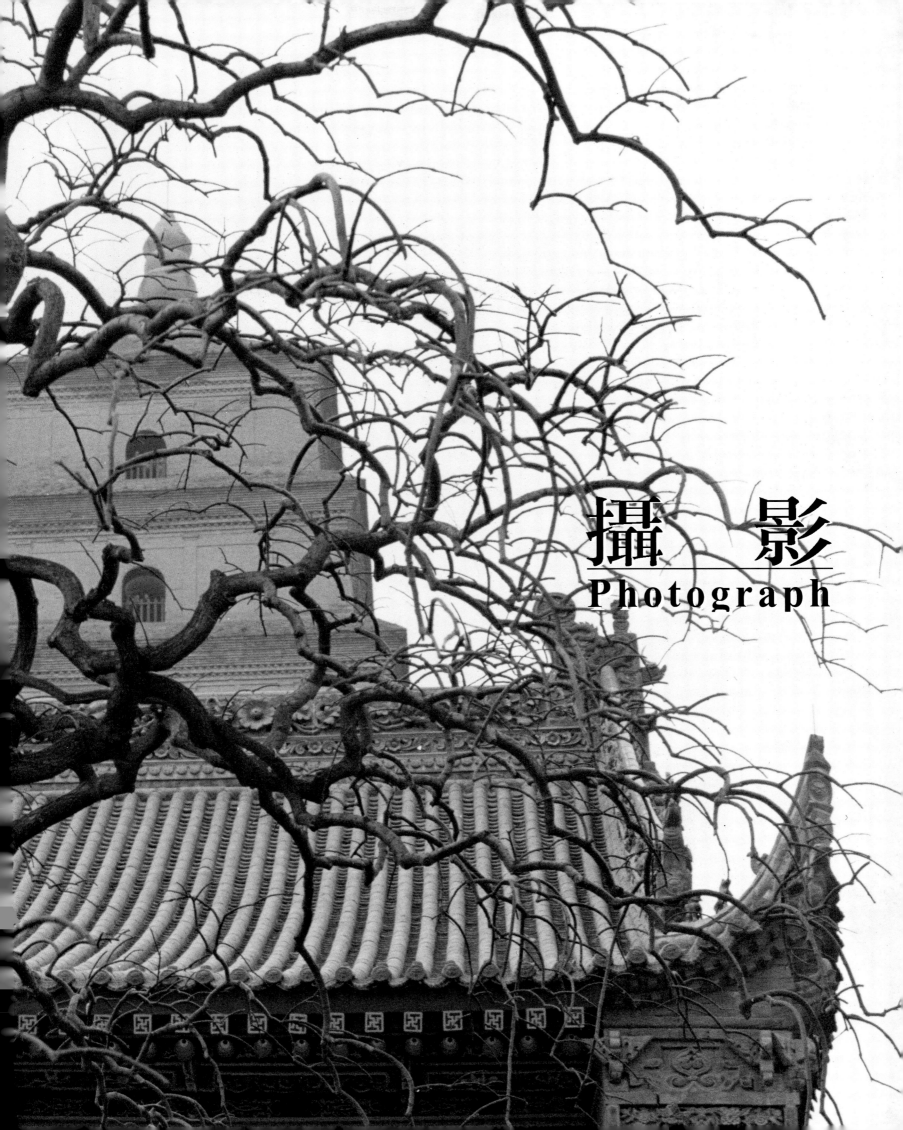

攝　　影
Photograph

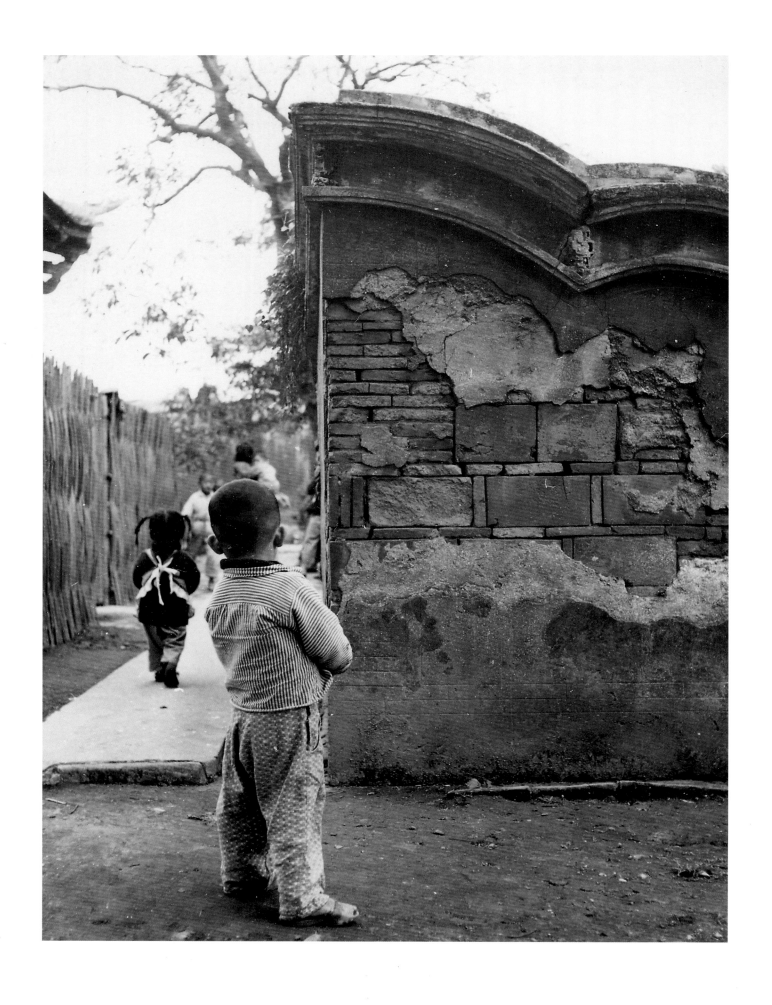

人物系列（一）　PORTRAIT SERIES（1）　約1950年代　攝影　11.8×8.8cm

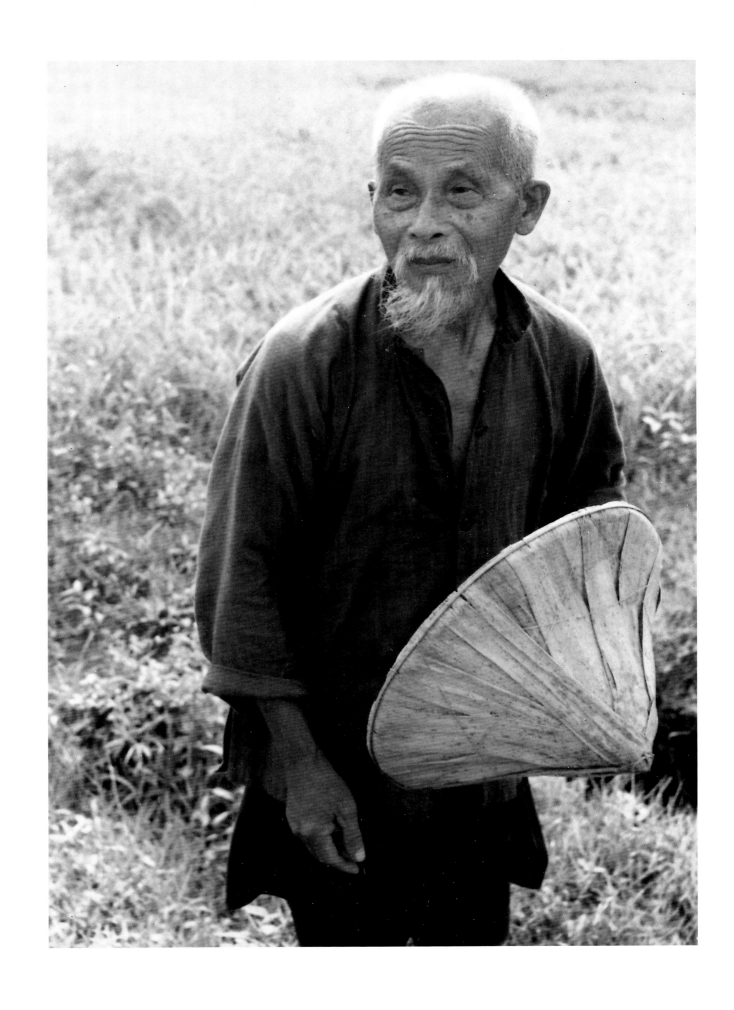

人物系列（二）　PORTRAIT　SERIES（2）　約1950年代　攝影　11×7.7cm

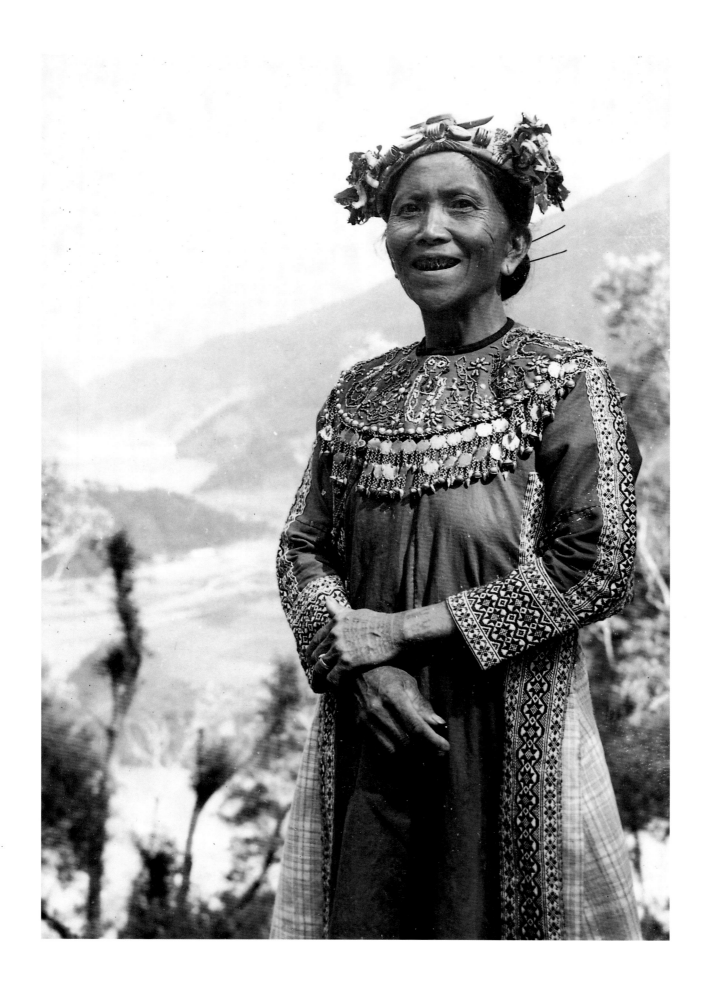

人物系列（三）　PORTRAIT　SERIES（3）　約1950年代　攝影　11×7.7cm

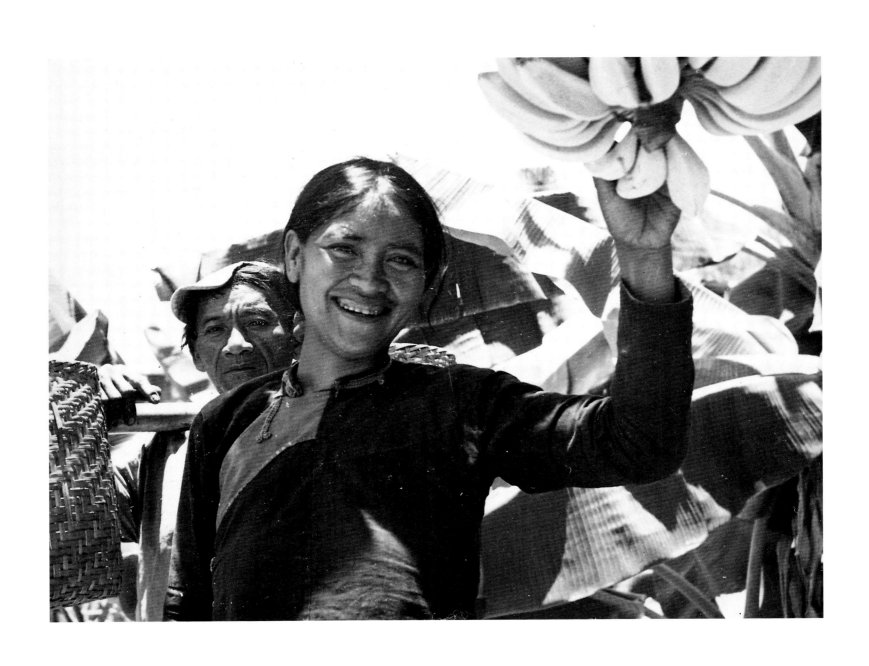

人物系列（四）　PORTRAIT　SERIES（4）　約1950年代　攝影　7.7×10.2cm

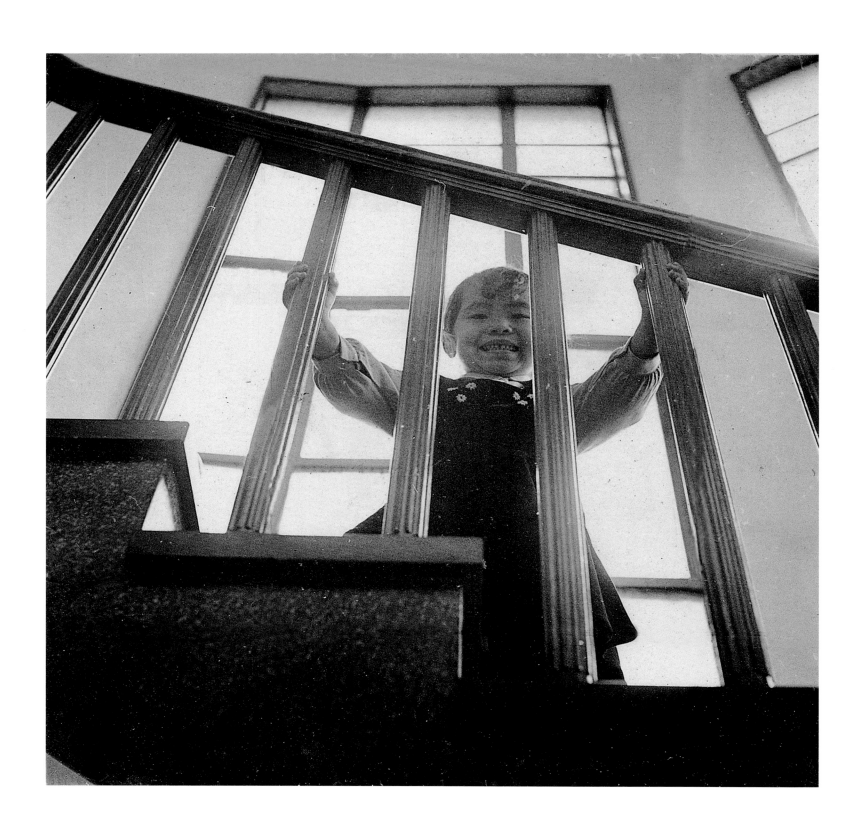

嬉　PLAY　1957　攝影　15.4×11.4cm
閒　FREE TIME　1957　攝影　15.1×11.5cm（右頁圖）

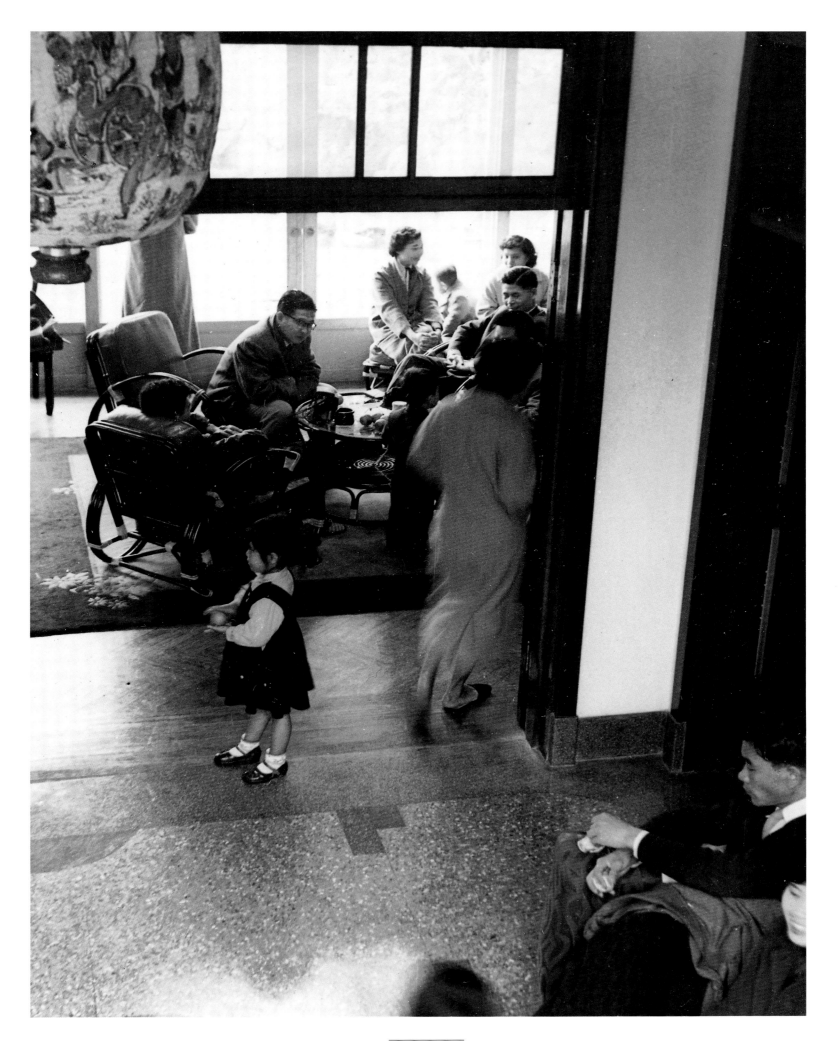

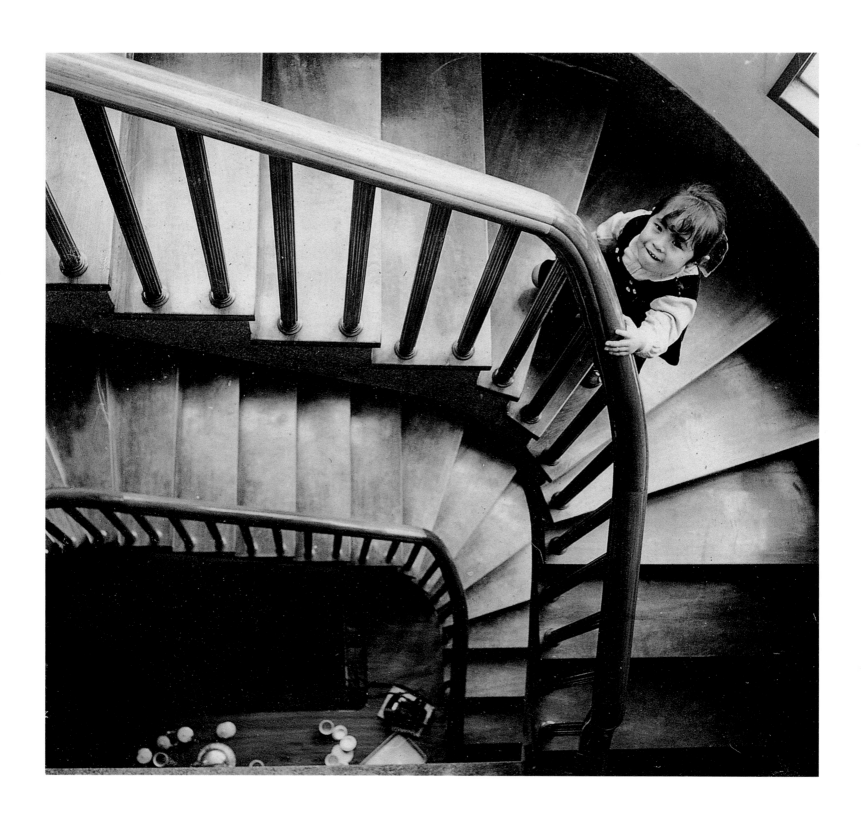

登　MOUNT　1957　攝影　5.3×5.4cm

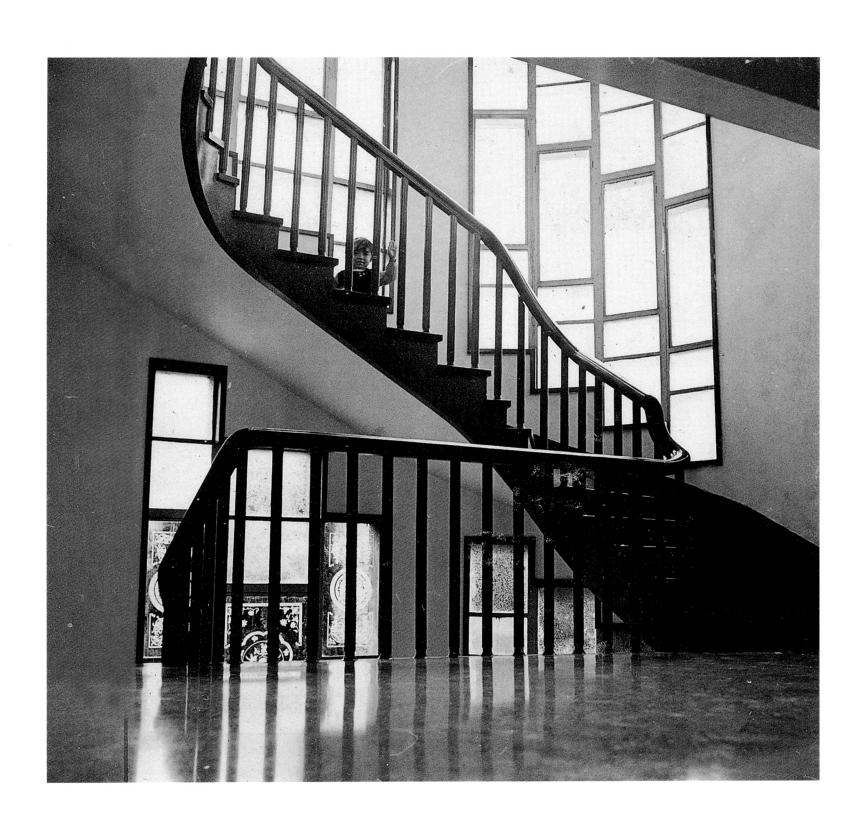

梯　STAIRS　1957　攝影　5.3×5.4cm

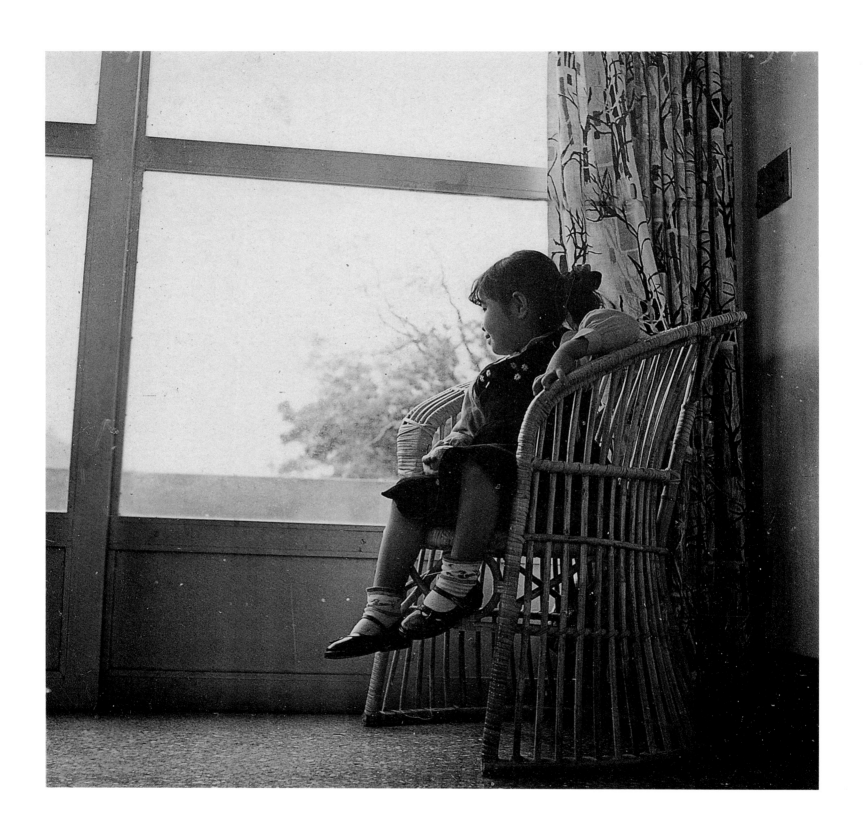

睇　SQUINT　1957　攝影　5.3×5.4cm

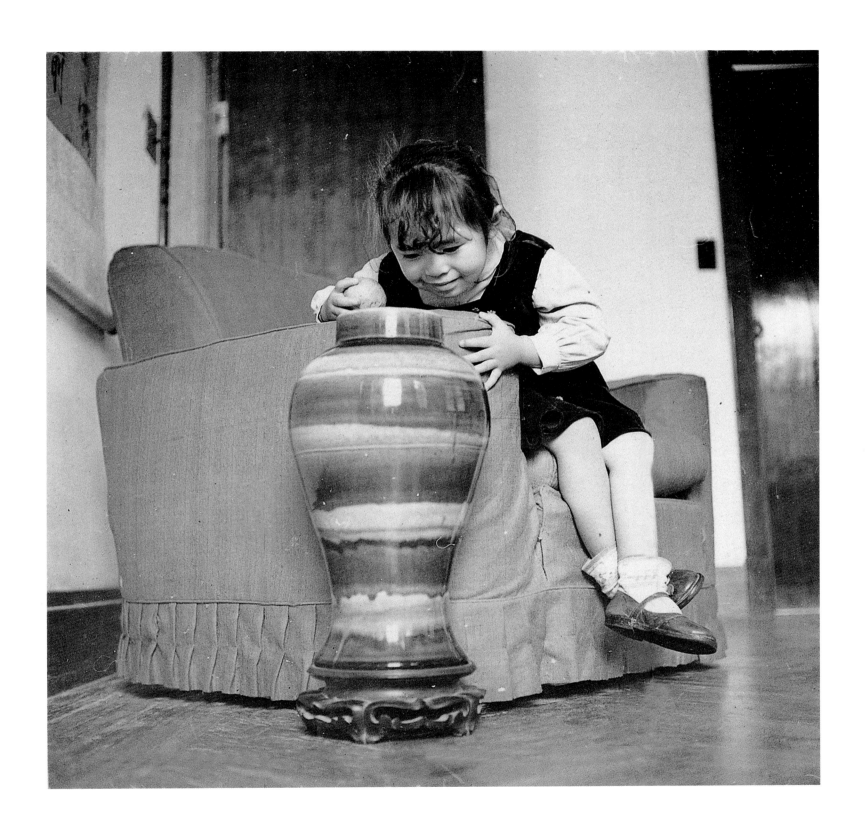

窺　PEEP　1957　攝影　5.3×5.4cm

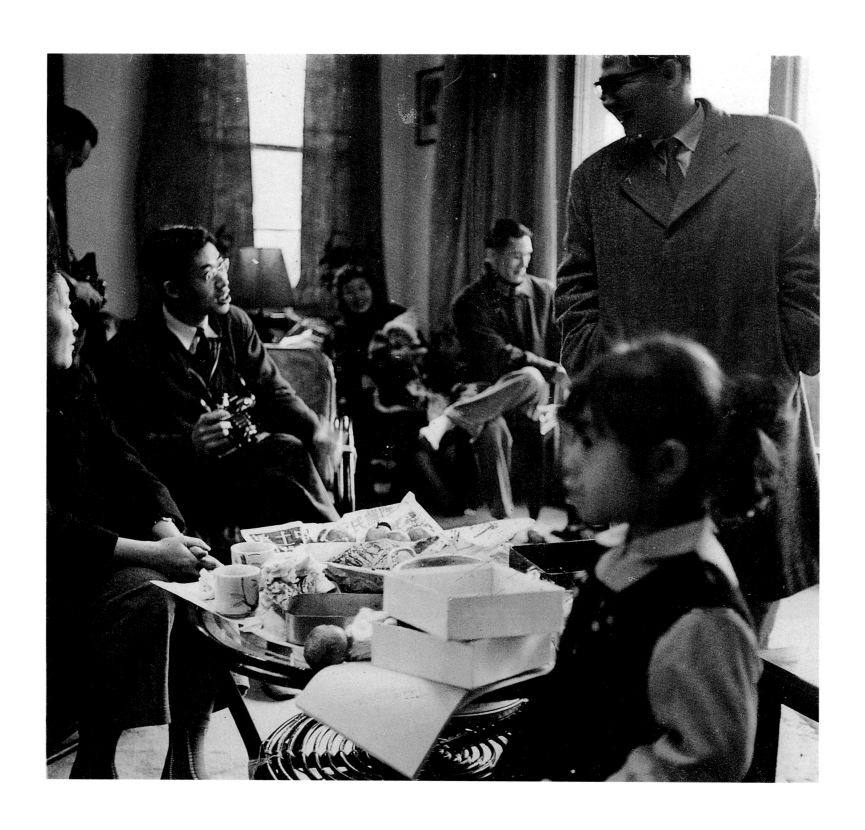

辯　ARGUE　1957　攝影　5.3×5.4cm

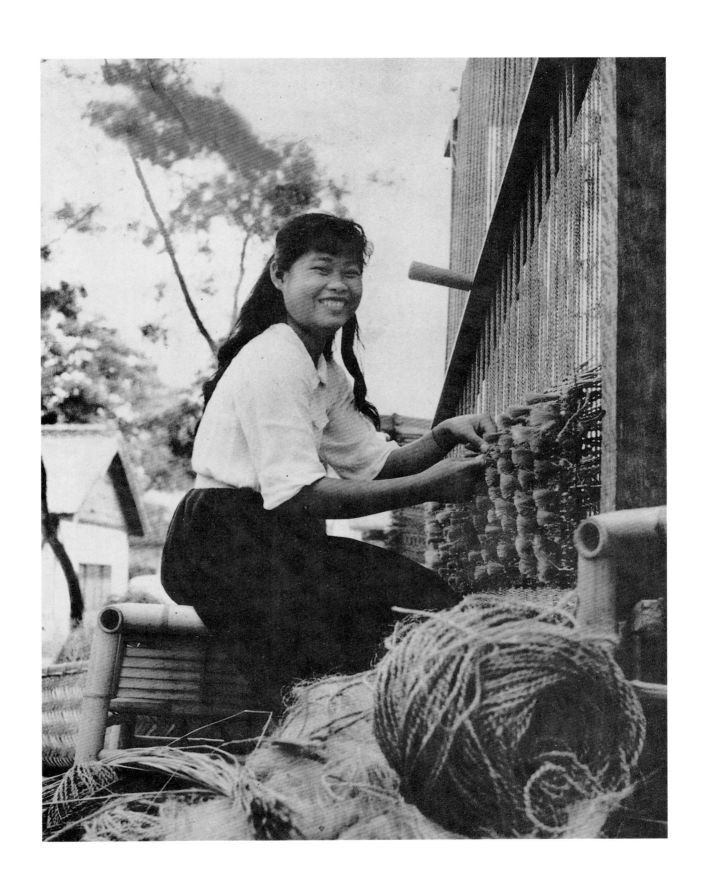

編織　WEAVE　1958　攝影　24.5×19.1cm

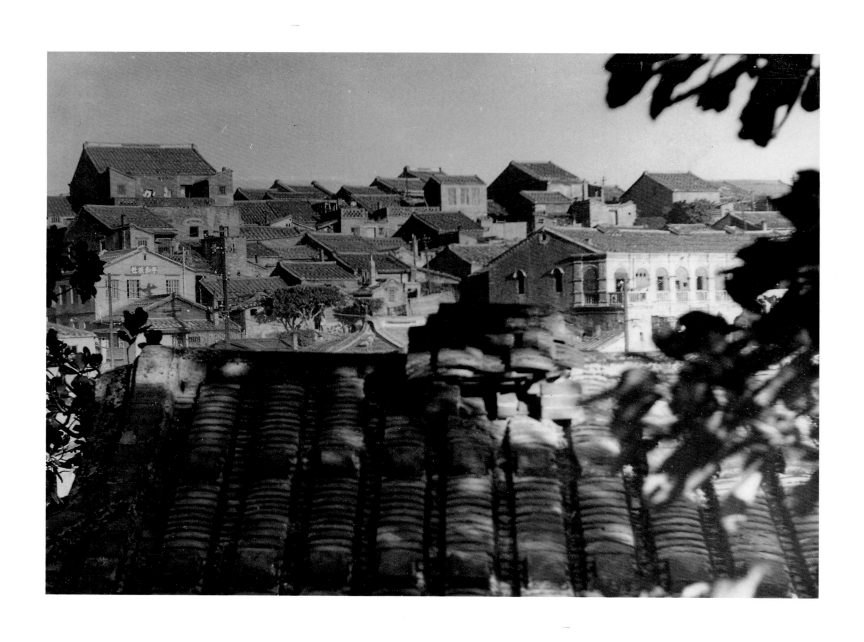

傳統建築系列（一）　TRADITIONAL ARCHITECTURE SERIES（1）　約1950年代　攝影　7.5×10.4cm

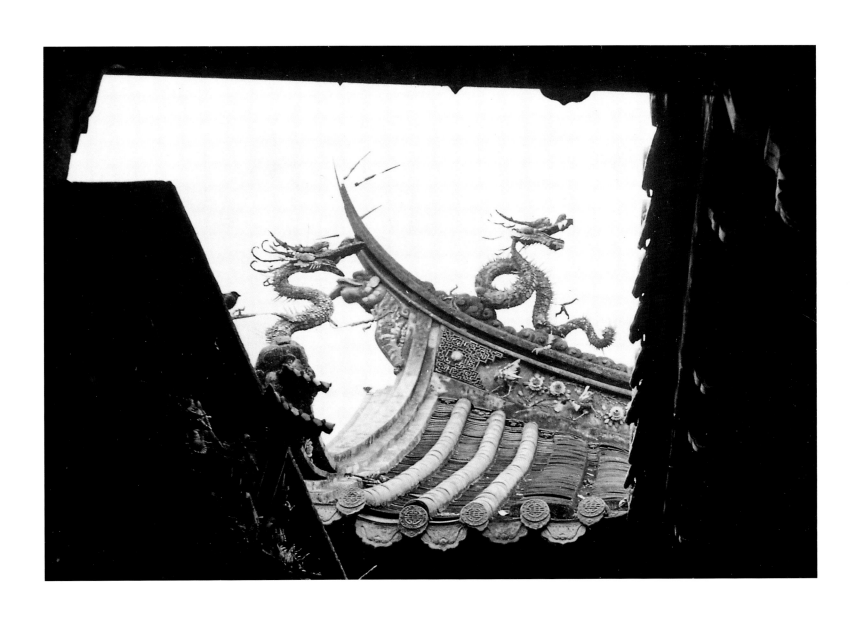

傳統建築系列（二）　TRADITIONAL ARCHITECTURE SERIES（2）　約1950年代　攝影　6.1×8.6cm

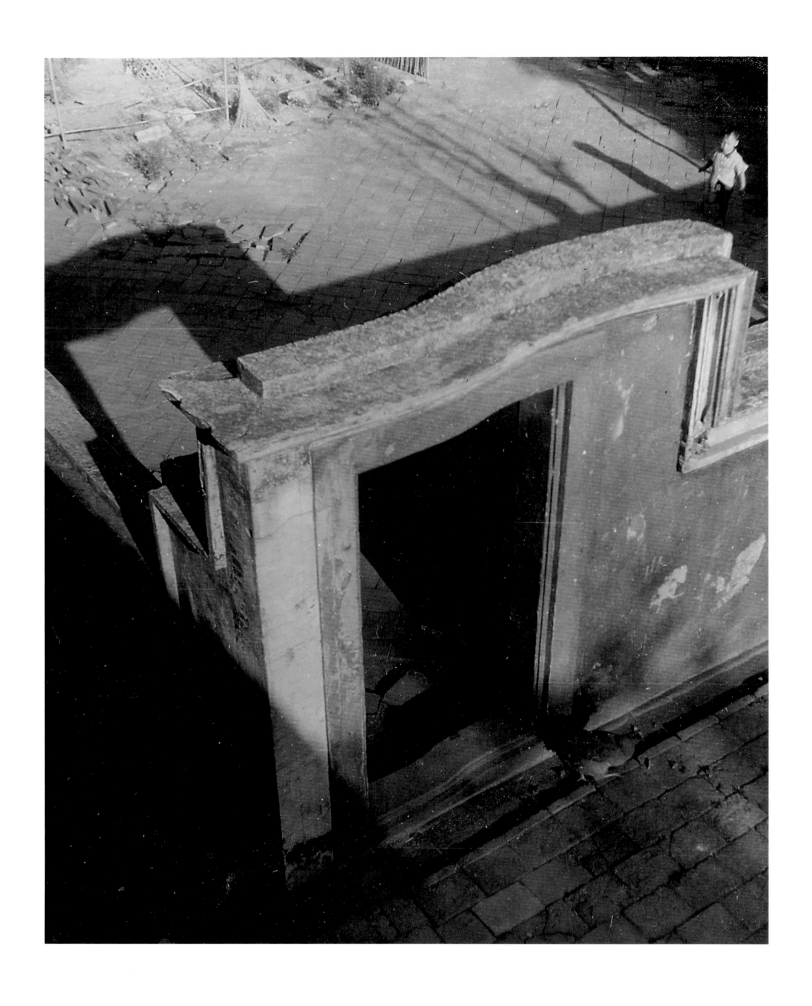

傳統建築系列（三）　TRADITIONAL ARCHITECTURE SERIES（3）　約1950年代　攝影　8×6.3cm

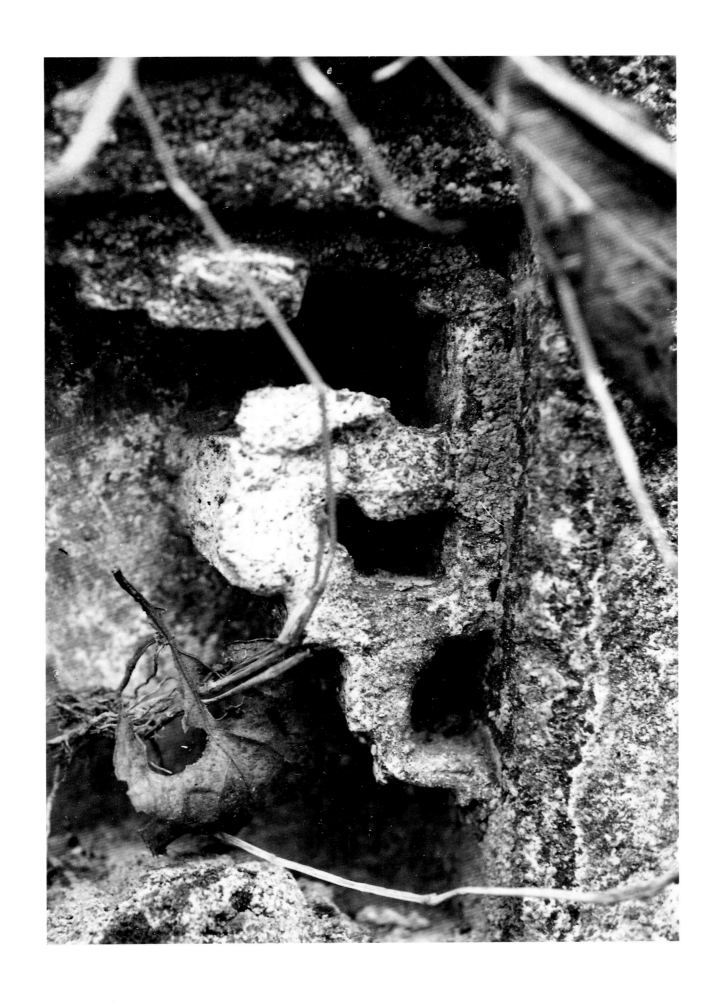

傳統建築系列(四)　TRADITIONAL ARCHITECTURE SERIES(4)　約1950年代　攝影　12.1×8.4cm

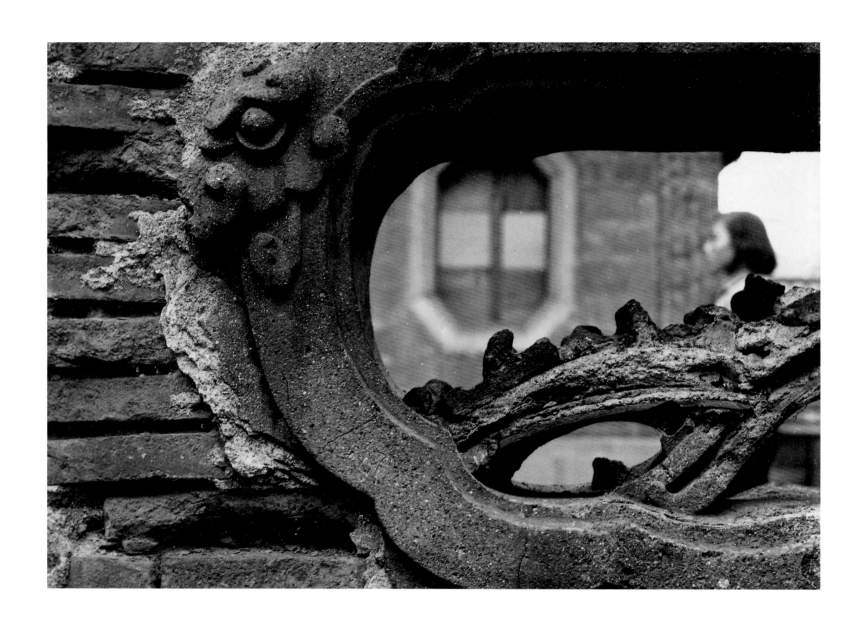

傳統建築系列（五）　TRADITIONAL ARCHITECTURE SERIES（5）　約1950年代　攝影　8.1×11.2cm

傳統建築系列（六）　TRADITIONAL ARCHITECTURE SERIES（6）　約1950年代　攝影　11.2×8.1cm（右頁圖）

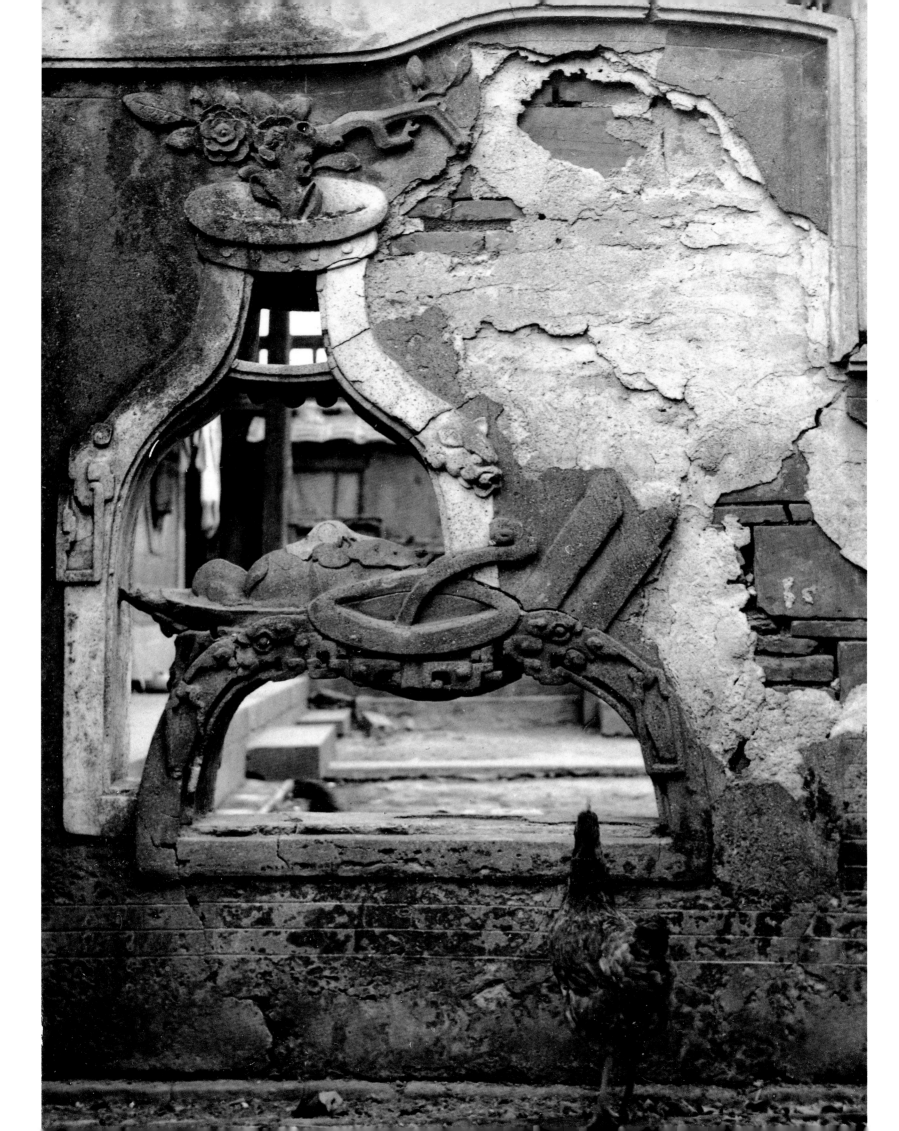

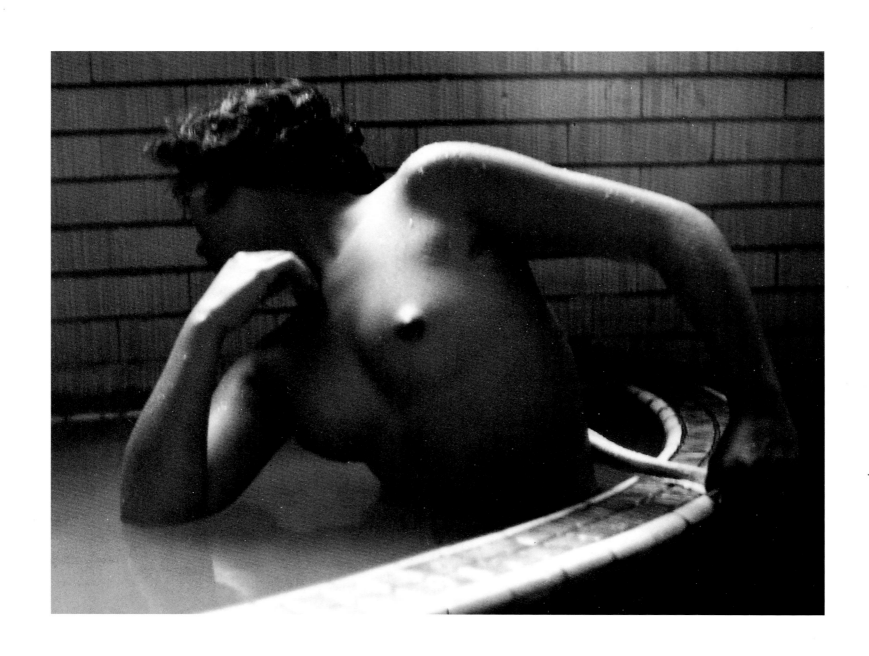

裸女系列：澡堂（一）　NUDE LADY SERIES : BATHROOM（1）　約1957　攝影　6.2×8.2cm

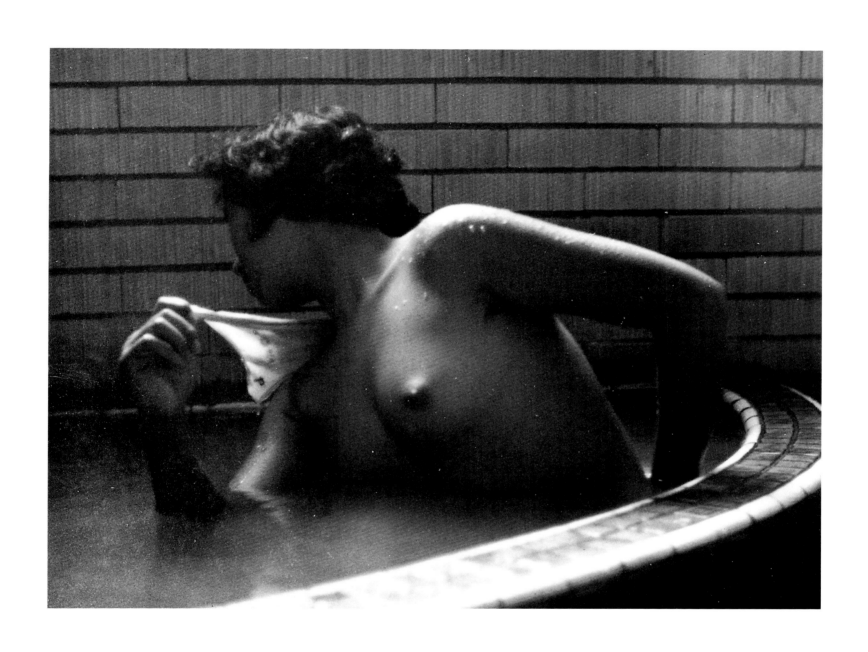

裸女系列：澡堂（二）　NUDE　LADY　SERIES：BATHROOM（2）　約1957　攝影　6.2×8.2cm

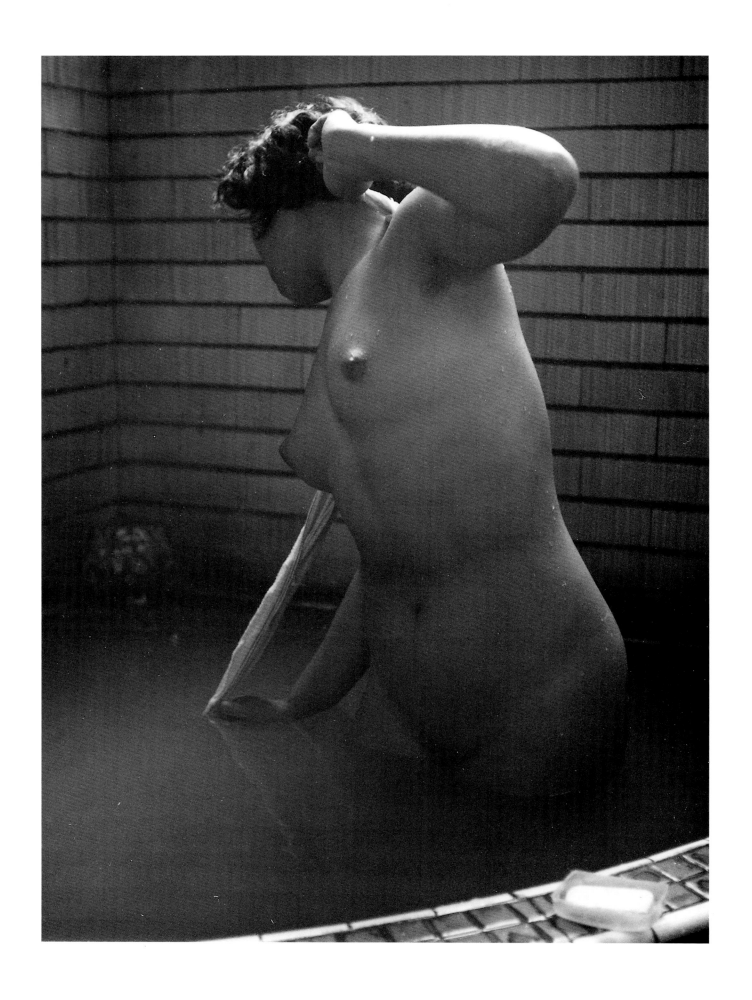

裸女系列：澡堂（三）　NUDE LADY SERIES：BATHROOM（3）　約1957　攝影　11.1×8.2cm

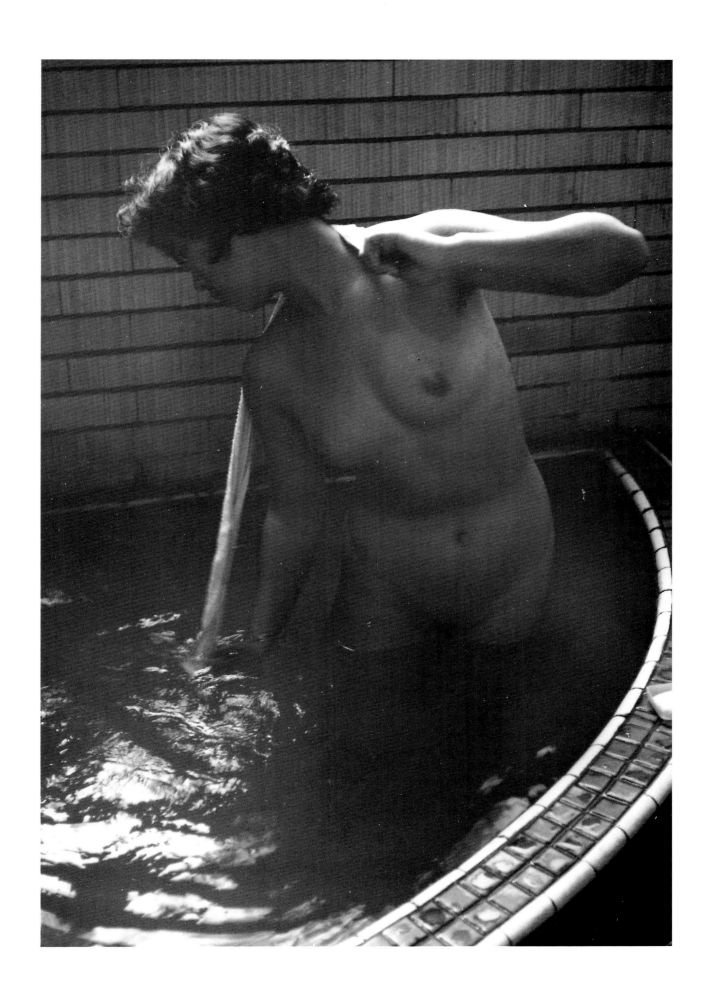

裸女系列：澡堂（四）　NUDE LADY SERIES：BATHROOM（4）　約1957　攝影　10.7×7.4cm

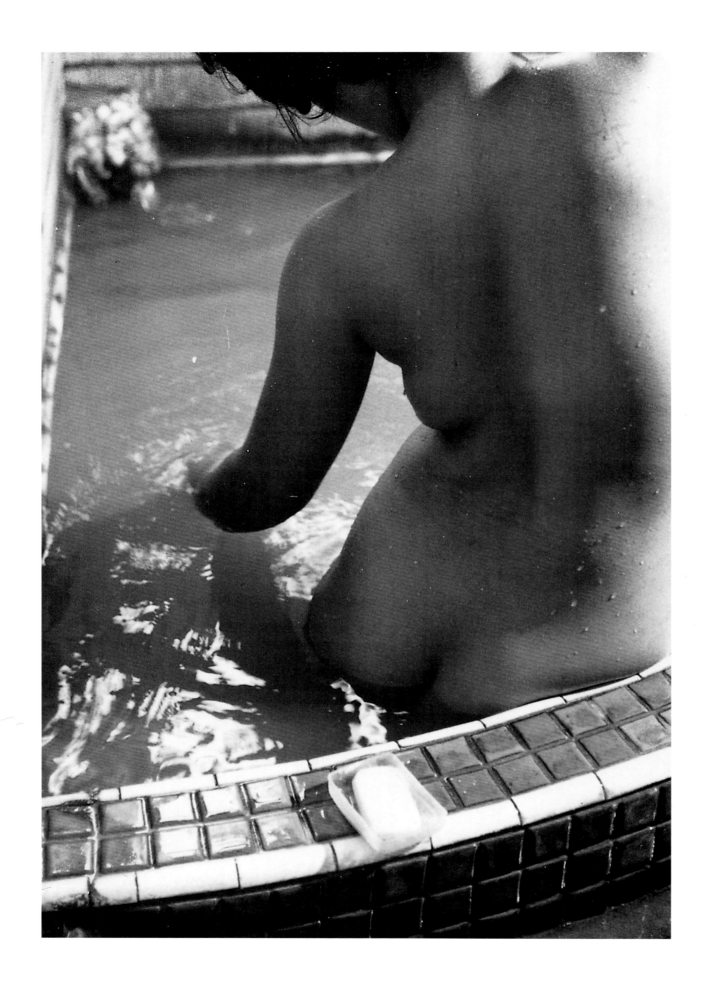

裸女系列：澡堂（五）　NUDE LADY SERIES：BATHROOM（5）　約1957　攝影　8×5.5cm

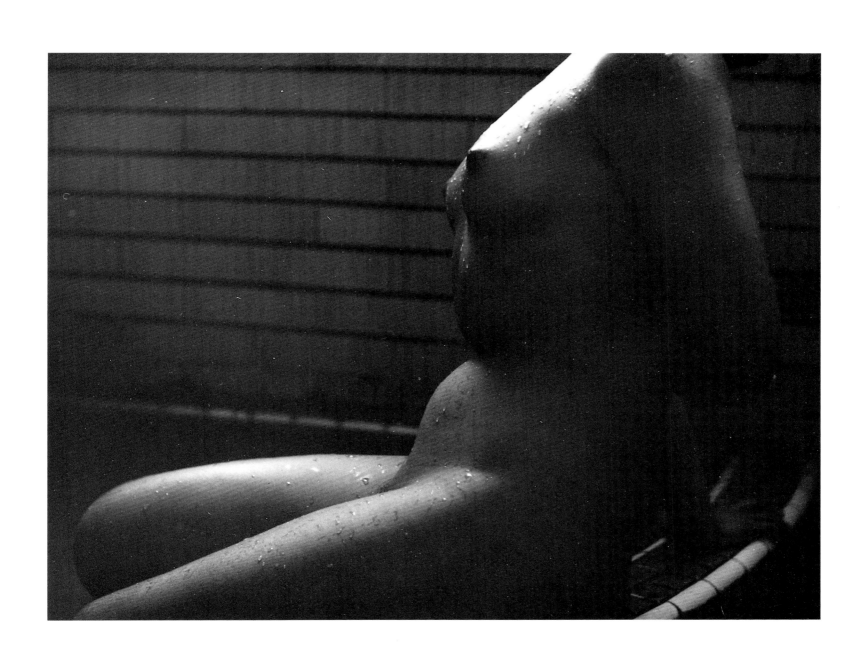

裸女系列：澡堂（六）　NUDE LADY SERIES : BATHROOM(6)　約1957　攝影　7.5×10cm

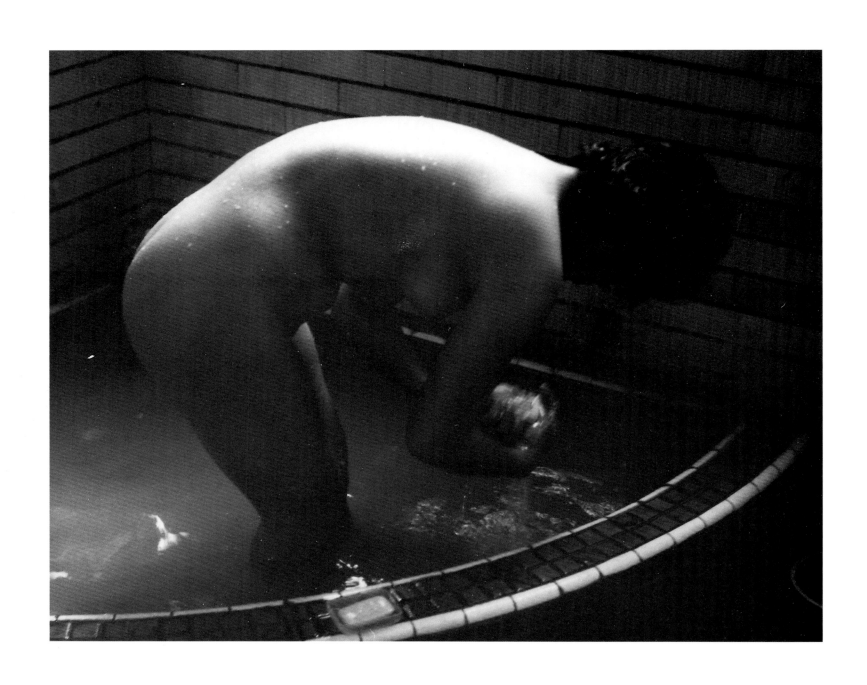

裸女系列：澡堂（七）　NUDE LADY SERIES：BATHROOM（7）　約1957　攝影　8.1×10.3cm

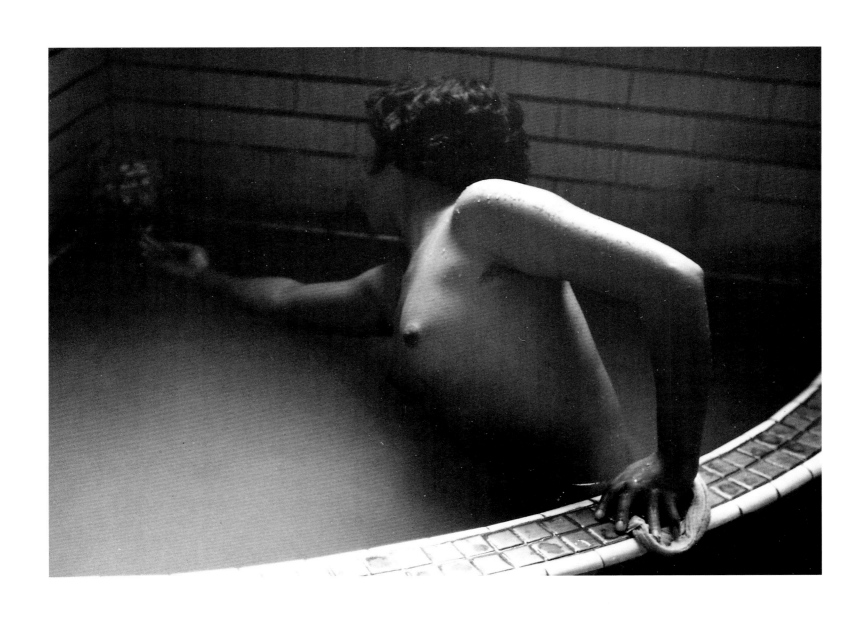

裸女系列：澡堂（八）　NUDE LADY SERIES：BATHROOM（8）　約1957　攝影　6.3×9.2cm

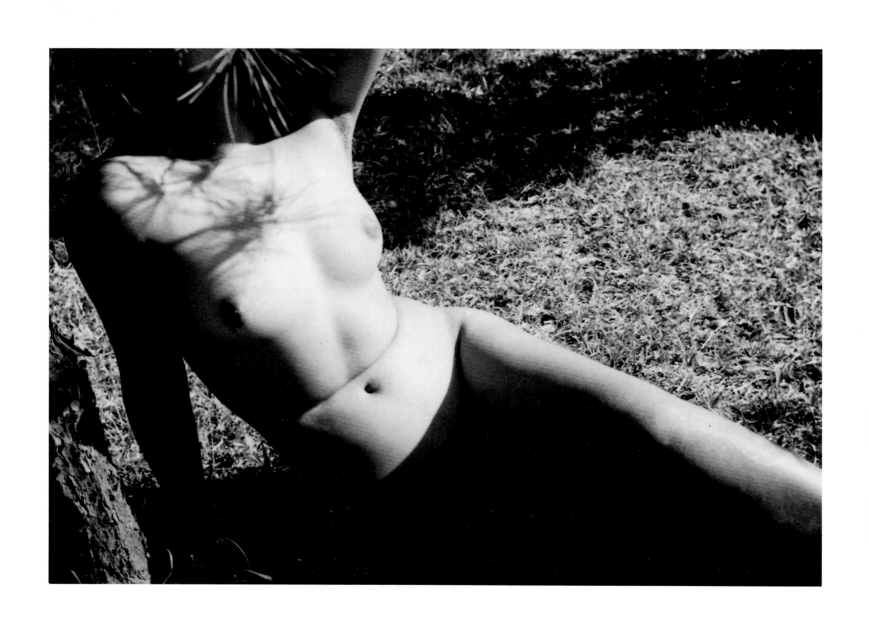

裸女系列：草地　NUDE LADY SERIES : LAWN　約1957　攝影　7.3×10.1cm

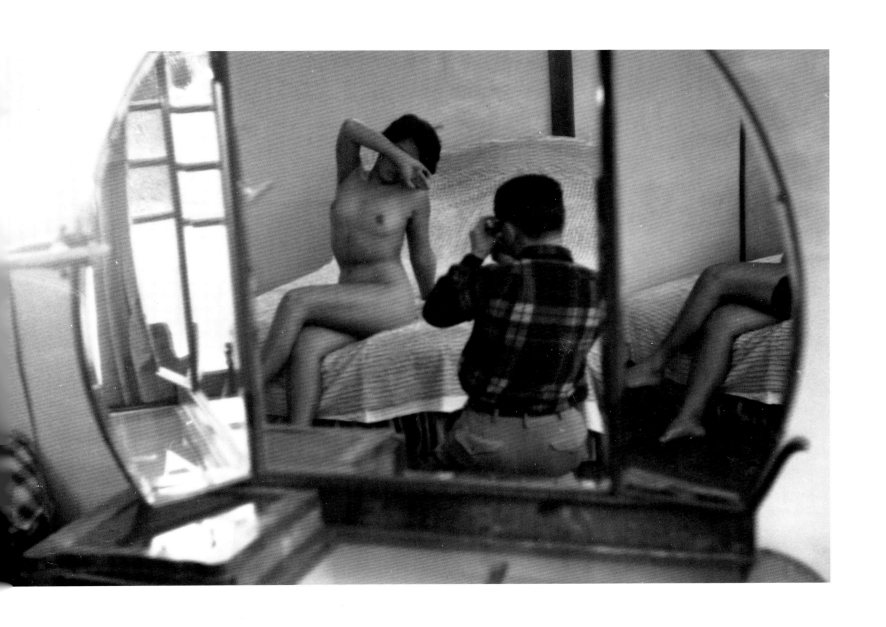

裸女系列：臥室（一）　NUDE LADY SERIES：BEDROOM（1）　約1957　攝影　7.1×10.2cm

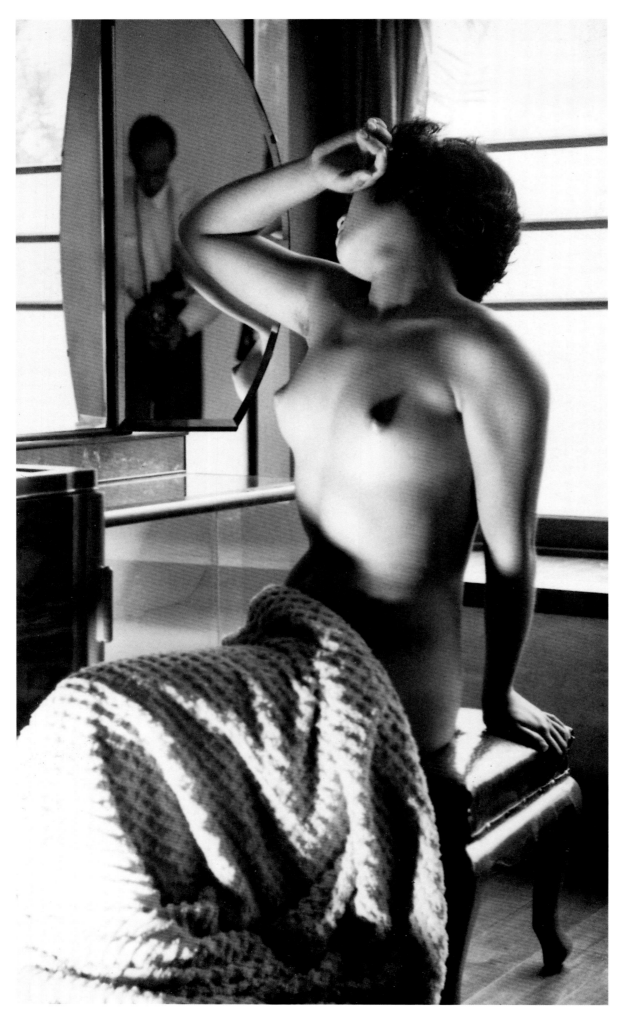

裸女系列：臥室（二）
NUDE LADY SERIES：
BEDROOM（2）
約1957　攝影
11.6×6.7cm

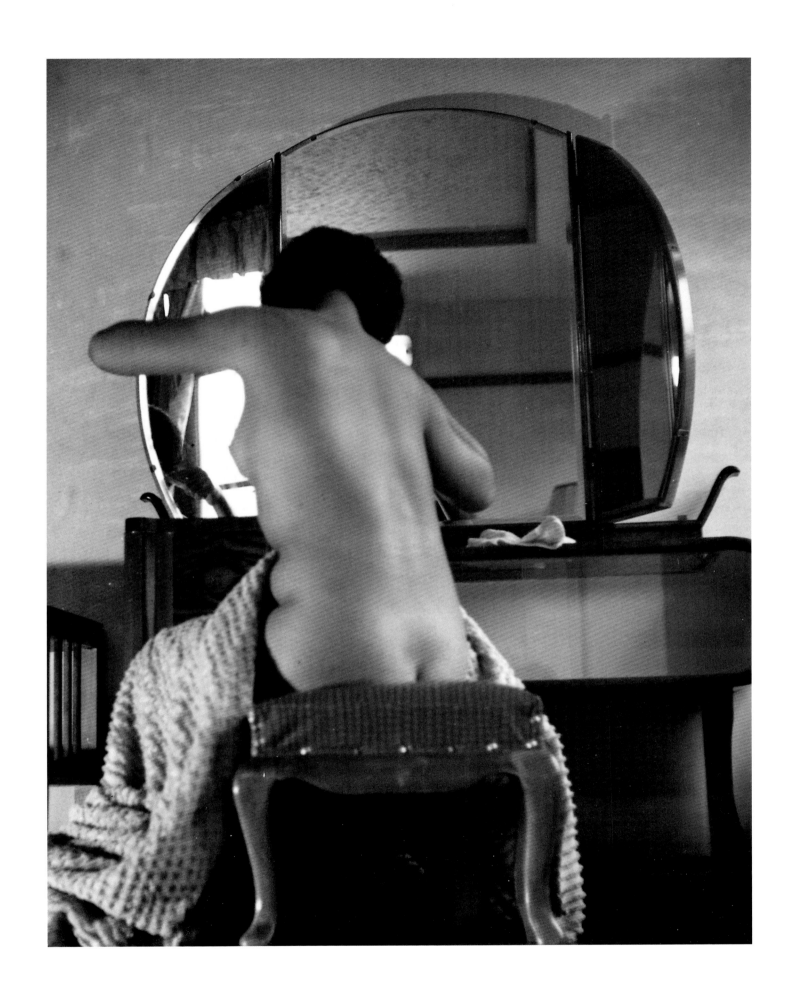

裸女系列：臥室（三）　NUDE LADY SERIES : BEDROOM（3）　約1957　攝影　11.5×8.8cm

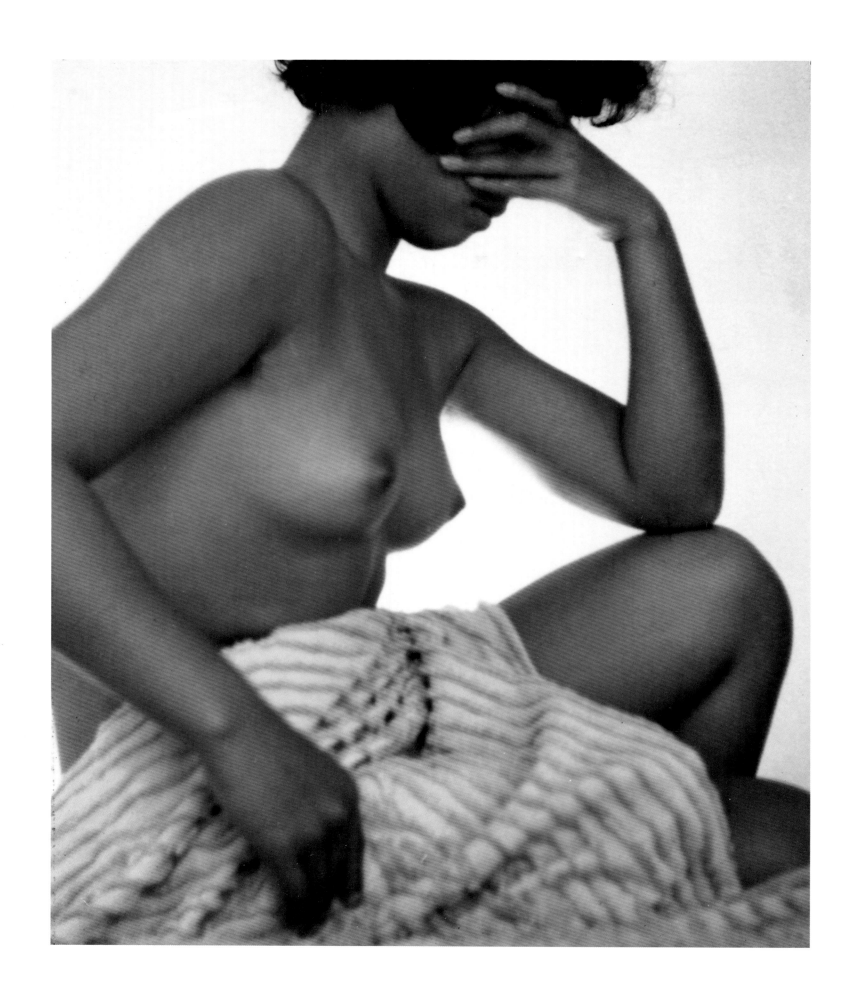

裸女系列：臥室（四）　NUDE LADY SERIES：BEDROOM（4）　約1957　攝影　8.3×6.8cm

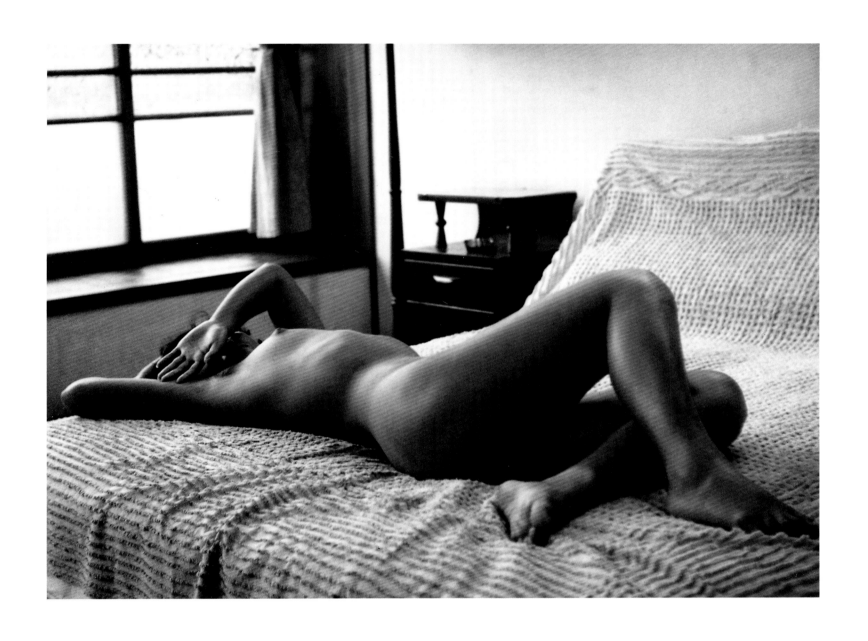

裸女系列：臥室（五）　NUDE LADY SERIES : BEDROOM（5）　約1957　攝影　8.6×11.5cm

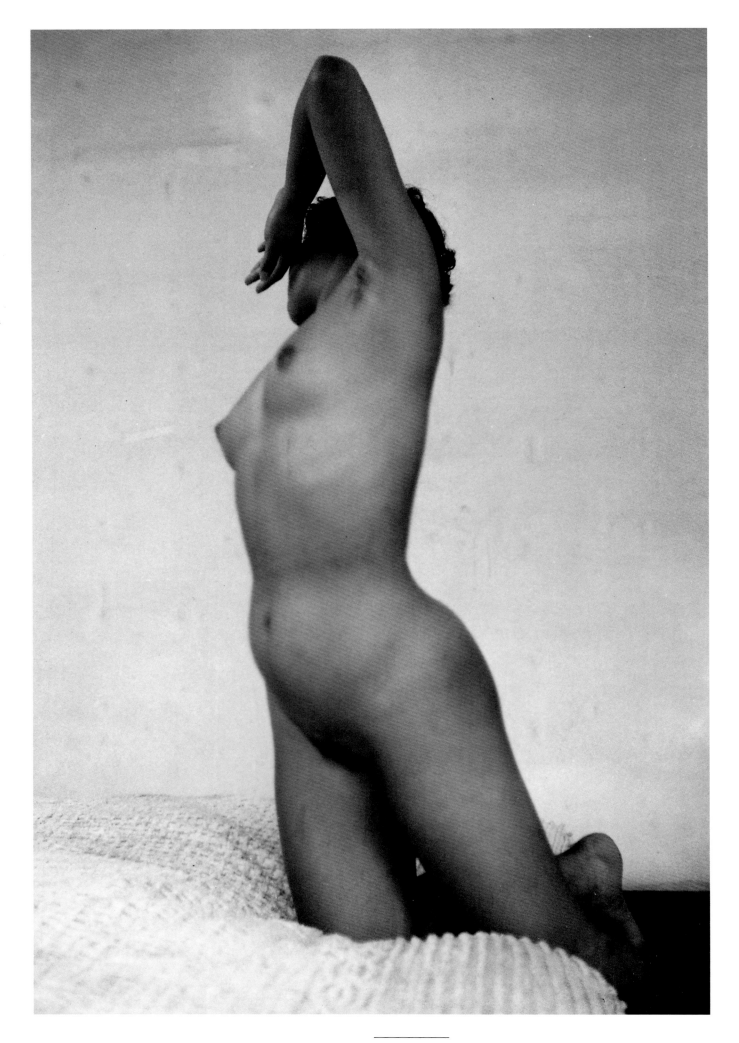

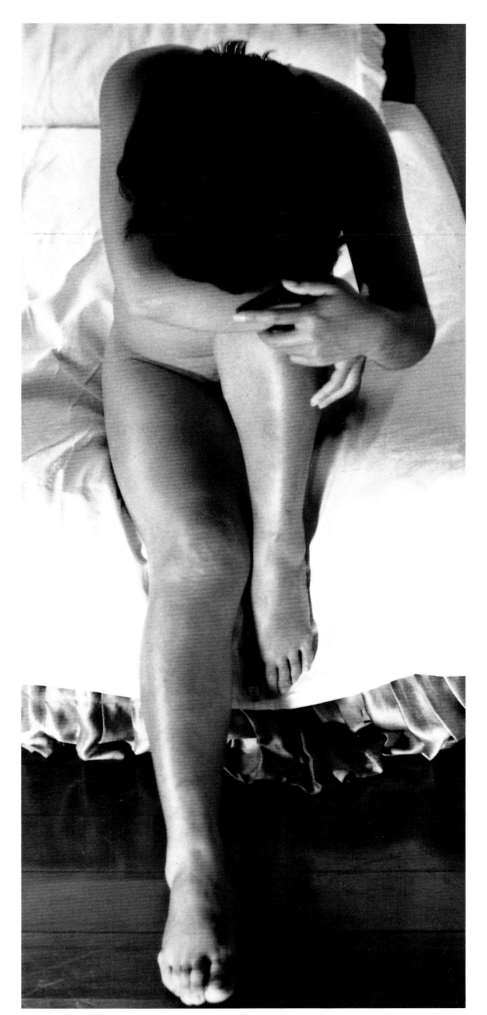

裸女系列：臥室（六）
NUDE LADY SERIES : BEDROOM（6）
約1957　攝影　11.5 × 7.5cm（左頁圖）

裸女系列：臥室（七）
NUDE LADY SERIES : BEDROOM（7）
約1957　攝影　11.5 × 8.9cm

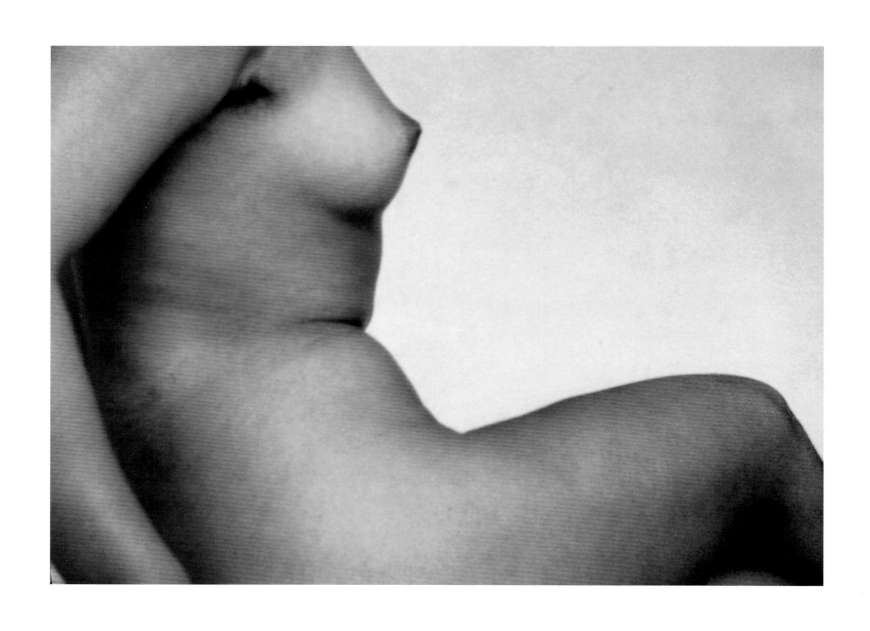

裸女系列：臥室（八）　NUDE LADY SERIES : BEDROOM（8）　約1957　攝影　11.5×5cm

裸女系列：臥室（九）　NUDE LADY SERIES : BEDROOM（9）　約1957　攝影　11.5×7cm（右頁圖）

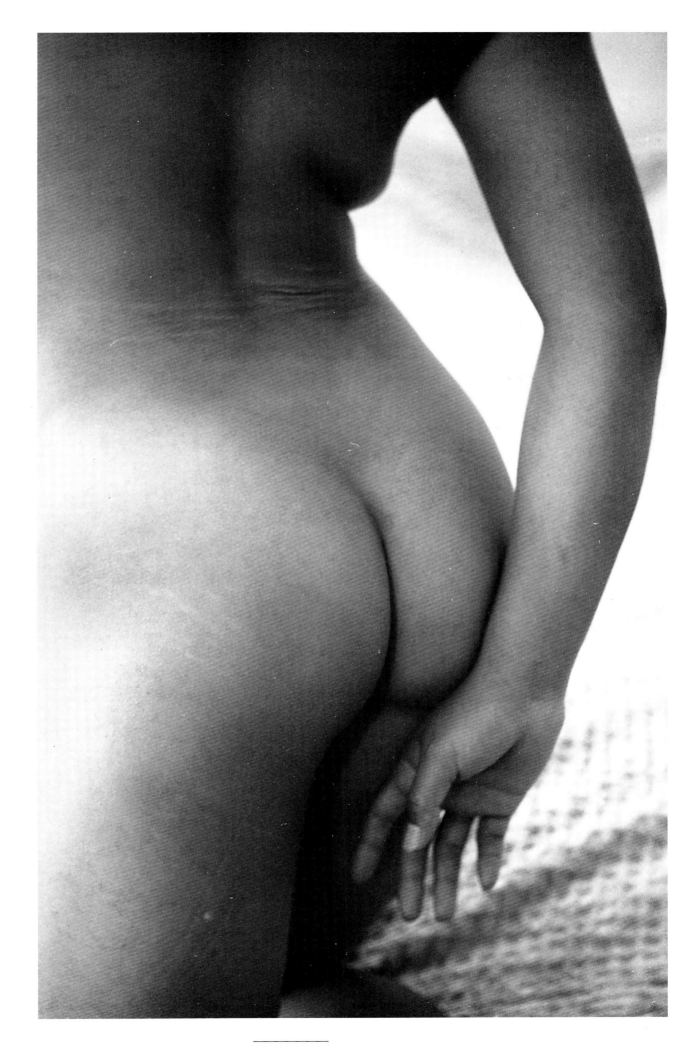

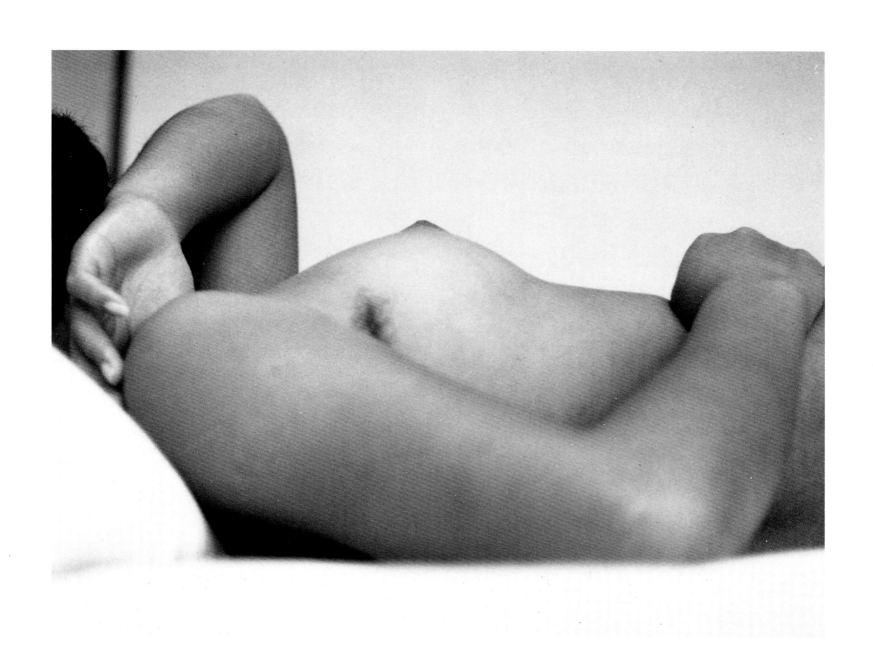

裸女系列：臥室（十）　NUDE LADY SERIES：BEDROOM（10）　約1957　攝影　6.8×8.7cm

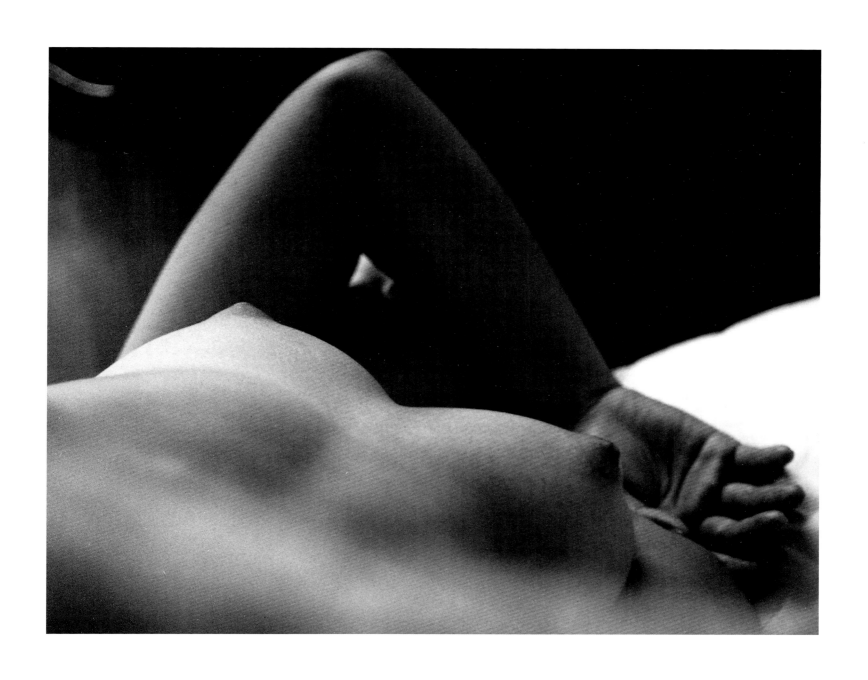

裸女系列：臥室（十一） NUDE LADY SERIES：BEDROOM（11） 約1957 攝影 9×11.7cm

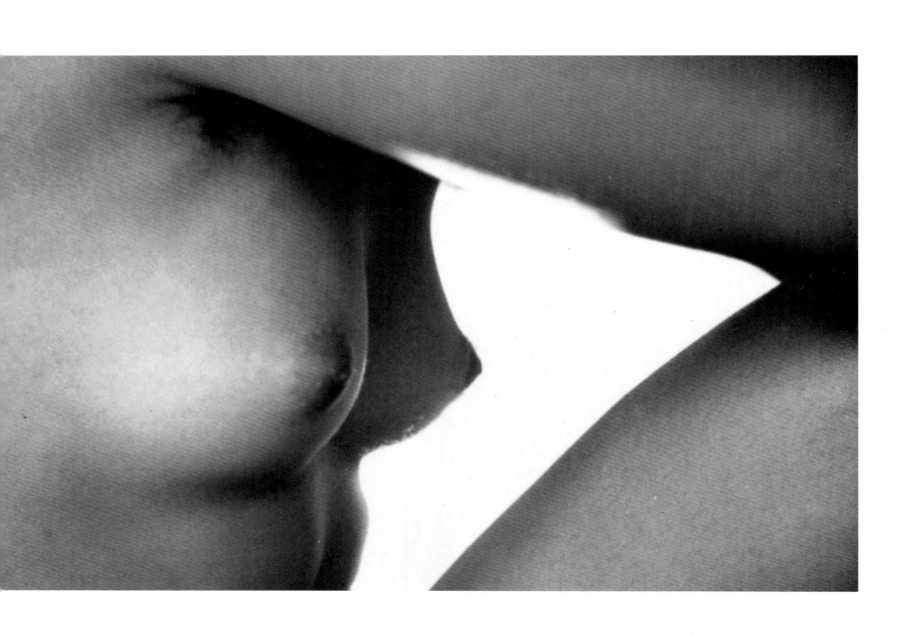

裸女系列：臥室（十二）　NUDE LADY SERIES：BEDROOM（12）　約1957　攝影　6.7×10.6cm

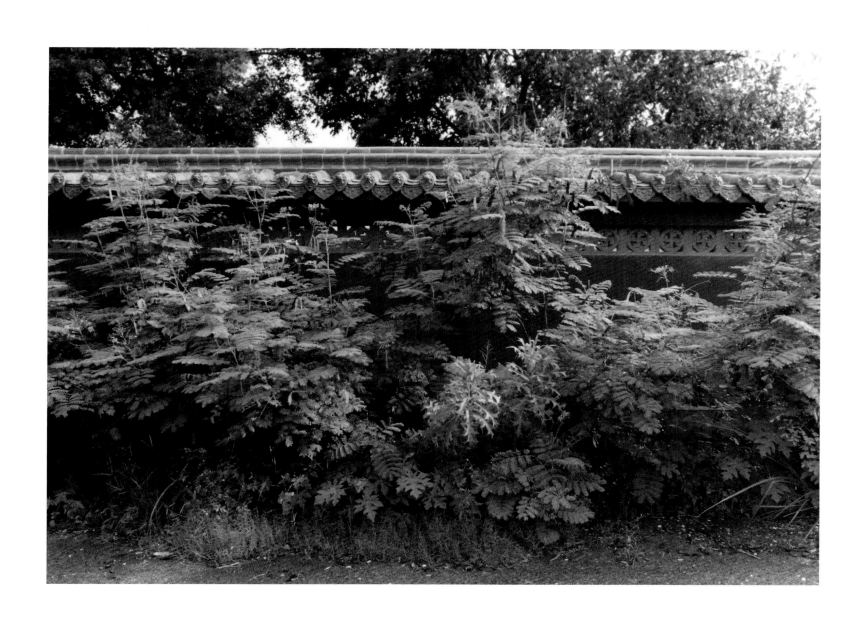

廟宇系列（一）　TEMPLE　SERIES（1）　年代未詳　攝影　17.9×24.9cm

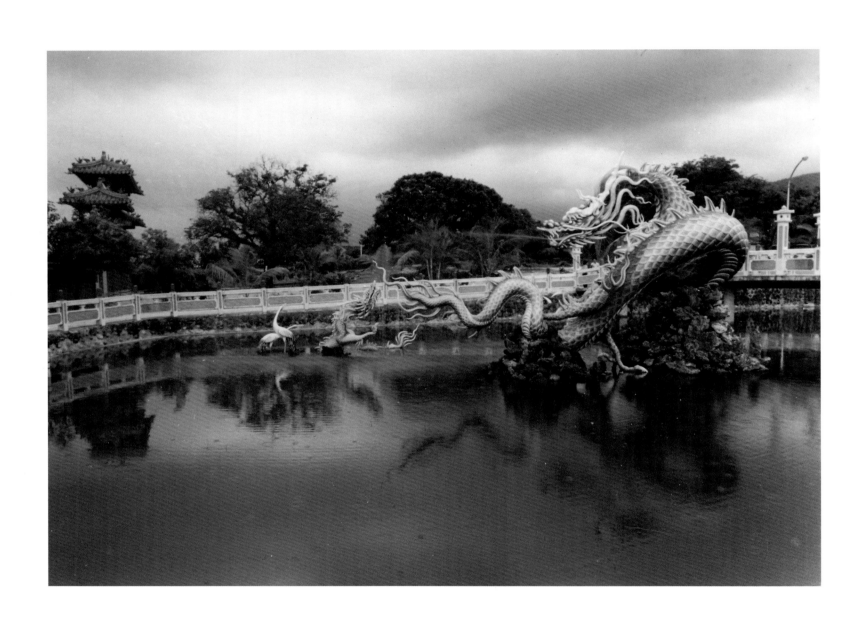

廟宇系列（二）　TEMPLE　SERIES（2）　年代未詳　攝影　18×24.9cm

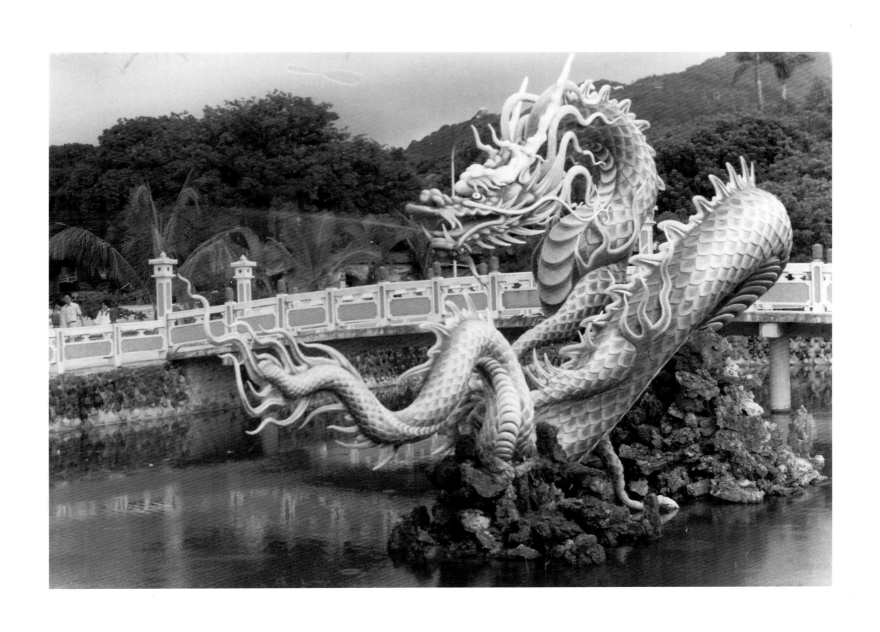

廟宇系列（三）　TEMPLE　SERIES（3）　年代未詳　攝影　17.8×25cm

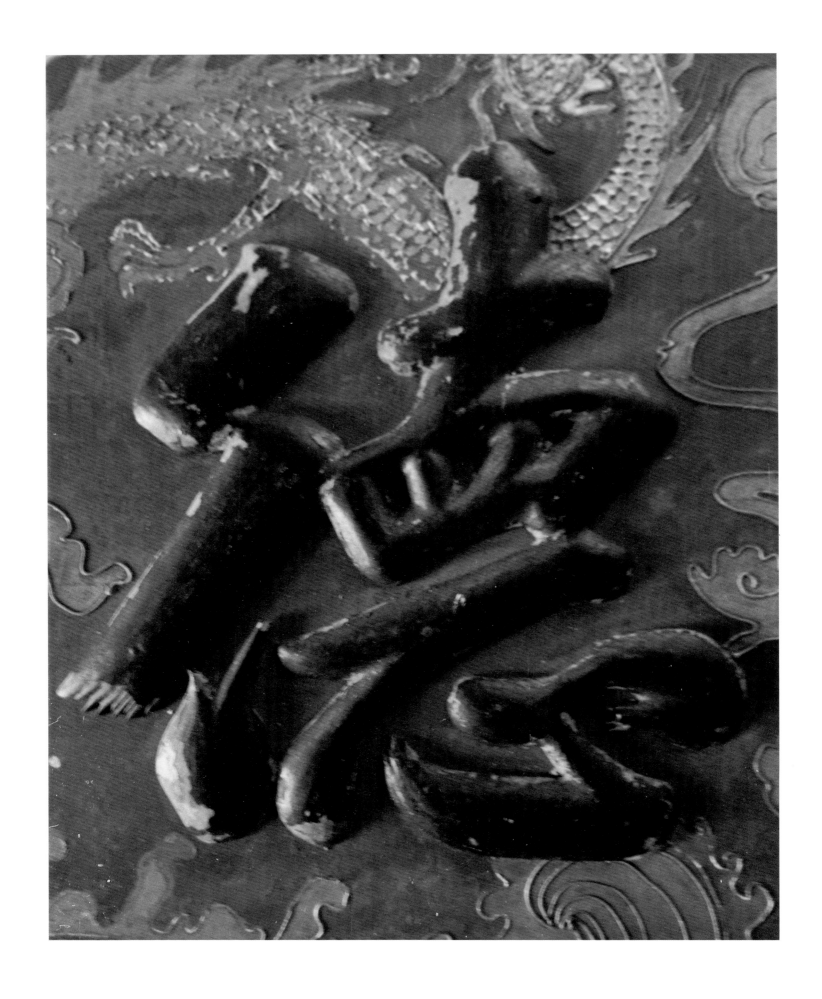

廟宇系列（四）　TEMPLE　SERIES（4）　年代未詳　攝影　25.3×20.3cm

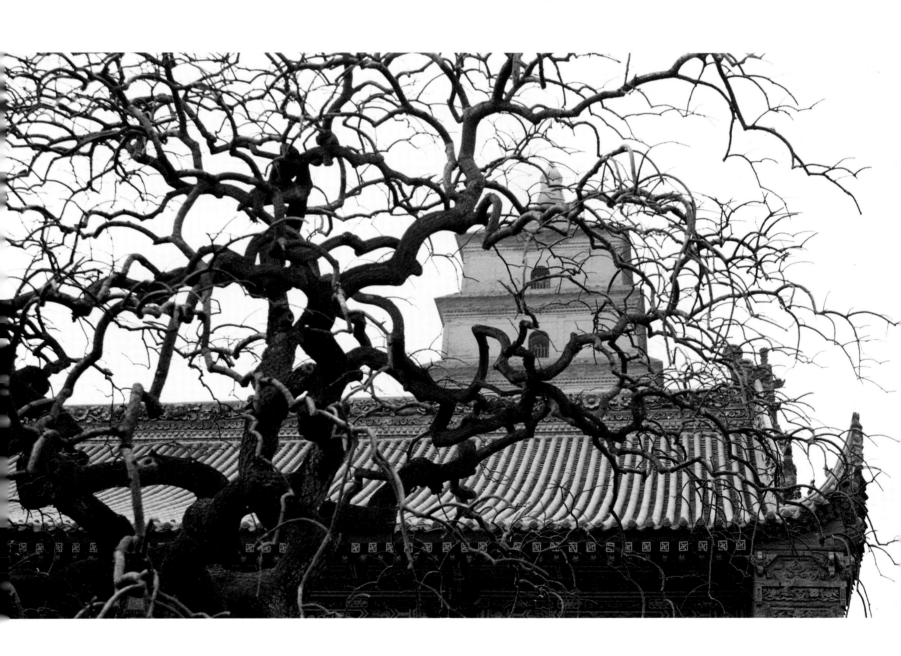

西安大雁塔　SIAN DAYAN TOWER　1989　攝影　25.2×38.4cm

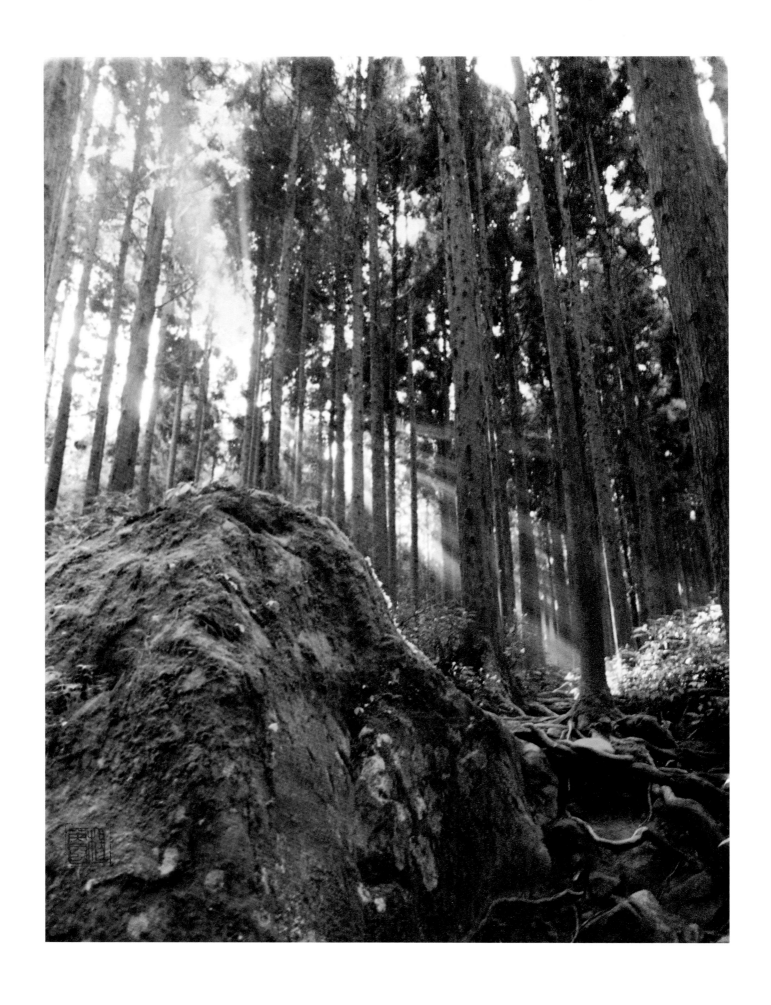

溪頭系列(一)　SI-TOU　SERIES(1)　1980　攝影　25×18.5cm

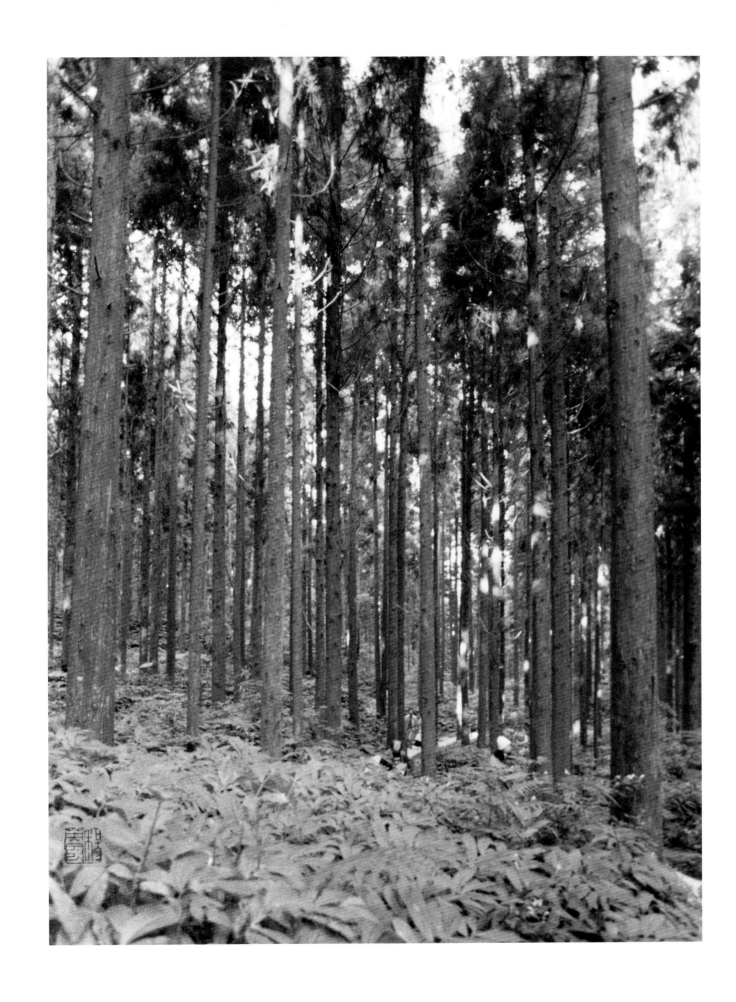

溪頭系列(二)　SI-TOU SERIES(2)　1980　攝影　25×17.7cm

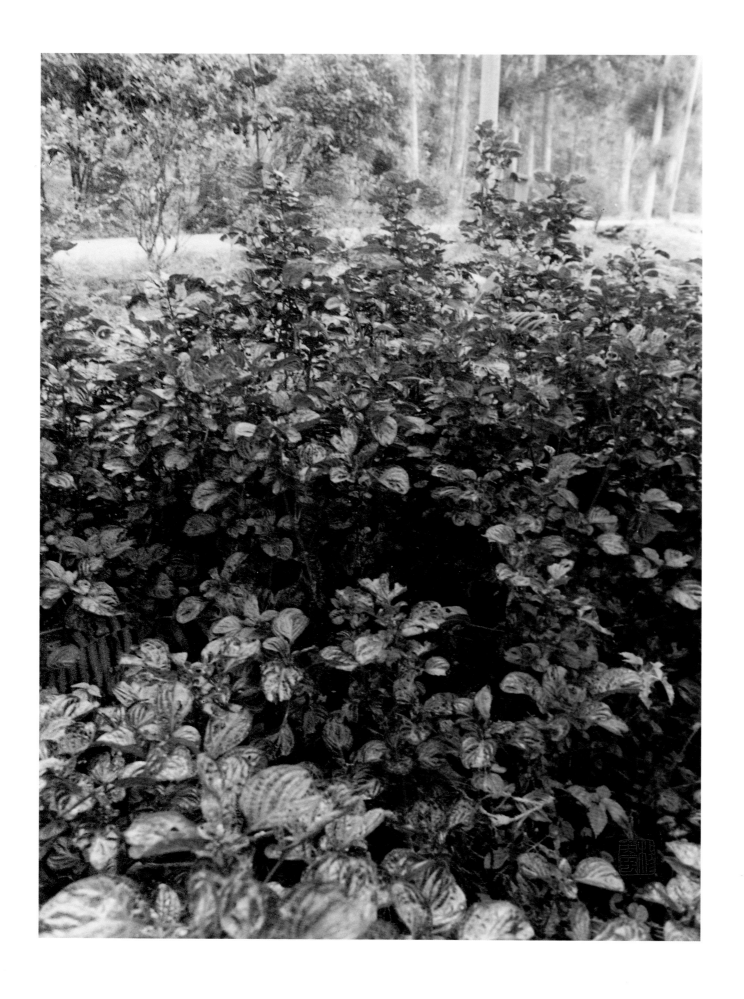

溪頭系列（三）　SI-TOU　SERIES（3）　1980　攝影　25×18cm

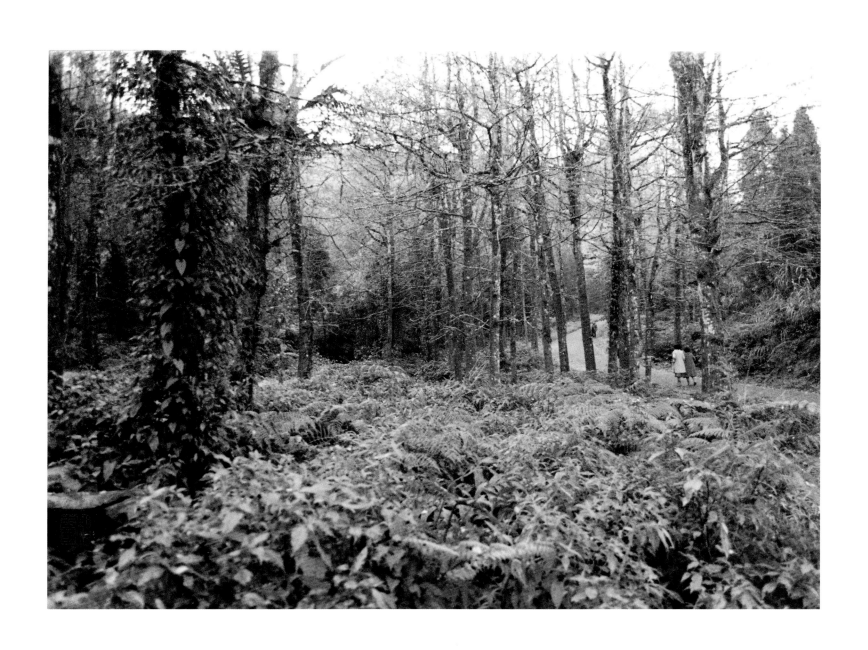

溪頭系列（四）　SI-TOU　SERIES（4）　1980　攝影　18.7×25cm

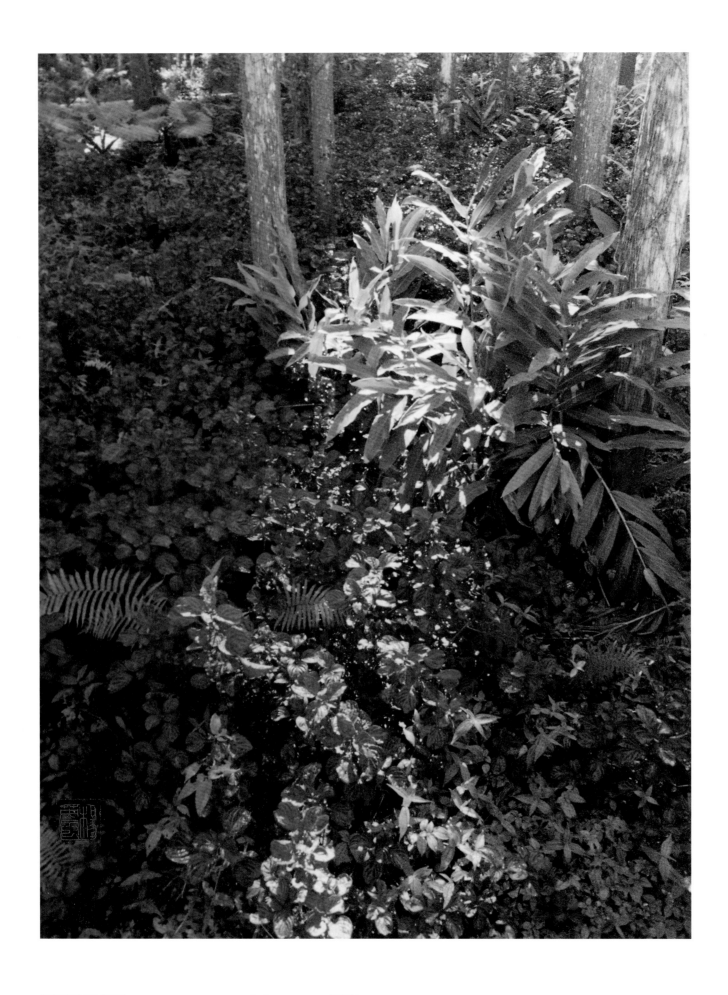

溪頭系列（五）　SI-TOU　SERIES（5）　1980　攝影　17.7×25cm

溪頭系列（六）　SI-TOU　SERIES（6）　1980　攝影　25.1×17.9cm(右頁圖)

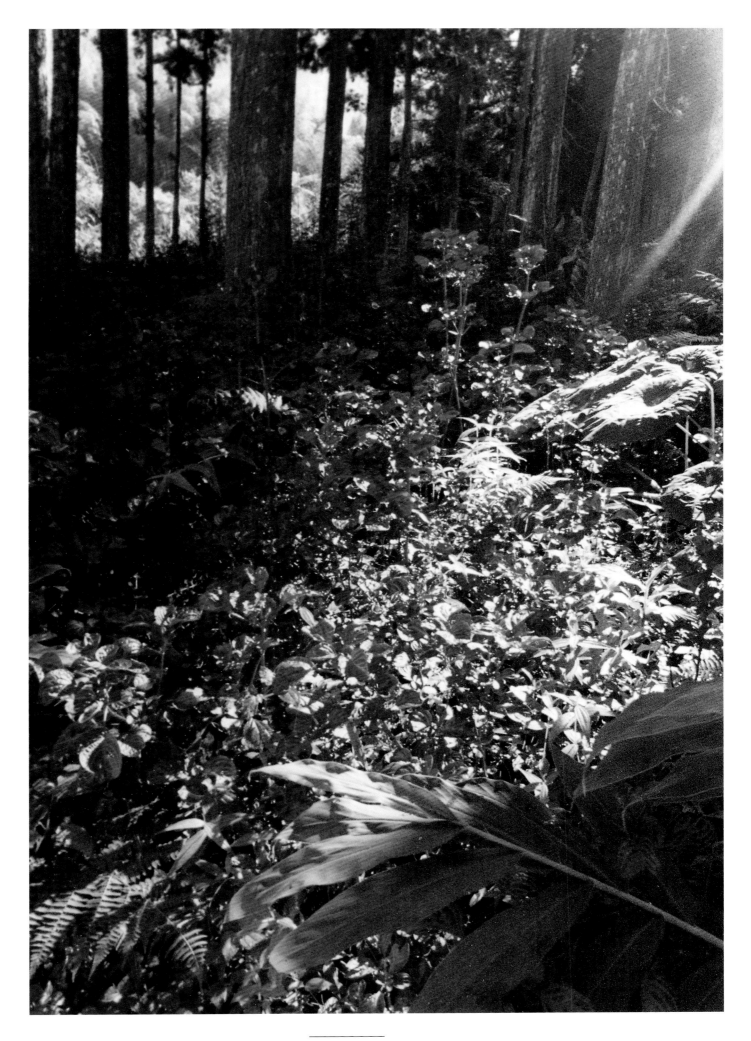

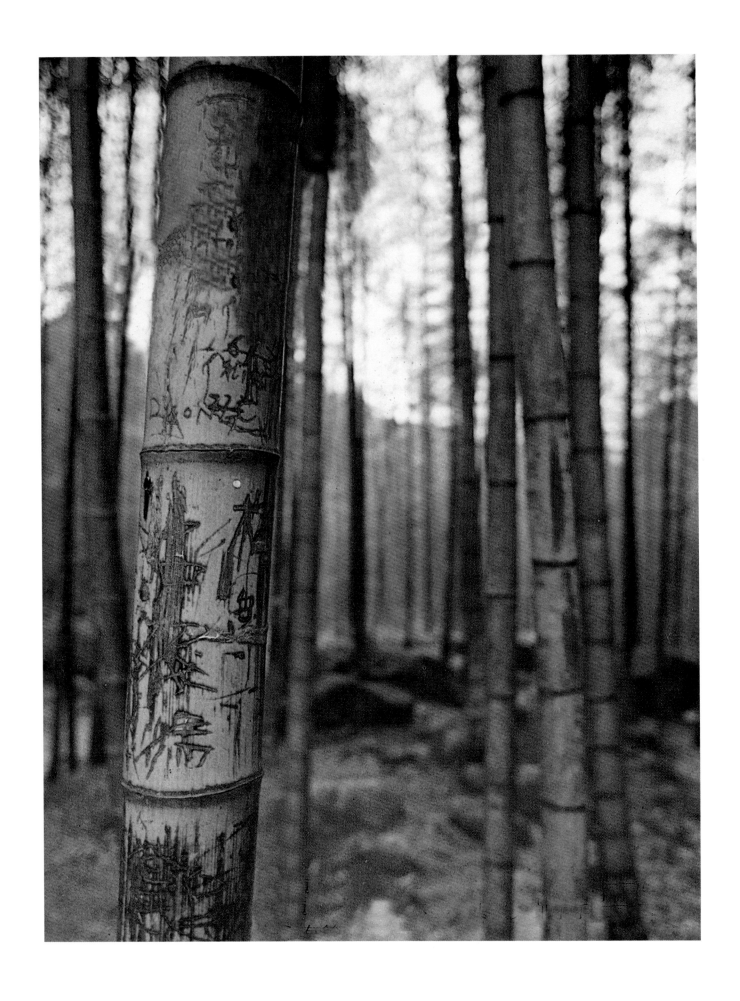

溪頭系列（七）　SI-TOU　SERIES（7）　1980　攝影　21.2×15cm

原野系列（一）　WILD-PLAIN SERIES（1）　約1980年代　攝影　12.4×17.6cm

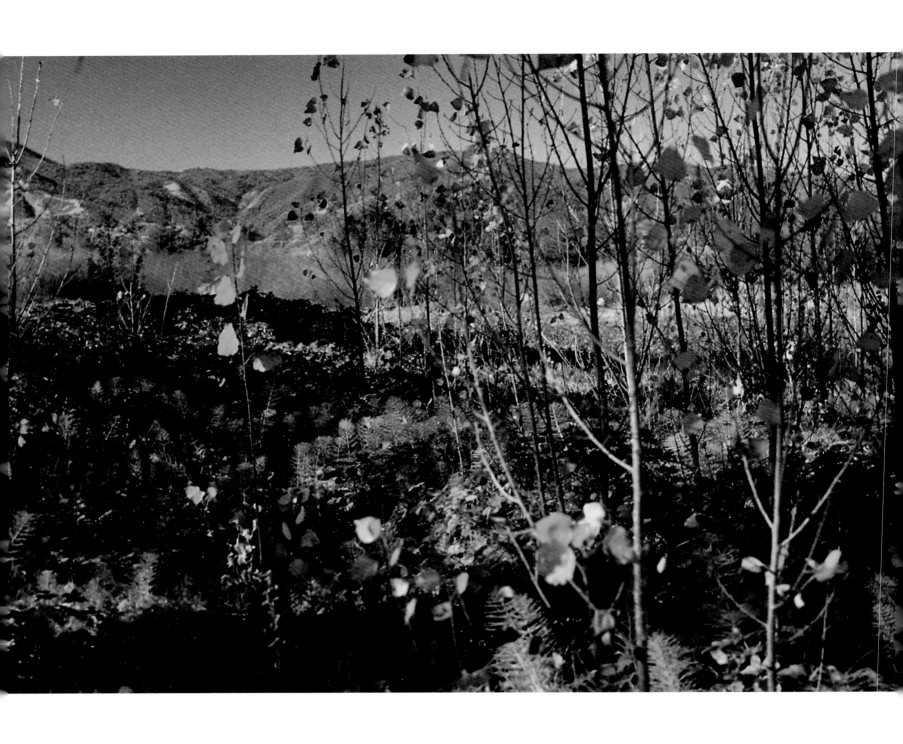

原野系列（二）　WILD-PLAIN　SERIES（2）　約1980年代　攝影　12.4×17.6cm

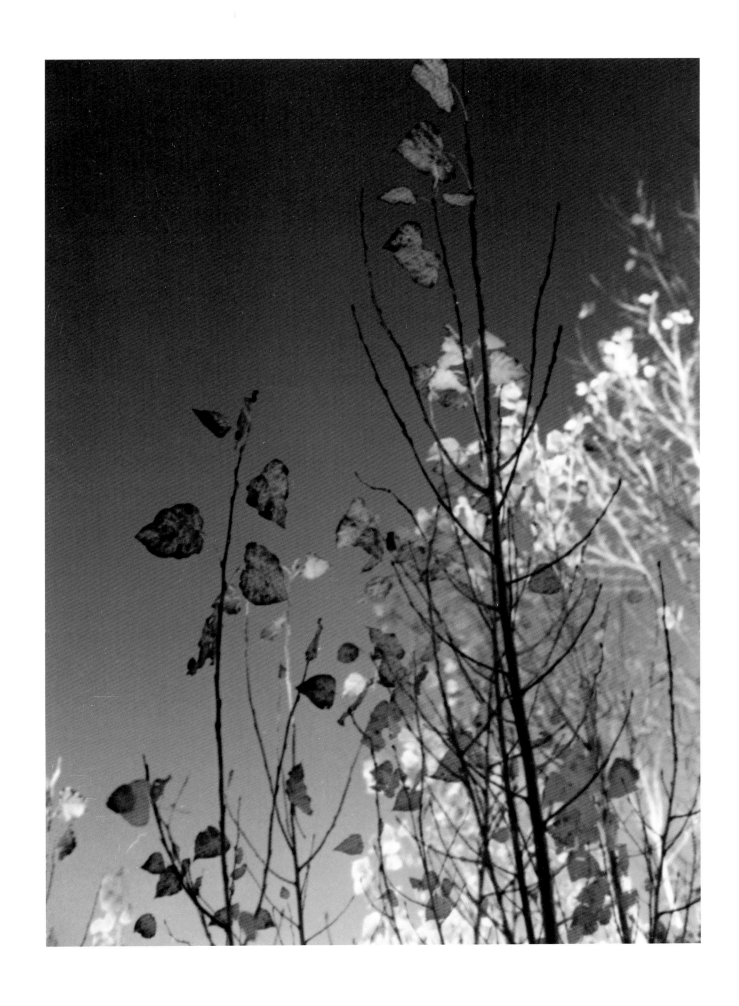

原野系列（三）　WILD-PLAIN SERIES（3）　約1980年代　攝影　17.6×12.5cm

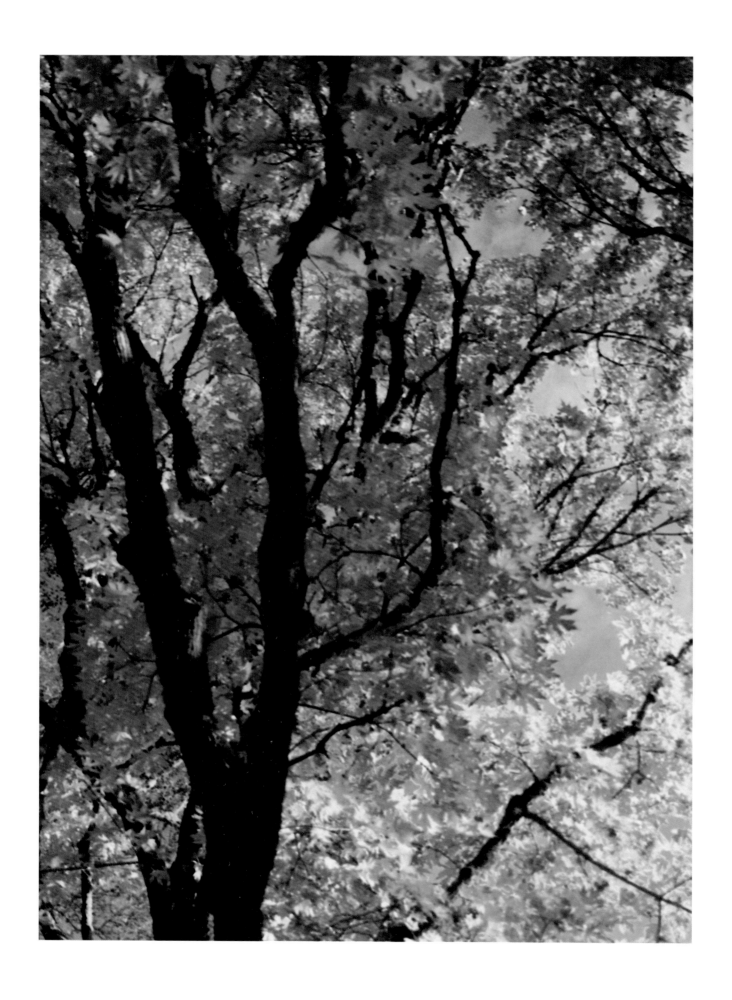

原野系列（四）　WILD-PLAIN　SERIES（4）　約1980年代　攝影　17.7×12.5cm

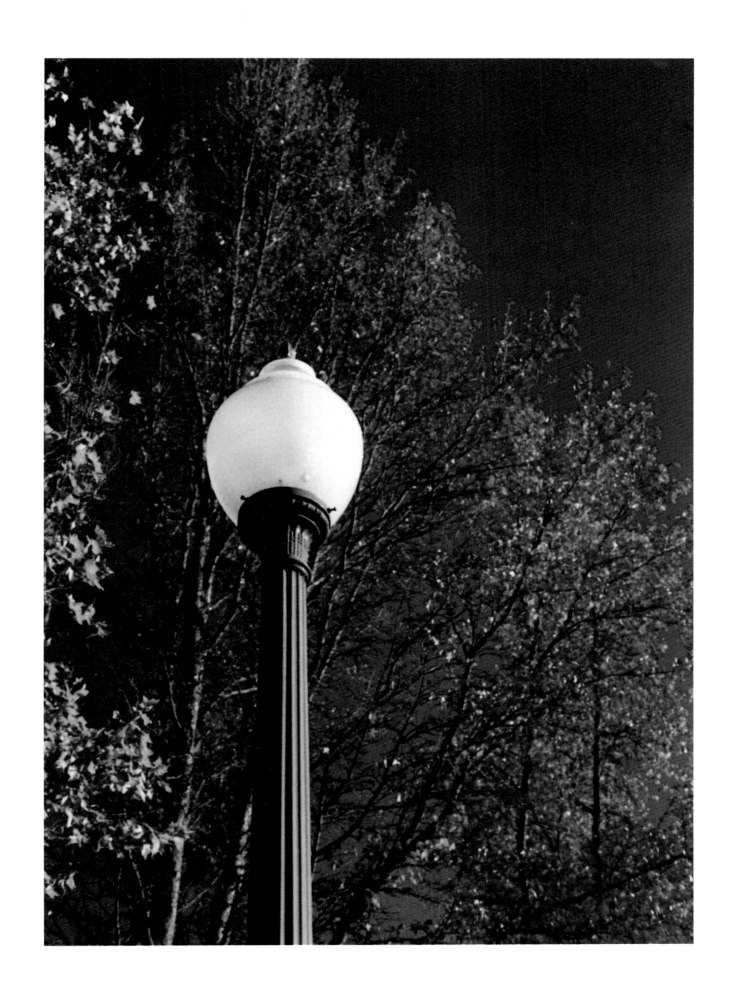

原野系列（五）　WILD-PLAIN SERIES（5）　約1980年代　攝影　17.7×12.4cm

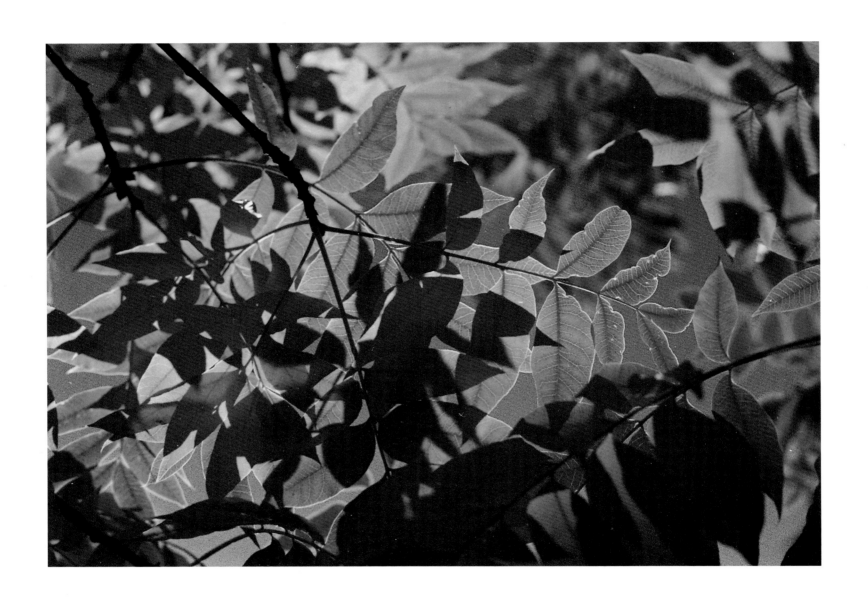

原野系列（六）　WILD-PLAIN SERIES（6）　約1980年代　攝影　12.4×17.6cm

原野系列（七）　WILD-PLAIN SERIES（7）　約1980年代　攝影　17.6×11.2cm（右頁圖）

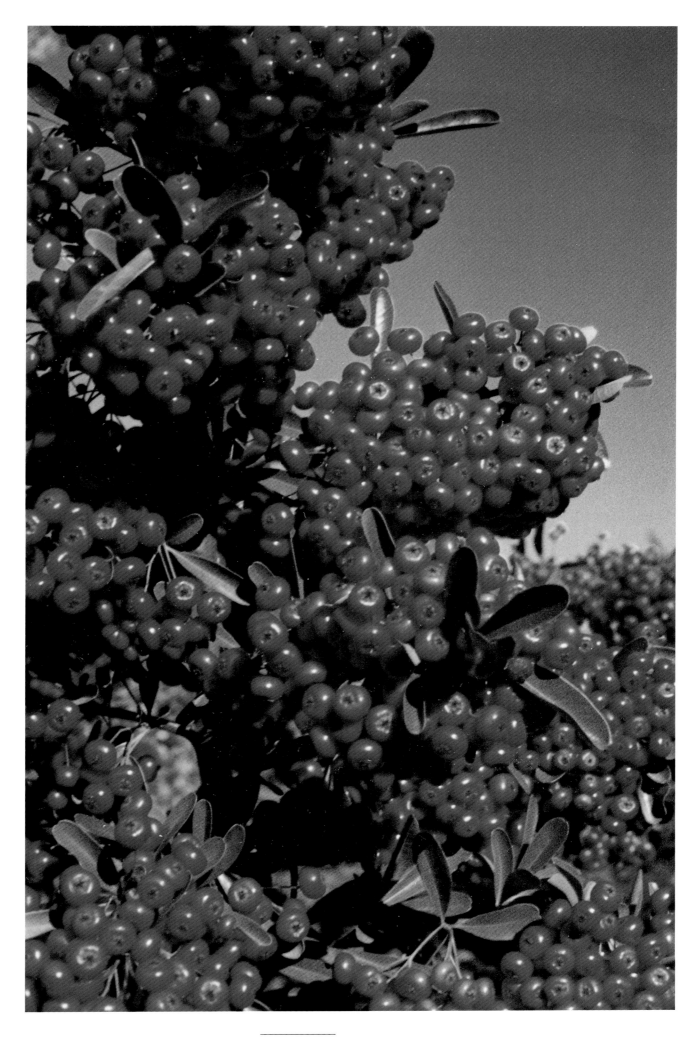

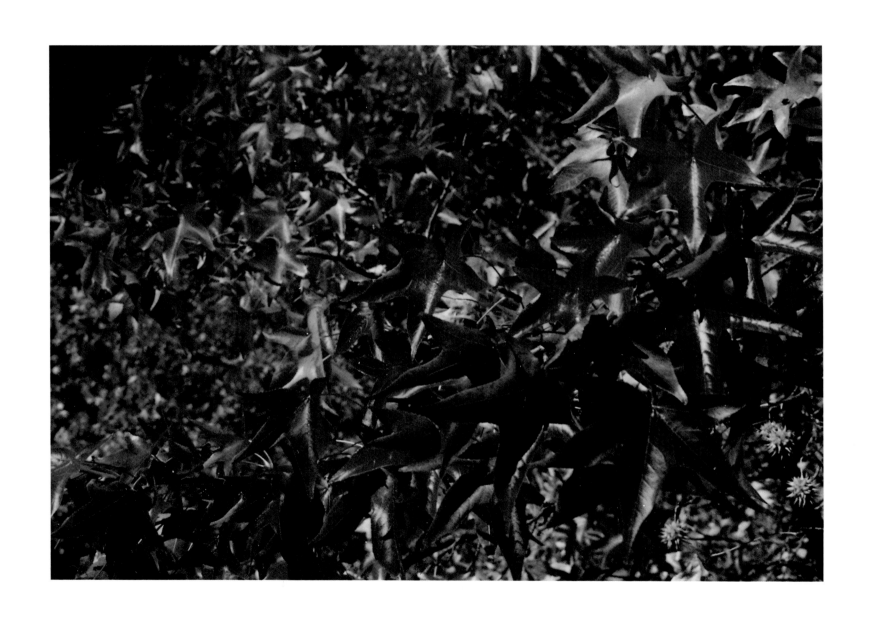

原野系列（八）　WILD-PLAIN　SERIES（8）　約1980年代　攝影　12.5×17.6cm

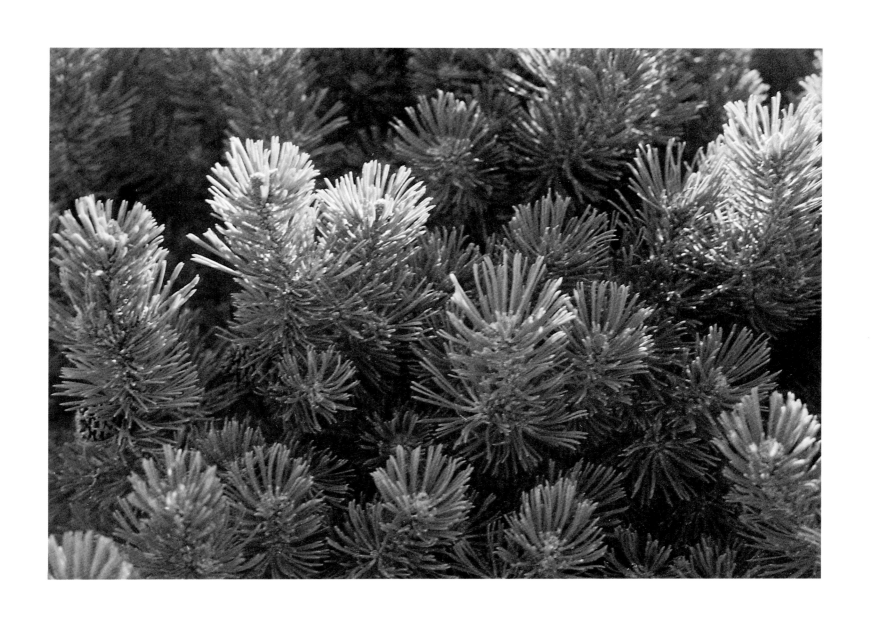

原野系列（九）　WILD-PLAIN　SERIES（9）　約1980年代　攝影　12.5×17.6cm

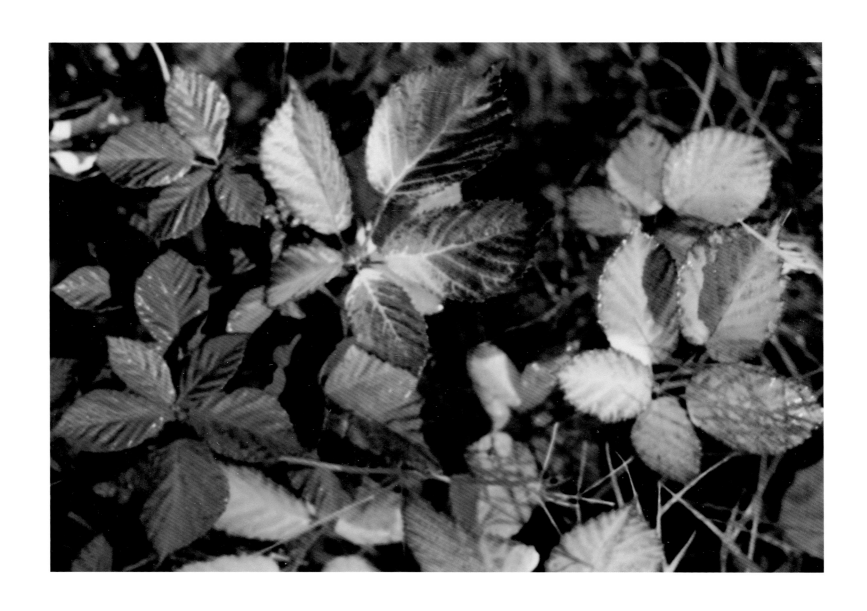

原野系列（十）　WILD-PLAIN　SERIES（10）　約1980年代　攝影　12.6×17.6cm

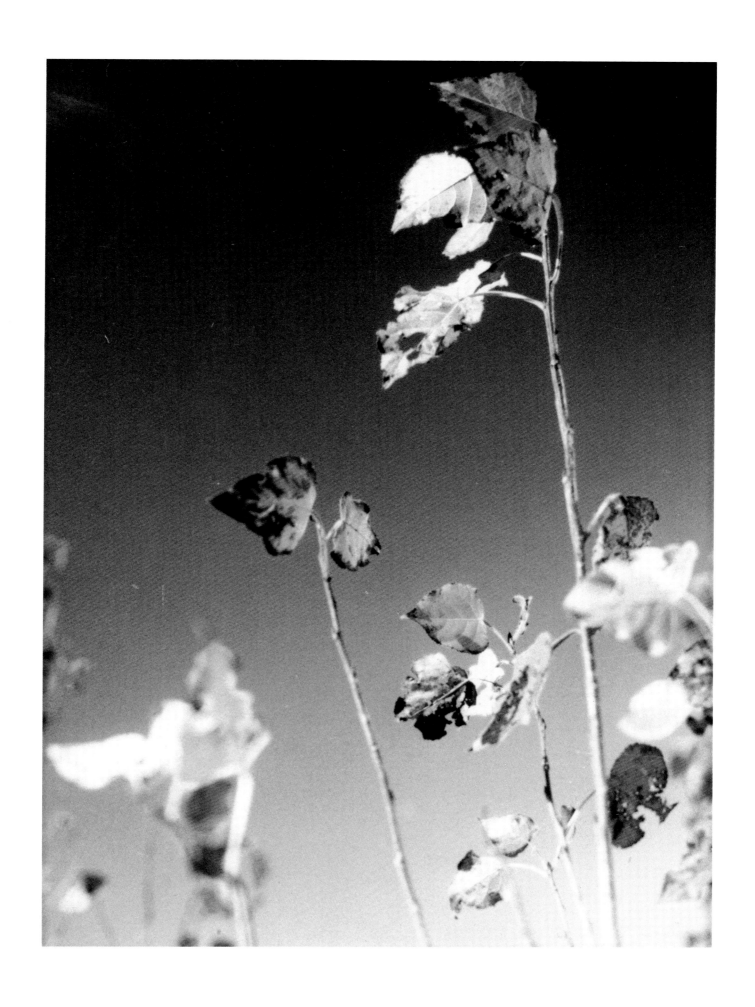

原野系列（十一）　WILD-PLAIN　SERIES（11）　約1980年代　攝影　11.4×8.2cm

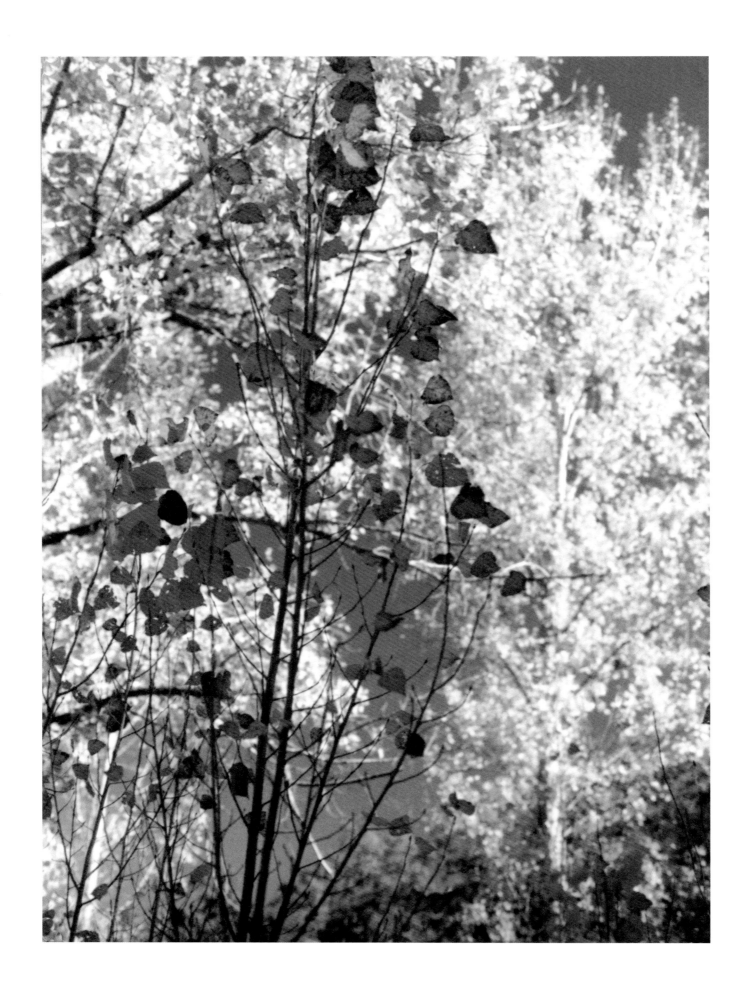

原野系列（十二） WILD-PLAIN SERIES（12） 約1980年代 攝影 12.4×8.8cm

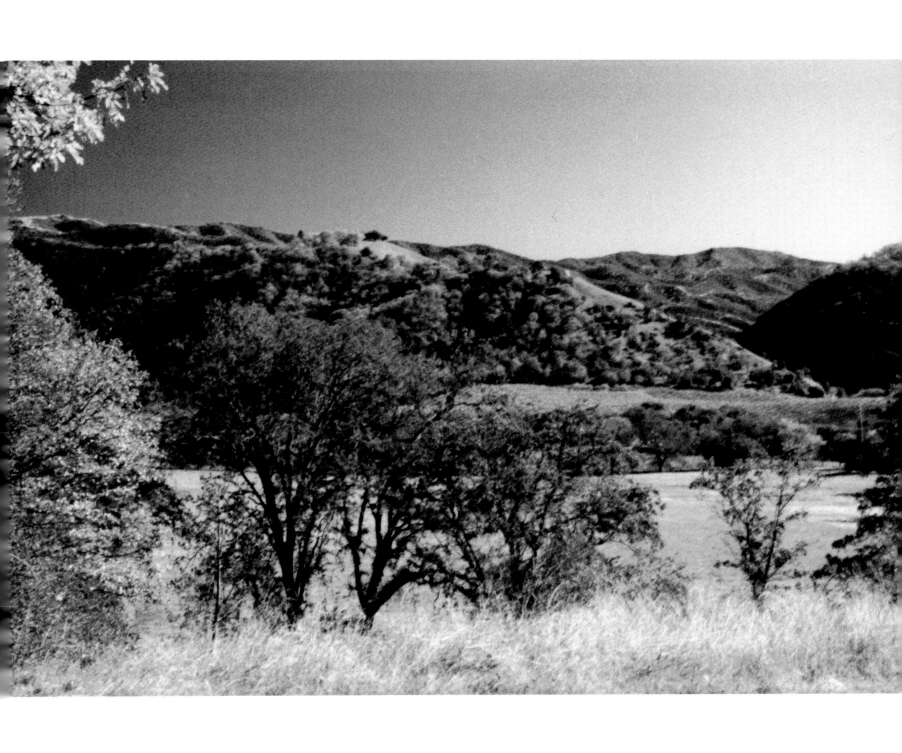

原野系列（十三）　WILD-PLAIN SERIES（13）　約1980年代　攝影　8.2×11.4cm

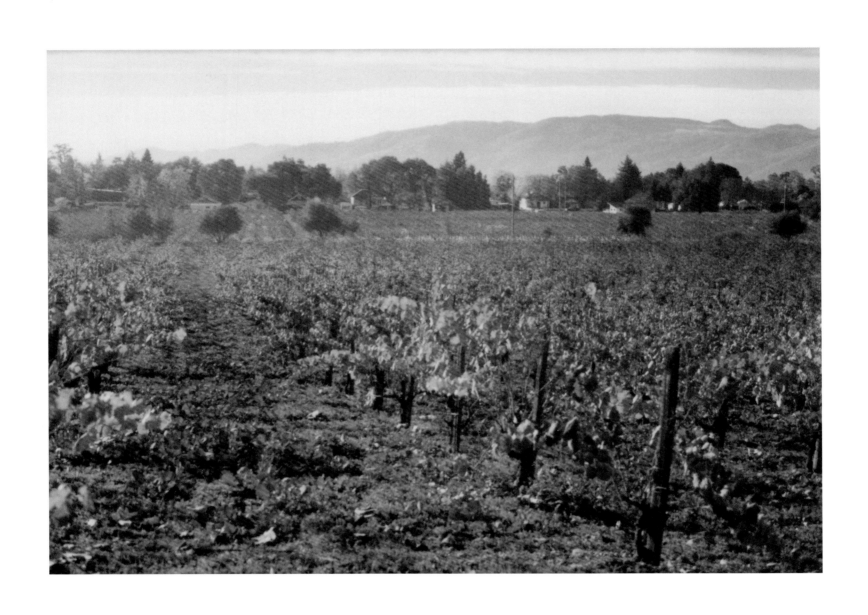

原野系列（十四） WILD-PLAIN SERIES（14） 約1980年代 攝影 8.2×11.4cm

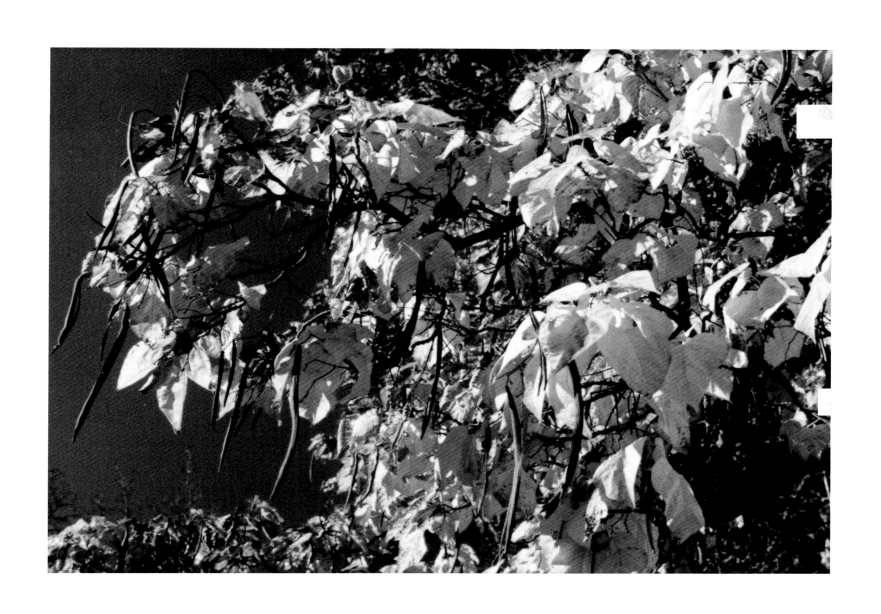

原野系列（十五）　WILD-PLAIN　SERIES（15）　約1980年代　攝影　8.2×11.4cm

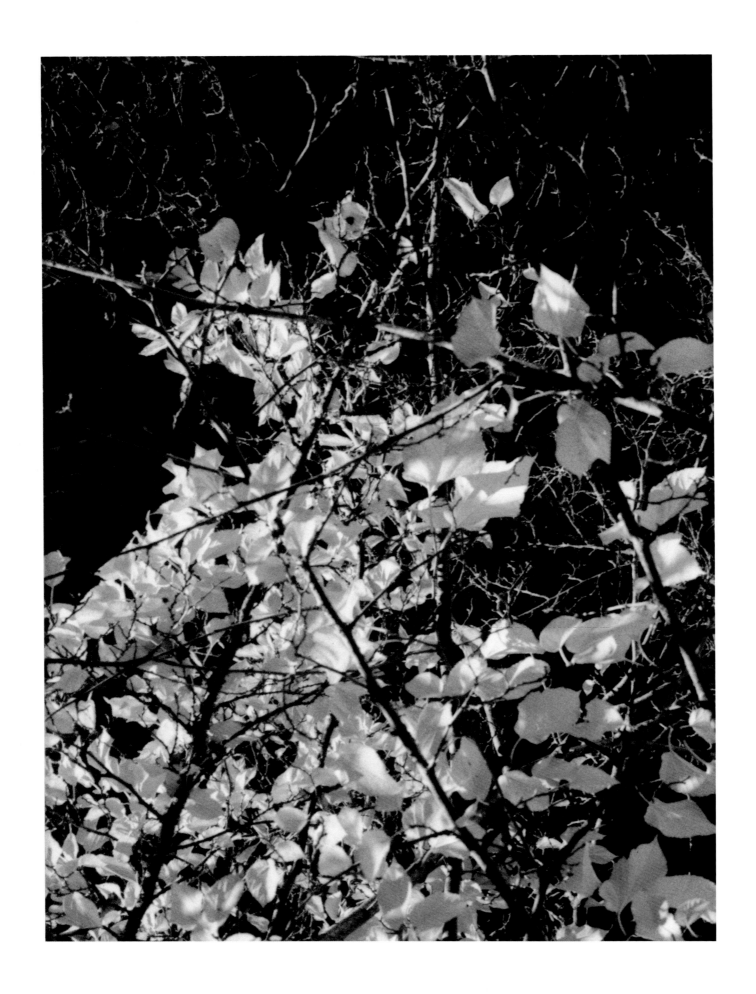

原野系列（十六）　WILD-PLAIN　SERIES（16）　約1980年代　攝影　11.4×8.2cm

蘭花　ORCHID　約1980年代　攝影　25.4×20.3cm（右頁圖）

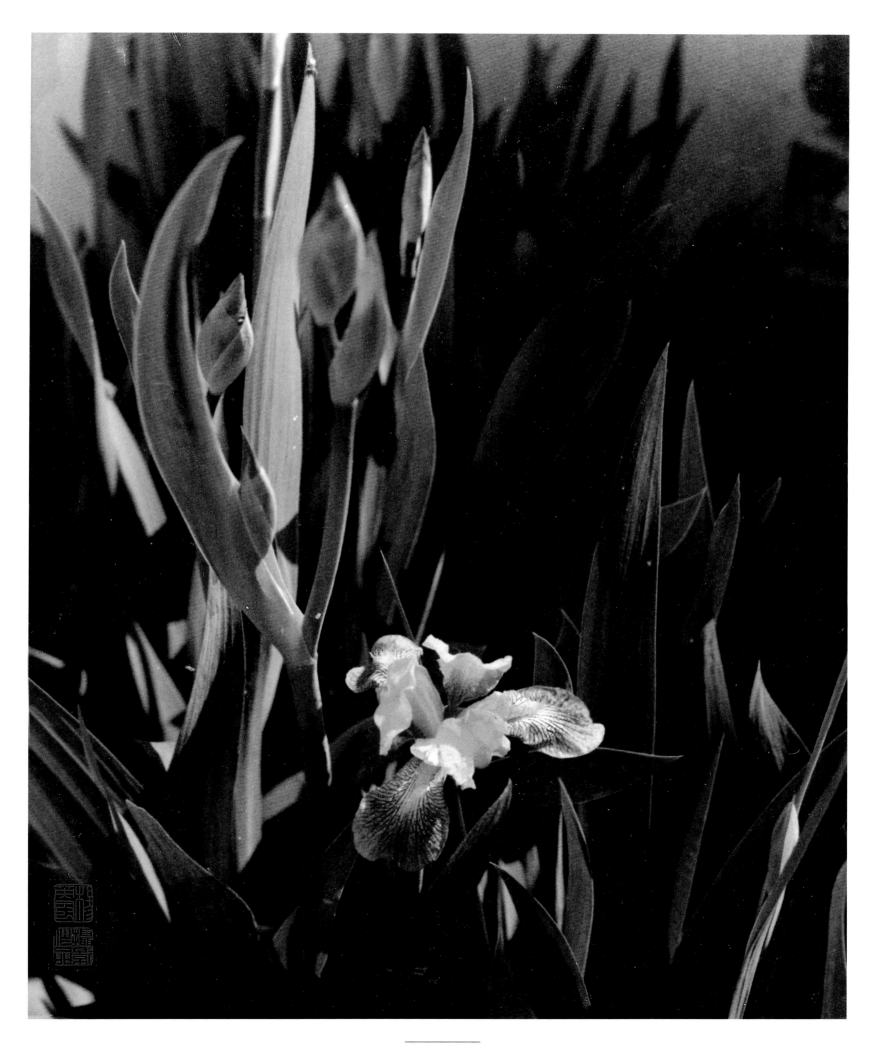

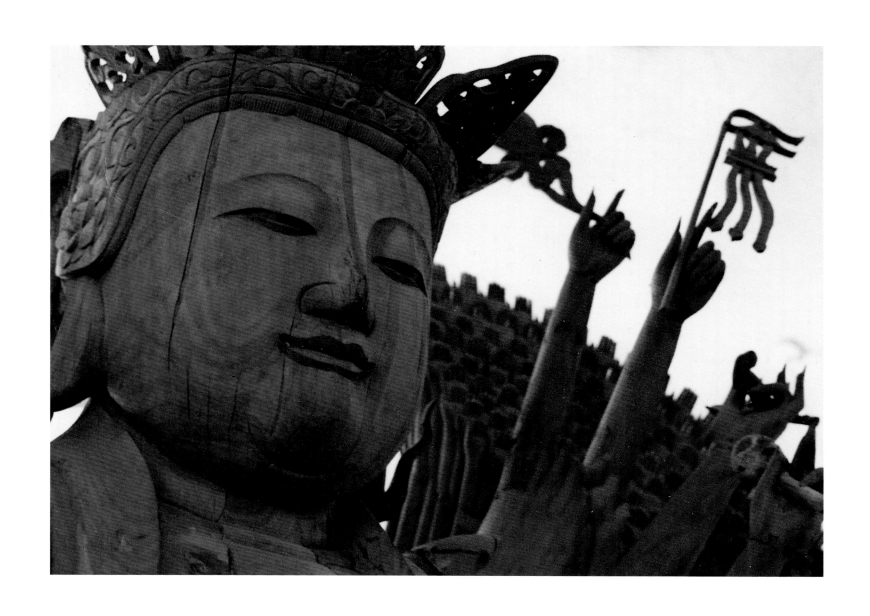

萬佛城系列(一) THE CITY OF TEN THOUSAND BUDDHAS SERIES(1) 約1980年代 攝影 12.4×17.6cm

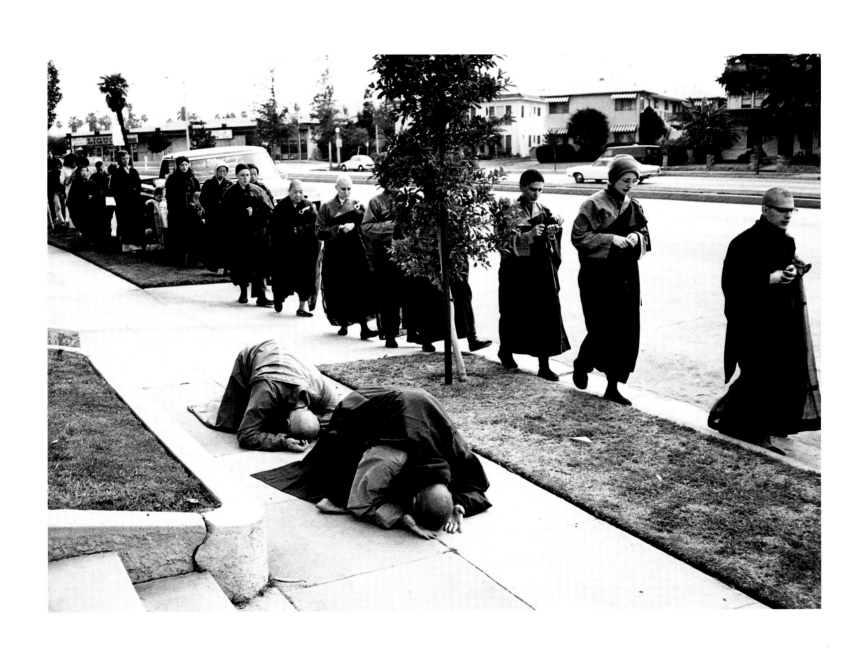

萬佛城系列(二)　THE CITY OF TEN THOUSAND BUDDHAS SERIES(2)　約1980年代　攝影　14.7×19.7cm

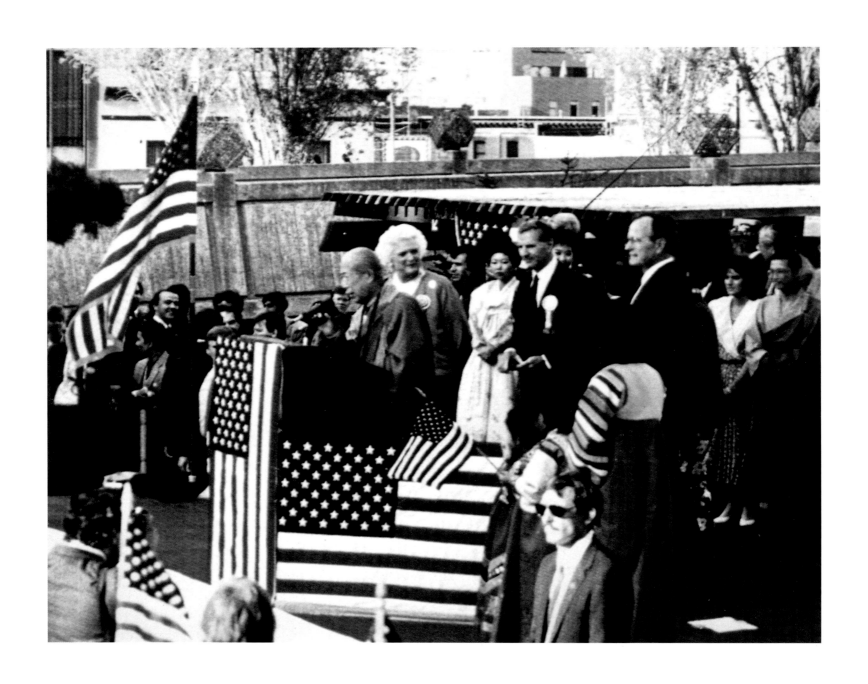

萬佛城系列（三） THE CITY OF TEN THOUSAND BUDDHAS SERIES（3） 約1980年代 攝影 20.7×25.9cm

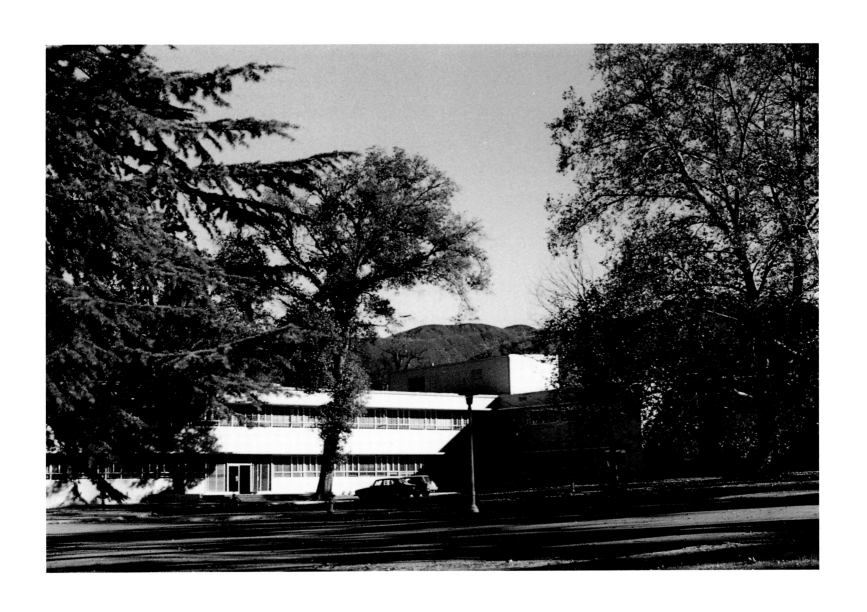

萬佛城系列(四)　THE CITY OF TEN THOUSAND BUDDHAS SERIES(4)　約1980年代　攝影　12.4×17.6cm

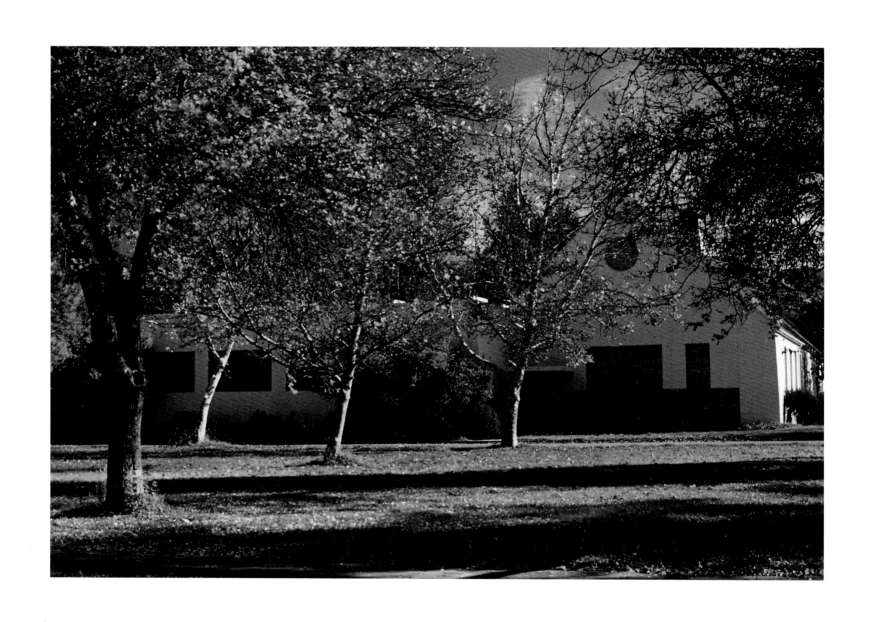

萬佛城系列（五）　THE CITY OF TEN THOUSAND BUDDHAS SERIES（5）　約1980年代　攝影　12.5×17.6cm

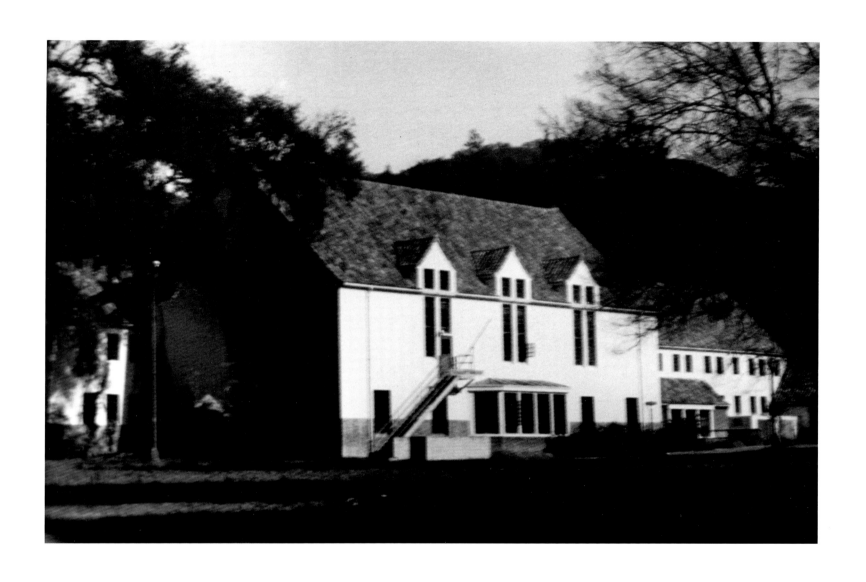

萬佛城系列(六)　THE CITY OF TEN THOUSAND BUDDHAS SERIES(6)　約1980年代　攝影　25.3×30.5cm

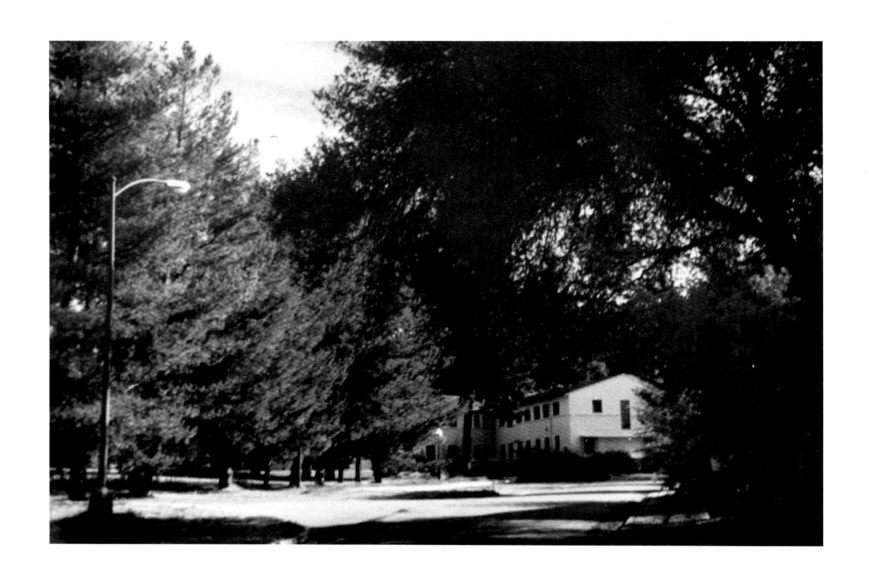

萬佛城系列（七）　THE CITY OF TEN THOUSAND BUDDHAS SERIES（7）　約1980年代　攝影　20.6×30.5cm

萬佛城系列（八）　THE CITY OF TEN THOUSAND BUDDHAS SERIES（8）　約1980年代　攝影　30.5×20.7cm（右頁圖）

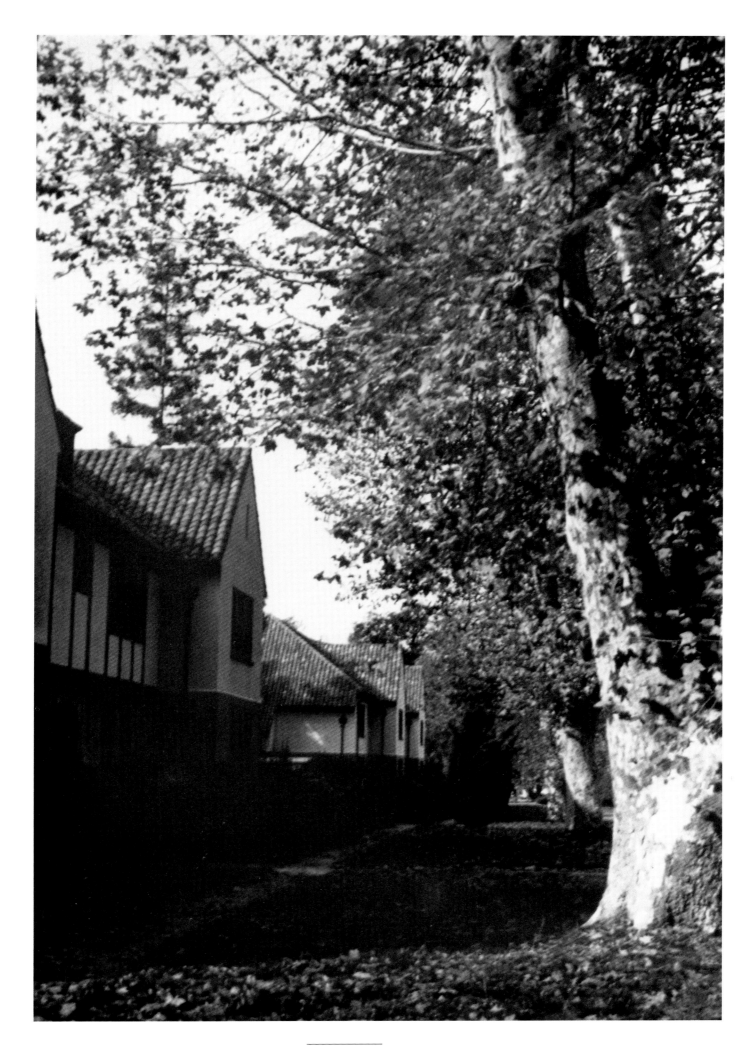

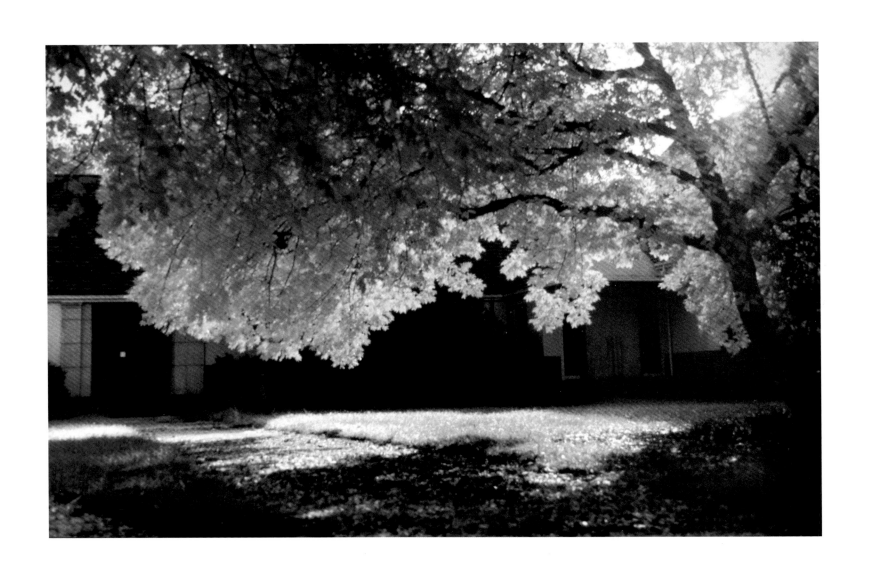

萬佛城系列(九)　THE CITY OF TEN THOUSAND BUDDHAS SERIES(9)　約1980年代　攝影　30.5×20.4cm

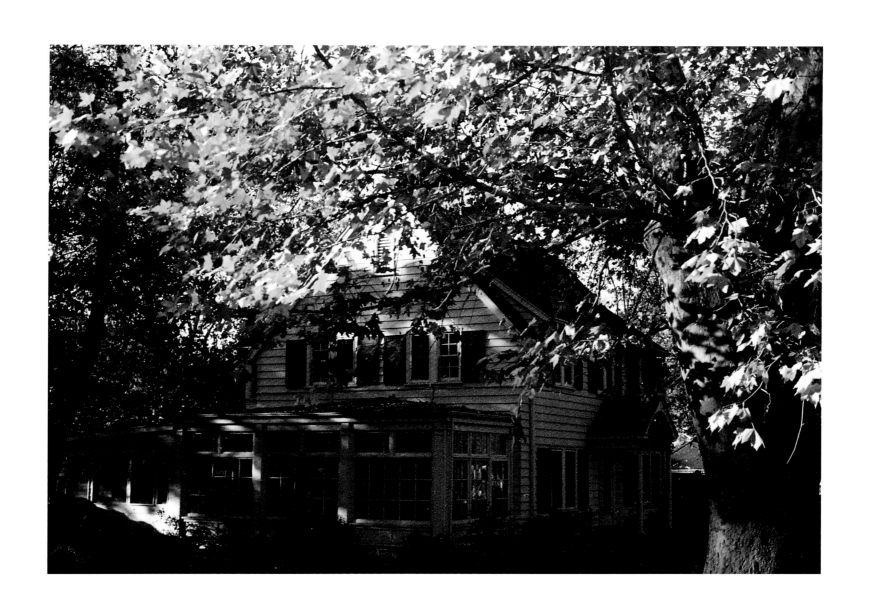

萬佛城系列（十）　THE CITY OF TEN THOUSAND BUDDHAS SERIES（10）　約1980年代　攝影　12.5×17.6cm

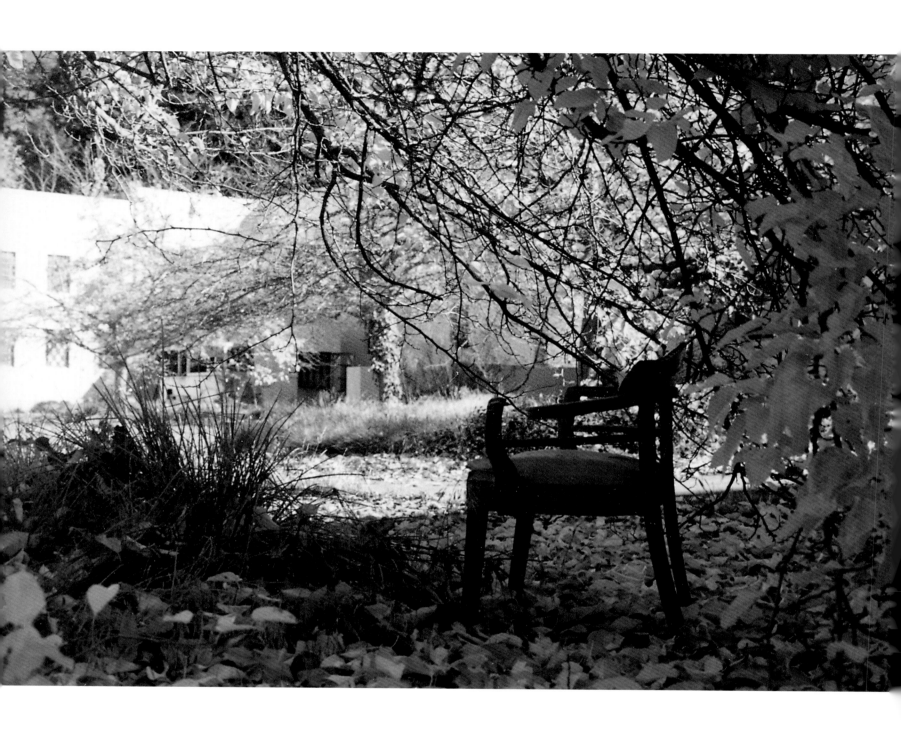

萬佛城系列（十一） THE CITY OF TEN THOUSAND BUDDHAS SERIES（11） 約1980年代 攝影 12.4×17.5cm

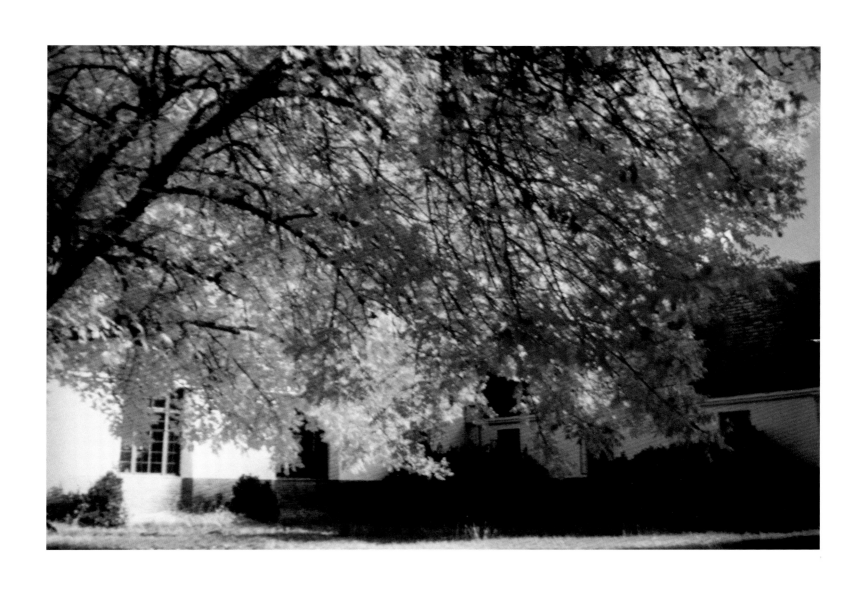

萬佛城系列（十二）　THE CITY OF TEN THOUSAND BUDDHAS SERIES（12）　約1980年代　攝影　20×30.5cm

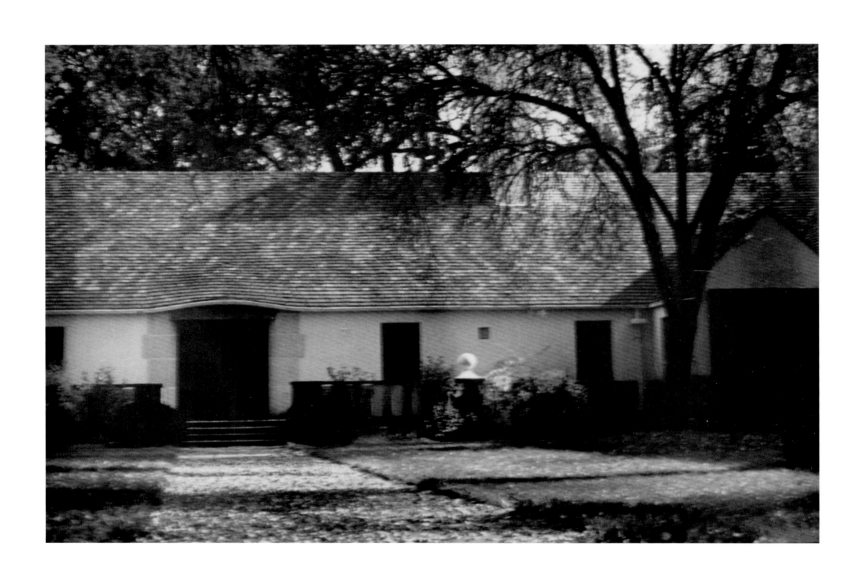

萬佛城系列（十三）　THE CITY OF TEN THOUSAND BUDDHAS SERIES（13）　約1980年代　攝影　20.6×30.5cm

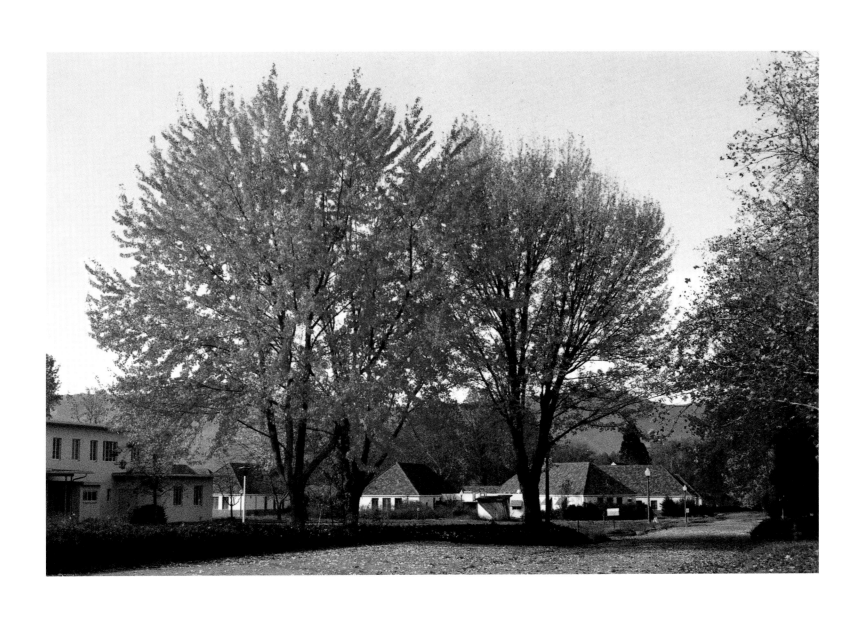

萬佛城系列（十四）　THE CITY OF TEN THOUSAND BUDDHAS SERIES（14）　約1980年代　攝影　21.5×30.5cm

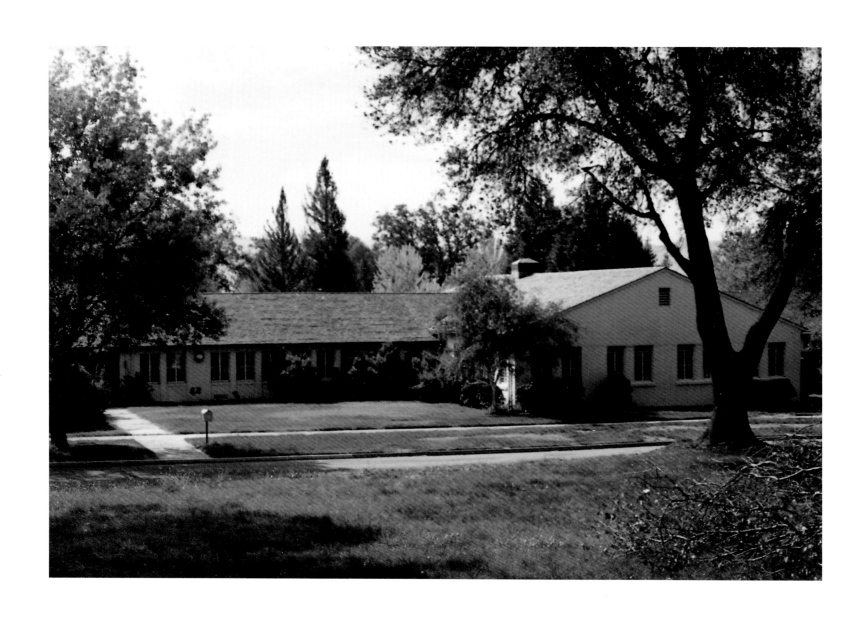

萬佛城系列（十五）　THE CITY OF TEN THOUSAND BUDDHAS SERIES（15）　約1980年代　攝影　12.5×17.6cm

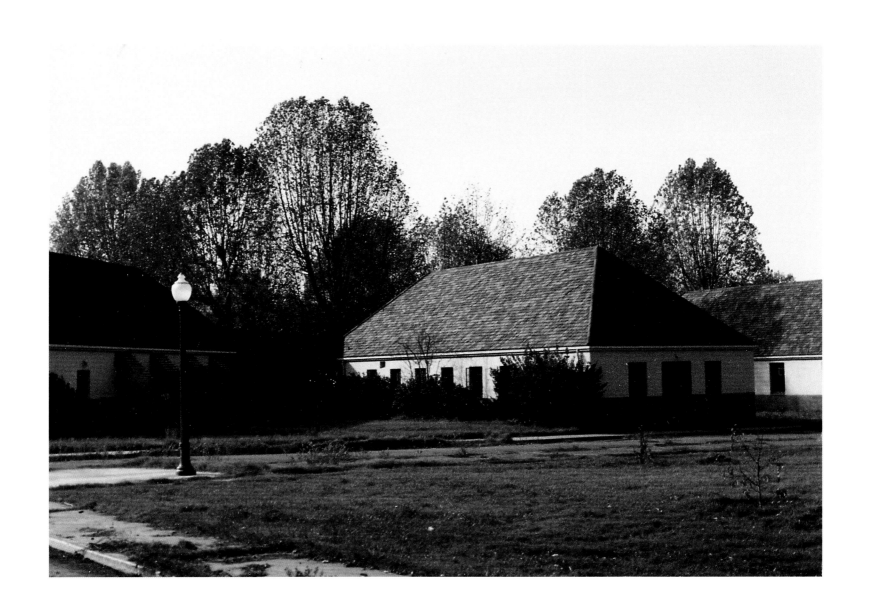

萬佛城系列（十六） THE CITY OF TEN THOUSAND BUDDHAS SERIES（16） 約1980年代　攝影　12.5×17.6cm

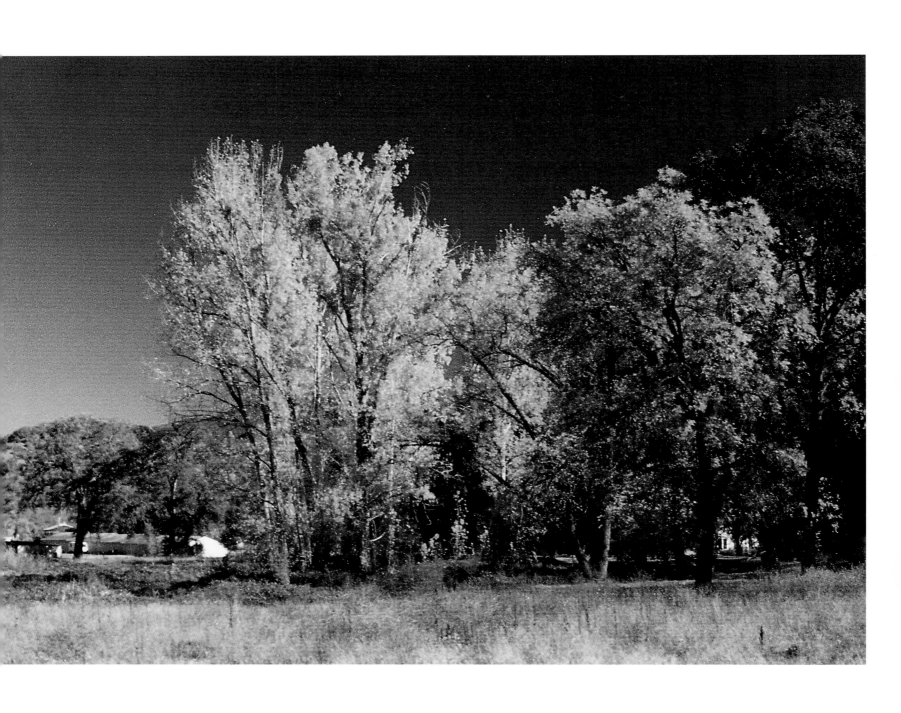

萬佛城系列（十七）　THE CITY OF TEN THOUSAND BUDDHAS SERIES（17）　約1980年代　攝影　12.5×17.5cm

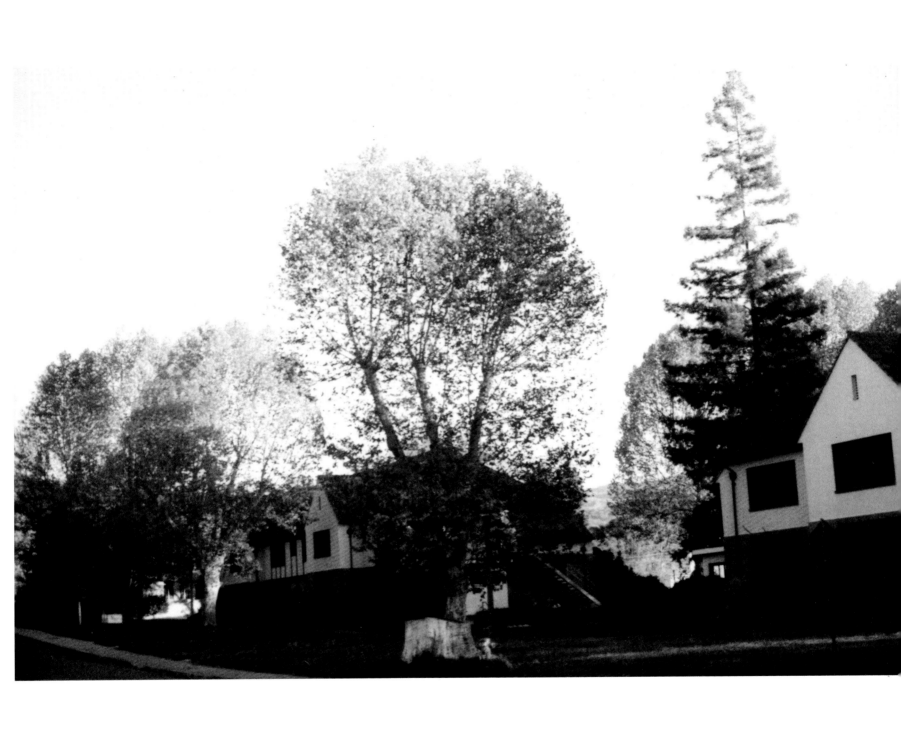

萬佛城系列（十八） THE CITY OF TEN THOUSAND BUDDHAS SERIES（18） 約1980年代 攝影 8.2×11.4cm

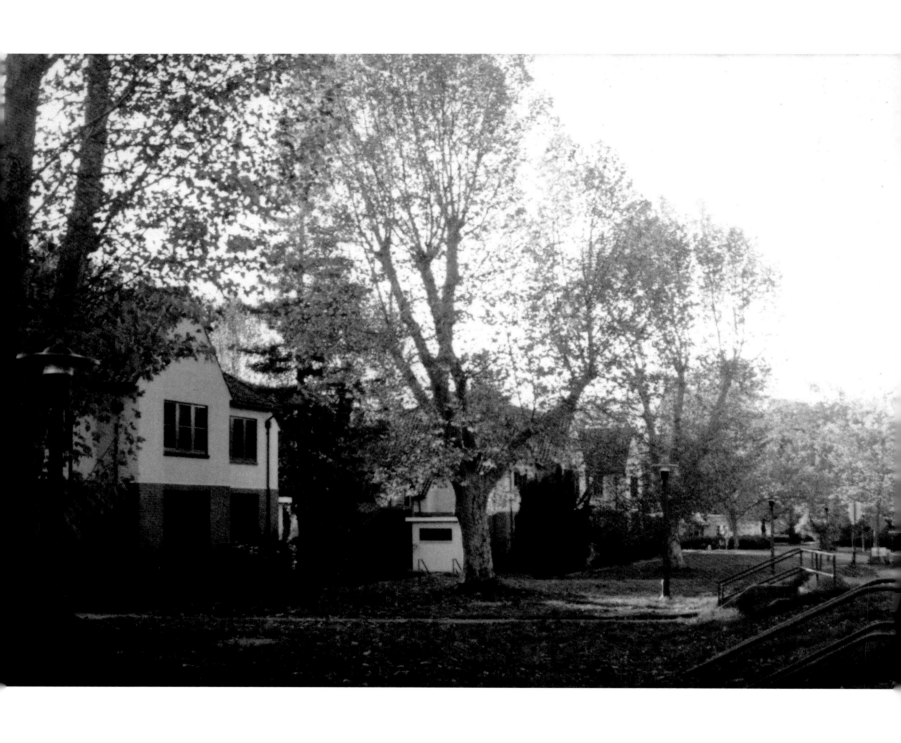

萬佛城系列（十九）　THE CITY OF TEN THOUSAND BUDDHAS SERIES（19）　約1980年代　攝影　8.2×11.4cm

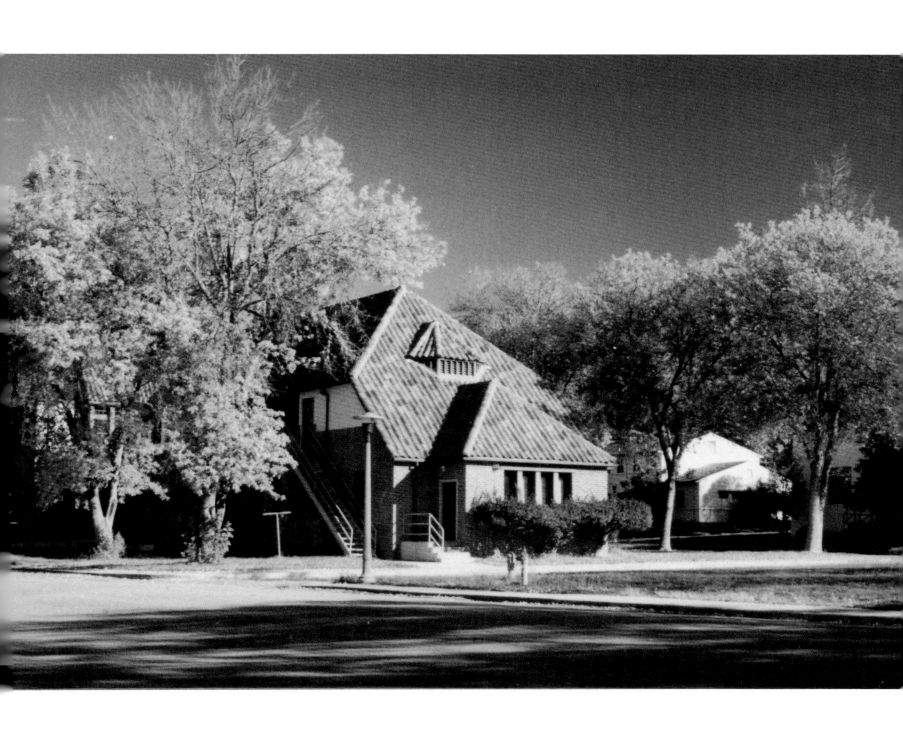

萬佛城系列（二十）　THE CITY OF TEN THOUSAND BUDDHAS SERIES（20）　約1980年代　攝影　8.2×11.4cm

萬佛城系列（二十一） THE CITY OF TEN THOUSAND BUDDHAS SERIES（21） 約1980年代　攝影　8.2×11.4cm

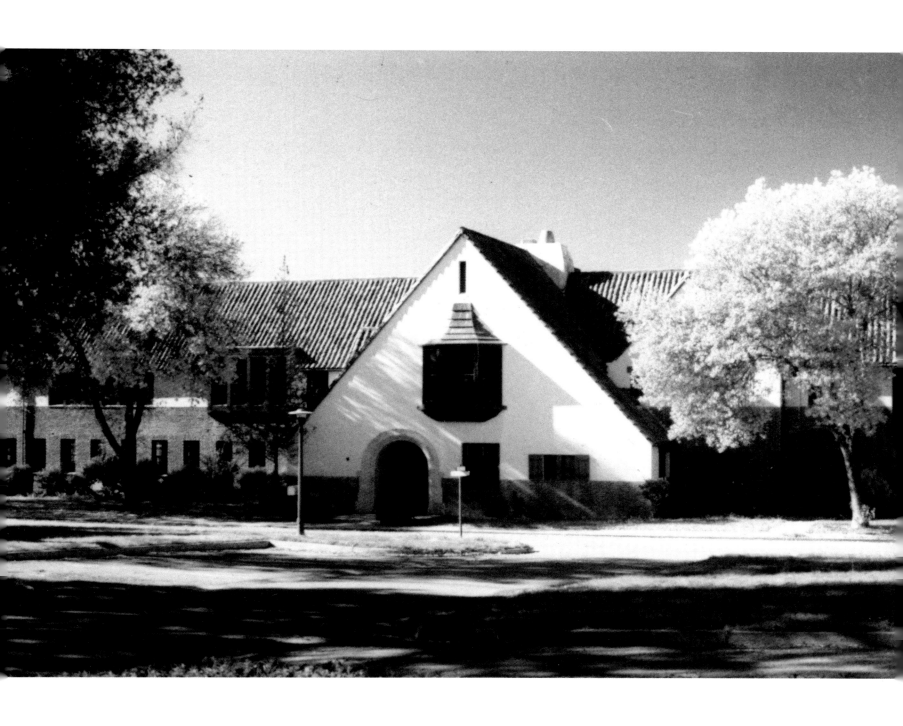

萬佛城系列（二十二）　THE CITY OF TEN THOUSAND BUDDHAS SERIES（22）　約1980年代　攝影　8.2×11.4cm

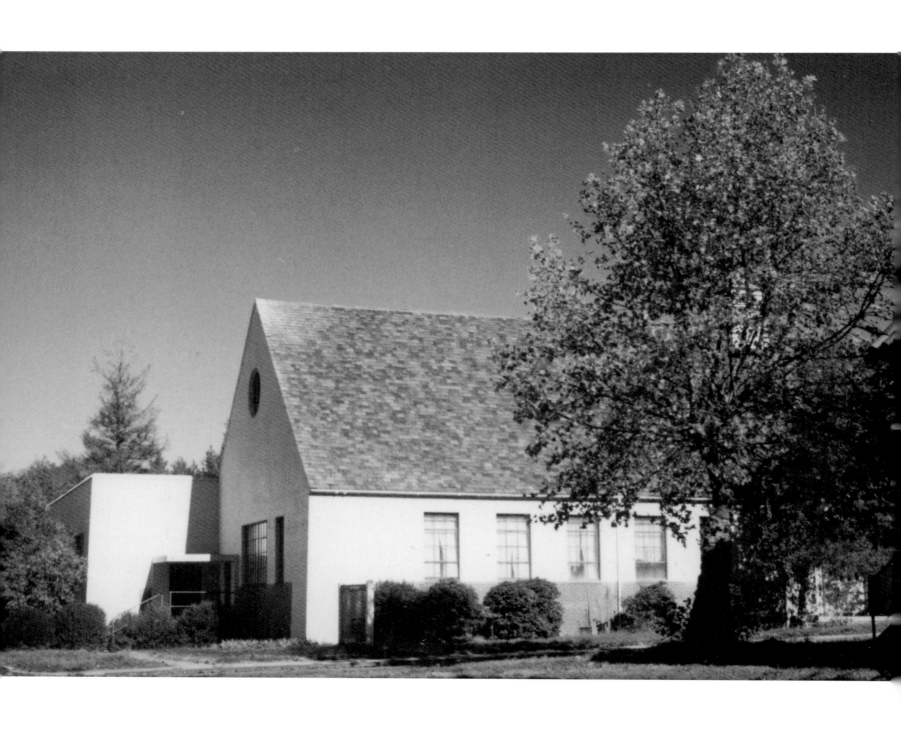

萬佛城系列（二十三）　THE CITY OF TEN THOUSAND BUDDHAS SERIES（23）　約1980年代　攝影　8.2×11.4cm
萬佛城系列（二十四）　THE CITY OF TEN THOUSAND BUDDHAS SERIES（24）　約1980年代　攝影　11.4×8.2cm（右頁圖）

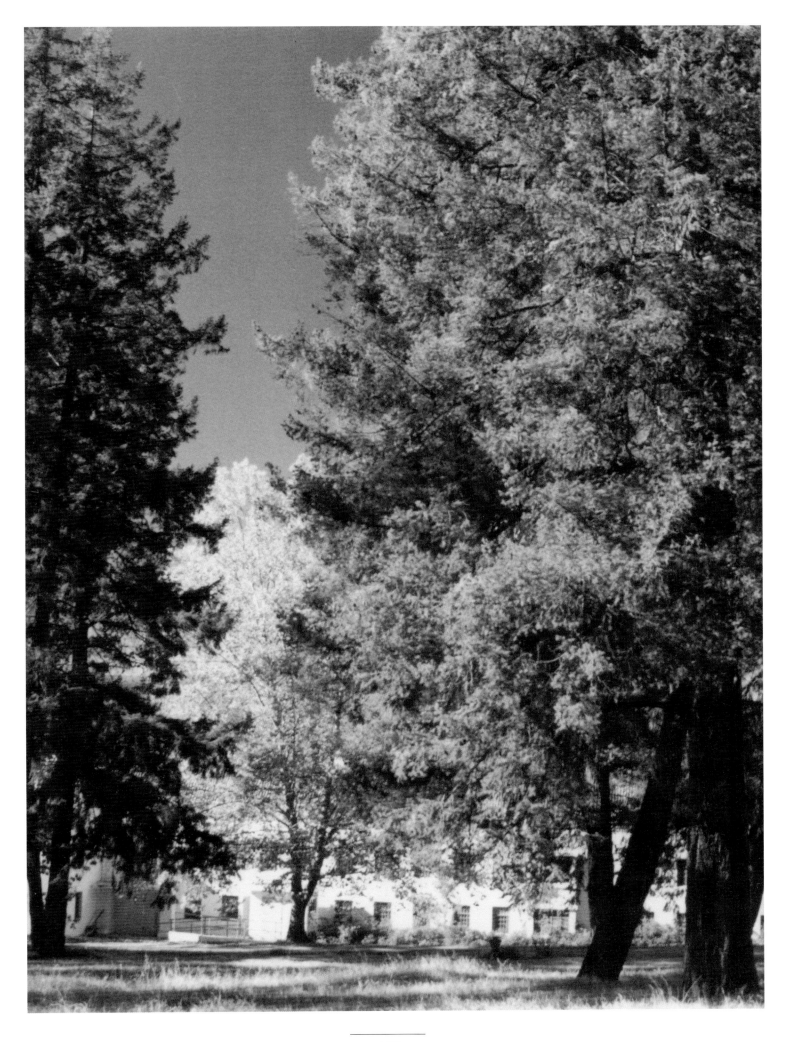

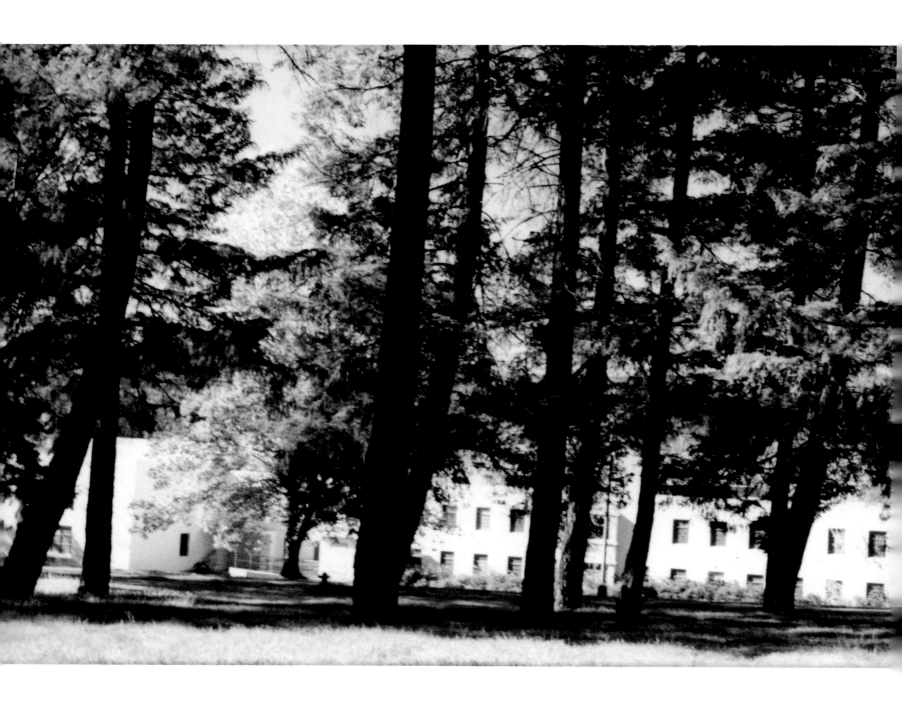

萬佛城系列（二十五）　THE CITY OF TEN THOUSAND BUDDHAS SERIES（25）　約1980年代　攝影　8.2×11.4cm

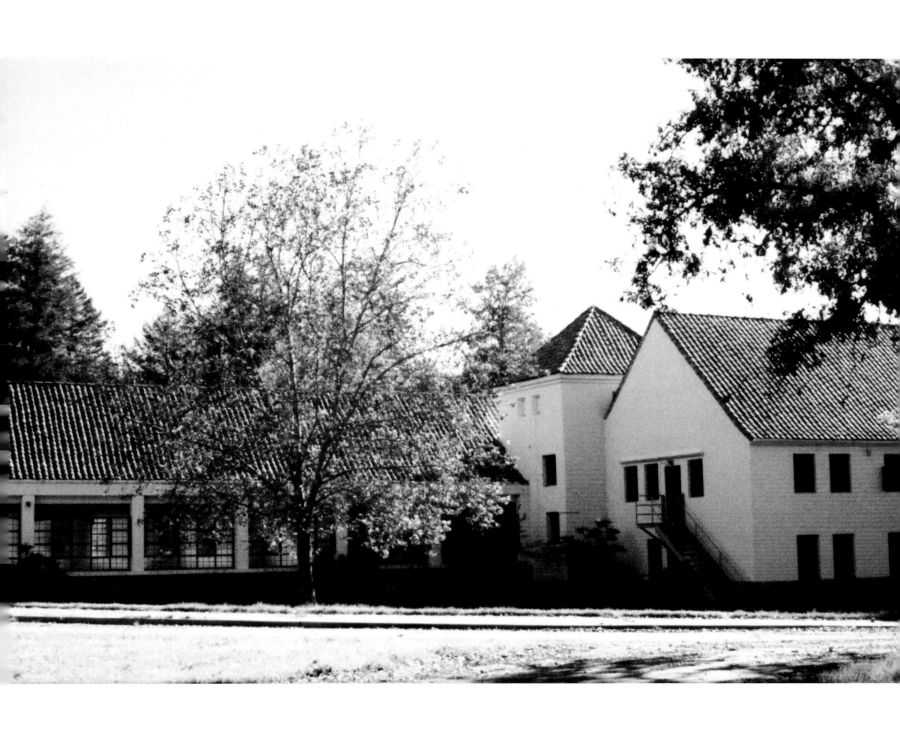

萬佛城系列（二十六）　THE CITY OF TEN THOUSAND BUDDHAS SERIES（26）　約1980年代　攝影　8.2×11.4cm

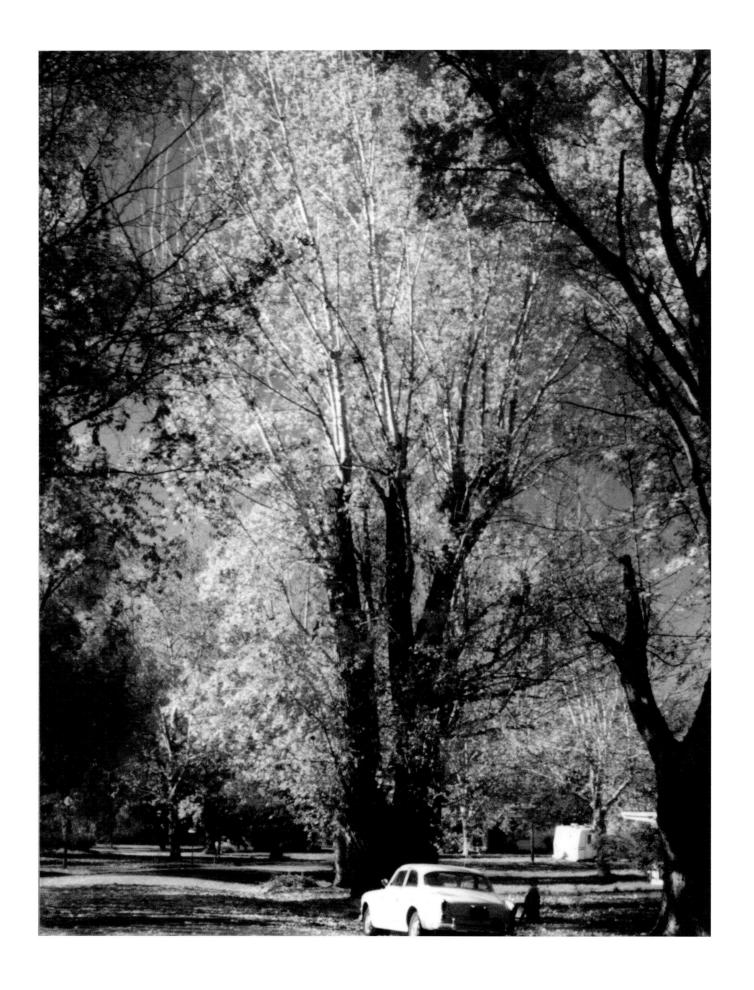

萬佛城系列（二十七）　THE CITY OF TEN THOUSAND BUDDHAS SERIES（27）　約1980年代　攝影　11.4×8.2cm
萬佛城系列（二十八）　THE CITY OF TEN THOUSAND BUDDHAS SERIES（28）　約1980年代　攝影　25.3×17.5cm(右頁圖)

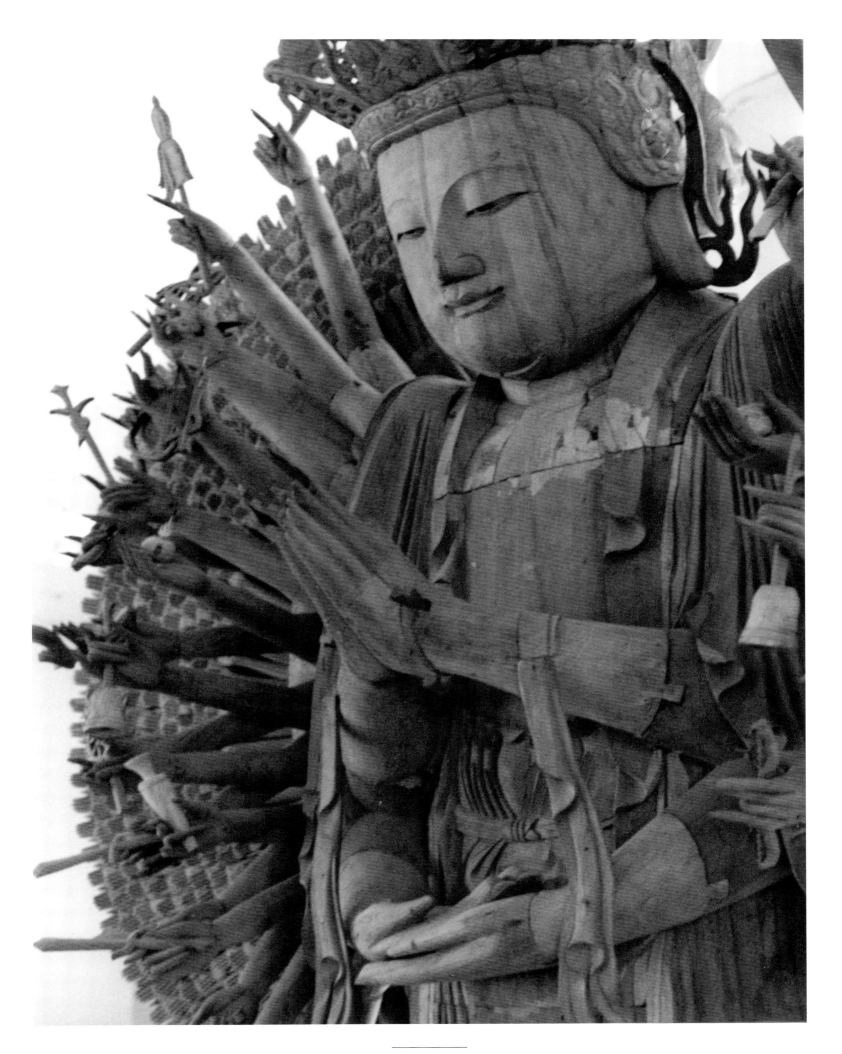

參考圖版
List of Illustration

作品名稱後有＊記號者，表示此作原缺名稱，此作品名稱係楊英風藝術教育基金會代為命名。

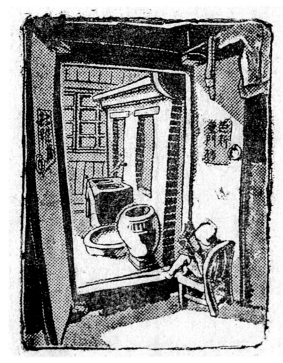

冬日之可愛　LOVELY WINTER DAY
1948　木刻版畫　12 × 10cm
刊於《和平日報》第 4 版，1948 年 11 月 22 日；刊於《學記》第 1 卷第 2 期，頁 7，19506 年月 24 日。另名〔我家〕、〔冬陽〕。

BA155

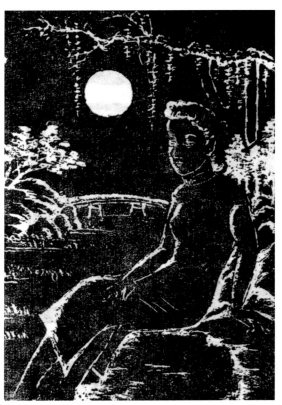

民謠　FOLK SONG　1953　木刻版畫　尺寸未詳
刊於《豐年》第 3 卷第 18 期，夾頁副刊，1953 年 9 月 15 日。

BA156

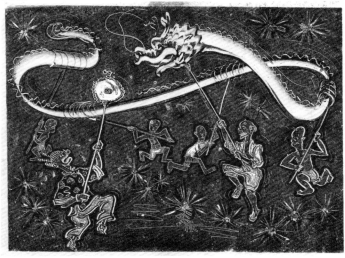

光復節　RETROCESSION DAY
1951　玻璃版畫　25 × 33.2cm
刊於《豐年》第 1 卷第 8 期，頁 11，1951 年 11 月 1 日。

BA157

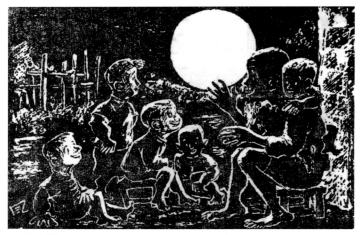

鄉下童聲　CHILDREN IN THE COUNTRY
1953　木刻版畫　尺寸未詳
刊於《豐年》第 3 卷第 18 期，夾頁副刊，1953 年 9 月 15 日。

BA158

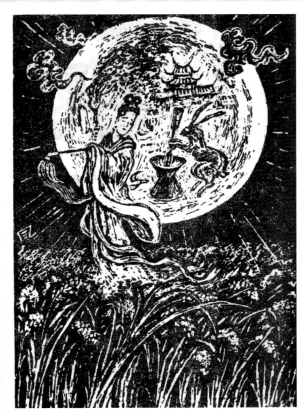

好中秋好晚稻　HARVEST AT MID-AUTUMN FESTIVAL
1953　木刻版畫　尺寸未詳
刊於《豐年》第3卷第18期，夾頁副刊，1953年9月15日。

BA159

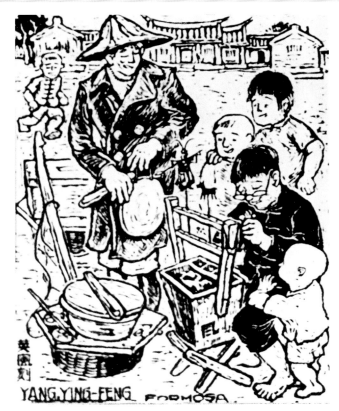

捏麵人　DOUGH DOLLS
1953　木刻版畫　尺寸未詳

BA160

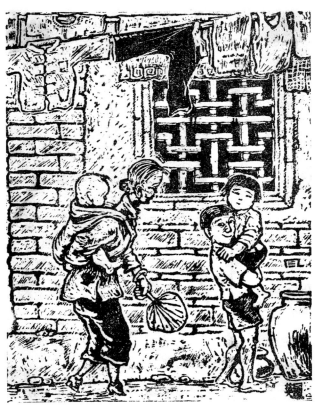

搖子歌　LULLABY　1953　木刻版畫　尺寸未詳
刊於《豐年》第3卷第18期，夾頁副刊，1953年9月15日。

BA161

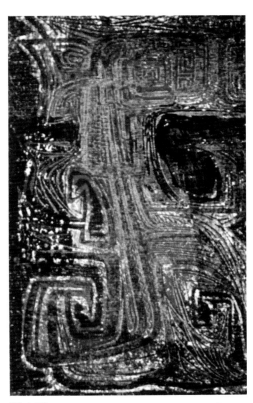

靜中動　TRANQUILITY IN MOTION
1959　木板版畫　尺寸未詳
曾參展1959年國立台灣藝術館「第二屆現代版畫展」；刊於
《良友》第43期，頁28，1960年3月。

BA162

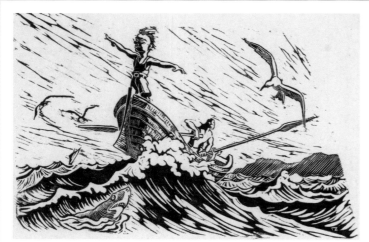

無題　NO TITLE　約1950年代　木刻版畫　17 × 25.5cm

AB163

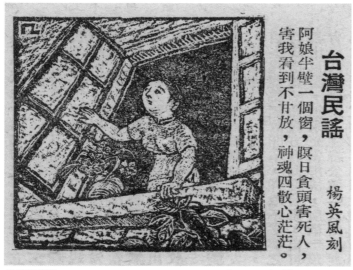

台灣民謠　TAIEAN FOLK SONG　約1950年代
木刻版畫　5 × 5cm

BA165

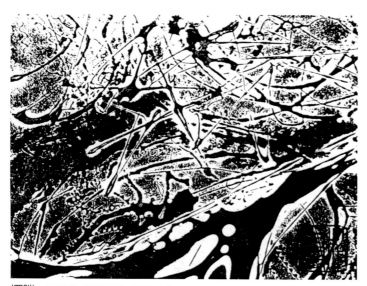

探勝　EXPLORING THE SCENERY
約1960　蔗板版畫　尺寸未詳
刊於《祖國》第30卷第8期，封面，1960年5月23日。

BA166

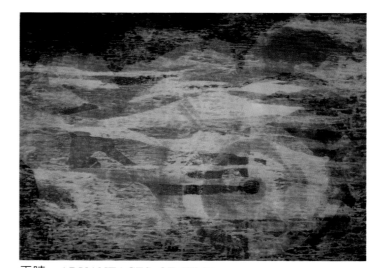

天時　ADVANTAGES OF TIME
1959　木板版畫　尺寸未詳
曾參展1959年國立台灣藝術館「第二屆現代版畫
展」（11月1日-6日）。

BA164

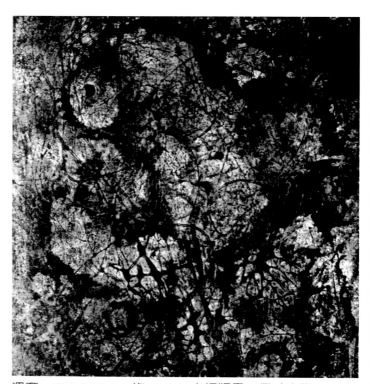

溫育　CULTURE　約1960　木板版畫　尺寸未詳
刊於《國際畫刊》第12期，頁23，1965年1月。

BA167

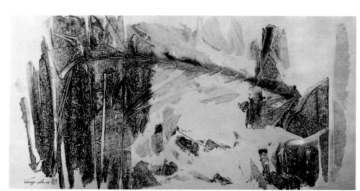

虛靜觀其反覆・羅第 9 號
CHANGES PRESERVED IN SILENCE：R.9
1964 複合版畫 60 × 120cm
義大利國立羅馬現代藝術館
另名〔靈靜觀其反覆〕；刊於《今天畫刊》第 10 期，頁 11，1967 年
7 月。

BA168

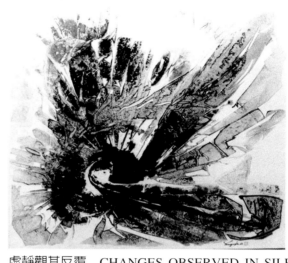

虛靜觀其反覆 CHANGES OBSERVED IN SILENCE
1966 複合版畫 尺寸未詳
曾參展 1966 年羅馬 BILICO 畫廊「楊英風個展」（2 月 3 日 -19 日）。

BA169

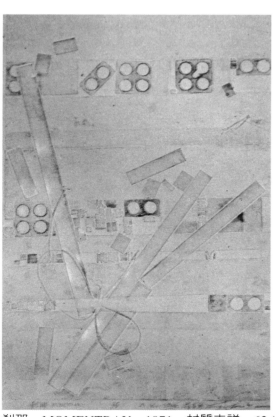

剎那 MOMENTRAY 1971 材質未詳 62 × 48cm
原載《美術雜誌》第 6 期，頁 6，1971 年 4 月。

BA170

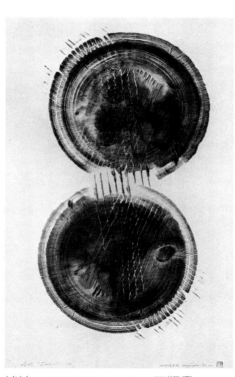

姊妹 SISTERS 1972 石版畫 121 × 72.5cm
曾參展 1977 年中韓現代版畫展；刊於《中韓現代版畫集》頁 39，
1977 年 9 月；《雄獅美術》第 79 期，頁 14，1977 年 9 月；《藝術
家》第 5 卷第 4 期（總號 28），頁 91，1977 年 9 月。

BA171

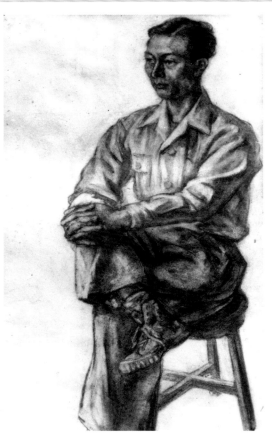

人物素描* PORTRAIT
1949 紙本鉛筆 尺寸未詳

BB051

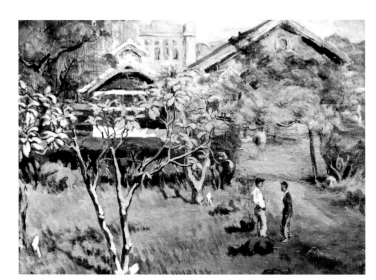

校園 CAMPUS 1949 布上油彩 尺寸未詳
獲1949年「台灣全省第四屆美術展覽會」洋畫部入選。

BB052

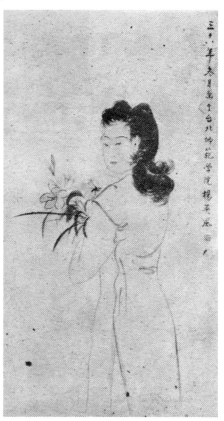

仕女 MADAM 1949 紙本水墨 尺寸未詳
曾參展1950年台北中山堂「台灣省立師範學院藝術系美術展覽
會」；刊於《新生報》星期畫刊，1950年1月1日。

BB053

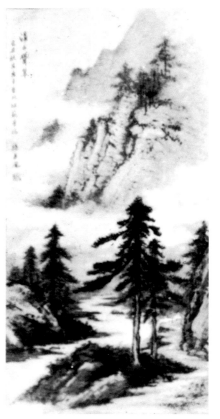

溪山聳翠 SCENERY OF GREEN MOUNTAIN AND CREEK
1949 紙本水墨 尺寸未詳
參展1950年台北中山堂「台灣省立師範學院藝術系美術展覽會」。

BB054

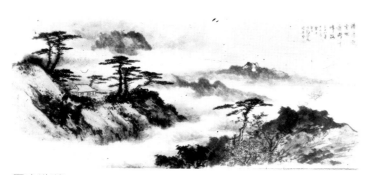

雲山浩蕩　GORGEOUS MOUNTAINS IN THE CLOUDS
約 1949　紙本水墨　尺寸未詳
參展 1950 年台北中山堂「台灣省立師範學院藝術系美術展覽會」。

BB055

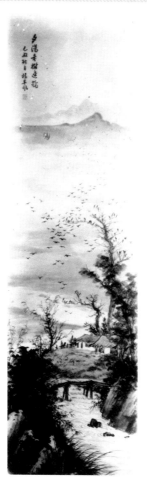

夕陽歸鴉
HOME-BOUNDING CROWS AT
THE SUNSET
1949　紙本水墨　尺寸未詳
參展 1950 年台北中山堂「台灣省立師範
學院藝術系美術展覽會」。

BB056

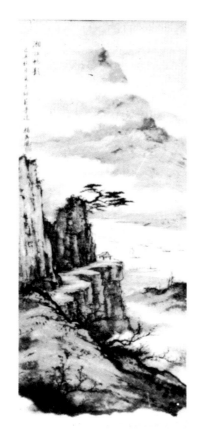

湘江帆影　SAILBOATS ON THE HSIAN RIVER
1949　紙本水墨　尺寸未詳
參展 1950 年台北中山堂「台灣省立師範學院藝術系美術展覽會」。

BB057

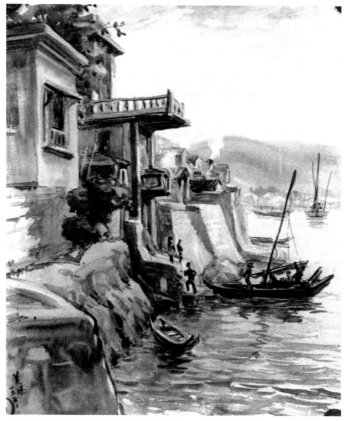

岸邊*　RIVER SIDE　1950　紙本水彩　尺寸未詳

BB058

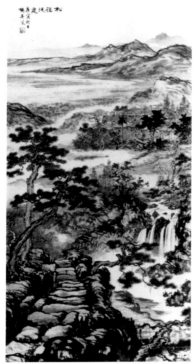

松徑流泉　RUNNING SPRING AND THE PATH THROUGH PINE WOODS
1950　紙本水墨　尺寸未詳
獲1950年「台灣全省第五屆美術展覽會」入選。

BB059

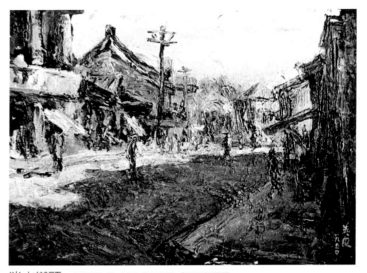

淡水街頭　THE DAN-SHUI STREET
1950　布上油彩　尺寸未詳
另名〔街景〕。

BB060

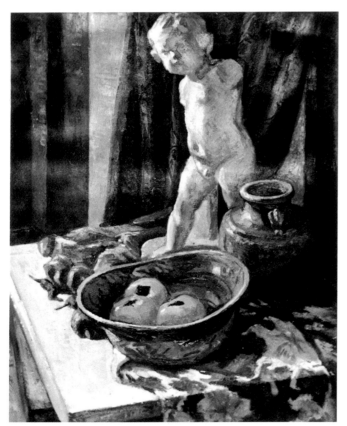

靜物　STILL LIFE　1950　布上油彩　尺寸未詳
獲1950年「台灣全省第五屆美術展覽會」西洋畫部入選。

BB061

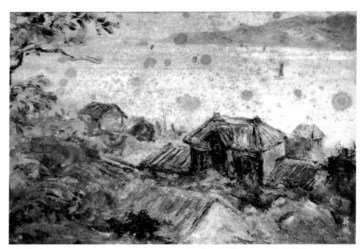

淡水*　DAN-SHUI　1951　布上油彩　尺寸未詳

BB062

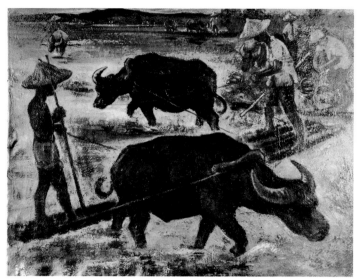

曉耕　TILLING IN EARLY MORNING
1951　布上油彩　尺寸未詳
獲1952年「自由中國美術展覽會」入選；刊於《自由中國美術選集》，頁55，1952年2月25日初版，台北：廿十世紀社。另名〔春耕〕。

BB063

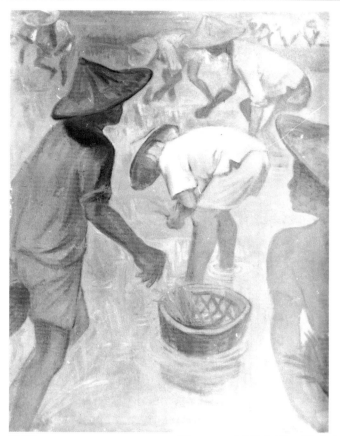

春霞　SPRING CLOUDS　約1952　材質未詳　尺寸未詳
獲1952年「台灣全省第七屆美術展覽會」入選。

BB064

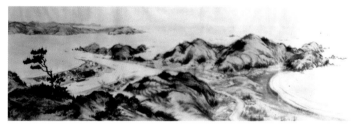

漁村　FISHING VILLAGE　約1952　水墨　尺寸未詳
獲1952年「台灣全省第七屆美術展覽會」國畫部主席獎第三名。

BB065

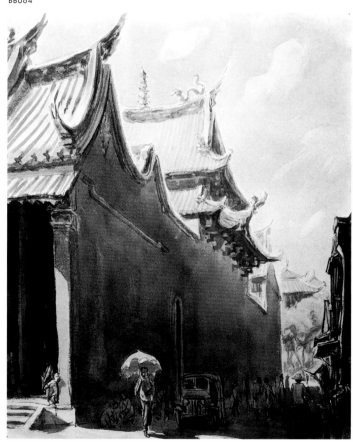

台南武廟　GENERAL KUAN'S TEMPLE IN TAINAN
1957　紙本水彩　尺寸未詳

BB066

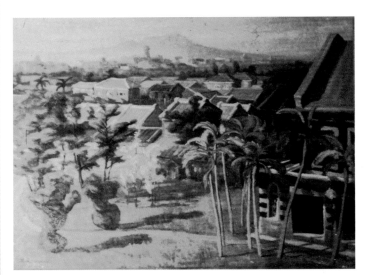

暮色* DUSK 約 1950 年代 紙本水彩 尺寸未詳

BB067

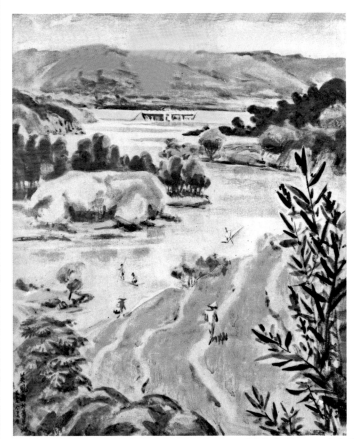

青草湖 GREEN GRASS LAKE 1957 紙本水彩 尺寸未詳
刊於《豐年》第 7 卷第 18 期，封面，1957 年 9 月 16 日。

BB068

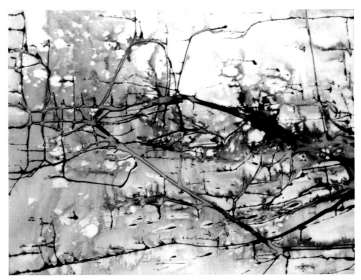

春 SPRING 約 1959 紙本水彩 尺寸未詳
曾參展 1959 年國立台灣藝術館「聯合西畫展」（10 月 17 日 -26 日）。

BB069

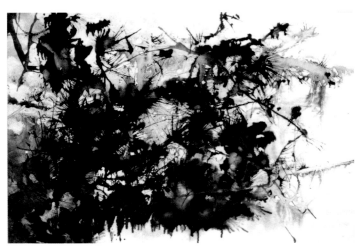

夏 SUMMER 約 1959 紙本水彩 尺寸未詳
曾參展 1959 年國立台灣藝術館「聯合西畫展」（10 月 17 日 -26 日）。

BB070

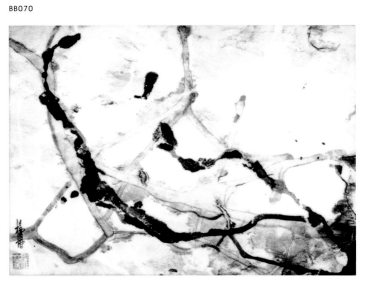

秋 AUTUMN 約 1959 紙本水彩 尺寸未詳
曾參展 1959 年國立台灣藝術館「聯合西畫展」（10 月 17 日 -26 日）。

BB071

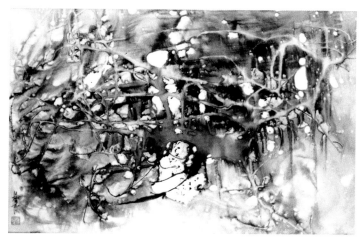

冬　WINTER　約 1959　紙本水彩　尺寸未詳
曾參展 1959 年國立台灣藝術館「聯合西畫展」（10 月 17 日 -26 日）。

BB072

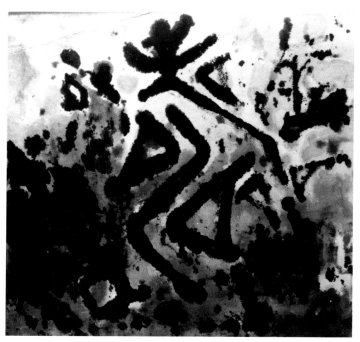

抽象繪畫60-02*　ABSTRACT　PAINTING　60-02
約 1960 年代　紙本水墨　尺寸未詳

BB075

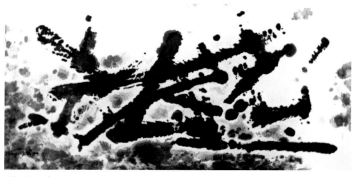

逆流而上　COUNTER-CURRENT
約 1960 年代　紙本水墨　尺寸未詳
曾參展 1962 年國立歷史博物館「現代繪畫赴美展覽預展」（5 月 22 日 -
27 日）；刊於《文星》第 56 期，五月畫展選粹，1962 年 6 月 1 日。

BB073

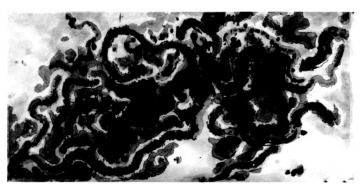

抽象繪畫60-01*　ABSTRACT　PAINTING　60-01
約 1960 年代　紙本水墨　尺寸未詳

BB074

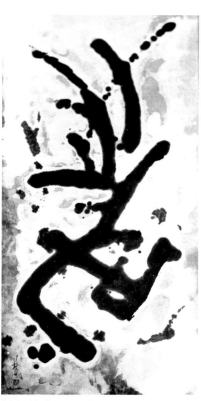

抽象繪畫60-03*　ABSTRACT　PAINTING　60-03
約 1960 年代　紙本水墨　尺寸未詳

BB076

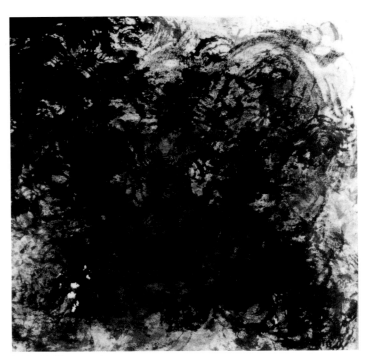

抽象繪畫60-04*　ABSTRACT PAINTING 60-04
約1960年代　紙本水墨　尺寸未詳

BB077

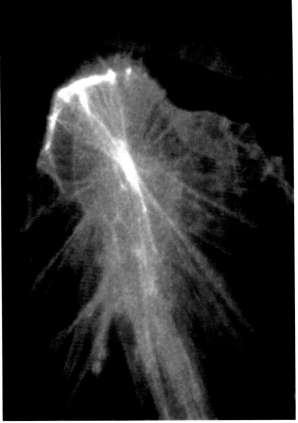

寶鏡　TREASURE MIRROR　1980　雷射
刊於《自然》第4卷第12期，頁12，1980年12月10日。

BC069

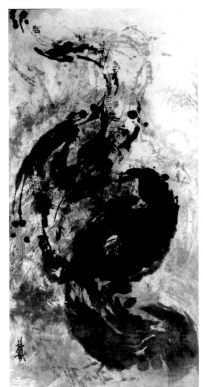

抽象繪畫60-05*　ABSTRACT PAINTING 60-05
約1960年代　紙本水墨　尺寸未詳

BB078

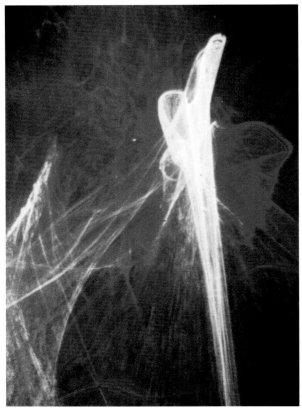

雄辯　ELOQUENCE　1980　雷射
刊於《自然》第4卷第12期，頁12，1980年12月10日。

BC070

圖版目錄
Catalogue

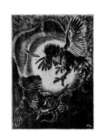

22
相依
刊於《豐年》第1卷第5期，頁11，1951年
9月15日；刊於《鄉曲》第2期，1950年4月
15日。另名〔愛〕、〔蜜語〕。

BA001

23
鬥雞

BA002

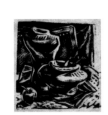
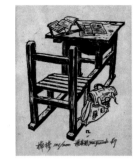

28
靜物
刊於《鄉曲》第2期，目錄，1950年4月15日。
另名〔壺〕。

BA007

29
桌椅

BA008

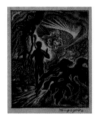
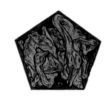

24
探索

BA003

25
邂逅
刊於《鄉曲》第2期，1950年4月15日。
另名〔雞鴨〕、〔兩性〕。

BA004

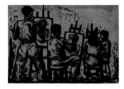
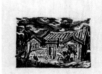

30
繪畫教室

BA009

31
台灣農家
刊於《中央日報》第7版，1950年5月24日；
《鄉曲》創刊號，頁3，1950年6月1日；《豐
年》第1卷第2期，頁2，1951年8月1日；
《豐年》第10卷第1期至12期合訂本封面。
另名〔豔陽天〕

BA010

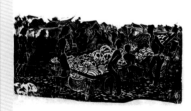

26
青果市場
刊於《中央日報》第7版，1950年6月7日。

BA005

27
校園走廊
另名〔豔陽〕。

BA006

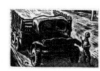
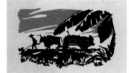

32
國軍
另名〔待令的卡車〕、〔補給〕、〔軍車〕。

BA011

33
歸
刊於《和平日報》第4版，1949年3月17日；
刊於《鄉曲》創刊號，頁7，1950年6月1日。
另名〔牛車破曉〕、〔健腳〕。

BA012

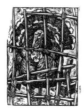
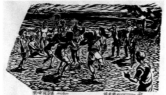

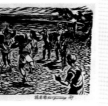

34

掙脫牢籠

刊於《豐年》第1卷第2期，頁6，1951年8月1日；刊於《鄉曲》第2期，1950年4月15日。另名〔火雞〕。

BA013

35

蘭嶼頭髮舞

曾參展1950年台北中山堂「臺灣省立師範學院藝術系美術展覽會」。刊於《中央日報》1950年1月1日，第26版；刊於《中央日報》第7版，1950年6月21日。另名〔青春舞〕。

BA014

40

嬉春

刊於《豐年》第4卷第3期，封面，1954年2月1日。

BA019

41

豐收

獲1952年「自由中國美術展覽會」木刻部入選。刊於《豐年》第3卷第24期，封面，1953年12月16日。另名〔農忙〕。

BA020

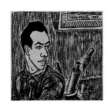

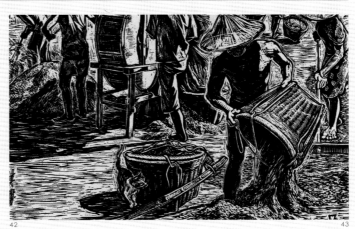

36

自刻像

BA015

37

石龍柱

刊於《鄉曲》創刊號，封面，1950年6月1日。

BA016

42

43

豐收（局部）

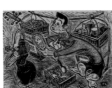

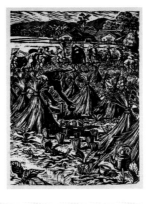

38

賣雜細

獲1952年「自由中國美術展覽會」木刻部入選。刊於《豐年》第1卷第7期，頁11，1951年10月15日；《自由中國美術選集》頁77，1952年2月25日初版。另名〔賣雜世〕。

BA017

39

豐年

BA018

44

間作

刊於《豐年》第5卷第22期，封面，1955年11月16日。另名〔收割〕。

BA021

45

後台

獲1959年「巴西聖保羅雙年展」入選。刊於《豐年》第6卷第6期，頁16，1956年3月16日；《豐年》第6卷第13期至24期合訂本封面。另名〔化裝〕。

BA022

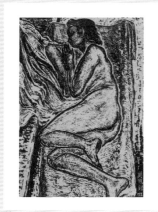 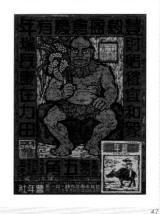

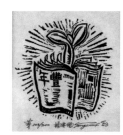

46

假寢

刊於《中外畫報》第31期，1959年2月，香港中日文版；《生活雜誌》第186期，頁14，1959年6月16日。另名〔臥〕、〔寢〕。

BA023

47

神農氏

為《豐年》雜誌製作之海報。

BA024

52

芽

BA029

53

聖誕夜

BA030

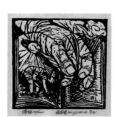 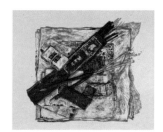

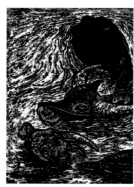 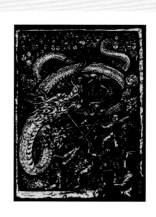

48

插秧

刊於《豐年》第5卷第1期至12期合訂本封面；《祖國》第12卷第10期，封面，1957年12月2日；《木刻選集》頁7，1958年4月，香港：友聯出版社。

BA025

49

糕仔金紙

刊於《豐年》第6卷第2期，頁16，1956年1月16日。

BA026

54

水牛

刊於《豐年》第6卷第5期，封面，1956年3月1日。

BA031

55

舞龍

刊於《豐年》第5卷第4期，封面，1955年2月16日。

BA032

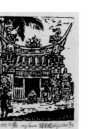

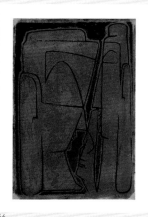 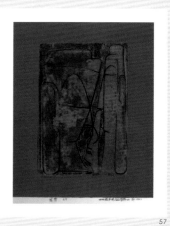

50

悠遊

刊於《豐年》第5卷第1期，頁13，1955年1月1日；《祖國》第12卷第5期，封面，1957年10月28日；《木刻選集》頁6，1958年4月，香港：友聯出版社。
另名〔勤讀〕、〔徜佯〕。

BA027

51

土地公廟

刊於《豐年》第5卷第1期，頁13，1955年1月1日。另名〔虔誠〕。

BA028

56

慈悲（一）

另名〔思古幽情〕、〔上下〕。

BA033

57

慈悲（二）

BA034

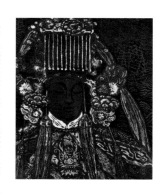

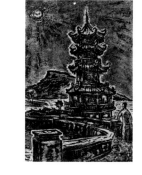

58
媽祖
刊於《豐年》第6卷第9期，封面，1956年5月
1日。

59
春秋閣

BA035

BA036

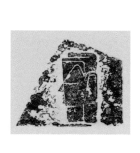

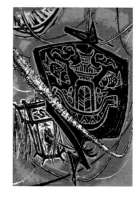

64
英風造佛供養

65
燈

BA041

BA042

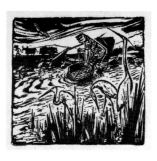

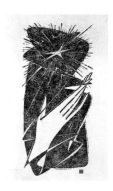

60
浸種
刊於《豐年》第8卷第1期至12期合訂本封面；
《中外畫報》第31期，1959年2月1日，香港
中日文版；《生活雜誌》第186期，頁14，1959
年6月16日。另名〔農村即景〕。

61
藍星
為「藍星詩社」所作。

BA037

BA038

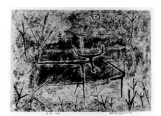

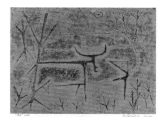

66
力田（一）

67
力田（二）

BA043

BA044

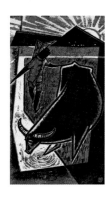

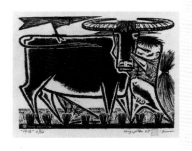

62
日出而作
刊於《豐年》第9卷第1期至12期合訂本封面。

63
伴侶
曾參展1957年教育部「第四次全國美術展覽
會」。刊於《自立晚報》1958年10月6日；
《幼獅》第9卷第2期，頁21，1959年2月；
《豐年》第7卷第13期至24期合訂本封面。
另名〔春牛圖〕。

BA039

BA040

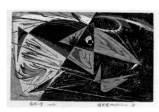

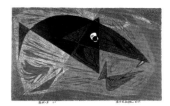

68
漏網之魚（一）

69
漏網之魚（二）

BA045

BA046

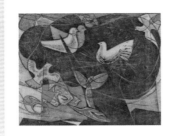
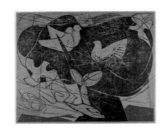

70

71

成長（一）　　　　　　　成長（二）

刊於《第一銀行紀要》封面，1958年2月；
《中外畫報》第31期，1959年2月，香港中日
文版；《幼獅》第9卷第2期，封面，1959年
2月。另名〔展望〕。

BA047　　　　　　　　BA048

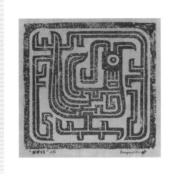
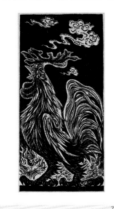

72

73

鳳凰生矣　　　　　　　司晨

　　　　　　　　　　　曾參展1962年越南「西貢第一屆國際美展」。

BA049　　　　　　　　BA050

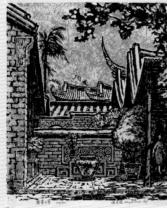
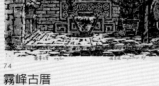

74

75

霧峰古厝　　　　　　　嬉

刊於《詩・散文・木刻》第2期，頁3，1961
年11月1日。另名〔霧峰林家庭院〕。

BA051　　　　　　　　BA052

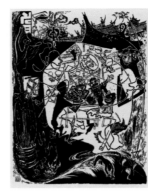

76

77

吃拜拜　　　　　　　　拜拜

刊於《豐年》第5卷第17期，頁16，1955年9
月1日。另名〔拜拜〕。

BA053　　　　　　　　BA054

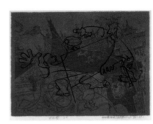

78

79

中元祭　　　　　　　　太空蛋（一）

刊於《藝術雜誌》第3卷第8期，頁15，1962
年6月1日。另名〔宇宙過客〕。

BA055　　　　　　　　BA056

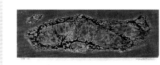

80

81

太空蛋（二）　　　　　太空蛋（三）

BA057　　　　　　　　BA058

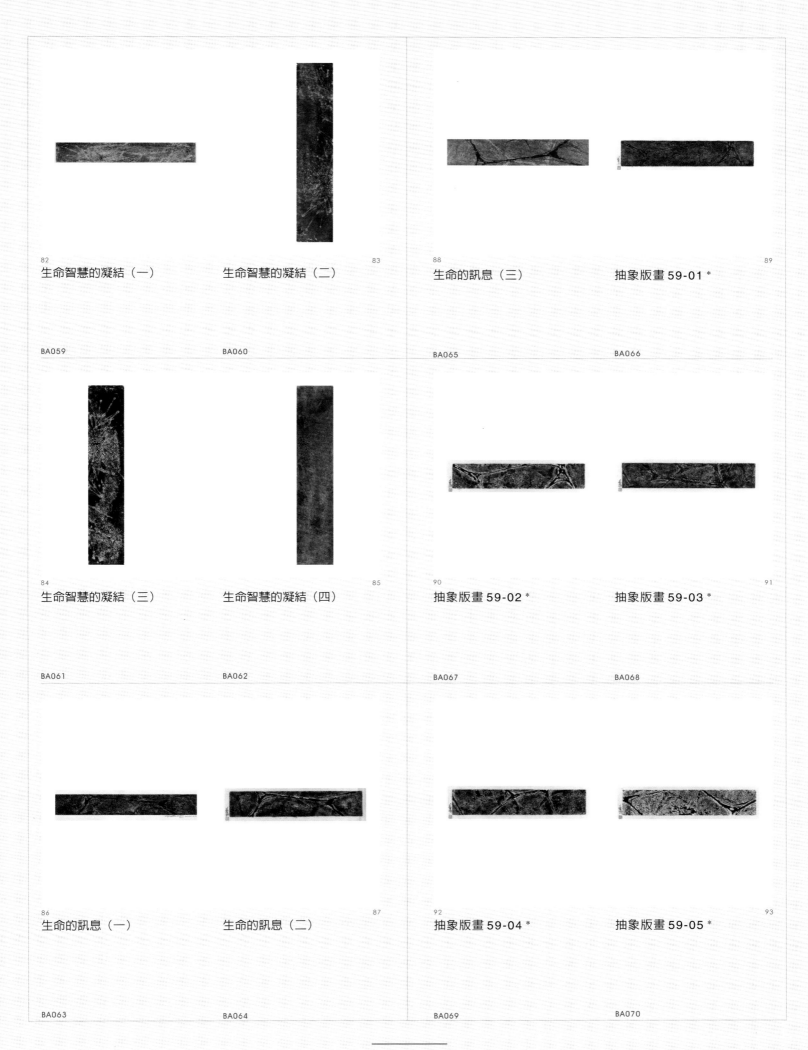

82
生命智慧的凝結（一）

83
生命智慧的凝結（二）

88
生命的訊息（三）

89
抽象版畫 59-01 *

BA059

BA060

BA065

BA066

84
生命智慧的凝結（三）

85
生命智慧的凝結（四）

90
抽象版畫 59-02 *

91
抽象版畫 59-03 *

BA061

BA062

BA067

BA068

86
生命的訊息（一）

87
生命的訊息（二）

92
抽象版畫 59-04 *

93
抽象版畫 59-05 *

BA063

BA064

BA069

BA070

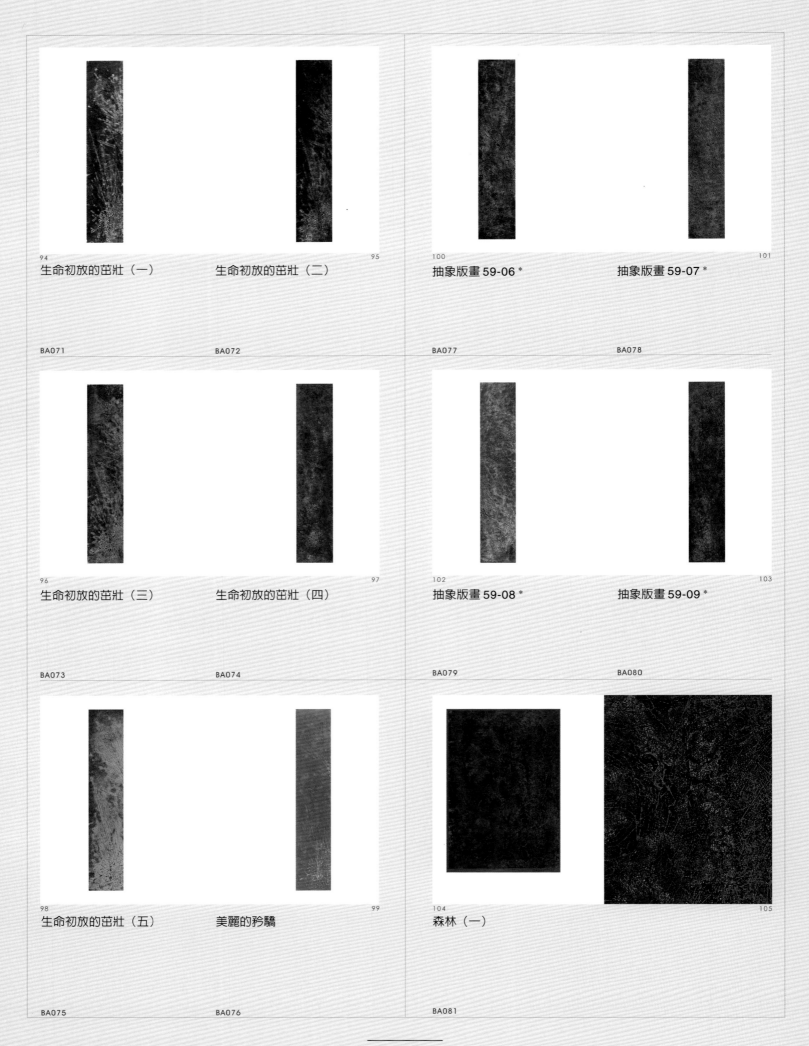

94   95   100   101

生命初放的茁壯（一）   生命初放的茁壯（二）   抽象版畫 59-06 *   抽象版畫 59-07 *

BA071   BA072   BA077   BA078

96   97   102   103

生命初放的茁壯（三）   生命初放的茁壯（四）   抽象版畫 59-08 *   抽象版畫 59-09 *

BA073   BA074   BA079   BA080

98   99   104   105

生命初放的茁壯（五）   美麗的矜驕   森林（一）

BA075   BA076   BA081

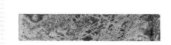

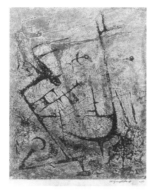

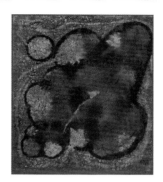

106
不眠之夜

107
雛鳳

刊於《良友》第43期，頁29，1960年3月。

112
抽象版畫 59-11 *

113
抽象版畫 59-12 *

BA082

BA083

BA088

BA089

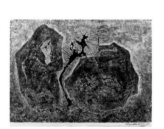

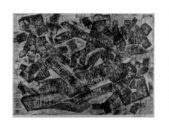

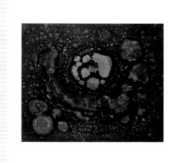

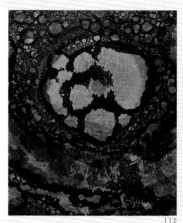

108
文化的起源

109
抽象版畫 59-10 *

獲香港第二屆國際美展銀碟獎。刊於《詩·散文·木刻》第6期，封底，1963年4月15日。相關報導參見《聯合報》第8版，1962年6月26日。

114
金

115

曾參展1959年國立台灣藝術館「第二屆現代版畫展」（11月1日-12日）。刊於《自由青年》第22卷第10期，頁10，1959年11月16日；刊於《良友》第43期，頁29，1960年3月。

BA084

BA085

BA090

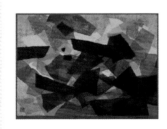

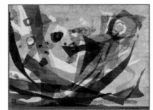

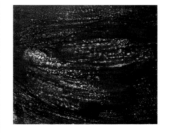

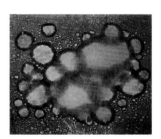

110
豐實的歡欣

111
節慶的喜悅

116
木

117
水

曾參展1959年國立台灣藝術館「第二屆現代版畫展」（11月1日-12日）。

曾參展1959年國立台灣藝術館「第二屆現代版畫展」（11月1日-12日）。

BA086

BA087

BA091

BA092

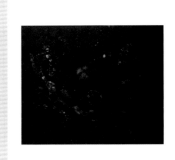 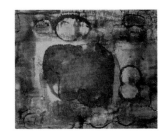 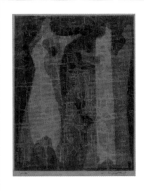 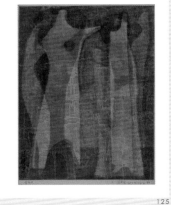

118
火
曾參展 1959 年國立台灣藝術館「第二屆現代版畫展」（11月1日-12日）。

119
土
曾參展 1959 年國立台灣藝術館「第二屆現代版畫展」（11月1日-12日）。

124
人和
曾參展1959年國立台灣藝術館「第二屆現代版畫展」（11月1日-6日）。刊於《攝影新聞》第2版，1959年11月6日。

125
傳教者
曾參展1963年九龍漆咸道雅苑畫廊「台灣‧作品‧畫家‧聯展」（5月1日-5日）。刊於《好望角》第5號，頁1，1963年5月5日。

BA093　　　　　　　BA094　　　　　　　BA099　　　　　　　BA100

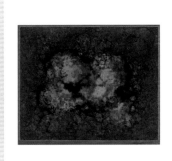 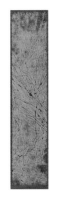 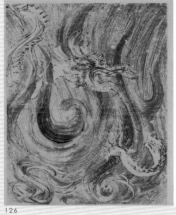

120
抽象版畫 59-13 *

121
抽象版畫 59-14 *

126
龍

127
幼獅

BA095　　　　　　　BA096　　　　　　　BA101　　　　　　　BA102

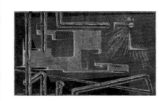 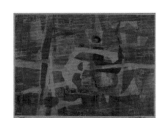 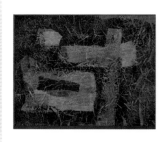 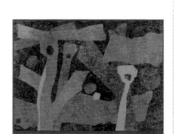

122
自由
曾參展 1959 年巴西現代美術博物館「五屆二年季極端新派之現代藝術國際競賽展覽」。另名〔奔向自由〕。

123
地利
曾參展 1959 年國立台灣藝術館「第二屆現代版畫展」（11月1日-6日）。

128
抽象版畫 60-01 *

129
抽象版畫 60-02 *

BA097　　　　　　　BA098　　　　　　　BA103　　　　　　　BA104

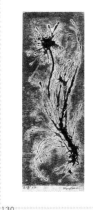
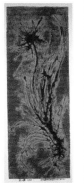
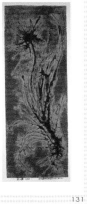
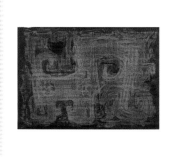
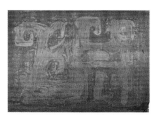

130

花之舞（一）

另名〔火之舞〕。

131

花之舞（二）

另名〔火之舞〕。

136

龍種

137

抽象版畫 62-01 *

BA105

BA106

BA111

BA112

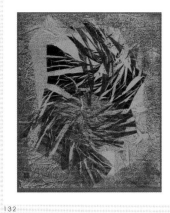

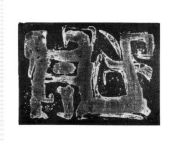
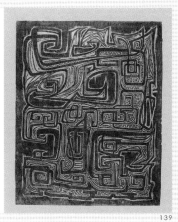

132

時代

刊於《民航公司雙月刊》第 13 卷第 3、4 期，
1960 年 3、4 月。

133

森林（二）

138

抽象版畫 62-02 *

139

抽象版畫 62-03 *

BA107

BA108

BA113

BA114

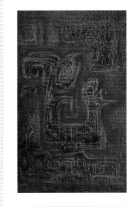
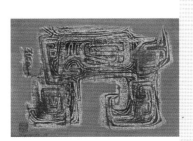
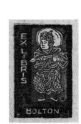

134

鳳凰生矣

135

動中靜

140

飛龍

141

狐狸的詭計

刊於楊寅賓著《狐狸的詭計》，封面。

BA109

BA110

BA115

BA116

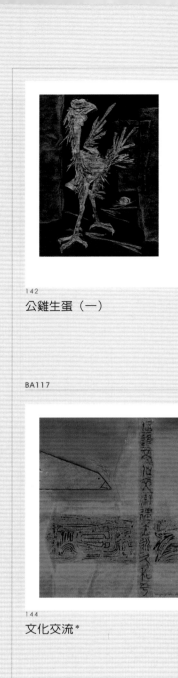

142
公雞生蛋（一）

公雞生蛋（二）
143

BA117

BA118

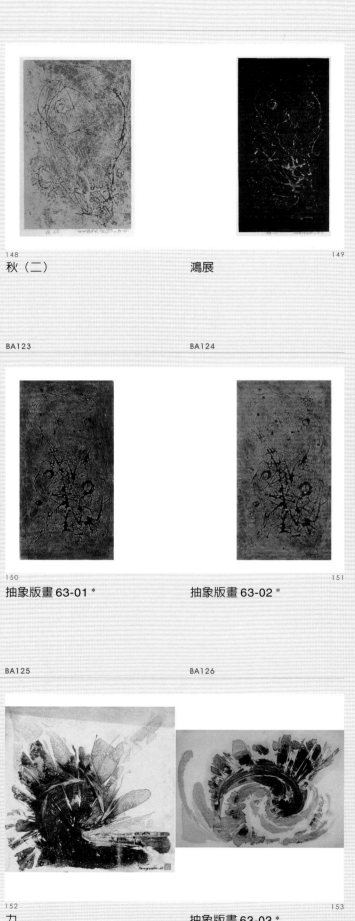

148
秋（二）

鴻展
149

BA123

BA124

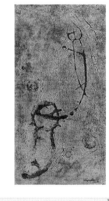

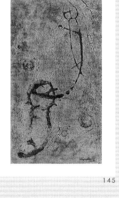

144
文化交流*

145
春（一）
此作與 1962 年曾參展國立歷史博物館「現代繪
畫赴美展覽預展」（5 月 22 日 -27 日）之作品〔古
生物之殘骸〕造形相似，惟「古生物之殘骸」已
佚失。

BA119

BA120

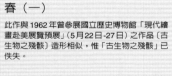

150
抽象版畫 63-01 *

151
抽象版畫 63-02 *

BA125

BA126

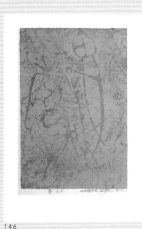

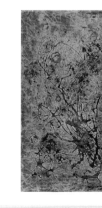

146
春（二）
原 1963 年蔗板版畫，1995 年電腦合成重製。

147
秋（一）
此作與 1962 年曾參展國立歷史博物館「現代繪
畫赴美展覽預展」（5 月 22-27 日）之作品〔秋之
旅〕造型相似，惟〔秋之旅〕已佚失。

BA121

BA122

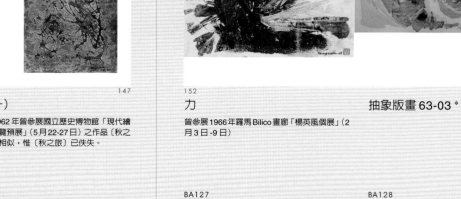

152
力
曾參展 1966 年羅馬 Bilico 畫廊「楊英風個展」（2
月 3 日 -9 日）

153
抽象版畫 63-03 *

BA127

BA128

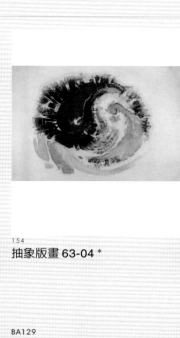
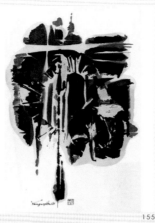
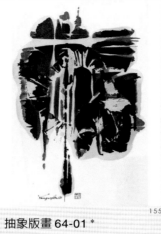

154 155
抽象版畫 63-04 * 抽象版畫 64-01 *

BA129 BA130

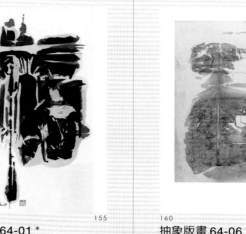
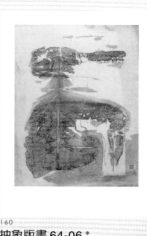
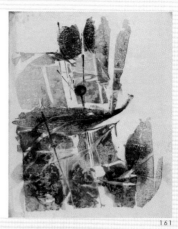

160 161
抽象版畫 64-06 * 抽象版畫 64-07 *

BA135 BA136

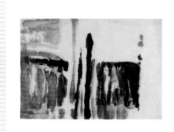
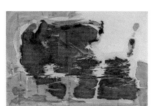
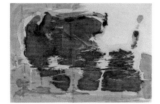

156 157
抽象版畫 64-02 * 抽象版畫 64-03 *

162 163
抽象版畫 64-08 *

BA131 BA132

BA137

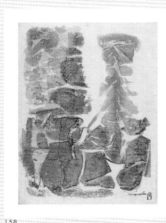
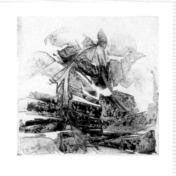
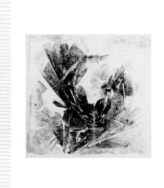
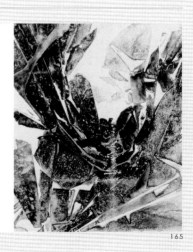

158 159
抽象版畫 64-04 * 抽象版畫 64-05 *

164 165
抽象版畫 64-09 *

BA133 BA134

BA138

433

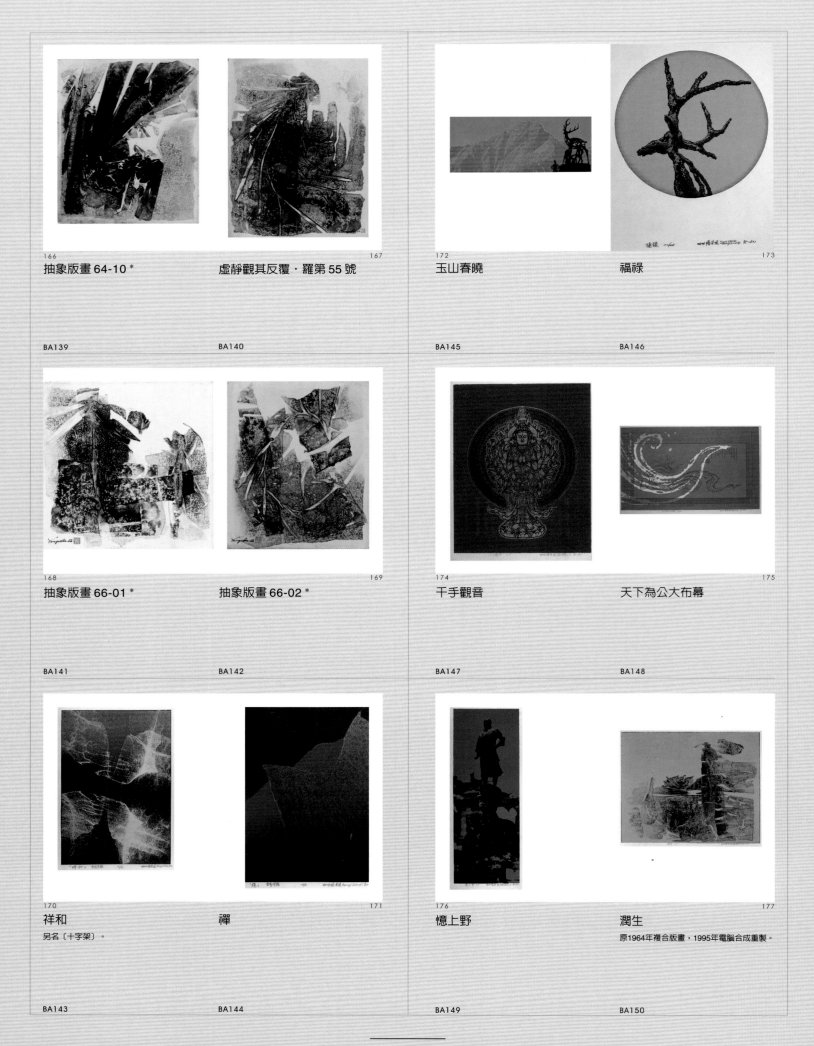

166
抽象版畫 64-10 *

167
虛靜觀其反覆‧羅第 55 號

BA139

BA140

172
玉山春曉

173
福祿

BA145

BA146

168
抽象版畫 66-01 *

169
抽象版畫 66-02 *

BA141

BA142

174
千手觀音

175
天下為公大布幕

BA147

BA148

170
祥和
另名〔十字架〕。

171
禪

176
憶上野

177
潤生
原1964年複合版畫，1995年電腦合成重製。

BA143

BA144

BA149

BA150

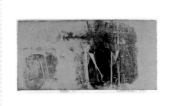
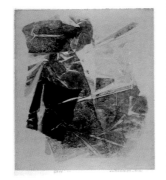
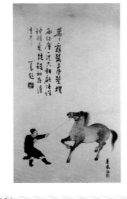
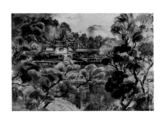

178
靜虛緣起
原1964年複合版畫，1995年電腦合成重製。
另名〔虛靜觀其反覆·羅第3號〕。

179
昂然千里
原1964年複合版畫，1995年電腦合成重製。

184
玉花驄圖
刊於《暢流》第18卷第3期，封面，1958年9
月16日。

185
風景*

BA151
BA152
BB001
BB002

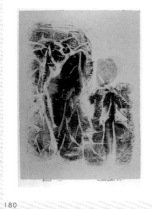
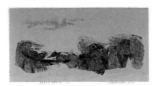
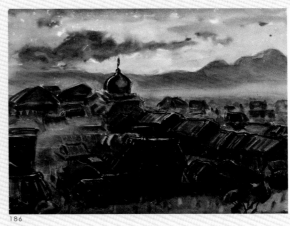

180
雪中送炭
原1964年複合版畫，1995年電腦合成重製。

181
島慶寒梅盛·砲響振天鳴
原1965年複合版畫，1995年電腦合成重製。

186
傍晚
獲1948年「第十一屆臺陽美術展覽會」入選。

187

BA153
BA154
BB003

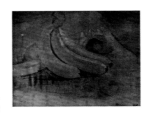
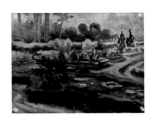

188
香蕉*

189
花園*

BB004
BB005

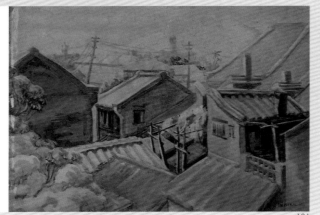

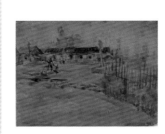

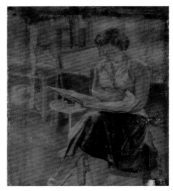

190
屋頂*

191

196
台灣農家

197
閱讀少女*

BB006

BB011

BB012

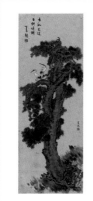

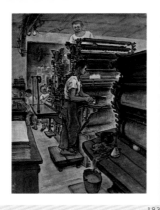

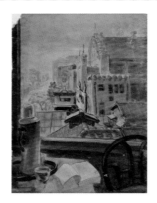

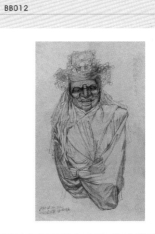

192
松鶴延齡
吳清源收藏。

193
印刷工人*
台灣區印刷工業同業工會七週年紀念特刊封面。

198
窗外*

199
台北霞海城隍廟之七爺

BB007

BB008

BB013

BB014

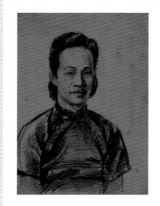

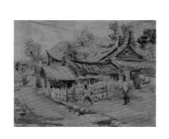

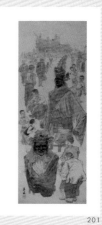

194
母親*

195
芝山巖農家

200
台北霞海城隍廟之八爺

201
范謝兩將軍
獲1954年「臺灣全省第九屆美術展覽會」國
畫部入選。

BB009

BB010

BB015

BB016

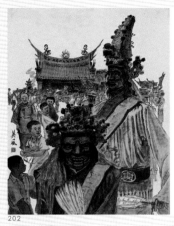

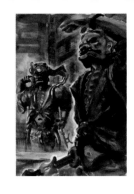

202
霞海城隍誕辰
刊於《豐年》第5卷第13期，封面，1955年7月1日。

ABB017

203
千里眼順風耳
刊於《豐年》第5卷第21期，頁16，1955年11月1日。

BB018

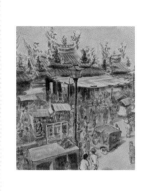

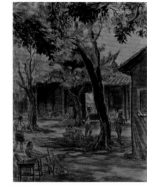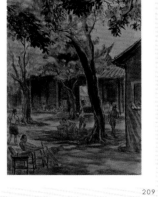

208
北港朝天宮

BB023

209
台南孔廟＊

BB024

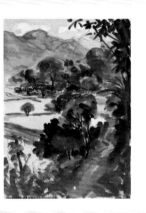

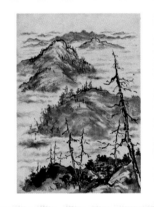

204
國姓鄉南港村林家全景

BB019

205
太平雲海
刊於《宜蘭勝蹟特刊》頁4，1956年4月。

BB020

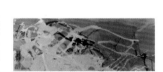

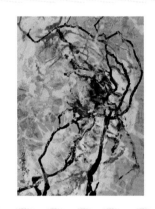

210
抽象繪畫59-01＊

BB025

211
抽象繪畫59-02＊

BB026

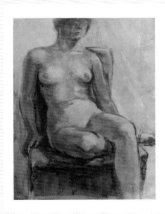

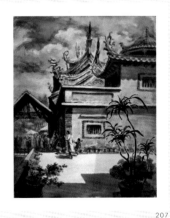

206
紅椅佳人

BB021

207
指南仙宮
曾參展1956年「第一屆全國書畫展覽會」。

BB022

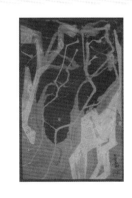

212
龍種
曾參展1959年國立台灣藝術館「聯合西畫展」
（10月17-26日）。

BB027

213
抽象繪畫59-03＊

BB028

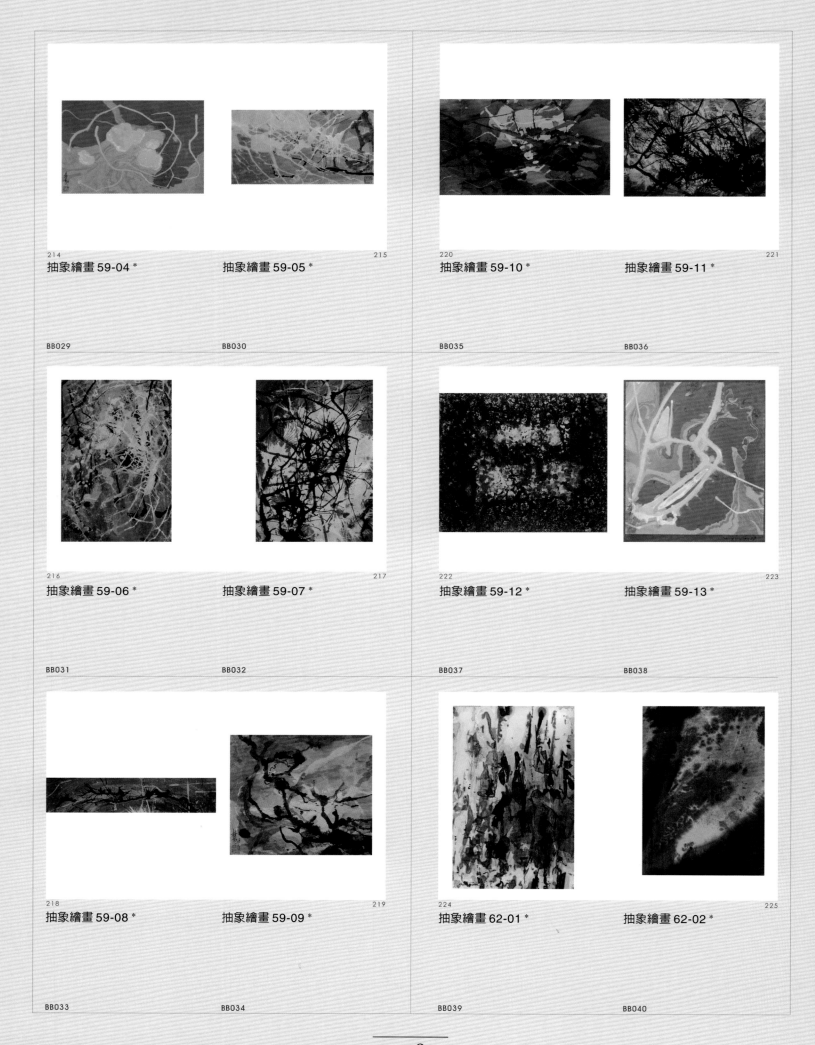

214
抽象繪畫 59-04 *

215
抽象繪畫 59-05 *

BB029

BB030

220
抽象繪畫 59-10 *

221
抽象繪畫 59-11 *

BB035

BB036

216
抽象繪畫 59-06 *

217
抽象繪畫 59-07 *

BB031

BB032

222
抽象繪畫 59-12 *

223
抽象繪畫 59-13 *

BB037

BB038

218
抽象繪畫 59-08 *

219
抽象繪畫 59-09 *

BB033

BB034

224
抽象繪畫 62-01 *

225
抽象繪畫 62-02 *

BB039

BB040

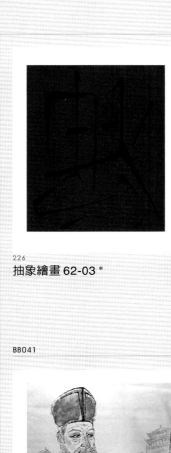

226

抽象繪畫 62-03 *

BB041

227

抽象繪畫 62-04 *

BB042

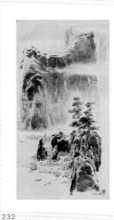

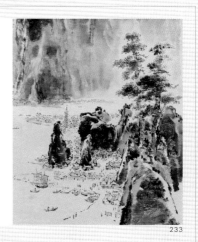

232

大地回春

233

BB047

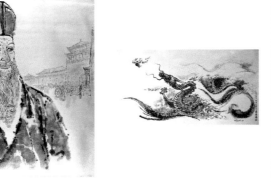

228

利馬竇在故宮

BB043

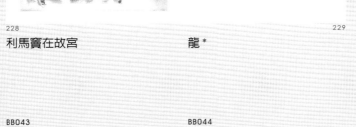

229

龍 *

BB044

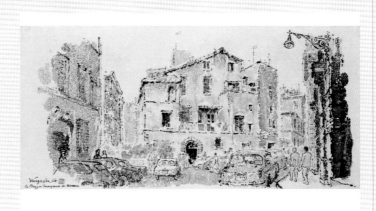

234

羅馬瑪歌娜廣場

235

BB048

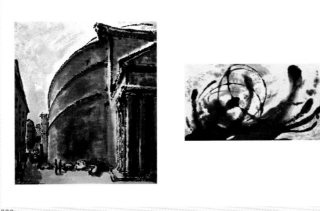

230

羅馬萬神殿

BB045

231

抽象繪畫 64-01 *

BB046

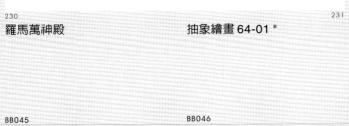

236

羅馬茶座

BB049

237

羅馬郊外

BB050

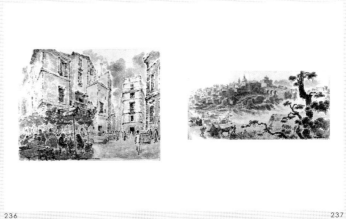

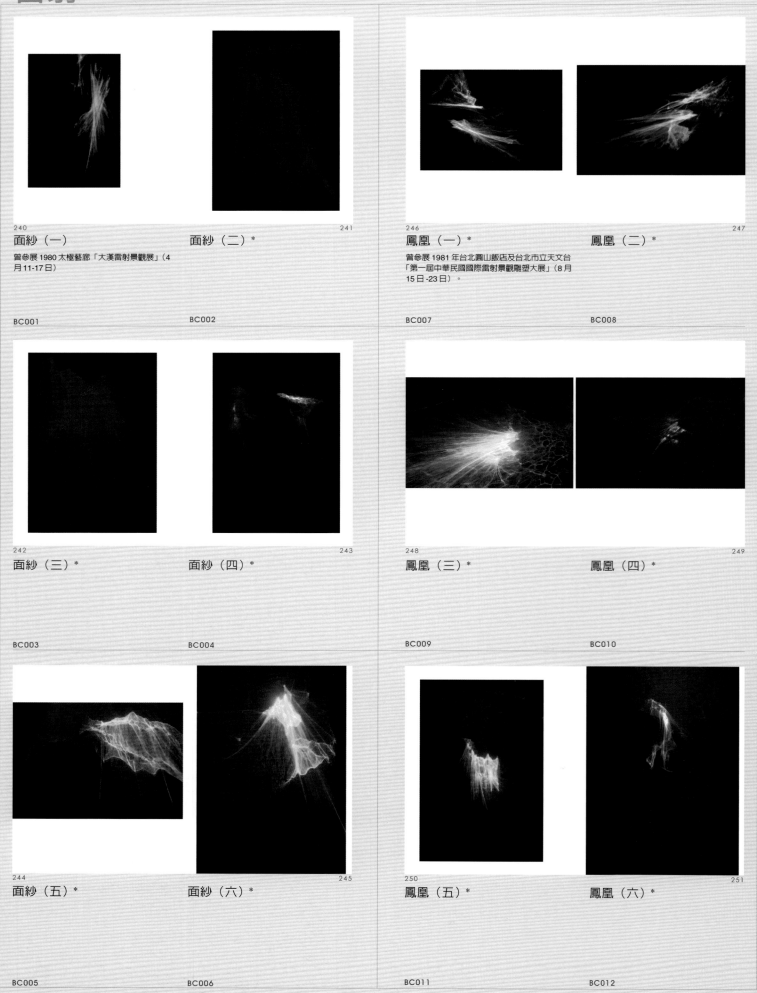

240
241

面紗（一）　　　　　　　面紗（二）＊

曾參展 1980 太極藝廊「大漢雷射景觀展」（4
月 11-17 日）

BC001　　　　　　　　　　BC002

246
247

鳳凰（一）＊　　　　　　鳳凰（二）＊

曾參展 1981 年台北圓山飯店及台北市立天文台
「第一屆中華民國國際雷射景觀雕塑大展」（8 月
15 日 -23 日）。

BC007　　　　　　　　　　BC008

242
243

面紗（三）＊　　　　　　面紗（四）＊

BC003　　　　　　　　　　BC004

248
249

鳳凰（三）＊　　　　　　鳳凰（四）＊

BC009　　　　　　　　　　BC010

244
245

面紗（五）＊　　　　　　面紗（六）＊

BC005　　　　　　　　　　BC006

250
251

鳳凰（五）＊　　　　　　鳳凰（六）＊

雷射 Laser ▼

BC011　　　　　　　　　　BC012

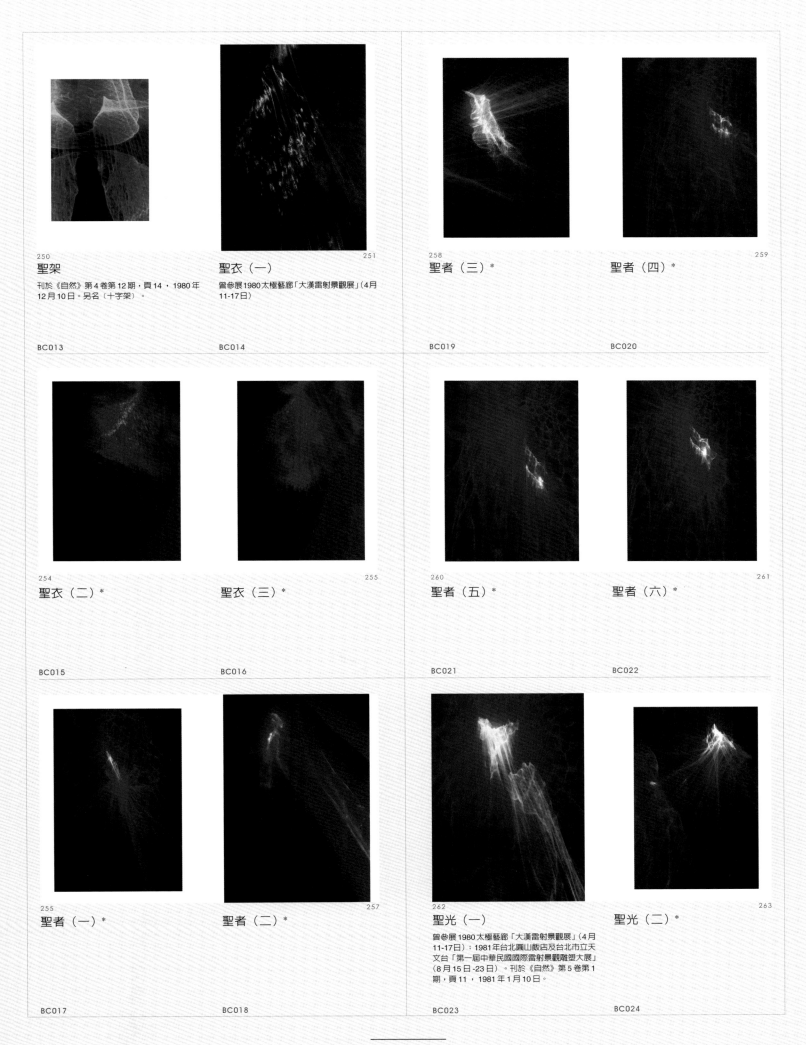

250
聖架
刊於《自然》第 4 卷第 12 期，頁 14，1980 年
12 月 10 日。另名〔十字架〕。

BC013

251
聖衣（一）
曾參展 1980 太極藝廊「大漢雷射景觀展」（4月
11-17日）

BC014

258
聖者（三）*

BC019

259
聖者（四）*

BC020

254
聖衣（二）*

BC015

255
聖衣（三）*

BC016

260
聖者（五）*

BC021

261
聖者（六）*

BC022

255
聖者（一）*

BC017

257
聖者（二）*

BC018

262
聖光（一）
曾參展 1980 太極藝廊「大漢雷射景觀展」（4月
11-17日）；1981 年台北圓山飯店及台北市立天
文台「第一屆中華民國國際雷射景觀雕塑大展」
（8 月 15 日 -23 日）。刊於《自然》第 5 卷第 1
期，頁 11，1981 年 1 月 10 日。

BC023

263
聖光（二）*

BC024

441

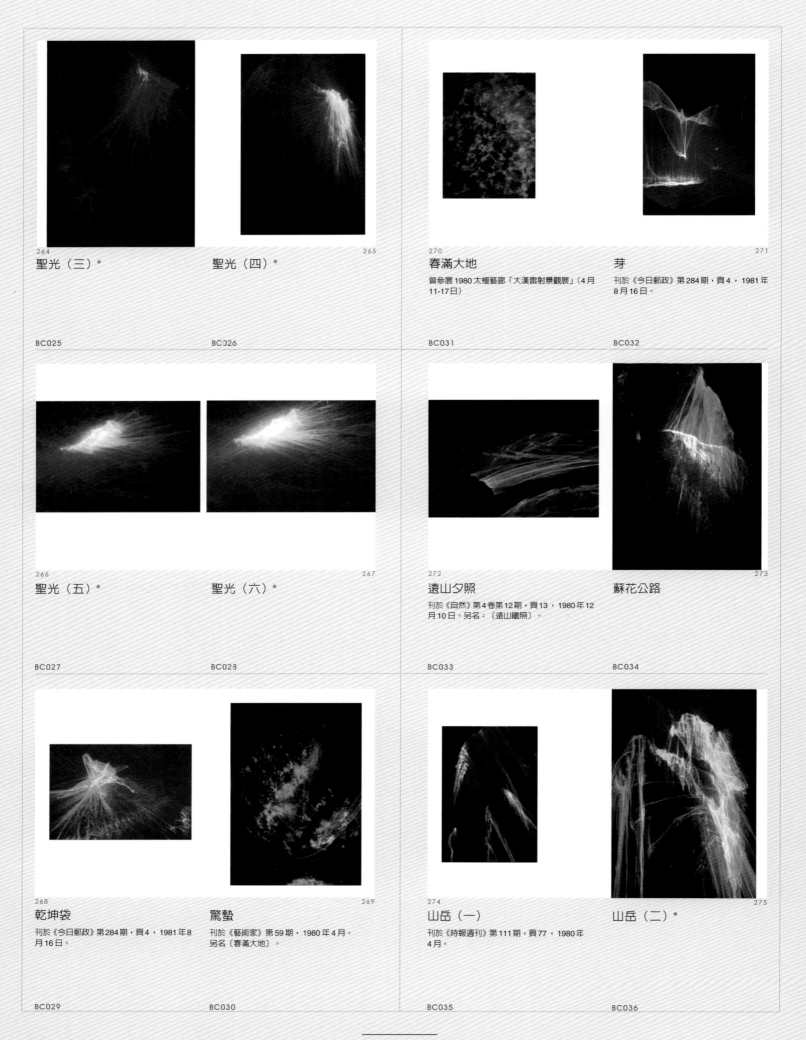

264
聖光（三）＊

265
聖光（四）＊

BC025

BC026

270
春滿大地

曾參展 1980 太極藝廊「大漢雷射景觀展」（4 月 11-17 日）

271
芽

刊於《今日郵政》第 284 期，頁 4，1981 年 8 月 16 日。

BC031

BC032

266
聖光（五）＊

267
聖光（六）＊

BC027

BC028

272
遠山夕照

刊於《自然》第 4 卷第 12 期，頁 13，1980 年 12 月 10 日。另名：〔遠山曦照〕。

273
蘇花公路

BC033

BC034

268
乾坤袋

刊於《今日郵政》第 284 期，頁 4，1981 年 8 月 16 日。

269
驚蟄

刊於《藝術家》第 59 期，1980 年 4 月。另名〔春滿大地〕。

274
山岳（一）

刊於《時報週刊》第 111 期，頁 77，1980 年 4 月。

275
山岳（二）＊

BC029

BC030

BC035

BC036

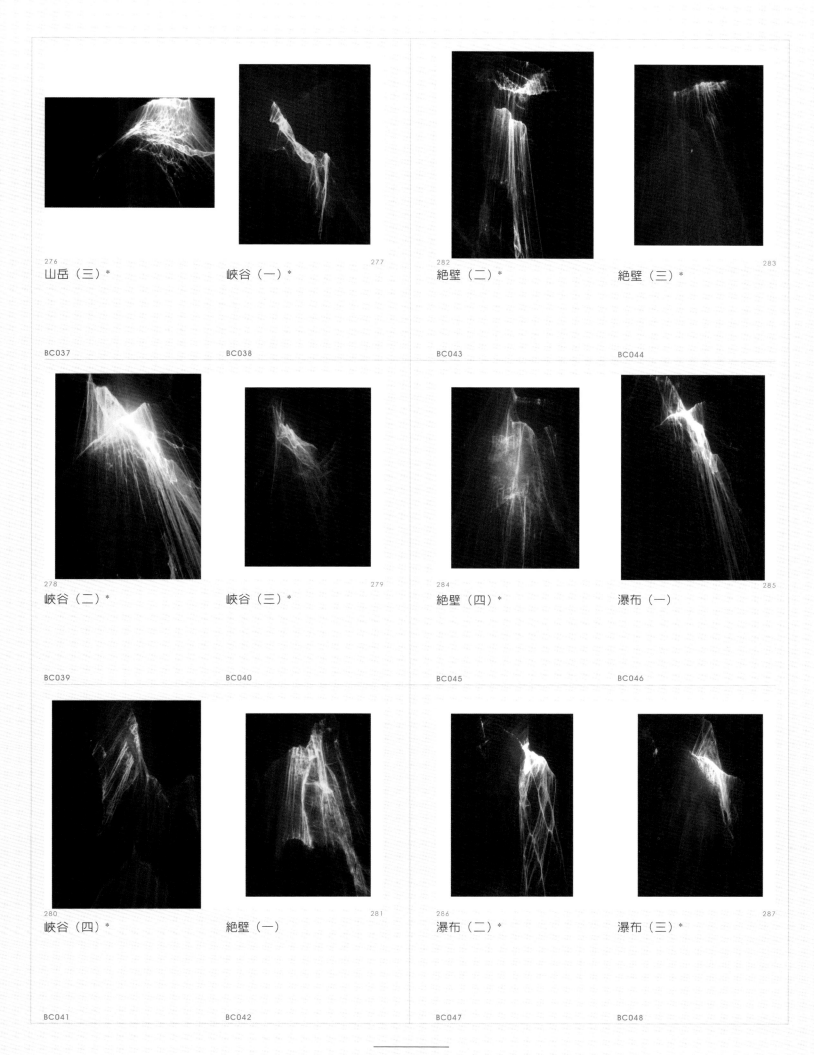

276
山岳（三）*

277
峽谷（一）*

282
絕壁（二）*

283
絕壁（三）*

BC037

BC038

BC043

BC044

278
峽谷（二）*

279
峽谷（三）*

284
絕壁（四）*

285
瀑布（一）

BC039

BC040

BC045

BC046

280
峽谷（四）*

281
絕壁（一）

286
瀑布（二）*

287
瀑布（三）*

BC041

BC042

BC047

BC048

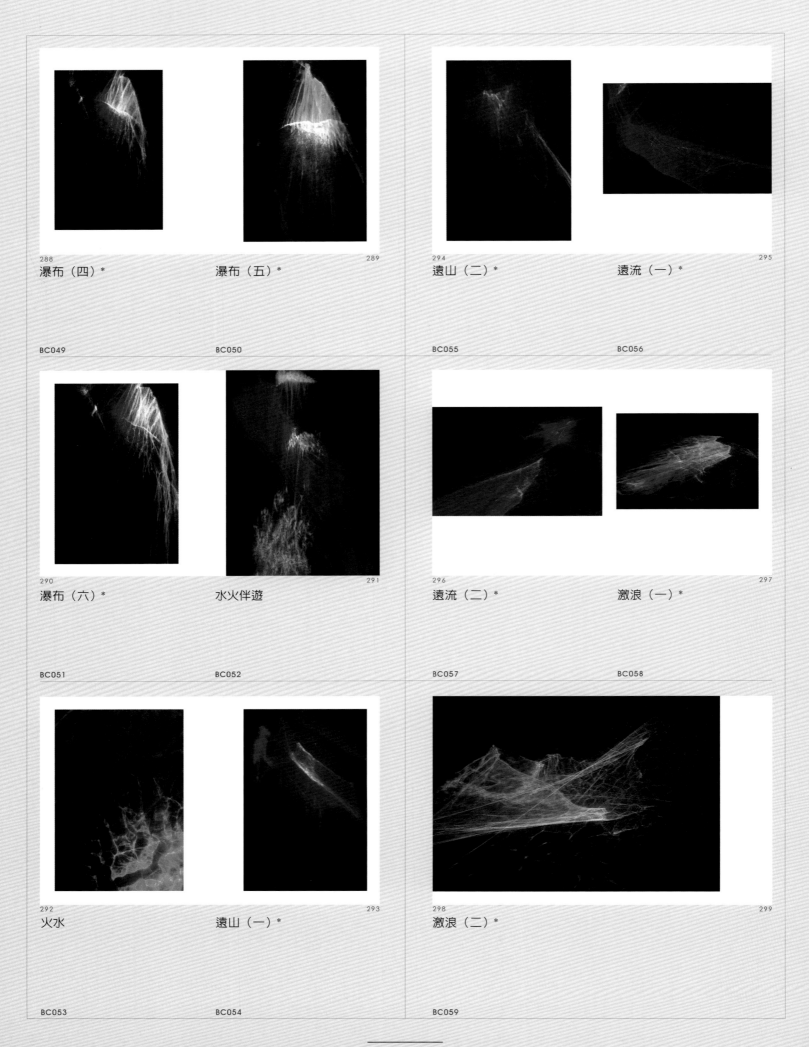

288
瀑布（四）*

289
瀑布（五）*

BC049

BC050

294
遠山（二）*

295
遠流（一）*

BC055

BC056

290
瀑布（六）*

291
水火伴遊

BC051

BC052

296
遠流（二）*

297
激浪（一）*

BC057

BC058

292
火水

293
遠山（一）*

BC053

BC054

298
激浪（二）*

299

BC059

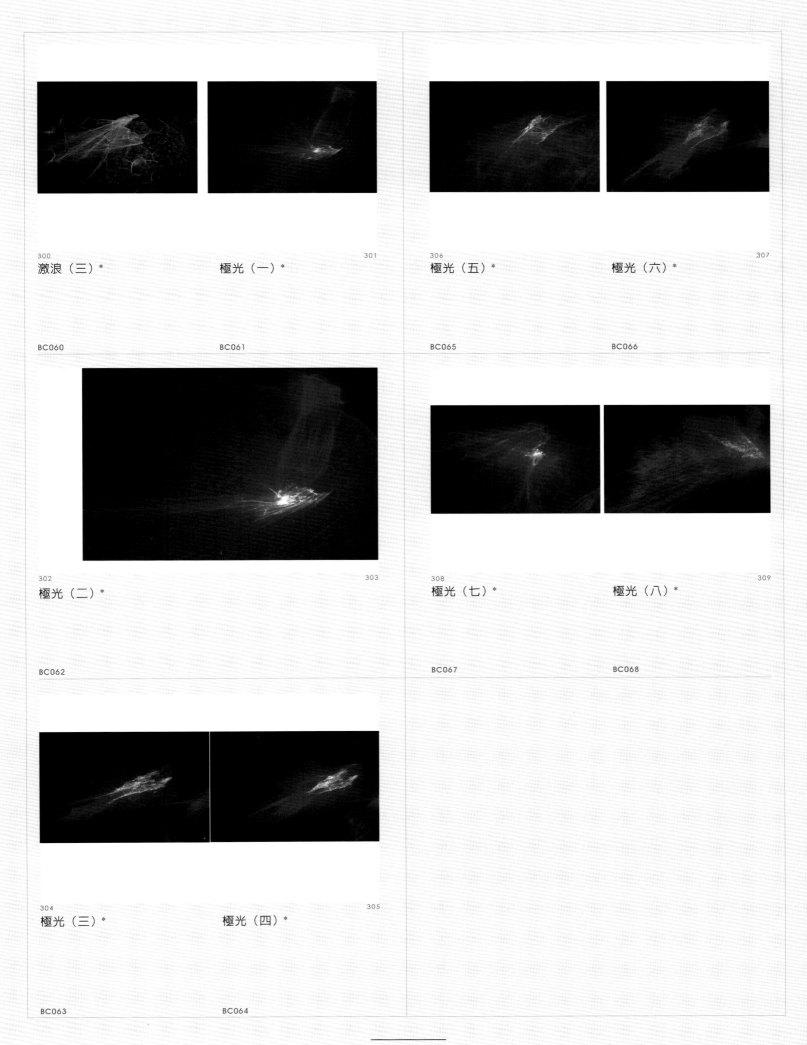

300
激浪（三）*

301
極光（一）*

BC060

BC061

306
極光（五）*

307
極光（六）*

BC065

BC066

302
極光（二）*

303

BC062

308
極光（七）*

309
極光（八）*

BC067

BC068

304
極光（三）*

305
極光（四）*

BC063

BC064

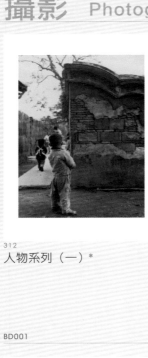
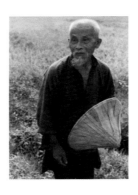

312 人物系列（一）*　　　313 人物系列（二）*

BD001　　　BD002

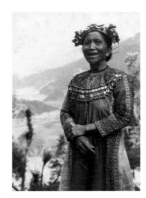
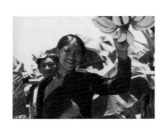

314 人物系列（三）*　　　315 人物系列（四）*

BD003　　　BD004

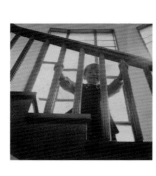
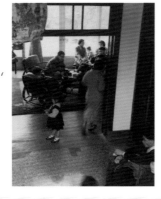

316 嬉　　　317 閒

BD005　　　BD006

318 登　　　319 梯

BD007　　　BD008

320 睇　　　321 窺

BD009　　　BD010

322 辮　　　323 編織

刊於《豐年》第8卷第16期，封面，1958年
8月16日。

BD011　　　BD012

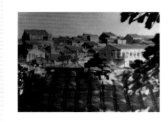 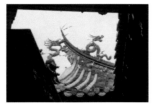 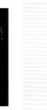 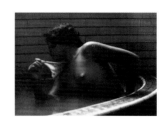

324 325　　　　　　　　　　　　　　330 331

傳統建築系列（一）*　　　傳統建築系列（二）*　　　裸女系列：澡堂（一）*　　　裸女系列：澡堂（二）*

BD013　　　　　　　　　BD014　　　　　　　　　BD019　　　　　　　　　BD020

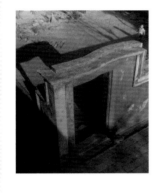 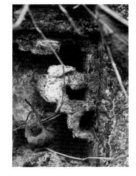 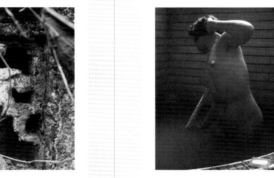 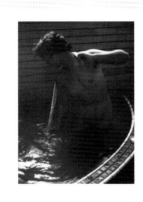

326 327　　　　　　　　　　　　　　332 333

傳統建築系列（三）*　　　傳統建築系列（四）*　　　裸女系列：澡堂（三）*　　　裸女系列：澡堂（四）*

BD015　　　　　　　　　BD016　　　　　　　　　BD021　　　　　　　　　BD022

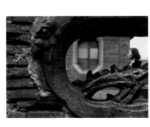 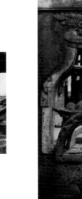 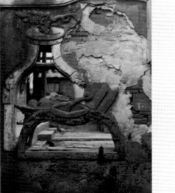 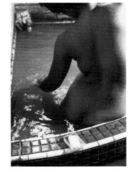 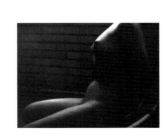

328 329　　　　　　　　　　　　　　334 335

傳統建築系列（五）*　　　傳統建築系列（六）*　　　裸女系列：澡堂（五）*　　　裸女系列：澡堂（六）*

BD017　　　　　　　　　BD018　　　　　　　　　BD023　　　　　　　　　BD024

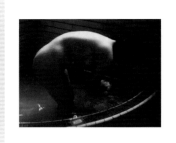 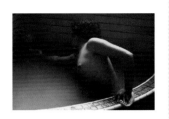 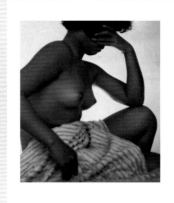 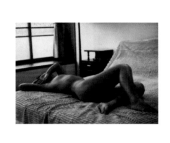

336	337	342	343
裸女系列：澡堂（七）*	裸女系列：澡堂（八）*	裸女系列：臥室（四）*	裸女系列：臥室（五）*
BD025	BD026	BD031	BD032

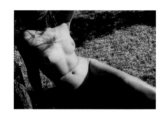 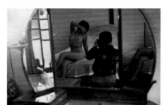 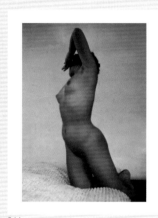 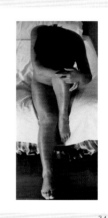

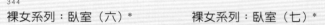

338	339	344	345
裸女系列：草地*	裸女系列：臥室（一）*	裸女系列：臥室（六）*	裸女系列：臥室（七）*
BD027	BD028	BD033	BD034

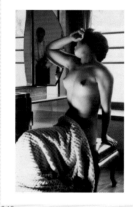 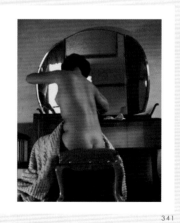 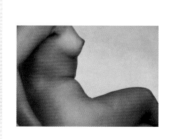 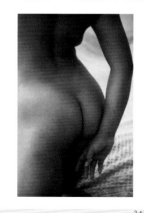

340	341	346	347
裸女系列：臥室（二）*	裸女系列：臥室（三）*	裸女系列：臥室（八）*	裸女系列：臥室（九）*
BD029	BD030	BD035	BD036

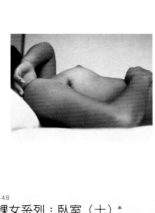

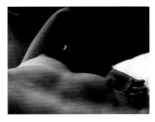

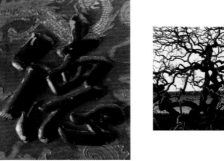

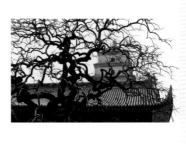

348
裸女系列：臥室（十）*

349
裸女系列：臥室（十一）*

354
廟宇系列（四）*

355
廟宇系列（五）*

BD037

BD038

BD043

BD044

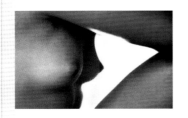

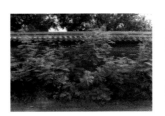

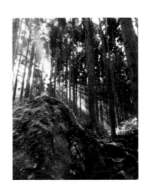

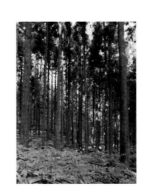

350
裸女系列：臥室（十二）*

351
廟宇系列（一）*

356
溪頭系列（一）*

刊於《自然》第4卷第11期，頁13，1980年
11月10日。

357
溪頭系列（二）*

刊於《自然》第4卷第11期，頁12，1980年
11月10日。

BD039

BD040

BD045

BD046

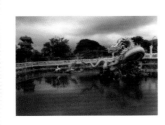

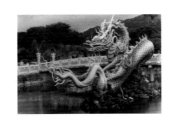

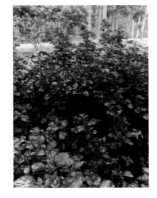

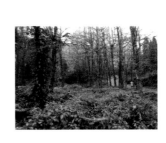

352
廟宇系列（二）*

353
廟宇系列（三）*

358
溪頭系列（三）*

刊於《自然》第4卷第11期，頁12，1980年
11月10日。

359
溪頭系列（四）*

刊於《自然》第4卷第11期，頁12，1980年
11月10日。

BD041

BD042

BD047

BD048

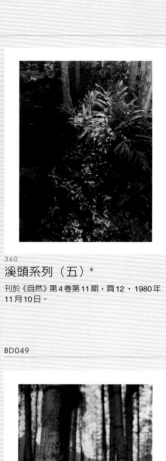

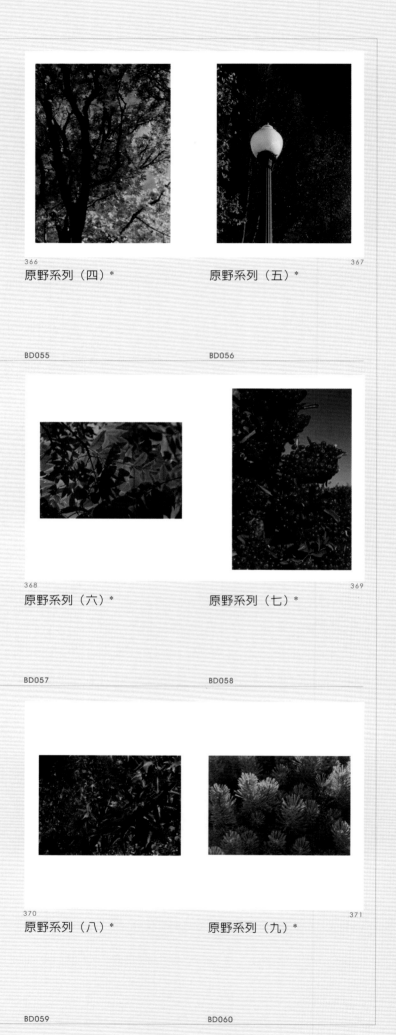

360
溪頭系列（五）*

刊於《自然》第4卷第11期，頁12，1980年
11月10日。

溪頭系列（六）*

361

366
原野系列（四）*

原野系列（五）*

367

BD049

BD050

BD055

BD056

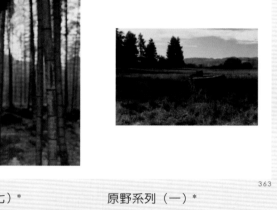

362
溪頭系列（七）*

刊於《關係我》秋季刊第1期，封面，1980年
10月10日。

原野系列（一）*

363

368
原野系列（六）*

原野系列（七）*

369

BD051

BD052

BD057

BD058

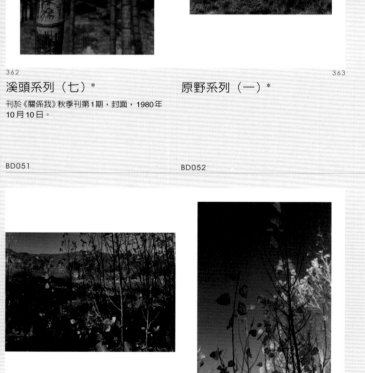

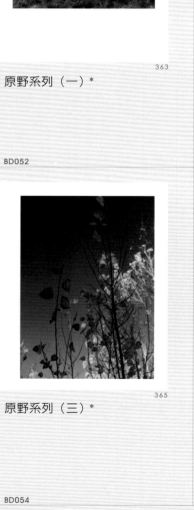

364
原野系列（二）*

原野系列（三）*

365

370
原野系列（八）*

原野系列（九）*

371

BD053

BD054

BD059

BD060

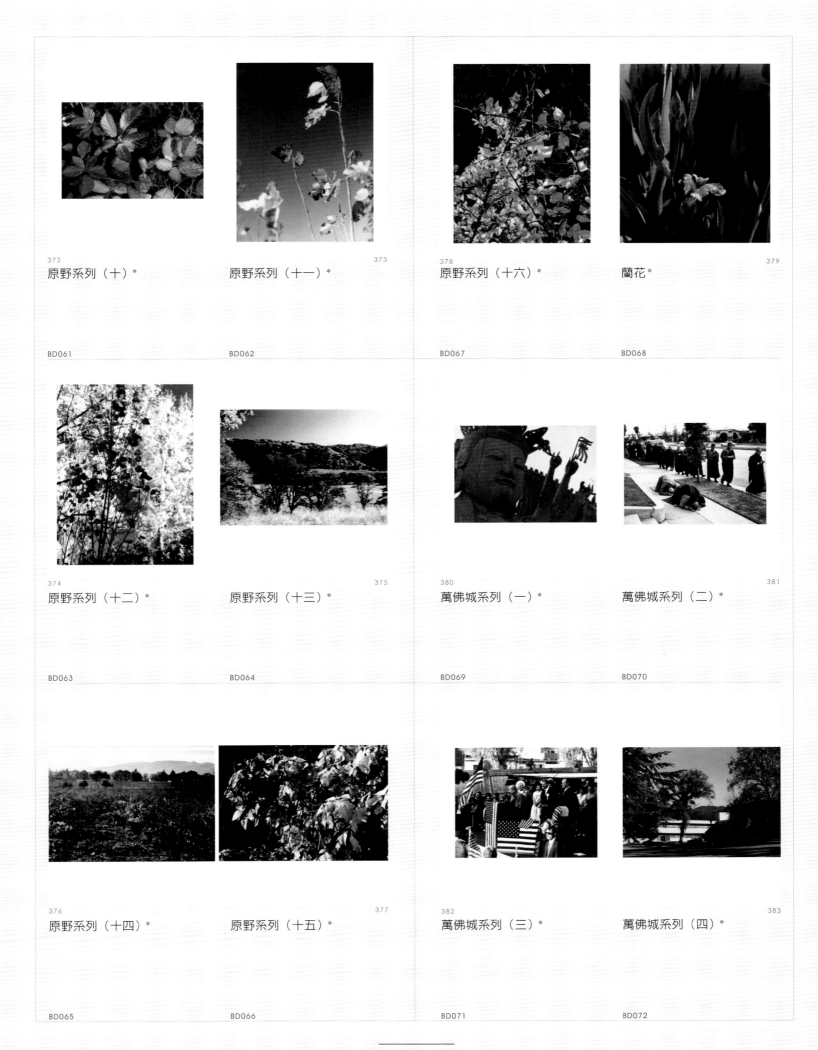

372
原野系列（十）*

373
原野系列（十一）*

BD061

BD062

378
原野系列（十六）*

379
蘭花*

BD067

BD068

374
原野系列（十二）*

375
原野系列（十三）*

BD063

BD064

380
萬佛城系列（一）*

381
萬佛城系列（二）*

BD069

BD070

376
原野系列（十四）*

377
原野系列（十五）*

BD065

BD066

382
萬佛城系列（三）*

383
萬佛城系列（四）*

BD071

BD072

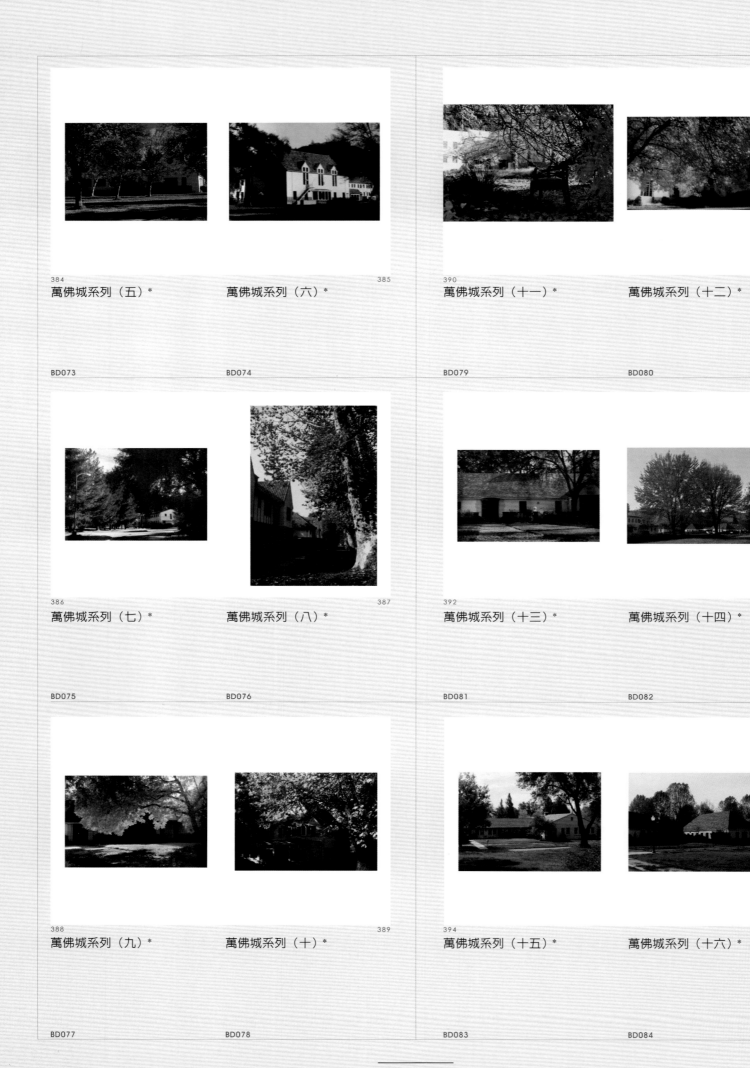

384
萬佛城系列（五）*

385
萬佛城系列（六）*

BD073

BD074

390
萬佛城系列（十一）*

391
萬佛城系列（十二）*

BD079

BD080

386
萬佛城系列（七）*

387
萬佛城系列（八）*

BD075

BD076

392
萬佛城系列（十三）*

393
萬佛城系列（十四）*

BD081

BD082

388
萬佛城系列（九）*

389
萬佛城系列（十）*

BD077

BD078

394
萬佛城系列（十五）*

395
萬佛城系列（十六）*

BD083

BD084

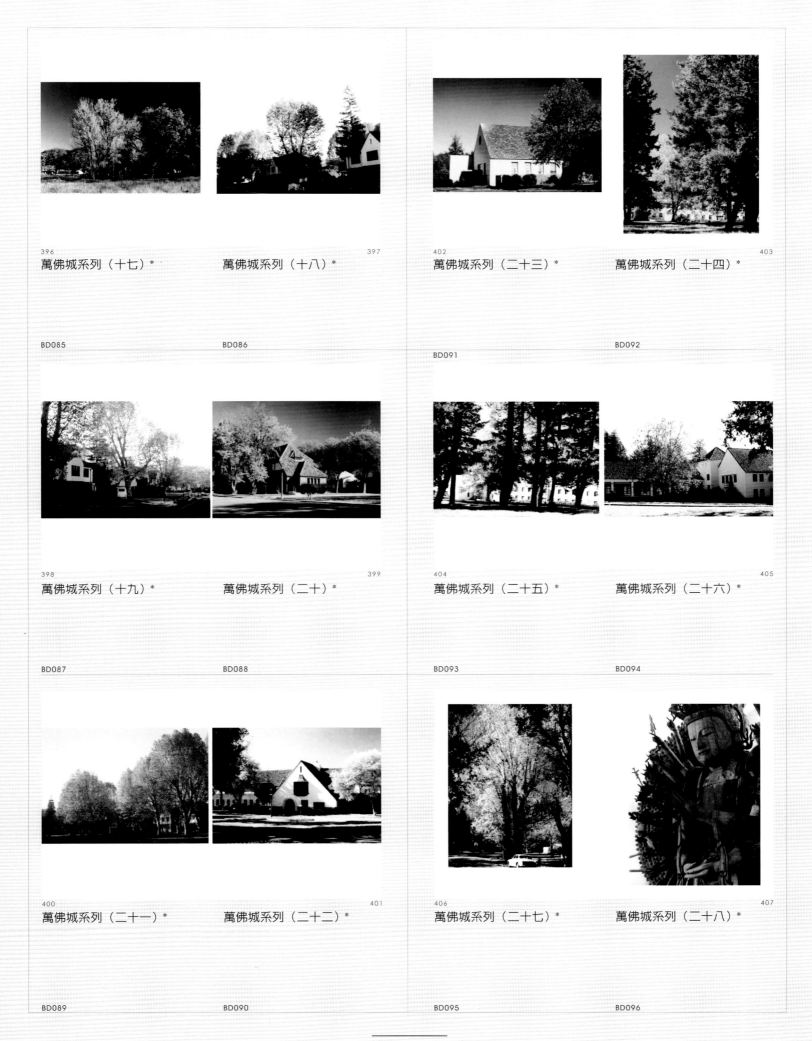

396
萬佛城系列（十七）*

397
萬佛城系列（十八）*

BD085

BD086

402
萬佛城系列（二十三）*

403
萬佛城系列（二十四）*

BD091

BD092

398
萬佛城系列（十九）*

399
萬佛城系列（二十）*

BD087

BD088

404
萬佛城系列（二十五）*

405
萬佛城系列（二十六）*

BD093

BD094

400
萬佛城系列（二十一）*

401
萬佛城系列（二十二）*

BD089

BD090

406
萬佛城系列（二十七）*

407
萬佛城系列（二十八）*

BD095

BD096

編後語

賴鈴如，成功大學歷史系畢業，現為楊英風藝術研究中心研究員。

在許多人的印象中，「楊英風」這三個字幾乎是與「雕塑」畫上等號，他更是被譽為繼黃土水之後，影響台灣雕塑界最大的藝術家。但卻很少人知道他的平面創作如繪畫、速寫、雷射、攝影、美術設計、漫畫、插畫等也很豐富。因此藉由楊英風全集的編輯，我們希望呈現的就是楊英風創作的全貌，而不是侷限在雕塑上的成就而已。第二卷至第四卷平面創作的編輯就是依此目標來進行的。在這一卷裡將楊英風平面創作依類型分成版畫、繪畫、雷射及攝影。

在編輯過程中，最困難的是早期資料的蒐集及整理，由於年代較早留存的資料相對的較少，因此在整理資料時，常常會遇到有作品名稱卻不知作品圖像為何，或是反過來只有作品圖像卻不知該作品的名稱，前者這種情形則將作品基本資料紀錄到作品清單中，後者則將作品圖像放入參考圖版中；此外，尚有同一個作品現在的名稱和早期的名稱不相同的情形，為了怕讀者混淆，我們擇一常用名稱做為作品的正式名稱，至於其他名稱就放置於作品的其他資料裡供讀者參考。

一本有質感的書冊，除了美編外，最重要的莫過於作品圖片的品質，因此，在編輯中必須慎選每一張圖片，希望所呈現出來的圖片可以將楊英風的作品表現到最好。由於1950年以前的作品資料留下的不多，且多為黑白的底片或照片，站在保存資料的立場，同時兼顧整個書冊的美觀，編輯時特別將這些作品放置於正式圖版之後，是為參考圖版，依此與正式圖版作區隔。此外，為了維持整個書冊簡潔美觀的風格，特別將作品其他資料如：展覽資料、作品出處或作者自述等等放置於書冊的最後面。

在這一卷書冊裡，版畫從1950年代中期以前的寫實風格，到中期以後抽象風格的轉變，是受到當時台灣藝壇大環境的影響，而至1994-1995年時則因電腦科技的進步，楊英風把他早期所做的部分版畫重製。編輯時為了讓讀者比較其差異，於是將圖案相同但用色、作品尺寸不同的作品，依創作年代的先後順序編排在一起；繪畫多是1960年代以前的，雖然數量不多，但材質卻是多樣的：有國畫、水彩、油畫等，可看出楊英風深厚的繪畫底子；而台灣雷射藝術的引進當推楊英風為第一人，他並在1981年舉辦「中華民國第一屆國際雷射景觀雕塑大展」於台北圓山飯店，可說是國內第一次大型的雷射景觀雕塑展，於是1980年代有相當多的雷射作品問世，書冊中所收集的雷射作品有70幅之多；攝影作品是第一次出現在正式的書冊中，楊英風對於攝影有莫大的興趣，雖然正式發表於報章雜誌上的作品不多，但我們還是將手邊收集到的資料全數放入書冊。由此可知，楊英風平面創作的類型包含多樣性，此外，尚有速寫、美術設計、漫畫、插畫作品，因為考慮到書冊的頁數及作品屬性不同所以留待第3卷、第4卷作介紹。

《楊英風全集》的出版可說是楊英風藝術研究中心所有同仁辛苦工作的成果，從原先堆積如山的資料到現在全集的編撰完成，最要感謝寬謙法師對於全集出版的執著、主編蕭瓊瑞教授悉心的指導及辛苦工作的同仁們，相信全集出版不但是完成了楊英風藝術研究中心階段性的計畫，也是台灣藝術界的創舉，我很高興也很榮幸可以參與其中！

Afterword

Ling-ju Lai, graduated from History Department of National Cheng Kung University. Currently Researcher at Yuyu Yang Art Research Center.

To many Yuyu Yang is synonymous with sculpture. He is praised as the greatest artist after Tu-shui Huang. But few knew of his other creative outputs in painting, sketch, laser, photograph, graphic design, comic and illustration. Thus the publishing of *Yuyu Yang Corpus* seeks to present the full repertoire of the artist rather than limited to the sphere of sculpture. Editing of his two-dimensional works under Volume II to IV is undertaken on such orientation. In this Volume, we sort Yuyu Yang's two-dimensional work by prints, paintings, laser and photographs.

The most challenging task in the course of the editing is the initial compiling and sorting: the earlier records are scantier; often available titles find no graphics, or vice versa. For the former, basic information is provided in the catalogue, and the latter photos are incorporated under reference. Another scenario is a piece of work having different titles at various stages; to deter confusion for the reader, a more frequently used version is adopted, and the other monikers are placed in the reference data.

A fine artwork publication apart from adroit art editing lies with the quality of the photography of works; hence every photo must be carefully scrutinized for optimum presentation of Yuyu Yang's creation. As photo records from pre-1950 are few and monochromatic in prints or negatives, from the standpoint of preserving record and considering overall publication aesthetics, these materials are arranged following formal plates as reference to distinguish from the plate proper. Moreover, in keeping a concise, neat style, data concerning works such as exhibition record, work source or author commentary are presented in the rear part.

In this volume the shift from representational style before mid 1950s to abstraction thereafter in prints was attributed to Taiwan's salient trend at the time. In 1994 to 1995, for the progress of computer technology, the artist reproduced some of his early prints. For the reader to compare the differences, prints of the same design but differ in coloration and size are organized chronologically. Paintings are mostly before 1960s, though not in great numbers, they are diverse in mediums, including Chinese ink painting, watercolour and oil. These works speak eloquently of Yuyu Yang's skillful draftsmanship. The introduction of laser art to Taiwan is irrefutably attributed to Yuyu Yang, who also organized the Laser Artland Taipei '81 at the Grand Hotel, the very first important laser art presentation in the nation. Consequently a lot of laser works was produced in the 1980s; seventy are included in the volume. His photographic productions are making their debut appearance in book publication. Yuyu Yang was very keen on photography. Although few have made it to newspaper or magazine publication, we have included all photo records found in the volume. Given Yuyu Yang's versatility in two-dimensional mediums and volume page limitation, the sketches, graphic designs, comics and illustrations are featured in the Volume III and IV.

The publication of *Yuyu Yang Corpus* owes to the efforts of the entire staff at Yuyu Yang Art Research Center who were involved from heaps of records and materials until the completion of editing, and Master Kuan Chian's full hearted resolve, chief editor Prof. Chong-ray Hsiao's able guidance and the many others that contributed to the project voluntarily. The availing of Complete Works of Yuyu Yang marks a phase completion for Yuyu Yang Art Research Center and an unprecedented undertaking for Taiwan art community. I am privileged to have been part of it.

國家圖書館出版品預行編目資料

楊英風全集・創作篇＝Yuyu Yang Corpus／蕭瓊
瑞總主編.　——初版.——台北市：藝術家，
2005〔民94〕
冊：24.5×31公分
ISBN 986-7487-98-2（精裝）
1.美術-作品集

902.2　　　　　　　　　　　94022348

楊英風全集 創作篇第二卷
YUYU YANG CORPUS

發　行　人／張俊彥、何政廣
指　　　導／行政院文化建設委員會
策　　　劃／國立交通大學
執　　　行／國立交通大學楊英風藝術研究中心
　　　　　　財團法人楊英風藝術教育基金會
諮詢委員會／召　集　人：張俊彥
　　　　　　副召集人：蔡文祥、楊維邦（按筆劃順序）
　　　　　　委　　　員：林保堯、施仁忠、祖慰、陳一平、張恬君、葉李華、
　　　　　　　　　　　　劉紀蕙、劉育東、顏娟英、黎漢林、蕭瓊瑞（按筆劃順序）
執 行 編 輯／總 策 劃：釋寬謙
　　　　　　策　　　劃：楊奉琛、王維妮
　　　　　　總 主 編：蕭瓊瑞
　　　　　　副 主 編：賴鈴如、陳怡勳
　　　　　　分冊主編：賴鈴如、陳怡勳、蔡珊珊、黃瑋鈴、潘美璟
　　　　　　美術指導：李振明、張俊哲
　　　　　　美術編輯：柯美麗
　　　　　　封底攝影：高　媛

出　版　者／藝術家出版社
　　　　　　台北市重慶南路一段 147 號 6 樓
　　　　　　TEL:(02) 23886715　FAX:(02) 23317096
　　　　　　郵政劃撥：01044798／藝術家雜誌社帳戶
總　經　銷／藝術圖書公司
　　　　　　台北市羅斯福路三段 283 巷 18 號
　　　　　　TEL:(02) 23620578、23629769
　　　　　　FAX:(02) 23623594
　　　　　　郵政劃撥：0017620~0 號帳戶
分　　　社／台南市西門路一段 223 巷 10 弄 26 號
　　　　　　TEL:(06) 2617268　FAX:(06) 2637698
　　　　　　台中縣潭子鄉大豐路三段 186 巷 6 弄 35 號
　　　　　　TEL:(04) 25340234　FAX:(04) 25331186

初　　　版／2006 年 3 月
定　　　價／新台幣 1800 元
I S B N　　986-7487-98-2（精裝）

法律顧問　蕭雄淋
行政院新聞局出版事業登記證局版台業字第 1749 號